THE STANDING STONES OF STENNIS. From an original drawing in the possession of the Author.

First Published as *Rude Stone Monuments* by
John Murray in 1872

This facsimile edition has been carefully scanned
and reprinted in the traditional manner by
THE LOST LIBRARY
5 High Street,
Glastonbury UK BA6 9DP

The LOST LIBRARY is a publishing house based in
Glastonbury, UK, dedicated to the reproduction
of important rare esoteric and scholarly texts for
the discerning reader.

Cataloguing Information
Old Stone Monuments
James Fergusson

ISBN 978 1 906621 07 0

Printed by Replika Press Pvt Ltd,
Haryana, India

**THE LOST
LIBRARY**

OLD STONE MONUMENTS

IN

ALL COUNTRIES;

THEIR AGE AND USES.

By JAMES FERGUSSON, D.C.L., F.R.S.,
V.P.R.A.S., F.R.I.B.A., &c.

Demi-Dolmen, Kerland.

WITH TWO HUNDRED AND THIRTY-FOUR ILLUSTRATIONS.

PUBLISHED BY

THE LOST LIBRARY

GLASTONBURY, ENGLAND

PREFACE

When, in the year 1854, I was arranging the scheme for the 'Handbook of Architecture,' one chapter of about fifty pages was allotted to the Rude Stone Monuments then known. When, however, I came seriously to consult the authorities I had marked out, and to arrange my ideas preparatory to writing it, I found the whole subject in such a state of confusion and uncertainty as to be wholly unsuited for introduction into a work, the main object of which was to give a clear but succinct account of what was known and admitted with regard to the architectural styles of the world. Again, ten years afterwards, while engaged in re-writing this 'Handbook' as a 'History of Architecture,' the same difficulties presented themselves. It is true that in the interval the Druids, with their Dracontia, had lost much of the hold they possessed on the mind of the public; but, to a great extent, they had been replaced by prehistoric myths, which, though free from their absurdity, were hardly less perplexing. The consequence was that then, as in the first instance, it would have been necessary to argue every point and defend every position. Nothing could be taken for granted, and no narrative was possible. The matter was, therefore, a second time allowed quietly to drop without being noticed. I never, however, lost sight of the subject, and I hoped some time or other to be able to treat of it with the fulness its interest deserves; and in order to forward this project, in July, 1860, I wrote an article in the 'Quarterly Review,' entitled 'Stonehenge,' in which I stated the views I had then formed on the subject; and again, ten years afterwards, in April of last year, another article, entitled 'Non-Historic Times' in the same

b

journal, in which I added such new facts and arguments as I had gathered in the interval. The principal object it was sought to attain in writing these articles, was to raise a discussion on the moot points which I hoped would have tended towards settling them. If any competent archæologist had come forward, and could have pointed out the weak point in the argument, he would have rendered a service to the cause; or if any leading authority had endorsed the views advocated in these articles, the public might have felt some confidence in their correctness. This expectation has not been fulfilled, but they have probably not been without their use in preparing the minds of others for the views advanced in them, while, as no refutation has appeared, and no valid objection has been urged against them, either in public or in private, I may fairly consider myself justified in feeling considerable confidence in their general correctness.

Till antiquaries are agreed whether the circles are temples or tombs or observatories, whether the dolmens are monuments of the dead or altars for sacrificing living men, and whether the mounds are tombs or law courts, it seems impossible, without arguing every point, to write anything that will be generally accepted. Still more, till it is decided whether they are really prehistoric or were erected at the periods where tradition and history place them, it seems in vain to attempt to explain in a simple narrative form either their age or uses. As a necessary consequence of all this confusion, it is scarcely practicable at present to compile a work which shall be merely a Historical and Statistical account of the Rude Stone Monuments in all parts of the world; but till something is settled and agreed upon, we must be content with one which to a certain extent, at least, takes the form of an argument. Many of its pages which would have been better employed in describing and classifying, are occupied with arguments against some untenable theory or date, or in trying to substitute for those usually accepted, some more reasonable proposition. Notwithstanding this, however, it is hoped that this work will be found to contain a greater number of new facts regarding Rude Stone Monuments, and of carefully selected illustrations extending over a larger area, than have yet been put together in a volume of the same extent.

It may fairly be asked, and no doubt will, how I dare to set up my opinions with regard to these monuments in opposition to those of the best informed antiquaries, not only in this country but on the Continent? The answer I would venture to suggest is, that no other antiquary, so far as I am aware, has gone so carefully and fully into the whole subject, or has faced all the difficulties with which the questions are everywhere perplexed. The books that have hitherto been written are either the work of speculative dreamers, like Stukeley, Higgins, or Vallancey, who having evolved a baseless theory out of their own inner consciousness, seek everywhere for materials to prop it up, and are by no means particular as to the inferences they draw from very obscure or slender hints: or they are, on the other hand, the works of local antiquaries, whose opinions are influenced mainly by what they find in their own researches. The works of such men are invaluable as contributions to the general stock of knowledge, but their theories must be received with caution, as based on too narrow a foundation either of facts or inferences ; for it need hardly be insisted upon that no amount of local experience can qualify any one to write on such a subject as this. It does not even seem sufficient that an author should be familiar with all the varieties of megalithic remains. Unless he has also mastered the other forms of architectural art, and knows in what manner and from what motives the styles of one people are adopted from or influenced by that of another race, he will hardly be able to unravel the various tangled problems that meet him at every step in such an investigation. When looked at, however, from the same point of view, and judged by the same laws as other styles, that of the dolmen builders does not appear either

PREFACE.

mythical or mysterious. They seem to be the works of a race o
men actuated by the same motives and feelings as ourselves, an
the phenomena of their arts do not seem difficult of explanation.

It is because I have spent the greater part of my life in studying
the architecture of all nations, and through all ages, that I believe
myself entitled to express an opinion on the perplexed question
connected with megalithic remains, though it differs widely from
that generally received, and that I dare to face the objection
which is sure to be raised that my work is based on too narrow
an induction, and that I have overlooked the evidences o
primæval man which exist everywhere. It is not, however
that I have neglected either the evidence from the drift
or from the caves, but that I have rejected them as irre
levant, and because I can hardly trace any connexion between
them and the megalithic remains, to the investigation o
which this work is specially devoted. I have also purposely
put on one side all reference to hut circles, Picts' houses
brochs, and other buildings composed of smaller stones, which
are generally mixed up with the big stone monuments. I
have done this, not because I doubt that many of these may
be coeval, but because their age being doubtful also, it would
only confuse and complicate the argument to introduce them, and
because, whenever the age of the great stones is determined these
minor monuments will easily fit into their proper places. At
present, neither their age or use throws any light either for
or against that of the great stones.

It need hardly be remarked, to anyone who knows anything
about the subject, that the difficulties in the way of writing
such a book as this are enormous, and I do not believe any
one could, in a first edition at all events, avoid all the pitfalls
that surround his path. The necessary information has to be
picked up in fragments from some hundreds of volumes of
travels, or the Transactions and Journals of learned Societies,
none of which are specially devoted to the subject, and very

few of which are indexed, or have any general résumé of their contents. Add to this that the older works are all untrustworthy, either from the theories they are twisted to support, or from bad drawing or imperfect knowledge; and too many of the modern examples are carelessly sketched and still more carelessly engraved. Another source of difficulty is, that it is rare with readers of papers and writers in journals to quote references, and sometimes when these are given they are wrong. I have thus been forced to limit the field from which my information is taken very considerably. I have tried hard to introduce no illustration I could not thoroughly depend upon, and I have not intentionally quoted a single reference I had not verified from the original authorities.

In one respect I cannot but feel that I may have laid myself open to hostile criticism. On many minor points I have offered suggestions which I do not feel sure that I could prove if challenged, and which, consequently, a more prudent man would have left alone. I have done this because it often happens that such suggestions turn the attention of others to points which would otherwise be overlooked, and may lead to discoveries of great importance; while if disproved, they are only so much rubbish swept out of the path of truth, and their detection can do no harm to any one but their author. Whatever my shortcomings, I am too much in earnest to look forward with any feelings of dismay to such a contingency.

Besides the usual motives which prompt the publication of such a work as this, there are two which seem to render its appearance at this time particularly desirable. The first is to promote enquiry by exciting interest in the subject; the second is to give precision to future researches. So long as everything is vague and mythical, explorers do not know what to observe or record: this work, however, presents a distinct and positive view of the age or use of the megalithic remains, and every new fact must tend either to upset or confirm the theory it seeks to establish. With this view, I need hardly add that I shall be extremely grateful for any new

facts or additional sources of information which may be communicated to me, either through the public press or privately. Numerous persons having local experience must know many things which
may have escaped me. It is very probable that these may induce
me to modify some of the details of this work; but so much is
now known, and the field from which my inductions are gathered
is so wide, that I have no fear that they will touch the main
arguments on which the theory of this work is founded.[1]

However this may be, I trust that this work may lay claim
to being, in one respect at least, a contribution to the cause of
truth regarding the much-disputed age and use of these Rude
Stone Monuments. It states distinctly and without reserve one
view of the mooted question, and so openly that any one who
knows better can at once pull away the prop from my house of
cards and level it with the ground. If one thing comes out more
clearly than another in the course of this investigation, it is that
the style of architecture to which these monuments belong is a
style, like Gothic, Grecian, Egyptian, Buddhist, or any other. It
has a beginning, a middle, and an end; and though we cannot
yet make out the sequence in all its details, this at least seems
clear—that there is no great hiatus; nor is it that one part is
prehistoric, while the other belongs to historic times. All belong
to the one epoch or to the other. Either it is that Stonehenge
and Avebury and all such are the temples of a race so ancient as
to be beyond the ken of mortal man, or they are the sepulchral
monuments of a people who lived so nearly within the limits of the

---

[1] What is really wanted now is, a
"Megalithic Monument Publication Society." After the meeting of the Prehistoric Congress at Norwich, a committee for this purpose was formed in
conjunction with the Ethnological Society. After several meetings everything was arranged and settled, but,
alas! there were no funds to meet the
necessary expenses, or, at least, risk of
publication, and the whole thing fell
through. To do what is wanted on a
really efficient scale a payment or a gua-
rantee of 1000*l.* would be necessary, and
that is far beyond what is attainable in
this poor country. If it could be obtained, the materials are abundant. Sir
Henry Dryden alone could fill a volume
with the materials he already possesses;
and Lieut. Oliver, Mr. Conwell, and
others, have drawings sufficient to keep
the society at work for a long time.

true historic times that their story can easily be recovered. If this latter view is adopted, the whole, it appears to me, hangs so perfectly together, and presents so complete and so rational an account of all the local or historical facts which are at present known concerning these remains, that I feel great confidence that it must eventually be adopted as the true explanation of the phenomena. If it is it will have this further advantage, that when any serious attempt is made to investigate either the history or the manners and customs of these ancient peoples, it is probable that these megalithic remains will be found to be the best and surest guide.

From the circumstances above detailed, this work would have been a much more meagre production than it is hoped it will be found, had it not been for the kindness of many friends who have assisted me in my undertaking. My chapter on Ireland, for instance, would have been much less full had not Sir W. Wilde, Mr. Eugene Conwell, and Mr. Moore assisted me with illustrations and information; and for my knowledge of Scotch antiquities I owe much to my friend John Stuart, of Edinburgh, while Sir Henry Dryden's invaluable collections have been of the utmost service to me both as regards Scotland and Brittany. Professor Säve and Mr. Hildebrand have materially aided me in Sweden, and M. Riaño in Spain; but the post apparently suppresses any correspondence on archæological subjects with France and Denmark. Without the kindness of Sir Bartle Frere and his elder brother in lending me drawings, or Colonel Collinson in procuring information, my account of the Maltese antiquities would have been very much less satisfactory than it is; and I also owe my best thanks to Mr. Walhouse, of the Madras Civil Service, and Mr. Burgess, of Bombay, for their assistance in respect to Indian antiquities. I have tried in the text to acknowledge my obligations to these and all other parties who have assisted me. If I have omitted any, I trust they will believe it has not been intentionally, but through inadvertence.

For myself, I hope I may be allowed to plead that I have spared no pains in investigating the materials placed at my disposal, and no haste in forming my conclusions; and I may also add, they are by no means those of predilection or that I wished to arrive at. When I first took up the subject, I hoped that the rude stone monuments would prove to be old,—so old, indeed, as to form the "incunabula" of other styles, and that we might thus, by a simple process, arrive at the genesis of styles. Bit by bit that theory has crumbled to pieces as my knowledge increased, and most reluctantly have I been forced to adopt the more prosaic conclusions of the present volume. If, however, this represents the truth, that must be allowed to be an ample compensation for the loss of any poetry which has hitherto hung round the mystery of the Rude Stone Monuments.

Langham Place, Dec. 1, 1871.

CONTENTS.

PAGE

INTRODUCTORY 1

CHAPTER II.

PRELIMINARY OBSERVATIONS. Tumuli—Dolmens—Circles—Avenues
—Menhirs 29

CHAPTER III.

ENGLAND. Avebury and Stonehenge 61

CHAPTER IV.

MINOR ENGLISH ANTIQUITIES. Aylesford—Ashdown—Rollright—
Penrith — Derbyshire — Stanton Drew — Smaller Circles —
Dolmens 116

CHAPTER V.

IRELAND. Moytura—Cemeteries—Boyne—Lough Crew—Clover
Hill—Dolmens 175

CHAPTER VI.

SCOTLAND. Orkney Stone Circles—Orkney Barrows—Maes-Howe
Dragon and Serpent-Knot—Holed Stone of Stennis—Callernish
—Aberdeenshire Circles—Fiddes Hill—Clava Mounds—Stone
at Aberlemmo—Sculptured Stones—Crosses in Isle of Man .. 239

CHAPTER VII.

PAGE

SCANDINAVIA AND NORTH GERMANY. Introductory — Battle-fields
— Harald Hildetand's Tomb — Long Barrows — Tumuli —
Dolmens — Drenthe: Hunebeds   275

CHAPTER VIII.

FRANCE. Introductory — Distribution of Dolmens — Age of Dolmens — Grottes des Fées — Demi-Dolmens — Rocking Stones
— Carnac — Locmariaker — Alignments at Crozon — Age of
the Monuments — What are these Monuments? — They must
be Trophies — Time of the Fight — M. Bertrand's List of
Dolmens in Thirty-one Departments of France   325

CHAPTER IX.

SPAIN, PORTUGAL, AND ITALY. Introductory — Dolmens — Portugal
— Italy   377

CHAPTER X.

ALGERIA AND TRIPOLI. Introductory — Bazinas and Chouchas —
Free-Standing Dolmens — Age of Dolmens — Circle near Bona
— The Nasamones — Origin of African Dolmen-Builders —
Tripoli: Trilithons — Buddhist Monument at Bangkok 395

CHAPTER XI.

MEDITERRANEAN ISLANDS. Malta — Sardinia — Balearic Islands   415

CHAPTER XII.

WESTERN ASIA. Palestine — Sinai — Arabia — Asia Minor — Circassia — The Steppes — Cabul 428

CHAPTER XIII.

PAGE

INDIA. Introductory — Eastern India — Khassia — Western India — Geographical Distribution — Age of the Stone Monuments — Comparison of Dolmens — Buddhism in the West 455

CHAPTER XIV.

AMERICA. North America — Central America — Peru 510

APPENDIX A.—Glens Columbkille and Malin 520

 „ B.—Oden's Howe, &c., Upsala 526

 „ C.—Antiquities of Caithness 527

INDEX 533

(xvii)

LIST OF ILLUSTRATIONS.

FRONTISPIECE.—Standing Stones of Stennis. VIGNETTE.—Demi-Dolmen at Kerland.

NO.		PAGE
1.	Section of Tomb of Alyattes ..	31
2.	Elevation of Tumulus at Tantalais	32
3.	Plan and Section of Chamber in Tumulus at Tantalais	32
4.	Section and Plan of Tomb of Atreus at Mycenæ	33
5.	View of Cocumella, Vulci	33
6.	View of principal Chamber in Regulini Galeassi Tomb	34
7.	Dolmen in Castle Wellan, Ireland	45
8.	Dolmen de Bousquet	46
9.	Tee cut in the Rock on a Dagoba at Ajunta	47
10.	Nine Ladies, Stanton Moor	49
11.	Chambered Tumulus, Jersey ..	51
12.	Avenues, Circles, and Cromlech, near Merivale Bridge, Dartmoor	55
13.	Lochcrist Menhir..	60
14.	View of Avebury restored	62
15.	Plan of Avebury Circle and Kennet Avenue	63
16.	Circle on Hakpen Hill..	76
17.	Section of Silbury Hill	78
18.	Iron Bit of Bridle, Silbury Hill ..	81
19.	Plan of Avebury	81
20.	Elevation of the Bartlow Hills ..	83
21.	Marden Circle	85
22.	General Plan of Stonehenge ..	90
23.	Stonehenge as at present existing	92
24.	Plan of Stonehenge restored ..	93
25.	Tomb of Isidorus, at Khatoura ..	100
26.	Country around Stonehenge ..	102
27.	Countless Stones, Aylesford ..	117
28.	The Sarsen Stones at Ashdown ..	122
29.	Sketch Plan of King Arthur's Round Table, with the side, obliterated by the road, restored	128
30.	Arbor Low	140
31.	Vases and Bronze Pin found in Arbor Low	141
32.	Section of Gib Hill	141
33.	Summit of Minning Low, as it appeared in 1786	142
34.	Plan of Chambers in Minning Low	143
35.	Fragment of Drinking Cup from Benty Grange	145

NO.		PAGE
36.	Fragment of Helmet from Benty Grange	145
37.	Circles at Stanton Drew	149
38.	View of the Circles at Stanton Drew	150
39.	Rose Hill Tumulus	155
40.	Snaffle-Bit found at Aspatria ..	156
41.	Side Stone, Aspatria Cist	157
42.	Mule Hill, Isle of Man, View of Cists	158
43.	Circle of Cists at Mule Hill ..	158
44.	Circles on Burn Moor, in Cumberland	160
45.	Boscawen Circles	161
46.	Park Cwn Tumulus	164
47.	Tumulus, Plas Newydd	167
48.	Entrance to Dolmen, in Tumulus, Plas Newydd	167
49.	Dolmen at Pentre Ifan	168
50.	Dolmen at Plas Newydd	169
51.	Arthur's Quoit, Gower	170
52.	Plan of Arthur's Quoit	171
53.	Hob Hurst's House, on Baslow Moor, Derbyshire	172
54.	Circle on Battle-field of Southern Moytura..	177
55.	Cairn on Battle-field of Southern Moytura..	178
56.	The Cairn of the "One Man," Moytura	179
57.	Urn in the Cairn of the "One Man," Moytura	179
58.	Battle-field of Northern Moytura	181
59.	Sketch Plan of Circle 27, Northern Moytura	182
60.	View of Circle 27, Northern Moytura	183
61.	Dolmen, with Circle, No. 7, Northern Moytura	183
62.	Rath na Riog, or, Cathair of Cormac, at Tara	194
63.	View of Mound at New Grange ..	201
64.	New Grange, near Drogheda ..	203
65, 66.	Ornaments at New Grange ..	206
67.	Branch at New Grange	207
68.	Sculptured mark at New Grange, of undecided character	207

NO.		PAGE
69.	Chambers in Mound at Dowth ..	208
70, 71.	Ornaments in Dowth	211
72.	Cairn T, at Lough Crew	214
73.	The Hag's Chair, Lough Crew ..	215
74.	Two Stones in Cairn T, Lough Crew	216
75.	Cell in Cairn L, at Lough Crew	217
76.	Stone in Cairn T, Lough Crew ..	222
77.	Stones in Sculptured Graves, Clover Hill	223
78.	Dolmen at Knockeen	229
79.	Plan of Dolmen at Knockeen ..	230
80.	Calliagh Birra's House, north end of Parish of Monasterboice ..	230
81.	Plan and Section of Chamber in Greenmount Tumulus	232
82.	Dolmen of the Four Maols, Ballina	233
83.	Sketch-Plan of Monument in the Deer Park, Sligo	234
84.	Circle at Stennis	242
85.	Dragon in Maes-Howe	245
86.	Wurm-Knot, Maes-Howe	245
87.	Plan and Section of Maes-Howe	246
88.	View of Chamber in Maes-Howe	247
89.	Monument at Callernish	259
90.	Circle at Fiddes Hill	264
91.	Plan of Clava Mounds	266
92.	View of Clava Mounds	266
93.	Stone at Coilsfield	267
94.	Front of Stone at Aberlemmo, with Cross	268
95.	Back of Stone at Aberlemmo ..	269
96.	Cat Stone, Kirkliston	272
97, 98.	Crosses in Isle of Man, bearing Runic Inscriptions	273
99.	View of Battle-field at Kongs-backa	279
100.	Part of the Battle-field of Braavalla Heath	281
101.	Harald Hildetand's Tomb at Lethra	282
102.	Long Barrow, Kennet, restored by Dr. Thurnam	284
103.	Long Barrow at Wiskehärad, in Halland	288
104.	Battle-field at Freyrsö	292
105.	Dragon on King Gorm's Stone, Jellinge	296
106.	Dolmen at Herrestrup	303
107.	Dolmen at Halskov	305
108.	Dolmen at Oroust	306
109.	Diagram from Sjöborg	307
110.	Dolmen near Lüneburg	308
111.	Double Dolmen at Valdbygaards	309
112.	Plan of Double Dolmen at Valdbygaards	309
113.	Triple Dolmen, Höbisch	309
114.	View of Interior of Chamber at Uby	311
115.	Plan of Chamber at Uby	311
116.	Dolmen at Axevalla	313
117.	Head-stone of Kivik Grave ..	314
118.	Graves at Hjortehammer	316
119.	Circles at Aschenrade	317
120.	Plan of Hunebed near Emmen ..	320
121.	Dolmen at Ballo	321
122.	Dolmen at Sauclières	335
123.	Dolmen at Confolens	337
124.	Plan of Dolmen at Confolens ..	337
125.	Dolmen near Mettray	342
126.	Dolmen at Krukenho	342
127.	Holed Dolmen, at Trie	344
128.	Dolmen of Grandmont	344
129.	Demi-dolmen, Morbihan	345
130.	Demi-dolmen, near Poitiers ..	346
131.	Demi-dolmen at Kerland	346
132.	Pierre Martine	347
133.	Pierre Martine, end view	348
134.	Pierre Branlante, near Huelgoat, in Brittany	348
135.	Map of Celtic Antiquities, near Carnac	352
136.	Carnac Antiquities, on enlarged Scale	353
137.	Head of Column at St.-Barbe ..	355
138.	Long Barrow at Kerlescant ..	356
139.	Hole between Two Stones at Kerlescant	357
140.	Entrance to Cell, Rodmarton ..	357
141.	Vases found at Kerlescant ..	357
142.	Plan of Moustoir-Carnac	358
143.	Section of Moustoir-Carnac ..	358
144.	Section of Chamber of Moustoir-Carnac	359
145. 146.	Sculptures at Mané Lud ..	361
147.	View of Dol ar Marchant	361
148.	End Stone, Dol ar Marchant ..	362
149.	Hatchet in Roof of Dol ar Marchant	362
150.	Stone found inside Chamber at Mané er H'roëk	364
151.	Plan of Gavr Innis	364
152.	Sculptures at Gavr Innis	365
153.	Holed Stone, Gavr Innis	365
154.	Alignments at Crozon	367
155.	View of the Interior of Dolmen at Antequera	383
156.	Plan of Dolmen called Cueva de Menga, near Antequera	384
157.	Dolmen del Tio Cogolleros.. ..	385
158.	Sepultura Grande	386
159.	Plan of Dolmen at Eguilar ..	387

NO.		PAGE
160.	Plan of Dolmen at Cangas de Onis	387
161.	Dolmen of San Miguel, at Arrichinaga	388
162.	Dolmen at Arroyolos	389
163.	Dolmen at Saturnia	392
164.	Bazina	397
165.	Choucha	398
166.	Dolmen on Steps	398
167.	Tumuli, with Intermediate Lines of Stones	399
168.	Group of Sepulchral Monuments, Algeria	399
169.	Plan and Elevation of African Tumulus	400
170.	Dolmen with Two Circles of Stones	401
171.	Dolmens on the Road from Bona to Constantine	402
172.	Four Cairns enclosed in Squares	402
173.	Tombs near Djidjeli	404
174.	Circle near Bona	405
175.	Trilithon at Ksaea	411
176.	Trilithon at Elkeb	412
177.	Buddhist Monument at Bangkok	413
178.	Giants' Tower at Gozo	417
179.	Plan of Monument of Mnaidra	419
180.	Section through Lower Pair of Chambers, Mnaidra	419
181.	Entrance to Chamber B, Mnaidra, showing Table inside	420
182.	North End of Left-hand Outer Chamber at Mnaidra	421
183.	Plan of Hagiar Khem, partially restored	423
184.	View of Madracen	424
185.	Nurhag	428
186.	Nurhag of Santa Barbara	428
187.	Section and Ground-plan of Nurhag of Santa Barbara	429
188.	Map of La Giara	430
189.	Talyot at Trepucò, Minorca	435
190.	Talyot at Alajor, Minorca	435
191.	Dolmens at Kafr er Wâl	441
192.	Holed Dolmen	447
193.	Holed Dolmen, Circassia	447
194.	Baba	449
195.	Four-cornered Grave	449
196.	Tumulus at Alexandropol	450

NO.		PAGE
197.	Uncovered Base of a Tumulus at Nikolajew	451
198.	Circle near Peshawur	452
199.	Circle at Deh Ayeh, near Darabgerd	453
200.	View in Khassia Hills	462
201.	Khassia Funereal Seats	463
202.	Menhirs and Tables	464
203.	Turban Stone, with Stone Table	464
204.	Trilithon	464
205.	Dolmen at Rajunkoloor	468
206.	Plan of Open Dolmen at Rajunkoloor	469
207.	Closed Dolmen at Rajunkoloor	469
208.	View of Closed Dolmen at Rajunkoloor	469
209.	Arrangement of Dolmens at Rajunkoloor	470
210.	Cairns at Jewurgi	471
211, 212.	Sections of Cairn at Jewurgi	471
213.	Double Dolmen, Coorg	473
214.	Tomb, Nilgiri Hills	473
215.	Sepulchral Circles at Amravati	474
216.	Iron Pillar at the Kutub, Delhi	481
217.	Sculpture on under side of capstone of Nilgiri Dolmen	483
218.	Dolmen at Iwullee	484
219.	Plan of Stone Monuments at Shahpoor	485
220.	Cross at Katapur	486
221.	Dolmen at Katapur	487
222.	Dolmen with Cross in Nirmul Jungle	488
223.	Lanka Ramayana Dagoba	490
224.	Dolmen at Pullicondah	491
225.	Rail at Sanchi, near Bhilsa	492
226.	View of the Senbya Pagoda, Burmah	497
227.	Enclosure in Newark Works, North America	511
228.	Plan of Uprights, Cromlech D I., Columbkille	521
229.	Position of Stones of D III.	522
230.	Plan of D VI.	522
231.	Plan of Cromlechs of Group E.	523
232.	Horned Cairn, Caithness	528
233.	Dolmen near Bona, Algeria	532

DIRECTION TO BINDER.

The MAP illustrating the distribution of Dolmens to be placed at the end of the Volume.

RUDE STONE MONUMENTS.

INTRODUCTORY.

So great and so successful has been the industry recently applied to subjects of archæological research that few of the many problems in that science which fifty years ago seemed hopelessly mysterious now remain unsolved. Little more than forty years have elapsed since Champollion's discoveries enabled us to classify and understand the wonderful monuments of the Nile Valley. The deciphering of the cuneiform characters has in like manner enabled us to arrange and affix dates to the temples and palaces of Babylon and Nineveh. Everything that was built by the Greeks and the Romans has been surveyed and illustrated; and all the mediæval styles that arose out of them have been reduced to intelligible sequences. The rock-cut temples of India, and her still more mysterious dagobas, have been brought within the domain of history, and, like those of Burmah, Cambodia, or China, shown to be of comparatively modern date. The monuments of Mexico and Peru may be said still to defy those who are endeavouring to wrest their secrets from them; but even for these a fairly approximate date has been obtained. But amidst all these triumphs of well-directed research there still remain a great group of monuments at our own doors, regarding whose uses or dates opinions are nearly as much divided as they were in the days of rampant empiricism in the last century. It is true that men of science do not now pretend to see Druids sacrificing their bleeding victims on the altar at Stonehenge, nor to be able to trace the folds of the divine serpent through miles of upright stones at Carnac or at Avebury; but all they have yet achieved is simple unbelief in the popular fallacies, nor have they hitherto ventured to supply anything better to take

B

their places. They still call the circles temples, but without being able to suggest to what god they were dedicated, or for what rites they were appropriate, and, when asked as to the age in which they were erected, can only reply in the words of the song, that it was "long long ago."

This state of affairs is eminently unsatisfactory, but at the same time to a great extent excusable. Indeed it is not at first sight easy to see how it is to be remedied. The builders of the megalithic remains were utterly illiterate, and have left no written records of their erection; nor are there any legible inscriptions on the more important monuments which would afford any hints to the enquirer. What is even more disheartening is that in almost every instance they are composed of rough unhewn stones, not only without any chisel marks, but even without any architectural mouldings capable of being compared with those of other monuments, or, by their state of preservation, of giving a hint as to their relative age.

"They stand, but stand in silent and uncommunicative majesty."

So silent, indeed, that it is hardly to be wondered at that fanciful antiquaries have supplied them with voices most discordantly and absurdly various, or, on the other hand, that the better class of enquirers have shrunk from the long patient investigations and thoughtful ponderings which are necessary to elicit even a modicum of truth from their stolid reticence.

If the investigation into the age and uses of the megalithic remains were a new subject which had for the first time been taken up some thirty or forty years ago, it is probable that a solution might have been obtained before now, or at all events would not be far off. When, however, an investigation gets into a thoroughly vicious groove, as this one has done, it is very difficult to rescue it from its false position. The careless are willing to accept any empirical solutions that are offered, however absurd they may be, and the thoughtful are deterred from meddling with an enquiry which has hitherto led only to such irrational conclusions.

The first of those who, in this country at least, led off the wild dance was the celebrated Inigo Jones, the architect of Whitehall.

It seems that when King James I. was on a visit to the Earl of Pembroke at Wilton, he was taken to see Stonehenge, and was so struck with its majesty and mystery that he ordered his architect to find out by whom it was built, and for what purpose. Whether the treatise containing the result of his enquiries was ever submitted to the King is not clear. It certainly was not published till after its author's death, and though it shows a very creditable amount of learning and research, the results he arrived at were very startling. After a detailed statement of the premises, his conclusions—as condensed in the Life prefixed to his treatise—were " That it was a Roman temple, inscribed to Cœlus, the senior of the heathen gods, and built after the Tuscan order."

This theory was attacked by Dr. Charleton, one of the physician of Charles II. He had corresponded for some time with Olaus Wormius, the celebrated Danish antiquary, and struck with the similarity in form and of construction that existed between the monuments in Denmark and those of this country, he came to the conclusion that Stonehenge and other similar monuments were erected by the Danes, and consequently after the departure of the Romans. This attack on the theory of Inigo Jones raised the wrath of a Mr. Webb, by marriage a relative, who replied in a very angry treatise, in which he reiterates all Jones's arguments, and then, adding a considerable number of his own, he concludes by triumphantly—as he supposes—restoring Stonehenge to the Romans.[1]

So far no great harm was done; but Dr. Stukeley, who next appeared in the controversy, was one of the most imaginative of men and one of the wildest of theorists. His studies had made him familiar with the Druids, whom classical authorities describe as the all-powerful priests of the Celtic race, but who had no temples; on the other hand, his travels made him acquainted with Stonehenge and Avebury, to the latter of which attention had just been called by the researches of his friend Aubrey. Here, then, were temples without priests. What could be so natural as to join

---

[1] These three treatises were afterwards republished in one volume, small folio, with all the plates, &c., in London, 1725. It is from this volume that the above is abstracted.

these two, though in most unholy matrimony. Our stone circles must be temples of the Druids! But there was still one difficulty. What divinities did they worship therein? Cæsar tells us that the Celts or Celtic Druids principally worshipped Mercury and some other Roman gods whom he named;[1] but no images of these gods are found in these temples, nor anything that would indicate a dedication to their worship. Unfortunately, however, Pliny[2] tells a very silly tale, how in Gaul the snakes meet together on a certain day and manufacture from their spittle an egg (*Anguinum*), which, when complete, they throw aloft, and if any one wants it, he must catch it in a blanket before it falls to the ground, and ride off with it on a fleet horse, for if the snakes catch him before he crosses a running stream, a worse fate than Tam o' Shanter's may befall him! He then goes on to add that this egg was considered as a charm by the Druids. From this last hint Dr. Stukeley concluded that the Druids were serpent-worshippers, and consequently that Stonehenge, Avebury, &c., were serpent temples—Dracontia, as he calls them, daringly assuming that a word, which in the singular was only the name of a plant, was actually applied by the ancients to serpent temples, of the form of which, however, they were as ignorant as the Doctor himself. Having advanced so far, it only remained to adapt the English circles to this newly discovered form of worship, and Avebury was chosen as the principal illustration. There was a small circle on Hakpen Hill, which had a stone avenue formed by six or eight stones running east and west; between West Kennet and Avebury there was another avenue leading to the circles, but trending north and south. By introducing a curved piece between these fragments, Hakpen became the head of the snake, the avenue its body; Avebury a convoluted part of it, and then a tail was added, a mile long, on the authority of two stones in the village, and a dolmen, called Long Stone Cove, about half-way between Avebury and the end of the tail! Stanton Drew and other circles were treated in the same way; curved avenues, for which there is not a shadow of authority, except in the Doctor's imagination, were added wherever required, and serpents manufactured wherever

---

[1] Cæsar, 'De Bell. Gal.' vi. 13-20.   [2] 'Hist. Nat.' xxix. 3

wanted. It never seems even to have occurred to the Doctor or his contemporaries to ask whether, in any time or place, any temple was ever built in the form of the gods to be worshipped therein or thereat, or how any human being could discover the form of the serpent in rows of stones stretching over hills and valleys, crossing streams, and hid occasionally by mounds and earthworks. On a map, with the missing parts supplied, this is easy enough; but there were no maps in those days, and in the open country it would puzzle even the most experienced surveyors to detect the serpent's form.

Had so silly a fabrication been put forward in the present day, it probably would have met with the contempt it deserves; but the strangest part of the whole is that it was then accepted as a revelation. Even so steady and so well informed an antiquary as Sir Richard Colt Hoare adopts Dr. Stukeley's views without enquiry. His magnificent works on 'Ancient and Modern Wiltshire,' which are not only the most splendid, but the most valuable works of their class which this country owes to the liberality and industry of any individual, are throughout disfigured by this one great blemish. He sees Druids and their Dragons everywhere, and never thinks of enquiring on what authority their existence rests.

It is not of course for one moment meant to contend that there were not Druids in Europe in ancient days. Cæsar's testimony on this point is too distinct, and his knowledge was too accurate to admit of any doubt on this point. It is true, however, that the description of them given by Diodorus,[1] and Strabo,[2] who mix them up with the bards and soothsayers, detracts somewhat from the pre-eminence he assigns to them : but this is of minor importance. The Druids were certainly the priests of the Celts, and had their principal seat in the country of the Carnutes, near Chartres, where, however, megalithic remains are few and far between. Neither Cæsar, however, nor any one else, ever pretended to have seen a Druid in England. Suetonius met "Druidæ" in the Island of Anglesea (Mona),[3] but none were ever heard of in Wiltshire, or Derbyshire, or Cumberland, where the principal monuments are

---

[1] 'Historia,' v. 31.   [2] 'Geographica,' iv. 273.   [3] Tacitus, 'Ann.' xiv. 29.

situated; nor in the Western Islands, or in Scandinavia. Still less are they known in Algeria or India, where these megalithic remains abound. According to the Welsh bards and Irish annalists, there were Druids in Wales and Ireland before the introduction of Christianity. But, even admitting this, it does not help us much; as even there they are nowhere connected with the class of monuments of which we are now treating. Indeed, it has been contended lately, and with a considerable show of reason, that the Celts themselves, even in France, had nothing to do with these monuments, and that they belong to an entirely different race of people.[1] It is not, in short, at all necessary to deny either the existence of the Druids or their power. The real difficulty is to connect them in any way, directly or indirectly, with the stone monuments: and it seems still more difficult to prove that the Celts ever worshipped the serpent in any shape or form.[2]

Notwithstanding all this, in the present century, an educated gentleman and a clergyman of the Church of England, the Rev. Bathurst Deane, adopts unhesitatingly all that Stukeley and his school had put forward. He took the trouble of going to Brittany, accompanied by a competent surveyor, and made a careful plan of the alignments of Carnac.[3] Like the avenues at Avebury, they certainly bore no resemblance to serpent forms, to eyes profane, but looked rather like two straight lines running nearly parallel to one another at a distance of about two miles apart. But may not an intermediate curvilinear piece some three miles long have existed in the gap and so joined the head to the tail? It is in vain to urge that no trace of it now exists, or to ask how any human being could trace the forms of serpents seven or eight miles long in an undulating country, and how or in what manner, or to what part of this strange deity or monster, he was to address his prayers.

It would be incorrect, however, to represent all antiquaries as

---

[1] See controversy between M. Bertrand and M. Henri Martin, in volume of 'Congrès préhistorique' (Paris, 1867), 193, 207, &c. See also 'Revue archéologique,' août, 1864, 144.

[2] For further information on the subject, the reader is referred to ' Tree and Serpent Worship,' by the author, p. 26 et seqq., where the subject is treated of at length.

[3] ' Archæologia,' xxv. 188 et seqq.

adopting the Ophite heresy. Another group have argued stoutly that Stonehenge was an observatory of the British Druids. This theory was apparently suggested by views published by Daniell and others of the observatories erected by Jey Sing of Jeypore at Delhi, Ougein, Benares, and elsewhere in India. All these, it is true, possess great circles, but each of all these circles contains a gnomon, which is as essential a part of such an astronomical instrument as it is of a sun-dial, and no trace of such a feature, it need hardly be said, occurs in any British circle. One antiquary, who ought to be better informed,[1] concluded that Stonehenge was an observatory, because, sitting on a stone called the Altar on a Midsummer morning, he saw the sun rise behind a stone called the Friar's Heel. This is the only recorded observation ever made there, so far as I know; and if this is all, it is evident that any two stones would have answered the purpose equally well, and as the Altar stone is sixteen feet long, it allows a latitude of observation that augurs ill for the Druidical knowledge of the exact sciences. Neither Mr. Ellis, however, nor Dr. Smith, nor the Rev. Mr. Duke,[2] nor indeed any of those who have taken up the astronomical theory, have yet pointed out one single observation that could be made by these circles that could not be made as well or better without them. Or, if they were orreries, as is sometimes pretended, no one has explained what they record or represent in any manner that would be intelligible to any one else. Till some practical astronomer will come forward and tell us in intelligible language what observations could be performed with the aid of the circles of Stonehenge, we may be at least allowed to pause. Even, however, in that case, unless his theory will apply to Avebury, Stanton Drew, and other circles so irregular as to be almost unmeasurable, it will add little to our knowledge.

It might be an amusing, though it certainly must be a profitless, task to enlarge on these and all the other guesses which have from time to time been made with regard to these mysterious remains. It is not, however, probable that theories so utterly

---

[1] Mr. Ellis, 'Gent. Mag.' 4th series, ii. 317.
[2] 'Proceedings of the Archæological Institute, Salisbury,' volume 113.

groundless will be put forward again, or, if promulgated, that they
will be listened to in future. The one excuse for them hitherto
has been that their authors have been deprived of all their usual
sources of information in this matter. It is not too much to assert
that there is not one single passage in any classical author which
can be construed as alluding directly or indirectly to the megalithic remains on these isles or on the continent. With all their
learning and industry, the antiquaries of the last century could
only find one passage which, with all their misapplied ingenuity,
they could pervert to their purposes. It was this—in his second
book, Diodorus, quoting from Hecatæus, mentions that in an island,
not less in size than Sicily, and opposite to Celtica, there existed
among the Hyperboreans a circular temple magnificently adorned.[1]
Stukeley and his followers immediately jumped to the conclusion
that the island not less than Sicily and opposite Gaul must be
England, and the circular temple Stonehenge, which was consequently dedicated to Apollo and the serpent Python, and our
forefathers were the Hyperboreans, and our intercourse with
Greece clear and frequent. It is marvellous what a super-
structure was raised on such a basis. But against it may be
urged that the whole of the second book of Diodorus is dedicated
solely to a description of Asia. In the preceding chapter he
describes the Amazons, who, if they ever existed, certainly lived
in that quarter of the globe. In the following chapters he
describes Arabia, and even in this one (xlvii.) he speaks of the
Hyperboreans as inhabiting the northern parts of Asia. By
the utmost latitude of interpretation we might assume this
island to have been in the Baltic—Œsel probably, Gothland
possibly, but certainly not further west. It is impossible Diodorus
could be mistaken in the matter, for in his fifth book he
describes the British Isles in their proper place, and with a
very considerable degree of accuracy.[2] But, after all, what does
it amount to? In this island there was a circular temple. We are
not told whether it was of wood or of stone, whether hypæthral, or
roofed, or vaulted, and certainly there is not a shadow of a hint
that it was composed of a circle of rude stones like those in this

---

[1] Diodorus, ii. 47.   [2] Ibid. v. 21 *et seqq.*

country with which the antiquaries of the last century tried to assimilate it.

It is little to be wondered at if all this rashness of speculation and carelessness in quotation should have produced a belief that the solution of the problem was impossible from any literary or historical data, or if consequently our modern antiquaries should have grasped with avidity at a scheme, first proposed by the Danes, which seemed at all events to place the question on a scientific basis. No country could well be more favourably situated for an enquiry of this sort than Denmark. It is rich in megalithic remains of all sorts. Its tumuli and tombs seem generally to have been undisturbed; and it was exceptionally fortunate in having a government with sufficient common sense to enact a law of treasure-trove, so just and, at the same time, so liberal as to prevent all metal articles from finding their way to the melting pot, and governors so intelligent as fully to appreciate the scientific value of these early remains. In consequence of all this, the museums at Copenhagen were soon filled with one of the richest collections of antiquities of this sort that was ever collected, and when brought together it was not difficult to perceive the leading features that connected them in one continuous sequence.

First it appeared that there was an age extending into far pre-historic times, when men used only implements of stone and bone, and were ignorant of the use of any of the metals; then that an age had succeeded to this when the use of bronze was known, and also probably that of gold; and, lastly, that there was a third age, when iron had been introduced and had superseded the use of all other metals for weapons of war and utilitarian purposes.

The Danish antiquaries were somewhat divided in opinion as to the exact period when bronze was first introduced, some carrying it back as far as 2000 B.C., others doubting whether it was known in Denmark more than 1000 or 1200 years B.C.; but all agreed that iron was introduced about the Christian era. Having satisfied themselves on these points, the Danish antiquaries proceeded at once to apply this system to the monuments of their country. Any tomb or tumulus which was devoid of any trace of metal was dated at once at least 1000, probably 2000, years before Christ, and might be 10,000, or 20,000 years old, or even still older. Any tomb containing bronze was at once set down as dating between the war of Troy and the Christian era; and if a trace of iron was detected, it was treated as subsequent to the last-named epoch, but still as anterior to the introduction of Christianity, which in Denmark dates about the year 1000 A.D.

This system seemed so reasonable and philosophical, compared with the wild theories of the British antiquaries of the last century, that it was instantly adopted both in the country of its birth and in England and France; and the succession of the three ages—stone, bronze, and iron—was generally looked upon as firmly established as any fact in chronology. Gradually, however, it has been perceived that the hard and fast line at first drawn between them cannot be maintained. At the last meeting of the International Archæological Congress, held at Copenhagen in the autumn of 1869, it was admitted on all hands that there was a considerable overlap between each of the three ages. Men did not immediately cease to use stone implements when bronze was introduced; and bronze continued to be employed for many purposes after the use of iron was well known.[1] Antiquaries have not yet made up their minds to what extent the overlap took place; but on its determination depends the whole value of the scheme as a chronometric scale.

If the Danes, instead of breaking up their "finds" and distributing them in cases according to a pre-conceived system, had kept and published a careful record of the places where the contents of their museums were found, and in what juxtaposition, we should not probably be in our present difficulty. Under the circumstances, it is perhaps fortunate that we had no central museum, but that our antiquaries have published careful narratives of their proceedings. Sir Richard Colt Hoare's great works are models of their class, but are scarcely to be depended upon

---

[1] The volume containing the account of the proceedings of the congress has not yet been published; so those who were not present cannot feel sure to what extent these modifications were carried or admitted. A short account of the Congress was published by Gen. Lefroy, in the 'Journal of the Archæological Institute,' Nov. 1869, p. 58 *et seqq.*

in the present instance, as the importance of flint and flint implements was not appreciated in his time to the extent it now is.[1] The explorations of the Messrs. Bateman in Derbyshire are more completely up to the mark of the science of the present day. A few extracts from one of their works will show how various and how mixed the contents of even a single group of tombs are, and will prove consequently how little dependence can be placed on any one class of objects to fix the age of these monuments.

In his 'Vestiges of the Antiquities of Derbyshire,' published in 1848 by Thomas Bateman, we find the following among other interesting facts, taking them as they are found arranged in his volume, without any attempt at classification :—

On Winster Moor (p. 20), a gold Greek cross—undoubtedly Christian, with a fibula of the same metal richly ornamented, and a quantity of glass and metal ornaments.

Pegges Barrow (p. 24). Several Anglo-Saxon ornaments, most probably of the seventh or eighth century.

In a barrow at Long Roods (p. 28) were found two urns, with calcined bones and a brass coin of Constantine, of the type " Gloria exercitus."

In Haddon Field Barrow (p. 30) were found 82 brass coins : among them Constantine 9, Constans 17, Constantius II. 9, family of Constantine 3, Urbs Roma 1, Constantinopolis 2, Valentinian 5, Valens 12, Gratian 3. The remainder illegible.

At Gib Hill, near Arbor Low (p. 31), of which more hereafter, there were found a flint arrow-head $2\frac{1}{2}$ inches long, and a fragment of a basaltic celt ; also a small iron fibula, and another piece of iron of indeterminable form.

On Cross Flatts (p. 35) the weapons found with the skeleton were an iron knife, the blade 5 inches long ; a piece of roughly chipped flint, probably a spear-head ; and a natural piece of stone of remarkable form. A similar iron knife and a stone celt were

---

[1] "According to an analysis made by Sir John Lubbock, of the contents of 250 tumuli described by Sir Richard Colt Hoare, in the first volume of his 'Ancient Wiltshire,' 18 only had any implements of stone, only 31 of bone, 67 of bronze, and 11 of iron, while one-half of them contained nothing to indicate their age ; but whether those that contained nothing are earlier or more modern is by no means clear."—*Prehistoric Times*, 2nd edit. p. 131.

afterwards found within a few yards of the barrow, probably thrown out and overlooked when first opened.

In Galley Lowe (p. 37), a very beautiful gold necklace set with garnets, and a coin of Honorius; but towards the outer edge of the Lowe, and consequently, as far as position goes, probably later, another interment, accompanied with rude pottery, a small arrow-head of grey flint, and a piece of ironstone.

In the great barrow at Minning Lowe (p. 39) were found coins of Claudius Gothicus, Constantine the Great, Constantine Junior, and Valentinian.

In a smaller barrow close by were found fragments of a coarse, dark-coloured urn, a flint arrow-head, a small piece of iron, part of a bridle-bit, and several horses' teeth ; lower down, a cist with an iron knife, with an iron sheath ; and on the outer edge another interment, accompanied by a highly ornamented drinking-cup, a small brass or copper pin, and a rude spear or arrow-head of dark grey flint.

In Borther Lowe (p. 48) were found a flint arrow-head much burnt and a diminutive bronze celt.

In Rolley Lowe (p. 55) were found a brass coin of Constantine, and a brass pin $2\frac{3}{4}$ inches long; and lower down a rude but highly ornamented urn, and with it two very neat arrow-heads of flint of uncommon forms; and in another part of the barrow a spear-head of coarse flint, with the fragments of an ornamented drinking-cup.

In a barrow on Ashford Moor (p. 57) were found, scattered in different parts, a small iron arrow-head and five instruments of flint.

In Carder Lowe (p. 63) were found several instruments of flint, amongst the latter a neatly formed barbed arrow-head; and lower down, with the primary interment, a splendid brass or bronze dagger; a few inches lower down a beautiful axe hammer-head of basalt. In another part of the barrow another interment was discovered, accompanied by an iron knife and three hones of sand-stone.

A barrow was opened at New Inns (p. 66), where, along with the principal interment, was found a beautiful brass dagger, with smaller rivets than usual; and in another part a skeleton, with two instruments of flint, and some animal teeth.

In Net Lowe (p. 68), close to the right arm of the principal interment, a large dagger of brass, with the decorations of its handle, consisting of thirty brass rivets; two studs of Kimmeridge coal. With the above-mentioned articles were numerous fragments of calcined flint, and amongst the soil of the barrow two rude instruments of flint.

At Castern (p. 73), in one part of the mound, an instrument was found, with a fine spear-head of flint, and a small arrow-head of the same. In other parts, but in apparently undisturbed earth, a circular instrument, and various chippings of flint, and the handle of a knife of stag's horn, riveted in the usual way on to the steel. A similar one is figured in Douglas's 'Nenia Britannica,' plate 19, fig. 4, as found with an interment in one of the barrows on Chartham Downs, Kent.

In Stand Lowe (p. 74), on digging towards the centre, numerous flint chippings and six rude instruments were found, and above the same place a broken whetstone. The centre being gained, an iron knife was found of the kind generally attributed to the Saxons. This was immediately followed by a bronze box and a number of buckles, fibulæ, and articles of iron, silver, and glass, all showing the principal interment to have been of very late date. Mr. Bateman adds—"the finding of instruments of flint with an interment of this comparatively modern description is rather remarkable, but by no means unprecedented."

In a barrow midway between Wetton and Ilam (p. 79) with the interment were found three implements of flint of no great interest, some fragments of an ornamented urn, and an iron pin, similar to the awl used by saddlers at the present day. Mr. Bateman adds—"one precisely similar was found in a barrow on Middleton Moor in 1824."

In a second barrow near the same place were found the remains of a coarse and rudely ornamented urn with its deposit of burnt bones. A third brass coin of Constantine the Great was also found on the summit, just under the surface.

In Come Lowe (p. 95), with an interment of a very late period, were found gold and iron ornaments and glass beads, as well as the usual chippings of flint and rats' bones.

In Dowe Lowe (p. 96) the most remote interment consisted of

two much decayed skeletons lying on the floor of the barrow about two yards from its centre; one was accompanied by a fluted brass dagger placed near the upper bone of the arm, and an amulet of iron ore with a large flint implement, which had seen good service, lying near the pelvis.

The other tumuli examined by this indefatigable explorer either contained objects generally of the same class or nothing that was of interest as marking their age. If his other works, or those of others, were abstracted in the same way, numerous examples of the same sort might be adduced. The above, however, are probably sufficient to show how little reliance can be placed on the hard and fast distinction between the flint, bronze, and iron ages which have hitherto been supposed to govern every determination of age in this science. If in a hundred short pages of one man's work so many instances of overlapping, and, indeed, of reversal of the usual order of things, can be found, it is easy to understand how many might be added if other works were also examined. All, however, that is wanted here is to show that the Danish system is neither perfect nor final, and that we must look for some other means of ascertaining the age of these monuments if we are to come to a satisfactory conclusion regarding them.

The fact is that, though a tomb containing only stone and bone implements may be 10,000 or 20,000 years old, unless it can also be shown that stone and bone were no longer used after the Christian era, it may also be as modern, or more so, than that epoch. Unless, also, it can be proved that stone implements were never used after iron was introduced, or that bronze was never employed down to a late period, this system is of no avail; and after the examples just quoted from the Bateman diggings, it seems the merest empiricism to assume that the use of each class of implements ceased on the introduction of another; and till it can be shown at what date their use did really cease, any argument based on their presence is of very little value. This, however, is a task to which no antiquary has yet applied himself; all have been content to fix the age of the monuments from the assumed age of their contents, empirically determined. It is a far more difficult task, however, to ascertain the age of the contents from that of the monument in which they are found; it is a task that requires an investigation into the history and circumstances of each particular example. With the scant materials that exist, this is by no means easy; but as it seems the only mode by which truth can be arrived at, it is the task to which we propose to devote the following pages; should it prove impossible, we may indeed despair.

It is curious to observe how different would have been the fate of this science, had the Scandinavians followed up the line of investigation commenced by their writers in the sixteenth century. Olaus Magnus, for instance, Archbishop of Upsala, writing in 1555, describes the megalithic remains of Sweden with the sobriety and precision with which a man in the present day might give an account of the cemeteries of Kensal-green or of Scutari. Some, he tells us, marked battle-fields, some family sepulchres, others the graves of greatly distinguished men.[1] In like manner, Olaus Wormius, in 1643, describes the tombs of the kings of Denmark as a writer in the present day might the Plantagenet sepulchres in Westminster Abbey.[2] Neither have any doubt or hesitation about the matter, and though Dr. Charleton was hasty in following this author too implicitly in applying his data to this country, still, so far as I can form an opinion, if that line of research had been steadily followed out, there would now have been as little doubt about the age of Stonehenge, as there is about that of Salisbury Cathedral. Stukeley, however, cut the vessel adrift from the moorings of common sense, and she has since been a derelict tossed about by the winds and waves of every passing fancy, till recently, when an attempt has been made to tow the wreck into the misty haven of prehistoric antiquity. If ever she reaches that nebulous

---

[1] "Veterum Gothorum et Suevorum antiquissimus mos est ut ubi acriores in campis seu montibus instituissent et perfecissent pugnas, illic erectos lapides quasi Egyptiacas pyramides collocare soliti sunt . . . Habent itaque hæc saxa in pluribus locis erecta longitudine x. vel xv. xx. aut xxx. et amplius et latitudine iv. vel vi, pedum, mirabili situ sed mirabiliori ordine et mirabilissimo charactere, ob plurimas rationes collocata literato, rectoque et longo ordine videlicet pugilarum certamina, quadrato, turmas bellantium, et spherico familiarum designantia sepulturas ac cuneato equestrium et pedestrium acies ibidem vel prope fortunatum triumphasse," &c. &c. — *De Gentibus Septentrionalibus*, &c. p. 48.

Or again :—"Quos humi recondere placuit honorabiles statuas lapidum excelsorum prout hodie cernuntur mira compagine in modum altissimæ et latissimæ januæ, sursum transversumque viribus gigantum erecta."—*Ibid.* 49.

[2] 'Danicorum Monumentorum,' libri sex, 22 *et seqq.*

region, she may as well be broken up in despair, as she can be of no further use for human purposes.

Whether this will or will not be her fate must depend on the result of the new impulse which has within the last ten or twelve years been given to the enquiry. Hitherto it seems certainly to be in a direction which, it is to be feared, is not likely to lead to any greater degree of precision in the enquiry. While the Danish "savans" were arranging their collections in the museums at Copenhagen, M. Boucher de Perthes was quietly forming a collection of flint implements from the drift gravels of the valley of the Somme, which far exceeded all hitherto found in antiquity. For many years his discoveries were ridiculed and laughed at, till in 1858 the late Hugh Falconer visited his museum at Abbeville, and being then fresh from his investigations at Kent's Hole and the Gower Caves,[1] he at once saw their value and proclaimed it to the world. Since then it has not been disputed that the flint implements found in the valley of the Somme are the works of man, and that from the position in which they are found their fabricators must have lived at a period on the edge of the glacial epoch, and when the configuration of the continent differed from what it now is, and when probably the British isles were still joined to France. Similar implements have before and since been found in Suffolk,[2] and other parts of England in analogous circumstances, and all allied with a fauna which was extinct in these parts before historic times.[3] If you ask a geologist how long ago the circumstances of the globe were such as these conditions represent, he will answer at once not less than a million of years! But they deal in large figures, and it is not necessary to investigate them now. It was a very long time ago.

Even more interesting than these for our present purposes was

---

[1] 'Memoirs of Hugh Falconer,' by Dr. Murchison, ii. p. 596.

[2] In 1797, Mr. John Frere found flint implements identical with those at Abbeville, and published an account of them, with engravings, in vol. xiii. of the 'Archæologia,' in 1800.

[3] In the first years of the last century a flint implement, together with some bones of the *Elephas primigenus*, were found in an excavation in Gray's Inn Lane. An engraving of it was published in 1715, and the implement itself is now in the British Museum.

the discovery a few years later of human remains in the valleys of the Dordogne and other rivers of the south of France. Here geology does not help us, but climatology does. At that time the climate of the south of France was so cold that the inhabitants of these caves had all the habits of people now dwelling in the Arctic regions. Their principal domestic animal was the reindeer, but they were familiar with the woolly-haired mammoth, the cave bear, and the aurochs. The climate was so cold that they could throw on one side the débris of their feasts, and floor their dwelling with marrow bones and offal without dreading pestilence or even suffering inconvenience. They were, in fact, in every respect, so far as we have the means of judging, identical with the Esquimaux of the present day, and must have inhabited a climate nearly similar to that of Arctic North America. How long ago was this? We know from the pictures in the tombs near the pyramids that the climate of Egypt was the same 5000 or 6000 years ago as it is now, and we have no reason to suppose that, while that of the southern shores of the Mediterranean remained unchanged, the northern would vary in any very different ratio. Clearing of forests may have done something, but never could have accounted for such a change as this. If we take 50,000 or 60,000 years instead of 5000 or 6000, it will not suffice for such a revolution, though geologists will be wroth if we assume only 100,000; as a convenient number this will answer our present purposes.

Having at least this space of time at their disposal, the tendency of modern antiquaries has been to sweep everything into this great gulf. Why, they ask, may not Stonehenge and Avebury be 10,000, 20,000, or 50,000 years old? Man then existed, and why may he not have erected such monuments as these? Of course he might, but there is no proof that he did, and as no single tangible reason has yet been adduced for supposing them so old, the mere presumption that they might be so cannot count for much.

To my mind the force of argument seems to tend the other way. If a race of men lived on the face of the globe for 100,000 years so utterly unprogressive as these cave men, incapable of discovering the use of metals for themselves during that long period, or even of adopting them from Egypt and the East, where bronze certainly, and most probably iron, were known at least 6000 or

7000 years ago; if this people used flint and bone during all this period, is it likely that they would adopt new-fangled implements and new customs the first time they were presented to them? The Esquimaux have been familiar with the Danish settlers in Greenland for some centuries, and could easily have procured improved implements and many of the advantages of civilization had they been so inclined. They have not been changed a hair's-breadth by the influence of the stranger. The red man of North America has been in contact with the white man for centuries now. Has he changed, or can he change? In Alaska, and to the northward of Vancouver's Island, there is a race of savages, called Hydahs, with all the artistic tastes and faculties of the men of the Dordogne caves, and with about the same degree of civilization.[1] All these are dying out, and may soon disappear, but they present at this day exactly the same phenomenon as we see in the south of France, say 10,000 years ago. They have been exterminated in all the civilized parts of Europe by the progressive Aryan races who have usurped their places; and it seems only too certain that, like them, their American kindred must perish before the growing influence of the white man, but they cannot change. In so far as we can judge from such facts as are before us, if any family of this old people still lurked among our hills or on any rocky island, their habits, or customs, and their implements, would be as like those of the cave men as those of the Esquimaux or Alaska savages are at the present day. It appears most unphilosophical to apply to those people the principles of progress that are found among the higher races of mankind, and to represent them as eagerly seizing on any improvement offered them, and abandoning their old faith and their old habits at the bidding of any wandering navigator that visited their shores.

This is not the place to enter on such an enquiry, but so far as can at present be seen, it seems that mankind has progressed not so much by advance within the limits of certain races as by the superposition of more highly organized races over those of an inferior class. Thus we have those stone men of the caves who possessed the world for 100,000 or a million of years, and

---

[1] For the last, and one of the best, accounts of the Hydahs, see 'Proceedings of the Royal Geographical Society,' vol. xiii. No. V. p. 386 et seqq., by Mr. Brown.

made no more progress in that period than the animals they were associated with. Even the progress from a chipped to a polished stone implement seems to have been taught them by a foreign bronze-using people. We have then such races as the Egyptian, the Chinese, or the Mexican, who can progress to a certain point, but stop and cannot go beyond; and, lastly, we have the Aryans, the last to appear in the field, but the most energetic, and the only truly progressive race. Our great error in reasoning with regard to the older races seems to be that we insist on applying to them the reasoning and principles which guide us, but which are wholly inapplicable to the less progressive races of mankind.

All this will be plainer in the sequel; but in the meanwhile it may safely be asserted that, up to this time, no royal road has been discovered that leads to an explanation of our megalithic antiquities. No one has yet been able so to classify the contents of cognate monuments as to construct a chronometric scale which is applicable for the elucidation of their dates; and no *à priori* reasoning has been hit upon that is of the smallest use in explaining either their age or their peculiarities. The one path that seems open to us is a careful examination of each individual monument, accompanied by a judicial sifting of all or any traditions that may attach to it, and aided by a comparison with similar monuments in other countries. By this means we have a chance of arriving at a fair proximate degree of certainty; for, though no one monument will tell its own tale directly, a multitude of whispers from a great number may swell into a voice that is clear and distinct and be audible to every one; while no system yet invented, and no *à priori* reasoning, can lead to anything but deepening the ignorance that now prevails on the subject. This is especially true with regard to the great megalithic circles in this country. With the rarest possible exceptions, no flint and no bronze or iron implements have been found within their precincts. They cannot be older than the invention of flint implements, and iron has been in continuous use since the art of smelting its ores was first discovered. If, therefore, they have no written or traditional history which can be relied upon, their age must for ever remain a mystery. The conviction, however, under which this book is written is that such a history does exist; that, when all the traditions attached to the monuments are sifted and weighed, they amount to such a mass of circumstantial evidence as suffices to prove the case and to establish the main facts of their history and use, wholly independently of any system or of any external testimony.

Direct literary evidence, in the sense in which the term is usually understood, cannot be said to exist. As before mentioned, no classical author alludes, either directly or indirectly, to these megalithic structures; yet they could not have been ignorant of them if they existed. When Cæsar and his army witnessed the fight between his galleys and the fleet of the Veneti in the Mor- bihan, he must have stood—if he occupied the best place—on Mont St. Michel, if it then existed, and among the stone avenues of Carnac. Is it likely that such an artist would have omitted the chance of heightening his picture by an allusion to the " standing stones" of Dariorigum? The Romans occupied Old Sarum probably during the whole time they remained in this island, and the Via Badonica passed so immediately under Silbury Hill that they could not have been ignorant of either Stonehenge or Avebury. Nor in France could they possibly have missed seeing the numerous dolmens with which the country is covered. Notwithstanding all this, the silence is absolute. The circular temple of the Hyperboreans is the only thing any one has ever pretended to quote against this; and that, for reasons given above being inadmissible, any argument based on it falls to the ground.

Neither Cæsar nor Tacitus, though describing the religious observances of our forefathers, make any mention of temples; nor, indeed, does any other classical author. Tacitus[1] tells us that the Germans worshipped only in groves; and though this is hardly to the point, his relations with Agricola were so intimate that had the Gauls and Britons had temples of stone, he could hardly have avoided alluding to them. The inference from Cæsar and all the other authors is the same, but there is no direct evidence either way.

There is no passage in any classical authors which connects the Druids, either directly or indirectly, with any stone temples or stones of any sort.

---

[1] 'Germania,' 9.

Dracontia are wholly the creation of Dr. Stukeley's very fertile imagination.

So far, therefore, as negative evidence goes, it is complete in showing that our megalithic circles did not exist in the time of the Romans, and that they were not temples. Unfortunately, however, no amount of negative evidence is sufficient to prove an affirmative, though it may suffice to establish a strong presumption in favour of a particular view, and, at all events, clears the way for the production of any direct evidence which we may have. The direct written evidence that has been adduced is, however, of the most shadowy character. It amounts to little more than this:—that every allusion to these monuments in mediæval authors, every local tradition, every scrap of intelligence we have regarding them, points to a post-Roman origin. No writer, of any age or country, suggested their being pre-historic or even pre-Roman before the age of Stukeley,—say 1700.

There is, so far as I know, only one paragraph in any classical author which mentions a French or British temple; but it belonged to so exceptional a community that it would hardly be safe to base an argument upon it. A "hieron," Strabo tells us, existed at the mouth of the Loire, inhabited by a colony of women who lived apart from their husbands, but the roof or thatch of the roof of whose temple was renewed annually :[1] a fact that shows, in the first place, that it had a roof, and in the second, that it was not a very dignified or permanent structure.

It would add very much to the clearness of our conception on this subject if the early Christian writers had left us some descriptions of the temples of the Britons when the missionaries first came among them. Though not quite so silent on the subject as the classical authors, their direct evidence is far from being so complete as might be wished. One of the passages most distinctly bearing on this question is found in a letter which Pope Gregory the Great addressed to the Abbot Millitus, then on a mission to England. In this letter he instructs him by no means to destroy the temples of the idols belonging to the English, but only the idols which are found in them ; and adds, "Let holy water be made, and

---

[1] Strabo, iv. p. 198.

sprinkled over them. Let altars be constructed, and relics placed
on them; insomuch as if these temples are well constructed, it is
necessary that they should be converted from the worship of dæmons
to the service of the true God. So that the people, seeing their
temples are not destroyed, may put away errors from their hearts,
and, acknowledging the true God and adoring Him, may the more
willingly assemble in the places where they were accustomed to
meet." [1] A little further on he adds, in order that no apparent
change may be made, "that on great festivals the people may
erect huts of boughs around those churches which have been converted (commutatæ) from temples."

The fair inference from this paragraph seems to be that there
was so little difference between the temples of the Pagans and
the churches of the Christians that a little holy water and a few
relics—as much esteemed in the West as in the East in those
days—were all that was required to convert the one into the other.

We gather the same impression from another transaction which
took place at Canterbury about the same time. After taking possession of the Cathedral, built of old by the Romans,[2] St. Augustine
obtained from the recently converted King Ethelbert the cession
of the temple in which he had been accustomed to worship his
idols, and without more ado dedicated it to St. Pancras, and
appropriated it as a burying place for himself and his successors
from the circumstance of its being outside the walls.[3] We further
learn from Gervaise[4] that it was so used till Cuthbert, the second
archbishop, got permission to allow burials within the walls, and
then erected the baptistry of St. John for this purpose, where

---

[1] Bede, 'Hist. Eccles.' i. 30.

[2] "Inibi antiquo Romanorum fidelium
opere factam," Bede, 'Hist. Eccles.' i. 32.

[3] Thorn, 'Dec. Script. Col.' 1760:—
"Erat autem non longe ab ipsa civitate
ad orientem quasi medio itinere inter
ecclesiam Sti. Martini et muros civitatis
Phanum sive ydolum situm ubi rex
Ethelbertus secundus ritum gentis suæ
solebat orare et cum nobilibus suis dæ-
moniis et non deo sacrificare. Quod
Phanum Augustinus ab iniquinamentis
et sordibus gentilium purgavit et simu-
lacro quod in eo erat infracto, synagogam

mutavit in ecclesiam, et eam in nomine
Sti. Pancratii martyris dedicavit."

Of this "Fane" we further learn from
Godselinus ('Leland Collect.' vol. iv.
p. 8), that "extat adhuc condita ex lon-
gissimis et latissimis lateribus more
Britannico ut facile est videre in muris
Verolamiensibus," and may now be seen
in this very church at Canterbury. "Basilica Sti. Pancratii nunc est ubi olim
Ethelbertus idolum suum coluit. Opus
exiguum structum tamen de more veterum Britannorum."

[4] Gervaise, 'Acc. Pont. Cant.' p. 1640.

apparently Becket's crown now stands. Afterwards the monastery of SS. Peter and Paul, now St. Augustine's, was erected "in fundo Templi"—whatever that may mean—but at that time St. Augustine seems to have accepted the Pagan temples as perfectly appropriate to Christian rites.

In like manner when King Redwald, after his conversion to Christianity was persuaded by his wife not rashly to forsake the faith of his forefathers, he set up two altars side by side in his temple (in fano), and dedicated the one to Christ, the other to the "victims of the dæmons."[1] The temple, apparently, was equally appropriate to either.

A still more instructive example is the description of the destruction of the church at Godmundingham by Coifi — the heathen priest — on his conversion to Christianity. He first desecrated it by throwing a spear into it—whether by the door or window we are not told—and then ordered his people to burn it to the ground with all its enclosures. These, therefore, must all have been in wood or some equally combustible material.[2]

All this is not much nor very distinct, but by these passages, and every hint we have on the subject, it would appear that the temples of the Pagans, between the departure of the Romans and the time of Alfred, were at least very similar to those of the Christians. Both were derived from the same model, which was the temple or basilica of the Romans, and both were apparently very rude, and generally, we may infer, constructed of wood. The word circular does not occur in any description of any Pagan temple yet brought to light, nor the word stone; nothing, in fact, that would in the remotest degree lead us to suppose that Bede, or any one else, was speaking or thinking of the megalithic monuments with which we are now concerned.

Although the classical authorities are silent regarding these rude stone monuments, and contemporary records help us very little in trying to understand the form of the temples in which our forefathers worshipped, till they were converted to Christianity, still the Decrees of the Councils render it quite certain that Rude

---

[1] Bede, 'Hist. Eccles.' ii. 15.

[2] "Succendere fanum cum omnibus septis suis," Bede, 'Hist. Eccles.' ii. 13.

Stone Monuments were objects of veneration—certainly in France, and, by implication, in England—down to the times of Charlemagne and Alfred, at least.

One often-quoted decree of a Council, held at Nantes, exhorts "Bishops and their servants to dig up, and remove, and hide in places where they cannot be found, those stones which in remote and woody places are still worshipped, and where vows are still made."[1] Unfortunately the date of this Council is not certain; but Richard places it in 658, which is probably at least nearly correct.[2] This, however, is of comparatively little consequence, as in 452 a Council at Arles decreed that "if, in any diocese, any infidel either lighted torches or worshipped Trees, Fountains, or Stones, or neglected to destroy them, he should be found guilty of sacrilege;"[3] and about a century later (567), a Council at Tours exhorts the clergy to excommunicate those who, at certain Stones or Trees or Fountains, perpetrate things contrary to the ordinances of the Church.[4]

Still another century further on (681), a Council held at Toledo admonishes those who worship Idols or venerate Stones, those who light torches or worship Fountains or Trees, that they are sacrificing to the devil, and subject themselves to various penalties, &c.[5] Another Council held in the same city, in the year 692, enumerates almost in the same words the various heresies which were condemned by the preceding Council.[6] A Council at Rouen, about the same time, denounces all who offer vows to Trees or Fountains

---

[1] Summo decertare debent studio episcopi et eorum ministri ut — *Lapides* quoque, quos in ruinosis locis et silvestribus, demonum ludificationibus decepti venerantur ubi et vota vovent et deferunt, funditus effodiantur, atque in tali loco projiciantur ubi nunquam a cultoribus suis inveniri possint et omnibus annunciatur quantum scelus est idolatria.—Labbeum, t. ix. 474.

[2] Richard, 'Analyse des Conciles,' i. 646.

[3] Si in alicujus episcopi territorio infideles, aut faculas accendunt, aut arbores, fontes vel *Saxa* venerentur si hoc eruere neglexerit, sacrilegii reum se esset cognoscat.—Labb., iv. 1013.

[4] Contestamur illam solicitudinem tam pastores quam presbyteros, gerere ut quemcunque in hac fatuitate persistere viderint, vel ad nescio quas *petras* aut arbores vel fontes, designata loca gentilium perpetrare, quæ ad ecclesiæ rationem non pertinent eos ab ecclesia sancta auctoritate repellant.—Baluz, i. 518.

[5] Cultores idolorum, veneratores *Lapidum*, accensores facularum excolentes sacra fontium vel arborum admonemus, &c.—Baluz, vi. 1234.

[6] Illi diversis suadelis decepti cultores idolorum efficiuntur, veneratores *Lapidum*, accensores facularum, excolentes sacra fontium vel arborum, &c.—Baluz, vi. 1337.

or Stones as they would at altars, or offer candles or gifts, as if any divinity resided there capable of conferring good or evil.[1]

Lastly, a decree of Charlemagne, dated Aix-la-Chapelle in 789, utterly condemns and execrates before God Trees, Stones, and Fountains, which foolish people worship.[2]

Even as late as in the time of Canute the Great, there is a statute forbidding the barbarous adoration of the Sun and Moon, Fire, Fountains, Stones, and all kinds of Trees and Wood.[3]

The above which are taken from Keysler[4] are not all he quotes, nor certainly all that could be added, if it were worth while, from other sources; but they are sufficient to show that, from Toledo to Aix-la-Chapelle—and from the departure of the Romans till the tenth, or probably the eleventh century—the Christian priesthood waged a continuous but apparently ineffectual warfare against the worship of Stones, Trees, and Fountains. The priests do not condescend to tell us what the forms of the Stones were which these benighted people worshipped, whether simple menhirs or dolmens, or " grottes des fées," nor why they worshipped them; whether they considered them emblems of some unnamed and unknown God, or memorials of deceased ancestors, in whose honour they lighted candles, and whom they propitiated with offerings. Nor do they tell us what the form of that worship was; they did not care, and perhaps did not know. Nor do we; for, except an extreme veneration for their dead, and a consequent ancestral worship,[5] mixed with a strange adoration of Stones, Trees, and Fountains, we do not know now what the religion was of these rude people. The testimony of these edicts is, therefore, not quite so

---

[1] Si aliquis vota ad arbores, vel fontes, vel ad *Lapides* quosdam, quasi ad altaria, faciat aut ibi candelam, seu quolibet munus deferet velut ibi quoddam Numen sit quod bonum aut malum possit inferre.—Baluz, l. 2, p. 210.

[2] Item de arboribus vel *Petris* vel fontibus ubi aliqui stulti luminaria vel aliquas observationes faciunt omnino mandamus, ut iste pessimus usus et deo execrabilis ubicunque invenitur tolletur et distruatur.—Baluz, t. i. p. 235.

[3] Barbara est autem adoratio, sive quas idola (puta gentium divos), Solem, Lunam, Ignem, Profluentem, Fontes, *Saxa*, cujusque generis arbores lignam coluerunt.—Keysler, ' Antiquitates Septemtrion.' (Hanoveræ, 1720), p. 18. He quotes also a canon of Edgar (967) to the same effect.

[4] ' Ant. Sept.' chap. ii.

[5] Laing in his wrath seems to have, by accident, very nearly guessed the truth, when, refuting the authenticity of Ossian, he accuses Macpherson of "having rendered the Highlanders a race of unheard-of infidels, who believed in no Gods but the ghosts of their fathers."

distinct as we might wish, and does not enable us to assert that
the Rude Stone Monuments, whose age and uses we are trying
to ascertain, were those alluded to in the preceding paragraphs.
But what it does seem to prove is, that down to the 11th century
the Christian Priesthood waged a continuous warfare against the
veneration of some class of Rude Stone Monuments, to which
the pagan population clung with remarkable tenacity, and many,
if not most of which may consequently have been erected during
that period. This is, at all events, infinitely more clear and
positive than anything that has been brought forward in favour of
their pre-historic antiquity. If, like the other branches of the
written argument, this is not sufficient to prove, by itself, that
the monuments were generally or even frequently erected after
the Christian era, it certainly entitles that assertion to a fair *locus
standi* in the argument we are attempting to develop.

If, however, the pen has been reticent and hesitating in its
testimony, the spade has been not only prolific but distinct. It
is probably not an exaggeration to say that three-fourths of the
megalithic monuments—including the dolmens, of course—have
yielded sepulchral deposits to the explorer, and, including the
tumuli, probably nine-tenths have been proved to be burial places.
Still, at the present stage of the enquiry, it would be at least
premature to assume that the remaining tenth of the whole, or the
remaining fourth of the stone section, must necessarily be sepulchral. Some may have been cenotaphic, or simply monuments,
such as we erect to our great men—not necessarily where the bodies
are laid. Some stones and some tumuli may have been erected to
commemorate events, and some mounds certainly were erected as
" Motes" or " Things"—places of judgment or assembly. In like
manner some circles may have been originally, or may afterwards
have been used as places of assembly, or may have been what
may more properly be called temples of the dead, than tombs.
These, however, certainly are the exceptions. The ruling idea
throughout is still of a sepulchre, with what exceptions, and
at what age erected, is the thesis which we now propose to
investigate.

At present these are mere assertions, and it is not pretended that they are more, and they are only brought forward in this place in order to enunciate the propositions it is hoped we may be able to prove as we advance in this enquiry. These are,—

First, that the Rude Stone Monuments with which we are concerned are generally sepulchral, or connected directly, or indirectly, with the rites of the dead.

Secondly, that they are not temples in any usual or appropriate sense of the term, and,

Lastly,—that they were generally erected by partially civilized races after they had come in contact with the Romans, and most of them may be considered as belonging to the first ten centuries of the Christian Era.

In stating these three propositions so broadly, it must be borne in mind, that the evidence on which their proof or disproof rests is eminently cumulative in its character; not perhaps with regard to the use to which the monuments were applied, that probably will be admitted as settled, as so large a proportion of the tumuli can be shown to have a fair title to a sepulchral character, and most of the stone monuments can equally lay claim to being erected for the same purpose to which one-half of them have been certainly proved to have been dedicated. This is the more clear, as, on the other hand, in spite of every surmise or conjecture, no one monument of the class we are treating of can be proved to have been erected as a temple, or as intended for any civic or civil purpose.

With regard to their age, the case is not quite so easily settled. Except such monuments as those of Gorm and Thyra, and one or two others, to be mentioned hereafter, few can produce such proof of their age as would stand investigation in a court of law. But when all the traditions, all the analogies, and all the probabilities of the case are examined, they seem to make up such an accumulation of evidence as is irresistible; and the whole appears to present an unbroken and intelligible sequence which explains everything. The proof of all this, however, does not rest on the evidence of two or three, or even of a dozen, of instances, but is based upon the multiplication of a great number of coincidences derived from a large number of instances, which taken together in the cumulative form, make up a stronger body of proof than

could be obtained from the direct testimony of one or two cases.
To appreciate this, however, the whole must be taken together.
To try to invalidate it by selecting one or two prominent cases,
where the proof is manifestly insufficient when taken by itself, is to
misunderstand and misrepresent the whole force of the argument.

One point, I fancy, there will be very little difficulty in proving,
which is, that the whole form one continuous group, extending in
an unbroken series, from the earliest to the latest. There is no
hiatus or break anywhere; and if some can be proved to belong
to the 10th century, it is only a question how far you can, by
extenuating the thread, extend it backwards. It can hardly be
much beyond the Christian era. It seems that such a date satis-
fies all the known conditions of the problem, in so far as the Stone
Monuments at least are concerned. There is, so far as I know
at present, absolutely no evidence on the other side, except what
is derived from the Danish system of the three ages: if that
is established as a rule of law, *cadit questio*, there is no more
to be said on the subject. But this is exactly what does not
appear to have yet been established on any sufficient or satisfactory basis. There need be no difficulty in granting that men
used stone and bone for implements, before they were acquainted
with the use of the metals. It may also be admitted, that they
used bronze before they learned the art of extracting iron from
its ores. But what is denied is, that they abandoned the use
of these primitive implements on the introduction of the metals;
and it is contended that they employed stone and bone simultaneously with bronze and iron, down to a very late period. The
real fact of the case seems to be, that the people on the shores of
the Baltic and the North Sea, were as remote from the centres of
civilization on the Mediterranean and to the eastward of it in the
earlier centuries of our era, and were as little influenced by them,
as the inhabitants of the islands in the Pacific and Arctic America
were by Europe in the last century. In the remote corners of the
world, a stone and bone age exists at the present day, only
modified by the use of such metal implements as they can obtain
by barter or exchange: and this appears to have been the state of
northern Europe, till, with their conversion to Christianity, the
new civilization was domesticated among its inhabitants.

CHAPTER II.

PRELIMINARY OBSERVATIONS.

BEFORE attempting to examine or describe particular instances—
in which, however, the main interest of the work must eventually
be centred—it would add very much to the clearness of what
follows if a classification could be hit upon, which would correctly
represent the sequence of forms. In the present state of our
knowledge such an arrangement is hardly possible, still the
following 5 groups, with their subdivisions, are sufficiently distinct
to enable them to be treated separately, and are so arranged as
roughly to represent what we know of their sequence, with
immense overlappings, however, on every joint.

I.—Tumuli ..	.. a. Or barrows of earth only.
	b. With small stone chambers or cists.
	c. With megalithic chambers or dolmens.
	d. With external access to chambers.
II.—Dolmens ..	.. a. Free standing dolmens without tumuli.
	b. Dolmens upon the outside of tumuli.
III.—Circles ..	.. a. Circles surrounding tumuli.
	b. Circles surrounding dolmens.
	c. Circles without tumuli or dolmens.
IV.—Avenues ..	.. a. Avenues attached to circles.
	b. Avenues with or without circles or dolmens.
V.—Menhirs ..	.. a. Single or in groups.
	b. With oghams, sculptures, or runes.

TUMULI.

The first three of the sub-divisions of the first class are so mixed
together that it is almost impossible in the present state of our
knowledge to separate them with precision either as to date or
locality, while, as they hardly belong to the main subject of this
book, it will not be worth while to attempt it here.

Without being too speculative, perhaps, it may be assumed that the earliest mode in which mankind disposed of the bodies of their deceased relatives or neighbours was by simple inhumation. They dug a hole in the earth, and, having laid the body therein, simply replaced the earth upon it, and to mark the spot, if the person so buried was of sufficient importance to merit such care, they raised a mound over the grave. It is difficult, however, to believe that mankind were long content with so simple a mode of sepulture. To heap earth or stones on the body of the beloved departed so as to crush and deface it, must have seemed rude and harsh, and some sort of coffin was probably early devised for the protection of the corpse,—in well-wooded countries, this would be of wood, which, if the mound is old, has perished long ago—in stony countries, as probably of stone, forming the rude cists so commonly found in early graves. That these should expand into chambers seems also natural as civilization advanced, and as man's ideas of a future state and the wants and necessities of such a future became more developed.

The last stage would seem to be when access was retained to the sepulchral chamber, in order that the descendants of the deceased might bring offerings, or supply the wants of their relative during the intermediate state which some nations assumed must elapse before the translation of the body to another world.

It is probable that some such stages as these were passed through by all the burying races of mankind, though at very various intervals and with very different details, while fortunately for our present subject it seems that the earliest races were those most addicted to this mode of honouring their dead. All mankind, it is true, bury their dead either in the flesh or their ashes after cremation. It is one of those peculiarities which, like speech, distinguish mankind from the lower animals, and which are so strangely overlooked by the advocates of the fashionable theory of our ape descent. All mankind, however, do not reverence their dead to the same extent. The peculiarity is most characteristic of the earlier underlying races, whom we have generally been in the habit of designating as the Turanian races of mankind. But if that term is objected to, the tomb-building races may be specified—beginning from the East—as the Chinese; the Monguls in Tartary, or Mogols, as they were called, in India; the Tartars in their own country, or in Persia; the ancient Pelasgi in Greece; the Etrurians in Italy; and the races, whoever they were, who preceded the Celts in Europe. But the tomb-building people, *par excellence*, in the old world were the Egyptians. Not only were the funereal rites the most important element in the religious life of the people, but they began at an age earlier than the history or tradition of any other nation carries us back to. The great Pyramid of Gizeh was erected certainly as early as 3000 years before Christ; yet it must be the lineal descendant of a rude-chambered tumulus or cairn, with external access to the chambers, and it seems difficult to calculate how many thousands of years it must have required before such rude sepulchres as those our ancestors erected—many probably after the Christian era—could have been elaborated into the most perfect and most gigantic specimens of masonry which the world has yet seen. The phenomenon of anything so perfect as the Pyramids starting up at once, absolutely without any previous examples being known, is so unique[1] in the world's history, that it is impossible to form any conjecture how long before this period the Egyptians tried to protect their bodies from decay during the pro-bationary 3000 years.[2]

Outside Egypt the oldest tumulus we know of, with an abso-lutely authentic date, is that which Alyattes, the father of Crœsus,

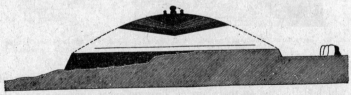

1.　　　　　Section of Tomb of Alyattes. From Spiegelthal. No scale.

king of Lydia, erected for his own resting-place before the year 561 B.C. It was described by Herodotus,[3] and has of late years

---

[1] It is so curious as almost to justify Piazzi Smyth's wonderful theories on the subject. But there is no reason what-ever to suppose that the progress of art in Egypt differed essentially from that elsewhere. The previous examples are lost, and that seems all.

[2] Herodotus, ii. 123; and Sir Gardner Wilkinson's 'Ancient Egyptians,' second series, i. 211; ii. 440 *et passim*.

[3] Herod. i. 93.

been thoroughly explored by Dr. Olfers.[1] Its dimensions are very considerable, and very nearly those given by the father of history. It is 1180 feet in diameter, or about twice as much as Silbury Hill, and 200 feet in height, as against 130 of that boasted monument. The upper part, like many of our own mounds, is composed of alternate layers of clay, loam, and a kind of rubble concrete. These support a mass of brickwork, surmounted by a platform of masonry; on this still lies one of Steles, described by Herodotus, and another of the smaller ones was found close by.

There is another group of tombs, called those of Tantalais, found near Smyrna, which are considerably older than those of Sardis, though their date cannot be fixed with such certainty as that last described. Still there seems no good reason for doubting that the one here represented may be as old as the eleventh or twelfth

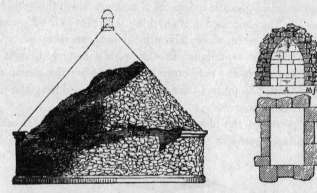

2.   Elevation of Tumulus at Tantalais. From Texier's   3.   Plan and Section of Chamber
          'Asie Mineure.' 100 ft. to 1 in.   in Tumulus at Tantalais.

century B.C., nor does it seem reasonable to doubt but these tumuli which still stand on the plain of Troy do cover the remains of the heroes who perished in that remarkable siege.[2]

A still more interesting group, however, is that at Mycenæ, known as the tombs or treasuries of the Atridæ, and described as such by

---

[1] 'Lydische Königsgräber,' Berlin, 1859.

[2] I am, of course, aware that the now fashionable craze is to consider Troy a myth. So far, however, as I am capable of understanding it, it appears to me that the ancient solar myth of Messrs. Max Müller and Cox is very like mere modern moonshine.

Pausanias.[1] The principal, or at least the best preserved of these, is a circular chamber, 48 feet 6 inches in diameter, covered by a

5 10 20 30 40 50 ft.

Section and Plan of Tomb of Atreus at Mycenæ.   Scale of plan 100 ft. to 1 in.

horizontal vault, and having a sepulchral chamber on one side. Dodwell discovered three others of the five mentioned by Pausanias,[2] and he also explored the sepulchre of Minyas at Orchomenos, which had a diameter of 65 feet.

Another group of tombs, contemporary or nearly so with these, are found in the older cemeteries of the Etrurians at Cœre, Vulci, and elsewhere. One of the largest of these is one called Cocumella, at Vulci, which is 240 feet in diameter, and must originally

5.   View of Cocumella, Vulci.

have been 115 to 120 feet in height. Near the centre rise two steles, but so unsymmetrically that it is impossible to understand why they were so placed and how they could have been grouped into anything like a complete design. The sepulchre, too, is placed on one side.

---

[1] Paus. ii. ch. 16 ; ' Dodwell's Pelasgic Remains in Greece and Italy,' pl. 11.
[2] Dodwell, l. c. p. 13.

A still richer and more remarkable tomb is that known as the
Regulini Galeassi Tomb at Cœre, the chamber of which is repre-

sented in the annexed
woodcut.

It is filled, as may be
seen, with vessels and
furniture, principally of
bronze and of the most
elaborate workmanship.
The patterns on these
vessels are so archaic,
and resemble so much
some of the older ones
found at Nineveh, whose
dates are at least ap-
proximately known, that
we may safely refer the
tomb to an age not later
than the tenth cen-
tury B.C.[1]

We have thus around
the eastern shores of the

6.   View of principal Chamber in Regulini Galeassi Tomb.

Mediterranean a group of circular sepulchral tumuli of well
defined age.   Some, certainly, are as old as the thirteenth century
B.C., others extend downwards to, say 500 B.C.   All have a podium
of stone.   Some are wholly of that material, but in most of them
the cone is composed of earth, and all have sepulchral chambers
built with stones in horizontal layers, not so megalithic as those
found in our tumuli, but of a more polished and artistic form of
construction.

The age, too, in which these monuments were erected was
essentially the age of bronze; not only are the ornaments and
furniture found in the Etruscan tombs generally of that metal, but
the tombs at Mycenæ and Orchomenos were wholly lined with
it.   The holes into which the bronze nails were inserted still

---

[1] More particulars and illustrations of these tombs will be found in the first
volume of my 'History of Architecture,' and they need not, therefore, be repeated
here.

exist everywhere, and some of the nails themselves are in the British Museum. It was also the age in which Solomon furnished his temple with all those implements and ornaments in brass— properly bronze—described in the Bible,[1] and the brazen house of Priam and fifty such expressions show how common the metal was in that day. All this, however, does not prove that iron also was not known then. In the Egyptian paintings iron is generally represented as a blue metal, bronze as red, and through- out they are carefully distinguished by these colours. Now, in the tombs around the pyramids, and of an age contemporary with them, there are numerous representations of blue swords as there are of red spear-heads, and there seems no reason for doubting that iron was known to the Greeks before the war of Troy, to the Israelites before they left Egypt (1320 B.C.), or to the Etruscans when they first settled in Italy. Hesiod's asser- tion that brass was known before iron may or may not be true.[2] In so far as his evidence is concerned we learn from it that iron was certainly in use long before his time (800 B.C.); so long indeed that he does not pretend to know when or by whom it was invented, and the modes of manufacturing steel—ἀδάμας— seem also to have been perfectly known in his day.

In India, too, as we shall see when we come to speak of that country, the extraction of iron from its ores was known from the earliest ages, and in the third or fourth century of our era reached a degree of perfection which has hardly since been surpassed. The celebrated iron pillar at the Kutub, near Delhi, which is of that age, may probably still boast of being the largest mass of forged iron that the world yet possesses, and attests a wonderful amount of skill on the part of those who made it.

When from these comparatively civilized modes of sepulture we turn to the forms employed in our own country, as described by Thurnam [3] or Bateman,[4] we are startled to find how like they are, but, at the same time, how infinitely more rude. They are either long barrows covering the remains of a race of dolicocephalic

---

[1] 1 Kings, vii. 13 et seqq.; 2 Chron. iv. 1 et seqq.
[2] Hesiod. 'Works and Days,' l. 150.
[3] 'Crania Britannica,' passim. 'Ar-

chæologia,' xxxviii.
[4] 'Vestiges of the Antiquities of Der- byshire,' 1848. 'Ten Years' Diggings,' 1861.

savages laid in rudely-framed cists, with implements of flint and bone and the coarsest possible pottery, but without one vestige of metal of any sort, or circular tumuli of a brachycephalic race shown to have been slightly more advanced by their remains being occasionally incinerated, and ornaments of bronze and spear-heads of that metal being also sometimes found buried in their tombs.

According to the usual mode of reasoning on these subjects, the long-headed people are older than the broad-pated race, the one superseding the other, and both must have been anterior to the people on the shores of the Mediterranean, for these were familiar with the use of both metals, and fabricated pottery which we cannot now equal for perfection of texture and beauty of design.

The first defect that strikes one in this argument is that if it proves anything it proves too much. We certainly have sepulchral barrows in this country of the Roman period, the Bartlow hills, for instance—of which more hereafter—and Saxon grave mounds everywhere; but according to this theory not one sepulchre of any sort between the year 1200 B.C. and the Christian era. All our sepulchres are ruder, and betoken a less advanced stage of civilization than the earliest of those in Greece or Etruria, and therefore, according to the usually accepted dogma, must be earlier.

It may be argued, however, that several are older than the Argive examples. That the Jersey tomb (woodcut No. 11), notwithstanding the coin of Claudius, is older, because more rude, than the Treasury at Mycenæ (woodcut No. 4); but that the Bartlow hills and the Derbyshire dolmens and tumuli above alluded to (page 11 et seqq.), containing coins of Valentinian and the Roman Emperors, are more modern. Such an hypothesis as this involves the supposition that there is a great gap in the series, and that after discontinuing the practice for a 1000 or 1500 years, our forefathers returned to their old habits, but with ruder forms than they had used before, and after continuing them for five or six centuries, finally abandoned them. This is possible, of course, but there is absolutely no proof of it that I know. On the contrary, so far as our knowledge of them at present extends, the whole of the megalithic rude stone monuments group together as one style as essentially as the Classical or

Gothic or any other style of architecture. No solution of continuity
can be detected anywhere. All are—it may be—prehistoric; or
all, as I believe to be the case, belong to historic times. The
choice seems to be between these two categories; any hypothesis
based on the separation into a historic and a prehistoric group,
distinct in characteristics as in age, appears to be utterly untenable.

The argument derived from the absence of iron in all our
sepulchres also proves more than is desirable. The Danish
antiquaries all admit that iron was not known in that country
before the Christian era. Our antiquaries, from the testimony of
Cæsar as to its use in war by the Britons, are forced to admit an
earlier date, but it is hardly, if ever, found in graves. It is, on the
other hand, perhaps correct to assume that its use was known in
Egypt 3000 years before Christ; even if this is disputed, it
certainly was known in the 18th dynasty, 15 centuries B.C., and
generally in the Mediterranean shortly afterwards. If, then, the
knowledge of the most useful of metals took 3000 or even 1500
years to travel across the continent of Europe, it seems impossible
to base any argument on the influence these people exercised
on one another, or on the knowledge they may have had of each
others' ways.

Or to take the argument in a form nearer home. When Cæsar
warred against the Veneti in the Morbihan, he found them in
possession of vessels larger and stronger than the Roman galleys,
capable of being manœuvred by their sails alone, without the use
of oars. Not only were these vessels fastened by iron nails, but
they were moored by chain cables of iron. To manufacture such
chains, the Veneti must have had access to large mines of the
ore, and had long familiarity with its manufacture, and they used
it not only for purposes on shore like the Britons, but in vessels
capable of trading between Brest and Penzance—no gentle sea
—and quite equal to voyages to the Baltic or other northern
ports, which they no doubt made; it is asserted that, in 50 B.C.,
the Scandinavians were ignorant of the use of iron, though
their country possessed the richest mines and the best ores of
Europe.

The truth of the matter appears to be that, a century or so

before Christ, England and Denmark were as little known to Greece and Italy, and as little influenced by their arts or civilization, as Borneo or New Zealand were by those of modern Europe at the beginning of the last century. Even now, with all our colonization and civilizing power, we have had marvellously little real influence on the native races, and were our power removed, all traces would rapidly disappear, and the people revert at once to what they were, and act as they were wont to do, before they knew us.

In like manner the North American Indians have been very little influenced by the residence of some millions of proselytizing Europeans among them for 200 years, and while this is so, it seems most groundless to argue because a few Phœnician traders may have visited this island to purchase tin, that, therefore, they introduced their manners and customs among its inhabitants; or because a traveller like Pytheas may have visited the Cimbrian Chersonese, or even penetrated nearly to the Arctic Circle, that his visit had, or could have, any influence on the civilization of these countries.[1] Civilization, as far as we can see, was only advanced in northern and western Europe by the extermination of the ruder races. Had this rude but effective method not been resorted to, we should probably have a stone-using people among us at the present day.

We may not know much of what happened in northern Europe before the time of the Romans, but we feel tolerably safe in asserting that none of the civilized nations around the Mediterranean basin ever colonized and settled sufficiently long in northern Europe to influence perceptibly the manners or usages of the natives. What progress was made was effected by migrations among themselves, the more civilized tribes taking the place of those less advanced, and bringing their higher civilization with them.

If these views are at all correct, it seems hopeless by any empirical theories founded on what we believe ought to have happened or on any analogies drawn from what occurred in other countries to arrive at satisfactory conclusions on the subject. It is at best reasoning from the unknown towards what we fancy

[1] See controversy between Sir George Cornewall Lewis in his 'Astronomy of the Ancients,' p. 467 et seqq. and Sir John Lubbock, in 'Prehistoric Times,' p. 59 et seqq. with regard to Pytheas and his discoveries.

may be found out. A much more satisfactory process would be to reason from the known backwards so far as we have a sure footing, and we may feel certain that by degrees as our knowledge advances we shall get further and further forward in the true track, and may eventually be able to attach at least approximative dates to all our monuments.

From this point of view, what concerns us most, in the first instance at least, is to know how late, rather than how early, our ancestors buried in tumuli. We have, for instance, certainly, the Bartlow Hills, just alluded to, which are sepulchres of the Roman period, probably of Hadrian's time ; and we have in Denmark the tumuli in which King Gorm and his English wife, Queen Thyra Danebode, were buried in A.D. 950. We probably also may be able to fill in a few others between these two dates, and add some after even the last. Thus, therefore, we have a firm basis from which to start, and working backwards from it may clear up some difficulties that now appear insuperable.

DOLMENS.

The monuments alluded to in the last section were either the rude barrows of our savage ancestors, with the ruder cists, or the chambered tumuli of a people who, when we first became acquainted with them, had attained nearly as high a degree of civilization as any Turanian people are capable of attaining. The people who erected such buildings as the Tombs of Mycenæ or Orchomenos must have reached a respectable degree of organization. They possessed a perfect knowledge of the use of metals, and great wealth in bronze at least, and had attained to considerable skill in construction. Yet it is not difficult to trace back—in imagination, at least—the various steps by which a small rude chamber in a circular mound, just capable of protecting a single body, may by degrees have grown into a richly-ornamented brazen chamber, 50 or 60 feet in diameter and of equal height. Nor is it more difficult to foresee what this buried chamber would have become, had not the Aryan occupation of Greece—figured under the myth of the return of the Heracleidæ—put a stop to the tomb-building propensities of the people. Before long it must have burst from its chrysalis state, and assumed a form of external beauty. It must have emerged from its earthen envelope, and taken a form which it did take in Africa[1] a thousand years after-wards,—a richly-ornamented podium, surmounted by a stepped cone and crowned by a stele. In Greece it went no further, and its history and its use were alike strange to the people who after-wards occupied the country.

In Italy its history was somewhat different. The more mixed people of Rome eagerly adopted the funereal magnificence of the Etruscans, and their tumuli under the Empire became magnified into such monuments as the Tomb of Augustus in the Campus Martius, or the still more gorgeous mausoleum of Hadrian, at the foot of the Vatican hill.

In like manner, it would not be difficult by the same process to trace the steps by which the rude tepés of the Tartar steppes bloomed at last into the wondrous domes of the Patan and Mogol Emperors of Delhi or the other Mahomedan principalities in the East. To do all this would form a most interesting chapter in the history of architecture, more interesting, perhaps, than the one we are about to attempt; but it is not the same, though both spring from the same origin. The people or peoples who eventually elaborated these wonderful mausoleums or domed structures affected, at the very earliest periods at which we become acquainted with them, what may be called Microlithic architec-ture. In other words, they used as small stones as they could use, consistently with their constructive necessities. These stones were always squared or hewn, and they always sought to attain their ends by construction, not by the exhibition of mere force. On the other hand, the people whose works now occupy us always affected the employment of the largest masses of stone they could find or move. With the rarest possible exceptions, they preferred their being untouched by a chisel, and as rarely were they ever used in any properly constructive sense. In almost every instance it was sought to attain the wished-for end by mass and the expression of power. No two styles of architecture can well be more different, either in their forms or motives, than these two. All that they

---

[1] In the Kubber Roumeia, in the Sahil, or the Madracen, near Blidah.

have in common is that they both spring from the same origin
in the chambered tumulus, and both were devoted throughout
to sepulchral purposes, but in form and essence they diverged at a
very early period. Long before we become acquainted with either ;
and, having once separated, they only came together again when
both were on the point of expiring.

The Buddhist Dagobas are another offshoot from the same source,
which it would be quite as interesting to follow as the tombs of
the kings or emperors; for our present purposes, perhaps, more
so, as they retained throughout a religious character, and being
consequently freed from the ever-varying influence of individual
caprice, they bear the impress of their origin distinctly marked
upon them to the present day.

In India, where Buddhism, as we now know it, first arose, the
prevalent custom—at least among the civilized races—was cremation. We do not know when they buried their dead ; but in
the earliest times of Buddhism they adopted at once what was
certainly a sepulchral tumulus, and converted it into a relic
shrine: just as in the early ages of Christianity the stone sarcophagus became the altar in the basilica, and was made to contain
the relics of the saint or saints to whom the church was dedicated.
The earliest monuments of this class which we now know are
those erected by the King Asoka, about the year 250 B.C.; but
there does not seem much reason for doubting that when the
body of Buddha was burnt, and his relics distributed among
eight different places,[1] Dagobas or Stupas may not then have
been erected for their reception. None of these have, however, been identified; and of the 84,000 traditionally said to
have been erected by Asoka, that at Sanchi[2] is the only one we
can feel quite sure belongs to his age; but, from that date to the
present day, in India as well as in Ceylon, Burmah, Siam, and
elsewhere, examples exist without number.

All these are microlithic, evidently the work of a civilized and
refined people, though probably copies of the rude forms of more
primitive races. Many of them have stone enclosures; but, like

---

[1] See Turnour in 'J. A. S. B.' vii. p. 1013.

[2] Cunningham, 'Bilsah Topes,' *passim;* and 'Tree and Serpent Worship,' by the
author, p. 87-148.

that at Sanchi, erected between 250 B.C. and 1 A.D., so evidently derived from carpentry that we feel it was copied directly, like all the Buddhist architecture of that age, from wooden originals. Whether it was from the fashion of erecting stone circles round tumuli, or from what other cause, it is impossible now to say; but as time went on the form of the rail became more and more essentially lithic, and throughout the middle ages the Buddhist tope, with its circle or circles of stones, bore much more analogy to the megalithic monuments of our own country than did the tombs just alluded to; and we are often startled by similarities which, however, seem to have no other cause than their having a common parent, being, in fact, derived from one primæval original. There is nothing in all this, at all events, that would lead us to the conclusion that the polished stone monuments of India were either older or more modern than the rude stone structures of the West. Each, in fact, must be judged by its own standard, and by that alone.

For the proper understanding of what is to follow the distinctions just pointed out should always be borne in mind, as none are more important. Half indeed of the confusion that exists on the subject arises from their having been hitherto neglected. There is no doubt that occasional similarities can be detected between these various styles, but they amount to nothing more than should be expected from family likenesses consequent upon their having a common origin and analogous purposes. But, except to this extent, these styles seem absolutely distinct throughout their whole course, though running parallel to one another during the whole period in which they are practised. If this is so, any hypothesis based on the idea that the microlithic architecture either preceded or succeeded to the megalithic at once falls to the ground. Nor, if these distinctions are maintained, will it any longer be possible to determine any dates in succession in megalithic art from analogies drawn from what may have happened at any period or place among the builders of microlithic structures. The fact which we have got to deal with seems to be that the megalithic rude stone art of our forefathers is a thing by itself—a peculiar form of art arising either from its being adopted by a peculiar race or peculiar group of races among mankind, or from its having been practised by people at a certain stage of civilization, or under peculiar circumstances, and this it is our business to try to find out and define. But to do this, the first thing that seems requisite is to put aside all previously conceived notions on the subject, and to treat it as one entirely new, and as depending for its elucidation wholly on what can be gathered from its own form and its own utterances, however indistinct they may at first appear to be.

Bearing this in mind, we have no difficulty in beginning our history of megalithic remains with the rude stone cists, generally called kistvaens, which are found in sepulchral tumuli. Sometimes these consist of only four, but generally of six or more stones set edgeways, and covered by a capstone, so as to protect the body from being crushed. By degrees this kistvaen became magnified into a chamber, the side stones increasing from 1 or 2 feet in height to 4 or 5 feet, and the capstone becoming a really mega-lithic feature 6 or 10 feet long, by 4 or 5 feet wide, and also of considerable thickness. Many of these contained more than one funeral deposit, and they consequently could not have been covered up by the tumuli till the last deposit was placed in them. This seems to have been felt as an inconvenience, as it led to the third step, namely, of a passage communicating with the outer air, and formed like the chambers of upright stones, and roofed by flat ones extending across from side to side. The most perfect example of this class is perhaps that in the tumulus of Gavr Innis in the Morbihan. Here is a gallery 42 feet long and from 4 to 5 feet wide, leading to a chamber 8 feet square, the whole being covered with sculptures of the most elaborate character.

A fourth stage is well illustrated by the chambers of New Grange, in Ireland, where a similar passage leads to a compound or cruciform chamber rudely roofed by converging stones. Another beautiful example of the same class is that of Maeshow in the Orkneys, which, owing to the peculiarity of the stone with which it is built, comes more nearly to the character of microlithic art than any other example. It is probably among the last if not the very latest of the class erected in these isles, and by a curious concatenation of circumstances brings the megalithic form of art very nearly up to the stage where we left its microlithic sister at Mycenæ some two thousand years before its time.

All this will be made clearer in the sequel, but meanwhile there are one or two points which must be cleared up before we can go further. Many antiquaries insist that all the dolmens[1] or cromlechs,[2] which we now see standing free, were once covered up and buried in tumuli.[3] That all the earlier ones were so, is more than probable, and it may since have been originally intended also to cover up many of those which now stand free; but it seems impossible to believe that the bulk of those we now see were ever hidden by any earthen covering.

Probably at least one hundred uncovered dolmens in these islands could be enumerated, which have not now a trace of any such envelope. Some are situated on uncultivated heaths, some on headlands, and most of them in waste places. Yet it is contended that improving farmers at some remote age not only levelled the mounds, but actually carted the whole away and spread it so evenly over the surface that it is impossible now to detect its previous existence. If this had taken place in this century when land has become so valuable and labour so skilled we might not wonder, but no trace of any such operation occurs in any living memory. Take for instance Kits Cotty House, it is exactly now where it was when Stukeley drew it in 1715,[4] and there was no tradition then of any mound ever having covered it. Yet it is contended that at some earlier age when the site was probably only a sheep-walk, some one carried away the mound for some unknown purpose, and spread it out so evenly that we cannot now find a trace of it. Or take another instance, that at Clatford Bottom,[5] also drawn by Stukeley. It stands as a chalky flat to which cultivation is only now extending, and which

---

[1] Dolmen is derived from the Celtic word *Daul*, a table—not *Dol*, a hole—and *Men* or *Maen*, a stone.

[2] *Crom*, in Celtic, is crooked or curved, and therefore wholly inapplicable to the monuments in question; and *lech*, stone.

[3] The most zealous advocate of this view is the Rev. W. C. Lukis, who, with his father, has done such good service in the Channel Islands. His views are em-

bodied in a few very distinct words in the Norwich volume of the ‘Prehistoric Congress,’ p. 218, but had previously been put forward in a paper read to the Wiltshire Archæological Society in 1861, and afterwards in the ‘Kilkenny Journal,’ v. N. S. p. 492 *et seqq.*

[4] ‘Iter Curiosum,’ pl. xxxii. and xxxiii.

[5] ‘Stonehenge and Avebury,’ pl. xxxii. xxxiii. and xxxiv.

certainly was a sheep-walk in Stukeley's time, and why, therefore, any one should have taken the trouble or been at the expense of denuding it is very difficult to understand, and so it is with nine-tenths of the rest of them. In the earlier days when a feeling for the seclusion of the tomb was strong, burying them in the recesses of a tumulus may have been the universal practice, but when men learned to move such masses as they afterwards did, and to poise them so delicately in the air, they may well have preferred the exhibition of their art to concealing it in a heap which had no beauty of form and exhibited no skill. Can any one for instance conceive that such a dolmen as that at Castle Wellan in Ireland

7.   Dolmen in Castle Wellan, Ireland. From a drawing by Sir Henry James.

ever formed a chamber in barrow, or that any Irish farmer would ever have made such a level sweep of its envelope if it ever had one? So in fact it is with almost all we know. When a dolmen was intended to be buried in a tumulus the stones sup-porting the roof were placed as closely to one another as possible, so as to form walls and prevent the earth penetrating between them and filling the chambers, which was easily accomplished by filling in the interstices with small stones as was very generally done. These tripod dolmens, however, like that at Castle Wellan, just quoted, never had, or could have had walls. The capstone is there poised on three points, and is a studied exhibition of a *tour de force*. No traces of walls exist, and if earth had been heaped upon it the intervals would have been the first part filled, and the

roof an absurdity, as no chamber could have existed. These tripod
dolmens are very numerous, and well worth distinguishing, as it
is probable that they will turn out to be more modern than the
walled variety of the same class. But with our present limited
knowledge it is hardly safe to insist on this, however probable it
seems at first sight.

The question, however, fortunately, hardly requires to be argued,
inasmuch as in Ireland, in Denmark,[1] and more especially in
France, we have numerous examples of dolmens on the top of
tumuli, where it is impossible they should ever have been covered
with earth. One example for the present will explain what is
meant. In the Dolmen de Bousquet in the Aveyron[2] the chamber

8.   Dolmen de Bousquet. From a drawing by E. Cartailhac.

is placed on the top of a tumulus, which from the three circles of
stone that surround it, and other indications, never could have
been higher or larger than it now is.

So far as I know, none of these dolmen-crowned tumuli have
been dug into, which is to be regretted, as it would be curious to
know whether the external dolmen is the real or only a simulated
tomb. My own impression would be in favour of the latter
hypothesis, inasmuch as a true and a false tomb are characteristic
of all similar monuments. In the pyramids of Egypt they co-
existed. In every Buddhist tope, without .exception, there is a
Tee, which is in every case we know only a simulated relic-casket.
Originally it may have been the place where the relic was deposited, and as we know of instances where relics were exposed to

---

[1] Madsen, 'Antiquités Préhistoriques,' pl. 6, 7, 8, 9, and 10.
[2] Norwich volume of 'Prehistoric Congress,' p. 355, pl. vi.

the crowd on certain festivals, it is difficult to understand where
they were kept, except in some external case like this.   In
every instance, however, in which
a relic has been found it has
been in the centre of the Tope
and never in the Tee.   A still
more apposite illustration, however, is found in the tombs
around Agra and Delhi.   In all
those of any pretension the body
is buried in the earth in a vault

9. Tee cut in the Rock on a Dagoba at Ajunta.

below the floor of the tomb and a gravestone laid over it, but on
the floor of the chamber, under the dome, there is always a
simulated sarcophagus, which is the only one seen by visitors.
This is carried even further in the tomb of the Great Akbar
(1556, 1605).   Over the vault is raised a pyramid surrounded,
not like this tumulus by three rows of stones, but by three rows
of pavilions, and on the top, exposed to the air, is a simulated
tomb placed exactly as this dolmen is.   No two buildings could
well seem more different at first sight, but their common parent-
age and purpose can hardly be mistaken, and it must be curious
to know whether the likeness extends to the double tomb also.

This, like many other questions, must be left to the spade to
determine, but, unless attention is turned to the analogy above
alluded to, the purpose of the double tomb may be misunderstood,
even when found, and frequently, I suspect, has already been mistaken for a secondary interment.

CIRCLES.

Circles form another group of the monuments we are about to
treat of, in this country more important than the dolmens to which
the last section was devoted.   In France, however, they are
hardly known, though in Algeria they are very frequent.   In
Denmark and Sweden they are both numerous and important,
but it is in the British Islands that circles attained their greatest
development, and assumed the importance they maintain in all
the works of our antiquaries which treat of megalithic art.

The cognate examples in the microlithic styles afford us very little assistance in determining either the origin or use of this class of monument. It might, nay has been suggested, that the podium which surmounts such a tumulus, for instance, that of the Cocumella (woodcut No. 5) would, if the mound were removed, suggest, or be suggested, by the stone circles of our forefathers. This podium, however, seems always to have been a purely constructive expedient, without any mystic or religious significance, for unless the base of an earthen mound is confined by a revêtement of this sort it is apt to spread, and then the whole monument loses that definition which is requisite to dignity.

The Rails of the Indian Buddhists at first sight seem to offer a more plausible suggestion of origin, but it is one on which it would be dangerous in the present state of our knowledge to rely too much; if for no other reason, for the one just given, that up to the time of Asoka, B.C. 250, they, like all the architecture of India, were in wood and wood only. Stone as a building material, either rude or hewn, was unknown in that country till apparently it was suggested to them by the Bactrian Greeks. Unless, therefore, we are prepared to admit that all our stone circles are subsequent, by a considerable interval of time, to the epoch of Asoka, they were not derived from India. My own impression is that all may ultimately prove to have been erected subsequently to the Christian Era, but till that is established we must look elsewhere than to India for our original form, and even then we have only got a possible analogy; and nothing approaching to a proof that any connexion existed between them.

The process in this country, so far as I can make out, was different, though tending to a similar result. The stone circles in Europe appear to have been introduced in supercession to the circular earthen mounds which surround the early tumuli of our Downs. These earthen enclosures still continued to be used, surrounding stone monuments of the latest ages, but, if I mistake not, they first gave rise to the form itself. Such a circle, for instance, as that called the Nine Ladies on Stanton Moor, I take to be a transitional example. The circular mound, which is 38 feet in diameter, enclosed a sepulchral tumulus, as was, no doubt, the case from time immemorial, but, in this instance, was further adorned and dignified by the circle of stones erected upon it. A century or so afterwards, when stone had become more recognized as a building material, the circular mound may have been disused, and then the stone circle would alone remain.

10.   Nine Ladies, Stanton Moor.   From a drawing by L. Jewitt.

These stone circles are found enclosing tumuli, as in the Dolmen de Bousquet (woodcut No. 8), in three rows, and sometimes five or seven rows are found. They frequently also enclose dolmens, either standing on the level plain or on tumuli, but often, especially in this country, they are found enclosing nothing that can be seen above ground. This has led to the assumption that they are "Things," comitia—or places of assembly—or, still more commonly, that they are temples, though, now that the Druidical theory is nearly abandoned, no one has been able to suggest to what religion they are, or were, dedicated. The spade, however, is gradually dispelling all these theories. Out of say 200 stone circles which are found in these islands, at least one-half, on being dug out, have yielded sepulchral deposits. One-quarter are still untouched by the excavator, and the remainder which have not yielded up their secret are mostly the larger circles. Their evidence, however, is at best only negative, for, till we know exactly where to dig, it would require that the whole area should be trenched over before we can feel sure we had not missed the sepulchral deposit. When, as at Avebury, the circle encloses an area of 28 acres,[1] and the greater part of it is occupied by a village, no blind digging is likely to lead to any result, or can be accepted as evidence.

Still the argument would be neither illegitimate nor illogical if, in the present state of the evidence, it were contended that all stone circles, up say to 100 feet diameter, were sepulchral, as nine-tenths of them have been proved to be, but that the larger circles were cenotaphic, or, if another expression is preferred, temples

---

[1] Sir H. Colt Hoare, 'Ancient Wiltshire,' ii, 71.

dedicated to the honour or worship of the dead, but in which no bodies were buried. But to admit—and it cannot now be denied —that all circles up to 100 feet are sepulchral, yet to assert that above that dimension they became temples dedicated to the sun, or serpents, or demons, or Druids, without any other change of plan or design but increased dimensions, appears a wholly untenable proposition.

All this will, it is hoped, be made more clear in the sequel when we come to examine particular examples, regarding which it is more easy to reason than merely from general principles; but in the meanwhile there is one other peculiarity which should be pointed out before proceeding further. It is that where great groups of circles are found, they—so far as is at present known— never mark cemeteries where successive generations of kings or chiefs were buried, but battle-fields. The circles, or dolmens, or cairns grouped in these localities seem always to have been erected by their comrades, to the memory of those who on these spots "fiercely fighting, fell," and are monuments as well of the prowess of the survivors as of those who were less fortunate. The proof of this also must depend on individual examples to be brought forward in the following pages. It does not, however, seem to present much difficulty, the principal point in the argument being that they are generally found in solitary places far removed from the centres of population, or are sometimes single and that they show no progression. Had they been cemeteries or sepulchres of kings, several would undoubtedly have been found grouped together; progression and individuality would have been observed; and lastly, they are just such monuments as an army could erect in a week or a month, but which the inhabitants of the spot could not erect in years, and could not use for any conceivable purpose when erected.

AVENUES.

It is somewhat unfortunate that no recognized name has yet been hit upon for this class of monument. Alignment has been suggested, but the term is hardly applicable to two rows of stones, for instance, leading to a circle. Parallellitha is, at best, a barbarous compound, and as such better avoided. Though therefore, the word avenues can hardly be called appropriate to rows of stones leading from nowhere to no place, and between which there is no evidence that anybody ever was intended to walk, still it seems the least objectionable expression that has yet been hit upon, and as such it will be used throughout.

These avenues are of two classes. First, those leading to circles. About the origin of this class there can be very little hesitation. They represent externally the passages in tumuli which lead to the central chamber; take, for instance, this example from a now

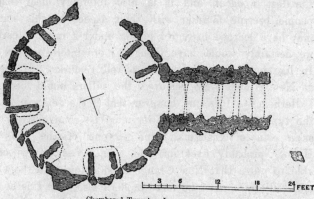

11.   Chambered Tumulus, Jersy.

destroyed[1] tumulus near St. Helier, in Jersey.[2] The circular chamber was 24 feet in diameter, and contained originally seven little cells, each roofed by a single slab of stone. This circular area was approached by an avenue, 17 feet long at the time of its destruction, which was roofed throughout the whole length with slabs of stone. The central chamber never, however, appears to have been vaulted, so that access to the tombs through this passage could never have been possible after the mound was finished. The chamber was found filled with earth, and the whole monument covered up by a tumulus of considerable extent. It need hardly be observed that it is more unlikely that any people should cover up such a monument at any subsequent age, than that they

---

[1] The stones of which it was composed were transported by General Conway to Park Place, near Henley-on-Thames, and re-erected there.

[2] 'Archæologia,' viii. p. 384.

should dig out such monuments and leave them standing without their envelopes, as is so generally assumed. The tumulus was removed, because the officer in command of the neighbouring fort wanted a level parade-ground. As it stood uncovered it was a miniature Avebury, and the position of its cells may give us a hint where the bodies may be found there—near the outer circle of stones, where they have not been looked for. But of this hereafter. It is meanwhile evident that while these monuments were in course of erection they stood as shown in the last woodcut, and it is also tolerably clear that when people became familiar with their aspect in this state, they may have learned to regret hiding under a heap of earth what we certainly would have thought more interesting as it was. In like manner, as John Stuart well remarks, "If the cairns at New Grange were removed, the pillars would form another Callernish."[1] It is true, however, that if the Jersey monument is the type of Avebury, the latter must be comparatively modern, as a coin of Claudius, found in one of the cells at St. Helier,[2] probably fixes its date. Again, as we expect to be able to prove that New Grange is subsequent to the Christian era, Callernish must be more modern also. Be this as it may, I think there can be very little doubt that these exposed circles, with their avenues, took their rise, as in the case of dolmens, from people becoming familiar with their forms before they were covered up, and eventually reconciling themselves to dispense with the envelope. In the case of the circles, the new plan was capable of infinitely greater extension than in that of the dolmens; but the process seems to have been the same in both instances.

Before leaving the Jersey circle, if any one will compare it with the chamber at Mycenæ (woodcut No. 4), they can hardly fail to perceive the close similarity and probable identity of destination that exists between them; but as the island example is very much ruder, according to the usual reasoning it must be the more ancient of the two. This, however, is the capital fallacy which has pervaded all reasoning on the subject hitherto. It is true that nothing can

---

[1] 'Sculptured Stones of Scotland,' ii. Introd. p. 25.   [2] 'Archæologia,' viii. p. 385.

be more interesting or more instructive than to trace the progress of
the Classical, the Mediæval, and the Indian styles through their
ever-changing phases, or to watch the influence which one style had
on the other. That progress was, however, always confined within
the limits of a nation, or community of nations, and the influence
limited to such nations as from similarity of race or constant
intercourse were in position to influence reciprocally not only the
architecture, but their arts and feelings. In order to establish
this in the present instance, we must prove that there was such
community of race and frequency of intercourse between the
Channel Islands and Greece 1000 years B.C., that the latter
would copy the other, or rather that 2000 years B.C. the Channel
Islanders gave the Greeks those hints which they were enabled
to elaborate, and of which the chambers at Mycenæ about the
time of the Trojan war were the result. Had this been the case
the influence could hardly have ceased as civilization and intercourse with other countries increased, and we ought to find Tholoi
in great perfection in these islands, and probably temples and
arts in all the perfection to which they were afterwards expanded
in Greece. In fact, we get into such a labyrinth of conjecture,
that no escape seems possible. It would be almost as reasonable
to argue that the images on Easter Island, which we know continued to be carved in our day, were prehistoric, because they
are so much ruder than the works of Phidias. The truth is, that
where we cannot trace community of race or religion, accompanied by constant and familiar intercourse, we must take each
people as doing what their state of civilization enabled them to
accomplish, wholly irrespective of what was doing or had been
done by any other people in any other part of the world. All
that it is necessary to assume in this case is, that a dead-revering
ancestral-worshipping people wished to do honour to the departed,
as they knew or heard was done by other races of their family of
mankind elsewhere, and that they did it in the best manner the
state of the arts among them admitted of—rudely, if they were
in a low state of civilization, and more perfectly if they had
advanced beyond that stage in which rude forms could be
tolerated.

It is much more difficult to trace the origin of the avenues which are not attached to circles, and do not lead to any important monuments. Nothing that is buried at all resembles them in form, and no erections in the corresponding microlithic style, either in the Mediterranean countries or in India, afford any hints which would enable us to suggest their purpose. We are thus left to guess at their uses solely from the evidence which can be gathered from their own form and position, and from such traditions as may exist; and these, it seems, have not hitherto been deemed sufficient to establish even a plausible hypothesis capable of explaining their intention.

Take, for instance, such an example as the parallel lines of stones near Merivale Bridge on Dartmoor. They certainly do not form a temple in any sense in which that word is understood by any other people or in any age with which we are acquainted. They are not procession paths, inasmuch as both ends are blocked up; and, though it is true the sides are all doors, we cannot conceive any procession moving along their narrow gangway, hardly three feet in width. The stones that compose the sides are only two and three feet high; so that, even if placed side by side, they would not form a barrier, and, being three to six feet apart, they are useless except to form an "alignment." There is no place for an image, no sanctuary or cell; nothing, in fact, that can be connected with any religious ceremonial.

If the inhabitants of the place had really wanted a temple, in any sense in which we understand the term, there is a magnificent tor, a few hundred yards off to the northward, where Nature has disposed some magnificent granite blocks so as to form niches such as human hands could with difficulty imitate. All that was wanted was to move the smaller blocks, lying loose in front of it, a few yards to the right or left, and dispose them in a semi-circle or rectangular form, and they would have one of the most splendid temples in England in which to worship the images which Cæsar tells us they possessed.[1] They, however, did nothing of the kind. They went to a bare piece of moorland, where there

---

[1] Deum maxime Mercurium colunt. Hujus sunt plurima simulacra. 'Bell. Gal.' vi. 16.

were no stones, and brought those we find there, and arranged them as shown on the plan; and for what purpose?

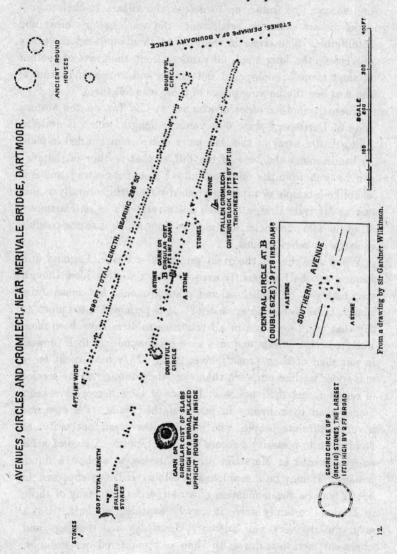

AVENUES, CIRCLES AND CROMLECH, NEAR MERIVALE BRIDGE, DARTMOOR.

From a drawing by Sir Gardner Wilkinson.

The only answer to the question that occurs to me is that these stones are intended to represent an army, or two armies, drawn up in battle array; most probably the former, as we can hardly understand the victorious army representing the defeated as so nearly equal to themselves. But if we consider them as the first and second line, drawn up to defend the village in their rear—which is an extensive settlement—the whole seems clear and intelligible. The circle in front would then represent the grave of a chief; the long stone, 40 yards in front, the grave of another of the "menu" people; and the circles and cromlech in front of the first line the burying-places of those who fell there.

There is another series of avenues at Cas Tor, on the western edge of Dartmoor,[1] some 600 yards in length, which is quite as like a battle array as this, but more complex and varied in plan. It bends round the brow of the hill, so that neither of the ends can be seen from the other, or, indeed, from the centre; and it is as unlike a temple or anything premeditated architecturally as this one at Merivale Bridge. There are several others on Dartmoor, all of the same character, and not one from which it seems possible to extract a religious idea.

When speaking of the great groups of stones in England and France, we shall frequently have to return to this idea, though then basing it on traditional and other grounds; but, meanwhile, what is there to be said against it? It is perhaps not too much to say that in all ages and in all countries soldiers have been more numerous than priests, and men have been prouder of their prowess in war than of their proficiency in faith. They have spent more money for warlike purposes than ever they devoted to the service of religion, and their pæans in honour of their heroes have been louder than their hymns in praise of their gods. Yet how was a rude, illiterate people, who could neither read nor write, to hand down to posterity a record of its victories? A mound, such as was erected at Marathon or at Waterloo, is at best a dumb witness. It may be a sepulchre, as Silbury Hill was supposed to be; it may be the foundation of a caer, or fort, as many of those in England certainly were; it may be anything, in short. But a savage might very well argue: "When any one sees how and where our men were drawn up when we slaughtered our enemies,

---

[1] Sir Gardner Wilkinson in 'Journal, Archæological Association,' xvi. p. 112, pl. 6 for Cas Tor, and pl. 7 for Merivale Bridge.

can he be so stupid as not to perceive that here we stood and fought and conquered, and there our enemies were slain or ran?" We, unfortunately, have lost the clue that would tell us who "we" and "they" were in the instance of the Dartmoor stones at least; but uncultivated men do not take so mean a view of their own importance as to fancy this possible.

This theory has at least the merit of accounting for all the facts at present known, and of being at variance with none, which is more than can be said for any other that has hitherto been proposed. Till, therefore, something better is brought forward, it must be allowed to stand at least as a basis to reason upon, in order to explain the monuments we have to describe in the following pages.

MENHIRS.

The Menhirs, or tall stones,[1] form the last of the classes into which we have thought it necessary for the present, at least, to divide the remains of which we are now treating. They occur in all the megalithic districts, but from their very singleness and simplicity, it is almost more difficult to ascertain their purpose than it is that of any more complicated monuments; nor do the analogies from the cognate microlithic styles help us much. The stones mentioned in the early books of the Old Testament, though often pressed into the service, were all too small to bear any resemblance to those we are now concerned with. Neither Greece nor Etruria help us in the matter, and though it is true that the Buddhists in India, from Asoka's time downward, were in the habit of setting up Lâts or Stambas, it seems with them to have been always, or nearly so, for the purpose of bearing inscriptions, which is certainly not a distinguishing characteristic of our Menhirs. It is true that we have in Scotland two stones. The Cat stone near Edinburgh, bearing the name of Vetta, the grandson of Hengist (who probably was slain in battle there),[2] and the Newton stone in Garioch, which is still

---

[1] From *Maen*, as before, stone, and *hir*—high. Minar is supposed to be the same word. It cannot, at least, be traced to any root in any Eastern language.

[2] 'Proceedings of the Society of Antiquaries of Scotland,' iv. 119 *et seqq.*

unread. We have also one in France near Brest,[1] equally illegible, and no doubt others exist. Perhaps these may be considered as early lispings of an infant, which certainly are the preludes of perfect speech, and only to be found where that power of words must afterwards exist. Here the analogy is, to say the least of it, remote.

There also are, especially in Ireland, but also in Wales and in Scotland, a great number of stones with Ogham inscriptions. So far as these have been made out they seem to be mere headstones of graves, intimating that A, the son of B, lies buried there. A custom, it need hardly be observed, that continues to the present day in every cemetery in the land. The fact seems to be that so soon as the use of stone was suggested and men were sufficiently advanced to be able to engrave Oghams, it was at once perceived that a stone pillar with an inscription upon it was not only a more durable but a more intelligent and intelligible record of a man's life or death than a simple mound of "undistinguishable earth." It in consequence rapidly superseded the barrow, and has continued in use to the present time, and been adopted by both Christians and Mahomedans, by all, in fact, who bury, as contradistinguished from those who burn their dead.

In Scotland the story of the stones is slightly different. A great many of these are no doubt cat stones or battle memorials, but as they have not even Ogham inscriptions, they tell no tale. It is doubtful, indeed, if an Ogham inscription could describe a battle, or anything more complex than a genealogy, and still more so if it did whether we could read it. But without it how can we say what they are? If, for instance, the battle of Largs had not been fought in historic times, how could we tell that the tall stone that now marks the spot was erected in the thirteenth century? Or how, indeed, can we feel sure of the history of any one? By degrees, however, in Scotland they faded into those wonderful sculptured stones which form so marked and so peculiar a feature of Pictland. Whether we shall ever get a key to the hieroglyphics with which these stones are covered is by no means clear, but even if we do they probably will not

---

[1] 'Freminville, Finistère,' pl. iv. p. 248.

tell us much. They certainly contain neither names nor dates, but even now their succession can be made out with tolerable distinctness. The probability seems to be that the figures on them are tribal marks or symbols of rank, and, as such, would convey very little information if capable of being read.

It is easy to trace the perfectly plain obelisk being developed into such as the Newton stones, which have only one or two Pagan symbols, but are certainly subsequent to the Christian era. From these we advance to those on the back of which the Christian cross timidly appears, and which certainly date after St. Columba's time (A.D. 563), and from that again to the erection of Sweno's stone, near Forres, in the first years of the eleventh century, where the cross occupies the whole of the rear, and an elaborate bas-relief supersedes the rude symbols in the front.

In Ireland the rude stones do not appear to have gone through the "symbol stage," but early to have ripened into the sculptured cross, for it was not from a timidly engraved cross as in Scotland that they took their origin. The Irish crosses at once boldly adopted the cross-arms, surrounded by a glory, with the other characteristics of that beautiful and original class of Christian monuments.

In France the menhir was early adopted by the Christians; so early that it has generally been assumed that those examples which we see surmounted by a cross were pagan monuments, on which at some subsequent time Christians have added a cross. This, however, certainly does not appear to have been always the case. In such a cross, for instance, as that at Lochcrist, the menhir and the cross are one, and made for one another, and similar examples occur at Cape St. Matthieu, at Daoulas, and in other places in Brittany.[1] In France the menhir, after being adopted by the Christians, does not seem to have passed through the sculptured stage[2] common to crosses in Scotland and Ireland, but to have bloomed at once into the Calvary so frequent in

---

[1] All these, and many others, are to be found illustrated in Taylor and Nodier's 'Voyage Pittoresque dans l'ancienne Bretagne;' but as the plates in that work are not numbered they cannot be referred to.

[2] I know only one instance of sculptured stone in France; it occurs near the Chapelle St. Marguerite in Brittany.

Brittany. Here the cross stands out as a tall tree, and the figures are grouped round its base, but how early this form was adopted we have no means of knowing.

13.   Lochcrist Menhir.

In Denmark the modern history of the Bauta stones, as the grave or battle stones are there called, is somewhat different. They early received a Runic as the Irish received an Ogham inscription, but Denmark was converted at so late an age to Christianity (the eleventh century) that her menhirs never passed through the early Christian stage, but from Pagan monuments sank at once into modern gravestones, with prosaic records of the birth and death of the dead man whose memory they were erected to preserve.

In all these instances we can trace back the history of the menhirs from historic Christian times to non-historic regions when these rude stone pillars, with or without still ruder inscriptions, were gradually superseding the earthen tumuli as a record of the dead. It is as yet uncertain whether we can follow back their history with anything like certainty beyond the Christian era. This, however, is just the task to which antiquaries should address themselves. Instead of reasoning as hitherto from the unknown to the known, it would be infinitely more philosophical to reason from the known backwards. By proceeding in this manner every step we make is a positive gain, and eventually may lead us to write with certainty about things that now seem enveloped in mist and obscurity.

CHAPTER III.

AVEBURY AND STONEHENGE.

IF there existed any acknowledged facts or accepted data with regard to the megalithic remains we are now treating of, the logical method of following out the subject would be to describe first their geographical distribution, and then their uses and dates. While, however, everything concerning them is considered as uncertain—in fact, as unknown, such a mode of treatment, though satisfactory to believers, would fail to carry conviction to the minds of those who doubt. It appears, therefore, that under the circumstances a preferable mode will be to take three or four of the principal and best known British groups, and to subject them to a tolerably exhaustive examination. If it is possible to dispel the errors that have grown up around them, and to fix their uses and dates on anything like a reasonable basis, the rest will be easy; but so long as men believe in Druids or Dragons, or even think it necessary to relegate these monuments to pre-historic antiquity, it is useless to reason regarding them. By the process it is proposed to follow, it is hoped at least to be able to dispel these mists. Others must judge whether the landscape their dispersion will reveal is either real, or pleasing to contemplate.

The first monument we propose selecting for examination is Avebury, as the largest, and in some respects the most important of the class in this country. Stonehenge might at first sight seem to have equal claims to precedence, but it is exceptional. It is the only hewn stone monument we possess, the only one where trilithons are found with horizontal architraves, and where the outer circle also possesses these imposts. It is, in fact, the megalithic monument which exhibits the most civilized forms, and to prove its age and use would not necessarily prove those of any rude stone monument found elsewhere. Avebury, on the contrary, though larger than the others, is constructed on precisely the same principle. It has the enclosing vallum, with its ditch inside, like Arborlow, Marden, Arthur's round table, at Penrith, and others we shall meet with further on, while its circle and avenues are identical, as far as we can judge, with numerous examples found elsewhere.

Before, however, proceeding to reason about Avebury, the first point is to ascertain what the group really consists of, which is a much more difficult task than would at first sight appear. Stukeley has introduced so many of his own fancies into his description of the place, and they have been so implicitly followed by all who have since written on the subject, that it is now no easy task to get back to the original form.

The principal monument at Avebury consists of a vallum of earth nearly, but not quite, circular in form, with an average

14.   View of Avebury restored. *a.* Silbury Hill. *b.* Waden Hill.

diameter of about 1200 feet. Close on the edge of its internal ditch stood a circle apparently originally consisting of about 100 stones, with a distance consequently of about 33 feet from centre to centre. Inside this were two other double circles, placed not in the axis of the great one, but on its north-eastern side. The more northern one was apparently 350 feet in diameter, the other 325 feet.[1] In the centre of the northern one stood what is here called a cove, apparently consisting of three upright stones supporting a capstone—a dolmen, in fact, such as we shall

---

[1] These particulars are taken from a careful survey made by Sir R. Colt Hoare, in 1812, and published in his 'Ancient Wilts,' vol. ii. pl. xiii. p. 70 *et seqq.*

frequently meet with in the following pages. In the southern circle there was only one stone obelisk or menhir. These facts we gather from Stukeley and Colt Hoare, for all is now so completely ruined and destroyed, that without their description no one could now make even an approximate plan of the place. The stones that comprise these inner as well as the outer circle are all the native Sarsens, which occur everywhere on these downs. In some places, such as Clatford Bottom, about a mile from Avebury, they lie still in numbers sufficient to erect a dozen Aveburys, and many are still to be seen in the Bottoms to the southward, and indeed in every place where they have not been utilized by modern civilization. No mark of a chisel is to be seen on any of the stones now standing here. For their effect they depend wholly on their mass, and that is so great as to produce an impression of power and grandeur which few of the more elaborate works of men's hands can rival.

From the outer vallum a stone avenue extended in a perfectly straight line for about 1430 yards, in a south-easterly direction. The centre was apparently drawn from the centre of the great 1200 feet circle, not from those of the smaller ones. This is called the Kennet Avenue, from its pointing towards the village of that name. I am

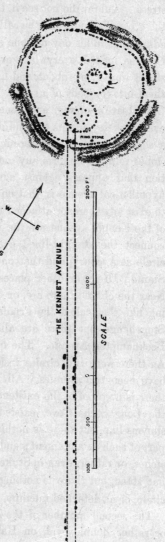

15. Plan of Avebury Circle and Kennet Avenue.
from Sir R. Colt Hoare.

extremely sceptical with regard to the existence of another, called
the Beckhampton Avenue, on which Dr. Stukeley lays so much
stress. Aubrey did not see it, though he saw the Long Stone Cove,
the "Devil's Quoits," as he called them; and Stukeley is obliged to
admit that in his day not one stone was standing.[1] It seems that
here, as, indeed, everywhere over this country, a number of Sarsen
stones were lying about, and his fertile imagination manufactured
them into the body of a snake. None, however, are shown in Sir R.
Colt Hoare's survey, and none exist now; and beyond the Cove
even Stukeley admits that he drew the serpent's tail only because
a serpent must have a termination of that sort. There were no
stones to mark its form any more then than now. The first objection that appears against admitting the existence of the very
hypothetical avenue is, that no curved avenue of any sort is known
to exist anywhere, or attached to any monuments. All the curves
of the Kennet avenue are the Doctor's own, introduced by him to
connect the straight-lined avenues which were drawn from the
circle at Avebury, and that on Hakpen Hill. There are none at
Stanton Drew, or other places where he audaciously drew them.
Near the church there are, or were, two stones placed in the opening like that called the Friar's Heel, and the prostrate stone at
Stonehenge, but these are all that probably ever existed of the
Beckhampton Avenue. The question is not, however, important.
As there were two circles inside the Avebury vallum, there may
have been two avenues. All that is here contended for is, that
there is no proof of the existence of the second. A dolmen, called
the Long Stone Cove, existed near where Stukeley draws its
sinuous line, but there is nothing to show that it ever formed any
part of such an alignment; and around it there were some standing
stones, or rather, even in Stukeley's time, stones which apparently
had stood, but there is nothing to show whether forming part of a
circle, or as detached menhirs, or as parts of an avenue.

The second member of the Avebury group is the double circle,
or rather double oval, on Hakpen hill—Haca's Pen;[2] this was,

---

[1] 'Stonehenge and Avebury,' p. 34.

[2] Haca, or Haco, according to Kemble,
was some mythical person with a very
Danish name which is found in Hamp-
shire and Berkshire, as well as here.
Pen seems to mean merely enclosure, as
it does now in English. See Kemble, in-
'Journal Arch. Inst.' xiv. p. 134.

according to Stukeley, 138 feet by 155 feet, and had an avenue 45 feet wide, as compared with 51 feet which Sir R. C. Hoare gives for those of the Kennet avenue of Avebury. The avenue is supposed to have extended in a perfectly straight line for above a quarter of a mile, pointing directly towards Silbury Hill, which is about one mile and a quarter distant.

The third member of the group is the famous Silbury Hill, about a mile distant due south from Avebury. That these two last named are of the same age, and part of one design, seems scarcely open to doubt; but it is quite an open question whether Hacas Pen belongs either to the same age or the same design. Its stones were very much smaller, its form different, and its avenue pointing towards Silbury looks as if that monument existed, and may have long existed before it was built; but of this hereafter.

Besides these three there are numerous barrows, both long and round, in the neighbourhood, and British forts and villages; but these we propose to pass over at present, confining our attention in the first instance to the three monuments above enumerated.

The first question that arises on looking at such a structure as Avebury, is whether it is a temple at all. It has already been attempted in the preceding pages to show what the temples of Britain were in the ages immediately succeeding the Roman occupation; but even if it is conceded that they were small basilicas, it will be contended that this is no answer to the question. If Avebury, it will be said, is a temple, it belonged to a mysterious, mythical, prehistoric people capable of executing such wonderful works before they came in contact with the Romans, but who, strange to say, were incapable of doing anything after the civilizing touch of that great people had left them feebler, and more ignorant than they were before!

If this question, What is Avebury? is addressed to one—brought up in the Druidical faith as most Englishmen have been—he at once answers, It is a temple of the Druids. If pressed and reminded of the groves and the oaks these sectaries delighted in, he will perhaps admit that no soil is so little likely to grow oaks as the chalk downs of Wiltshire, and that there is no proof that any oaks ever grew in the neighbourhood. But this is not a complete answer, for it may be contended that for some reason we cannot comprehend, the Druids may have dispensed with trees on this occasion. The real difficulty is, as before mentioned, that no stones or stone structures are ever mentioned in connection with Druids.

If an educated man whose mind is free from prejudice or pre-conceived ideas is asked the question, he runs over in his own mind what he knows of the temples of other peoples—Egypt, Assyria, Greece, Rome, in the ancient or the middle ages. They produced nothing of the sort. Persia, India, China, or the countries in the Eastern seas are all equally unsuggestive; nor will Mexico or Peru help him. The first conclusion, therefore, that he inevitably arrives at is, if these were the temples of the Britons, they must indeed have been a "Peculiar people," unlike any other race that lived at any time in any part of the world.

If they were temples, to what god or gods were they dedicated? It could hardly have been Mercury, or Apollo, or Mars, Jove, or Minerva, mentioned by Cæsar,[1] as the gods worshipped by the Druids—and though perhaps these were only the nearest synonyms of Roman gods applied to Celtic divinities, still there must have been such resemblances as to have justified these appellations. We know of what form the temples of these gods were, and cer-tainly they were not built after the fashion of the circles at Avebury. Some antiquaries have timidly suggested a dedication to the Sun. But there is certainly no passage in any author, classical or mediæval, which would lead us to suppose that our forefathers were addicted to the worship of a deity so unlikely to be a favourite in such a climate as ours. But again, what is a sun temple? Does one exist anywhere? Had the Wiltshire shepherds attempted it, they probably would have found the same difficulty that beset the fire-worshipping Persians of old. It is not easy to get the sun into a temple fashioned by human hands, and his rays are far more available on high places or on the sea-shore than inside walls or enclosures of any sort.

Even putting aside the question to what god it was dedicated, what kind of worship could be performed in such a place? It

---

[1] 'Bell. Gall.' vi. 17.

could not be for speaking in. Our largest cathedrals are 600 feet long, and no man would attempt from the altar of the lady chapel to address a crowd beyond the west door; still less would he in the open air attempt to address a crowd in a circle 1200 feet in diameter, and where from the nature of the arrangements one half of the audience must be behind him. Still less is it fitted for seeing. The floor of the area is perfectly flat, and though people talk loosely of the crowd that could stand on the vallum, or on the berm, or narrow ledge between the internal ditch and the foot of the rampart, they forget that only one row of persons could stand on a sharp-pointed mound, and that the berm is on the same level as the rest of the floor, and is the last place any one would choose, as 100 great stones were put up in front of it as if especially designed to obstruct the view. This was, in fact, the case with all the stones. Assuming the ceremony or action to take place in the centre of either of the two inner circles, the double row of stones which surround them is so placed as to obstruct the view in every direction to the utmost possible extent. It may be suggested that the priest might climb on to the cap-stone of the cove, in the northern circle, and there perform his sacrifice in sight of the assembled multitude. It would be difficult to conceive any place so ill suited for the purpose; and even then, how would he manage on the point of the obelisk in the centre of the southern circle? No place, in fact, can be so ill adapted for either seeing or hearing as Avebury; and those who erected it would have been below the capacity of ordinary idiots if they designed it for either purpose. Besides this, it has none of the ordinary adjuncts of a temple. There is no sanctuary, no altar, no ark, no procession path, no priests' house, nothing that is found more or less prominently forming a part of every temple in every part of the world.

Why so hypæthral? Are we to understand that the climate of the Wiltshire downs is so perfect and equable that men can afford to dispense with roofs or the ordinary protection against weather? or are we to assume that the men who could move these masses of stone and raise these mounds were such utter savages that they could not erect an enclosed building of any sort?

Egypt possesses the finest and most equable climate in the

world; yet all her temples are roofed in a more careful manner and more stately than our mediæval cathedrals, and so are all those of India and the Eastern climes where shelter is far less wanted than here. In all these countries and climes the temples of the gods are the dwellings or halls of men, enlarged and improved. What they did well for themselves, they did better for their deities. Are men therefore to assume that the Wiltshire shepherd slept on the snow in winter, with no other protection than a circle of widely spaced stones, and had no idea of a roof? Yet, if he were not hardened by some such process, it is difficult to see why he should build a temple so exposed to the inclemency of the weather that no ceremony could be properly performed in it for one half of the days of the year.

Another objection to the temple theory that would strike most people, if they would think about it, is the enormous size of Avebury. Its area is at least five times that of St. Peter's at Rome; 250,000 people could easily be seated within its vallum, and half a million could stand. Men generally try to adapt the size of their buildings to the amount of accommodation required. But where should such a multitude as this come from? How could they be fed? How could they be lodged? There is no reason to suppose that in any ancient time before the introduction of agriculture, the pastoral population on these downs could ever have been greater than, or so great as, that which now exists there. When Doomsday Book was compiled, there were only two hides of arable land in the manor, and they seem to have belonged to the church. A fair inference from which seems to be that, but for the superior knowledge and influence of the priesthood, the inhabitants of these downs might, in the eleventh century, have remained in the same state of pastoral barbarity in which there is every reason to believe they were sunk in pagan times. How a few shepherds, sparsely scattered over these plains, could have erected or have required such a temple as this, is the mystery that requires to be explained. A very small parish church now suffices for their spiritual wants; and if 10,000 pilgrims, even at the present day, when agriculture has been extended to every available patch of ground, visited the place for a week, many of them would be starving before it was over.

It would be easy to adduce fifty other arguments of this sort. Many more must indeed occur to any one who will give himself the trouble to think of the matter; but to those who are accustomed to such investigations the two most convincing probably are, first, that there is no evidence whatever of progress in the design of Avebury. It was built and finished as first designed. The second is, that in it there is a total absence of ornament. In India, we have temples as big as Avebury; but their history is written on their faces. The first step in the process is generally that a small shrine, with a narrow enclosure and small gateway, becomes from some cause or other, sacred or rich, and a second enclosure is added to contain halls for the reception of pilgrims or the ceremonial display on festal occasions. But no god in that pantheon can live alone. New shrines are added for other deities, with new halls, new residences for priests, and more accommodation for all the thousand and one requisites of a great idol establishment. This requires a third or fourth new enclosure, up even to a seventh, as at Seringham. But in all this there is progress: 200 or 300 years are required, and each century—sometimes each decade—leaves its easily recognised mark as the work progresses. In like manner, the great temple at Karnac, though covering only one-third the area of Avebury, took the Egyptians three centuries to build, and every step of its progress can be easily traced. The works of the earlier Thotmes differ essentially from those of Manepthah and Rameses, and theirs again from those of Seshonk; and these again differ essentially from the little shrine of Osortasen, which was the germ of the whole.

So it was with all our cathedrals. The small Saxon church was superseded by the Norman nave with a small apsidal choir. This was enlarged into the Early English presbytery, and beyond this grew the lady chapel, and as the ill-built Norman work decayed, it was replaced by Tudor constructions. But there is nothing of the sort at Avebury. Had the temple been built or begun by the sparse inhabitants of these downs, we should have seen something to show where the work began. They must have brought one stone one year and another the next, and inevitably they would have employed their leisure hours, like the inhabitants of Easter Island, in carving these stones either with ornaments or symbols, or fashioning them into idols. There is absolutely no instance in the whole world where some evidence of care and of a desire after ornament of some sort is not to be traced in the temples of the people. Nothing, however, of the sort occurs here. Indeed, if there is one thing more evident than another about Avebury, it is that, as it was begun, so it was ended. There is no hesitation, no sign of change: the same men, to all appearance, who traced its plan saw its completion; and as they designed it, so they left it. There is no sign of any human hand having touched it from that hour henceforward till the sordid greed of modern farmers set to work to destroy it, to build with its materials the alehouse and the village which now occupies a small portion of the enclosure.

So too with regard to ornament. This structure, we may fairly assume, if a temple, must have been in use for some centuries; but during that time, or any shorter time that may be assumed, no man had the skill or the inclination to adorn the greatest temple of his native land either with carving or emblems or ornament of any kind. The men who could conceive the great design—so great and noble—could do nothing more. Their hands drooped in listless idleness by their sides, and they were incapable of further exertion! Such a state of affairs, if not impossible, is certainly unparalleled. No such example exists anywhere else with reference to any temple, so far as we know, in any part of the world. Tombs do show these peculiarities at times, temples never.

If these reasons are sufficient to prove that Avebury was not a temple, there are more than can be required, to show that it was not a place of meeting of ancient Britons. Whatever may be thought of the extent of prehistoric assemblies, it will hardly be contended that it was necessary to provide accommodation for the 250,000 men who could be seated in the great circle. Even supposing it were intended only to accommodate 12,000 or 13,000 lords and as many commons in the two subordinate rings, they would hardly have arranged an inner circle of great stones in the middle of each assembly, or placed a spiked obelisk for a woolsack in the one or a tall dolmen under or behind the Speaker's chair in the other. Nothing in fact could be conceived so utterly unsuited for the purpose as these rings, and unless these primeval men

were very differently constituted from ourselves, any assembly
of elder-men who were likely to meet at Avebury would have preferred a room however rude, and of one-hundredth part of the
extent, for their deliberations to the unsheltered and unsuitable
magnificence of the Big Stones. Of course, among all rude people,
and often also among those more civilized, open-air assemblies of
the people will take place; but then these will always be near the
great centres of population.   Men will go into the desert for religious purposes, but they prefer talking politics nearer home.   In
some communities a Campus Martius or a Thing field may be set
apart for the purpose ; but the first requisite of such a place of
assembly is that it shall be open and free from encumbrance of
any sort. A Mote hill too, like the terraced Tynwald Mount in
the Isle of Man, is an intelligible arrangement, not for a delibera-
tive assembly, but as a rostrum from which to proclaim law.   We
can also understand why Shire courts should be held on barrows,
as seems often to have been the case. For here the judge occupied
a dignified position on the summit. His assessors stood behind him,
and the pleaders and people in front.   Instances are also known in
the fourteenth and fifteenth centuries where local courts were sum-
moned to meet at the "standing stones," or in circles, in Scotland
at least;[1] but in all these instances it was apparently to settle
territorial disputes on the spot, and the stones or mounds were
merely indicated as well-known marks and, consequently, convenient
trysting-places. Even if this were not so, it would not be at all
to be wondered at that in the middle ages sepulchral circles or
mounds were habitually used as meeting-places. They were then
old enough to be venerable; and their antiquity must have con-
ferred on them a dignity suitable to the purpose, whatever their
original destination may have been. But all this is very different
from erecting as a place of assembly so huge and inconvenient
a place as Avebury is, and always must have been.

It seems needless to follow this line of argument further, for unless
it can be shown that the people who erected Avebury were so differently constituted from ourselves that no reasoning derived from our
experience can be applied to them, the answer seems inevitable.

---

[1] 'Sculptured Stones of Scotland,' ii. p. xli.

That no such Temple, nor has any such meeting-place, been
built or attempted by any set of men in any part of the world.
But is there any reason for supposing that the inhabitants of these
downs differed so essentially from ourselves?   Dr. Thurnam
has examined with care some hundreds of skulls gathered from
the grave-mounds in this neighbourhood, and has published
decades on decades of them.[1] Yet the most learned craniologists
cannot detect—except perhaps in degree—any difference that
would lead us to suppose that these ancient men were not actuated
by the same motives and governed by the same moral influences as
ourselves. If this is so, Avebury certainly was not erected either
as a temple or a place of assembly, in any sense of the word which
we can understand, and those who insist that it was either are bound
to explain what the motives or objects could have been which
induced the inhabitants of the Wiltshire downs to act in a manner
so entirely opposed to all we know of the actions or feelings of all
other nations in all other parts of the world.

If, therefore, Avebury was neither a temple nor a place of
assembly, what was it? The answer does not seem far to seek. It
must have been a burying-place, but still not a cemetery in the
ordinary sense of the term. The inhabitants of these downs could
never have required a bigger and more magnificent burying-place
than any other community in Great Britain, and must always
have been quite unequal to raise such a monument. But what is
more important than this, a cemetery implies succession in time
and gradations in rank, and this is exactly what is most conspi-
cuously wanting at Avebury. It may be the monument of one
king or two kings, but it is not a collection of the monuments
of individuals of various classes in life, or of a series of individuals of the same rank, erected at different intervals of
time. As before remarked, it is in one design—" totus teres
atque rotundus," erected with no hesitation and no shadow of
change.

If, however, we assume that Avebury was the burying-place of
those who fell in a great battle fought on the spot, every difficulty

---

[1] Thurnam, 'Crania Britannica;' London, 1856 to 1865.

seems at once to vanish. It is now admitted that men did bury in stone circles or under dolmens, and beside headstones and within earthen enclosures, and what we find here differs only in degree from what we find elsewhere. It seems just such a monument as a victorious army of say 10,000 men could, with their prisoners, erect in a week. The earth is light, and could easily be thrown up into the form of the vallum, and the Sarsen stones lay all over the downs, and all on a higher level than Avebury, which perhaps for that very reason is placed on the lowest spot of ground in the neighbourhood. With a few rollers and ropes, 10,000 men would very soon collect all the stones that ever stood there, and stick them up on their ends. They probably would have no skilled labour in their ranks, and no leisure, if they had, to employ it in ornamentation of any sort. Without this, it is just such a monument as might and would be raised by an illiterate army wishing to bury with honour those who had fallen in the fight, and having at the same time no other means of leaving on the spot a record of their own victory.

On theoretical grounds, there seems to be no argument that can be urged against this view; and during the ten years that it has been constantly before the public none have been brought forward that deserve notice. It is urged, however, that the evidence is not complete, and that nothing written serves to confirm this view. Those who make the objection forget that one of the first conditions of the problem is that those who erected such a monument should be illiterate. If they could have written to any primeval 'Times,' they would not have taken such pains to lithograph their victory on the spot. Had they been able either to read or write, an inscription would have done more than the 200 or 300 stones of Avebury; but because they could not write, they raised them, and, for that reason also, left us the problem of finding out why they did so.

We are not, however, wholly without evidence on this subject. Many years ago Mr. Kemble printed a charter of King Athelstan, dated in 939, which, describing the boundaries of the manor of Overton, in which Avebury is situated, makes use of the following expression:—" Then by Collas barrow, as far as the broad road to Hackpen, thence northward up along the Stone row, thence to the burying-places."[1] It does not seem to be a matter of doubt that the stone row here mentioned is the Kennet Avenue, nor that the burying-places (byrgelsas) are the Avebury rings; but it may be urged that the Saxon surveyor did not know what he was talking about; and as, unfortunately, he does not say who were buried there, and gives no corroborative evidence, all we learn from this is that they were so considered in the tenth century.

Something more tangible was nearly obtained shortly before Stukeley's time, when Lord Stawell levelled the vallum next the church, where the great barn now stands. The original surface of the ground was " easily distinguishable by a black stratum of mould on the chalk. Here they found large quantities of buckhorns, bones, oyster-shells, and wood-coals. An old man who was employed on the work says there was a quantity of a cartload of horns, that they were very rotten, and that there were very many burned bones among them."[2] On the same page, Dr. Stukeley adds: "Besides some Roman coins accidentally found in and about Abury, I was informed that a square bit of iron was taken up under one of the great stones upon pulling it down." Other Roman coins have, I understand, been found there since, but there is no authentic record of the fact which can be quoted. This is to be regretted; for the presence, if ascertained, of these coins would go far to prove that the erection of the monument was after their date, whatever that may be.

Unfortunately no scientific man saw these bones, so no one was able to say whether they were human or not; but the presumption is that they were, for why should burned bones of animals be placed in such a situation? The answer to this is that the Wiltshire Archæological Society have made some excavations at Avebury, and found nothing. In 1865, they tapped the vallum in various places, and dug one trench to its centre, and, as they found nothing, concluded that nothing was to be found. But in a mound 4442 feet long, according to Sir R. Colt Hoare, there must be many vacant spots, especially if the bodies were burnt; and such negative evidence cannot be considered as conclusive, nor as suffi-

---

[1] 'Codex diplomaticus Ævi Saxonici,' v. p. 238, No. 1120.
[2] Stukeley, 'Stonehenge and Abury,' p. 27.

cient to disprove the evidence acquired in Lord Stawell's diggings. Stukeley's honesty in recording facts of this sort is hardly to be suspected, though the inferences he draws from his facts are generally to be received with the extremest caution. The Society also dug in the centre of the northern circle, where the dolmen stood, and penetrated to the original chalk, but found nothing except the ruins of the stones which had been destroyed by fire, and express great disappointment at finding "no human bones whatever."[1] If the bodies were burnt—as we should be led to infer from what Lord Stawell found under the vallum—what they probably would have found, had the "Cove" been complete, would have been a vase or urn with ashes. The barbarians who destroyed the stones are scarcely likely to have spared so worthless a piece of crockery; and if it were broken at the time, it would be in vain a hundred years afterwards to look either for it or for bones that in all probability were never laid there. Nor need better results have been expected from their trench, 60 feet long. A man must know very exactly what he is looking for, and where to look for it, who expects to find an object like an urn, a foot in diameter, in a 28-acre field. Judging from the experience obtained at Crichie, in Scotland, where a funereal deposit was obtained at the foot of every one of a circle of stones that stood inside a ditch like the internal one at Avebury, it is there we should expect to find the deposit.[2] That is just where nobody has thought of looking at Avebury, though nothing would be easier. There are fifty or sixty empty holes, and any one might without difficulty be enlarged, and if there were a deposit at the foot of each, it would then inevitably be found.

To this we shall return presently. Meanwhile let us see what evidence, if any, is to be obtained from the circle on Hakpen Hill.

As before mentioned, this monument consists of two ovals, according to Dr. Stukeley the outer one was 138 by 155 feet and

---

[1] The particulars are taken from a pamphlet entitled 'Excavations at Avebury, under the direction of the Secretary of the Wiltshire Archæol. and Nat. Hist. Society,' printed at Devizes, but, so far as I know, not yet published.

[2] 'Sculptured Stones of Scotland,' vol. i. introd. p. xx.

the inner 45 by 51 feet. He does not give the dimensions of the stones; but Aubrey calls them from 4 to 5 feet in height, which

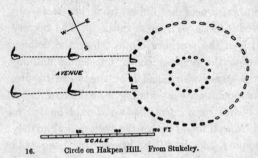

16.   Circle on Hakpen Hill.   From Stukeley.

is confirmed by the Doctor's engraving; and, altogether, they do not seem to average one-quarter the size of those at Avebury. Of the avenue, only four stones are shown in the plan woodcut (No. 16), and the same number is shown in the view (plate xxi.). In both instances, the avenue is represented as perfectly straight, and as trending rather to the southward of Silbury Hill.[1] It extended, according to Aubrey, a quarter of a mile— say 440 yards.

The most curious circumstance, however, connected with this circle is that, at the distance of about 80 yards from the outer oval, there were found two rows of skeletons, laid side by side, with their feet towards the centre of the circles. In a curious letter, written by a Dr. Toope, of Oxford, dated 1st December, 1685, addressed to Mr. Aubrey, and published by Sir R. Colt Hoare,[2] it is said:—" I quickly perceived them to be human." " Next day dugg up many bushells, with which I made a noble medicine. The bones are large and nearly rotten, but the teeth extream and wonderfully white. About 80 yards from where the bones were found, is a temple 40 yards diameter, with another 15 yards ; round about bones layd so close that scul toucheth scul. Their feet all round turned towards the temple, 1 foot below the surface of the ground. At the feet of the first order lay the head of the next row, the feet always tending towards the temple." Further

[1] A plan of it was published about Stukeley's time by a Mr. Twining, in a pamphlet, which was written to prove that this group of monuments was erected by Agricola, to represent a map of England! A plan accompanies it, which shows all the avenues as straight; but what weight can possibly be attached to any evidence coming from a man with such a theory as this?

[2] 'Ancient Wiltshire,' ii. p. 63.

on Aubrey asserts that a ditch surrounded the temple, which Stukeley denies; but there seems no difficulty in reconciling the two statements. The destruction of the monument had commenced before Aubrey's time. For it is impossible to conceive bodies lying for even 1000 or 1200 years in so light a soil, at the depth of 1 foot or even 2 feet, exposed to the influence of rain and frost, without their being returned to earth. Most probably there was a ditch, and where there was a ditch there must have been a mound, and that, if heaped over the bodies, might have protected them. The vallum had disappeared in Aubrey's time; the ditch was filled up before Stukeley's, and stones and all had been smoothed over in Sir R. Colt Hoare's; so that now the site can hardly be defined with certainty. A trench, however, cut across it, if it can be traced, might lead to some curious revelations, for there can be no doubt whatever with regard to the facts stated in Dr. Toope's letter. He was a medical man of eminence, and knew human bones perfectly, and was too deeply interested in the diggings, from which he drew "his noble medicine," and to which he frequently returned, to be mistaken in what he stated.

Meanwhile, however, what interests us more at this stage of the enquiry are the differences as well as the similarities of the two monuments. The circles at Hakpen are on a very much smaller scale both as to linear dimensions and the size of the stones than the circles at Avebury; and the difference between burning and burying, which, so far as the evidence goes, seems to have prevailed in the two places, is also remarkable. Do they belong to two different ages, and, if so, which is the elder? The evidence of the tumuli is uniform that the inhabitants of this island buried before they burnt. But can these bones be so old as this would force us to admit they were? So far as the evidence at present goes, it seems impossible to carry the burials on Hakpen Hill back to the earliest period of prehistoric interments; the condition of the bones is sufficient to render such an hypothesis untenable. Unless the phosphates and other component adjuncts remained in them, they would have been as useless for medicine as for manure, and the exposed position in which they lay would have reduced these to dust or mud in a very few centuries. From the descriptions we have, the bodies certainly were not in the contracted doubled-up position usual in the so-called bronze age, and there were no traces of the cremations apparently introduced by the Romans, and practised for some time after they left. All appear to have been laid out in the extended position afterwards adopted and continued to the present day. In fact everything would lead us to suppose that Camden was not far wrong in saying that these were the bones of the Saxons and Danes slain at the battle of Kennet in A.D. 1006.[1] Even then, unless there was a mound over them, they could hardly have lasted 600 years in the state in which they were found. If we do not adopt this view, but insist that Hakpen and Avebury are contemporary monuments, and part of one great plan, the only hypothesis that occurs to me that will at all account for their peculiarities is that the victorious army burnt and buried their dead at Avebury, and that the defeated force got permission to bury their dead more modestly on Hakpen Hill.

Silbury Hill, which forms the third member of our group, is situated nearly due south from Avebury, at a distance of 1200 yards from the outside of the ring, of the former, to the foot of

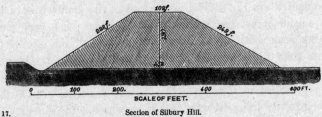

17.　　　　　　　　　　　Section of Silbury Hill.

the hill, or, as nearly as may be, one Roman mile from centre to centre. Mr. Rickman[2] based an argument on the latter fact, as if it proved the post-Roman origin of the group; and like the many recurring instances of 100 feet and 100 yards, which run through all the megalithic remains, it may have some value, but, as a single instance, it can only be looked upon as a co-incidence.

The dimensions of the hill, as ascertained by the Rev. Mr. Smith,

---

[1] Camden, 'Britannia,' 127.　　　[2] 'Archæologia,' xxviii. p. 399 et seqq.

of Yatesbury,[1] are that it is 130 feet in height, 552 feet in diameter, and 1657 feet in circumference; that the flat top is 104 feet or 102 feet across,[2] according to the direction in which it is measured; this last being another Roman coincidence, as the top has no doubt both sunk and spread. The angle of the slope of the sides is 30 degrees to the horizon.

In the year 1777 a shaft was sunk from the top of the mound to the base, by order of the then Duke of Northumberland and Colonel Drax, but no record has been preserved of what they found, or rather did not find, for had they made any discovery of the least importance, it certainly would have been communicated to some of the learned societies of the day. Subsequently, in 1849, a shaft was driven nearly horizontally from the southern face on the level of the original soil to the centre, where it met the Duke's shaft; and subsequently a circular gallery was carried round the centre, but in vain; nothing was found in these excavations that would show that the mound had ever been used for sepulchral purposes, or that threw any light whatever on its history or destination.[3]

Judging from the analogies gathered from our knowledge of the parallel Indian series, we ought not to be surprised if this really were the only result. From the accounts of the Chinese travellers who visited India in the fifth and seventh centuries, we learn that about one-half of the topes they saw and described were erected to commemorate events, and not to contain relics, or as simulated tombs. Wherever Buddha or any of his followers performed any miracles, or where any event happened of sufficient importance to make it desirable that the memory of the locality where it happened should be preserved, there a Tope was erected. To take an example as bearing more directly than usual on our present subject. When Dutthagamini, king of Ceylon (161 B.C.),

---

[1] 'Journal Wiltshire Archæol. and Nat. Hist. Society,' vii. p. 1861.

[2] Curiously enough these dimensions are almost identical with those of the mound erected by the Belg'c-Dutch, to commemorate the part they did not take in the battle of Waterloo. Its dimensions are 130 feet high, 544 feet in diameter, and 1632 feet in circumference. The angle of the slope of the sides is lower, being 27½ degrees, owing to the smaller diameter of the flat top, which is only 40 feet.

[3] Douglas, 'Nenia Brit.' p. 161. See also Salisbury volume of the Archæological Institute, p. 74.

defeated the usurper Ellala, and restored the true faith, "he erected near the capital a dagoba in commemoration of his victory. A stone pillar marks the spot where the action commenced, and another stone pillar exists there with an inscription to the effect that it marks the spot rendered sacred by the death and blood of Ellala."[1] The dagoba is a simple mound of earth, and, so far as known, has never been opened. In Afghanistan, many of the topes opened by Messrs. Masson and Honigberger were found to be what they call "blind topes," but they were not able to detect by any external sign whether their researches were likely to be rewarded with success or to end in disappointment.[2]

Whether these analogies are worth anything or not, nothing appears, at first sight at least, more probable than that, if the fallen chiefs of a victorious army are buried at Avebury, the survivors should have employed their prisoners as slaves to erect a mound on the spot probably where the chiefs were slain and the battle decided. The tradition, however, having been lost, the mound stands silent and uncommunicative, and it is not easy now to read its riddle.

It is very premature, however, to speculate either on these analogies or on the negative results of the explorations made into the hill: these last were undertaken, like the diggings at Avebury, on the empirical assumption that the principal deposit would be found in the centre, and at Silbury on the ground level, which is exactly the place where almost certainly it was not. Supposing that there is a low-level sepulture at Silbury, it probably will be found within 30 or 40 yards of the outer face of the mound, on the side looking towards Avebury, if it is connected with that monument. But the knowledge we have acquired, as will be afterwards detailed, from the examination of the Minning Lowe, Arbor Lowe, Rose Hill tumuli, and other monuments of this class, would lead us to expect to find the principal deposit near the summit. The bit of a bridle (woodcut No. 18) and the traces of armour which were found in Stukeley's time, near the summit, mark in all

---

[1] 'Journal Royal Asiatic Soc.' xiii. p. 164; and Major Skinner's plan of Anurajapura.
[2] Wilson, 'Ariana Antiqua,' p. 41; and Masson's 'Memoir,' passim.

probability the position of the principal graves, and nothing would surprise me less than if five or six entombments were found arranged around the upper plateau at a small depth below the surface. We shall be in a better position to judge how far this is probable when we have finished this chapter; but till the evidence is adduced, it is useless to speculate on its effect.

18. Iron Bit of Bridle.   Found in Silbury Hill.

At one time I hoped that the Roman road might be found to have passed under the hill, and if this were the case, it would settle the question as to whether it were pre- or post-Roman. In order to ascertain this, some excavations were made into the hill in 1867, and simultaneously on the high ground to the southward of it. As traces which seemed undoubtedly to mark the existence of the road running past the hill, at about 50 to 100 yards to the southward, were found there, the excavations into the hill were discontinued, and the line of the road considered as established. Owing to various mishaps, no plan of these discoveries has yet been published, but the annexed woodcut, which is traced from

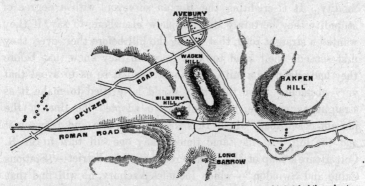

19.   Plan of Avebury, from Ordnance Survey.   The line of the Roman road is hatched throughout.

the Ordnance Survey sheet, will suffice to explain its bearing on the question.

Standing on Silbury Hill and looking westward, the road coming from Bath over the downs seems to come direct at the hill. After passing the Devizes road, it trends to the southward, and shortly

G

again resumes its original direction. About a mile before it reaches the hill, it again resumes its southward direction, and passes it at a distance of between 50 to 100 yards, making, apparently, for the spot where the bridge over the Kennet now exists, and may have existed in Roman times. Those who contend for the pre-Roman antiquity of the hill rest their case on the assumption that the Romans always made or wished to make their roads perfectly straight, and that this being deflected to the south, it was in consequence of the hill being there at the time the road was made. This, however, is singularly contradicted by the line of this very road westwards from the Devizes road. According to the Ordnance Survey, it is set out in a curve for 3½ miles till it meets the Wands-dyke. Why this was done is not clearer than why the road should have been curved to the eastward of the Devizes road. But, on the other hand, supposing the hill to have been where it now stands, and the Romans wished the road to be straight, nothing in the world was so easy as for them to set out a line mathematically straight between the Devizes road and the point where it passes the hill. The country is and was perfectly open, and quite as flat as any Roman road-maker could desire, and signals could have been seen throughout with perfect facility. It is crediting the Roman surveyors with a degree of stupidity they certainly did not show elsewhere, to say, if they wanted a straight road, that seeing the hill before their eyes, they first set out their road towards it, when they knew that before they had advanced a mile, they must bend it so as to avoid that very obstacle. Even then they would have tried to make it as straight as possible, and would have adopted the line of the present coach-road, which runs inside their line and between it and the hill. At the same time, if any one will turn to Sir R. Colt Hoare's map of the Roman roads in this district—"Stations Calne and Swindon"—which includes Avebury, he will find that all are set out in lines more or less curvilinear, and sometimes violently so, when any object was to be gained by so doing. Though, therefore, as a general rule, it is safe to argue on the presumption of the straightness of Roman roads, it may lead to serious error to rely on such evidence in every instance.

The inference drawn from the piece of the Roman road further eastward on Hakpen Hill is the same. It is perfectly distinct and quite straight for about a mile, but if it had been continued in that line, it would have passed the hill at a distance of at least 200 yards to the southward, and never have joined the other piece till long after it had passed the Devizes road. It was deflected northward in the village of Kennet, apparently to reach the bridge, and then to join the piece coming from Bath.

The result of all this seems to be, that the evidence of the Roman road is inconclusive either way and must be withdrawn. Taking the point where it passes the Devizes road, and the piece which is found on Hakpen hill as fixed points, to join these it must have passed considerably to the southward of the hill; whether it did so in a mathematically straight line or in one slightly curved, was a matter for the judgment of the surveyor; but till we know his motives, it is not in our power to found any argument upon them.

If, however, the Roman road refuses to give evidence in this cause, the form of the hill offers some indications which are of value. As before mentioned, it is a truncated straight-lined cone, sloping at an angle of 30° to the horizon, while all the British

20.   Elevation of the Bartlow Hills.   From the 'Archæologia,' xxx.

barrows known are domical or, at least, curvilinear in section. In all his experience, Sir R. Colt Hoare met with only one straight-lined monument of this class, which consequently he calls the Conical Barrow. Whether it was truncated or not is not quite clear. There are bushes, or weeds, growing out of the top, which conceal its form.[1] Nothing was found in the barrow to indicate its age except a brass (bronze?) spear-head, but it was attached to a British village, apparently of the Roman period, inasmuch as iron nails and Roman pottery were found in it.[2] Be this as it may, there are a range of tumuli at Bartlow, on the

---

[1] Sir R. C. Hoare, 'Ancient Wiltshire,' i. pl. ii. fig. 8.   [2] Ibid. i. p. 191.

boundary between Essex and Cambridgeshire, which are all truncated cones, and are undoubtedly of Roman origin. A coin of Hadrian was found in the chamber of one of them, and Mr. Gage, and the other archæologists who were present at the opening, were all agreed that all the four opened were of about the same age.[1] We may therefore feel assured that they were not earlier than the time of Hadrian, though from the style of workmanship of the various articles found, I would feel inclined to consider them somewhat more modern, but that is of little consequence. The point that interests us most is, that the angle of the Conical Barrow quoted above is 45° to the horizon, that of the principal tumuli at Bartlow 37½°, and that of Silbury Hill 30°. Here we certainly have a sequence not long enough to be quite satisfactory, but still of considerable value, as an indication that Silbury hill was post-Roman.

On the other hand, we have undoubted evidence that the truncated conical form was common in post-Roman times. We have one, for instance, at Marlborough, close by, and if that place was Merlin's bury, as Sir R. Colt Hoare would fain persuade us it was, it assists us considerably in our argument. Without insisting on this, however, Mr. George Clark, in his most valuable paper on Ancient English Castles,[2] enumerates ninety truncated cones erected in England, he considers, between the Roman times and the Norman conquest. "These earthworks," he says, "may be thus described: First was cast up a truncated cone of earth, standing at its natural slope from 50 feet to 100 feet in diameter at the top, and from 20 feet to 50 feet high."[3] Mr. Clark does not believe that these were ever sepulchral, nor does it occur to him that they might be memorial. I should, however, be disinclined to accept the first conclusion as absolute till excavations had been made into some of them, at least, where I fancy we may find indications rather tending the other way. Whether they were memorial or not must depend on traditions that have not hitherto been looked for. Mr. Clark's contention was that all had at some time or other been used for resi-

---

[1] 'Archæologia,' xxx. p. 300 et seqq.   [2] 'Arch. Journ.,' xxiv. pp. 92 and 319.
                        [3] Ibid. p. 100.

dential purposes, and as fortifications, and many are recorded
as having been erected as castles. All this is probably quite
correct, but the point that interests us here is, that there are
nearly one hundred examples of truncated cones of earth thrown
up in England after the Roman times, and not one before. If this
is so, the conclusion seems inevitable that Silbury Hill must belong
to the latter age. Whether this conclusion can be sustained or
not, must depend on what follows from the other monuments we
are about to examine. The evidence of the monument itself,
which is all we have hitherto had an opportunity of bringing
forward, may be sufficient to render it probable, but not to prove
the case. Unless other examples can be adduced whose evidence
tends the same way, the case cannot be taken as proved, however
strong a *primâ facie* presumption may be established.

Though a little distant, it may be convenient to include the
Marden circle in the Avebury group. It is situated in a village
of that name seven miles
south of Silbury Hill.
When Sir R. Colt Hoare
surveyed it fifty years ago,
the southern half of the
vallum had been so com-
pletely destroyed, that it
could not be traced, and
he carried it across the
brook, making the whole
area about fifty-one acres.[1]
My impression is that this
is a mistake, and that the

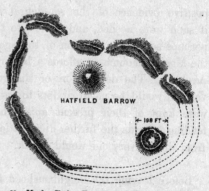

HATFIELD BARROW

|← 196 FT →|

21. Marden Circle. From Sir R. C. Hoare. No Scale.

area of the circle was only about half that extent. The rampart
was of about the same section as Avebury, and the ditch was inside
as there. Within this enclosure were two mounds, situated unsymmetrically, like the circles at Avebury. The greater one was
opened with great difficulty, owing to the friable nature of the
earth of which it was composed; and Mr. Cunnington was con-

---

[1] 'Ancient Wiltshire,' ii. 5. Unfortunately there is no scale attached to the plan
of the Marden Circle, and no dimensions quoted in the text.

vinced that it was sepulchral, and contained one or more burials by cremation; but Sir R. Colt Hoare was so imbued with the Druidical theory as to Avebury, that he could not give up the idea that so similar a monument must be also a Druidical altar, and the whole a temple. The second barrow was too much ruined to yield any results, and on revisiting the spot, it was found to have been cleared away. A great part of the vallum had also been removed, but in it was found at least one skeleton of a man who had been buried there.[1] How many more there may have been it is impossible to say. The destroyers of these antiquities were not likely to boast of the number of bodies they had disturbed.

The great interest of this circle is that it contains in earth the counterpart of what was found at Avebury in stone; not that this necessarily betokens either an earlier or a later age. There are no stones to be found at Marden, which is on the edge of the chalk, while the country about Avebury was and is covered with Sarsens to this day. It may, however, be considered as very positive evidence of the sepulchral nature of that monument, if such were needed, and if it were thoroughly explored, might perhaps settle the question of the age of both. In this respect, the Marden monument affords a better field for the explorer than Avebury. The destruction or disfigurement of its mound, or vallum, would be no great loss to antiquaries, if a proper record were kept of their present appearance; while to do anything tending towards the further dilapidation of Avebury is a sacrilege from which every one would shrink.

Before leaving the neighbourhood it now only remains to try and determine who the brave men were who were buried at Avebury, and who the victors who raised the mound at Silbury, assuming that the one is a burying place, and the other a trophy. Some years ago I suggested it was those who fell in Arthur's last and greatest battle of Badon Hill, fought somewhere in this neighbourhood in the year A.D. 520,[2] and nothing that has since

[1] 'Ancient Wiltshire,' p. 7.

[2] I adopt Dr. Guest's dates for this part of the subject, not only because I think them most probable, but because I think, from his knowledge and the special attention he has bestowed on the subject, he is most likely to be right. See *Salisbury Volume Arch. Journal*, p. 62.

occurred has at all shaken my conviction in the correctness of this determination,[1] but a good deal has tended to confirm it.

The authors of the 'Monumenta Britannica' fix the site of this battle at Banesdown, near Bath, which is the generally received opinion.[2] Carte, and others, have suggested Baydon Hill, about thirteen miles west by north from Avebury, while Dr. Guest carries it off to Badbury, in Dorset,[3] a distance of forty miles. Unfortunately, Gildas, who is our principal authority on this matter, only gives us in three words all he has to say of the locality in which it was fought—" Prope Sabrinum Ostium";[4] and it has been asserted that these words are an interpolation, because they are not found in all the ancient MSS. If they are, however, an insertion, they are still of very ancient date, and would not have been admitted and repeated if they had not been added by some one who knew or had authority for introducing them. As the words are generally translated, they are taken to mean near the mouth of the Severn, a construction at once fatal to the pretensions of Bath, which it is impossible any one should describe as near that river, even if any one could say where the mouth of that river is. It is most difficult to determine where the river ends and the estuary begins, and to a mediæval geographer, especially, that point must have been much nearer Gloucester than even Bristol. This, however, is of little consequence, as the words in the text are not "Sabrinæ ostium," but "Sabrinum ostium"; and as the river is always spoken of as feminine, it is not referred to here, and the expression can only be translated as "near the Welsh gate." Nor does it seem difficult to determine where the Welsh gate must have been.

The Wandsdyke always seems to have been regarded as a barrier erected to stop the incursions of the Welsh into the southern counties, and that part of it extending from Savernake forest westward, for ten or twelve miles, seems at some comparatively recent period to have been raised and strengthened[5] (either by the Belgæ or Saxons) to make it more effectual for that purpose. According as an army is advancing northward from Winchester, or Chichester

---

[1] 'Athenæum Journal,' Dec. 13, 1865.
[2] 'Mon. Brit.' p. 15.
[3] 'Salisbury Vol.' p. 63.
[4] 'Mon. Brit.' p. 15.
[5] Colt Hoare, 'Ancient Wiltshire,' ii. p. 22.

to the Severn valley, or is marching from Gloucester or Cirencester towards the south, the rampart either protects or bars the way. In its centre, near the head-waters of the Kennet, the Saxons advanced in 557 to the siege of Barbury Castle, and having gained that vantage ground, they again advanced in 577 to Deorham, and fought the battle that gave them possession of Glewanceaster, Cyrenceaster, and Bathanceaster.[1] What they then accomplished they seem to have attempted unsuccessfully thirty-seven years earlier, and to have been stopped in the attempt by Arthur at Badon Hill. If this is so, there can be very little difficulty in determining the site of the Welsh gate as that opening through which the road now passes 2½ miles south of Silbury Hill, in the very centre of the strengthened part of the Wandsdyke. If this is so, the Saxons under Cerdic must have passed through the village of Avebury, supposing it then existed, on their way to Cirencester; and if we assume that they were attacked on Waden hill by Arthur, the whole history of the campaign is clear. If we may rely on a nominal similarity the case may be considered as proved. Waden is the name by which the hill between Avebury and Silbury is called at the present day by the people of the country, and it is so called on the Ordnance survey sheets, and etymologically Waden is more like Badon than Baydon, or Badbury, or any other name in the neighbourhood. The objection to this is that Waden Hill is not fortified, and that Gildas speaks of the " Obsessio Montis Badonici." It is true there is no trace of any earthworks on it now, but in Stukeley's time there were tumuli and earthen rings (apparently sepulchral) on its summit, which are represented in his plates; but no trace of these now remains. The hill was cultivated in his day, and in a century or so beyond his time all traces of ramparts may have been obliterated, supposing them to have existed. The true explanation of the difficulty, however, I believe to be found in Jeffrey of Monmouth's account of these transactions. He is a frail reed to rely upon; but occasionally he seems to have had access to authorities now lost, and their testimony at times throws considerable light on passages of our history otherwise obscure. According to him there was both a

---

[1] Saxon Chronicle, in 'Mon. Brit.' p. 304.

siege and a battle; and his account of the battle is so circumstantial and so probable, that it is difficult to believe it to be a pure invention. If it is not, every detail of his description would answer perfectly to an attack on an army posted on Waden Hill.[1] The siege would then probably be that of Barbury Hill, which Cerdic would be obliged to raise on Arthur's advance; and retreating towards the shelter of the Wandsdyke, he was overtaken at this spot and defeated, and so peace was established for many years between the Brits and the Saxons. It may be true that the written evidence is not either sufficiently detailed or sufficiently precise to establish the fact that the battle was fought on this spot. It must, however, be conceded that nothing in all that is written contradicts what is here advanced, and when to this we add such a burying place, Avebury at one end of Waden Hill, and such a monument as Silbury Hill at the other, the proofs that it was so seem to me to amount as nearly to certainty as we can now expect to arrive at in such matters.

Those who believe, however, that all these monuments are absolutely prehistoric, will not, of course, be convinced by any argument derived from a single monument; but if it should turn out that even a more certain case can be made out for the equally modern age of others, that point must eventually be conceded. When it is, I feel no doubt that it will come eventually to be acknowledged that those who fell in Arthur's twelfth and greatest battle were buried in the ring at Avebury, and that those who survived raised these stones and the mound at Silbury in the vain hope that they would convey to their latest posterity the memory of their prowess.

STONEHENGE.

Although from its exceptional character Stonehenge is not so valuable as some others for evidence of the age or uses of the rest of the monuments of this class, it is in some respects even more important for our argument, inasmuch as it possesses a more complete

---

[1] 'Jeffrey of Monmouth,' ix. p. 4.

mediæval history than almost any other of the series. It must be confessed that this history is neither so clear nor so complete as might be wished; but, with the other evidence that can be adduced, it makes up a case so strong as to leave little to be desired. Before, however, proceeding to this, it is necessary to ascertain what Stonehenge really is, or rather was, for strange

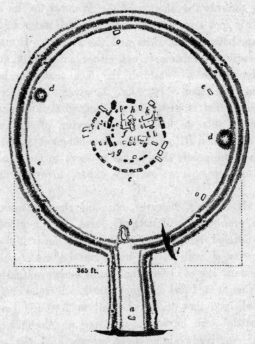

22.   General Plan of Stonehenge.   From 'Knight's Old England.'

to say, though numberless restorations of it have been published, not one is quite satisfactory. There is very little discrepancy of opinion with regard to the outer circle or the five great central trilithons, but there is the greatest possible variety of opinion as to the number and position of the smaller stones inside the central or between the two great circles.

There seems to be no doubt that the outer stone circle originally consisted of thirty square piers, spaced tolerably equally in the circle. Though only twenty-six can now be identified, either standing or lying in fragments on the ground, it seems equally certain that they were all connected by a continuous stone impost or architrave, though only six of these are now in *situ*.[1] The diameter of the circle is generally stated to be about 100 feet, and as this has been suggested as a reason for its being considered as post-Roman, it is important to know what its exact dimensions are. It turns out that from the face of one pier to that of the opposite one, where both are perpendicular, the distance is 97·6, or exactly 100 Roman feet. The distance from the outer face of these piers to inside of the earthen vallum that surrounds the whole is again 100 feet, though that cannot now be ascertained within a foot or two, or even more; but as this makes up the 100 yards and the 100 feet which recur so often in these monuments, these dimensions can hardly be considered accidental, and "valeant quantum" are an indication of their post-Roman date.[2]

Inside these outer circles stand the five great trilithons. Since the publication of Sir R. Colt Hoare's plan, their position and plan may be considered as settled. According to him, the height of the outer pair is 16·3, of the intermediate pair 17·2, and of the great central trilithon as it now stands 21·6. In their simple grandeur they are perhaps the most effective example of megalithic art that ever was executed by man. The Egyptians and Romans raised larger stones, but they destroyed their grandeur by ornament, or by their accompaniments; but these simple square masses on Salisbury plain are still unrivalled for magnificence in their own peculiar style.

---

[1] The history of the plan given on page 92, and from which all the dimensions in the text are quoted, is this. When I was staying with my friend, Mr. Hawkshaw, the eminent engineer, at Eversley, I was complaining of the incorrectness of all the published plans, when he said, "I have a man in my office whose plans are the very essence of minute accuracy. I will send him down to make one for you." He did so, and his plan —to a scale of 10 feet to 1 inch, is before me. I afterwards took this plan to Stonehenge, and identified the position and character of every stone marked upon it.

[2] I am almost afraid to allude to it even in a note, lest some one should accuse me of founding any theory upon it, like Piazzi Smyth's British inches in the Pyramids, but it is a curious coincidence that nearly all the British circles are set out in two dimensions. The smaller class are 100 feet, the larger are 100 mètres in diameter. They are all more than 100 yards. The latter measure is at all events certainly accidental, so far as we at present know, but as a nomenclature and "memoria technica," the employment of the terms may be useful, provided it is clearly understood that no theory is based upon it.

All the stones in these two great groups are Sarsens, as they are locally called, a peculiar class of silicious sandstone that is found as a local deposit in the bottoms of the valleys between Salisbury and Swindon. It is the same stone as is used at Avebury, the difference being that there the stones are used rough in their natural state, here they are hewn and fitted with very considerable nicety. Each of the uprights has a tenon on its surface, and the undersides of the architrave, or horizontal piece, have each a mortice, or rather two mortices, into which these tenons fit with considerable exactness.

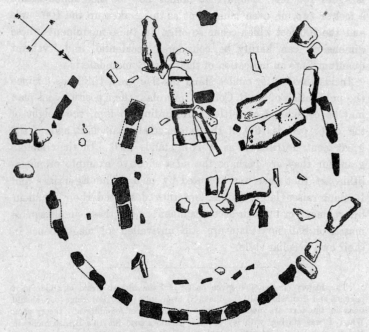

23.   Stonehenge as at present existing, from Mr. Hawkshaw's plan.

Besides these there are even now eleven stones, some standing, others thrown down, but still existing, within the inner circle. These are of a different nature, being all cut from igneous rocks, such as are not to be found nearer than Cornwall or even Ireland. It has not been exactly ascertained whence they came; indeed, they seem to be of various kinds, and consequently must have been brought from different places. Locally they are called Blue stones, and it may be well to adopt that short title for the present, as involving no theory, and as sufficing to distinguish them from the local Sarsens.

None of the blue stones are large; one of the finest (23 in Sir R. Colt Hoare's plan) is 7 feet 6 inches high, 2 feet 3 inches wide at base, tapering to 1 foot on top. The others are generally smaller. One blue stone opposite 23 is grooved with a channel from top to bottom, though for what purpose it is not easy to guess. On the most cursory glance, it is evident that these stones generally stood

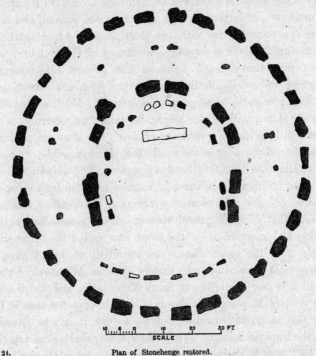

24.   Plan of Stonehenge restored.

in pairs, about 3 feet apart; but some are so completely over-thrown and displaced, that it is not quite clear whether this can be predicated of all. Entering the choir on the left hand we find one that seems to stand alone. But we may infer that this was not always so, from the circumstance that there lies close by it an impost stone with two mortice holes in it, only 3 feet 6 inches apart, which must have belonged to a smaller order of trilithons, and is just such as would fit a pair of blue stones. The next pair on the left is very distinct, and stands between the two great trilithons. The next pair is also similarly situated. On the opposite side there are two pairs, but situated, as far as can be made out, in front of, and not between the trilithons; and again, there are two blue stones behind the stone called the Altar stone, but so displaced by the fall of the great trilithon behind them, that it is impossible to make out their original position with certainty.

It will probably be impossible to determine whether all the pairs of the stones were miniature trilithons or not, till we are able to turn over all the stones that now strew the ground, and see if there is a second stone with two mortices 3 or 4 feet apart. In the meanwhile there is a passage in Henry of Huntingdon's work which may throw some light on the subject. He describes "Lapides miræ magnitudinis in modum portarum elevati sunt, ita ut portæ portis superpositæ videantur." [1] With a very little latitude of translation, this might be taken as referring to the great trilithons towering over the smaller; but if we are to adhere to the literal meaning of the words, this is inadmissible. Another explanation has therefore been suggested. The impost stone of the great trilithon has apparently mortice holes on both sides. If those on one side are not mere wearings of the weather, this must indicate that something stood upon it. If we assume two cubical blocks, and raise on them the stone now called the Altar stone, which is of the exact dimensions required, we would have an arrangement very similar to that of the Sanchi gateway, [2] a cast of which is now exhibiting at South Kensington, and which would fully justify Huntingdon's words. If it is objected that it is a long way to go to Sanchi to look for a type, it may be answered that the Imperial coins of Cyprus show a very similar construction, and both may be derived from a common centre. On the whole, however, I am inclined to the first explanation. There certainly were large and small trilithons, and too great accuracy of description is not to be expected from a Latin writer in the middle ages.

A good deal of astonishment has been expressed at the labour

---

[1] 'Historia,' in 'Mon. Brit.' 694.   [2] 'Tree and Serpent Worship,' by the author, plates iii. et seqq.

it must have required to transport these blue stones from Cornwall or Wales and to set them up here.. If we refer them to the pre-Roman times of our naked blue painted ancestors, the difficulties are, of course, considerable. But after Roman times, the class of vessels they were in the habit of building in these islands must have made their transport by sea easy, even if they came from Ireland, as I believe they did. And any one who has seen with what facility Chinese coolies carry about monolithic pillars 10 feet and 12 feet long, and thick in proportion, will not wonder that twenty or thirty men should transport these from the head of Southampton water to Stonehenge.[1] With the works the Romans left, and the modicum of civilization the natives could not fail to have imbibed from them, the whole was simple, and must have been easy.

Still more wonder has been expressed at the mass of the stones composing the great trilithons themselves, and speculations have been rife as to how our forefathers could, without machinery, drag these masses to the spot, and erect them as they now stand. A good deal of this wonder has been removed, since it was understood that the Sarsens of which they are composed are a natural deposit, found on the surface on all the bottoms in the Wiltshire downs. Owing to the progress of civilization, they have disappeared about Salisbury, but they are still to be seen in hundreds in Clatford bottom, and all about Avebury, and in the northern portion of the downs. The distance, therefore, that the stones of Stonehenge had to be dragged was probably very small; and over a hard, even surface of chalk down, with a few rollers and ropes, must have been a task of no great difficulty. Nor would the process of blocking them up with a temporary mound composed of wood and chalk be one that would frighten a rude people with whom time was no object. After all, Stonehenge is only child's play as compared with the monolithic masses the Egyptians quarried, and carved, and moved all over their country, long before Stonehenge was thought of, and without machinery in the sense in which we understand the term. In India, our grandfathers might have seen far more wonderful things done before we

---

[1] Twenty Chinese coolies would carry any one of them up in a week.

crushed all feeling and enterprise out of the people. The great gateway, for instance, at Seringham is 40 feet high, 21 feet wide, and 100 feet deep. The four door posts are each of a single block of granite, more, consequently, than 40 feet in length, for they are partially buried in the earth. The whole is roofed by slabs of granite, each more than 21 feet long, and raised to the height of 40 feet; and all of these, though of granite, are elaborately carved. Yet the building of the gateway was stopped by our quarrel with the French for the possession of Trichinopoly in the middle of the last century. The Indians in those days had no machinery, but with plenty of hands and plenty of leisure mountains may be raised; and it is on this principle that barbarous nations act and by which they achieve such wonders. The masses of Stonehenge are not, however, so very great after all, but they impose by their simplicity. To use an apparent paradox, it is one of the most artistic buildings in the world from its very want of art. The 40 feet monoliths of Seringham do not impress as much as the 20 feet stones of Stonehenge, because the one is covered with sculpture, the other more nearly in a state of nature, and the effect on the mind is immensely enhanced by the monolithic simplicity of the whole.

Strange to say, this very grandeur and apparent difficulty is one of the most common reasons adduced for its pre-Roman antiquity. Few can escape from an ill-defined impression that what is great and difficult must also be ancient, though the probability is, that if the feeling were analyzed it would be found to have arisen from the learning we imbibed in the nursery, and which told us of the giants that lived in the olden time. If, however, we turn from the teachings of nursery rhymes to the pages of sober history, what we learn is something very different. Without laying too much stress on the nakedness and blue paint of our ancestors, all history, and the testimony of the barrows, would lead us to suppose that the inhabitants of this island, before the Romans occupied it, were sparse, poor in *physique*, and in a very low state of civilization. Though their national spirit may have been knocked out of them, they must have increased in number, in physical comfort, and in civilization during the four centuries of peaceful prosperity of the Roman domination, and therefore in so far as that argument goes, became infinitely more capable of erecting such a monument as Stonehenge after the departure of the Romans than they had been before their advent.

It certainly appears one of the strangest inversions of logic to assume that the same people erected Stonehenge who, during the hundreds, or it may be the thousands, of years of their occupation, could attempt nothing greater than the wretched mole-hills of barrows which they scraped up all over the Wiltshire downs. Not one of those has even a circle of stone round its base; nowhere is there a battle stone or a stone monument of any sort. Though the downs must have been covered with Sarsens, they had neither sense nor enterprise sufficient even to set one of those stones on end. Yet we are asked to believe that the same people, in the same state, erected Stonehenge and Avebury, and heaped up Silbury Hill. These monuments may be the expression of the feelings of the same race; but if I am not very much mistaken, in a very different and much more advanced state of civilization.

We shall be in a better position to answer a question which has frequently been raised, whether or not the blue stones were a part of the original structure, or were added afterwards, when we have discussed the materials for the history of its erection; meanwhile we may pass from these, which are the really interesting part of the structure, to the circle which is generally supposed to have existed between the outer circle of Sarsens and the inner choir of great stones.

With regard to this nothing is certain, except in respect to eight stones, which stretched across the entrance of the choir, and may consequently be called the choir screen. Of the four on the right hand side only one has fallen, but it is still there; on the left hand only two remain, and only one is standing, but the design is perfectly clear. The two central stones are 6 feet high, and the stones fall off by regular gradation right and left to 3 feet at the extremities. They are rude unhewn Sarsen stones, but there is nothing to indicate whether they were, or were not, a part of the original design.

Beyond this, between the two great Sarsen circles, there exist some nine or ten stones, but whether they are in *situ* or not, or

H

whether they were ever more numerous, it seems impossible to determine. On the left hand, near the centre, are a pair that may have been a trilithon, but the rest are scattered so unsymmetrically that it would be dangerous to hazard any conjecture with regard to their original arrangement. It seems, however, most improbable that while the choir screen is so nearly entire even now, that this circle, if it ever existed, should have been so completely destroyed. Had it been complete, it would probably have consisted of 40 stones (excluding, of course, the choir screen), and of these only 10, if so many, can be said to belong to it. These are rude unhewn stones, and of no great dimensions.

In addition to these, there are two stones now overthrown lying inside the vallum, unsymmetrically with one another, or with anything else. Here again the question arises, were there more? There is nothing on the spot to guide us to our answer, and as nothing hinges upon it, I may perhaps be allowed to suggest that each of these marks a secondary interment. At the foot of each, I fancy urns or bones, or some evidence of a burial might be found, and if the place had continued for a century as a burying place, it might have been surrounded by its circle of stones, like Avebury, or Crichie, or Stanton moor. The place, however, may have become deserted shortly after these two were erected, and none have been added since.

There are still two other stones, one standing, one lying in the short avenue that leads up to the temple. Their position is exactly that of the two stones, which are all that is visible of the so-called Beckhampton avenue, at Avebury. But what their use is it is difficult to guess. Were either of the places temples, they would have been placed opposite one another on each side of the avenue, so that the priests in procession and people might pass between, but being placed one behind the other in the centre of the roadway, they must have had some other meaning. What that may have been I am unable to suggest. The spade may tell us if judiciously applied, but except from the spade I do not know where to look for a solution of the riddle.

Those who consider that Stonehenge was a temple have certainly much better grounds for such a theory than it would be possible to establish in respect to Avebury. Indeed, looking at the ground

plan above, there is something singularly templar in its arrangement. In the centre is a choir, in which a dignified service
could be performed, and a stone lies now just in such a
position as to entitle it to the appellation it generally receives
of the altar stone. Unfortunately for this theory, however, it lies
flush with the ground, and even if we assume that the surface has
been raised round it, its thickness is not sufficient to entitle it
to be so called, judging from any analogous example we know of
elsewhere. Around the choir is what may fairly be considered
the procession path; and if its walls had only been solid, and
there were any indications that the building had ever been roofed,
it would be difficult to prove that it was not erected as a temple,
and for worship. As, however, it has no walls, and it is
impossible to believe that it was ever intended to be roofed,
all the arguments that apply to Avebury in this respect are
equally applicable here, with this one in addition. Unless its
builders were much more pachydermatous, or woolly, than their
degenerate descendants, when they chose this very drafty and
hypæthral style of architecture, they would certainly have selected
a sheltered spot on the banks of the Avon close by, where, with
trees and other devices, they might have provided some shelter
from the inclemency of the weather. They never would have
erected their temples on the highest and most exposed part of
an open chalk down, where no shelter was possible, and no service could be performed except at irregular intervals, dependent
on the weather throughout the year. As, however, it differs
not only in plan but in construction—being hewn and having
imposts—from all the rude stone circles we are acquainted with
elsewhere, no theory will be quite satisfactory that does not
account for this difference. My belief is, that this difference
arises from the fact that alone of all the monuments we know
of its class, it was erected leisurely and in time of peace by a
prince retaining a considerable admixture of Roman blood in
his veins. All, or most of the others, seem to be records of
battles erected in haste by soldiers and unskilled workmen: but
of this hereafter.

Owing to its exceptional character, the usual analogies apply
less directly to Stonehenge than to almost any other monument.

We shall be better able to judge how far those derived from India apply, when we have described the monuments of that country. In Europe the trilithon is certainly exceptional, and its origin not easily traced. My own impression is, that it is only an improved dolmen, standing on two legs instead of three, or four; but if that is so, the intermediate steps are wanting which would enable us to connect the two in a logical manner. They were not, however, quite unknown in the Roman world. Several exist in Syria, for instance; three of these are engraved in De Vogüé's work. One (the tomb of Emilius Reginus, A.D. 195) consists of two Doric columns, with an impost; another (woodcut No. 25) is

the tomb of a certain Isidorus, and is dated A.D. 222, and is more like our Salisbury example; both these last-named are situated near Khatoura.[1] The bearing of such an example as this on the question of the age of these monuments admits of a double interpretation. According to the usual and specious mode of reasoning, the ruder form must be the

25.   Tomb of Isidorus, at Khatoura.

earliest, and the architectural one copied from it. But this theory I believe to be entirely at variance with the facts, as observed. The rudeness or elaboration of a monument will probably be found in all instances to be an index of the greater or less civilization of the people who erected it, but seldom or ever a trustworthy index of time. What interests us more at present

---

[1] 'Syrie Centrale,' by Comte Melchior de Vogüé. Though this work was commenced some ten years ago, and subscriptions obtained, it is still incomplete. No text has yet been published, and no maps, which makes the identification of the places singularly difficult.

is the knowledge that these Syrian examples are certainly
sepulchral, and their form is thus another argument in favour of
the sepulchral character of Stonehenge, if any were needed. More
satisfactory than this, however, is the testimony of Olaus Magnus,
archbishop of Upsala, quoted above.[1] He describes and figures
"the most honourable monuments of the great of his country as
erected with immense stones, and formed like great gates or
trilithons" (in modum altissimæ et latissimæ januæ sursum transversumque viribus gigantum erecta). There is no reason for
supposing that this author ever saw or even heard of Stonehenge,
yet it would be difficult to describe either the purpose or the
mode of construction of that monument more correctly than he
does; and in so far as such testimony is considered valuable, it
is decisive as to both the age and use of the monument.

Passing on from this branch of the enquiry to such local indications as the spot affords, we find nothing very relevant or very
important either for or against our hypothesis. It has been argued,
for instance, that the number of tumuli that stud the downs within
a few miles of Stonehenge, is a proof that this temple stood there
before the barrows were erected, and that they gathered round its
sacred precincts. The first objection to this view is, that it is
applying a Christian precedent to a Pagan people. Except the
Jews, who seem to have buried their kings close to their temples,[2]
I do not know of any people in ancient or modern times except
Christians who did so, and we certainly have no hint that the
ancient Britons were an exception to this universal rule.

Assuming, however, for the sake of argument, that this were
otherwise, we should then certainly find the barrows arranged
with some reference to Stonehenge. Either they would have
gathered closely around its precincts, or ranged in rows alongside
the roads or avenues leading to it. Nothing of the sort, however, occurs, as will be seen from the woodcut in the following page.
Within 700 yards of the monument there is only one very insignificant group, eight in number (15 to 23 of Sir R. Colt Hoare's
plan). Beyond that they become frequent, crowning the tops of
the hills, or clustering in the hollows, but nowhere with the

---

[1] Vide *ante*, footnote, p. 15.   [2] ' Topography of Jerusalem,' by the Author, p. 58.

least apparent reference to Stonehenge. If any one will take the Ordnance Survey maps, or Sir R. Colt Hoare's plans, he will

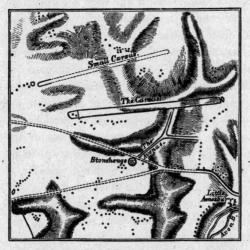

find the barrows pretty evenly sown all over the surface of the plain, from two or three miles south of Stonehenge as far as Chidbury camp, eight miles north of it. Indeed, if Sir R. Colt Hoare's plans are to be trusted, they were thicker at the northern end of the plain than at the southern;[1] but as the Ordnance

26. Country around Stonehenge. From Ordnance Survey maps.
Scale 1 inch to 1 mile.

maps do not bear this out, it must not be relied upon. Nowhere over this large area (say 10 miles by 5 miles) is there any trace of system as to the mode of placing these barrows. Indeed, from Dorchester up to Swindon, over a distance of more than seventy miles, they are scattered either singly or in groups so completely without order, that the only feasible explanation seems to be, that each man was buried where he lived; it may possibly have been in his own garden, but more probably in his own house. The hut circles of British villages are in grouping and in form so like the barrows, that it is difficult not to suspect some connexion between them. It may have been that when the head of a family died, he was buried on his own hearth, and an earthen mound replaced the hut in which he lived. Be this as it may, there is one argument that those overlook who contend that the barrows came to Stonehenge. It is admitted that Stonehenge belongs to the so-called Bronze age,[2] but one half of the barrows

---

[1] 'Ancient Wiltshire,' i. p. 178, plan vi.
[2] Sir John Lubbock, 'Prehistoric Times,' p. 116.

contain only flint and stone, and consequently were there before Stonehenge was built. Nor is it by any means the case that the nearest it were those which contained bronze or iron, it is generally quite the contrary; with all his knowledge, even Sir R. Colt Hoare never could venture to predict from the locality whether the interment would be found to belong to one class or to another, nor can we now.

One of the most direct proofs that this argument is untenable is found in the fact, that the builders of Stonehenge had so little respect for the graves of their predecessors, that they actually destroyed two barrows in making the vallum round the monument. Sir R. C. Hoare found an interment in one, and from this he adds, "we may fairly infer that this sepulchral barrow existed on the plain, I will not venture to say before the construction of Stonehenge, but probably before the ditch was thrown up." [1]

It seems needless, however, to pursue the argument further. Any one who studies carefully the Ordnance Survey sheet must, I think, perceive that there is no connexion between the earthen and the stone monuments. Or if this fail to convince him, if he will ride from Stonehenge over Westdown to Chidbury camp,[2] he can hardly fail to come to the conclusion that Stonehenge came to the barrows, not the barrows to Stonehenge.

One other indication drawn from the barrows has been thought to throw some light on the subject. In one of those (No. 16) near Stonehenge, about 300 yards off, were found chippings of the same blue stones which form the inner circle of the monuments; but there was nothing else in this barrow to indicate its age except a spear-head of brass in fine preservation, and a pin of the same metal, which seemed to indicate that it belonged to the bronze age. In another (No. 22) a pair of ivory tweezers were found. From this discovery it was inferred, and not without some show of reason, that the barrows were more modern than Stonehenge; and if we are to believe that all barrows are pre-Christian, as some would try to persuade us, there is an end of the argument. But is this so? We have just seen that the

---

[1] Sir R. Colt Hoare, 'Ancient Wiltshire,' i. p. 145.
[2] The name is written as Sidbury in the Ordnance maps.

Bartlow hills were certainly Roman. We know that the Saxons buried in hows in the country, down at least to Hubba the Dane,[1] who was slain in 878, and in Denmark, as we shall presently see, to a much later period; and we do not know when the Ancient Britons ceased to use this mode of interment. Whoever they were that built Stonehenge, they were not Christians; or, at all events, it is certainly not a Christian building, and we have no reason to assume that those men who were employed on its erection, and who had for thousands of years been burying in barrows, changed their mode of sepulture before their conversion to Christianity. It is infinitely more probable that they continued the practice very long afterwards; and till we can fix some time when we feel sure that sepulture in barrows had ceased, no argument can be drawn from this evidence. That the chief mason of Stonehenge should be buried in his own house, or own workshop, appears to us the most natural thing in the world; and that a village of barrows, if I may use the expression, may be contemporary with the monument I regard also as probable; but unless from some external evidence we can fix their age, their existence does not seem to have any direct bearing on the points we are now discussing.

The diggings inside the area of Stonehenge throw more light on the subject of our enquiry than anything found outside, but even they are not so distinct or satisfactory as might be desired. The first exploration was undertaken by the Duke of Buckingham, and an account of it is preserved by Aubrey. He says, "In 1620 the duke, when King James was at Wilton, did cause the middle of Stonehenge to be digged, and this underdigging was the cause of the falling down and recumbencie of the great stone there," meaning evidently the great central trilithon. In the process of digging they "found a great many bones of stagges and oxen, charcoal, batter dashes (whatever that may mean), heads of arrows, and some pieces of armour eaten out with rust. Bones rotten, but whether of stagges or of men they could not tell."[2] He further adds "that Philip Earl of Pembroke did say that an altar stone was found in the middle of the area here, and that it

---

[1] 'Archæologia,' vii. pp. 132-134.　　　[2] 'Ancient Wiltshire,' i. p. 154.

was carried away to St. James'." What this means it is not easy to discern, for Inigo Jones distinctly describes as the altar the stone now known by that name, which measures, as he says, 16 feet by 4. It seems impossible that any other could have existed without his knowing it, and if it existed it would have favoured his views too distinctly for him not to mention the fact.

As the digging above referred to must have taken place between what is now called the altar stone and the great trilithon, it is of considerable interest to us. But strange to say it leaves us in ignorance whether the bones found there were human or not; one thing, however, seems tolerably certain, that the arrow-heads and armour were of iron, from the state of rust they are described as being in, and this so far is indicative of a post-Roman date.

Another curious fact is mentioned by Camden. In his plate (page 122), half plan, half elevation—at a spot marked C outside the vallum, men are represented as making an excavation, and the reference is " Place where men's bones are dug up." This is of no great value in so far as Stonehenge itself is concerned, but it is curious from its analogy with the place where the bones were found on Hakpen Hill, and may serve as an indication to the spot where the bones may yet be found in Avebury. As we shall see further on, there are strong reasons for believing that the principal interment at least was not inside the circle, but situated externally on one side.

In more modern times, Sir R. Colt Hoare adds—" We have found, in digging (within the circle), several fragments of Roman as well as coarse British pottery, parts of the head and horns of deer and other animals, and a large barbed arrow-head of iron," thus confirming what Aubrey tells us of the Duke of Buckingham's excavation to the fullest extent. Mr. Cunnington also dug near the altar to a depth of nearly 6 feet, and found the chalk had been moved to that depth. At about the depth of 3 feet he found some Roman pottery. Soon after the fall of the great trilithon, in 1797, he dug out some of the earth that had fallen into the excavation, and " found fragments of fine black Roman pottery, and since then another piece on the same spot."[1]

---

[1] 'Ancient Wiltshire,' i. p. 150.

No excavation in the area has been undertaken since Sir R. Colt Hoare's day, but as both he and Mr. Cunnington were experienced diggers, and perfectly faithful recorders of what they found, it seems impossible to doubt, from the finding of iron armour and Roman pottery in such places, and at such depths that the building must have been erected after the Romans settled in this island. As no one now will probably be found to adopt Inigo Jones' theory that it was built by the Romans themselves, we must look to some date after their departure to which we may assign its erection.

For the written history of Stonehenge we are unfortunately forced to rely principally on Jeffrey of Monmouth, who, though a recorder of historical events, was also a fabulist of the most exuberant imagination. It is consequently easy to throw discredit on his testimony, and some consider themselves justified in putting it aside altogether. If, however, we are to reject every mediæval author who records miracles, or adorns his tale with fables, we may as well shut up our books at once, and admit that, between the departure of the Romans and the arrival of the Normans, the history of England is a mere confused jumble, in which may be found the names of some persons and of the battles they fought with one another, but nothing more. It is an easy process, and may be satisfactory to some minds. The attempt to separate the wheat from the chaff is a more tedious and laborious task, surrounded by difficulties, and open to criticism, but it is one that must be undertaken if truth is to be arrived at. In the present instance the choice of difficulties seems to be clear. Either we must reject the history of Jeffrey as entirely fabulous and unworthy of credit, or admit his principal statement that Stonehenge was erected by Aurelius Ambrosius as a monument to the memory of the British chiefs treacherously slain by Hengist.

The first account we have of the event which led to its erection is in Nennius, who lived much nearer to the time of the occurrence than Jeffrey, who copied his narrative. It is as follows:—The Saxons having been defeated in several actions on the coast of Kent by Vortimir, were shut up in Thanet and forced to wait till they could summon succour from home. When these arrived,

Hengist, before attempting open force, had recourse to stratagem, and at a feast held at the palace or monastery at Amesbury, to which it was agreed all should come unarmed, three hundred British nobles were treacherously slain by the followers of Hengist, who had concealed their weapons under their cloaks. War ensued on this, and lasted apparently for four years, when Ambrosius, who had succeeded to Vortigern, forced the Saxons to sue for peace.[1] That being established, Jeffrey represents him as erecting Stonehenge by the aid of Merlin as a monument to those who were so treacherously slain by Hengist. The massacre took place apparently in the year 462, and the erection of Stonehenge consequently may have been commenced about the year 466, and carried on during the following years, say down to 470 A.D. If he had been content to tell the story in as few words as are used here, it probably never would have been doubted; but Merlin, in the first place, has a bad character, for he is mixed up with the mediæval romances which made the story of Arthur famous but fabulous, and the mode in which he is represented by Jeffrey as bringing the stones from Ireland is enough to induce incredulity in all sober minds.[2] As I understand the narrative, it is this—there existed on a mountain in Ireland a monument something like Stonehenge, which Merlin, when consulted, advised the King to copy. This certainly is the view taken of the matter by Geraldus Cambrensis in 1187, inasmuch as he tells us, that in the spot referred to "similar stones, erected in a similar manner, were to be seen in his day," though in the same sentence he tells us, that they, or others like them, were removed to Salisbury Plain by Merlin.[3] As he probably speaks of what he saw with his own

---

[1] Nennius, in 'Mon. Brit.' p. 69.

[2] Jeffrey, viii. c. 9.

[3] "Fuit antiquis temporibus in Hibernia lapidum congeries admiranda, quæ et Chorea gigantum dicta fuit, quia gigantes eam ab ultimis Africæ partibus in Hiberniam attulerunt et in Kildariænes planicie non procul a Castro Nasensi, tam ingenii quam virium opere mirabiliter erexerunt. Unde et ibidem lapides quidam aliis simillimi similique modo erecti usque in hodiernum conspi-

ciuntur. Mirum qualiter tanti lapides tot etiam et tam magni unquam in unum locum vel congesti fuerint vel erecti: quantoque artificiis lapidibus tam magnis et altis alii superpositi sint non minores; qui sic in pendulo et tanquam in inani suspendi videntur ut potius artificum studio quam suppositorum podio inniti videantur. Juxta Britannicam historiam lapides istos rex Britonum Aurelius Ambrosius divina Merlini diligentia de Hibernia in Britanniam advehi pro-

eyes, his words furnish tolerably clear evidence that Merlin had not removed what still remained at Kildare so many centuries after his death. It is also evidence, however, that the design of the monument was brought from Ireland, and even copied from a circle, the remains of which may probably still, if looked for, be found. So far as we know there was nothing like Stonehenge existing in England, nor in France, in the 5th century. But, as we shall presently see, there probably may have been in Ireland. The only trilithons I know of elsewhere are three in a monument in the Deer Park near Sligo. They are small and simulate portals, but they are more like Stonehenge than any else now known. At the age we are now speaking of Ireland had contrived to nurse her old traditions uninfluenced by Roman or foreign examples, and had attained to that stage in art which would enable her to elaborate such a style of architecture. While in England it is most improbable that anything so purely original could have been elaborated during the Roman occupation of the island. Still a monument like this must have had a prototype, and unless we can prove its existence here before Cæsar's time, it is to Ireland or some foreign country that we must look for the model that suggested the design. But, after all, are we not fighting with a shadow? May it not be that the tradition of a monument being brought from Ireland applies only to the blue stones? I have been assured by competent geologists, though I have not seen the fact stated in any form I can quote, that these belong to rocks not found in Great Britain, but which are common in Ireland. If this is so, there would be no greater difficulty in bringing them from the Sister Island than from Wales or Cornwall. Once on board ship the difference of distance is nothing. If they did come from Ireland nothing is more likely than that, after a lapse of eight or ten centuries, the facts belonging really only to a part should be applied to the whole; and in that case the aid of

---

curavit; et ut tanti facinoris egregium aliquod memoriale relinqueret eodem ordine et arte qua prius in loco constituit ubi occultis Saxonum cultris Britanniæ flos occidit et sub pacis obtentu nequitiæ telis male tecta regni juventus occubuit."—*Topogr. Hiberniæ*, vol. ii. ch. xviii.

If we could trust Ware, they still existed in the beginning of the last century. He speaks of "Saxa illæ ingentia et rudia quæ in planitie non longe a Naasa in agro Kildariensi et alibi visuntur."—*Hist. Hib.*, xxiv. 103.

Merlin or of some equally powerful magician would certainly have become indispensable. In that age, at least, I do not know any other agency that could have accomplished the transference, and I am not at all surprised, under the circumstances, that Jeffrey arrived at the same conclusion.

The true explanation of the mystery seems to be, that the design of Stonehenge may have come from Ireland, the native style of art having been in abeyance in England during the Roman occupation, and that the blue stones most probably came from the Sister Island, which is quite enough to account for the Merlin myth; but of all this we shall be better able to judge when we have discussed the Irish antiquities of the same age.

To return to our history, however, a little further on Jeffrey asserts that Aurelius himself was buried "near the convent of Ambrius within the Giant's Dance (chorea gigantum), which in his lifetime he had commanded to be made."[1] As far as it goes, this is a distinct assertion that the place was used for burial, otherwise from the context we would gather that the Britons slain by Hengist were buried in the cemetery attached to the monastery, and that Stonehenge was consequently a cenotaph and not a monument. But again, in recording the life of Constantine, the nephew and successor of Arthur, after relating how he defeated the Saxons and took vengeance on the nephews of Mordred, he goes on to say—" Three years after this he was killed by Conan, and buried close to Uther Pendragon, within the structure of stones which was set up with wonderful art, not far from Salisbury, and called in the English tongue Stonehenge."[2] This last event, though no date is given, must have occurred some time between 546, or four years after Arthur's death, and 552, the date of the battle of Banbury Hill, where Conan his successor commanded. Assuming for the moment that this may be the case, may it not suffice to explain one of the mysteries of Stonehenge, the presence of the pairs of blue stones inside the choir? Why may we not suppose that these were erected in memory of the kings or others who were buried in front of them? Why may not Aurelius and Constantine have been buried in front of the two small

---

[1] 'Hist. Brit.' viii. ch. xvi.   [2] 'Hist. Brit.' xi. ch. iv.

pairs at either end of the so-called altar stone? If this were so, and it appears to me extremely probable that it was, the last remains of the mist that hangs over the uses of this monument would be dispersed.

From the time of Jeffrey (1147) all subsequent mediæval historians adopt the account of these events given by him, with occasional but generally slight variations, and even modern critics are inclined to accept his account of Constantine and Conan, as his narrative can be checked by that of Gildas, who was cotemporary with these kings. Similar statements are also found in the triads of the Welsh bards, which some contend are original and independent authorities.[1] My own impression is that they may be so, but I do not think their independence has been so clearly established as to enable us to found any argument upon it. On the other hand, the incidental allusion of Jeffrey to the erection of Stonehenge as a cenotaph to the slain nobles, and the subsequent burial there of the two kings, seems so likely and natural that it is difficult to see why they should be considered as inventions. The two last-named events, at all events, do not add to the greatness or wonder of the kings, or of his narrative, and are not such things as would be inserted in the page of history, unless they were currently known, or were recorded somewhere in some writing to which the historian had access.

Before quitting Stonehenge there is one other antiquity connected with it, regarding which it is necessary to say a few words. Both in Sir R. Colt Hoare's plan and the Ordnance Survey, there are marked two oblong enclosures called the greater and lesser " Cursus," and along which the antiquaries of the last century amused themselves by picturing the chariot races of the Ancient Britons, though as they ascribed the introduction of races to the Romans, they admitted that they must have been formed after the subjection of the island by that people.[2] The greater cursus is about a mile and three-quarters long, by 110 yards wide. The smaller is so indistinct that only its commencement can be identified; but even as concerns the larger, I walked twice

---

[1] This is the principal argument of Herbert's 'Cyclops Christianus.'

[2] 'Ancient Wiltshire,' i. p. 158. See also woodcut No. 26, p. 102. The dotted part of the smaller cursus is a restoration of my own.

across it without perceiving its existence, though I was looking for it, and no one I fancy would remark it if his attention were not turned to it. Its boundary mounds never could have been 3 feet high, and now in many places are very nearly obliterated.

That these alignments were once race-courses, appears to me one of the most improbable of the various conjectures which have been hazarded with regard even to Stonehenge. No Roman race-course, that we know of, omitted to provide for the horses returning at least once past the place they started from, and no course was even a mile, much less a mile and three-quarters long. What sort of horse-races the British indulged in before the Conquest I don't know, nor will I hazard an opinion on the subject; but if they wanted the races to be seen, there are several beautiful and appropriate spots close at hand where they could have laid out a longer course along one of the bottoms, where tens of thousands might conveniently have witnessed the sport from the sloping banks on either hand, whereas here only the front rank could have seen the race at all, and that imperfectly. It may also be remarked that the east end of the cursus is closed by a mound which must have been a singularly awkward position for the judges, though that is the place assigned to them by Sir Richard; and the west end is cut off also by an embankment, behind which are several tumuli on the course, which seems a very unlikely racing arrangement.

But if not race-courses, what were they? If any one will turn back to woodcut No. 12, p. 55, representing the alignments at Merivale bridge, and compare them with the cursus as shown in woodcut No. 26, p. 102, representing the ground about Stonehenge, I think he must perceive that the two cursus, if complete, would occupy exactly the same relative position with regard to Stonehenge—on a much larger scale of course—as those at Dartmoor do to the circle there. The arrangements are so similar that the purposes can hardly be different. At first sight this seems to tell against the battle theory. We know of no battle fought on Salisbury Plain. This, however, is the merest negative assumption possible. We know that the massacre at Amesbury was followed by a four years' war, between Ambrosius and the Saxons.[1]   Battles there must have been, and many, and what so likely as that the crowning victory should have been fought in the immediate proximity of the capital of one of the contending parties.   If these cursus do mark the battle-field, it will at once account for the somewhat anomalous position of Stonehenge.   What is so likely as that the victor should have chosen the field of his final victory to erect there a monument to the memory of those whose treacherous slaughter had been the cause of the war?   Of course this is only an hypothesis, and it is only put forward as such, but it seems to me infinitely nearer the truth than that of the gratuitous suggestion of a race-course, and looks like one of the coincidences sure to occur when the investigation is on the right path towards the true solution.

The first impression that the narrative of the preceding pages will convey to most readers, will probably be that there must be something more to be said on the subject, or that something important is left out.   If, it may be argued, the case is so clear as here stated, it could never have been doubted, and must have been accepted long ago.   All I can say in answer is, that if anything is omitted I am not aware of it.   Everything I know of has been stated as fully and as fairly as seemed necessary for its being clearly understood.   In this instance it must be remembered that the usual arguments drawn from the division into stone, bronze, and iron ages hardly come into play.   Nothing has been found inside Stonehenge but iron and Roman pottery.   Even admitting the barrows in the immediate proximity of Stonehenge to be coeval, before their testimony can be of any avail, it must be ascertained when men ceased to be buried in barrows, and when a man might not wish a bronze spear-head to be entombed with him as a relic, even if he did not fight with it in his lifetime.   Even then, however, the evidence would be too indistinct to outweigh that of the finds inside the circle.

If, after what has been said above, any one still maintains that Stonehenge is a temple, and not sepulchral, we have no common ground from which to reason, and need not attempt it.   Or if any

---

[1] *Vide ante*, p. 107.

one as familiar with the locality as I am personally, or who has studied the Ordnance maps with the same care, likes to argue that the barrows came to Stonehenge, and not Stonehenge to the barrows, we see things with such different eyes that we equally want a common basis for argument.

In a case like the present, however, the great difficulty to be overcome is not so much cool argument and close reasoning, as a certain undefined feeling that a monument must be old because we know so little about it. "Omne ignotum pro antiquo" is a matter of faith with many who will listen to no argument to the contrary, and in the case of Stonehenge the false notion has been so fostered by nearly all those who have written about it since the time of James I., that it will be very difficult now to overthrow it. Those who adhere to it, however, hardly realize how dark the ages were between the departure of the Romans and the time of Alfred the Great, and how much may have been done in that time without any record of it coming down to our day. Even if we give them all the megalithic monuments we possess, it is very little indeed for so large a population in so long a time.

Even at a much later period of English history than we are now occupied with, it is wonderful how little we should know of our monuments if we depended on the "litera scripta" for our information. Any one who is familiar with the guide-books of the last, or beginning of the present century, will see what dire confusion of dates existed with regard to the erection of our greatest cathedrals and mediæval monuments. Saxon and Norman were confounded everywhere, and the distinction of any of the styles between Early English and Perpendicular was not appreciated, and frequently the dates were reversed. In fact, it was not till Rickman took the matter in hand that order emerged out of chaos, and he succeeded because his constructive knowledge enabled him to perceive progressive developments which formed true sequences, and he was thus able to supply the want of written information. Every tyro now can fix a date to every moulding in any of our mediæval buildings, but if we had only written history to depend upon, in nine cases out of ten he could not prove that the building was not erected by the Romans or the Phœnicians, or anybody else. If

I

this is the case in an age when writing was so common as between the Conquest and the Reformation, should we be surprised if we find matters so much darker between the departure of the Romans and Alfred, when written history hardly helps us at all? But Rickman's method will, when applied to Stonehenge and similar monuments, if I am not very much mistaken, render their dates nearly as clear as those of our mediæval monuments have been rendered by the same method.

None but those who have had occasion specially to study the subject can be aware how devoid of all literary records the period is of which we are now treating. So meagre and so scarce are they, that many well-informed persons doubt whether such a person as King Arthur ever lived; and scarcely one of his great actions is established by anything like satisfactory contemporary testimony. Yet, in all ages, and in all countries where histories either written or oral exist, they are filled with the exploits of favourite national heroes—as Arthur was—which, even where they are fullest and most diffuse, it is the rarest possible thing to find in them a record of the building of any temple or tomb. From the building of the Parthenon to the completion of Henry VIII.'s Chapel, the notices of buildings in general histories are as few and meagre as may be, and are comprised in a few paragraphs scattered through many hundred volumes. No one, I am convinced, who has thought twice on the subject, would expect to find any notice of buildings in the few pages which are all we possess of history between the departure of the Romans and the time of the Venerable Bede; yet the absence of record is the argument which, if I am not mistaken, has had more influence on the popular mind than almost any other. Too generally it is assumed that, as we know nothing about them, they must be old. To me, on the contrary, nothing appears so extremely improbable as that the builders, while leaving no record of their exploits, should have left any written account of the erection of the Rude Stone Monuments.

One other point seems worth alluding to before concluding this chapter, which is that nothing has been advanced, so far as I know, that would lead us to suppose that the people of this island were, before the time of the Romans, either more numerous or more powerful, and consequently more capable of erecting such monuments as Stonehenge and Avebury, than they were after that people had resided for four centuries among them. All our existing knowledge seems to tend to a diametrically opposite conclusion, and now that the day for vague declamation and *à priori* reasoning is past, if any proof to the contrary can be brought forward, it would be well that it were now adduced, for otherwise judgment may go by default. If we mistake not, the case must be strong and clear that is to outweigh the evidence just brought forward in reference to the two monuments the use and age of which we have just been discussing.

CHAPTER IV.

MINOR ENGLISH ANTIQUITIES.

AYLESFORD.

THE detailed examination of these groups at Avebury and Stonehenge will probably be deemed sufficient to establish at least a
primâ facie case in favour of the hypothesis that these monuments
were sepulchral—that at least some of them marked battle-fields,
and lastly, that their antiquity was not altogether prehistoric. If
this is so, it will not be necessary to repeat the same evidence in
treating of those monuments or groups we are about to describe.
Incidentally the latter will, if I am not mistaken, afford many
confirmations of those propositions, but it will not be necessary to
insist or enlarge on them to the same extent as has been done
in the previous pages.

Among the remaining groups of stones in England, one of the
most important is—or rather was—that in front of Aylesford in
Kent. The best known member of this group is that known as
Kit's Cotty—or Coity-house, which has, however, been so often
drawn and described that it is hardly necessary to do much
more than refer to it here. It is a dolmen, composed of four
stones, three upright; the two side stones being about 8 feet
square and 2 in thickness, the third somewhat smaller; these
form three sides of a chamber, the fourth side being — and
apparently always having been—left open. These three support
a cap stone measuring 11 feet by 8 feet. If we can trust
Stukeley's drawing,[1] it was an external dolmen standing on the
end of a low long barrow. At the other end of the mound lay an
obelisk, since removed, but in Stukeley's time it was said to mark
"the general's grave." The mound has since been levelled by the

---

[1] 'Iter Curiosum,' pl. xxxiii.

plough, but the whole forms an arrangement so common both in England and in Scandinavia, that I am inclined to place faith in the drawing. So little, however, hinges on it here that it is not worth while insisting on it, but a trench across the site of the barrow might lead to interesting results. Nearly due south of Kit's Cotty-house, at the distance of about 500 yards, is another monument of the same class, popularly known as the Countless Stones, but so ruined—apparently by searchers after treasure—that its plan cannot now be made out. In Stukeley's time, however, it was more perfect, and as his pencil is always more to be trusted than his pen, it may be worth while to reproduce his drawings,[1] for the arrangement of the stones was peculiar, but

27.   Countless Stones, Aylesford. From a drawing by Stukeley.

may have analogies elsewhere. Between these two a third dolmen is said to have existed within the memory of man, but no trace of it is now to be found. In the rear of these groups, nearer the village, there exists, or existed, a line of great stones, extending from a place called Spring Farm, in a north-easterly direction, for a distance of three-quarters of a mile, to another spot known as Hale Farm,[2] passing through Tollington, where the greater number of the stones are now found. In front of the line near the centre at Tollington lie two obelisks, known to the country

[1] 'Iter Curiosum,' p. xxxii.

[2] When I was there four years ago I was fortunate enough to find an old man, a stonemason, who had been employed in his youth in utilizing these stones. He went over the ground with me, and pointed out the position of those he remembered.

people as the coffin-stones—probably from their shape. They are 12 feet long by 4 to 6 broad, and about 2 or 3 feet thick.[1] They appear to be partially hewn, or at least shaped, so as to resemble one another.

Besides these stones, which are all on the right bank of the river, there are several groups at or near Addington, about five miles to the westward of Aylesford. Two of these in the park at Addington have long been known to antiquaries, having been described and figured in the 'Archæologia' in 1773.[2] The first is a small circle, about 11 feet in diameter, the six stones comprising it being 19 feet high, 7 wide, and 2 in thickness. Near it is the larger one of oval form, measuring 50 paces by 42 paces. The stones are generally smaller than those of the other circle. The other groups or detached stones are described by Mr. Wright,[3] who went over the ground with that excellent and venerable antiquary the Rev. L. B. Larking. They seem to have adopted the common opinion that an avenue of such stones existed all the way from Addington to Aylesford, but it seems to me that there is no sufficient evidence to justify this conclusion. Many of the stones seem natural boulders, and in no place is any alignment distinctly perceptible.

In addition to these, Mr. Wright found, and attempted to excavate some smaller monuments of a sepulchral character, near Kit's Cotty House, but situated on the brow of the hill immediately above it. These " consist generally of groups of stones buried partly on the ridge of the hill, but evidently forming, or having formed, small sepulchral chambers." "Each group," he adds, "is generally surrounded by a circle of stones."[4]

There only now remains the question, why were all these stones placed here, and by whom? Mr. Wright is far too sober and too well-informed an antiquary to repeat the usual nonsense about such monuments having been Druid temples or altars. The conclusion at which he arrives (p. 183) is that Kit's

---

[1] It is extremely difficult to be precise about the dimensions. One is almost wholly buried in the earth, and its dimensions can only be obtained by probing; the other is half buried.

[2] 'Archæologia,' ii. 1773, p. 107.

[3] 'Wanderings of an Antiquary;' London, 1854, p. 175 et seqq.

[4] loc cit. 175.

Cotty-house, and the cemetery around it, with that in the parish of Addington, together formed the grand necropolis of the Belgian settlers in this part of the island. Against this it must be observed that the Belgians erected no such monuments in their own country, Gallia Belgica being exactly that part of France in which no stone monuments are found, and it is very unlikely that the Belgians should have done here what they did not do at home. But another objection is, that the theory is wholly gratuitous, no shadow of tradition, no analogy, and no reason being adduced to show why it should be so, and, to say the least of it, it is most unlikely. If a straight line were drawn from the mouth of the Humber to the head of Southampton Water, this is the only group of this class of monuments to the eastward of the line, and what possible reason can we have for supposing that the princes or people of that vast district chose this place, and this only, for their necropolis? Had it been some vast plain like Salisbury, or some gloomy valley, or the site of some ancient sacred city, the choice might have been intelligible, but a more unromantic, unlikely spot than the valley of the Medway could hardly have been chosen. It is neither central nor accessible, and neither history nor tradition lends any countenance to the suggestion.

Suppose, on the other hand, we assume that these erections are a record of the battle which, according to the Saxon chronicle,[1] was fought on this spot between Vortigern and Hengist and Horsa, in the year 455, and in which Catigren was slain on the side of the British, and the redoubted Horsa fell on that of the Saxons. This at least has the merit of accounting for all we see—the line of stones at Tollington is just such a position as the British army would take up, to cover the ford at Aylesford against an enemy advancing from Thanet. The two obelisks in front would represent the position of the two chiefs; Kit's Cotty-house would become the tomb of Catigren, which tradition always represented it to be; the circles at Addington would become the graves of chiefs who were wounded in the battle, and taken to the rear and buried with due honours, at or near the

---

[1] 'Mon. Hist. Brit.' p. 299.

spot where they died; and lastly the tumulus at Horstead would also in accordance with ancient tradition be the grave of Horsa.

So much depends on this last determination, that last year through the kindness of Colonel Fisher, R.E., the assistance of a party of sappers was procured from Chatham, and the mound was thoroughly explored. It was found that a cremation (it is presumed of a human body) had taken place on the natural surface of the ground, and that a tumulus had been raised over it. The chalk was dug down to some depth and found quite undisturbed, but no ornament or implement was found anywhere. At first this seemed disappointing; but on Mr. Godfrey Faussett, who was present at the digging, referring to certain passages in 'Beowulf,' it appears to be exactly what should have been expected. The poem, in the first place, is about the best authority we could have, inasmuch as, according to Kemble, "it gave accounts of exploits not far removed, in point of time, from the crossing of Hengist and Horsa into Britain, and the poem was probably brought hither by some of those Anglo-Saxons, who, in 495, accompanied Cerdic and Cyneric."[1] After Hengist's conflict with Fin, the body was burnt (l. 2232-2251); but after Beowulf's death not only cremation is mentioned, but a splendid mound is raised over the spot where the funeral pile stood, "ad on Eorthen" (l. 6266), on the surface of the ground. At Beowulf's funeral, vases, and arms, and jewels of all kinds, were thrown upon the pile and burnt with him; and no wonder, considering the wealth just rescued from the guardianship of the "Wurm" by the victorious hero. Poor Horsa died defeated, and all his friends could expect would be to be allowed to bury him under a flag of truce, with such rites as would ensure his proper reception in the next world. Had they attempted to bury any treasures with him, they probably would have been appropriated by the victorious Brits.

Bede's expression that Horsa's tomb was situated in "orientalibus partibus Cantiæ,"[2] has more than once been quoted to disprove this identification. But what did Bede mean by "eastern

---

[1] 'Beowulf: an Anglo-Saxon Poem,' translated by J. W. Kemble, 1835, preface, p. xix.   [2] 'Mon. Hist. Brit.' p. 121.

parts"? May it not have been that in his day the Medway divided Kent into east and west? Or he may have spoken without sufficient local knowledge. But that Horsa fell at Aylesford, is as well authenticated as any fact in that age : he most probably was buried near the battle-field; and the village where the mound is situated has probably ever since been called Horstead, as it is at this day.

All this, it appears to me, makes so strong a case, that I cannot help thinking it might be accepted till, at least, something is advanced against it. At present I am not aware of any argument to the contrary that seems to me entitled to any serious consideration. No flint, or bronze, or iron implement of any sort, so far as I know, have been found on the spot—this may be only because they have not been looked for; but as the case at present stands, the Danish system cannot be pleaded for or against this view.

The real difficulty to be feared in obtaining acceptance of this explanation of the stone at Aylesford, is its extreme simplicity. After all that has been written about the unfathomable mystery and the primæval antiquity of this class of monuments, to be told that these are merely the memorials of a battle fought on the spot in the year 455, is too terribly prosaic to be tolerated, nor ought it perhaps to be accepted if it stood alone. If, however, it proves to be only one of many instances, the ultimate admission of the above views can hardly be doubtful.

ASHDOWN.

In the neighbourhood of Uffington, in Berkshire, there are three monuments, two at least of which still merit a local habitation and a name in our history. One of these is the celebrated white horse, which gives its name to the vale, and the scouring of which is still used by the inhabitants of the neighbourhood on the occasion of a triennial festival and games, which have been so graphically described by Mr. Thomas Hughes.

The second is a cromlech, known as Wayland Smith's Cave, and immortalized by the use made of it by Sir Walter Scott in the novel of 'Kenilworth.' The third is as remarkable as either, but still wants its poet. The annexed woodcut will give a fair idea of its nature and extent.[1] It does not pretend to be minutely accurate, and this in the present instance is fortunately of no great

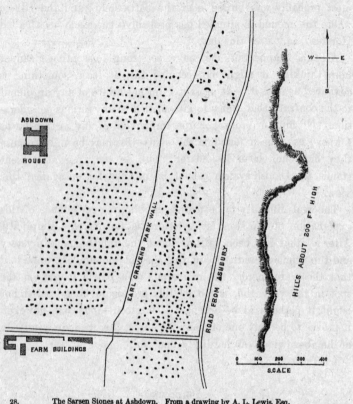

28.   The Sarsen Stones at Ashdown.   From a drawing by A. L. Lewis, Esq.

consequence. All the stones are overthrown: some lie flat on the ground, some on their edges, and it is only the smallest that can be said to be standing. The consequence is, that we cannot feel sure that we know exactly where any of them stood, nor whether they were arranged in lines, like those at Carnac; nor if so, in

---

[1] This woodcut is copied literally from one by Mr. Lewis published in the 'Norwich Volume of the International Prehistoric Congress,' and the figures and facts I am about to quote are mostly taken from the paper that accompanied it. The inferences, however, are widely different.

how many rows, or whether they always had the confused appearance they now present. They are spread over an area of about 1600 feet north and south, and of half that distance east and west. The gap in the centre was made purposely to clear the view in front of the house when it was built, and many of the stones it is feared were employed in the erection. They are the same Sarsens as are used at Avebury and Stonehenge, and the largest are about 10 feet long from 6 to 9 wide, and from 3 to 4 feet high (in their present recumbent position); but there are few so large as this, the majority being from 2 to 4 feet in length and breadth, and from 1 to 3 high.[1]

No one has yet attempted to give any explanation of the monument beyond repeating the usual Druidical formulæ. To me it appears almost incontestable that it is a memorial of the battle fought here between the Saxons and the Danes in the year 871. From Asser we learn that the Pagans, advancing from Reading, occupied the higher ground. It is sometimes supposed that Uffington Castle was thrown up by them on the occasion, which is by no means impossible. Advancing eastward, they then attacked the Christians under Alfred, who occupied the lower ground. This, and the ill-timed fit of devotion on his brother's part, nearly lost the Christians the day; but Alfred's skill and intrepidity prevailed, and the victory was complete.[2] This being so, nothing appears more probable than that the victorious army, either by themselves or with the assistance of the peasantry, should have collected together the Sarsens in the neighbourhood, and have arranged them as Alfred and his army stood, when he first received the shock of the Pagans. It seems also probable that he would have engraved the emblem of the white horse on the side of the hill where the Pagans had encamped the night before the battle, and where probably the fight ended on the following day.

The question whether Weyland Smith's Cave belongs to the same group, or to an earlier date, is not so easily settled. My impression is that it is older. It is a three-chambered dolmen

---

[1] 'Norwich Volume of the International Prehistoric Congress,' p. 37.
[2] Asser, in 'Mon. Hist. Brit.' p. 476.

almost identical in plan with Petrie's No. 27, Carrowmore, to be described in the next chapter, but with this difference, that whereas the circle of stones in the Irish example contained thirty-six or thirty-seven stones, and was 60 feet in diameter, this one contained probably only twenty-eight, and was only 50 feet in diameter. This and the fact of the one consisting of Sarsens—the other of granite blocks—account so completely for all the difference between them, that I cannot believe that so great a lapse of time as eight centuries could have taken place between the erection of the two. I fancy it must have been erected for the entombment of a local hero in the early centuries of the Christian era; but of this we will be better able to judge when we are further advanced in our survey of similar monuments.

ROLLRIGHT.

At Rollright, between Chipping Norton and Long Compton, in Oxfordshire, there is a circle, which, from what has been written about it, has assumed an importance in the antiquarian world, which is certainly not due either to its dimensions or to any traditions that attach to it. Every antiquary, from Camden down to Bathurst Deane, has thought it necessary to say something about this splendid temple of the Druid priesthood, so that the traveller, when he visits it, is sure to be dreadfully disappointed. It is an ordinary 100-foot circle, the entrance to which is apparently from the south opposite to the five largest stones, which are placed in juxtaposition on the north, the tallest in the centre being about 5 feet in height. The others average about 3 or 4 feet, but are uneven in height and irregularly spaced, but with a tendency to form groups of threes, which is a peculiarity observable in some similar circles on Dartmoor.

Across the road, at a distance of about 50 yards, stands a single obeliscal stone, about 10 feet high, on a mound which appears to be artificial. If it is so, however, it was raised with the materials taken out of a pit, which still exists on one side, and not from a ditch surrounding it, as is usual in such cases. In another direction, about a quarter of a mile from the circle, stands a dolmen, which is the finest feature in the group. The cap stone, which has fallen, measures 8 feet by 9, and is of considerable thickness; and three of the supporting stones are 7, 8, and 10 feet in height respectively.

This circle appears to have been examined by Ralph Sheldon, but without results.[1] The mound, so far as is known, is yet untouched, and the dolmen could not now be explored without causing its complete ruin; I presume no one will contest its being sepulchral. It would be difficult now to bring to the test of experiment the question whether the circle is so or not, as some forty or fifty years ago, it and the plot round it were planted with larch trees, whose roots have spread over the surface and could with difficulty be now got rid of. This is to be regretted, as from its isolated position the group affords an excellent opportunity of testing the usual theories regarding these monuments. If it was a temple, it gives us a very low idea of the religious state of our ancestors, that for a district of from twenty to thirty miles' radius they should have possessed only one single small enclosure, surrounded by a low imperfect wall, 3 or 4 feet high. If any other had ever existed, traces of it must have been found, or why has this one remained so complete, for not one stone apparently is missing. It is also strange that, as in other instances, it should be situated on the highest and bleakest part of the surrounding country. It is, in fact, not only the unlikeliest form, but the most inconvenient site for a temple. It also gives us a very low idea of their civilization. The circle at Rollright is a sort of monument that the boys of any of our larger schools could set up in a week, supposing the stones to be found lying about, at no great distance, which there is little doubt was the case when it was erected. The dolmen might require a little contrivance to get the cap stone hoisted; but there is nothing that the villagers in the neighbourhood could not now complete in a few days, if so inclined, and certainly nothing that a victorious army, of say even 1000 men, could not complete between sunrise and sunset in a summer's day. Even if the sepulchral character of the group is admitted, it can hardly be the buryingground of a chief, or clan, or family. In that case, instead of one

[1] Stukeley, 'Avebury,' p. 12; Borlase, p. 210.

dolmen there must have been several, smaller it may be, but in succession. The chief must have had ancestors, or successors, or relations, and they would not be content that one, and one only, of their family should possess an honoured tomb, and that they themselves should rest in undistinguished graves. As in other cases, unless we are prepared to admit that it marks the site of a battle, I know of nothing that will explain the situation and the form of the group; nor do I see why we should reject Camden's explanation of the circumstances under which it was erected: "These would, I verily think, to have been the monument of some victory, and haply erected by Rollo the Dane, who afterwards conquered Normandy." "In what time he with the Danes troubled England with depredations we read that the Danes joined battle with the English thereby at Hock Norton, a place for no one thing more famous in old time than for the woful slaughter of the English on that foughten field, under the reign of King Edward the Elder."[1] This last, however, is apparently a mistake, for it was Eadward (901-923) who was really the contemporary of Rollo. He was also the contemporary of Gorm the Old, of Denmark, of whose tumulus and Pagan habits we shall hear hereafter.

This again will appear a very prosaic anti-climax to those who are nursed on ideas of the hoar antiquity and wondrous magnificence of such monuments as Ashdown and Rollright. A visit to them is sufficient to dispel one part of that illusion, and a little common-sense applied to the other will probably show that the more moderate view meets perfectly all the real exigencies of the case.

PENRITH.

In the neighbourhood of Penrith in Cumberland there is a group, or perhaps it should be said there are three groups of monuments, of considerable importance from their form and size, but deficient in interest from the absence of any tradition to account for their being where we find them. They extend in

---

[1] Camden, 'Britannia,' i. p. 285. See also Charleton's 'Stonehenge restored to the Danes,' p. 36.

a nearly straight line from Little Salkeld on the north to Shap on the south, a distance of fourteen miles as the crow flies, Penrith lying a little to the westward of the line, and nearer to its northern than its southern extremity.

About half a mile from the first named village is the circle known popularly as Long Meg and her Daughters, sixty-eight in number, if each stone represents one. It is about 330 feet (100 metres) in diameter, but does not form a perfect circle. The stones are unhewn boulders, and very few of them are now erect. Outside the circle stands Long Meg herself, of a different class of stone from the others, about 12 feet high, and apparently hewn, or at all events shaped, to some extent.[1] Inside the circle, Camden reports "the existence of two cairns of stone, under which they say are dead bodies buried; and indeed it is probable enough," he adds, "that it has been a monument erected in honour of some victory."[2] No trace of these cairns now remains, nor am I aware that the centre has ever been dug into with a view of looking for interments. My impression, however, is that the principal interment was outside, and that Long Meg marks either the head or the foot of the chief's grave.

Close to Penrith is another circle called Mayborough, of about the same dimensions—100 metres—as that at Little Salkeld, but of a very different construction. The vallum or enclosure is entirely composed of small water-worn stones taken from the beds of the Eamount or Eden rivers. The stones are wonderfully uniform in size, and just about what any man could carry without inconvenience. This enclosure mound is now so mined that it is extremely difficult to guess what were its dimensions. It may have been from 15 feet to 20 feet high, and twice that in breadth at its base. The same cause makes it difficult to determine the dimensions of the internal area. The floor of the circle I calculated as 290 feet from the foot of one slope to the foot of the opposite one, and consequently the whole as from 320 feet

---

[1] On this stone Sir Gardiner Wilkinson traced one of those circles of concentric rings which are so common on stones in the north of England. I did not see it myself, but assuming it to be true—which I have no doubt it is—it will not help us much till we know when and by whom these circles were engraved.

[2] 'Brit.' p. 1021.

to 340 feet[1] from crest to crest; but these dimensions must be taken as only approximative till a more careful survey is made than it was in my power to execute. Near, but not quite in the centre, stands a single splendid monolith; it may be 12 feet in height, but is more than twice the bulk of Long Meg. In Pennant's time there were four stones still standing in the centre, of which this was one, and probably there may originally have been

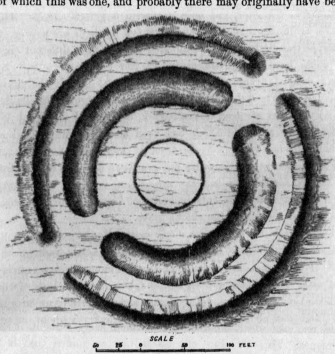

SCALE

50   25   0   50   100 FEET

29. Sketch Plan of King Arthur's Round Table, with the side, obliterated by the road, restored.

several more forming a small circle in the centre.[2] In his day also he learned that there were four stones—two pairs—standing in a gap in the vallum looking like the commencement of an avenue. The place, however, is too near Penrith, and stone is there too valuable to allow of such things escaping, so that nothing now remains which would enable us to restore this monument with certainty.

Close by this is a third circle known as Arthur's Round Table.

---

[1] Pennant in his text calls the diameter 88 yards, but the scale attached to his plan makes it 110 yards nearly.   [2] 'Tour in Scotland, 1772,' pl. xxxvii. p. 276.

It consists, or consisted, of a vallum of earth, as near as can be made out, 300 feet from crest to crest; but about one-third of the circle being cut away to form a road, it is not easy to speak with certainty. Inside the rampart is a broad berm, then a ditch, and in the centre a plateau about 170 feet in diameter, slightly raised in the centre. No stone is visible on the surface, though the rampart when broken into shows that it is principally composed of them. There is now only one entrance through the rampart and across the ditch, but as both entrances existed in Pennant's time (1772), and are figured in his plan of the monument, I have not hesitated to restore the second accordingly.[1] The distance between Mayborough and King Arthur's Round Table is about 110 yards, and at about the same distance from the last-named monument, a third circle existed in Pennant's time. It seems, however, to have been in his day at least only a circular ditch, and has now entirely disappeared.

Owing to their more ruined state, the remains at Shap are more difficult to describe. They were, however, visited by Stukeley in 1725, but he complains it rained all the time that he was there, and rain on a bleak exposed moor like Shap is singularly inimical to antiquarian pursuits.[2] The remains were also described by Camden,[3] but not apparently from personal observation, and others have described them since, but the destruction has been so rapid, the village being almost entirely built out of them, that it is now extremely difficult to ascertain what they really were. All, however, are agreed that the principal monument was an alignment, according to some of a double row of stones, of which others can only trace a single row. So far as I could make out on the spot, it commenced near a spot called the Thunder-stone, in the north, where there are seven large stones in a field; six are arranged as a double row; the seventh seems to commence a

---

[1] Near Lochmaben, in Annandale, a circle exists, or existed, called Wood Castle, which, in so far as the plan and dimensions are concerned, is identical with this. It is figured in General Roy's ' Military Antiquities of the Romans,' pl. viii. I would not hesitate in quoting it as a monument of this class, but for the view which I distrust excessively, but which makes it look like a fortification. As I have no means of verifying the facts, I can only draw attention to them.

[2] ' Iter Boreale,' p. 42.

[3] ' Brit.,' Gough edit. iii. p. 401.

single line, from this all the way to a place at the southern
extremity of the village, called Karl Lofts, single stones may be
traced at intervals, in apparently a perfectly straight line and
still beyond this, at a farmyard called Brackenbyr, Mr. Simpson
fancied he could, in 1859, trace the remains of a circle 400 feet in
diameter, with a large obelisk in the centre.[1] I confess I was not
so fortunate in 1869, and I also differ from him as to the position
of the stone row. He seems to fancy, from the description of
Stukeley, that it was situated to the southward of Karl Lofts,
though he could not detect any traces of it. My impression is that
it commenced with the circle at Brackenbyr, immediately south of
Karl Lofts, and proceeded in a north-westerly direction for nearly
a mile and a half to the Thunder-stone, as before mentioned.
Rather more than half a mile due south of Brackenbyr stands a
portion of what was once a very fine circle. It was partially
destroyed by the railway, but seems to have been a hundred-
foot circle, and to have stood considerably in advance of the
line of the avenue, in the same relative position to the stone
row as the circle at Merivale Bridge (woodcut No. 12), or as
Stonehenge to its cursus (woodcut No. 26), whether we assume
that it was continued in this direction, or terminated as above
indicated. In front of the circle is a noble tumulus, called Kemp
How, in which the body of a man of gigantic stature is said to
have been found.[2]

According to the popular tradition the stone avenue originally
extended to Muir Divock, a distance of rather more than five
miles, to which it certainly points. Though this is most
improbable, it is not wholly without reason, as on Muir Divock
there are five or six circles of stone and several tumuli. The
circles have most of them been opened recently, and in all
instances were found to contain cists or other evidence of interments.[3] Immediately over the Muir stands a commanding hill,
1747 feet high, marked on the Ordnance Survey as Arthur's Pike.
Besides these, on the hill behind Shap, to the eastward, are
several stone circles, some single, some double, but none are of

---

[1] 'Archæological Journal,' xviii. p. 29.   [2] *Ibid.*, xviii. p. 37.
[3] I am not aware that any account of these diggings has been published. The
facts I ascertained on the spot.

any great size, or composed of stones of very large dimensions. The whole aspect of the country is that of a district used as a burying-place to an extent far beyond anything that the usual inhabitants of the locality could have required, for a bleaker and more ungenial spot is not inhabited in any part of these islands.

So far as I know, no credible tradition attaches to these monuments so as to connect them with any historical or local incident. We are, therefore, left almost wholly to their intrinsic forms, or to analogies, to determine either their history or their purposes.

No one will now probably be found seriously to maintain that the long stone row at Shap was a temple either of the Druids or of any one else. At least if these ancient people thought a single or even a double row of widely-spaced stones, stretching to a mile and a half across a bleak moor, was a proper form for a place to worship in, they must have been differently constituted from ourselves. Unless they possessed the tails, or at least the long-pointed ears with which Darwin endows our ancestors, they would have adopted some form of temple more nearly similar to those used in all other countries of the world. Nor was it a tomb. Not only have no sepulchral remains been found here, but nowhere else has any trace of such a purpose been found connected with such alignments. Even, however, if it is contended that it is sepulchral, it certainly was not the burying-place of the hamlet of Shap, or of its neighbourhood, for a more miserable spot for habitation does not exist in England, and it cannot be that Shap, like Avebury, should require the most magnificent cemeteries in the island, while nothing of the sort exists near the great centres of population. Had the country been as thickly inhabited as China, we might fancy the people seeking waste uncultivable spots in which to bury their dead, but even at the present day Woking is the only cemetery that has been selected on this principle in England, and at any previous time to which we can look back, the idea appears too absurd to be entertained for a moment.

If, therefore, the alignment at Shap was sepulchral, it must

K 2

have been the burying-place of those that fell in some battle on the spot; this in fact brings us to the only suggestion I am aware of that seems at all tenable: that it marks a battle-field like those on Dartmoor (*ante*, p. 54), and others we shall meet with hereafter.

Excavations have proved that all the smaller circles which abound in the neighbourhood are graves, and if those from 60 feet to 100 feet in diameter are so, all analogy must lead us to the inference that the 100-metre circles are so also. Direct proof has not, however, yet been obtained of this, but that may arise first from the difficulty of excavating so large an area; or it may be that the bodies were buried outside the circle, as at Hakpen (*ante*, p. 76), or at the foot of the stones, as at Crichie (*ante*, p. 75) or in those circles which have no erect stones in a similar position—at the toe of the inner slope of the rampart—and these are just the places where they have not been looked for. Meanwhile the cairns in the inside of the circle of Long Meg's Daughters seem to favour this view of their sepulchral purpose. But if sepulchres, certainly they were not family or princely tombs. If that was their destination they would not be found only in two or three groups in the wildest and most remote parts of the country, but in far greater numbers, and nearer those places where men most do congregate. We are in fact driven to Camden's suggestion, that they may have been made to celebrate some victory; but, if so, what victory? It looks like riding a hobby very hard to make the same suggestion as was made with regard to Avebury, but I confess I know no other that can be brought forward with so much plausibility as that of considering them to be memorials of Arthur's campaigns against the Saxon invaders.

The first objection that will naturally be raised to this hypothesis is, that King Arthur was a myth, and never fought any battles at all. It was not necessary to examine this when speaking of Avebury. All that was then required was to know if Waden Hill was Badon Hill. If it was the site of that famous battle, there was no further enquiry necessary. Arthur, and he only, commanded there; and if we admit the fact of the battle being fought, we admit at the same time the existence of him who commanded there. But with regard to the other eleven battles mentioned by Nennius[1] the case is not so clear, and according to the present fashionable school of historical criticism it is thought reasonable to reject the whole as a myth, because the evidence is not such as would stand examination in a court of law, and also because the story as it now stands is so mixed up with incredible fables as to throw discredit on the whole. It is very much easier to heap ridicule on the silly miracles which Merlin is said by mediæval minstrels to have performed, and to laugh at the marvellous exploits of Arthur and the Knights of his Round Table, than to attempt to glean the few facts which their wild poetry has left unobscured. But if any one will attempt the same process with one of the many 'Lhystoires du noble et vaillant roy Alexandre le grand,' he will find exactly the same difficulties. Aristotle and his master have been rendered quite as fabulous persons as Merlin and Arthur, and the miracles of the one and the feats of the other are equally marvellous. In Alexander's case we fortunately have Arrian and Curtius, and others, who give us the truth with regard to him; but Arthur had no contemporary history, and instead of living in a highly civilized state that continued for ages after him, he was the last brilliant light of his age and race, and after him all was gloom for centuries. It was not till after a long eclipse that his name was seized upon in a poetical and an uncritical age as a peg for bards whereupon to hang their wild imaginings.

This is not the place to examine so large a question. It will be sufficient to state what I believe to be the main facts. Those who do not admit them need not read further. Arthur, it seems to me, was born the prince of one of the smaller states in the West of England, probably Cornwall, and after the death of Ambrosius, in or about the year 508, took up the struggle the latter had carried on with varying success against the hordes of Saxons and others who were gradually pushing the Bryts out of England. My impression is, that even before the Romans left, Jutes, Angles, and Danes had not only traded with, but had

---

[1] Here, again, I quote from the copy in the 'Mon. Hist. Brit.' p. 47 *et seqq.*, to which it will not be necessary to refer every time the name is mentioned.

settled, both on the Saxonicum littus of Kent, and on the coast of Yorkshire, Northumberland, and the Lothians; and that during the century that elapsed between the departure of the Romans and the time of Arthur, they were gradually pushing the British population behind the range of hills which extends from Carlisle to Derby and forms the back-bone of England. It was in the plains behind this range and further south that all Arth r's battles seem to have been fought. With Cumberland, Wales, and Cornwall behind him, he was not only sure of support from the native population in his rear, but had a secure retreat in case of adverse fortune overtaking him. In all this range of country I do not know any spot so favourable strategically for a defender of his country to take up as the high land about Shap, or the open country extending from thence to Salkeld. The ridges at Shap protected his right against an enemy advancing by Lancaster, the Caledonian Forest and a very rugged country covered his left, and in front there was only a wild inhospitable tract by which the invader from the opposite coast could advance against him, while by a single day's march to his rear he was among the inaccessible mountains and lakes of Cumberland.

I am afraid to lay much stress on the fact of one of the circles at Penrith and the hill opposite Shap bearing Arthur's name, because in the last few years we have seen two hard-headed sober-minded Scotchmen proving, to their own satisfaction, that Arthur was born north of the Tweed—that all his battles were fought and all his exploits performed in the northern portion of the island. Even Ganora—the faithless Guinevere—if not a Scotchwoman, was at all events buried in Miegle churchyard under a stone, which some pious descendant sculptured some centuries later.[1] Even here, however, I fancy I can perceive a difference between the two cases. In the middle ages the Scotch had historians like Boece and Fordun, who recorded such fables for the edification of their countrymen, and with proper patriotism were willing that their country should have as large a share of the world's greatness or great men as they could well appropriate. They were followed

---

[1] Stuart Glennie, 'King Arthur.' 1867. L. W. Skene. 'Ancient Books of Wales,' i. 52 et seqq.

by an educated class throughout the country, who were actuated by the same motives, and did exactly what Stukeley and his followers did with English monuments. They found Druids who had no temples, and remains which they supposed to be temples with no priests; so, putting the two together, they made what they fancied was a perfect whole out of two incongruous halves. So the Scotch, having a rich repertory of fables on the one hand, and on the other having hills without names and sculptured stones without owners, joined the two together, and went on repeating in the same manner their inventions till, from dire reiteration, they took the likeness of fact.

. The case was, if I mistake not, very different in Cumberland. The boors of that land had no literature—no learning, and none of that ardent patriotism which enabled the Scotch poets and pedants to manufacture a quasi history for themselves out of other people's doings. It is difficult to fancy the inhabitants of Cumberland troubling themselves with Arthur and his affairs, and wishing to apply his name to their hills or antiquities, unless some ancient tradition had made it probable, and, " valeat quantum," these names may therefore be considered as suggesting a real connexion between the place and the man.

Owing to the extreme brevity of the record in Nennius,[1] there are few things about which greater discrepancy of opinion exists even among the believers in Arthur than the localities of his battles. Taking them in the order in which they are mentioned, the first is said to have been fought on the river Glem of Glein, which the editors of the 'Monumenta Historica Britannica' suggest may be a river of that name in Northumberland. The river indicated is so small a brook that it is difficult to fancy its name should be attached to so important an event.

If we must go so far north, I would rather feel inclined to place it at Wood Castle, near Lochmaben, in Dumfriesshire, where there is a circular enclosure identical in plan and dimensions with King Arthur's Round Table at Penrith.[2] Strategically, it is a much more likely spot than the exposed east coast of Northumberland;

---

[1] 'Mon. Hist. Brit.' p. 73.
[2] General Roy's 'Mil. Ant. of the Romans,' pl. viii.

but, except the plan of Wood Castle, I know of no authority for placing this battle-field in Annandale.

There is no indication where the second, third, or fourth battles were fought; but for the fifth we have this important designation that it was fought "super aliud flumen quod vocatur Duglas vel Dubglas quod est in regione Linuis," or in another MS. Linnuis. A marginal note suggests Lindesay, in Lincolnshire, but for no other reason apparently than from the first three letters being the same in both. There is a River Duglas flowing past Wigan, in Lancashire, which Whittaker, in his 'History of Manchester,' boldly adopts as the place indicated, and others have been inclined to accept his determination. After going carefully over the ground, I confess no spot appears to me more unlikely for a great battle than the banks of this river, nor does any local evidence of their having been so now remain. One cannot but feel that if Arthur ever allowed himself to be pushed into such a corner, with nothing but the sea behind him to retreat upon, he certainly was not the general that made so successful a stand against the Saxons. I am much more inclined to believe that Linnuis is only a barbarous latinization of Linn, which in Gaelic and Irish means sea or lake. In Welsh it is Lyn, and in Anglo-Saxon Lin, and if this is so, "In regione Linnuis" may mean "In the Lake Country."

The name of the river does not appear to me at all an insuperable difficulty. All the rivers about Penrith, the Lowther, the Eamount, and the Eden, have names that were certainly given to them by the Saxons, but they must have had Celtic names before they came; and Dubh as an adjective is dark or black, and Glas, green or grey, is used as a substantive to denote the sea, in Irish. Such an epithet would apply admirably to the Lowther; and if it could be identified with the river mentioned by Nennius, our difficulties would be at an end. These speculations, however, must of course be taken for what they are worth. There is, so far as known, no authority for the name Duglas or Dubhglas being applied to the Lowther or Eden.

The sixth battle was on a river called Bassas. It has been suggested that this means the Bass Rock in the Frith of Forth; but it need hardly be objected that a rock is not a river, and there is an extreme improbability that Arthur ever saw the Lothians. In Derbyshire there is a Bas Lowe[1] in a neighbourhood where, as we shall presently see, there is reason to believe Arthur fought one or more of his battles, but I am not aware of any river so called in that neighbourhood.

The seventh war was in Silva Calidonis, "id est Cat Coit Celidon." The Cat in the last name is evidently Cat or Cath, "a battle," which we frequently meet with, and shall again in describing these matters. Coit, only so far as the dictionaries tell us, means coracle, and would seem to indicate a struggle in boats. The Caledonian Forest, is what will really determine the locality. Generally it is understood to be the forest that extended from Penrith to Carlisle; and, if so, any one of our Penrith circles might be assumed to mark the site of the seventh battle. Most probably in that case it would be the Salkeld circle, or it might be one known as the Grey Yawds, near Cumrew, about eight or nine miles further north.[2]

The eighth battle was in Castello Guinnion, or Guin, which, from the sound of the name, can hardly escape being in Wales or the Welsh border, unless indeed we assume that these Welsh appellations were common to the whole country before the Saxons re-named many of the places. In that case we have nothing to guide us as to where the battle was fought.

The ninth battle was " in Urbe Legionis." This may be either Chester or Caerleon in South Wales. It most probably was the latter, as in another MS. it is added "quæ Britannice Karlium dicitur," or Cair lin in another.

The tenth war was on the shores of a river which was called Ribroit. Though this is spelt in various MSS. Tribruit, Trathreuroit, and Trattreuroit, it seems impossible to identify it. But it must have been a large river, or the expression "in littore" would hardly have been used.

The eleventh battle "fuit in Monte quod dicitur Agned Cath-

---

[1] Bateman, 'Ten Years' Diggings,' p. 87.

[2] I have not seen this circle myself, though I made a long journey on purpose. It is said to consist of eighty-eight stones, and one larger than the rest, standing outside the circle, at a distance of about five yards, or exactly as Long Meg stands with reference to her daughters.

regonnon;" and in different MSS. this is spelt Cathregomion, Cabregonnon, Catbregonnion, and in one it is added, "in Somersetshire quem nos Cathbregion appellamus." No such name seems now to be known in that country; but as we shall presently, I hope, see reason for believing, the spot is probably that now known as Stanton Drew.

The twelfth battle was that of Mount Badon, the position of which, as we have already pointed out, may almost certainly be fixed in the immediate neighbourhood of Avebury.

All this is indistinct enough, it must be confessed, and much of it depends on nominal similarities, which are never very satisfactory; still the general impression it leaves seems worthy of acceptance. It would lead us to think that Arthur commenced his struggles with the invaders in the north of England, probably in the time of Ambrosius, and fought his way southwards, till after twelve campaigns, or twelve battles, he reached his crowning victory at Badon Hill, which gave him peace for the rest of his days. At all events, with respect to the first seven battles, there seems no reason why we should not appropriate any of them except perhaps the first—to our Cumberland circles. The proof of whether or not it is reasonable to do so will of course depend on the case we can make out for the other circles we have to examine, and on the general interdependence which the whole series can be shown to have on one another.

At present it may be allowed to stand on an hypothesis, which certainly has the merit of explaining the facts as now known; but the probability or disproof of which must depend on the facts and arguments to be adduced hereafter.

DERBYSHIRE.

The next group of monuments with which we have to deal is perhaps as interesting as any of those hitherto described. As before mentioned, when speaking of the labours of William and Thomas Bateman, the north-western portion of the county is crowded with barrows, but none apparently of so ancient a character as those excavated by Canon Greenwell in Yorkshire, and most of them containing objects of so miscellaneous a character as to defy systematic classification. As these, however, hardly belong to the subject of which we are now treating, it is not necessary to say more about them at present; and the less so, that the group which falls directly in with our line of research is well defined as to locality, and probably also as to age.

The principal monument of this group is well-known to antiquaries as Arbe or Arbor Low,[1] and is situated about nine miles south by east from Buxton, and by a curious coincidence is placed in the same relative position to the Roman Road as Avebury. So much is this the case, that in the Ordnance Survey —barring the scale—the one might be mistaken for the other if cut out from the neighbouring objects. Minning Low, however, which is the pendant of Silbury Hill in this group, is four miles off, though still in the line of the Roman road, instead of only one mile, as in the Wiltshire example. Besides, there is a most interesting Saxon Low at Benty Grange, about one mile from Arbor Low. Gib Hill, Kens Low, Ringham Low, End Low, Lean Low, and probably altogether ten or twelve important mounds covering a space five miles in one direction, by one and a half to two miles across.

Arbor Low consists of a circular platform, 167 feet in diameter, surrounded by a ditch 18 feet broad at bottom, the earth taken from which has been used to form a rampart about 15 feet to 18 feet high, and measuring about 820 feet in circumference on the top.[2] The first thing that strikes us on looking at the plan (woodcut No. 30) is that, in design and general dimensions, the monument is identical with that called "Arthur's Round Table," at Penrith. The one difference is that, in this instance, the section of the ditch, and consequently that of the rampart, have been increased at the expense of the berm; but the arrangements of both are the same, and so are the internal and external dimensions. At Arbor Low there are two entrances across the ditch, as there was in the Cumberland and Dumfriesshire

---

[1] First described in the 'Archæologia,' vol. viii. p. 131 et seqq., by the Rev. S. Pegge, in 1783.

[2] These dimensions, as well as the plan, are taken from Sir Gardner Wilkinson's paper in the 'Journal of the Archæological Association,' xvi. p. 116, and may consequently be thoroughly depended upon.

examples. As mentioned above, only one is now visible there, the other having been obliterated by the road, but the two circles are

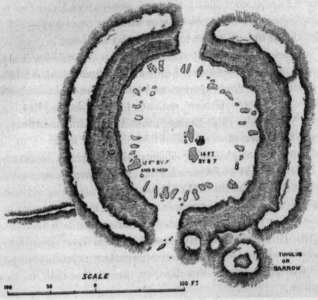

SCALE

100   50   0   100 FT

30.   Arbor Low. From a drawing by Sir Gardner Wilkinson.

in other respects so similar as to leave very little doubt as to their true features.

The Derbyshire example, however, possesses, in addition to its earthworks, a circle of stones on its inner platform, originally probably forty or fifty in number; but all now prostrate, except perhaps some of the smallest, which, being nearly cubical, may still be in *situ*. In the centre of the platform, also, are several very large stones, which evidently formed part of a central dolmen.

There is another very interesting addition at Arbor Low, which is wanting at Penrith, this is a tumulus attached unsymmetrically to the outer vallum. This was, after repeated attempts, at last successfully excavated by the Messrs. Bateman, and found to contain a cist of rather irregular shape, in which were found among other things two vases [1] one of singularly elegant

---

[1] Bateman, 'Vestiges,' p. 65.

shape, the other less so. In themselves these objects are not sufficient to determine the age of the barrow, but they suffice to show that it was not very early. One great point of interest in this discovery is its position with reference to the circle. It is identical with that of Long Meg with reference to her daughters, and perhaps some of the stones outside Avebury, supposed to be the commencement of the avenue, may mark the principal places of interment.

31.   Vases and Bronze Pin found in Arbor Low.

Attached to Arbor Low, at a distance of about 250 yards, is another tumulus, called Gib Hill, apparently about 70 to 80 feet in diameter.[1] It was carefully excavated by Mr. T. Bateman in 1848; but after tunnelling through and through it in every direction on the ground level and finding nothing, he was surprised at finding, on removing the timber which supported his galleries, that the side of the hill fell in, and disclosed the cist very near the

32.   Section of Gib Hill.   No scale.

summit. The whole fell down, and the stones composing the cist were removed and re-erected in the garden of Lumberdale House. It consisted of four massive blocks of limestone forming the sides of a chamber, 2 feet by 2 feet 6 inches, and covered by one 4 feet square. The cap stone was not more than 18 inches below the turf. By the sudden fall of the side a very pretty vase was crushed, the

---

[1] These dimensions are taken from Sir Gardner Wilkinson's plan. The Batemans, with all their merits, are singularly careless in quoting dimensions.

fragments mingling with the burnt bones it contained; but though restored, unfortunately no representation has been given. The only other articles found in this tumulus were " a battered celt of basaltic stone, a dart or javelin-point of flint, and a small iron fibula, which had been enriched with precious stones."[1]

Though Gib Hill is interesting as the first of the high-level dolmens which we have met with in this country, Minning Low is a still more striking example of that class which we hinted at before as common in Aveyron (*ante*, woodcut No. 8), and which we shall meet with frequently as we proceed. When it first attracted the attention of antiquaries in 1786, Minning Low seems to have been a straight-lined truncated cone, about 300 feet in diameter, and the platform on its summit measured

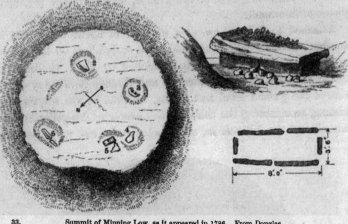

33.   Summit of Minning Low, as it appeared in 1786. From Douglas.

80 feet across.[2] Its height could not be ascertained.[3] It was even then planted over with trees, so that these dimensions, except the breadth of the platform, are hardly to be depended upon, and since then the whole mound has been so dug into and ruined, that they cannot now be verified. On the platform

[1] *Ante*, p. 11.

[2] Douglas, 'Nenia Brittanica,' p. 168, pl. xxxv.

[3] If we knew its height we might guess its age. If it was 65 feet high, its angle must be 30 degrees, and its age probably the same as that of Silbury Hill. If 100 feet, and its angle above 40 degrees, it must have been older.

at the top in 1786 there stood five kistvaens, each capable of
containing one body; and, so far as can be made out from
Douglas' plates and descriptions, the cap stone of these was flush
with the surface, or possibly, as at Gib Hill, they may have been
a few inches below the surface, and, becoming exposed, may have
been rifled as they were found; but this is hardly probable, because
unless always exposed, it is not likely they would have been either
looked for in such a situation, or found by accident.   Below them
—at what depth we are not told—a stone chamber, or rather three
chambers, were found by Mr. Bateman, apparently on the level of

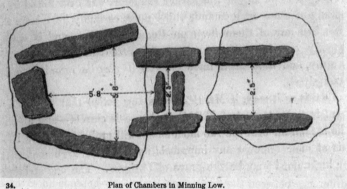

34.   Plan of Chambers in Minning Low.

the ground on the south side of the Barrow.[1] To use Mr. Bateman's
own words ('Vestiges,' &c., p. 39): " On the summit of Minning
Low Hill, as they now appear from the soil being removed from
them, are two large cromlechs, exactly of the same construction as
the well-known Kit's Cotty-house, near Maidstone, in Kent.   In
the cell near which the body lay were found fragments of five
urns, some animal bones, and six brass Roman coins, viz., one of
Claudius Gothicus (270), two of Constantine the Great, two
of Constantine, junior, and one of Valentinian.   There is a
striking analogy between this and the great Barrow at New
Grange, described by Dr. Ledwich, of which a more complete
investigation of Minning Low would probably furnish additional
proofs."   Mr. Bateman was not then aware that a coin of Valen-

---

[1] ' Ten Years' Diggings,' p. 82.

tinian had been found in the New Grange mound,[1] which is one similarity in addition.

The fact of these coins being found here fixes a date beyond which it is impossible to carry back the age of this mound, but not the date below which it may have been erected. The coins found in British barrows seem almost always those of the last Emperors who held sway in Britain, and whose coins may have been preserved and to a certain extent kept in circulation after all direct connexion with Rome had ceased, and thus their rarity or antiquity may have made them suitable for sepulchral deposits. No coin of Augustus or any of the earlier Emperors was ever found in or on any of these rude tumuli, which must certainly have been the case had any of them been pre-Roman. This mound is consequently certainly subsequent to the first half of the fourth century, and how much more modern it may be remains to be determined.

Be this as it may, if Mr. Bateman's suggestion that this monument is a counterpart of Kit's Cotty-house is correct—and no one who is familiar with the two monuments will probably dispute it—this at once removes any improbability from the argument that the last-named may be the grave of Catigren. The one striking difference between the two is, that Kit's Cotty-house is an external free-standing dolmen, while Minning Low is buried in a tumulus. This, according to the views adopted in these pages, from the experience of other monuments, would lead to the inference that the Kentish example was the more modern of the two. It is not, however, worth while arguing that point here; for our present purpose it is sufficient to know that both are post-Roman, and probably not far distant in date.

Another barrow belonging to this group is at Benty Grange, about a mile from Arbor Low, which, though of a different character, may be connected with the others. One body only was buried in it, of which no trace, however, remained but the hair.[2] There was apparently little more than 2 feet of earth over it. The first thing found was a leather drinking-cup, ornamented in silver

---

[1] 'Petrie's Life,' by Stokes, p. 234.

[2] The complete disappearance of the body of this undoubted Saxon chief ought to make us cautious in ascribing remote antiquity to many comparatively fresh bodies we find elsewhere.

with stars and crosses.   Two circular enamels were also there,
adorned with that interlacing pattern found in the earliest Anglo-
Saxon or Irish MSS. of the sixth or seventh centuries, or it may be
a little earlier; a helmet also was found, formed of iron bars, with

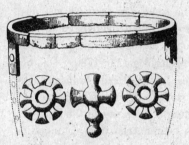

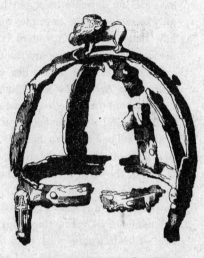

35. Fragment of Drinking Cup from Benty Grange.   36. Fragment of Helmet from Benty Grange.

bronze and silver ornaments, and surmounted by what Mr. Bateman
assures us was a perfectly distinct representation of a hog.   He
then quotes from Beowulf several passages, in which the poet
describes: "The boar an ornament to the head, the helmet lofty
in wars" (l. 4299). . . . "They seemed a boar's form to bear over
their cheeks" (l. 604). . . . "At the pile was easy to be seen, the
mail-shirt covered with gore, the hog of gold, the boar hard as
iron" (l. 2213).   As Beowulf lived, as shown above, probably
in the fifth century, the poem may be taken as describing perfectly the costume of the warriors of his day; and nothing could
answer more completely his description than the contents of this
tomb.

In Kenslow Barrow, between Minning Low and Arbor Low,
were found a few implements of flint and bone; but on clearing
out the grave in the rock, which had been examined before in 1821,
Mr. S. Bateman found some portions of the skeleton undisturbed,
and with them a small neat bronze dagger, and a little above these

L

an iron knife of the shape and size usually deposited in Anglo-Saxon interments.[1] Of course the theory of successive interments is called on to explain away these disturbing facts; but there seems nothing here to justify any other inference than that in this case all the deposits belonged to the same age. This, therefore, may be added to the examples quoted from the 'Vestiges,' to show how little the Danish system is really applicable to the class of monuments of which we are treating.

On Stanton Moor, four miles east from Kenslow, and about five miles from Arbor Low and Minning Low respectively, there are many monuments, both of earth and stone, which, though on a smaller scale, seem to belong to the same age as those just described. They seem to have been very much overlooked by the Batemans, but a very detailed account of them is given by Mr. Rooke in the sixth volume of the 'Archæologia,' in 1780. One of them, called the Nine Ladies, has been given already (ante, p. 49); but westward of it stands or stood a stone, called the King Stone, at a distance of 34 yards, thus suggesting a similarity to the Salkeld circle. Half a mile west from this, nearer Arbor Low, is another group of nine stones, the tallest 17 feet in height, and 75 yards southward two stones of smaller dimensions; 200 yards from this an oval ring, the major axis of which measures 243 feet, the minor 156 feet. It has what Mr. Rooke calls a double ditch, a rampart outside the ditch as well as one inside; it is, in fact, a less-developed example of that form of which Arbor Low and Arthur's Round Table are finished examples. On the east side of the Moor were three tall isolated stones, which in Rooke's time the natives still called Cat Stones, showing clearly that the tradition still remained of a battle fought there, but when or by whom no tradition lingers on the spot to enlighten us.

All these monuments and many more which it would be tedious and uninteresting to particularize, are contained within a circle, which may be described with a radius of about three miles, the centre being half way between Henty Grange and Stanton Moor. It would perhaps be too much to assert that they are all of one age; but there is certainly a very strong family likeness

---

[1] Bateman, 'Ten Years' Diggings,' p. 21.

among them, and they cannot differ much either in age or purpose. It may also perhaps be conceded that they are not the tombs or temples of the inhabitants of the moors on which they stand. The country where they are situated is a bleak inhospitable tract, only not quite so bad as Shap, but hardly more able to support a large population, if left only to their own resources, than the Wiltshire Downs. These three localities could never consequently have been so much richer in this class of monuments than settlements in the more fertile parts of the island. Strangers must have erected them, and to determine who these strangers were, is the task to which antiquaries have now to apply themselves.

Whatever may be determined on the point, one thing, I think, must and will be conceded, which is, that Arthur's Table at Penrith, Arbor Low, and Avebury, are monuments of the same age, and were dedicated to the same purposes. The first is a simple earthen monument, of a certain design and with certain dimensions; the second has the same design and dimensions, with the addition of a circle of stones and dolmen in the centre; the third has all the features that the other two possess, with the addition of increased dimensions, and the internal circles being doubled. But the internal ditch, the rampart, and the character of the circle and other features, are so like each other, and so unlike what are found elsewhere, that they must stand or fall together. If any one of these belonged to the age of Arthur, all three certainly did. If, on the other hand, any one of the three can be proved to belong to another age, the other two will hardly be able to maintain their position. The circles at Cumrew, Salkeld, and Mayborough, present so many points of similarity, that they, too, must probably be classed with these three, though there is not the same evidence to justify their being classed together. The stone avenue at Shap is also most probably the counterpart of that at Kennet; but the destruction of the circle at Brackenbyr, and the limited knowledge we have of it, prevent anything very definite being predicated regarding it.

If we may consider Gib Hill as the analogue of Silbury Hill, its place and position may throw some light on the mystery attaching to the latter. The relative distances of these satellites to their primaries is nearly proportional to the diameter of the circles, and they both present the peculiarity that they have no interment in their base. The Archæological Institute in 1849 did exactly what the Batemans had done before them. They tunnelled and explored the base of Gib Hill, and gave it up in despair, when an accident revealed to them the grave over their heads, within 18 inches of the surface. The antiquaries were not so fortunate at Silbury; but judging from the analogy of Gib Hill, and still more from that of Minning Low, the graves may be expected to be found arranged around the plateau on the summit, probably six or seven in number, and as probably within a few feet of the surface. There was none in the centre of the platform at Minning Low, though there was in the smaller tumulus of Gib Hill; and this may account for the Duke of Northumberland's ill-success when he dug into the hill in 1776. Poor Stukeley was very much laughed at for prizing a very modern-looking iron bit, belonging to a bridle that was found on the top of the hill[1] (woodcut No. 18); yet it may turn out to be the only real fact he brought away from the place. Nothing but an iron sword was found in the kistvaen, on the top of Minning Low, but it was nearly perfect;[2] why should not the bridle be found, for we know that horses were frequently buried with the warriors they had borne in battle?

Omitting Cornwall for the present, the circles at Stanton Drew form the only other group of any importance in England for which it remains to find a purpose and a name; and I confess I see no reason for separating them from those just named. There are so many points of similarity, that they can hardly be of an age far apart, and their purpose certainly is the same. If there is anything in the arguments adduced above, they must mark a battle-field. They are certainly not a family or a princely sepulchre,

---

[1] "In 1723 the workmen dug up the body of a great king buried there in the centre, a very little below the surface. The bones were extremely rotten, and, six weeks after, I came luckily to rescue a great curiosity which they took out there—an iron chain, as they called it. It was the bridle buried along with the monarch. There were deer horns and an iron knife, with a bone handle, too, all excessively rotten, taken up along with it."—Stukeley's 'Stonehenge and Avebury,' pp. 41-42. The bridle is figured, pl. xxxvi.

[2] Douglas, 'Nenia Brit.' p. 168.

still less a local cemetery, nor need it now be added, certainly not
a temple.

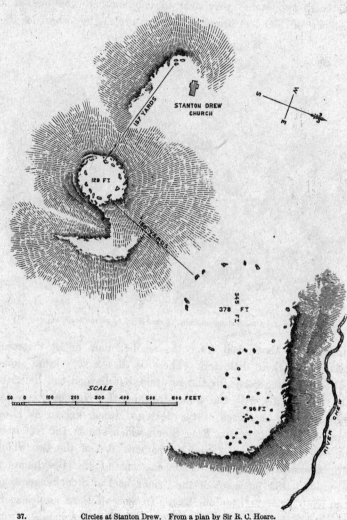

37.   Circles at Stanton Drew. From a plan by Sir R. C. Hoare.

Their arrangement will be understood from the annexed woodcut (No. 37). The group consists of one first-class circle or oval,
378 feet (?) by 345 feet—100 metres; and two of the second class,
one 96 feet, the other 129; and a dolmen near the church, at

a distance of 157 yards from the last-named.[1]   Attached to the
two principal circles are short straight avenues, pointing apparently to two stones very near to one another—the one at a
distance of 300 feet from the large circle, the other at the

88.   View of the Circles at Stanton Drew.   From a sketch by Percy Shelton, Esq.

distance of about 100 from the smaller one, or at distances
relative to their diameters. There is also a very large stone,
called the King Stone, by the roadside, but beyond the limits of
the plan. This, with the stones to which the avenues point, are
probably the analogues of the detached stone, known as Long
Meg, at Salkeld, or the Ring Stone, which stands 180 feet from
one of the circles at Avebury; perhaps also of the two which
are assumed to be the commencement of the Beckhampton
avenue at that place, or of the Friar's heel at Stonehenge, or of
the King Stone at Stanton Moor. In fact, all these circles seem
to have detached stones standing at some little distance from

---

[1] Nothing can exceed the effrontery
with which Stukeley inserted curved
avenues between these circles, so as to
make the whole into a serpent form.
Nothing of the kind exists, nor existed
in 1826, when Mr. Croker made, for Sir
R. C. Hoare, the survey from which the
woodcut is copied, with Sir Gardner
Wilkinson's corrections.

them outside. It is there that I would look for the principal interments, rather than in the circles themselves; but this is one of the questions that the spade, and the spade only, can decide. There is, however, also attached to the smaller of the two circles at Stanton Drew a heap of stones which is apparently the ruins of a dolmen, and these may mark the real place of interment, as does the tumulus attached to Arbor Low, which corresponds with them in position.

The only recorded tradition with regard to this monument at Stanton Drew represents Keyna, a holy virgin in the fifth century, the daughter apparently of a Welsh prince, obtaining a grant of the land on which the village of Keynsham now stands from the prince of the country. She was warned, however, of the insecurity of the gift, in consequence of the serpents of a deadly species that infested the place. She accepted the gift notwithstanding, and by her prayers converted the serpents into the stones we now see there,[1] so at least Stukeley and Bathurst Dean assure us.

Such a tradition is only valuable as indicating the date that is popularly ascribed to the monument. In this instance the fifth century is suggested, which may be 50 or even 100 years earlier than I would be inclined to assign it to, but such data are of little consequence. The date is also shadowed forth in the incident related; for not only in Ireland, but in France, and frequently also in England, the early struggles of the first Christian missionaries are represented as victories over the snakes or snake worshippers. St. Hilda, for instance, at Whitby signalized the establishment of Christianity in the seventh century by converting the Yorkshire snakes into Ammonites, which are still found there in quantities, which in the eyes of the peasantry are much more like stone snakes than the stones into which St. Keyna transformed her Somersetshire enemies.

Whatever the value of these and such like traditions, one thing seems quite certain, that every local tradition which has yet been quoted represents these monuments as erected subse-

---

[1] 'Archæologia,' xxv. p. 189.

quently to Roman times, and generally as belonging to that transitional age when Christianity was struggling with Paganism for the mastery. The common people are generally willing enough to amuse themselves with fables about giants and demi-gods, and to wander back into prehistoric times; but with regard to these monuments they do not seem to have done so. I do not recollect a single tradition that ascribes any stone circle to the pre-Roman period.

If, however, I am correct in assuming that these great groups of circles belong to the Arthurian age, we have no difficulty in assigning to this one its proper place in the series of his battles. The ninth, as we have seen above, was probably fought at Caerleon on the Usk; which would seem to indicate that, at a certain point in his career, Arthur was forced back quite out of England into South Wales; but his return on that hypothesis is easily traced. The tenth battle was on the shore of some large river, which ought in consequence to be the Severn, though the name given in the text lends no countenance to this supposition; the eleventh was "In monte quod dicitur Agned in Somersetshire," which would answer perfectly, except in name; for Stanton Drew, in that case, would be in the direct line of advance to Badon Hill, where the twelfth and crowning victory was fought.

The name here, as throughout, creates the difficulty, but Stanton on the Stones, or Stone Town, is simply an epithet applied to all these groups by the Saxons at some period subsequent to that of which we are speaking, when the memory of their purpose was lost, or little cared for by those of a different race, and speaking a different language, who had succeeded to the Bryts, who had erected them. Unless we assume that Stonehenge, Stanton Drew, the circles on Stanton Moor, and the stones at Stennis, and others, were erected by the Saxons themselves, they must originally have borne Celtic names, and it would be these names that Nennius would quote, and which consequently could not be those by which they are now known.

The expression "in monte" is singularly confirmatory of this determination, inasmuch as one of the remarkable features of the locality is the fortified hill known as Maes[1] Knoll, which literally looks into Stanton Drew, and is the most remarkable feature seen from it, and a fight on its ridge is as probable an operation as any likely to be undertaken in this quarter.

If the above were all the evidence that could be produced in support of the hypothesis that all these great circles belonged to the Arthurian age, it might be admitted to be sufficient to establish not a conclusion but a fair *primâ facie* case. The reasonableness, however, of what has been here advanced will, it is hoped, become more and more apparent as we proceed. Absolute mathematical or logical proof it is to be feared, in the present state of the evidence, is not available. Till attention is fairly turned to a certain definite line of argument, the experiments are not made, and the authorities are not read, which bear upon it, or if made or read are not understood; but when the arguments are examined with the earnest desire to prove or disprove them, new light springs up from every quarter, and before long there may be grounds for a positive answer.

Meanwhile it may be well to point out, before going further, that this class of circles is peculiar to England. They do not exist in France or in Algeria. The Scandinavian circles are all very different, so too are the Irish. The one circle out of England that at all resembles them is that at Stennis, or rather Brogar, in the Orkneys, which will be described in detail further on. There we have a great 100-metre circle, with a ditch (but no rampart), a smaller 100-foot circle, with a ruined dolmen in its stone circle, as at Stanton Drew, and we have the Maes Knoll for the Maes How. The Stennis group has also the detached stones, though it wants the rudimentary avenues, and some minor peculiarities, and it may be more modern, but it is very similar; whereas those in Cornwall and elsewhere are small and irregular, and totally wanting in the dignity belonging to those which we have ventured to call Arthurian.

---

[1] What is the meaning of the word "Maes"? It is singular that the Maes How, in Orkney, should bear the same relative position to the Standing Stones of Stennis, in Orkney, that Maes Knoll does to the group of circles. I do not know of the name occurring anywhere else. According to the dictionaries, it merely means "plain" or "field." In Irish "Magh" pronounced "Moy;" but that can hardly be the meaning here.

The arguments adduced in the preceding pages will probably be deemed sufficient to make out a strong case to show that these great circles were erected, at all events, after the departure of the Romans, and if this is so, it confines the field for discussion within very narrow limits. Either they must have been erected by the Romanized Britons before they were so completely Christianized as to be entirely weaned from their Pagan habits, or they were the works of the Saxons or Danes. We shall be in a better position to judge how far it is likely that the latter were the authors, when we have examined the rude stone monuments of Scandinavia or Friesland, from which countries the Northmen descended on our shores. When this is done, we shall probably come to the conclusion that, as they erected Dolmens as burying-places for their dead, and Menhirs or Bauta Stones and circles in their battle-fields, there is no improbability of their having done so also here. The question, however, is, did they erect these great 100-metre circles? These are unique, so far as I know; a class quite by themselves, and so similar, whether found in Cumberland or Derbyshire, or in Wilts or Somersetshire, that, with the probable exception of the Orkney group, they must be the work of one people, and also nearly of the same age. If, in fact, they do not mark the battle-fields to which I have attempted to ascribe them, they must mark something nearly approximating to them in date, and as nearly analogous in intention and purpose.

SMALLER CIRCLES.

It would be as tedious as unprofitable to attempt to enumerate all the smaller circles existing in various parts of England; but there are two or three which are curious in themselves, and interesting as illustrating the large circles of which we have just been treating. The first to be mentioned is one situated in Englewood Forest, near Rose Hill, and therefore nearly equi-distant from Cumrew, Salkeld, and Carlisle. Locally, therefore, it belongs to the Cumberland group, described above, and may do so in date also. It is a low platform, it can hardly be called a tumulus, as it is only 12 feet high. It is circular, and measures 63 feet across. On the platform stand, or at least stood in 1787,

three bilithons, or groups of two tall stones standing side by side,
like those in the inner circle at Stonehenge.   Mr. Rooke dug in
front of one of these, with the intention of seeing how deep it was
in the ground, but to his astonishment he found a cist formed of
six perfectly well fitted hewn stones, but measuring little more
than 2 feet each way.   In front of the other outside group he
found a similar cist, but a little larger, 2 feet 10 inches by 2 feet
2 inches, and further removed from the central pair of upright

39.   Rose Hill Tumulus.   From the Archæologia,' vol. x.

stones, and nearer the centre of the circle, a third cist, formed
equally of hewn and well fitted stones.   In all three of these were
found human bones, fragments of skulls, teeth, &c., but no implements or ornaments of any sort, only under one head a metallic
lump, with apparently particles of gold in it.[1]   This was sent to
the Society of Antiquaries for examination, but with what result

---

[1] 'Archæologia,' x. pl. xi. p. 106.

is not stated.[1] According to the plan, it would appear as if there were originally six interments in the mound. In fact, that it was the counterpart of the top of Minning Low, with the addition of the pairs of obelisks. Mr. Rooke was, however, so much puzzled at finding Druids buried six feet below the floor of their own temple, that he did not seek further. But if the mound still exists, it would be very interesting to know if any more cists exist in the mound, or any burial deeper down below them, as in the Derbyshire example. It might contain coins, and if so, would be interesting as another example of its date; but meanwhile its truncated conoidal form and arrangement of graves, and of trilithons, are sufficient to show that it was cotemporary with Minning Low and Stonehenge, or at all events not far from their date.

In the same paper in which Mr. Rooke describes the Rose Hill tumulus he gives an account of an excavation at a place called Aspatria, a little farther westward, and near St. Bees. They cleared away a barrow about 90 feet in diameter, and at 3 feet below the original surface of the ground found a cist in which lay the skeleton of a man of gigantic stature. As he lay extended, he measured 7 feet from the head to the ankle. His feet were decayed and rotted off. At his side, near the shoulder-blade, was an iron sword 4 feet in length, the handle elegantly ornamented with inlaid silver flowers; a gold fibula or buckle was also found,

40.   Snaffle-Bit found at Aspatria.

with portions of the shield and his battle-axe. One of the most curious things found was the bit of a snaffle-bridle, which is so modern-looking that it would not excite interest if seen on a stall in Seven Dials. The main interest resides in its similarity to that which Stukeley found at Silbury Hill (woodcut No. 18, p. 81). He cleaned and polished his one carefully. Mr. Rooke had his engraved with all the rust upon it, so, at first sight, they are not so similar as they are in reality. The fact of this one being found in an undoubtedly

---

[1] It probably may have been a piece of iron pyrites, and may have been used for striking a light.

ancient grave, takes away all *primâ facie* improbability from the
suggested age of the other. From its form, Stukeley's appears
to be the older of the two; but we have no chronometric scale
for bridle-bits.

All these things make this grave look as if it were very modern;
but on the outside of the stones forming the cist were engraved a
variety of figures which are of interest as a means of comparison
with the Irish and Danish engravings we shall meet with hereafter. They are not very artistically drawn, and are probably
worse engraved; but it is easy to recognize the cross in the circle

41.   Side Stone, Aspatria Cist.

There are the concentric circles with dots in the centre and
straight lines proceeding from them and other figures found on
rocks and elsewhere, which antiquaries have hitherto been
inclined to ascribe to a primæval antiquity, but which this tomb
would bring down at least to the Viking age—of which more
hereafter.

The circle of cists on Mule Hill, in the Isle of Man, are interesting from another cause; for unfortunately they all have been
laid bare and rifled before any antiquary took cognisance of them,
and we have consequently nothing by which their date can be
even guessed at. Their interest lies in their arrangement, which is
that of eight cists arranged in a circle, with, it would seem, others
at right angles at certain intervals.[1] From simple inspection it is

---

[1] 'Archæologia Cambriensis,' third
series, vol. xii. p. 54. A fancy plan of
the same circle appears in the same
volume, but is utterly untrustworthy.
It is reproduced by Waring, 'Mon.' &c.
pl. xli.

evident that these cists must at one time have been covered with earth. They are not dolmens, or anything that would do for self-

42.   Mule Hill, View of Cists.

standing monuments. If covered with earth, they would form a circular mound 45 feet in diameter internally, and 65 feet across

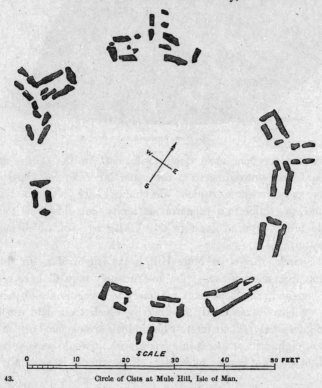

SCALE

0   10   20   30   40   50 FEET

43.   Circle of Cists at Mule Hill, Isle of Man.

to the foot of the outer slope, and, as far as one example can go, would tend to prove that the circular vallum at Avebury and many other places was a place for the deposit of bodies. Except in the instance spoken of in describing the circle at Marden, I am not aware of bodies having been found in England under these ramparts; but they have not been sought for. Of one thing we may feel certain, that nothing is unique in these matters, and that what occurred once, occurred frequently, and will no doubt be found when looked for.

Another peculiarity of this circle is worth observing. There are two gaps or openings in the circle opposite one another, as at Arbor Low and Penrith. One must not rely too much on this, as the gaps here may arise from the removal of cists; but the coincidence is at least curious, and if we restored this monument in the sense just indicated, and could rely on that restoration, the secret of the vallum surrounding Avebury and other similar monuments would no longer be a mystery. To my mind it has not been so for many years past; but though I dare not yet ask others to follow at once, I trust sufficient evidence has been accumulated in the preceding pages to render it probable that they were only continuous tumuli.

The circle or rather circles, on Burn Moor, near Wast Water, Cumberland, are described by Mr. Williams as consisting of a 100-foot circle, formed of forty-four stones, beyond which, at a distance of 25 feet is an outer circle of fourteen large stones. A niche or square enclosure on one side of the inner circle contains a cairn 25 feet in diameter, and within the circle are four others, irregularly spaced, and measuring 21 to 25 feet in diameter; each like the circle itself, surrounded by fourteen stones. These, on being opened, were found to contain a rude chamber formed of five stones, in which were found remains of burnt bones, horns of stags, and other animals.[1]

One point of interest in this monument is, that it explains the existence of a similar square enclosure on one side of a well-known 100-foot circle near Keswick. There is no sign of a cairn there now; it may have been removed, as those at Salkeld were, or it may be that the body was interred without this external indication; but that it lies, or lay, in this enclosure seems certain. The

---

[1] 'Proceedings of the Society of Antiquaries,' iii. p. 225.

principal reason for referring to it here is that it is undoubtedly
sepulchral. We shall find many examples equally so further on,
but it is well, in the meanwhile, to illustrate one which certainly
was neither a temple nor place of assembly, and which contains,
besides, several peculiarities to which we shall have occasion to
advert hereafter.

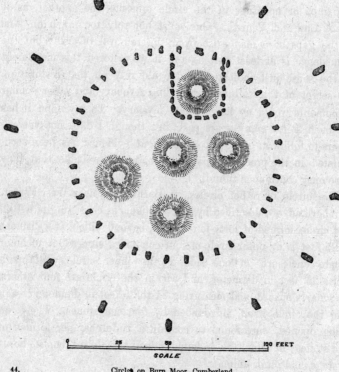

Circles on Burn Moor, Cumberland.

It seems almost equally clear that the Boscawen circles, with
which we close our illustrations of English circles for the present,
were neither Temples nor Things. It is very difficult to see how
any one could fancy that anything so confused as the centre of
these circles is, could be a temple, still less a place of assembly.
But Borlase, though generally admitting the sepulchral nature of
the circles, maintains that this one was a temple, and describes the

position of the serving Druids and all the ceremonies down to
the minutest particulars. The circles are small, the largest being
only 75 feet in diameter, and the whole group only 200 feet across,
neither are the stones by any means of imposing dimensions.

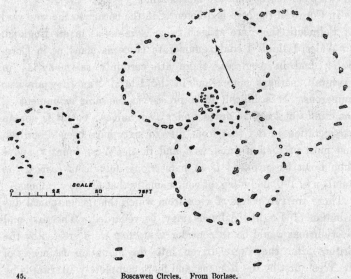

45.   Boscawen Circles. From Borlase.

Another circumstance worthy of being noticed, is that there are
detached stones in front of the principal circles. Interesting
results might be obtained by excavating at their bases, as, for
reasons above stated, it seems as if the principal interment might
be found at their feet.

DOLMENS.

As stated above, England seems to be the native country of
the great circles, no 100-metre circles having yet been found
anywhere out of England, excepting, of course, that at Stennis.
France, on the contrary, seems to be the native country of the
dolmens. They exist there in numbers far beyond anything we
can show, and of dimensions exceeding anything we can boast
of. In England proper, when we have enumerated Kit's Cotty-
house, the dolmen in Clatford Bottom, Wayland Smith's Cave,
that at Rollright, and one at Drewsteignton, in Devonshire, our

M

list is nearly exhausted. There may be heaps of stones which seem dolmens, or something like them; and chambered tumuli, whose internal kistvaens, if exposed, might be entitled to rank with dolmens; but, taking the word in its broad sense, it is difficult to carry our list beyond the half-dozen.

In Cornwall the case is different. In the corner to the westward of Falmouth there are at least twice as many as in all England. In Wales, I think I could enumerate twice as many as in Cornwall; and in Anglesea[1] there are certainly as many as in Cornwall, perhaps more; and in the Isle of Man they are also numerous. It is difficult to be precise, as the same monument is, sometimes at least, recorded under two names; but it is not an exaggeration to say that from fifty to sixty have been described, and most of them figured, as found in the West country, and I should not be surprised if an industrious statistician carried the number to 100, including, of course, many that are now ruinous.

There are two points of view from which this geographical distribution of English dolmens may be regarded. The first and most obvious would be to consider that they were erected by the Britons after they were driven into the mountain fastnesses of the West, first by the Romans, and more completely afterwards by the Saxons. The other view would be that they are the work of a different race, who, we have every reason to believe, occupied the western country in the time of the Romans. Tacitus is particularly explicit on this point. He divides the inhabitants of the country into three classes. The red-haired Caledonians, resembling the Germans and inhabiting the north; the Silures, of dark complexion and curling hair, and whom he describes as living in that part of the country which is opposite Spain, and he suggests that the ancient Iberians crossed over and occupied these regions; and he then adds: "Those nearest to Gaul are similar to the inhabitants of that country."[2] There is so much in the present aspect of the people of this country to confirm this general classification that there seems very little reason for doubting its general correctness; and as all these

---

[1] The Hon. W. C. Stanley enumerates by name twenty-four in Anglesea.— 'Archæologia Cambrensis,' fourth series, vol. i. p. 58.

[2] Tacitus, 'Vita Agricolæ,' chap. v.

dolmens are found in the country of the Silures it may be argued that they belong to them. If he had joined the Aquitanians to Iberians he would probably have expressed more completely the whole facts of the case as we now know them.

Admitting, however, this ethnographic view of the case to the fullest possible extent—which I am prepared to do, it still leaves the question of date wholly unsettled. It would be answered if we dared to assume that the Silures were driven from the fertile parts of the valley of the Severn, which we have reason to suppose they occupied in Agricola's time, to the mountain fastnesses, and that it was then only that they began to repeat in stone what previously they had only erected in earth. If this could be established, we should get both an ethnographical and a chronological determination of no small value; but of this we shall be better able to form an opinion after discussing the monuments of France.

Meanwhile there is one point bearing upon the subject to which it may be as well to draw attention. In Wales and Anglesea, which we may assume to have been the country of the Silures or that to which they were driven, there are no circles, but only dolmens. In Cornwall, where the blood was certainly more mixed, there are both circles and dolmens, and the same is the case at the other extremity of the western district in the Isle of Man.

If it is contended that, being nearer to Spain or Aquitaine than Wales, Cornwall must have been earliest and most exclusively inhabited by the dark race, the answer is, that though it may originally have been so, the races in Cornwall had been mixed with Celtic and other blood before the age of the stone monuments; while in the Isle of Man we shall probably see reason for believing that northern blood was infused into the veins of the people, at a very early age, when few, if any, monuments of this class existed, and certainly before all had been completed.

Even a cursory examination of these West Coast dolmens would, I think, be sufficient to prove to any one that the theory that all were originally covered with earthen mounds is utterly untenable. That such chambered graves as those at Uley in Gloucestershire,[1]

---

[1] 'Somerset Archæo. Soc. Proceedings,' viii. p. 51.

or Stoney Littleton in Somersetshire,[1] were always intended to be so covered up is clear enough. So was this one at Park Cwn, in the peninsula of Gower, recently opened and described by Sir John Lubbock.[2] It is of the same type as Uley and Stoney Littleton, but has only four chambers arranged on each side of the

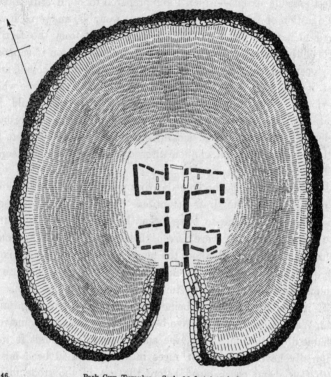

46. Park Cwn Tumulus. Scale 16 feet to 1 inch.

central passage. One of its most remarkable characteristics is the beautiful masonry of the retaining walls on each side of the funnel-shaped passage leading to the cells. These are so carefully built that it is evident that they were meant to be seen, and the entrance to be kept open. Indeed, unless we fancy it was the monument of some fight, which there seems no reason for supposing,

---

[1] 'Archæologia,' xix. p. 43 et seqq.
[2] 'Journal of the Ethnological Society,' January, 1871, p. 416.

it is evident it must have been kept open till forty deaths had occurred in the family of the chief to which it served as sepulchre, as at least that number of bodies were found in the chambers, but in a dreadfully confused condition, as if the grave had been rifled before, but no implements or trace of metal were left to indicate even approximately its age.

At Uley, in Gloucestershire, half way between Berkeley and Tetbury, there is a tumulus which, in its internal arrangement, is very similar to that last described. The entrance is of the same form, and there are four side-chambers; but those at Uley are grouped more artistically in the centre, instead of being separated by a passage, as at Park Cwn. Externally the differences are more apparent; the Gloucestershire example being oblong, or rather heart-shaped, while that in Gower is more circular in form. The Uley tumulus was first opened by a Mr. Baker, in 1821, but subsequently examined with great care by Dr. Thurnam; and a very careful account, resulting from his own observation compared with the records of Mr. Baker's, published by him in the 'Archæological Journal.'[1] The bodies in the chambers, which were numerous, had been disturbed and were lying in disorder, as at Park Cwn; but among them was found a vessel resembling a Roman lachrymatory, and some pottery which may have been either Romano-British or Mediæval. There were also found some fragments of flint implements, apparently arrow-heads, and outside two stone axes—one of flint. Near the summit of the mound, exactly over the easternmost chamber, there had been another interment, and beside the skeleton were found three brass coins of the sons of Constantine the Great.

On this evidence, Dr. Thurnam, with the approval probably of every antiquary in England, comes to the conclusion that the original erection of the chambered tumulus belongs to the long prehistoric past; that the pottery, &c., were accidentally introduced; and that the coins belong to a secondary post-Roman interment. The only evidence for this being the presence of the flints above mentioned, and the assumptions based on them; they having become articles of faith with antiquaries which it is rank

---

[1] Vol. xi. p. 315 *et seqq.*

heresy to dispute. As I have already stated, till some one can show at what period flint ceased to be used in any particular locality, this evidence is worthless. With regard to the secondary interments, it appears to be inconceivable that, after the lapse of 500 or 600 years at least, and the civilizing influence of the Roman occupation, any one should choose the top of one of the mounds of the long-forgotten pagan savages for a burying-place. If burying in barrows had been the fashion in Gloucester-shire, as it was on the wolds of Yorkshire or the downs of Wiltshire, something might be said in favour of such an hypo-thesis if we could also assume that the races had been undisturbed in the interval. But there are hardly half-a-dozen tumuli in the whole county. They, like Uley, Rodmarton,[1] Stoney Littleton,[2] are all chambered tumuli of one class and apparently of one age. All too, it may be remarked, are close to Roman stations and surrounded by evidences of Roman occupation.

In the previous pages we have already met with several instances of summit interments, as at Gib Hill, Minning Low, &c., which are certainly not secondary, and we have reason to suspect that more will be found when looked for; and the finding of Roman coins on or near the top of tumuli is too frequent to be acci-dental, and occurs even in Ireland, where the Romans never went.

We shall have occasion to recur to this subject when speaking of the tomb of King Harald Hildetand at Lethra, and then propose to treat it more in detail; but meanwhile it seems clear that the evidence of the coins and the pottery must be allowed to outweigh that of the flints; and if this is so, not only Uley but all the chamber-tumuli in Gloucestershire or Somerset belong either to the Romano-British, or rather to the post-Roman period of British history.

Another and even more interesting example of this class has recently been brought to light by the Hon. W. O. Stanley, at Plas Newydd, not far from the great dolmen represented on woodcut No. 50.[3] It is a chamber or cist, 3 feet 3 inches

---

[1] 'Pro. Soc. Ant.,' second series, ii. 275. Thurnam, 'Archæologia,' xlii. 217.

[2] 'Archæologia,' xix. p. 43.

[3] 'Archæologia Cambrensis,' fourth series vol. i. p. 51 et seqq.

wide by about 7 feet long, and covered by two slabs. Before being disturbed, the supporting slabs must have formed nearly

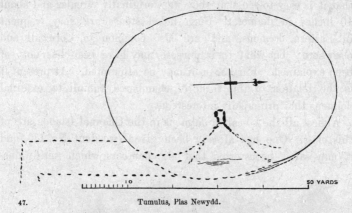

47.   Tumulus, Plas Newydd.

perfect walls, thus distinguishing the cist from those standing on widely-spaced legs. Its principal point of interest, however, is the

48.   Entrance to Dolmen, in Tumulus, Plas Newydd.

widely-splayed avenue of stones leading up to it, showing that it was always intended to be visited; and still more curious are the

two holes that were pierced in the slab that closed the entrance.
The upper part of this slab is now broken off, but so much remains
that it is easy to see that they were originally circular and about
10 inches in diameter. Such holed stones are very frequent
in Eastern dolmens, and are also common in Cornwall and
elsewhere;[1] but what their purpose may have been has not yet
been explained. Further on it may be attempted. At present it
is the relation of this form of chambered tumuli to external
dolmens that principally interests us.

Almost all the so-called dolmens in the Channel Islands are of
this class. One has already been given (woodcut No. 11), and
it may safely be asserted that all chambers which were wains-

49.   Dolmen at Pentre Ifan.   From 'Archæologia Cambrensis.'

coted with slabs, so as to form nearly perfect walls, and all that
had complicated quasi-vaulted roofs were, or were intended to be,
covered with mounds—more especially those that had covered passages leading to them. There is, however, a very wide distinction
between these sepulchral chambers and such a monument as this
at Pentre Ifan, in Pembrokeshire.[2] The top stone is so large
that it is said five persons on horseback have found shelter under

---

[1] For Rodmarton, see 'Proceedings Soc. Ant.' *l. s. c.*; for Cornish, see paper by
M. Brash, 'Gent. Mag.,' 1864.
[2] 'Archæologia Cambrensis,' third series, xi. p. 284.

it from a shower of rain. Even allowing that the horses were only Welsh ponies, men do not raise such masses and poise them on their points for the sake of hiding them again. Besides that, the supports do not and could not form a chamber. The earth would have fallen in on all sides, and the connexion between the roof and the floor been cut off entirely, even before the whole was completed. Or, to take another example, that at Plas Newydd, on the shore of the Menai Strait. Here the cap stone is an enormous block, squared by art, supported on four stone legs, but with no pretence of forming a chamber. If the cap stone were

50.   Dolmen at Plas Newydd.   From 'Archæologia Cambrensis.'

merely intended as a roofing stone, one a third or fourth of its weight would have been equally serviceable and equally effective in an architectural point of view, if buried. The mode of architectural expression which these Stone men best understood was the power of mass. At Stonehenge, at Avebury, and everywhere, as here, they sought to give dignity and expression by using the largest blocks they could transport or raise—and they were right; for, in spite of their rudeness, they impress us now; but had they buried them in mounds, they neither would have impressed us nor their contemporaries.

As before mentioned, however, the great argument against the theory of their having been always covered up is the impossibility of accounting for the disappearance of the tumuli. If they had been situated on fertile plains where the land was valuable for agricultural purposes, it might be assumed that a civilized people with highly cultivated antiquarian tastes might have been at the trouble and expense of removing the tumuli for the sake of the land, and of preserving the dolmens for their historical value. But that the rude peasantry of Cornwall and Wales should have done this is inconceivable, more especially as by far the greater number of these monuments are situated on bleak moorlands of no agricultural value whatever. Still more inconceivable is it that they should have done it so neatly and so carefully that no trace of the mound can now be found either around the stones or in the neighbourhood.

If any history were attached to these Western dolmens, or any remains had been found under them which would enable us to fix their dates, even approximately, or to arrange them in any intelligible sequence, it might be worth while recapitulating their names or illustrating their forms. Nothing of the sort, however, has yet been attempted; and apparently no materials exist from which any such series could be elaborated.

Only one dolmen in Wales, so far as I know, bears a name; but

LINE OF LEVEL 14 FT.

51.   Arthur's Quoit, Gower.   From a drawing by Sir Gardner Wilkinson.

it is the illustrious one of King Arthur. The dolmen bearing his name is situated in the peninsula of Gower, on the northern slopes of the bleak Bryn Cefn, about ten miles west from Swansea.[1]   It forms the centre of a very extensive group of monuments—eighty cairns, at least, are still to be counted in an area less than half a mile in length, by a quarter of a mile in width.   These are mostly small, 12 to 15 feet in diameter; one, 20 feet across, was opened by Sir Gardner Wilkinson, but proved to contain no interment. The largest is 68 feet in diameter, but has not been opened.   About 350 feet from this is the dolmen.   The cap stone is 14 feet 6 inches in length, 7 feet 5 inches in height, and 6 feet 8 inches in breadth

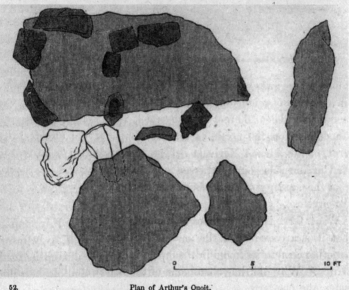

52.   Plan of Arthur's Quoit.

even now, but a very large piece has been broken off, and now lies beside it, measuring upwards of 3 feet in thickness; and another piece seems to have been broken off on the other end, so that when complete it must have weighed between 35 and 40 tons.   It rested originally on ten or eleven upright stones, two of which, however, have fallen, and only four now touch the cap stone.   Sir Gardner is of opinion that it once was covered with a tumulus; but this

---

[1] The following particulars are taken from a paper by Sir J. Gardner Wilkinson, in the first volume, fourth series, of the 'Archæologia Cambrensis,' 1870. It is not only the last, but the best description which I know, and, being from the pen of so accurate an observer, I have relied on it exclusively.

appears very doubtful. The slight mound, backed up with large stones, that now surrounds it, with a diameter of 73 to 74 feet, seems an enclosure more like that of Hob Hurst's House (woodcut No. 53) than the remains of a tumulus, and till some further evidence is adduced, we must be allowed to doubt whether any cap

53. Hob Hurst's House, on Baslow Moor, Derbyshire. From a drawing by Thomas Bateman.[1]

stone on legs was ever so treated. Sir Gardner traced, doubtfully, an avenue, of which, however, only five stones now remain, extending to about 500 feet in a direction that would have passed the dolmen on the north, as that at Shap did the circle at its front, or the lines at Merivale Bridge, the circle still found there; Sir Gardner also points out some small circular enclosures, which, from the analogy of those found on Dartmoor, he assumes to be hut-circles.

What, then, is this group of monuments? Sir Gardner assumes that it is a cemetery of the ancient Britons; but, if so, why are not other cemeteries found in the fertile valleys and plains in South Wales? Why did they choose one of the barest and bleakest hill-sides, and one farthest removed from their habitations as a place in which to bury their dead? Why did they not, like the inhabitants of Salisbury Plain, disperse their graves pretty equally over an area of 30 miles by 10? Why crowd them into less than half-a-mile? Without reverting to my previous suggestion of a battle-field, I do not see how these questions can be answered; and if so, I do not think we have far to go to look for its name? As hinted above, Arthur's eighth battle must have been fought in Wales. The name of the place is written Guin (Gwyn), Guinon, Guinnon, Gunnion,[2] which certainly is Welsh; and when we find it imme-

---

[1] 'Ten Years' Diggings,' p. 87.   [2] Dare one suggest Gower?

diately preceding the battle of Caerleon on the Usk, and the principal monument still bearing Arthur's name, we may fairly, I think, adopt the suggestion till, at least, a better is offered.

Be this as it may, I think all antiquaries will agree with Sir Gardner Wilkinson in assuming that this is the stone of Cetti [1] mentioned in the Welsh triads. 'The 84th Triad' speaks of the Cor of Emmrys in Caer Caradawg (another name for Salisbury), and the 88th of the three mighty achievements of the Isle of Britain, the raising of the stone of Cetti, the building of the work of Emmrys, and the heaping of the pile of Cyvragnon.[2]　The work of Emmrys (Ambrosius) is generally admitted to be Stonehenge. If this is the stone of Cetti, which I see no reason for doubting, it only remains to identify the third. Most antiquaries suggest Silbury Hill; and, if I am correct in placing these three monuments so near one another in date, this seems also extremely probable, and so far as it goes, is a satisfactory confirmation of what has been advanced above from other sources.

From my ignorance of the Welsh language I am not in a position to say what amount of reliance should be placed in the evidence of these triads. But Herbert and other competent scholars consider it undoubted that Emmrys is Ambrosius, and the 'Work' referred to certainly Stonehenge. If this is so, it fixes its date beyond question, and as the other two are mentioned in the same breath it is probable they were not distant in date. All this may be, I believe certainly is so, but the circumstantial evidence adduced above seems to me so much clearer and so much more to be relied upon, that it derives very little additional force from the utterance of the Welsh bards. It is, however, no doubt satisfactory that their evidence coincides with everything that has been brought forward above, as bearing directly or indirectly on their age or use.

Before proceeding, it may be as well to revert for one moment to Hob Hurst's House. It is quoted here to show how a tumulus, with a dolmen on the top of it, may be connected with a low ram-

---

[1] Is this the same word as "Cotty," as applied to Kit's Cotty-house, in Kent? It looks very like it.—Coity?　　　[2] Herbert, 'Cyclops Christianus,' p. 35.

part so as not to conceal it, exactly, I believe, as is the case with Arthur's Quoit. But the name of the place where it is situated may afford a hint which may lead to something hereafter. It will be recollected that Arthur's sixth battle was fought "super flumen quod vocatur Bassas." This mound is situated on "Bas" Moor, the Low being merely the name of the mound itself. These nominal similarities are too treacherous to be relied upon; but the more the whole group is looked at the more does it appear that there are coincidences of name, or form, or purpose, between those monuments here called Arthurian, which cannot all be accidental. Individually they may not be able to resist hostile criticism, but in their cumulative form they appear to me to make up a very strong case indeed.

If any of the other dolmens in the West had even so good a title to a date as Arthur's Quoit, it might be possible to arrange them in a series; but as none have even traditional dates, all we can now do is to suggest that the dolmen at Plas Newydd (woodcut No. 50) is of about the same age as Arthur's Stone: perhaps something more modern, as it is more carefully squared; but this may arise from the one being a battle-stone, the other a peaceful sepulchre. In like manner it would seem that such an exaggerated form as Pentre Ifan (woodcut No. 49) is a "tour de force" of a still more modern date; and if we could get one certainly older than any of these, a tentative scheme could be constructed which might lead us to satisfactory results.

I by no means despair of being able eventually to construct such a scheme of classification, and, even before this Work is concluded, to make it tolerably clear that the thing is possible, and then it will only remain, if one or two fixed or probable dates can be ascertained, to bring the whole within the range of historical investigation.

CHAPTER V.

IRELAND.

———◦———

MOYTURA.

IT is probable, after all, that it is from the Irish annals that the greatest amount of light will be thrown on the history and uses of the Megalithic monuments. Indeed, had not Lord Melbourne's Ministry in 1839, in a fit of ill-timed parsimony, abolished the Historical Commission attached to the Irish Ordnance Survey, we should not now be groping in the dark. Had they even retained the services of Dr. Petrie till the time of his death, he would have left very little to be desired in this respect. But nothing of the sort was done. The fiat went forth. All the documents and information collected during fourteen years' labour by a most competent staff of explorers were cast aside—all the members dismissed on the shortest possible notice, and our knowledge of the ancient history and antiquities of Ireland thrown back half a century, at least.[1]

Meanwhile, however, a certain number of the best works of the Irish annalists have been carefully translated and edited by John O'Donovan and others, and are sufficient to enable any one not acquainted with Irish to check the wild speculations of antiquaries of the Vallancy and O'Brien class, and also to form an opinion on the value of the annals themselves, though hardly yet sufficient to enable a stranger to construct a reliable scheme of chronology or history out of the heterogeneous materials presented to him. We must wait till some second Petrie shall arise, who shall possess a sufficient knowledge of the Irish language and literature, without losing his Saxon coolness of judgment, before we can hope to possess a reliable and consecutive account of ancient Ireland.

---

[1] Stokes, 'Life of Petrie;' London, 1868, p. 99 *et seqq.*

When this is done, it will probably be found that the Irish possess a more copious literature, illustrative of the eocene period of their early history, than almost any other country of Europe. Ireland may also boast that, never having been conquered by the Romans, she retained her native forms, and the people their native customs and fashions, uninterrupted and uninfluenced by Roman civilization, for a longer time than the other countries of Europe which were subjected to its sway.

As most important and instructive parts of the Irish annals, it is proposed first to treat of those passages descriptive of the two battles of Moytura[1] (Magh Tuireadh), both of which occurred within a period of a very few years. A description of the fields on which they were fought will probably be sufficient to set at rest the question as to the uses of cairns and circles; and if we can arrive at an approximative date, it will go far to clear up the difficulties in understanding the age of the most important Irish antiquities.

The narrative which contains an account of the battle of Southern Moytura, or Moytura Cong, is well known to Irish antiquaries. It has not yet been published, but a translation from a MS. in Trinity College, Dublin, was made by John O'Donovan for the Ordnance Survey, and was obtained from their records above alluded to by Sir William Wilde. He went over the battle-field repeatedly with the MS. in his hand, and has published a detailed account of it, with sufficient extracts to make the whole intelligible.[2] The story is briefly this:—At a certain period of Irish history a colony of Firlolgs, or Belgæ, as they are usually called by Irish antiquaries, settled in Ireland, dispossessing the Fomorians, who are said to have come from Africa. After possessing the country

---

[1] In the following pages it is proposed to follow the popular and pronounceable spelling of Irish proper names. One half of the difficulty of following the Irish annals is the unfamiliar and uncouth mode in which proper names are spelt, and which we learn, from Eugene O'Curry's lectures, never represents the mode in which they are pronounced. In a learned work intended for Irish scholars, like the 'Annals of the Four

Masters,' the scientific mode of spelling is, of course, the only one that could be adopted, but in such a work as this it would be only useless and prejudicial pedantry.

[2] 'Lough Corrib, its Shores and Islands.' Dublin, 1867. Sir William possesses a residence on the battle-field, where I was hospitably entertained for some days when I visited that neighbourhood last year.

for thirty-seven years, they were in their turn attacked by a colony of Tuatha de Dananns coming from the north, said to be of the same race and speaking a tongue mutually intelligible. On hearing of the arrival of these strangers, the Firbolgs advanced from the plains of Meath as far as Cong, situated between Lough Corrib and Lough Mask, where the first battle was fought, and, after being fiercely contested for four days, was decided in favour of the invaders.[1]

The second battle was fought seven years afterwards, near Sligo, under circumstances which will be detailed more fully below, and resulted equally in favour of the Tuatha de Dananns, and they in consequence obtained possession of the country, which, according to the Four Masters, they held for 197 years.[2]

The field on which the four-days' battle of Southern Moytura was fought extends from five to six miles north and south. Near the centre of the space, and nearly opposite the village of Cong, is a group of five stone circles, one of which, 54 feet in diameter, is represented in the annexed woodcut (No. 54). Another, very

54.　　　Circle on Battle-field of Southern Moytura. From Sir W. Wilde.

similar, is close by; and a third, larger but partially ruined, is within a few yards of the first. The other two can only now be traced, and two more are said to have existed close by, but have entirely disappeared. On other parts of the battle-field there are six or seven large cairns of stone, all of them more or less ruined,

---

[1] These, and all the particulars of the battle of South Moytura, are taken from the eighth chapter of Sir W. Wilde's book, pp. 211-248, and need not, there-fore, be specially referred to.

[2] 'Annals of the Four Masters,' translated by J. O'Donovan,' i. p. 23.

the stones having been used to build dykes, with which every
field is surrounded in this country; but none of them have been
scientifically explored. One is represented (woodcut No. 55). Sir
W. Wilde has identified all of these as connected with incidents
in the battle, and there seems no reason to doubt his conclusions.
The most interesting, however, is one connected with an incident
in the battle, which is worth relating, as illustrating the manner
in which the monuments corroborate the history. On the morning
of the second day of the battle, King Eochy retired to a well to
refresh himself with a bath, when three of his enemies looking
down, recognised him and demanded his surrender. While he

55.   Cairn on Battle-field of Southern Moytura.

was parleying with them, they were attacked by his servant
and killed; but the servant died immediately afterwards of his
wounds, and, as the story goes, was interred with all honours in
a cairn close by. In the narrative it is said that the well where
the king had so narrow an escape is the only open one in the
neighbourhood. It is so to the present day; for the peculiarity of
the country is, that the waters from Lough Mask do not flow into
Lough Corrib by channels on the surface, but entirely through
chasms in the rock underground, and it is only when a crack in
the rock opens into one of these that the water is accessible. The
well in question is the only one of these for some distance in
which the water is approached by steps partly cut in the rock,
partly constructed. Close by is a cairn (woodcut No. 56), called
to this day the "Cairn of the One Man." It was opened by Sir
W. Wilde, and in its chamber was found one urn, which is now

deposited in the Museum of the Royal Academy at Dublin, the excavation thus confirming the narrative in the most satisfactory manner.

"The battle took place on Midsummer day. The Firbolgs were

56.   The Cairn of the "One Man," Moytura.

defeated with great slaughter, and their king, who left the battle-field with a body-guard of 100 brave men in search of water to allay his burning thirst, was followed by a party of 150 men, led by the three sons of Nemedh, who pursued him all the way to the strand, called Traigh Eothaile, near Ballysadare, in the county of Sligo. Here a fierce combat ensued, and King Eochy (Eochaidh) fell, as well as the leaders on the other side, the three sons of Nemedh."[1] A cairn is still pointed out on a promontory jutting into the bay, about a mile north-west of the village of Ballysadare, which is said

57. Urn in the Cairn of the "One Man," Moytura.

to have been erected over the remains of the king, and bones are also said to have been found between high and low water on the strand beneath, supposed to be those of the combatants who fell in the final struggle. It

---

[1] Eugene O'Curry's 'Materials for Ancient Irish History,' p. 246.

may be otherwise, but there is a consistency between the narrative and the monuments on the spot which can hardly be accidental, and which it will be very difficult to explain except in the assumption that they refer to the same events.

In fact, it would be difficult to conceive anything more satisfactory and confirmatory of the record than the monuments on the plain; and no one, I fancy, could go over the field with Sir William's book in his hand, without feeling the importance of his identifications. Of course it may be suggested that the book was written by some one familiar with the spot, to suit the localities. The probability, however, of this having been done before the ninth century, and done so soberly and so well, is very remote, and the guess that but one urn would be found in the cairn of the "One Man," is a greater piece of luck than could reasonably be expected. Even, however, if the book was written to suit the localities, it will not invalidate the fact that a great battle was fought on this spot, and that these cairns and these circles mark the graves of those who fell in the fight.

The collection of monuments on the battle-field of Northern Moytura is even more interesting than that on Moytura Cong, and almost justified the assertion of Petrie "that, excepting the monuments at Carnac, in Brittany, it is, even in its present state of ruin, the largest assemblage of the kind hitherto discovered in the world."[1] They have also this advantage, that the principal group, consisting of some sixty or seventy monuments, are situated on an elevated table-land, and in an area extending not more than a mile in one direction, and about half a mile in another. The country, too, is much less stony than about Cong, so that the monuments stand out better and have a more imposing look. Petrie examined and described sixty-four monuments as situated in or around this space, and came to the conclusion that originally there could not have been less than 200.[2] My impression is that there may have been 100, but hardly more, though, of course, this is only a guess, and the destruction of them is going on so rapidly that he may be right after all.

In the space above described almost every variety of Megalithic

---

[1] Stokes, 'Life of Petrie,' p. 253.   [2] l. c. p. 242.

art is to be found. There are stone cairns, with dolmens in their interiors—dolmens standing alone, but which have been evidently always exposed; dolmens with single circles; others with two or three circles of stones around them; and circles without dolmens or anything else in the centres. The only form we miss is the avenue. Nothing of the sort can now, at least, be traced, nor does it seem that any of the circles possessed such appendages.

58.   Battle-field of Northern Moytura.
Scale 6 inches to 1 mile.

The annexed woodcut (No. 58) will explain the disposition of the principal group. It is taken from the Ordnance Survey, and is perfectly correct as far as it goes, but being only on the 6-inch scale, is too small to show the form of the monuments.[1] In the centre is, or rather was, a great cairn, called Listoghil. It is marked by Petrie as No. 51, but having for years been used as a quarry for the neighbourhood, it is now so mined that it is difficult to make out either its plan or dimensions. Petrie says it is 150 feet in

---

[1] I regret very much that the state of my health, and other circumstances, prevented my mapping and drawing these remains, but I hope some competent person will undertake the task before long. Carrowmore is more easily accessible than Carnac. The inns at Sligo are better than those at Auray, the remains are within three miles of the town, and the scenery near Sligo is far more beautiful than that of the Morbihan; yet hundreds of our countrymen rush annually to the French megaliths, and bring home sketch-books full of views and measurements, but no one thinks of the Irish monuments, and no views of them exist that are in any way accessible to the public.

diameter; I made it 120. It was surrounded by a circle of great
stones, within which was the cairn, originally, probably, 40 or 50 feet
high. All this has been removed to such an extent as to expose
the kistvaen or dolmen in its centre. Its cap stone is 10 feet
square and 2 feet thick, and is of limestone, as are its supports.
All the other monuments are composed of granite boulders.
"Those who first opened it assert that they found nothing within
but burnt wood and human bones. The half-calcined bones of
horses and other animals were and are still found in this cairn
in great quantities" (Petrie, p. 250). In a note it is said that a large
spear-head of stone (flint?) was also found in this cairn.

The annexed woodcut (No. 59) will give an idea of the general
disposition of a circle numbered 27 by Petrie.[1] It is of about the

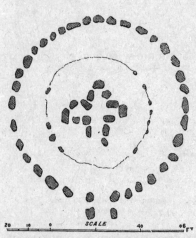

medium size, being 60 feet
in diameter. The general dimensions of the circles are 40,
60, 80, and one (No. 46) is 120
feet in diameter. The outer
circle of No. 27 is composed of
large stones, averaging 6 feet
in height, and some 20 feet
in circumference. Inside this
is a circle of smaller stones,
nearly obliterated by the
turf, and in the centre is a
three-chambered dolmen, of
which fifteen stones still
remain; but all the cap
stones, except that of the

59. Sketch-plan of Circle 27, Northern Moytura.

central inner chamber, are gone, and that now stands on its edge
in front of its support.

The general appearance of this circle will be understood from the
annexed view (woodcut No. 60), taken from a photograph. It does
not, however, do justice to its appearance, as the camera was placed
too low and does not look into the circle, as the eye does. In the

---

[1] It is unfortunately only an eye-
sketch, hurriedly taken, and thus not to
be implicitly depended upon. The two

stones outside, that look like the rudi-
ments of the avenue, I take to mark
only an external interment.

distance is seen the hill, called Knock na Rea, surmounted by the so-called Cairn of Queen Meave, of which more hereafter.

60.   View of Circle 27, Northern Moytura. From a photograph.

Another of these circles, No. 7, is thus described by Petrie:— "This circle, with its cromlech, are perfect. Its diameter is 37 feet, and the number of stones thirty-two. The cromlech is about 8 feet high, the table-stone resting on six stones of great magnitude: it is 9 feet long and 23 feet in circumference." Its general appearance will be seen in the annexed view from a photograph (woodcut

61.   Dolmen, with Circle, No. 7, Northern Moytura. From a photograph.

No. 61); though this, as in the last instance, is far from doing justice to its appearance.[1]

No. 37 is described by Dr. Petrie (p. 248) as a triple circle. The inner one 40 feet in diameter. The second of twelve large stones, and of 80 feet, the third as a circle of 120 feet in diameter. " The cromleac is of the smallest size, not more than 4 feet in height. The circumference of the stone table is 16 feet, and it rests on five supporters."

---

[1] These, and several other photographs of the field and localities near it, were specially made for me by Mr. A. Sleater, 26, Castle-street, Sligo, who executed my commission both cheaply and intelligently.

Excavations were made into almost all these monuments either by Mr. Walker, the proprietor of the ground, or by Dr. Petrie, and, with scarcely one exception, they yielded evidence of sepulchral uses. Either human bones were found or urns containing ashes. No iron, apparently, was found in any. A bronze sword is said to have been found, forty years ago, in 63; but generally there was nothing but implements of bone or stone. At the time Petrie wrote (1837) these were not valued, or classified, as they have since been; so we cannot draw any inference from them as to the age of the monuments, and no collection, that I am aware of, exists in which these "finds" are now accessible. Indeed, I am afraid that Petrie and those who worked with him were too little aware of the importance of these material points of evidence, to be careful either to collect or to describe the contents of these graves; and as all or nearly all have been opened, that source of information may be cut off for ever.

Besides these monuments on the battle-field, there are two others, situated nearly equi-distant from it, and which seem to belong to the same group; one known as the Tomb of Misgan Meave, the celebrated Queen of Connaught, who lived apparently contemporaneously with Cæsar Augustus, or rather, as the annalists insist, with Jesus Christ;[1] though, according to the more accurate Tighernach, her death occurred in the 7th year of Vespasian, in A.D. 75.[2] It is situated on the top of a high hill known as Knock na Rea (woodcut No. 60), at a distance of two miles westward from the battle-field. It was described by the Rt. Hon. William Burton, in 1779, as an enormous heap of small stones, and is of an oval figure, 650 feet in circumference at the base, 79 feet slope on one side and 67 feet on the other. The area on the top is 100 feet in its longest diameter and 85 feet in its shortest. When Petrie visited it in 1837, it was only 590 feet in circumference, and the longest diameter on the top only 80 feet. It had in the interval, in fact, been used as a quarry; and I have no doubt but that the flat top originally measured the usual 100 feet, and was circular. "Around its base," says Petrie, "are

---

[1] O'Curry's 'Materials for Ancient Irish History,' Appendix xxv. p. 41.
[2] "Meaba Regina occisa est a Furba dio filio Concobari 7 Vespasiano," ii. p. 23.

the remains of many sepulchral monuments of lesser importance, consisting of groups of large stones forming circular or oval enclosures. A careful excavation within these tombs by Mr. Walker resulted in the discovery not only of human interments, but also of several rude ornaments and implements of stone of a similar character to those usually found in sepulchres of this class in Ireland, and which, being unaccompanied by any others of a metallic nature, identify this group of monuments as of contemporaneous age with those of Carrowmore, among which no iron remains are known to have been discovered, and mark them as belonging to any period of semi-civilized society in Ireland." [1]

From their situation, it seems hardly possible to doubt that these smaller tombs are contemporaneous with or subsequent to the Great Cairn; and if this really were the tomb of Queen Meave, it would throw some light on our subject. The great cairn has not, however, been dug into yet; and till that is done the ownership of the tomb cannot be definitely fixed. There are several reasons, however, for doubting the tradition. In the first place, we have the direct testimony of a commentary written by Moelmuiri, that Meave (Meahbh) was buried at Rathcroghan, which was the proper burying-place of her race; "her body having been removed by her people from Fert Medhbha; for they deemed it more honourable to have her interred at Cruachan." [2] As the Book of the Cemeteries confirms this, there seems no good reason for doubting the fact, though she may have first been laid in this neighbourhood, which may have given rise to the tradition.

If, on the other hand, we may trust Beowulf's description of a warrior's grave, as it was understood in the 5th century, no tomb in these islands would answer more perfectly to his ideal than the Cairn on Knock na Rea :—

> " Then wrought
> The people of the Westerns
> A mound over the sea.
> It was high and broad,
> By the sea-faring man
> To be seen afar."

---

[1] Stokes, 'Life of Petrie,' p. 256.   [2] Petrie's 'Round Towers,' p. 107.

That an Irish queen should be buried on a mountain-top over--
looking the Western Ocean seems most improbable, and is opposed
to the evidence we have; but that a Viking warrior should be so
buried, overlooking the sea and a battle-field, seems natural; but
who he may have been is for future investigators to discover.

The other cairn is situated just two miles eastward from the
battle-field, on an eminence overlooking Loch Gill. It is less in
height than the so-called Queen's Tomb, but the top is nearly
perfect, and has a curious saucer-like depression, as nearly as can
be measured, 100 feet in diameter. It has never been dug into,
nor, so far as I could learn, does any tradition attach to it.

The history of the Battle of Northern Moytura, as told in the
Irish Annals, is briefly as follows :[1]—

Nuada, who was king of the Tuatha de Dananns when the battle
of Southern Moytura was fought, lost his arm in the fight. This,
however, some skilled artificers whom he had with him skilfully
replaced by one made of silver; so that he was always afterwards
known as Nuada of the Silver Hand. Whether from this cause
or some other not explained, he resigned the chief sovereignty to
Breas, who, though a Fomorian by birth, held a chief command
in the Tuatha de Danann army. Owing to his penurious habits
and domineering disposition, Breas soon rendered himself very
unpopular with the nobles of his Court; and, at a time when
the discontent was at its height, a certain poet and satirist,
Cairbré, the son of the poetess Etan, arrived at his Court. He
was treated by the king in so shabby a manner and with such dis-
respect, that he left it in disgust; but, before doing so, he wrote
and published so stinging a satire against the king, as to set the
blood of the nobles boiling with indignation, and they insisted on
his resigning the power he had held for seven years. "To this
call the regent reluctantly acceded; and, having held a council
with his mother, they both determined to retire to the Court of
his father Elatha, at this time the great chief of Fomorian pirates,
or Sea Kings, who then swarmed through all the German Ocean
and ruled over the Shetland Islands and the Hebrides."

---

[1] It will be found at more length in E. O'Curry's 'Materials for Ancient Irish
History,' pp. 247-250.

Elatha agreed to provide his son with a fleet to conquer Ireland for himself from the Tuatha de Danann, if he could; and for this purpose collected all the men and ships lying from Scandinavia westwards for the intended invasion, the chief command being entrusted to Balor of the Evil Eye, conjointly with Breas. Having landed near Sligo, they pitched their tents on the spot— Carrowmore—where the battle was afterwards fought.

Here they were attacked by Nuada of the Silver Hand, accompanied by the great Daghda, who had taken a prominent part in the previous battle, and other chiefs of note. The battle took place on the last day of October, and is eloquently described. The Fomorians were defeated, and their chief men killed. King Nuada was slain by Balor of the Evil Eye, but Balor himself fell soon after by a stone flung at him by Lug his grandson by his daughter Eithlenn.

After an interval of forty years, according to the 'Annals of the Four Masters,' the Daghda succeeded to the vacant throne, and reigned eighty years.[1]

From the above abstract—all the important passages of which are in the exact words of the translation—it is evident that the author of the tract considered the Fomorians and the Tuatha de Danann as the same people, or at least as two tribes of the same race, the chiefs of which were closely united to one another by intermarriage. He also identifies them with the Scandinavian Vikings, who played so important a part in Irish history down to the Battle of Clontarf, which happened in 1014.

This may at first sight seem very improbable. We must not, however, forget the celebrated lines of Claudian:[2] "Maduerunt

---

[1] It was, according to the same authorities, "during this interval that Lugh, the then reigning king, established the fair at Tailtean, in commemoration of his foster-mother, the daughter of Magh Mor, king of Spain," "This fair," adds Dr. O'Donovan, "continued famous down to the time of Roderic O'Conor, last monarch of Ireland; and the traditions of it are still so vivid, that Telltown was till recently resorted to by the men of Meath for hurling, wrestling, and manly sports." It would be a wonderful instance of the stability of Irish institutions if a fair, established in a miserable inland village eighteen centuries before Christ, should flourish through the middle ages, and hardly now be extinct! It may have been established about the Christian era, but certainly not before, and thus becomes another piece of evidence as to the date of the events we are describing.—'Annals of the Four Masters,' p. 23.

[2] 'Mon. Hist. Brit.' xcviii.

Saxone fuso Orcades: incaluit Pictorum sanguine Thule: Scotorum cumulos flevit glacialis Ierne." This, it may be said, was written three or even four centuries after the events of which we are now speaking; but it was also written five centuries before the Northmen are generally supposed to have occupied the Orkneys or to have interfered in the affairs of Ireland, and does point to an earlier state of affairs, though how much anterior to the poet's time there is nothing to show.

It has been frequently proposed to identify the Dananns with the Danes, from the similarity of their names. Till I visited Sligo, I confess I always looked on this as one of those random guesses from identity of mere sound which are generally very deceptive in investigations of this sort. The monuments, however, on the battle-field correspond so nearly to those figured by Madsen in his 'Antiquités prehistoriques du Danemark,'[1] and their disposition is so similar to that of the Braavalla feld[2] and other battle-fields in Scandinavia, that it will now require very strong evidence to the contrary to disprove an obvious and intimate connection between them.

In concluding his account of the battle, Mr. O'Curry adds: "Cormac Mac Cullinan, in his celebrated Glossary, quotes this tract in illustration of the word *Nes*; so that so early as the ninth century it was looked upon by him as a very ancient historic composition of authority."[3] If this is so, there seems no good reason for doubting his having spoken of events and things perfectly within his competence, and so we may consider the account above given as historical till at least some good cause is shown to the contrary.

It now only remains to try and find out if any means exist by which the dates of these two battles of Moytura can be fixed with anything like certainty. If we turn to the 'Annals of the Four Masters,' which is the favourite authority with Irish antiquaries, we get a startling answer at once. The battle of Moytura Cong, according to them, took place in the year of the world 3303, and the second battle twenty-seven years afterwards.[4] The twenty is

---

[1] Madsen, 'Antiquités prehistoriques du Danemark.' Copenhagen, 1869.

[2] Sjöborg Samlingar för Nordens Fornälskare,' i. p. 12.

[3] 'Materials for Ancient Irish History,' p. 250.

[4] 'Annals of the Four Masters,' translated by J. O'Donovan, i. p. 21.

a gratuitous interpolation. This is equivalent to 1896 and 1869 years before Christ. Alphabetical writing was not, as we shall presently see, introduced into Ireland till after the Christian Era, the idea therefore that the details of these two battles should have been preserved orally during 2000 years, and all the intermediate events forgotten, is simply ridiculous. The truth of the matter seems to be that the 'Four Masters,' like truly patriotic Irishmen in the middle of the seventeenth century, thought it necessary for the honour of their country to carry back its history to the Flood at least. As the country at the time of the Tuatha de Dananns was divided into five kingdoms,[1] and at other times into twenty-five, they had an abundance of names of chiefs at their disposal, and instead of treating them as cotemporary, they wrote them out consecutively, till they reached back to Ceasair—not Julius—but a granddaughter of Noah, who came to Ireland forty days before the Flood, with fifty girls and three men, who consequently escaped the fate of the rest of mankind, and peopled the western isle. This is silly enough, but their treatment of the hero of Moytura is almost as much so. Allowing that he was thirty years of age when he took so prominent a part in the second battle, in 3330, he must have been seventy-one when he ascended the Irish throne, and, after a reign of seventy-nine years, have died at the ripe old age of 150, from the effects of a poisoned wound he had received 120 years previously. The 'Four Masters' say eighty years earlier, but this is only another of their thousand and one inaccuracies.

When we turn from these to the far more authentic annals of Tighernach, who died 1088 A.D., we are met at once by his often quoted dictum to the effect that " omnia Monumenta Scotorum usque Cimboeth incerta erant."[2] It would have been more satisfactory if he could have added that after that time they could be depended upon, but this seems by no means to have been the case. As, however, Cimboeth is reported to have founded Armagh, in the year 289 B.C., it gives us a limit beyond which we cannot certainly proceed without danger and difficulty. We get on surer ground when we reach the reign of Crimthann, who, according to

---

[1] O'Curry, ' Materials for Ancient Irish History,' p. 246.
[2] O'Connor, ii. p. 1. O'Curry, ' Materials for Ancient Irish History,' p. 63.

Tighernach, died in the year of our era 85, after a reign of 16 years.[1] The 'Four Masters,' it is true, make him contemporary with Christ; but even Dr. O'Donovan is obliged to confess that all these earlier reigns, after the Christian era, are antedated to about the same extent.[2] Unfortunately for our purpose, however, Tighernach's early annals are almost wholly devoted to the chronicles of the kings of Emania or Armagh, and it is only incidentally that he names the kings of Tara, which was the capital both of the Firbolgs and Tuatha de Dananns, and he makes no allusion to the battles of Moytura. Though our annalist, therefore, to a certain extent deserts us here, there are incidental notices of the Daghda and his friends in Irish manuscripts referring to other subjects, which seem sufficient to settle the question. The best of these were collected together for another purpose by Petrie, in his celebrated work on the Round Towers, and, as they are easily accessible there, it will not be necessary to quote them in extenso, but merely the passages bearing directly on our subject.[3]

The first extract is from a very celebrated work known as the 'Leabhar na l'Uidhre,' written apparently before 1106, which is given by the 'Four Masters' as the date of the author's death. Speaking of Cormac, the son of Art and grandson of Conn of a Hundred Battles:—" Before his death, which happened in 267, he told his people not to bury him at Brugh, on the Boyne, where the kings of Tara, his predecessors, were buried, because he did not adore stones and trees, and did not worship the same god as those interred at Brugh, for he had faith," adds the monkish chronicler, " in the one true God according to the law."

The tract then goes on to say that " the kings of the race of Heremon were buried at Cruachan until the times of Crimthann, who was the first king of them that was buried in Brugh." The others, including Queen Meave, were buried at Cruachan, because they possessed Connaught. " But they were interred at Brugh from the time of Crimthann to the time of Leoghaire, the son of Niall (A.D. 428), except three persons, namely Art the son

[1] 'Tighernachi Ann.' O'Connor, p. 11-23.

[2] 'Annals of the Four Masters,' i. p. 99.

[3] 'Essay on the Ancient Architecture of Ireland,' by G. Petrie, pp. 97-109.

of Conn, and Cormac the son of Art, and Niall of the Nine Hostages." A little further on we have the following paragraph: —"(101.) The nobles of the Tuatha de Danann were used to bury at Brugh, *i.e.*, the Dagdha with his three sons, and also Lughaidh and Oe, and Ollam and Ogma, and Etan the poetess, and Corpre the son of Etan, and Crimthann followed them because his wife was one of the Tuatha Dea, and it was she that solicited him that he should adopt Brugh as a burying-place for himself and his descendants."

In the 'Book of Ballymote' (p. 102) it is said, " Of the monument of Brugh here, viz., The Bed of daughter of Forann. The monument of the Daghda. The mound of the Morrigan. The Barc of Crimthann in which he was interred. The Carnail (stone cairn) of Conn of a Hundred Battles," &c. In a second passage we recognise the following names rather more in detail: " The Bed of the Dagdha first, the two paps of the Morrigan, at the place where Cermud Milbhel, the son of the Dagdha was born [1]—(the monuments of) Cirr and Cuirrell wives of the Dagdha—there are two hillocks; the grave of Aedh Luirgnech, son of the Dagdha." Again, in a prose commentary on a poem which Petrie quotes, we have the following apparently by Moelmuori. The chiefs of Ulster before Conchobar (he is said to have died 33 [2]) were buried at Talten . . . The nobles of the Tuatha de Dananns, with the exception of seven who were interred at Talten, were buried in Brugh, *i.e.*, Lugh and Oe, son of Ollamh and Ogma, and Carpre the son of Etan, and Etan (the poetess herself), and the Daghda and her three sons, and a great many others besides of the Tuatha de Danann, Firbolgs, and others."

There is no doubt but that many similar passages to these might be found in Irish MSS., if looked for by competent scholars, but these extracts probably are sufficient to prove two things. First, that the celebrated cemetery at Brugh, on the Boyne, six miles west from Drogheda, was the burying-place of the kings of Tara from Crimthann (A.D. 84) till the time of St.

---

[1] Could this be the great Rath close to the Netterville domain? See Sir W. Wilde, 'The Boyne and the Blackwater,' p. 211.

[2] Tighernach, O'Connor, ii. p. 23, " Carcobarus filius Nessæ obiit hoc anno —33."

Patrick (A.D. 432), and that it was also the burying-place of all those who were concerned—without being killed—in the battles of Moytura. We are not, unfortunately, able to identify the grave of each of these heroes, though it may be because only one has been properly explored, that called New Grange, and that had been rifled before the first modern explorers in the seventeenth century found out the entrance. The Hill of Dowth has only partially been opened. The great cairn of Knowth is untouched, so is the great cairn known as the Tomb of the Dagdha. Excavations alone can prove their absolute identity; but this at least is certain, we have on the banks of the Boyne a group of monuments similar in external appearance at least with those on the two Moytura battle-fields, and the date of the greater number of those at Brugh is certainly subsequent to the Christian era.[1]

The second point is not capable of such direct proof, but seems equally clear. It is that the kings of the race of Crimthann immediately succeeded to the kings of the Tuatha de Danann, who fought at Moytura. If, indeed, we could trust the assertion that Crimthann was the first king that was buried at Brugh, we should be obliged to find a place for the Daghda under some pseudonym afterwards, and it is possible that may be the case,[2] but for the present it seems more reasonable to assume that he preceded him at a very short interval.

According to the 'Four Masters,' the Tuatha de Danann had been extinct for nearly 2000 years when we find Crimthann marrying a princess of that race, and one of sufficient influence to induce him to adopt what appears literally to have been the family burying-place of the Dagdha for that of himself and his race; and it seems impossible to believe that when this took place it could have been old, or neglected, or deserted.

---

[1] In the 'Annals of the Four Masters' (i. p. 89) there is a king called Eochaid Aireamb. "Ideo dictus," says Lynch, translating Keating, "quod tumulos effodi primus in Hibernia curavit." I have no doubt the etymology is correct, and the fact also; but it would hardly do to base our argument upon it, though it accords perfectly with the conclusion I have arrived at from other circumstances. He lived, according to the 'Four Masters,' 118 B.C. According to the more correct Tighernach, 45 B.C.

[2] The real name of the Daghda was, according to the 'Four Masters,' Eochaidh Ollathair; and Eochaid, or Eochy, is one of the most common names in Irish history, and constantly recurring.

According to the 'Four Masters,' the Firbolgs reigned thirty-seven years only, so that they do not in this case seem to err on the side of exaggeration, and the Tuatha de Danann 196 years. From this, however, we must deduct the twenty years they unnecessarily interpolated between the two battles, and we must take something from the eighty years the Dagdha reigned after he was ninety-one years of age. If we allow, then, a century, it will place the battles of Moytura 20 to 30 B.C., and the arrival of the Firbolgs about the middle of the first century B.C. This, with a small limit of error either way is, I am convinced, pretty nearly the true date of these events.[1]

If we turn to the celebrated Hill of Tara, about ten miles off, where those resided who were buried at Brugh-na-Boinne, we find a great deal to confirm the views expressed above. When Petrie was attached to the Ordnance Survey, he had a very careful plan made of the remains on that hill, and compiled a most elaborate memoir regarding them, which was published in the eighteenth volume of the 'Transactions of the Royal Irish Academy.' It concludes with these words (p. 231): "From the historical allusions deduced it will be seen that, with the exception of the few last described,[2] they are all nearly contemporaneous and belong to the third century of the Christian era. The era of the original Tuatha de Danann Cathair belongs to the remote period of uncertain tradition. The only other monuments of ascertained date are those of Conor Mac Nessa and Cuchullim, both of whom flourished in the first century. These facts are sufficient to prove that before the time of Cormac Mac Art,[3] Tara had attained to no distinguished celebrity."

---

[1] Since the above was written I have been gratified to find so eminent an authority as Dr. Henthorn Todd, late President of the Royal Irish Academy, arriving, by a very different road, at very nearly the same conclusion:—"The Firbolgs, or Belgæ," he says, "invaded Ireland, not from France, but from Britain—Dumnonii, or Devon." "The conquest of Ireland was not much older than Cæsar's time, if it were not a good bit later, and was the first influx of civilization, rude, indeed, but much su-

perior to that of the Hiberni."—*Irish Nennius*, translated by J. H. Todd, D.D., Appendix C.

[2] The principal one of these is the rath of Queen Meave, at some distance off. She, according to Tighernach, was slain by her stepson, in the seventh year of Vespasian, A.D. 75.

[3] According to Tighernach, Cormac, the grandson of Conn of a Hundred Battles, commonly called Cormac Mac Art, reigned 218-266 A.D.

The only difficulty in this passage is the allusion to the Tuatha de Danann. At the time Petrie wrote it he, like most Irish antiquaries, had been unable to emancipate himself from the spell of the 'Four Masters,' and, struck by the pains they had taken, and the general correctness of their annals after the Christian era, had adopted their pre-Christian chronology almost without question. The Cathair here alluded to is only an undistinguishable part of the Rath of Cormac, to which tradition attaches that name, but neither in plan, nor materials, nor construction can be separated from it. That the Dananns had a Cathair on this hill is more than probable if, as I suppose, they immediately preceded the Crimthann dynasty, who certainly resided here. It may also well be that they occupied this site, which is the highest on the hill, and that their palace was afterwards enlarged by Cormac. The plan of it is worth referring to (woodcut No. 62), from its curious

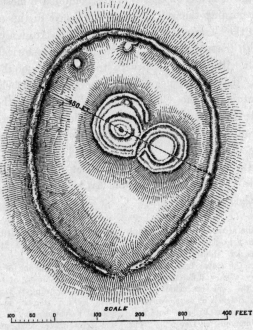

62.   Rath na Riogh, or, Cathair of Cormac, at Tara.

resemblance to that of Avebury; what was here done in earth was afterwards done in stone in Wiltshire, and it seems as if, as is so often the case, the house of the dead was copied from the dwelling of the living.

The Dagdha had apparently no residence here. From the context I would infer that he resided in the great Rath, about 300 feet diameter, at Dowth, where his son, apparently, was born, and near to which, as above shown, he also was buried. If, however, he had no residence on the Royal hill, his so-called spit was one of the most celebrated pieces of furniture of the palace. It was a most elaborate piece of ironmongery, and performed a variety of cooking operations in a very astonishing manner, and shows, at all events, that the smith who made it had no little skill in the working of iron, of which metal it was principally composed.[1]

The Rath of Leoghaire (429-458 A.D.) is interesting to us, not only as the last erected here, but from the circumstances of its builder being buried in its ramparts. It seems that, in spite of all the preaching and persuasions of St. Patrick, who was his contemporary, Leoghaire refused to be converted to the Christian religion; but like a grand old Pagan, he ordered that he should be buried standing in his armour in the rampart of his Rath, and facing the country of the foes with whom he had contended during life. That this was done is as well authenticated as any incident of the time, perhaps even better;[2] and I cannot help fancying from the appearance of the Raths, that some others of the kings were interred here also. Be that as it may, this circumstance ought to prevent our feeling any surprise at the actual discovery of the skeleton of a man under the rampart at Marden (*ante* p. 86), or if human bones were still found under the vallum at Avebury, in spite of the negative evidence of the partial explorations of the Wiltshire Archæological Society.

There is still another point of view from which this question may be regarded, so as to throw some light on the main issue of the age of the monuments in question. If we can ascertain when the art of writing was first practised in Ireland, we may obtain an approximate date before which no detailed history of any events could be expected to exist. Now all the best antiquaries of Ireland

---

[1] 'Hist. and Ant. of Tara Hill.'—'Trans. R. I. A.' xviii. p. 212.
[2] *Ibid.* xviii. pp. 81, 137, 170, &c.

are agreed that no alphabetic writing was used in Ireland before the reign of Cormac Mac Art, A.D. 218-266. There seems to be evidence that, as above mentioned, he was converted to Christianity by some Romish priest; and though it is unlikely that he himself acquired the art of writing, he seems to have caused certain tracts to be compiled. None of these, it is true, now exist, but they are referred to and quoted from an ancient Irish MS. in a manner that leaves little doubt that some books were written in Ireland in the third century, but almost certainly there were none before that time. It is true, however, that Eugene O'Curry pleads hard for some kind of Ogham writing having existed in Ireland before that time, and even before the Christian era.[1] But though we may admit the former proposition, the evidence of the latter is of the most unsatisfactory description. Even, however, if it could be established it would prove very little. It would be as difficult to write a connected history in Ogham as it would be in Exchequer tallies, and so far as is known, it never was attempted. The utmost Ogham ever did, or could do, was to record genealogies; and such detailed histories as we possess of the Moytura battles are quite beyond its powers. On the other hand, Mr. O'Curry's own account of Senchan's difficulties in obtaining copies of the celebrated 'Táin Bó Chuailgne,' or 'Cattle Spoil of Cooley,' after the year 598, shows how little the art was then practised. No copy of this poem, which contains the life and adventures of Queen Meave, in the first century, then existed in Ireland. A mission was consequently sent to Italy to copy one said to have existed there, and though the missionaries were miraculously spared the journey,[2] the inference is the same, that no written copy of their most celebrated work existed in Ireland in the year 600.

Petrie is equally clear on the subject. In his history of Tara he states that the Irish were unacquainted with letters till the introduction of Christianity in the fifth century, with the doubtful exception of the writings ascribed to Cormac Mac Art. He consequently believes that the authentic history of Ireland commences only with Tuathal, A.D. 130, 160, in which he is probably correct.[3]

---

[1] 'Materials for Ancient Irish History,' Appendix ii. p. 463 et seqq.
[2] Ibid. p. 29 et seqq.   [3] 'Hist. and Ant. of Tara.'—'Trans. R. I. S.' xviii. p. 46.

But here the question arises—Before the introduction of writing into a country, how long could so detailed a narrative as that which we possess of the Battles of Moytura, and one so capable of being verified by material evidences on the spot, be handed down orally as a plain prose narrative? Among so rude a people as the Irish avowedly then were, would this period be one century or two, or how many? Every one must decide for himself. I do not know an instance of any rude people preserving orally any such detailed history for a couple of centuries. With me the great difficulty is to understand how the memory of the battles was so perfectly preserved, assuming them to have taken place so long ago as the first century B.C. As it is not pretended that the narratives were reduced to writing so early as the time of Cormac, I should, from their internal evidence, be much more inclined to assume that the battles must have taken place one or two centuries after the birth of Christ. At all events, it seems absolutely impossible that the date of these battles can be so remote as the Four Masters place them, or even as some Irish antiquaries seem inclined to admit.

The truth of the matter appears to be that, in the Eocene period of Irish history or in the one or two centuries that preceded the introduction of writing, we have a whole group of names so inextricably mixed together that it is impossible to separate them. We have the Dagdha and his wives and their sons. We have Etan the poetess and her ill-conditioned son. There is Queen Meave of the Cattle Raid, and her husband Conchobhar McNessa. There is Cumbhail, the Fingal of Macpherson and Cuchullin; and then such semi-historical persons as Tuathal the Accepted, and Conn of a Hundred Battles. All these lived almost together in one capital, and were buried in one cemetery, and form a half-historic, half-mythic group, such as generally precedes written history in most parts of the world. Many of their dates are known with fairly approximate certainty, whilst that of others cannot be fixed. There seems, however, enough to justify us in almost positively affirming that the Battle of Moytura, which raised the Dagdha to fame, happened within the fifty years that preceded or the fifty that followed the birth of Christ. My own impression is in favour of the former as the more probable date.

To some this may appear an over-laboured disquisition to prove an insignificant point. It is not, however, one-tenth part of what might be advanced on the subject from translated and printed documents, and, certainly, it would be difficult to exaggerate its importance with reference to the subject matter of this work. If the two groups of monuments at Cong and Carrowmore can be proved to be the monuments of those who fell in the two battles of Southern and Northern Moytura, we have made an immense step towards a knowledge of the use of these monuments; and if it can be shown that they date from about the Christian Era, we gain not only a standpoint for settling the age of all other Irish antiquities, but a base for our reasoning with reference to similar remains in other countries.

No Irish antiquary, nor indeed of any other country, so far as I know, has ventured to hint a doubt that they mark the battle-fields. Nor, in the present state of the evidence, do I see any reason for questioning the fact; and, for the present at least, we may assume it as granted. The second proposition is more open to question. Irish antiquaries generally will dissent from so serious a reduction in the antiquity of these two great battles. But, after the most earnest attention I have been able to give to all that has been written and said on the subject and a careful comparison of the monuments on these fields with those of other countries, I would, on the whole, be inclined to bring them forward a century or two, if I could find a gap to throw them into, rather than date them earlier. They look older and more tentative than the English circles described in the last chapter, but not so much so as to lead us to expect a difference of four or five centuries. On the other hand, they are so like those on the Bravalla field, and other monuments in Scandinavia, to be described hereafter, that it is puzzling to think that seven or ten centuries elapsed between them. But, taking all the circumstances of the case into consideration, the conclusions above arrived at appear fair and reasonable, and in conformity, not only to what was said in the last chapter, but to the facts about to be adduced in the following pages.

Cemeteries.

Although Irish antiquaries have succeeded in identifying the localities of a considerable number of the thousand and one battles which, as might be expected, adorn at every page the annals of a Celtic race; yet, as none of these are described as marked with circles or cairns, like those found on the two battle-fields of Moytura, they are of no use for our present purpose, and our further illustrations must be drawn from the peaceful burying-places of the Irish, which are, however, of singular interest.

In the history of the Cemeteries, eight are enumerated;[1] but of these only the first three can be identified with anything like certainty at the present day. But as the antiquities of Ireland have never yet been systematically explored, others may yet be found, and so also may many more stone-marked battle-fields. Meanwhile our business is with

> " The three cemeteries of the idolaters :
> The Cemetery of Tailten the select,
> The Cemetery of the ever fair Cruachan,
> And the Cemetery of Brugh."[2]

The two last are known with certainty. The first is most probably the range of mounds at Lough Crew, recently explored by Mr. Conwell; but, as some doubt this identification, we shall take it last, and speak first of those regarding which there is more certainty.

Cruachan, or Rathcrogan, is situated five miles west from Carrick-on-Shannon, and consists, according to Petrie, of a circular stone ditch,[3] now nearly obliterated, 300 feet in diameter. Within this "are small circular mounds, which, when examined, are found to cover rude sepulchral chambers, formed of stone, without cement of any kind, and containing unburnt bones." The monument of Dathi (428 A.D.), which is a small circular mound with a pillar-stone of Red Sandstone, is situated outside the enclosure, at a short distance to the east, and may be identified from the following notice of it by the celebrated antiquary Duald Mac Firbis. " The body of Dathi was brought to Cruachan, and was interred at

---

[1] Petrie, 'Round Towers,' 100 *et seqq.*
[2] L. c. 105.
[3] The Irish use ditch, as the Romans used vallum, or the Scotch dyke, to designate either a rampart or the hollow from which it was taken.

Relig na Riogh, where most of the kings of the race of Heremon were buried, and where to this date the Red Stone pillar remains on a stone monument over his grave, near Rath Cruachan, to this time (1666).[1]

Here, therefore, we have the familiar 300-foot circle, with the external burial, as at Arbor Low, and external stone monument as at Salkeld and elsewhere. The chief distinction between this and our English battle-circles seems to be the number of cairns, each containing a chamber, which crowd the circle at Rath Crogan, and it is possible that if these were opened with great care, a succession might be discovered among them; but at present we know little or nothing of their contents.

At present there are only two names that we can identify with certainty as those of persons buried here. Queen Meave, who, as before mentioned, was transferred from Fert Meave—or Meave's Grave, her first burying-place, to this Rath, about the end of the first century, and Dathi, at the beginning of the fifth. Whether any other persons were interred here before the first-named queen seems doubtful. From the context, it seems as if her being buried in her own Rath had led to its being consecrated to funereal rites, and continuing to be so used till Christianity induced men to seek burying-places elsewhere than in the cemeteries of the idolaters.

By far the best known, as well as the most interesting, of Irish cemeteries is that which extends for about two miles east and west on the northern bank of the Boyne, about five miles from Drogheda. Within this space there remain even now some seventeen sepulchral barrows, three of which are pre-eminent.[2] They are now known by the names of Knowth for the most westward one, Dowth for that to the east, and about half-way between these two, that known as New Grange. In front of the latter, but lower down nearer the river, is a smaller one, still popularly known as that of the Dagdha, and others bear names with more or less certainty; but no systematic exploration of the group has yet been made, so that we are very much in the dark as to their succession, or who the kings or nobles may be that lie buried within their masses.

---

[1] Quotation from 'Book of Geneal,' p. 251. Petrie, 'Round Towers,' p. 107.
[2] Sir W. Wilde, 'The Boyne and the Blackwater,' 1849, p. 188.

That at Knowth has never been carefully measured, nor, so far as I know, even described in modern times. At a guess, it is a mound 200 feet in diameter, and 50 to 60 feet in height, with a flat top not less than 100 feet across. It is entirely composed of small loose stones, which have been extensively utilized for road making and farm buildings, so that the mound has now a very dilapidated appearance, which makes it difficult to ascertain its original form; and so far as is known, its interior has not been accessible in modern times. Petrie identifies it (p. 103) with "the cave of Cnodhba, which was searched by the Danes on an occasion (A.D. 862), when the three kings, Amlaff, Imar, and Auisle, were plundering the territories of Flann, the son of Conaing. If this is so, its entrance ought not to be difficult to find, but the prospect of the explorers being rewarded by any treasure or object of value is very small indeed.

Less than a mile from this one is the larger and more celebrated mound of New Grange. It is almost certainly one of the three

63.   View of Mound at New Grange.   From a drawing by Colonel Forbes Leslie.

plundered by the Danes 1009 years ago. No description of it has anywhere been discovered, prior to the time when Mr. Llwyd, the keeper of the Ashmolean Museum at Oxford, mentioned it in a letter dated Sligo, 1699.[1] He describes the entrance, the passage, and the side chapels, and the three basins as existing then exactly as they do now, and does not allude to the discovery of the entrance as being at all of recent occurrence, though

---

[1] Rowland's 'Mona Antiqua,' p. 314.

Sir Thomas Molyneux, in 1725, says it was found apparently not
long before he wrote, in accidently removing some stones.[1] The
first really detailed account, however, is that of Governor Pownall,
in the second volume of the 'Archæologia' (1770). He employed
a local surveyor of the name of Bouie to measure it for him, but
either he must have been a bungler, or the engraver has misunderstood his drawings, for it is almost impossible to make out
the form and dimensions of the mound from the plates published.
In the 100 years that have elapsed since his survey was made,
the process of destruction has been going on rapidly, and it
would now require both skill and patience to restore the monument to its previous dimensions. Meanwhile the accompanying
cuts, partly from Mr. Bouie's plates, partly from personal observations, may be sufficient for purposes of illustration, but they
are far from pretending to be perfectly accurate, or such as one
would like to see of so important a monument.

Its dimensions, so far as I can make out, are as follows: it has
a diameter of 310 to 315 feet for the whole mound, at its junction
with the natural hill, on which it stands. The height is about
70 feet, made up of 14 feet for the slope of the hill to the floor
of the central chamber, and 56 feet above it. The angle of external
slope appears to be 35 degrees, or 5 degrees steeper than Silbury
Hill, and consequently if there is anything in that argument, it
may, at least, be a century or two older. The platform on the
top is about 120 feet across, the whole being formed of loose stones,
with the smallest possible admixture of earth and rubbish.

Around its base was a circle of large stone monoliths (woodcut
No. 63). They stand, according to Sir W. Wilde, 10 yards apart,
on a circumference of 400 paces, or 1000 feet. If this were so, they
were as nearly as may be 33 feet from centre to centre, and their
number consequently must originally have been thirty, or the same
number as at Stonehenge. From Bouie's plan I make the number
thirty-two, but this is hardly to be depended upon. From this disposition it will be observed that if the tumulus were removed, or
had never been erected, we should have here exactly such a circle
—333 feet in diameter—as we find at Salkeld or at Stanton Drew,

---

[1] 'Philosophical Transactions,' Nos. 335-336.

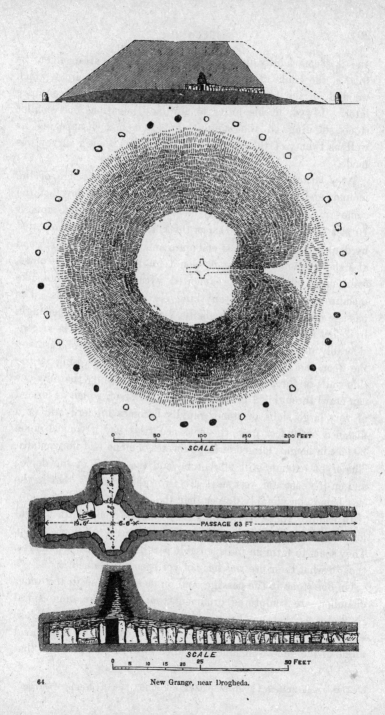

PASSAGE 63 FT

19.6"   6.6"   7.9"

SCALE
0   50   100   150   200 FEET

SCALE
0   5   10   15   20   25   50 FEET

64.   New Grange, near Drogheda.

and it seems hardly doubtful but that such an arrangement as this on the banks of the Boyne gave rise to those circles which we find on the battle-fields of England two or three centuries later. Llwyd, in his letter to Rowland, mentions one smaller stone standing on the summit, but that had disappeared, as well as twenty of the outer circle, when Mr. Bouie's survey was made.

At a distance of about 75 feet from the outer edge of the mound, and at a height of 14 or 15 feet above the level of the stone ring, is the entrance to the crypt. The threshold stone is 10 feet long by about 18 inches thick, and is richly ornamented by double spirals of a most elaborate and elegant character;[1] and at a short distance above it is seen a fragment of a string-course, even more elaborately ornamented with a pattern more like modern architecture than anything else on these mounds. The passage into the central chamber is, for about 40 feet, 6 feet high, by 3 feet in width, though both these dimensions have been considerably diminished, the first by the accumulation of earth on the floor, the second by the mass of the mound pressing in the side walls of the passage, so that it is with difficulty that any one can crawl through. Advancing inwards, the roof, which is formed of very large slabs of stone, rapidly becomes higher; and at a distance of 70 feet from the entrance, rises into a conical dome 20 feet in height, formed of large masses of stone laid horizontally. The crypt extends still 20 feet beyond the centre of the dome; and on the east and west sides are two other recesses, that in the east being considerably deeper than the one opposite to it.

In each of these recesses stands a shallow stone basin of oval form 3 feet by 3 feet 6 or 7 inches across, and 6 to 9 inches deep. They seem to form an indispensable part of these Irish sepulchres, though what their use was has not yet been ascertained.

On one stone in the passage, and on most of those in the inner chamber, are sculptured ornaments, mostly of the same spiral character as that on the stone at the threshold, but hardly so elaborately or carefully executed. One stone on the right hand angle of the inmost chamber has fallen forward (see plan), so that

---

[1] This is well illustrated in Sir W. Wilde's Look, p. 192, by a woodcut by Wakeman.

by creeping behind it, it is possible to see the reverse of some of the neighbouring stones, and it is found that several of these are elaborately carved with the same spiral ornaments as their fronts, though it is quite impossible that, situated as they are, they could have been seen after the mound was raised. To account for this, some have asserted that they belonged to an older building before having been used in this; but it hardly seems necessary to adopt so violent an hypothesis. It may have been that the stones were carved before being used, and at a time when no plans or drawings existed, may have been found unsuited in size or form for the places for which they were first intended, and consequently either turned round or used elsewhere. Or it may be that as the crypt must have been built and tolerably complete before the mound was raised over it, the king may have had it ornamented externally while in that state. Labour was of little value in those days, and it is dangerous to attempt to account for the caprices of kings in such a state of society as must then have existed. The identity of the style and character of the ornaments both on the hidden and the visible parts of these stones excludes the idea that they were the work of different epochs. A removal from an older building implies a desecration and neglect which must have been the work of time; and, having regard to their identity, it is improbable that a time considerable enough would have elapsed to admit of a building being so desecrated and neglected as that its stones should be carried away and used elsewhere.

The position of the entrance so much within the outline of the Tumulus, is a peculiarity at first sight much more difficult to account for. As it now stands, it is situated at a distance of about 50 feet horizontally within what we have every reason to believe was the original outline of the mound. Not only is there no reason to believe that the passage ever extended further, but the ornamented threshold, and the carved string-course above, and other indications, seem to point out that the tumulus had what may be called an architectural façade at this depth. One mode of accounting for this would be to assume that the original mound was only about 200 feet in diameter at the floor level, and that the interior was then accessible, but that after the death of the king who erected it, an envelope 50 feet thick was added by his successors, forming the broad platform at the top, and effectually closing and hiding the entrance to the sepulchre. If this were so, we may easily fancy that many of his family, or of his followers, were buried in this envelope, and formed the secondary but nearly contemporary interments which are so frequently found in English mounds. The experience of Minning Lowe

65.   Ornament at New Grange. From a rubbing.

(woodcut No. 33), Rose Hill (woodcut No. 39), and other English tumuli, goes far to countenance such an hypothesis; and there is much besides to be said in its favour, but it is one of those questions which can only be answered satisfactorily by a careful examination of the mound itself. Meanwhile, however, I am rather inclined to adopt the hypothesis that the mound had a funnel-shaped entrance like Park Cwn tumulus (woodcut No. 46), and that at Plas Newydd (woodcut No. 47), and shown in dotted lines in the woodcut No. 64. The reason for this will be more apparent when we come to examine the Lough Crew

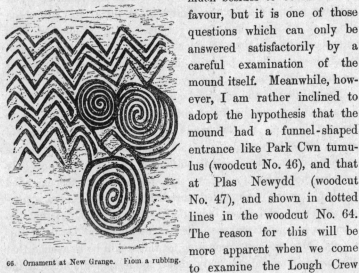

66.   Ornament at New Grange. From a rubbing.

tumuli, but the apparent ease with which Amlaff and his brother Danes seem to have robbed these tombs in the ninth century, seems to indicate that the entrances were not then difficult to find.

The ornaments which cover the walls of the chambers at New Grange are very varied, both in their form and character. The most prevalent design is that of spirals variously combined, and often of great beauty. They seem always to have been drawn by the hand, never outlined with an instrument, and never quite regular either in their form or combination. The preceding woodcuts from rubbings give a fair idea of their general appearance, though many are much more complex, and some more carefully cut. The most extensive, and perhaps also the most beautiful, is that on the external doorstep.[1] These spirals are, however, seldom alone, but more frequently are found combined with zigzag ornaments, as in (woodcut No. 66), and in lozenge-shaped patterns; in fact, in every conceivable variety that seemed to suit the fancy of the artist, or the shape of the stone he was employed upon. In one instance a vegetable form certainly was intended.

67. Branch at New Grange. From a rubbing.

There may be others, but this one most undoubtedly represents either a palm branch or a fern; my impression is that it is the former, though how a knowledge of the Eastern plant reached New Grange is by no means clear. One other example of the sculptures is worth quoting, if not for its beauty, at least for its interest (woodcut No. 68). It is drawn full size in the second volume of the 'Archæologia,' p. 238, and Governor Pownall, after a learned disquisition, concludes that the characters are Phœnician but only numerals (p. 259).

68. Sculptured mark at New Grange, of undecided character.

General Vallancey and others have not been so modest; but one thing seems quite clear, that it is not a character in any alphabet

---

[1] Wakeman, 'Handbook of Irish Antiquities,' p. 25.

now known. Still it can hardly be a mere ornament. It must
be either a mason's mark, or a recognizable symbol of some sort,
something to mark the position of the stone on which it is
engraved, or its ownership by some person. Similar marks are
found in France, but seem there equally devoid of any recognizable meaning.

The third of these great tumuli on the Boyne is known as
that of Dowth. Dubhad if Petrie is right in identifying it
with the third sepulchre plundered by the Danes in 862. It was
dug into by a Committee of the Royal Irish Academy in 1847,

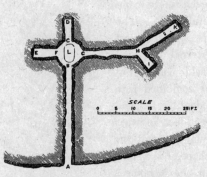

69.   Chambers in Mound at Dowth.   From a MS. plan.

but without any satisfac-
tory results. A great gash
was made in its side to its
centre, which has fearfully
disfigured its form,[1] but
without any central cham-
ber being reached; but
on the western side a
small entrance was dis-
covered leading to a pas-
sage which extended 40
feet 6 inches (from A to D)
towards the interior. At the distance of 28 feet from the entrance
it formed a small domical chamber, with three branches, very
like that at New Grange, but on a smaller scale. In the centre
of this apartment was one large flat basin (L), similar in form,
and, no doubt, in purpose, to the three at New Grange, but
far larger, being 5 feet by 3 feet. The southern branch of the
chamber extends to K in a curvilinear form for about 28 feet, where
it is stopped for the present by a large stone, and another partially
obstructs the passage at 8 feet in front of the terminal stone.

The Academy have not yet published any account of their
diggings, nor does any plan of the mound exist, so far as I know,
anywhere. Even its dimensions are unknown. Pending these

---

[1] In extenuation of this disfigurement,
it must be explained that these Irish
cairns are extremely difficult to explore
without destroying them. Being wholly
composed of loose stones, it is almost
impossible to tunnel into them, and
almost as difficult to sink shafts through
them. The only plan seems to be to cut
into them, and, when this is done, disfigurement is inevitable.

being ascertained, it does look as if this chamber was in an envelope similar to that just suggested as having existed at New Grange. In that case the original tumulus was probably 120 feet in diameter, and with its envelope 200 feet.

The walls of the chambers of this tomb are even more richly and elaborately ornamented than those of the chambers at New Grange, and are in a more delicate style of workmanship. Altogether I should be inclined to consider it as more modern than its more imposing rival.

One other small tumulus of the cemetery is open. It is situated in the grounds of Netterville House. It is, however, only a miniature repetition of the central chambers of its larger compeers, but without sculptures or any other marked peculiarity.

The mound called the Tomb of the Dagdha and the ten or twelve others which still exist in this cemetery, are all, so far as is known, untouched, and still remain to reward the industry of the first explorer. If the three large mounds are those plundered by the Danes, which seems probable, this is sufficient to account for the absence of the usual sepulchral treasures, but it by no means follows that the others would be equally barren of results. On the contrary, there being no tradition of their having been opened, and no trace of wounds in their sides, we are led to expect that they may be intact, and that the bones and armour of the great Dagdha may still be found in his honoured grave.

Nothing was found in the great mounds at New Grange and Dowth which throws much additional light either on their age or the persons to whom they should be appropriated. Two skeletons are said to have been discovered at New Grange, but under what circumstances we are not told, and we do not consequently know whether to consider them as original or secondary interments. The finding of the coin of Valentinian is mentioned by Llwyd in 1699, but he merely says that they were found on the top, or rather, as might be inferred, near the top, when it was uncovered by the removal of the stones for road-making and such purposes. Had it been found in the cell, as at Minning Low, it would have given us a date, beyond which we could not ascend, but when and under what circumstances the coin of Theodosius was found, does not appear, nor what has become of either. A more important find was made

by Lord Albert Cunyngham in 1842. Some workmen who were
employed to dig on the mound near the entrance discovered two
splendid gold torques, a brooch, and a gold ring, and with them
a gold coin of Geta[1] (205-212 A.D.). A similar gold ring was
found about the same time in the cell, and is in the possession
of Mrs. Caldwell, the wife of the proprietor. Although we might
feel inclined to hesitate about the value of the conclusions to be
drawn from the first discovery of coins, this additional evidence
seems to be conclusive. Three Roman coins found in different
parts, at different times, and with the torques and rings, are, it
seems, quite sufficient to prove that it cannot have been erected
before 380, while the probable date for its completion may be
about 400 A.D. It may, however, have been begun fifty or sixty
years earlier. It is most likely that such a tomb as this was
commenced by the king whose remains it was destined to
contain; but the mound would not be heaped over the chamber
till the king himself, and probably his wives and sons, were laid
there, and a considerable period may consequently have elapsed
between the inception and the completion of such a monument.

At Dowth there was the usual miscellaneous assortment of
things. A great quantity of globular stone-shot, probably sling-
stones; and in the chamber fragments of burned bones, many of
which proved to be human; glass and amber beads of unique
shape, portions of jet bracelets, a curious stone button, a fibula,
bone bodkins, copper pins, and iron knives and rings. Some
years ago a gentleman residing in the neighbourhood cleared out
a portion of the passage, and found a few iron antiquities, some
bones of mammals, and a small stone urn, which he presented to
the Irish Academy.[2] In so far as negative evidence is of value,
it may be remarked that no flint implements and nothing of
bronze—unless the copper pins are so classed—was found in any
of these tumuli.

The ornaments found inside the chambers at Dowth are similar
in general character to those at New Grange, but, on the whole,
more delicate and refined. Assuming the progressive nature of

---

[1] 'Archæologia,' xxx. pl. xii. p. 137.
[2] Sir W. Wilde, 'The Boyne and the Blackwater,' p. 209.

Irish art, which I see no reason for doubting, they would indicate a more modern age, and this, from other circumstances, seems more than probable.

Though spirals are frequent, the Dowth ornaments assume more of free-traced vegetable forms. It is not so easy to identify the figures in the annexed woodcut (No. 70), as in the palm - branch in NewGrange (woodcut No.

70.   Ornament in Dowth. From a rubbing.

67), but there can be little doubt that the intention was to simulate vegetable nature. At other times forms are introduced which a fanciful antiquary might suppose were intended for serpents, or writing, or, at all events, as having some occult meaning. The annexed from a rubbing is curious, as some-

71.   Ornament in Dowth. From a rubbing.

thing very similar occurs on a stone at Coilsfield, in Ayrshire, and may really be intended to suggest an idea, but of what nature we are not yet in a position to guess. It is not so like an alphabetical character as those at New Grange (woodcut No. 68), and till that is shown to have a meaning, it is hardly worth while speculating with regard to this one. We shall be in a better position to judge of the value or importance of these ornaments, in an artistic or chronometric point of view, when we have examined those at Lough Crew and elsewhere; but even irrespectively of such considerations, no one can examine the monuments on the banks of the Boyne without being struck with the elegance as well as the endless variety of the ornaments which cover their walls.

If, however, the material proofs are deficient, the written evidence is clearer and more satisfactory than with regard to any group of tombs in the three kingdoms. In the passage above quoted, it is said "that they"—the kings of Ireland—"were interred at Brugh from the time of Crimthann (A.D. 76) to the time of Leoghaire, the son of Niall (A.D. 458), except three persons, namely, Art the son of Conn, and Cormac the son of Art, and Niall of the nine hostages,"—the father of Leoghaire. The reason given why Art and Cormac were not buried here was that they had embraced Christianity. Art was buried at a place called Treoit; Cormac on the right bank of the Boyne at a place called Ros-na-righ, opposite Brugh; and Niall at Ochaim. But having disposed of these three, we have still some twenty-seven kings to find graves for, and only seventeen mounds can now be traced at Brugh; and, besides these, we have to find the tombs of the Dagdha, and his three sons, and Etan the poetess and her son Corpre, and Boinn, the wife of Nechtan, "who took with her to the tomb her small hound Dabilla," and a vast number of nobles of Tuatha de Danann and others. It is impossible to find places for all these persons in the graves now visible, if each was buried separately. It may be, however, that the great mounds contained several sepulchres. The form and position of the chambers at Dowth (woodcut No. 69) perhaps countenances such a supposition; but many may have been buried under smaller cairns, long since removed to make way for agricultural improvements, and many may yet be discovered if the place be carefully and systematically explored, which does not yet seem to have been done. Before, however, anything like certainty could be arrived at as to the distribution of these graves, it would be necessary that the great mounds should be thoroughly explored, and this, from the nature of their material, will practically involve their destruction, which would be very much to be regretted. Meanwhile, if I may be allowed to offer a conjecture, I would say that New Grange might be the " Cumot or Commensurate grave of Cairbre Lifeachair." He, according to the Four Masters, reigned from 271 to 288—but probably fifty or sixty years later—and seems to have been a king deserving of a right royal sepulchre; and I feel great confidence that the unopened tumulus near the river may be what tradition says it is—the grave of the Great Dagdha, the hero of Moytura. With regard to the others, it would not be safe to hazard any opinion in the present state of our knowledge. For the present it is sufficient to feel sure that we have a group of monuments all, or very nearly all of which were erected in the first four centuries of the Christian era, and from this basis we may reason with tolerable certainty regarding the other groups which we may meet with in the course of this enquiry.

Lough Crew.

At a distance of twenty-five miles nearly due west from Brugh na Boinn, and two miles south-east from Oldcastle, is a range of hills, called on the Ordnance map Slieve na Calliagh—the hags' or witches' hill. It is upwards of 200 feet above the level of the sea, and the most conspicuous elevation in that part of the country. On the ridge of this range, which is about two miles in extent, are situated from twenty-five to thirty cairns, some of considerable size, being 120 to 180 feet in diameter; others are much smaller, and some so nearly obliterated that their dimensions can hardly be now ascertained. Till seven or eight years ago this cemetery was entirely unknown to Irish antiquaries, and the positions of the cairns were hardly even indicated in the Ordnance Survey; but in 1863 they attracted the attention of Mr. Eugene Conwell, of Trim. In the years 1867-8 he was enabled, with the assistance and co-operation of the late Mr. Naper, of Lough Crew, the proprietor of the soil, to excavate and explore the whole of them. A brief account of the results which he obtained was submitted to the Royal Irish Academy in 1868, and afterwards printed by him for private circulation in 1868; but the greater work, with plans and drawings, in which he intends fully to illustrate the whole, is still in abeyance, owing to want of encouragement. When completed it will be one of the most valuable contributions to our archæological knowledge that we have received of late years. Meanwhile the following meagre particulars are derived from Mr. Conwell's pamphlet and the information I picked up during a personal visit which I made to the spot in his company in the Autumn of last year. The illustrations are all from his drawings.

One of the most perfect of these tumuli is that distinguished by Mr. Conwell as Cairn T (woodcut No. 72). It stands on the highest

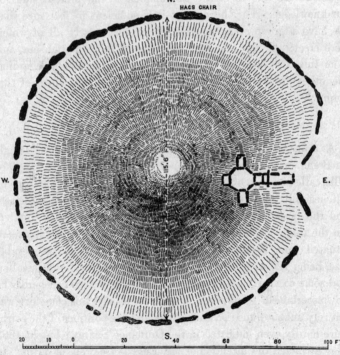

72.   Cairn T, at Lough Crew.—From a plan by E. Conwell.

point of the hill, and is consequently the most conspicuous. It is a truncated cone, 116 feet in diameter at base, and with a sloping side, between 60 and 70 feet in length. Around its base are thirty-seven stones, laid on edge, and varying from 6 to 12 feet in

length. They are not detached, as at New Grange, but form a
retaining wall to the mound. On the north, and set about 4 feet
back from the circle, is a large stone, 10 feet long by 6 high, and
2 feet thick, weighing consequently above 10 tons. The upper
part is fashioned as a rude seat, from which it derives its name of
the Hag's Chair (woodcut No. 73), and there can be little doubt
but that it was intended as a seat or throne; but whether by the

73.   The Hag's Chair, Lough Crew.—From a drawing by E. Conwell.

king who erected the sepulchre, or for what purpose, it is difficult
now to say.

On the eastern side of the mound the stones forming the peri-
phery of the cairn curve inwards for eight or nine yards on each
side of the spot where the entrance to the chamber commences.
It is of the usual cruciform plan, and 28 feet long from the entrance
to the flat stone closing the innermost cell; the dome, consequently, is not nearly under the centre of the tumulus, as at New
Grange, and lends something like probability to the notion that the
cell at Dowth (woodcut No. 69), was really the principal sepulchre.
Twenty-eight of the stones in the chamber were ornamented with
devices of various sorts. Two of them are represented on the accompanying woodcut (No. 74), which, with the drawings on the
Hag's Chair give a fair idea of their general character. They are
certainly ruder and less artistic than those on the Boyne, and so far
would indicate an earlier age. Nothing was found in the chambers

of this tomb but a quantity of charred human bones, perfect human teeth, mixed with the bones of animals, apparently stags, and one bronze pin, $2\frac{1}{2}$ inches long, with a head ornamented and stem slightly so, and still preserving a beautiful green polish.

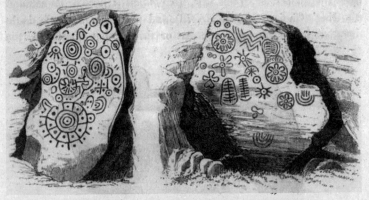

74.   Two Stones in Cairn T, Lough Crew.—E. Conwell.

Cairn L (woodcut No. 75), a little further west, is 135 feet in diameter, and surrounded by forty-two stones, similar to those in Cairn T. The same curve inwards of these stones marks the entrance here, which is placed 18 feet from the outward line of the circle. The chamber here is nearly of the same dimensions as that last described, being 29 feet deep and 13 across its greatest width. In one of the side chambers lies the largest of the mysterious flat basins that have yet been discovered, 5 feet 9 inches long by 3 feet 1 inch broad, the whole being tooled and picked with as much care and skill as if executed by a modern mason. This one has a curious nick in its rim, but as it does not go through, it could hardly be intended as a spout. Till some unrifled tomb is found, or something analogous in other countries, it is extremely difficult to say what the exact use of these great stone saucers may have been. That the body or ashes were laid on them is more than probable, and they may then have been covered over with a lid like a dish-cover, such as are found on tombs in Southern Babylonia.[1] Under this basin were found great quan-

---

[1] 'Journal Royal Archæological Society,' xv. p. 270.

tities of charred human bones and forty-eight human teeth, besides a perfectly rounded syenite ball, still preserving its original polish, also some jet and other ornaments. In other parts were found quantities of charred bones, some rude pottery and bone implements, but no objects in metal. The woodcut representing the cell, with large basin, gives a fair idea of the general style of sculpture in this and the neighbouring cairns. The parts cross-hatched seem to have been engraved with a sharp metal

75.   Cell in Cairn L, at Lough Crew.—E. Conwell.

tool. The ordinary forms, however, both here and on the Boyne are picked; but whether they were executed with a hammer, or pick direct, or by a chisel driven by a hammer, is by no means clear. My own impression is, that it would be very difficult indeed to execute these patterns with a hammer of any sort, and that a chisel must have been used, but whether of flint, bronze, or iron, there is no evidence to show.

Cairn H, though only between 5 and 6 feet in height and 54 feet

in diameter, seems to have been the only one on the hill not previously rifled, and yielded a most astonishing collection of objects
to its explorer. The cell was of the usual cruciform plan, 24 feet
from the entrance to the rear, and 16 feet across the lateral
chambers. In the passage and crypts of this cairn Mr. Conwell
collected some 300 fragments of human bones, which must have
belonged to a considerable number of separate individuals;
14 fragments of rude pottery, 10 pieces of flint, 155 sea-shells in
a perfect condition, besides pebbles and small polished stones,
in quantities.

The most remarkable part of the collection consisted of 4884
fragments, more or less perfect, of bone implements. These are
now in the Dublin Museum, and look like the remains of a
paper-knife-maker's stock-in-trade. Most of them are of a knife
shape, and almost all more or less polished, but without further
ornamentation; but 27 fragments appear to have been stained,
11 perforated, 501 engraved with rows of fine lines; 13 combs
were engraved on both sides, and 91 engraved by compass with
circles and curves of a high order of art. On one, in cross-hatch
lines, is the representation of an antlered stag, the only attempt to
depict a living thing in the collection.

Besides these, there were found in this cairn seven beads of
amber, three small beads of glass of different colours, two fragments, and a curious molten drop of glass, 1 inch long, trumpet-
shaped at one end, and tapering towards the other extremity; six
perfect and eight fragments of bronze rings, and seven specimens
of iron implements, but all, as might be expected, very much cor-
roded by rust. One of these presents all the appearance of being
the leg of a compass, with which the bone implements may have
been engraved, and one was an iron punch, 5 inches long, with
a chisel-shaped point, bearing evidence of the use of the mallet
at the opposite end.

Cairn D is the largest and most important monument of the
group, being 180 feet in diameter, and though it is very much
dilapidated, the circle of fifty-four stones which originally surrounded it can still be traced. On its eastern side the stones curve
inwards for about twelve paces, in the form universal in these
cairns; but though the explorers set to work industriously to follow

out what they considered a sure "find," they could not penetrate the mound. The stones fell in upon them so fast, and the risk they ran was so great, that they were forced to abandon the idea of tunnelling, and though a large body of men worked assiduously for a fortnight trying to work down from above, they failed to penetrate to the central or any other chambers. It still, therefore, remains a mystery if there is a blind tope, like many in India, or whether its secret still remains to reward some more fortunate set of explorers. If it has no central chamber, the curving inwards of its outer circle of stones is a curious instance of adherence to a sacred form.

The other monuments on the hill do not present any features worth enumerating in a general summary like the present, though they would be most interesting in a monograph. Though differing greatly in size and in richness of ornamentation, they all belong to one class, and apparently to one age. For our present purpose one of the most interesting peculiarities is that, like the group on the banks of the Boyne, this is essentially a cemetery. There are no circles, no alignments, no dolmens, no rude stone monuments, in fact. All are carefully built, and all more or less ornamented; and there is a gradation and progression throughout the whole series widely different in this respect from the simplicity and rudeness of the English monuments described in the last chapter.

It now only remains to try to ascertain who those were who were buried in these tumuli, and when they were laid there to their rest. So far as the evidence at present stands it hardly seems to me to admit of doubt but that this is the cemetery of Talten, so celebrated in Irish legend and poetry:—

> "The host of Great Meath are buried
> In the middle of the Lordly Brugh;
> The Great Ultonians used to bury
> At Talten with pomp.

> "The true Ultonians, before Conchobar,
> Were ever buried at Talten,
> Until the death of that triumphant man,
> Through which they lost their glory."[1]

---

[1] Petrie's 'Round Towers,' p. 105.

The distance of the spot from Telltown, the modern representative of Talten, is twelve miles, which to some might appear an objection, but it must be remembered that Brugh is ten miles from Tara, where all the kings resided, who were buried there; and as Dathi and others of them were buried at Rath Croghan, sixty-five miles off, distance seems hardly to be an objection. Indeed, among a people who, as evidenced by their monuments, paid so much attention to funeral rites and ceremonious honours to their dead, as the Pagan Irish evidently did, it must have mattered little whether the last resting-place of one of their kings was a few miles nearer or further from his residence.

It must not, however, be forgotten, that the proper residence of the Ultonians, who are said to have been buried at Talten, was Emania or Armagh, forty-five miles distant as the crow flies. Why they should choose to be buried in Meath, so near the rival capital of Tara, if that famed city then existed, is a mystery which it is not easy to solve; but that it was so, there seems no doubt, if the traditions or Books of the Irish are at all to be depended upon. If their real residence was so distant, it seems of trifling consequence whether it was ten or twelve miles from the place we now know as Telltown. There must have been some very strong reason for inducing the Ultonians to bury so far from their homes; but as that reason has not been recorded, it is idle to attempt to guess what form it took. What would appear a most reasonable suggestion to a civilized Saxon in the nineteenth century would in all probability be the direct antithesis of the motive that would guide an uncivilized Celt in the first century before Christ, and we may therefore as well give up the attempt. Some other reason than that of mere proximity to the place of residence governed the Irish in the choice of the situation of their cemeteries; what that was we may hereafter be able to find out,— at present, so far as I know, the materials do not exist for forming an opinion. If, however, this is not Talten, no graves have been found nearer Telltown, which would at all answer to the descriptions that remains to us of this celebrated cemetery; and, till they are found, these Lough Crew mounds seem certainly entitled to the distinction. I cannot see that the matter is doubtful.

If this is so, there is little difficulty in determining who were buried here. Besides the testimony of the poem just quoted, it is stated in the Book of the 'Cemeteries'—"At Tailten the kings of Ulster were used to bury vig^t Ollamh Fodhla with his descendants down to Conchobhar, who wished to be carried to a place between Slea and the sea, with his face to the east, on account of the faith which he had embraced." This conversion of Conchobhar is one of the most famous legends in Irish ancient history. He was wounded in the head by a ball that remained there, and was ordered by his physician to remain quiet and avoid all excitement as his only chance of surviving. For seven years he followed this advice; but when he saw the eclipse of the sun, and felt the great convulsion that came over nature, the day that Christ was crucified, he turned to his Druid and asked, "What is this?" To which Bacrach, the Druid, replied: "It is true, indeed, Christ, the Son of God, is this day crucified by the Jews." "At the recital of this enormity, Conchobhar felt so indignant that he went nearly mad: his excitement was so great that the ball burst from his head, and he died on the very Friday on which the crucifixion took place."[1] All this may be silly enough, as the electric telegraph was not then in use, but it is worth quoting here, as it seems that it was to establish this synchronism that the chronology of the period was falsified to the extent of half a century at least. Conchobhar and Crimthann were the two kings of the two great dynasties then reigning in Ireland whom the annalists strive to synchronize with Christ, and though they fail in that, they establish beyond much doubt that those kings were contemporaries. If to this we add the fact so often repeated by the authorities quoted above, that Conchobhar was the last of his race buried at Talten, and that Crimthann was the first of his line buried at Brugh, we obtain a tolerably clear idea of the history of these cemeteries. Brugh, in fact, succeeded to Talten on the decline of the Ultonian dynasty and the rise of Tuatha de Danann after the victories at Moytura had established their supremacy and they had settled themselves at Tara.

The character of the sculptures in the two groups of monu-

---

[1] O'Curry's 'Materials for Irish History,' p. 636 *et seqq.* So, too, even Tighernach adds, in the year 33:—" Concobares filius Nessæ obiit hoc anno."—*Ann.* p. 18.

ments fully bears out this view. The carvings at Lough Crew are ruder and less artistic than those at Brugh. They are more disconnected, and oftener mere cup markings. The three stones represented in the preceding and following woodcuts (Nos. 75 and 76), are selected from a great many in the Conwell portfolios as fair average specimens of the style of sculpture common at Lough Crew, and with the woodcut No. 73, representing the Hag's Chair, and No. 75, the chamber in cairn L, will convey a fair notion of the whole. In no one instance does it seem

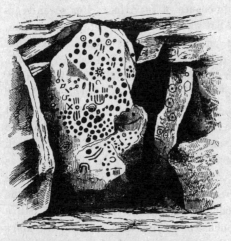

possible to guess what these figures were meant to represent. No animal or vegetable form can be recognized, even after allowing the utmost latitude to the imagination; nor do the circles or waving lines seem intended to convey any pictorial ideas. Beauty of form, as a decoration, seems to have been all the old Celt aimed at, and he may have been thought successful

76. Stone in Cairn T. Lough Crew.—E. Conwell.

at the time, though it hardly conveys the same impression to modern minds. The graceful scrolls and spirals and the foliage of New Grange and Dowth do not occur there, nor anything in the least approaching to them. Indeed, when Mr. Conwell's book is published, in which they will all be drawn in more or less detail, I believe it will be easy to arrange the whole into a progressive series illustrative of the artistic history of Ireland for five centuries before the advent of St. Patrick.

It would be an extremely dangerous line of argument to apply this law of progressive development to all countries. In India, especially, it is very frequently reversed. The rudest art is often much more modern than the most refined, but in Ireland this apparently never was the case. From the earliest scratchings on pillar stones, down to the English conquest, her art seems to have been unfalteringly progressive; and, beginning with these two cemeteries, which are probably the oldest incunabula of her art, its history might be written without a gap, or halt, till it bloomed in those exquisite manuscripts and crosses and works of gold and metal which still excite such unqualified admiration.

There may be, and no doubt are, many other sculptured graves in Ireland, but they have not yet been explored, or, at least, published. One, however, deserves notice; not, certainly, on account of its magnificence, but for several points of interest which its peculiarities bring out. It is situated in a field near Clover Hill, not far from Carrowmore, the battle-field of northern Moytura.[1] It measures only 7 feet by 5, and is $4\frac{1}{2}$ feet deep. Its cap-stone was originally flush with the earth, and no cairn or circle of stones marks it externally, nor is there any tradition of any such ever having existed. The carvings on the stones forming the chamber are shallow, and now very indistinct, from being overgrown with lichens and moss, but their general character will be understood from the annexed woodcut. Its character is something between the sculptures of Talten and Brugh, which would agree very

77. Stones in Sculptured Graves, Clover Hill.
From a sketch by the Author.

well with its date if we suppose it connected with the battle-field. This, however, is very doubtful, for there are few things that come out more prominently in the investigation than the fact that all those monuments which are directly or indirectly connected with battle-fields are literally rude and untouched by the chisel, but that all, or nearly all those which are in cemeteries, or have been erected leisurely by, or for, those who occupy them, are more or less ornamented. It may, however, be that some one

---

[1] 'Petrie's Life,' by Stokes, p. 256.

connected with the battle wished to be buried near his companions who fell there, and prepared this last resting-place for himself, but we must know more before such speculations can be of much value.

One other point is of interest regarding this tomb. If the minor sepulchres at Brugh were like the one flush with the surface, we cannot guess how many may yet be there undiscovered, and equally difficult to say how they are to be disinterred.

DOLMENS.

It is extremely difficult to write anything that will be at all satisfactory regarding the few standing solitary dolmens of Ireland. Not that their history could not be, perhaps, easily ascertained, but simply because every one has hitherto been content to consider them as pre-historic, and no one has consequently given himself the trouble to investigate the matter. The first point would be to ascertain whether any of them exist on any of the battle-fields mentioned in the Irish annals. My impression is that they do not: but this question can only be answered satisfactorily by some one more intimately acquainted with the ancient political geography of Ireland than I can pretend to be. No connexion has, however, yet been shown to exist between them and any known battle-fields, and till this is done, we must be content to consider them as the graves of chiefs or distinguished individuals whose ashes are contained in the urns which are generally found under them.

A still more important question hinges on their geographical distribution. Nothing can be more unsafe than to found any important deductions on what is known on this subject at present. If all those which are described in books and in journals of learned societies were marked on a map, the conclusion would be that the most of them are found on the east coast of Ireland; a dozen or so in Waterford and Wexford; as many in Dublin and Meath, and an equal number in County Down. But this knowledge may merely mean that the east coast, possessing roads and towns, has consequently been more frequented by tourists and antiquaries than the remote or inaccessible west.

Among the records, however, of the Ordnance survey, and in the Du Noyer drawings, there are probably sufficient materials for the purpose. Both are deposited in the Library of the Royal Irish Academy at Dublin; but any person who would attempt to use these materials for the purpose of such an investigation, must be not only an enthusiast, but have his whole time at his disposal. The disarray in which they now exist renders them utterly useless to any ordinary student of Irish antiquities.

The Irish themselves seem to have only one tradition regarding their dolmens. They call them all " Beds of Diarmid and Graine," and that is the name applied to them in the sheets of the Ordnance Survey. The elopement of Diarmid with Graine, the daughter of Cormac Mac Art, whose date, according to the Four Masters, was A.D. 286, is one of the most celebrated of Irish legends.[1] The story is, that being pursued all over Ireland by Finn, the disappointed suitor, they erected these as places of shelter, or for hiding in. This is, of course, absurd enough; but it shows that, in the opinion of the Irish themselves, they belong to the period which elapsed between the birth of Christ and the conversion of the people to Christianity. There is no hint in any Irish book that any of them were erected before the Christian era, nor anything that would lead us to suppose that any are more modern than the time of St. Columba.

The most extensive group of free standing dolmens known to exist in Ireland, is that in or near Glen Columbkille, at the extreme western point of Donegal. No account of these has been published—so far as I know—in any book or journal, and I am indebted for all I know about them to my friend, Mr. Norman Moore, who paid a visit to the spot this autumn to obtain the information I wanted, and it is from his descriptions that the following is abstracted.[2]

The principal groups are situated in Glen Malin More, a small valley running parallel to that of Columbkille, about two miles to the southward of it. There are three groups on the north side of this valley and two on the south, extending from about half a mile

---

[1] Eugene O'Curry, 'Materials,' &c., 314, 597.
[2] This most valuable contribution, with his permission, is printed *in extenso* in Appendix A.

from the sea-shore to about three miles inward. The finest group is that next the sea on the south side, and consists of six dolmens, situated nearly in a row, about 50 or 100 feet apart, and is accompanied by some cairns, but so small as hardly to deserve the name of Tumuli. The stones of the dolmens range from 6 to 12 feet in height, and their cap-stones are still there, though some have been displaced.

The second group, a little way up the glen, consists of ten dolmens arranged in two parallel rows, but they are neither so large nor so perfect as those nearer to the sea.

Nearly opposite the first-named group on the shore, but on the north side of the stream, are two dolmens so nearly contiguous to each other that they may almost be considered as one structure. About half a mile to the east of this is a fourth group, consisting of four dolmens, accompanied by cairns, and two at least of the former are of considerable magnificence. The group farthest up the glen consists of five or six dolmens, but all except one in a ruinous state.

The number of dolmens in Glen Columbkille is not given by Mr. Moore; but, from the context, there must be five or six, making up twenty to thirty for the whole group. So far as can be judged from the description, the group in Glen Columbkille seems to have better fitted and more complete chambers; consequently, I should infer it to be more modern than the others. It would, however, require careful personal inspection to classify them; though I have no doubt it could be done, and that, with a little care, these six groups could be arranged into a consecutive series, whatever the initial or final date may turn out to be.

The general construction and appearance of these tombs is that of the so-called Calliagh Birra's house in Meath, described further on (woodcut No. 80). From its situation and appearance, there seems little reason for doubt that the Meath example belongs to the fifth or the sixth century; and if this is so, as little for doubting that these dolmens in Donegal are of about the same age, or, in other words, that this mode of interment continued to be practised in certain parts of Ireland, especially near the coasts, down to the entire conversion of the inhabitants to Christianity.

There are no other traditions, so far as I know, attached to anything in this glen, except those that relate to St. Columba, who, it is understood, long resided here, attempting to convert the inhabitants to Christianity. Whether he was successful or not is not clear. He certainly left Ireland in disgust, and settled in the first island whence the shores of his detested native land could not be seen. The only other tradition that seems to bear on the subject relates to St. Patrick, who, being unable to convert the "Demons" about Croagh Patrick, in Mayo, drove them into the sea; but, instead of perishing, as they ought to have done, when he threw his bell after them, they reappeared, and settled on this promontory.[1] The meaning of this fable seems to be, that some tribe—not Celtic, for the Celts accepted Christianity whenever and wherever it was preached to them, but, it may be of Iberian origin—refusing to accept the doctrine, was expelled by force from their seats in Mayo, and sought refuge with kindred tribes in this remote corner of the island, and here remained till St. Columba took up his abode among them. If we might assume that the Columbkille group belongs to a time immediately preceding their conversion, and that the other five groups in Malin More extended back to a date two, three, it may be four centuries before St. Columba's time, and that they belonged to an Iberian or Celtiberian race, we should have an hypothesis which at least would account for all their peculiarities. Though in sight of Carrowmore, on the southern side of Sligo Bay, it is certain that these monuments have no affinity with them or with the works of any of the Northern circle-building nations. Spanish or French they must be; and we can hardly hesitate between the two. In Elizabeth's time, and as far back as history reaches, we have Spaniards settled in Galway, and on the western coast of Ireland. Such colonisation, if lasting, is not the work of any sudden impulse or of a long past time; and the probability is that Iberians, before they learned to talk Latin,

---

[1] "Croagh Patrick, a mountain in Mayo, is famous in legendary records as the scene of St. Patrick's final conflicts with the demons of Ireland. From its summit he drove them into the ocean, and completed their discomfiture by flinging his bell among their retreating ranks. Passing northward they emerged from the deep, and took up their abode in the savage wilds of Seang Cean, on the south-west of Donegal. Here they remained unmolested till our Tirconellian saint (Columba) was directed by an angel to rid the place of its foul inhabitants. After a violent struggle he completely routed them. His name was thenceforth associated with the tract, and the wild parish of Glen Columbkille preserves, in its topography and traditions, a living commentary on the legend of St. Columba," &c. — Reeves, *Vita St. Adam.*, p. 206.

were settled here from a very early age. It is also probable from what we know of them and their monuments in the Peninsula, that they would refuse for a longer period than the Celts to be converted, and that they should use dolmens for their sepulchres in preference either to tumuli or circles.

Be this as it may, there are at least two points which we may assume negatively with regard to these dolmens. The first is, that they do not mark battle-fields : they have none of the appearance of such monuments. The second is, that as there is no capital or fertile country in their neighbourhood, they are not a royal cemetery; they are not, indeed, claimed, even in the remotest manner, by any of the royal races of Ireland. They are, so far as we can see, the sepulchres of a foreign colony settled on this spot. Whether this is probable or not must, of course, depend on a comparison of these monuments with those in the countries from which they are supposed to have come. But, in the meanwhile, it may be assumed, as an hypothesis which at least accounts for the phenomena as we find them in Ireland, even when judged of by their own internal evidence alone.

One of the most interesting of the Irish dolmens is that known as the Giant's Grave, near Drumbo, about four miles south from Belfast. The interest attached to this monument does not, however, arise so much from the grandeur of the structure itself, though it may be considered a first-class example and very tolerably perfect, but from its standing solitary in the centre of the largest circle in these islands, Avebury only excepted. The circle is about 580 feet in diameter, and consequently more than six acres in extent, and is formed, not as at Avebury or Arbor Low, by a ditch dug inside, and the earth so gained being used to form a rampart, but by the top of a hill being levelled and the earth removed in so doing being thrown up so as to form a circular amphitheatre. Although, consequently, the rampart is not so high outside as at Avebury, the whole surface internally having been lowered, the internal effect is very much grander.[1]

---

[1] I cannot help thinking that the great rath at Dowth was formed by a similar process. It may not, therefore, after all, be a residential rath, as suggested above, but we are not yet in a position to speak positively on such matters.

What, then, was the object of this great earthwork with one solitary dolmen in the centre? Was it simply the converse of such a mound as that at New Grange? Was it that, instead of heaping the earth over the sepulchral chamber, they cleared it away and arranged it round it, so as to give it dignity? Or was it that funereal games or ceremonies were celebrated round the tomb, and that the amphitheatre was prepared to give dignity to their performance? These are questions that can only be answered when more of these circles are known and compared with one another, and the whole subject submitted to a more careful examination than has yet been the case. My impression is that it is the grave of a chief, and of him only, and that it is among the most modern of its class.

At about the same distance west from Belfast is another dolmen, which, in itself, is a much finer example than this Grave of the Giant. Its cap-stone is said to weigh 40 tons, and is supported by five upright stones of considerable dimensions. It has, however, no circle or accompaniments. The Celtic name of the district in which it stands was 'Baille clough togal,' *i. e.* the Town of the Stone of the Strangers, which

78.   Dolmen at Knockeen.

would seem to indicate that it was not very old, nor its origin quite forgotten.

At Knockeen, county Waterford, there is a remarkable dolmen (woodcut No. 78), though it neither has any surroundings nor any tradition attached to it.[1] It is interesting, however, as it looks as if we were approaching the form out of which Stonehenge grew, which, I have not a doubt, could be found in Ireland if looked for. It is also interesting as showing in plan (woodcut

---

[1] 'Journal Kilkenny Archæo. Soc.' v. N. S. p. 479.

No. 79), an arrangement which is peculiar, I believe, to Irish dolmens. The cell is well formed, but in front of it is a demi-cell, or ante-chamber, which looks as if it might have been used for making offerings to the dead after the cell was closed.

One other dolmen deserves being illustrated before going further, as it belongs to a class of monuments common in Brit-

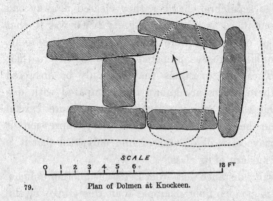

SCALE
0 1 2 3 4 5 6 12 FT

79. Plan of Dolmen at Knockeen.

tany, hitherto unknown in Great Britain. It consists of a cell 12 feet 8 inches long internally, with a width of 4 feet at the

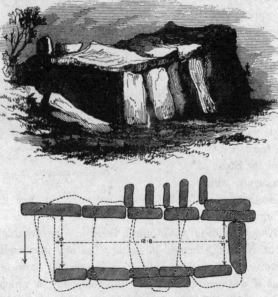

80. Calliagh Birra's House, north end of Parish of Monasterboice.

entrance, but diminishing to 3 feet at its inner end. It is situated near Monasterboice, at the northern limit of the parish, and not far, consequently, from New Grange, and close to Greenmount. Locally it is known as the house or tomb of Calliagh Vera, or Birra,[1] the hag whose chair is illustrated in woodcut No. 73, and whose name is indissolubly connected with the Lough Crew tombs. According to the traditions collected by Dr. O'Donovan and Mr. Conwell, she broke her neck before completing the last tumulus, and was buried, close to where she died,[2] in the parish of Diarmor, where, however, nothing remains to mark the spot.

From the mode in which it is constructed, it seems hardly doubtful that the original intention was to cover it with a tumulus; but probably it never was occupied. If I am correct in my surmise as to its age, its builder may have been converted to Christianity before he had occasion for it. But, be that as it may, its exposed position may serve to explain how a king or chief who had erected such a structure for his burying-place might very well have amused himself, if his life were prolonged, in adorning both the interior and exterior with carvings. I cannot believe that the internal ornaments were ever executed by artificial light, and both, therefore, must have been completed before the chamber was buried.

Last year, General Lefroy excavated a tumulus at Greenmount, Castle Bellingham, about five miles north of Calliagh Birra's so-called house.[1] In it he found a chamber, 21 feet long by about 4 feet wide and 5 feet high, enclosed by two parallel walls built of small stones, and closed at each end by similar masonry.

---

[1] If, instead of this silly legend, we could connect this tomb with Brendanus Biorro, the founder of the monastery of Birra, now Parsonstown, it would be a step in the right direction. His date would accord perfectly with the architectural inferences; for, according to Tighernach, he died 573.* The difficulty is to believe that a Christian "propheta," as he is called, could have thought of so pagan a form of supulchre. It is not easy, however to eradicate long-established habits, and his countrymen may not, within a century of St. Patrick's time, have invented and become reconciled to a new mode of burial. The Danes certainly buried in howes for centuries after their conversion, and the Irish may have been equally conservative. It is, however, hardly worth while arguing the question here, as we have nothing but a nominal similarity to go upon, which is never much to be relied upon.

[2] Eugene Conwell's pamphlet descriptive of the Lough Crew Tumuli, p. 2.

---

* Reeves, 'Vita Adamnani,' p 210.

The roof was formed of slabs in two rows, the lower projecting as brackets and the upper stretching across beyond the walls

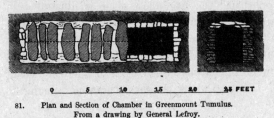

on each side. In plan, therefore, it was identical with the Birra's house, though longer and larger. But, from the mode

81.   Plan and Section of Chamber in Greenmount Tumulus.
From a drawing by General Lefroy.

in which it was constructed, it was evidently more modern,—the most modern, in fact, of all the chambered sepulchral tumuli yet discovered in Ireland.

Nothing was found in the chamber: it had been rifled before, but by whom and at what period there was nothing to show. At 9 or 10 feet below the summit, but still 6 or 7 feet above the floor of the chamber, a bronze monument was found with a Runic inscription on it, which, with the assistance of the Danish antiquaries, the General decides to belong to the ninth century (852?). The one question is, is it coeval with the building of the tomb or its destruction? The name Domnal, or Domhnall, being Irish, and the position in which it was found seem to prove that it belongs to the period of the raising of the mound, not to that of its being rifled; and if so, this grave approaches the age to which Maeshowe in the Orkneys may belong.

The circumstance, however, which interests us most at present is the similarity of the Greenmount Chamber to the Lady Birra's tomb. Being locally so close to one another, and so like in plan, they cannot be very distant in date, though the more southern is, from its megalithic character, undoubtedly the more ancient of the two. If we allow two òr three centuries it is a long stretch, though even that takes us far away from any connexion with the monuments at Lough Crew, and barely allows of it following very close on those at Brugh na Boinne.

---

[1] The following particulars are taken from a paper by General Lefroy, in the 'Archæological Journal,' No. 180, 1870, pp. 284 et seqq.

The similarity of this tomb with those at Glen Columbkille has already been pointed out, and no doubt others exist in Ireland, and will be brought to light as soon as attention is directed to the subject. But meanwhile they seem, so far as we can at present judge, to make up an extensive group of pagan or semi-pagan monuments, extending from the time of St. Patrick to that of St. Columba, and, as such, are among the latest, and certainly among the most interesting, monuments of the class in Ireland.

Vague as all this may probably appear, there is one dolmen in Ireland which seems to have a date. The great grandson of Dathi, whose red pillar-stone at Rath Croghan, erected A.D. 428, we have already pointed out, was named Ceallach. He was murdered by his four foster-brothers through envy about the sovereignty. They were hanged for their crime at a spot known as Ard-na-Riagh, near Ballina, and were buried on a hill on the opposite side of the river, where a dolmen still stands, and is pointed out as the grave of the four Maols, the murderers. These particulars are related in the Dinnsenchus, in the Book of Lecan, and in the Annals of the Hy Fiachrach, translated by Dr. O'Donovan (p. 35), who, in a note, adds

82. Dolmen of the Four Maols, Ballina.

that " this evidence, coupled with the description of the situation on the other side of the Moy, opposite Ard-na-Riagh, leaves no doubt of its identity."

The dolmen in question has nothing very remarkable about it. The cap-stone, which measures 9 feet by 7 feet, is hexagonal in form, and is supported on three uprights, arranged similarly to those of Kit's Cotty House. It is perfectly level, and stands about 4 feet above the level of the soil. The cap-stone may have been fashioned into its present form by art; but there is no sign of chiselling, and, altogether there is nothing that would attract especial attention.[1] The interest rests with its date. If it can be

---

[1] My attention was first directed to this monument by Mr. Samuel Ferguson, Keeper of the Records, Dublin. He con- sidered it then as the only cromlech in Ireland with an authenticated date; but, as he has not published this, I must not

established that it belongs to the beginning of the sixth century, which I see no more reason for doubting than Dr. O'Donovan does, it is a point gained in our investigation, in so far at least as dates are concerned.

It would be tedious to enumerate the other dolmens in Ireland which have neither dates nor peculiarities to distinguish them from others of this class, but there is one monument of a megalithic character in Ireland which must be described before leaving the country, though it certainly is not a dolmen, and its date and use are both mysterious at present.

It stands in the deer park of the Hazlewood domain, about four miles east of Sligo. It is entered from the south, and consists first of an enclosure 54 feet by 24 feet. To the westward of this is a smaller apartment, about 30 feet by 12 feet, divided

83.   Sketch-Plan of Monument in the Deer Park, Sligo.
Scale 40 feet to 1 inch.

into two by two projecting stones. At the east end are two similar apartments side by side, but smaller, the whole length of the structure measuring about 115 feet.[1] The three entrances from the central to the side apartments are trilithons of squared and partially dressed stones, and would remind us of Stonehenge, were they not so small. They are only 3 feet under the lintel, and you must bow low indeed to pass under them. Indeed, when speaking of these enclosures as apartments, it must be borne in mind that one can enter anywhere by passing between the stones, and stepping over the walls, which are composed of stones hardly ever touching each other, the highest being only 3 or

be considered as committing him to anything except beyond the desire of putting me on the scent of an interesting investigation.

[1] There is a model of this curious structure in the Royal Academy Museum, Dublin, but not a correct one; and the woodcut in their catalogue, taken from the model, has still less pretensions to accuracy.

4 feet high. Many of them, though massive, have only half that height.

What, then, is this curious edifice? It can hardly be a tomb, it is so unlike any other tomb which we know of. In plan it looks more like a temple; indeed, it is not unlike the arrangement of some Christian churches: but a church or temple with walls pervious, as these are, and so low that the congregation outside can see all that passes inside, is so anomalous an arrangement, that it does not seem admissible. At present it is unique; if some similar example could be discovered, perhaps we might guess its riddle.

It is situated on the highest plateau of the hill. A little lower down is a very fine stone Cathair, or circular fort, with an L-shaped underground apartment of some extent in its centre; and on a neighbouring eminence are several round tumuli, which, looking like the burying-places of the "Castellani," increase the improbability of the upper building being a sepulchre.

Before leaving this branch of the subject, it may be as well to allude to a point which, though not very distinct in itself, may have some influence with those who are shocked at being told that the rude stone monuments of Ireland are so modern as from the preceding pages we should infer they were. It is that every allusion to Ireland, in any classical author, and every inference from its own annals, lead us to assume that Ireland, during the centuries that elapsed between the Christian era and St. Patrick, was in a state of utter and hopeless barbarism. The testimony of Diodorus[1] and Strabo[2] that its inhabitants were cannibals is too distinct to be disputed, and according to the last named authority, they added to this an ugly habit of eating their fathers and mothers. These accusations are repeated by St. Jerome[3] in the fourth century with more than necessary emphasis. All represent the Irish as having all their women in common, and as more barbarous than the inhabitants of Britain,[4] indeed, than any other people of Europe. Nor can it be pleaded that

---

[1] Diodorus, v. p. 32.　　[2] 'Geo.' iv. p. 201.　　[3] Ed. Valersii, i. p. 413; ii. p. 335.
[4] Tacitus, 'Agricola,' p. 24.

these authors wrote in ignorance of the state of the country, for
Ptolemy's description of the coasts and of the interior, of the
cities and tribes shows an intimate acquaintance with the island
which could only be derived from observation.[1] Their own annals
do not, it is true, repeat these scandals; but nothing we now
have can be said to have been reduced to writing in anything
like the form in which we now possess it before the time of
St. Patrick; and even that has passed through edition after edition
at the hands of patriotic Irishmen before it assumed the form in
which we now find it. Even these tell of nothing but fighting
and assassination, and of crimes of every sort and kind. Even
the highest title of one of their greatest kings, Conn "of a
hundred battles," is sufficiently indicative of the life which he
led, and the state of the country he governed. As we have
every reason to believe that the progress of Ireland was steadily
and equably progressive, it is evident that if it was so, a very short
time prior to what we find in the early centuries of Christianity
would take us back to the present state of the natives of
Australia, and we should find a condition of society when any
combined effort was impossible. So evident is this, not only from
history, but from every inference that can be gathered from the
state of Ireland in subsequent ages, that the wonder really is how
such a people could have erected such monuments as those we
find on the banks of the Boyne in the early centuries of our
epoch. The answer is, of course, that the idleness of savages
is capable of wonderful efforts. A nation of men who have no
higher ambition than to provide for their daily wants, and who
are willing to submit to any tyrant who will undertake to
supply these in order to gratify his own pride or ambition, may
effect wonders. The pyramids of Egypt and the temples of
southern India are examples of what may be done by similar
means. But to effect such things, the people must be sufficiently
organised to combine, and sufficiently disciplined tò submit; and
we have no reason to suppose that in Ireland they were either
before the Christian era, and it is even very difficult to understand how they came to be so far advanced even in the time

---

[1] Mercator, 'Geogra.' p. 31.

of St. Patrick. That they were so their works attest; but if
we had to trust to indications derived from history alone, the
inference certainly would be that the monuments are considerably
more modern than the dates above assigned to them; while it
seems barely possible they should be carried back to any earlier
period.

There may be other rude stone monuments in Ireland besides
those described or alluded to in the preceding pages, but they
can scarcely be very numerous or very important, or they could
hardly have escaped notice. They are not, consequently, likely
to disturb any conclusion that may be arrived at from the
examination of those which are known. From these, we may
safely conclude that all, with perhaps the exception of the Hazlewood monument, are certainly sepulchral; and all, unless I am
very much mistaken, were erected subsequently to the building
of Emania by Eochaidh Ollamh Fodlha in the third century B.C.
There may be cairns, and even dolmens, belonging to the earlier
Hiberni before the Scoti were driven from the Continent, by the
Punic or Roman wars, to seek refuge and repose in the green
island of the West, but they must be insignificant, and probably
must remain for ever unrecognizable.

From the date, however, of the founding of Emania we seem
to have a perfectly consecutive and intelligible series commencing
with the smaller and ruder cairns of Lough Crew, and rising at
last to the lordly sepulchres of Brugh na Boinne. Between these
two stand the monuments on the battle-fields of Moytura, and
contemporary with the last are the Raths on the far-famed hill of
Tara. Beyond these we seem to have the tomb of the four Moels,
the so-called house of Calliagh Birra, and the dolmens of Glen-
columbkille, all apparently belonging to the sixth century. The
tumulus at Greenmount is later than any of these, but hardly
belongs to our Irish series.

From these we pass by easy gradations to the beehive cells
and oratories of the early Christians. No such stone dwellings
probably existed before the time of St. Patrick, or we should
have found traces of them at Tara, or Armagh, or Telltown; but
as none such existed in these royal seats of the Scots, we may

fairly assume that for domestic purposes wood and turf alone were used. But as soon as the use of stone became prevalent for such purposes, as was the case with the introduction of Christianity, we soon find the round towers, with their accompanying churches, springing up in every corner of the land, and Irish architecture progressing steadily in a groove of its own, till its forms were modified, but not obliterated, by the changes introduced by the English conquerors. The history of their style from St. Patrick to the English conquerers has been so well written by Petrie, that little now remains to be said about that division. But the history of the preceding seven centuries still remains for some one with the leisure requisite to explore the country, and with patience and judgment sufficient to read aright the many enigmas which are still involved in it, although the main outlines of the story seem sufficiently clear and intelligible. If it were written out in detail and fully illustrated, it would prove a most valuable commentary on the dark period of the history of Ireland before the introduction of Christianity, and when the concomitant introduction of alphabetic writing first rendered her annals intelligible and trustworthy.

In one other respect the study of these early monuments of Ireland seems to afford a subject of most engrossing interest. It is in Ireland that we first begin to perceive the threefold division, which, if it can be established, will lead to the most important ethnographical determinations. It appears that in this island the stone circles of the Scandinavians were introduced simultaneously with the dolmens of the Iberians or Aquitanians, and we can trace the rude barrows of the Celts growing up between them till they expanded into the great mounds of the Boyne. That these three forms ever were at any one time absolutely distinct is most unlikely, and equally so that they should have long remained so in the same country, even if it could be shown that at any one time they belonged to three separate races. Generally, however, it seems hardly doubtful that they do point to ethnographic peculiarities, which may become most important. Combined with their history and a knowledge of their uses, these monuments promise to rescue from oblivion one of the most curious chapters of Irish history, which without them might remain for ever unwritten.

CHAPTER VI.

SCOTLAND.

WHATEVER may be the case as regards Ireland, it is probable that the megalithic remains of Scotland are all known and have been described more or less in detail. Such descriptions, however, as exist are scattered through the pages of ponderous statistical compilations, or in the transactions of learned societies in England and Scotland, or in local journals, so that it is extremely difficult to acquire a connected grasp of the whole subject, or to feel sure you do know all that is required, and still more difficult to convey to others a clear view of its outlines. Had any one done for the unsculptured stones of Scotland what John Stuart has done for those that have devices in them, the case would be widely different. Except Daniel Wilson's 'Pre-historic Annals of Scotland'—whatever that may mean—no general account is available, and that work is too brief and too sparsely illustrated to be of much use. The introductory matter, however, in Mr. Stuart's two volumes,[1] with Mr. Wilson's book, may suffice for most purposes ; but a complete knowledge can only be obtained by wading through the volumes of the Scotch and English Archæologias, and the transactions and proceedings of the various antiquarian societies of both countries.[2]

---

[1] 'The Sculptured Stones of Scotland.' Two vols. quarto. Published by the Spalding Club. 1856 and 1867.

[2] A few years ago the late Mr. Rhind, of Sibster, left an estate worth more than 400*l.* per annum, to endow a Professorship of Archæology in Scotland, who was also to act as curator of the monuments themselves, but unfortunately left it encumbered by a life interest to a relative. Two years ago an attempt was made to get the Government to anticipate the falling in of the life interest, and appointing Mr. Stuart to the office at once. It was, perhaps, too much to expect so enlightened an act of liberality from a Government like ours. But their decision is to be regretted ; not only because we may thereby lose altogether the services of the best qualified man in Scotland for the purpose, but more so because the monuments are themselves fast disappearing without any record of them being preserved. Agriculture is very merciless towards a big stone or a howe that stands in the way of the plough, and in so improving a country as Scotland, very little may remain for the next generation to record.

Putting aside for the present the sculptured stones as hardly belonging to our subject, and the "cat" or battle stones, their predecessors, though they are numerous, as might be expected among the pugnacious Celtic races who inhabited the country, the remaining rude stone monuments are not numerous. The free-standing dolmens are few and far. between, some half-dozen for the whole country, and none of them with histories or traditions attached to them. The circles, however, are numerous and important, and to some extent are calculated to throw light on our investigations. If we exclude the two battle-fields of Moytura, they are infinitely more numerous than those found in all Ireland and Wales put together, although there is only one group, that at Stennis in the Orkneys, that can compare with the great English examples.

Their distribution too is interesting. No stone circles exist in the lowlands or south of the Frith of Forth and Clyde; and dolmens are rare in these regions, though this may arise from the extent to which cultivation is carried on there. Until, however, a statistical account is compiled, accompanied with a map, it is difficult to speak confidently on such a subject, but the general impression is that the lowlands are not, and never were, a region of megalithic remains; and if this is so, it is one of the many proofs that the dolmens are neither pre-Roman nor Celtic. At least we have no reason to believe that the Teutonic races who now occupy that country were settled there in the time of Agricola. But if the Celts or Picts who then inhabited that land had been in the habit of raising megalithic structures, we would have been more likely to find traces of them in that densely inhabited country than in the bleak uplands of Aberdeenshire, or the bare pastures of the Orkney Islands.

The district of Scotland where these circles and rude stone monuments most abound is on either side of a straight line drawn direct from Inverness to Aberdeen, which is a locality where sculptured stones are also found in considerable numbers, but the rude stone monuments are not found in Angus or Fife, where their sculptured successors are most numerous. The district of the circles *par excellence* in Scotland, however, is not on the mainland at all, but in the northern and western isles. The principal group is in the

Orkneys; next in importance are those in Lewes. They are found in Skye and Kantyre. There are several in Arran, and thence the transition is easy to the Isle of Man, where they meet the English group in Cumberland.

The larger circles in the Orkneys are four in number; three of these stand on a long slip of land that divides the loch of Harra from that of Stennis. The fourth is at some little distance from the others, and separated from them by a narrow strait connecting the two lochs. Besides these there are several smaller earthen circles and numerous tumuli. The largest circle, known as the Ring of Brogar,[1] is 340 feet (100 metres) in diameter between the stones. These originally were sixty in number, ranging from 6 and 7 to 15 feet in height; outside the stones runs a ditch about 30 feet in width, and 6 in depth, but with no perceptible rampart on either side. Two causeways cross the ditch as at Penrith or Arbor Low (woodcuts No. 29 and 30) opposite to one another, but neither square with the axis of the spit of land on which the circle is situated, nor facing any of the four cardinal points of the heavens.

Next in importance to this is the circle at Stennis, about three-quarters of a mile distant. It consisted originally of twelve stones 15 to 18 feet in height. Only two are now erect, but a third was so not many years ago; and the fourth, of which now only a fragment remains, is represented as standing when the drawing, which forms the frontispiece to this work, was made.[2] The remains of a dolmen still exist within the circle, not however in the centre, but close to its side, one of the stones of the circle apparently acting as head-stone to it. Beyond the stone circle which measures 104 feet

---

[1] The account of these monuments is abstracted from a paper by Lieutenant Thomas, of H. M.'s surveying vessel *Woodlark*. It is the most detailed and most correct survey we have of any British group. It was published in the 'Archæologia,' xxxiv. p. 88 *et seqq.*

[2] Four stones are represented as standing when Barry's view of the monument was published in 1807, and four are represented as standing in a series of etchings made by the Duchess-Countess of Sutherland from her own drawings, in 1805. If the elbow in the bridge shown in the drawing in the frontispiece is not a licence permitted to himself by the artist, my drawing is earlier than either of these. When I first purchased it I believed it to be by Daniel. His tour, however, took place in 1815. From the internal evidence this drawing must be anterior to 1805.

in diameter is a ditch 50 feet wide, making the whole diameter of the monument to the outward edge of the surrounding mound about

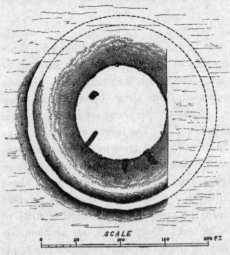

SCALE

84. Circle at Stennis. From Lieutenant Thomas's plan.

240 feet. Not far from this circle, and close to the bridge of Brogar, stands a single monolith 18 feet in height, which is the finest and highest stone of the group; and in another direction a lesser one, with a hole through it. Though only 8 feet high, 3 feet broad, and 9 inches thick, this stone has become more famous than the others, from the use Sir Walter Scott makes of it in the 'Pirate,' and because, till a very recent period, an oath taken with hands joined through the hole in the Stone of Woden, was considered even by the courts in Orkney as more than usually solemn and binding.[1]

No excavations, so far as I know, have been attempted in the circle of Stennis, but its ruined dolmen is probably sufficient to attest its sepulchral character. Some attempts at exploration were made in the larger Ring at Brogar, but without success. This is hardly to be wondered at, for a man must feel very sure where to look, who expects to find a small deposit in an area of two acres. The diggings are understood to have been made in the centre. There, however, the ground looks very like the undisturbed surface of the original moor, and as if it had never been levelled or used either for interment or any other human purpose, and slopes away irregularly some 6 feet towards the loch. My impression is that the deposits, if any exist, will be found near the outer circum-

---

[1] 'Archæologia,' xxxiv. p. 89.

ference of the circle, either at the foot of the stones as at Crichie,
or outside the ditch as at Hakpen or Stonehenge. In the
smaller circles the diameter of which does not exceed 100 feet,
the deposit seems either to have been in the centre; or, if at the
sides, the stones were so arranged as to mark its place. In the
larger, or 100-metre circles, we have not yet ascertained where to
look. Accident may some day reveal the proper spot, but till it
is ascertained either scientifically or fortuitously, no argument can
be based on the negative evidence which our ignorance affords.

In the neighbourhood of these stone circles are several bowl-
shaped barrows similar to those in the neighbourhood of Stonehenge, not only externally but internally. When opened they
were almost all found to contain interments by cremation and
rude half-burnt pottery. It is not here, however, that these barrows
are found in the greatest numbers. In the neighbouring parish of
Sandwick they exist in hundreds, and scattered exactly as on the
Wiltshire downs, here and there, singly or in pairs, without any
apparent arrangement or grouping. It is said that there are at
least 2000 of these mole-hill barrows in the islands.[1] Here, as
there, it would seem, that where a man lived and died there he
was buried, without any reference to anything existing, or that
had existed. None of these barrows have stone circles of any
sort attached to them. Indeed, the only rude stone monuments
in Orkney of the class we are discussing are those just described,
and they are all confined to one remote inhospitable-looking
spot. Close to these, however, Lieutenant Thomas enumerates
six or seven conoid barrows, whose form and contents are of a
very different nature. The bodies in them had been buried entire
without cremation, and with their remains were found silver
torques and other ornaments, similar as far as can be made out—
none are engraved—to those found in Skail Bay, along with coins
of Athelstane, 925, and of the Caliphs of Bagdad, of dates from
887 to 945.[2] That these conoid graves here, as well as others
found in the islands, are of Scandinavian origin, can hardly be
doubted, and their juxta-position to the circles is at least sug-

---

[1] 'Archæologia,' xxxiv. p. 90.
[2] The greater part of this find, with
all the coins, is in the Museum of the

Society of Antiquaries, Edinburgh. The
dates on the coins were kindly copied for
me by Mr. Stuart.

gestive. If the circles were monuments of the Celts, whom they despised, and in fact had even then exterminated, they would hardly choose a burying-place so close to them.

The most important, however, of all the tumuli, not only in this neighbourhood, but in the islands, is known as the Maes-Howe. It was opened in 1861, in the presence of a select party of antiquaries from Edinburgh, who had hoped from its external appearance to find it intact: in this, however, they were disappointed. It would seem that men of the same race as those who erected it, but who in the meanwhile had been converted to Christianity, had apparently in the middle of the twelfth century broken into this sepulchre of their Pagan forefathers, and despoiled it of its contents. As some compensation for this, they have written their names in very legible Runes on the walls of the tomb, and recorded, in short sentences, what they knew and believed of its origin.[1]

From these Runes we learn, in the first place, that the robbers were Christian pilgrims on their way to the Holy Land—Iorsala Farer—from which Professor Munch infers that they must have formed part of the expedition organized for that purpose by Jarl Ragnvald, 1152. Beyond this it is not possible to lay much stress on what these Runes tell us. In the first place, because the learned men to whom they have been submitted differ considerably in their interpretation,[2] and the record, even in the best of them, is indistinct. In one or two respects the evidence of the inscriptions may be considered satisfactory. Their writers all seem to have known so perfectly what the tomb was, and to whom it belonged, that no one cared to record, except in the most poetic fashion, what every one on the spot probably knew perfectly well. At all events, there is no allusion in these inscriptions to any other or earlier race. Every expression, whether intelligible or not, bears a northern stamp. Lothbrok, Ingeborg, and all the other names introduced are Scandinavian, and all the allusions have a Northern twang. Though this is merely negative evidence, it certainly goes

---

[1] 'Notice on the Runic Inscriptions discovered during Recent Excavations in the Orkneys.' By James Farrer, M.P. 1862.　　[2] 'Proc. Soc. Ant. Scot.' v, p. 70.

some way to show that the robbers were aware that the Howe was originally erected by people of their own race. If, however, the direct evidence of these inscriptions is inconclusive, there is
one engraving on a pillar facing
the entrance which looks as if
it were original, both from its
position and character. It represents a dragon (woodcut No.
85) of a peculiar Scandinavian
type. A similar one is found on
a stone attached to the tumulus
under which King Gorm was
buried, at Jellinge, in Denmark, in the middle of the tenth
century. Making allowance for

85.   Dragon in Maes-Howe.

the difference in drawing, they are so like that they cannot be very distinct in date. A third animal of this species is found at Hunestadt, in Scania,[1] and dating about the year 1150, but very different, and very much more
modern-looking than this one. Had
the Jerusalem pilgrims drawn this
dragon, it would probably have been
much more like the Hunestadt example. On the other hand, if the one
at Maes-Howe is original, the age of
the tomb can hardly be half a century distant from that of King Gorm's
Howe, which in other respects it very
much resembles. It is, however, very
unlikely that Christian pilgrims would
draw a dragon like this, and still less
that they would accompany it with a

86.   Wurm-Knot, Maes-Howe.

Wurm, or Serpent-knot, like that found on the same pillar; both look like Pagan emblems, and seem to belong to the original decorations of the tomb.

---

[1] Olaus Wormius, 'Monumenta Danica,' p. 188, fig. 6.

Among the inscriptions in Maes-Howe is one which, from its apparent insignificance, none of the interpreters have condescended to notice. It will be observed on one of the loose stones lying in the foreground on woodcut No. 88, it consists of only four letters, and reads either HIAI or IKIH, according as it is turned one way or another. As it is impossible to make a recognisable word, much less sense out of such a combination, it is no wonder it was thrown aside; but it is just because it is unintelligible that it may turn out to be valuable as an index to the age of the monument. Nothing is more unlikely than that a Iorsala Farer would

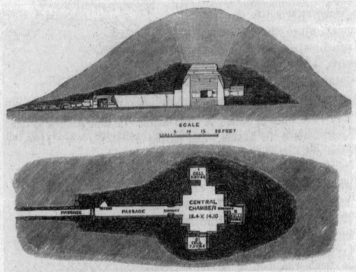

87.   Plan and Section of Maes-Howe.   From Mr. Farrer's work.

have idly engraved these Runes on a loose stone, but nothing more likely than that a mason who hewed the stone and fitted it to close the "loculus" exactly, would have put a mark upon it to show that it belonged to the right-hand chamber in which A or B was to be buried. The inscription is on the inner edge of the stone, where it would be hid when the stone was *in situ*, and most probably was engraved on the stone before it was originally used to close the opening.

This, at least, is an explanation of its meaning better than any other which has yet been suggested, and if it is the correct one, this inscription with the Dragon and the Wurm-knot are among the original sculptures of the tomb; and, if so, it will be difficult to assign it to an earlier age than the tenth century, which, from the circumstances to be mentioned hereafter, seems on the whole the most probable date.

The architecture of the tumulus, though offering some indications of great value, hardly possesses any features sufficiently marked to fix its date with certainty. Externally it is a truncated cone (woodcut No. 87), about 92 feet in diameter, by 36 feet in height, and is surrounded at a distance of about 90 feet by a ditch 40 feet wide, and 6 feet deep, out of which the earth seems to have been taken which was required to form the mound. Internally it contains a chamber slightly cruciform in plan, measuring 15 feet 4 inches, by 14 feet 10 inches, and, when complete, probably 17 feet in height.

88.　View of Chamber in Maes-Howe.　From a drawing by Mr. Farrer.

On each of three sides of the chamber is a sepulchral loculus, entered by a small opening 3 feet from the ground. The largest of these, that on the right as you enter, is 7 feet by 4 feet 6 inches, and the central one 5 feet 6 inches by 4 feet 6 inches. Each of these was closed by a single stone carefully squared, so as to fit the opening. The passage leading into the central chamber was 3 feet wide by 4 feet 6 inches in height, and originally closed, apparently by a doorway at 2 feet 6 inches from the chamber. Beyond this it is lined by two slabs 18 feet long, reaching nearly to a recess, which seems arranged as if to receive the real door which closed the sepulchre, probably a large stone. Beyond this the passage still extends some 20 feet to the present entrance, but is of very inferior class of masonry, and how much of it is modern is not clear.

The first thing that strikes any one on examining this mound is that it certainly is the lineal descendant of the great cairns on the banks of the Boyne, but separated from them by a very long interval of time. It is not easy to determine what interval must have elapsed before the side chambers of those tombs merged into the "loculi" of this, or how long it must have been before their rude unhewn masses were refined into the perfectly well-fitted masonry of this one. Some allowance must, however, be made for the difference of material. The old red sandstone of the Orkneys splitting easily into self-faced slabs, offers wonderful facilities for its use, but still the way in which the angle-buttresses of the chamber were fitted, and the cells finished, and the great slabs line the entrance, all show a progress in masonic science that must have required centuries, assuming, of course, that they were built by the same people. But was this so? So far as we at present know, these islands, when conquered by Harold Harfagar in 875, were inhabited by two races called Pape and Peti. The former were generally assumed to have been colonies of Irish missionaries and their followers, who settled here after the conversion of the Picts by St. Columba in the middle of the sixth century. The Peti, it is also generally assumed, were the Pechts, or Picts.[1] It will not be easy to ascertain now whether they were so or not, as, according to Bishop Tulloch, they were so entirely exterminated by the Northmen, that of their "posteritie there remained nocht." But if the Pape, or Papas were Irish missionaries, they were Christians, and whatever else Maes-Howe may be, it certainly is not a place of Christian burial. Nor is it Pictish. If it were, we certainly should find something like it in Pictland proper; but nothing that can be at all compared with it is found in Fife or Forfar, or in any of

---

[1] Barry's 'History of Orkney,' p. 399. See also 'Archæologia,' xxxiv. p. 89.

those countries which were occupied by the Picts in the days of their greatness; and it is most improbable that a people who could not, or at least did not, erect any such sepulchre in the fertile and populous lands which they occupied on the mainland, would erect such a one as this on a comparatively barren and sparsely inhabited island. On the other hand, there seems every reason for believing that the 2000 little barrows above alluded to are the graves of the Picts, or original inhabitants of the island before they were exterminated by the Northmen. These barrows, however, have absolutely no affinity with Maes-Howe. None of them have chambers, none have circles of stone round them; all are curvilinear, and none, indeed, show anything to induce the belief that in any length of time they would be developed into such a sepulchre as that which we have been describing. It is in fact the story of Stonehenge and its barrows over again. A race of Giants superseding a nation of Pigmies with which they certainly had no blood affinities, and erecting among their puny sepulchres monuments dedicated, it may be, to similar purposes, but as little like them in reality as the great cathedrals of the middle ages are to the timber churches of the early Saxons.

Only one hypothesis seems to remain, which is that it is a tomb of the northern men who conquered these islands in the ninth century. This may seem a very prosaic descent from the primæval antiquity some are inclined to ascribe to these monuments, but it certainly is not improbable; in the first place, because we have what seems undoubted testimony that Thorfin, one of the Jarls (940 to 970 A.D.) "was buried on Ronaldshay under a tumulus, which was then known by the name of Haugagerdium, and is perhaps the same as that we now call the How of Hoogsay," or Hoxay.[1] I have not been able to ascertain whether this is literally true or not, but have reason to believe that it was not in the How of Hoxay that Thorfin was buried, but in a mound close by.[2] The fact of his being buried in a Howe is, however, all that

---

[1] Barry, 'History of the Orkneys,' p. 124.

[2] Mr. George Petrie has recently at my request made some excavations in these mounds, but the results have not been conclusive. He is of opinion that one of the mounds he explored may be the grave of Thorfin, but it is too much ruined to afford any certain indication.

is at present demanded. Another important barrow is mentioned by Professor Munch,[1] known as Halfdan's Barrow, in Sandy, and raised by Torf Einar (925 to 936). So that we know of at least two important barrows belonging to the Norwegian Jarls in the tenth century, though only one has been identified with absolute certainty. As before mentioned, it is quite certain that King Gorm (died 950) and Thyra of Denmark were buried in tumuli in outward appearance very similar to Maes-Howe. That of Queen Thyra has alone been opened. It is a chamber tomb, similar to Maes-Howe, except in this, that the chamber in Denmark is formed with logs of wood, in the Orkneys with slabs of stone, but the difference is easily accounted for. At Jellinge stone is rare, and the country was covered with forests. At Stennis self-faced slabs of stone were to be had for the lifting, and trees were unknown. The consequence was, that workmen employed the best material available to carry out their purpose. Be that as it may, the fact that kings of Denmark and Jarls of Orkney were buried in Howes in the tenth century, takes away all *à priori* improbability from the hypothesis that Maes-Howe may be a sepulchre of one of those Northmen.

If this is so, our choice of an occupant lies within very narrow limits. We cannot well go back beyond the time of Harold Harfagar (876 to 920), who first really took possession of these islands, as a dependency of Norway, and created Sigurd the elder first Jarl of Orkney in 920. Nor can we descend below the age of the second Sigurd, who became Earl in 996, as we know he was converted by Olaus to Christianity, and was killed at Clontarf in 1014.[2] Within these seventy-six years that elapsed between 920 and 996 there is only one name that seems to meet all the exigencies of the case, and in a manner that can hardly be accidental. Havard "the happy," one of the sons of Thorfin, who was buried at Hoxay, was slain at Stennis in 970. Havard had married Raguhilda, the daughter of Eric Blodoxe, prince of Norway, and widow of his brother Arfin, but she, tired of her second husband, stirred up one of his nephews against him, and a battle was fought at

---

[1] 'Mémoires des Ant. du Nord,' iii. p. 236.

[2] These dates are taken from Barry, p. 112 *et seqq.*, but they seem undisputed, and are found in all histories.

Stennis, on a spot, says Barry, "which afterwards bore the name
of Havardztugar, from the event or the slaughter."[1] The same
story is repeated by Professor Wilson as follows, "Olaf Tryguesson,
says Havard, was then at Steinsnes in Rossey. There was meeting
and battle about Havard, and it was not long before the Jarl
fell. The place is now called Havardsteiger. So it was called,
and so M. Petrie writes me, it is still called by the peasantry to
the present day."[2] Professor Munch, of Christiania, who visited
the place in 1849, arrived at the conclusion "that most of the
grave mounds grouped around the Brogar circle are, probably,
memorials of this battle, and perhaps one of the larger that of
Havard Earl."[3] In this I have no doubt he is right, but that
larger one I take to be Maes-Howe, which is in sight of the circle,
though not so close to it as those he was speaking of.

One circumstance which at first sight renders this view of the
case more than probable is, that Maes-Howe is, so far as we at
present know, unique. Thorfin's grave, when found, may be a
chambered tumulus, so may Halfdan's Barrow, when opened, but no
others are known in Orkney. If it had been the tomb of a king or
chief of any native dynasty, similar sepulchres must have been as
numerous as they were on the banks of the Boyne or Blackwater.
There must have been a succession of them, some of greater, some
of less magnificence. Nothing of the sort, however, occurs, and till
more are found, the Stennis group cannot be ascribed to a dynasty
that lasted longer than the seventy-six years just quoted. That
brief dynasty must also have been the most splendid and the most
powerful of all that reigned in these islands, as no tomb there
approaches Maes-Howe in magnificence. If such a description
suits any other race than that of the Norwegian Jarls, I do not
know where to look for an account of it.

Assuming for the present that this is so, we naturally turn to
the Runic inscriptions on the walls of the tomb to see how far they
confirm or refute this view. Unfortunately there is nothing in
them very distinct either one way or the other. The only recognizable names are those of Lothbrok and Ingiborg. The former,

[1] 'History of Orkney.' p. 125.
[2] 'Pre-Historic Annals of Scotland,' p. 112. 'Archæologia,' xxxiv. p. 89.
[3] 'Mémoires des Antiquaires du Nord,' iii. p. 250.

if the Lothbrok of Northumbrian notoriety, is too early; the Ingiborg, if the wife of Sigurd the Second, is too late, though, as the first Christian countess of Orkney, her name may have got mixed up in some way with the tomb of the last Pagan Jarl. But should we expect to find any sober record of the date and purposes of the Howe in any of the scribblings on the walls? The English barbarians who write their names and rhymes on the walls of the tombs around Delhi and Agra do not say this is the tomb of Humayoon, or Akbar, or of Etimad Doulah, or Seyed Ahmed. They write some doggerel about Timour the Tartar, or the Great Mogul, or some wretched jokes about their own people. The same feeling seems to have guided the Christian Northmen in their treatment of the tomb of their Pagan predecessor, and though, consequently, we find nothing that can fairly be quoted as confirming the view that it is the tomb of Havard, there is nothing that can be assumed as contradicting it.

One inscription may, however, be considered as throwing some light on the subject. In XIX. XX. it is related, though in words so differently translated by the various experts to whom it was submitted, that it is difficult to quote them, that "much fee was found in the Orkhow, and that this treasure was buried to the north west," adding, "happy is he who may discover this great wealth."[1] A few years ago a great treasure was found to the north-west of Maes-Howe, in Skail Bay, just in such a position as a pirate on his way to the Holy Land would hide it, in the hope, on his return, to dig it up and take it home; but shipwreck or fever may have prevented his doing this. With this treasure were found, as mentioned above, coins of Athelstane of the date of 925, and of the Caliphs of Bagdad, extending to 945, just such dates as we should expect in a tomb of 970, recent, but not the most recent coins. Connecting these with the silver torques found in the conoid barrows around the Ring of Brogar, we seem to have exactly such a group of monuments as the histories above quoted would lead us to expect, and which with their contents belong almost certainly to the age above assigned to them.

Had Maes-Howe been an old sepulchre of an earlier race, when

---

[1] Farrer, ' Inscriptions in the Orkneys,' p. 37.

the Northmen ravaged the western islands in the early part of the ninth century, it is most improbable that they would have neglected to break into the "Orkhow." The treasures which Amlaff and his Danes found in the mounds on the banks of the Boyne would certainly have stimulated these explorers to see what was contained in the Orcadian tumulus. Had they done this, the Jerusalem pilgrims would not, three centuries later, have been able to record that "much fee" was found in the tomb, and was buried to the north-west, apparently in Skail Bay. The whole evidence of the inscriptions, in so far as it goes, tends to prove that the tomb was intact when broken into in the twelfth century. If this is so, nothing is so unlikely as that it could have remained unrifled if existing before the year 861, as a Celtic sepulchre. On the other hand, nothing seems more probable than that Christian Northmen would have plundered the grave of one of their Pagan ancestors, whom they knew had been buried "with much fee" in this tumulus two centuries before their time. Two hundred years, it must be recollected, is a very long time among an illiterate people. A long time, indeed, among ourselves, with all our literary aids; and when we add to this the change of religion that had taken place among the Northmen in the interval, we need not be surprised at any amount of ignorance of history or contempt for the customs of their Pagan forefathers on the part of the Jerusalem pilgrims. The time, at all events, was sufficiently long fully to justify Christian robbers in helping themselves to the treasures of their Pagan forefathers.

Even assuming, however, that Maes-Howe is the tomb of Havard, or of some other of the Pagan Norwegian Jarls of Orkney, the question still remains whether it has any, and, if any, what connexion with the two circles in the immediate neighbourhood?[1]

---

[1] A few years ago such a question would have been considered answered as soon as stated; but, as Daniel Wilson writes in a despairing passage in his Introduction,* "This theory of the Danish origin of nearly all our native arts, though adopted without investigation, and fostered in defiance of evidence, has long ceased to be a mere popular error. It is, moreover," he adds, "a cumulative error; Pennant, Chambers, Barry, Mac Culloch, Scott, Hibbert, and a host of other writers might be quoted to show that theory, like a snow-ball, gathers as it rolls, taking up indiscriminately whatever chances to be in its erratic course."

* 'Pre-Historic Annals of Scotland,' p. xv.

Locally, the Howe and the circles certainly form one group. No such tumuli, and no such circles exist in other parts of the islands, and the spot is so inhospitable, so far from any of the centres of population in the island, that it is difficult to conceive why it should have been chosen, unless from the accident of being the scene of some important events. If Havard was slain here, which there seems no reason for doubting, nothing seems more probable than that one of his surviving brothers, Liotr or Laudver, should have erected a tumulus over his grave, meaning it also to be a sepulchre for themselves. On the other hand, it is extremely unlikely that the six or seven other tumuli which are admitted to be of Scandinavian origin should have gathered round the Ring of Brogar if it had been a Pagan fane of the despised Celts, who preceded them in the possession of the island. It cannot be necessary here to go over the questions again, whether a few widely spaced stones stuck up around a circle one hundred metres in diameter was or was not a temple. It is just such a monument as 1000 victorious soldiers could set up in a week. It is such as the inhabitants of the district could not set up in years, and would not attempt, because, when done, it would have been absolutely useless to them for any purpose either civil or religious; and if it is not, as before said, a ring in which those who fell in battle were buried, I know not what it is. The chiefs, in this case, would be buried in the conoid barrows close around, the Jarl in the neighbouring howe.

As Stennis is mentioned in the Sagas that give an account of Havard's death, it probably existed there, and was called by the simple Scandinavian name which the Northmen gave to all this class of stone monuments. None, so far as I know, have retained a Celtic denomination. Assuming it to be earlier, it still can hardly be carried back beyond the year 800. The earliest date of

---

In spite of his indignation, however, I suspect it will be found to have gathered such force, that it will be found very difficult to discredit it. Since, too, Alexander Bertrand made his onslaught on the theory, that the Celts had anything to do with the megalithic monuments, the ground is fast being cut away from under their feet; and though the proofs are still far from complete, yet according to present appearances the Celts must resign their claims to any of the stone circles certainly, and to most of the other stone monuments we are acquainted with, if not to all.

the appearance of the Northmen in modern times is in the year 793 in the 'Irish Annals,' where mention is made of a "vastatio omnium insularum a Gentibus.[1] In 802, and again in 818, they harried Iona,[2] and from that time forward seem constantly to have conducted piratical expeditions along these coasts, until they ended by formally occupying the Orkneys under Harold Harfagar. Though smaller in diameter, Stennis has a grander and a more ancient look than Brogar, and may even be a century or two older, and be a monument of some chief who fell here in some earlier fight. That it is sepulchral can hardly be a matter of doubt from the dolmen inside its ring.

Connected with the circle at Stennis is the holed stone[3] alluded to above, which seems to be a most distinct and positive testimony to the nationality of this group of monuments.

It is quite certain that the oath to Woden or Odin was sworn by persons joining their hands through the hole in this ring stone, and that an oath so taken, although by Christians, was deemed solemn and binding. This ceremony was held so very sacred in those times, that the person who dared to break the engagement made there was accounted infamous and excluded from society.[4] Principal Gordon, in his 'Journey to the Orkney Islands' in 1781, relates the following anecdote:—"The young man was called before the session, and the elders were particularly severe. Being asked by the minister the cause of so much severity, they answered, 'You do not know what a bad man this is; he has broken the promise of Odin,' and further explained that the contracting parties had joined hands through the hole in the stone."[5]

Such a dedication of a stone to Woden seems impossible after their conversion of the Northmen to Christianity about the year 1000, and most improbable if the monument was of Celtic origin, and existed before the conquest of the country 123 years earlier. If the Northmen had not hated and despised their predecessors they would never have exterminated them; but while engaged in this work is it likely they would have adopted one of their

---

[1] 'Annales Innisfal.' in O'Connor. 'Rerum. Hib. Scrip.' ii. p. 24. 'Annales Ulton.' *Ibid.* iv. p. 117.

[2] Duke of Argyll's 'Iona,' p. 100.

[3] On the left of the view in the Frontispiece.

[4] 'Archæologia Scot.' iii. p. 119.

[5] 'Archæologia,' xxxiv. p. 113.

monuments as especially sacred, and followed up one of their customs, supposing this to have been one, though there is absolutely no proof in a holed stone being used in any Celtic cemetery for any such purpose? The only solution seems to be that the monument, with this accompaniment, was erected between the conquest of the country and the conversion of the conquerors, and, like many ancient rites, remained unchanged through ages, not as adopted from the conquered races, but because their forefathers had practised it from time immemorial in their native land. On any other hypothesis it seems impossible that so purely Pagan a rite could have survived through eight centuries of Christianity, and still be considered sacred by those whose ancestors had worshipped Wodin in the old times many centuries before these stones were erected in the islands.

All this seems so clear and consistent, that it may be assumed that this group of monuments were erected between the year 800 and 1000 A.D., till, at least, some argument is brought forward leading to a certain conclusion. At present I know of only one which tends to make me pause: it is a curious one, and arises from the wonderful similarity that exists between this and some of the greater English groups. Take, for instance, Stanton Drew (ante, p. 149). It consists of a great circle 340 feet in diameter, the same as the Ring of Brogar, and of a smaller circle within three feet of the dimensions of that of Stennis (101 against 104), both the latter possess a dolmen, not in the centre, but on its edge, the only essential difference being that the great ring at Stanton had twenty-four stones, and the smaller one eight, as against sixty and twelve in the northern example; this, however, may arise from the one being in a locality so much more stony than the other, and it must be confessed the Stanton stones look older, but this also may arise from the different nature of the rocks from which they were taken.

The Ring of Bookan answers to the circle in the orchard; the Watch or King Stone at Stennis to Hautville's Quoit. Even the names are the same, "ton" and "ness" being merely descriptive of the townland, and the long slip of land on which they are respectively situated, and Maes-Knoll looks down on the one, and Maes-Howe into the other. The only thing wanted is a ring stone in the Somersetshire example, but that might easily have disappeared, and there is one at Avebury. Some of these coincidences may, of course, be accidental, but they are too numerous and too exact to be wholly so. If at all admitted, they seem to force us to one of two conclusions: either the time which elapsed between the ages of the two monuments is less than the previous reasoning would lead us to suppose, or the persistence in these forms, when once adopted, was greater than, on other grounds, it seems reasonable to expect. Three or four centuries seem a long time to have elapsed between buildings, the style of which is so nearly identical. If, however, their dates are to be brought nearer to one another, it seems much more reasonable to bring Stanton Drew down, than to carry Stennis back. It is much more consistent with what we know, to believe that Stanton Drew was erected by Hubba and his Danes, than that the Orkney circles and Maes-Howe could have been the work of the wretched Pape and Peti, who inhabited the island before the invasion of the Northmen.

As this is the last of the great groups containing first-class circles, which we shall have to deal with in the following pages, it may be well to try and sum up, in as few words as possible, the points of the evidence from which we arrive at the conclusion that it may be of the date above assigned to it :—

1. History is absolutely silent either for or against this theory. In so far as the *litera scripta* is concerned, it may either have been erected by the Phœnicians or in the time of the Stuarts.

2. The Danish theory is of no avail. No flint, bone, or bronze or iron implements have been found in a position to throw any light on its age.

3. There are in the islands some thousands of small mole-hill barrows—insignificant, stoneless, unadorned.

4. All parts of the Stennis group show design and power, and produce an effect of magnificence.

5. It seems evident that the circles and the barrows belong to two different peoples.

6. If so, the barrows belong to the Peti and Pape ; the large howes and the stone monuments to the Northmen.

7. If this is so, the latter belong to the two centuries comprised between 800 and 1000 A.D.

8. Maes-Howe, being unique, must have belonged to the shortest, but most magnificent dynasty in the Island.

9. With regard to Havard. He was killed on, or close to the spot where Maes-Howe now stands.

10. His father, Thorfin, was buried in a howe in Ronaldshay. His contemporary, Gorm, was buried in a howe at Jellinge.

11. A dragon and serpent were carved in Gorm's tomb. Similar representations were found in Maes-Howe.

12. The four Runic letters on the closing stone of the right-hand loculus, date probably from its first erection.

13. All the subsequent inscriptions on the tomb acknowledge it as a Scandinavian monument.

14. The mention of treasure being found in it in 1152 goes far to show that it did not exist in 861, or it would then have been robbed by the Northmen, as the Irish tombs were.

15. It is extremely probable that the Skail Bay " find " is part of this treasure, which is not earlier than 945, and may be twenty or forty years later.

16. The torques found in the six large tumuli at Brogar belong to the same age.

17. The Holed Stone at Stennis was certainly set up by Northmen and by them dedicated to Woden, and it certainly forms part of the group.

18. The name Havard's Steigr, attaching to the place at the present day, is important.

Against this, I know of only one argument: *Omne ignotum pro antiquo ;* which, for reasons, given above, I reject.

If such a case were submitted to anyone, regarding a monument of which we had never heard before, no one would probably hesitate in considering the case as proved, till, at least, something more to the point could be brought forward on the other side. Such, however, is the effect of education, and so strong the impression on the minds of most Englishmen with regard to Phœnicians and Druids, that nine people out of ten will probably reject it; some alleging that it must be an unfair, others that it is an inconclusive statement. Let them try and state their view in as few words, and I do not believe it will be difficult to judge between the two cases.

CALLERNISH.

The next in importance after those of Stennis among the Scottish group of circles is that at Callernish, in the Isle of Lewis. They are situated at the inner end of Loch Roag, on the western coast of the island, and consequently more remote from the routes of traffic or the centres of Pictish or Celtic civilization than even the Orcadian groups. The country, too, in their neighbourhood is of the wildest and most barren description, and never could have been more densely inhabited than now, which is by a sparse population totally unequal to such monuments as these.

The group consists of three or four circles, situated near to one another, at the head of the bay. They are of the ordinary form, 60 to 100 feet in diameter, and consequently not remarkable for their dimensions, nor are they for the size of the stones of which they are composed. One of them, which had been covered up with peat-moss, was excavated some years ago, and a number of holes were found, filled, it is said, with charcoal of wood;[1] but the account is by no means satisfactory. About a mile to the westward of the three, on the northern shore of Loch Roag, stands the principal monument. This consists of a

SCALE

80 40 30 20 10 0   50   100   150

89.   Monument at Callernish. From a plan by Sir Henry James.

circle[2] 42 feet in diameter. In the centre of this is a tall stone, about 17 feet high, which forms the headstone of a grave of a somewhat

---

[1] 'Proceedings Soc. Ant. of Scotland,' iii. p. 213.

[2] These dimensions and the plan are taken from Sir Henry James's work on 'Stonehenge, Turuschan,' &c.

cruciform plan; but it is in fact only the tricameral arrangement common in tumuli in Caithness and other parts of the north of Scotland.[1] It apparently was covered originally by a little cairn of its own; but this had disappeared, and the tomb emptied of its contents at some period anterior to the formation of the peat which had accumulated round the stones, and which was removed a few years ago by Sir James Matheson when this grave was first discovered. From the central stone a double avenue extends 294 feet, and from the same point southward, a single row for 114 feet; making the whole length of the avenues 408 feet; while two arms extend east and west, measuring 130 feet across the whole.

I believe it was John Stuart that first made the remark:— " Remove the cairn from New Grange, and the pillars would form another Callernish;"[2] and there seems little doubt but that this is the true explanation of the peculiar form of the monument. Nor is it difficult to see why this should be the case; for it must be borne in mind that the whole of the chambers and the access to them must have been constructed, and probably stood, naked for some time before they began to heap the cairn over them. Calliagh Birra's tomb (woodcut No. 80), and the numerous "Grottes des fées" we meet with in France and elsewhere I look on as chambers, some of which it was intended should be buried in tumuli, which, however, never were erected : others, when men had become familiar with the naked forms, were like many dolmens, never intended to be hidden. It may be a mere fancy; but I cannot escape from an impression that, in ·many instances at least, the chambers were constructed during their lifetime by kings or chiefs as their own tombs, and that the cairn was not raised over them till the bodies were deposited in their recesses. This, at least, is the case in the East, where most of the great tombs were erected by those who were to lie in them. During their lifetime they used them as pleasure-houses, and only after their death were the entrances walled up and the windows obscured, so as to produce the gloom supposed to be appropriate to the residences of the dead. Another point is worth observing. It seems most improbable that sculptures,

---

[1] Anderson, on horned Tumuli in Caithness, 'Proc. Soc. Ant. of Scotland,' vi. p. 442 et seqq., and vii. p. 480 et seqq.

[2] 'Sculptured Stones of Scotland,' ii. p. xxv.

such as are found in the Irish and French chambered tumuli, could have been executed by artificial light. Either the stones were sculptured before being put into their places—which, to say the least of it, is very unlikely; or they were sculptured while the light could still penetrate through the interstices of the stones forming the walls. In any case, however, the naked forms of these chambers must have been perfectly familiar with those who used them; and there is no difficulty in understanding why, as at Carrowmore or Callernish, they should have repeated the same forms which were certainly never intended to be covered up.

From the occurrence of a similar form at Northern Moytura (woodcut No. 59), used externally also, it may be argued that this may be of the same age. The Irish example, as explained above, is probably of the same age as the great chambered tumuli of Meath; but there seems to be a difference between the two, which would indicate a very different state of affairs.

At Moytura, the covering stones, though thrown down, still exist, and there is every appearance of direct imitation. At Callernish, the size, the wide spacing, the pointed form of the stones, and the whole structure exhibit so marked a difference from anything that could be intended to be covered up, that it certainly appears as if a long time had passed before the original use of the form could have been so completely overlooked as it has been in this instance. Everyone must determine for himself how many centuries he would interpose between New Grange and Callernish. To me it appears that an interval of very considerable duration must have elapsed between them.

At Tormore, on the west coast of the Isle of Arran, there is a third group of these monuments, more numerous, but not on so large a scale as those of Stennis or Callernish. These were all carefully examined by Dr. Bryce, of Glasgow, assisted by a party of archæologists, in 1864, and the results recorded in the 'Proceedings of the Scottish Antiquaries,'[1] and also in a small work on the Geology of Arran.[2] All were found to contain sepulchral remains, except one which had been rifled, but there the cist still remained. The principal circle is now represented by only three

---

[1] Vol. iv. p. 499.   [2] Glasgow, 1865, p. 186 et seqq.

upright stones, from 18 to 20 feet in height; but they originally formed parts of a circle 60 feet in diameter. Two other circles can be traced, and two kistvaens of considerable dimensions, and two obelisks on the high ground, which apparently formed parts either of circles or of some other groups of stones.

Though not so large as the other two groups named above, this one at Tormore is interesting because it affords fair means of testing whether these groups were cemeteries, or marked battle-fields. Here the two principal circles are situated on a peat moss which extends to some feet, at least, below the bottom of the pillars, and the sepulchral deposits were found in the peat. Others of these Tormore monuments are situated where the peat joins the sandy soil, and others are situated on the summit of the sandy hills, which here extend some way in from the shore. Now it seems hardly probable that such a diversity of taste should have existed in any line of princes. If the peat was chosen as a resting-place for some, it probably would have been for all. If elevated sandy hillocks were more eligible for that purpose, why should some have chosen the bog? and if a cemetery, why not all close together? They extend for about half a mile east and west at a distance of about a mile from the shore, and on about as desolate a plain as one could find anywhere. If a battle was fought here against some enemy who had landed in the bay, and those who were killed in it were interred where they fell, all the appearances would be easily explained; but it is difficult to guess who the chiefs or princes could be who were buried here, if they had leisure to select their last resting-place, or why they should have been buried in this scrambling fashion.

There are the remains of two other circles and one obelisk in Brodick Bay, on the other side of the island, but widely scattered, and with nothing to indicate their purpose. There are also other circles and detached standing stones in the Mull of Cantyre, up to the Crinan Canal; but the published maps of the Ordnance Survey do not extend so far, and such accounts as have been pub-lished are too vague to admit of any conclusions being drawn from them either as to their age or uses.

The Aberdeenshire circles, above alluded to, differ in some respects from those found in other parts of the country, and are thus described by Colonel Forbes Leslie, in a Paper read to the British Association this year:—" The principal group of stones in these circles always contains one stone, larger than the rest, which in different monuments varies from 11 to 16 feet in length, and from 2 to 6 in breadth. It is never placed upright; but close at each end of this recumbent monolith stand two columnar stones; these vary in height from 7 to 10 feet, and have generally been selected of a pyramidal form. From the face, and near the ends of the recumbent stone, two stones project about 4 feet into the circle, and the recess thus formed is occupied by a stone laid flat on the ground.

" In several of these circles a raised platform, 5 or 6 feet broad, and 18 or 24 inches high, can be traced. This has been supported on the outer side by a low wall connecting the columnar stones, which are disposed at equal distances on the circumference. The inner side of the platform has been supported by stones little more than its height, placed near each other.

" Circles of this sort are found at Aquhorties, Tyrebagger, Balquhain, Rothiemay, Parkhouse, near Deer, Daviot, New Craig, Dunadeer, &c., in Aberdeenshire. There is also a circle on the " Candle Hill of Old Rayne," [1] within sight of which, on the slope of a ridge about a mile distant, stood the two sculptured stones now at Newton,—on one of which is the unique alphabetical inscription; and on the other a serpent, with the broken sceptre, surmounted by the double disk, usually called the Spectacle Ornament."

Their general arrangement will be understood from the woodcut overleaf, representing one at Fiddes Hill, figured in the fifth volume of 'Archæologia,' which may be taken as a type of the rest. The sepulchral deposit here, is no doubt, in the raised part, in front of the great stone, and not in the centre,— a peculiarity we have already had occasion to remark upon in the smaller circles at Stanton Drew and Stennis. This, however, does not seem to have been always the case. The circle, for instance, at Rayne, above alluded to, was excavated under the

---

[1] In the 'Archæologia,' vol. xxii. pp. 200 and 202, are plans and views of six Aberdeenshire circles, and two more are given in the same volume further on.

superintendence of Mr. Stuart,[1] and found to contain in its centre a pit, in which were "a quantity of black mould, incinerated bones, and some bits of charcoal. Fragments of small urns were also found, and all the usual accompaniments of a sepulchral deposit." In concluding his account of it, Mr. Stuart says:— "It is worthy of remark, that on the 2nd of May, 1349, William, Bishop of Aberdeen, held a court at the Standing Stones of

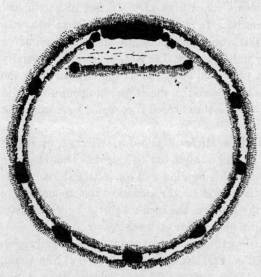

90.   Circle at Fiddes Hill, 46 feet in diameter.

Rayne, at which the King's Justiciar was present " (' Regst. Episc. Aberd.' vol. i. p. 79, Spald. Club). Thus clearly proving not only the sepulchral nature of the circles, but the use that was subsequently made of them.

If we may connect these stones at Rayne with the Newton stones, as Colonel Forbes Leslie is inclined to do, we obtain a proof of a post-Christian date for this sepulchral circle, as well as a mediæval use; and though I have no doubt that all this is correct, the mere juxtaposition of the sculptured stones and the circle hardly seems sufficient to rely upon.

In the Appendix to the Preface of the first volume of the ' Sculptured Stones,' Mr. Stuart records excavations made in some fourteen circles, similar, or nearly so, to this one at Rayne; and in all sepulchral deposits, more or less distinct, were found. In some, as in that of Crichie, before alluded to, a sepulchral deposit was found at the foot of each of the six stones which surrounded

---

[1] ' Sculptured Stones of Scotland,' vol. i. p. xxi.

it. Like many of our English circles, this last was surrounded by a moat, in this instance 20 feet wide and 6 feet deep, crossed by two entrances, as is Arbor Low and the Penrith circle, and within the moat stood the stones. As a general rule, it may be asserted that all the Scotch circles, having a diameter not exceeding 100 feet, when scientifically explored, have yielded evidences of sepulchral uses. Such, certainly, is the result of Mr. Stuart's experience, as detailed above; of Dr. Bryce's, in Arran; of Mr. Dyce Nicol[1] and others, in Kincardine; and elsewhere. Colonel Forbes Leslie informs me that he has not been so fortunate in some of those he mentioned in his lecture, which he either opened himself or learnt the details of on the spot. Some of these he admits, however, had been opened before, others disturbed by cultivation; and altogether his experiences seem to be exceptional, and far from conclusive. The preponderance of evidence is so overwhelming on the one side, that we may be perfectly content to wait the explanation of such exceptional cases as these.

The Aberdeenshire circles are all found scattered singly, or at most in pairs, in remote and generally in barren parts of the country; so that it is evident they neither marked battle-fields nor even cemeteries, but can only be regarded as the graves of chiefs, or sometimes, it may be, family sepulchres. There is one group, however, at Clava, about five miles east from Inverness, which is of more than usual interest, but regarding which the published accounts are neither so full nor so satisfactory as could be wished.[2]

According to Mr. Innes, the ruins of eight or nine cairns can

---

[1] In September, 1858, Mr. Dyce Nicol, with a party of experienced archæologists, excavated four circles situated in a row, and extending for nearly a mile, on the road from Aberdeen to Stonehaven, and about 1½ mile from the sea. The first and last had been disturbed before, but the second, at King Caussie, and the third, at Aquhorties, yielded undoubted evidences of their sepulchral origin. The conclusion these gentlemen arrived at was, that "whatever other purposes these circles may have served, one use of them was as a place of burial." —*Proceedings Soc. Ant. Scot.* v. p. 134.

[2] I regret much that I have been unable to visit this place myself. It was, however, carefully surveyed by Captain Charles Wilson, when he was attached to the Ordnance Survey at Inverness. He also made detailed plans and sketches of all the monuments, but, unfortunately, sent them to the Ordnance Office at Southampton, and they consequently are not accessible nor available for our present purposes.

still be distinguished, though the whole of the little valley or depression in which they are situated seems strewn with blocks which may have belonged to others, but which the advancing tide of cultivation has swept away. The most perfect of those now remaining are three at the western end of the valley, the

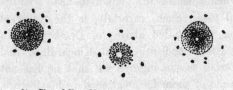

91.   Plan of Clava Mounds.   From Ordnance Survey.
25 inch scale.

two outer and larger cairns stand about 100 yards apart. They are of stone, about 70 feet in diameter, surrounded by a circle of upright stones measuring 100 feet across.

The intermediate one is smaller, being only 50 feet, with a circle 80 feet in diameter.[1] The two extreme ones have been opened, and found to contain circular chambers about 12 feet in diameter, and 9 in height, with passages leading to them about 15 feet long and 2 feet wide; and in two or three instances the stones in them were adorned with cup-marking, though it does not appear

92.   View of Clava Mounds.   From a drawing by Mr. Innes.

that they were otherwise sculptured.[2]   In that to the west two sepulchral urns were found, just below the level of the original soil. They were broken, however, in extracting them; and they do not appear to have been put together again or drawn, so that no conclusions can be deduced from them as to the age of the cairns.

Meagre as this information is, it is sufficient to show that Clava

---

[1] These dimensions are taken partly from the Ordnance Survey Sheet, 25-inch scale, and partly from Mr. Innes's paper in 'Proceedings Soc. Ant.' iii. p. 49 et seqq.

[2] Ibid. Appendix, vi. pl. x.

does not mark a battle-field. Carefully-constructed chambers with horizontally-vaulted roofs are not such monuments as soldiers erect in haste over the graves of their fallen chiefs. It evidently is a cemetery; and, with the knowledge we have acquired from the examination of those in Ireland, there cannot be much hesitation in ascribing it to that dynasty which was represented by King Brude, when St. Columba, in the sixth century, visited him in his "Munitio," on the banks of the Ness.[1] If King Brude were really converted to Christianity by Columba, it is by no means improbable that the small square enclosure at the west end of the "heugh," which is still used as the burying-place of Pagan, or at least unbaptized babies, marked the spot where he and his successors were laid after the race had been weaned from the more noble burial-rites of their forefathers.

It would be extremely interesting to follow out this inquiry further, if the materials existed for so doing; as few problems are more perplexed, and at the same time, of their kind, more important, than the origin of the Picts, and their relations with the Irish and the Gaels. Language will not help us here: we know too little of that spoken by the Picts; but these monuments certainly would, if any one would take the trouble to investigate the question by a careful comparison of all those existing in Scotland and Ireland.

93.   Stone at Coilsfield.

In the south of Scotland, for instance, we find such a stone as this at Coilsfield, on the Ayr,[2] which, taking the difference of drawing into account, is identical with that represented in woodcut No. 71. There is the

[1] Reeves, 'Adamnan. Vita St. Columb.' p. 150.
[2] Wilson's 'Prehistoric Annals,' p. 332.

same circle, the same uncertain, wavy line, and generally the same
character.   Another was found at Annan-street, in Roxburghshire,
and is so similar in pattern and drawing that if placed in the

94.   Front of Stone at Aberlemmo, with Cross.

chamber in the tumuli of New Grange, or Dowth, no one would
suspect that it was not in the place it was originally designed

for.[1] But no sculptures of that class have yet, at least, been brought to light in Pictland, or, in other words, north of the Forth, on the east side of Scotland.

95.   Back of Stone at Aberlemmo.

[1] An amusing controversy regarding the existence of this stone will be found in the 'Proceedings Scot. Ant.' iv. p. 524 et seqq. It seems absolutely impossible that any man, even under the inspiration of some primordial whisky, to have drawn by accident a sculpture so like what his ancestors did fifteen centuries before his time.

The sculptured stones of the Picts are, however, quite sufficient
to prove a close affinity of race between the two peoples, but
always with a difference, which is evident on even a cursory
examination. To take one instance. There is a very beautiful
stone at Aberlemmo, near Brechin, which is said to have been put
up to record the victory gained over the Danes at Loncarty, in
the last years of the tenth century.[1] Be this as it may, there seems
no reason for doubting that it is a battle-stone, and does belong
to the century in which popular tradition places it. On the front
is a cross, but, like all in Scotland, without breaking the outline of
the stone, which still retains a reminiscence of its Rude form.
In Ireland, the arms of the cross as invariably extend beyond the
line of the stone, like those at Iona, which are Irish, and these
are generally joined by a circular Glory. The ornaments on the
cross are the same in both countries, and generally consist of
that curious interlacing basket-work pattern so common also in
the MSS. of that age in both countries, but which exist nowhere
else, that I am aware of, except in Armenia.[2] The so-called
" key " ornament on the horizontal arms of the cross at Aberlemmo seems also of Eastern origin, as it is found in the Sarnath
Tope, near Benares, and elsewhere, but is common to both
countries; as is also the dragon ornament on the side of the
cross, though this looks more like a Scandinavian ornament than
anything that can claim an origin further east.

Among the differences it may be remarked that the figure-
subjects on Irish crosses almost invariably refer to the scenes of
the Passion, or are taken from the Bible. On the Scotch stones,
they as constantly refer to battle or hunting incidents, or to what
may be considered as events in civil life. The essential difference,
however, is, that, with scarcely an exception, the Pictish stones
bear some of those emblems which have proved such a puzzle to
antiquaries. The so-called broken sceptre, the brooch, and the
altar, are seen in the Aberlemmo stone; but in earlier examples

---

[1] Gordon, ' Iter Septemtrionale,' p. 151.

[2] In my 'History of Architecture,'
ii. p. 345, I ventured timidly to hint
that this Armenian ornament would be
found identical with that in the Irish
and Pictish crosses. Since then I have
seen a series of photographs of Armenian
churches, which leave no doubt in my
mind that this similarity is not accidental, but that the one country borrowed it from the other.

they are far more important and infinitely various.[1] It may also
be worthy of remark that the only two real round towers out of
Ireland adorn the two Pictish capitals of Brechin and Abernethy.
All this points to a difference that can well make us understand
why St. Columba should have required an interpreter in speaking
to the Picts;[2] but also to a resemblance that would lead us to
understand that the cemetery at Clava was the counterpart of
that on the banks of the Boyne, with the same relative degree
of magnificence as the Kings of Inverness bore to those of Tara;
and if we do not find similar tumuli at Brechin or Abernethy, it
must be that the kings of these provinces—if there were any—
were converted to Christianity before they adopted this mode of
burial. It may be suggested that, as Maes-Howe is certainly the
lineal descendant of the monuments on the Boyne, it too must
be a Celtic or Pictish tomb. For the reasons, however, given
above, such a theory seems wholly untenable; but thus much
may be granted, that such a tomb would probably not have been
erected, even by a Northman, in a country where there was not
an underlying Celtic or Pictish population.

Before leaving these sculptured stones, it may be as well to
point out one of those anomalies which meet us so frequently
in these enquiries, and show how little ordinary probabilities
suffice to guide to the true conclusion. Among the sculptured
stones of Scotland, one of the oldest is probably the Newton
stone. It has at least an Oghan inscription on its edge; and
most antiquaries will admit that Oghan engravings on stone were
discontinued when alphabetic writing was introduced and generally understood. It also has an alphabetic inscription on its
face, but the letters are not Roman. They may be bad Greek, but
certainly they appear to be pre-Roman, and therefore probably the
earliest Scotch inscription known. There is another stone at Kirkliston, near Edinburgh, which has a Latin inscription on it. It is
a " cat " or battle-stone, and records the name of Vetta, the son of
Victis, in good Latin. Whether this Vetta is, or is not, the
grandfather of Hengist and Horsa, as Sir James Simpson con-

---

[1] See Stuart's 'Sculptured Stones,' and Colonel Forbes Leslie's 'Early Races of
Scotland,' *passim*.   [2] Reeves, 'Adamnan. Vita St. Columb.' pp. 65 and 145.

tended,[1] is of no great consequence to our present argument.
It is of about their age, and therefore as old as any of the other

96.　　Cat Stone, Kirkliston.

stones in Scotland; and there is
also a third at Yarrow,[2] with a later
inscription, which seems about the
same age as the Lothian example.
Now the curious part of this matter
is, that having begun with alphabetic writing, they entirely discontinued it, and during the six or
seven centuries through which these
sculptured stones certainly extend,
it is the rarest possible thing to
find one with an alphabetic inscription; and why this should be so
is by no means clear. Take, for
instance, the Aberlemmo stone just
quoted. The people who erected it were Christians,—witness the
cross: the ornaments on it are almost identical with those found
in Irish MSS. of the seventh and eighth centuries.[3] It is thus
evident that the persons who drew these ornaments could write,
and being able to write and carve with such exquisite precision,
it seems strange they never thought of even putting the name
of the persons who erected the stone or some word expressive of
its purpose. The Irish probably would have done so; and the
Scandinavians would have covered them with Runes, as they did
those they erected in the Isle of Man, though probably at a somewhat later date. In the instance of the two crosses illustrated in
the woodcuts, Nos. 97 and 98, the first bears an inscription to
the effect that "Sandulf the Swarthy erected this cross to his wife,
Arnbjörg." From their names, both evidently of Scandinavian
origin. The inscription on the side of the second runs thus: "Mal
Lumkun erected this cross to his foster-father Malmor, or
Mal Muru."[4] Both names of undoubted Gaelic derivation, thus

---

[1] 'Proceedings Soc. Ant. Scot.' iv. p.
119 et seqq.

[2] Ibid. iv. p. 524.

[3] Westwood, 'Facsimiles of Irish MSS.'

plates 4-28.

[4] These two woodcuts are borrowed
from Worsaae, 'The Danes and Northmen.' London, 1852.

showing that at that age at least any ethnographic theory that
would give these stones exclusively to either race can hardly
be maintained. The two races seem
then to have followed the fashion
of the day as they did in ruder
times. Except in the instance of the
St. Vigean's stone on which Sir James
Simpson read the name of Drosten,[1]
ascribing it with very fair certainty
to the year 729 A.D., none of the 101
stones illustrated in the splendid
volumes of the Spalding Club contains hardly a scrap of alphabetic
writing. Throughout they preferred
a strange sort of Heraldic symbolism,
which still defies the ingenuity of
our best antiquaries to interpret. It

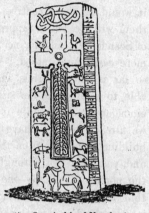

97.   Cross in Isle of Man, bearing
Runic Inscription.

was a very perverse course to pursue, but while men did so,
probably as late as Sueno's time, A.D. 1008,[1] it is needless to ask
why men set up rude stones to commemorate events or persons
when they could have carved or inscribed
them; or why, in fact, as we would insist
on doing, they did not avail themselves
of all the resources of the art or the
learning which they possessed?

The other rude-stone monuments of
Scotland are neither numerous nor important. Daniel Wilson enumerates some
half-dozen of dolmens as still existing in
the lowlands and in parts of Argyllshire,
but none of them are important from their
size, nor do they present any peculiarities
to distinguish them from those of Wales
or Ireland; while no tradition has attached

98.   Cross in Isle of Man, bearing
Runic Inscription.

itself to any of them in such a manner as to give a hint of their
age or purpose. Besides these, there are a number of single stones

---

[1] 'Sculptured Stones of Scotland,' ii. p. 70.   [2] Camden, 'Brit.' 1268.

T

scattered here and there over the country, but there is nothing to indicate whether they are cat stones or mark boundaries, or merely graves, so that to enumerate them would be as tedious as it would be uninstructive. What little interest may attach to them will be better appreciated when we have examined those of Scandinavia and France, which are more numerous, as well as more easily understood. When, too, we have mastered them in so far as the materials available enable us to do, we shall be able to appreciate the significance of much that has just been enunciated. Meanwhile it may be as well to remark that what we already seem to have gained is a knowledge that a circle-building race came from the north, touching first at the Orkneys, and, passing down through the Hebrides, divided themselves on the north of Ireland—one branch settling on the west coast of that island, the other landing in Cumberland, and penetrating into England in a south-easterly direction.

In like manner we seem to have a dolmen-building race who from the south first touched in Cornwall, and thence spread northwards, settling on both sides of St. George's Channel, and leaving traces of their existence on the south and both coasts of Ireland, as well as in Wales and the west of England generally. Whether these two opposite currents were or were not synchronous is a question that must be determined hereafter. We shall also be in a better position to ascertain what the races were who thus spread themselves along our coasts, when we have examined the only countries from which it is probable they could have issued.

CHAPTER VII.

SCANDINAVIA AND NORTH GERMANY.

———◆◇◆———

INTRODUCTORY.

So much has been said by the Danes and their admirers of the services that they have rendered to the study of prehistoric archæology that it is rather disappointing to find that, when looked into, almost less is known regarding their megalithic monuments than regarding those of any other country in Europe. No work has yet been published giving anything like a statistical account of them, and no map exists showing their distribution. What little information can be obtained regarding the Danish dolmens, and other similar monuments, is scattered through so many volumes of transactions and detached essays that it is extremely difficult to arrive at any connected view of them— almost, indeed, impossible for any one who is not locally familiar with the provinces in which they are found. The truth seems to be that the Danish antiquaries have been so busy in arranging their microlithic treasures in glass cases that they have totally neglected their larger monuments outside. They have thus collected riches which no other nation possesses, and have constructed a very perfect grammar and vocabulary of the science. But a grammar and a dictionary are neither a history nor a philosophy; and though their labours may eventually be most useful to future enquirers, they are of very little use for our present purposes. They have indeed up to this time been rather prejudicial than otherwise, by leading people to believe that when they can distinguish between a flint or bronze or iron implement they know the alpha and omega of the science, and that nothing further is required to determine the relative date of any given monument. It is as if we were to adopt the simple chemistry of the ancients, and divide all known substances into earth, water, fire, and air: a division not only convenient but practically so true that there is very little to be said against it. It is not, however, up to the mark of the knowledge of the day, and omits to take notice of the fact that earths can occasionally be converted into gases, and airs converted into liquids or solidified. Instead of their simple system, what is now wanted is something that will take into account the different races of mankind—some progressive, some the reverse—and the different accidents of success and prosperity, or disaster and poverty: the one leading to the aggregation of detached communities into great centres, and consequent progress; the other leading to dispersion and stagnation, if not retrocession, in the arts of life which tend towards what we call civilization. At the International Congress of Prehistoric Archæology, held at Copenhagen in the autumn of 1869, it was understood that many of the best Northern antiquaries were inclined to abandon, to a very considerable extent, the hard and fast lines of their first system, and to admit not only that there may be considerable overlapping, but even, in some instances, that its indications were not in accordance with the facts. More than two years have elapsed since the Congress was held, but the volume containing the account of its proceedings is not yet published; when it is, we may probably be in a position to speak much more favourably not only of their views but of the extent of their knowledge of the antiquities in question.

Under these circumstances, we may congratulate ourselves in possessing such a work as that of Sjöborg.[1] He wrote, fortunately, before the Danish system was invented, but, unfortunately, before drawing and engraving had reached the precision and clearness which now characterize them. In consequence of the last defect, we cannot always feel sure of our ground in basing an argument on his drawings; but, generally speaking, he is so honest, so free from system, that there is very little danger in this respect. The work has also the merit of being as free from the speculations about Druids and Serpents which disfigure the contemporary works of English antiquaries, as it is from the three ages of the Danes; though, on the other hand, he relegates all

---

[1] 'Samlingar för Norders Fornalskare,' Stockholm, 1822-1830.

the dolmens and such like monuments to a prehistoric "Joter," or giant race, who preceded, according to his views, Odin and his true Scandinavians, to whom he ascribes all the truly historic monuments.

In addition to the difficulties arising from the paucity of information regarding the monuments, the Scandinavians have not yet made up their minds with regard to their early chronology. Even the vast collections contained in the ponderous tomes of Langebeck and Suhm [1] are far from sufficing for the purpose; and such authors as Saxo Grammaticus [2] write with an easy fluency too characteristic of our own Jeffrey of Monmouth, and others who bury true history under such a mass of fables as makes it extremely difficult to recover what we are really seeking for. Patient industry, combined with judicious criticism, would, no doubt, clear away most of the obscurities which now disfigure this page of mediæval history; but, meanwhile, the Scandinavian annals are as obscure as the Irish, and more uncertain than the contemporary annals of England.

Of the history of Scandinavia anterior to the Christian era, absolutely nothing is known. It is now no longer admissible to believe in a historic Odin, whom all the mediæval historians represent as living in the first century B.C., and as the founder of those families who play so important a part in the subsequent histories of our own as well as of the whole group of Northern nations. The modern school of Germans has discovered that Odin was a god who lived in the sky in pre-Adamite times, and never condescended to visit our sublunary sphere. It is now rank heresy to assume that during the thousand years which elapsed between his pretended date and that of our earliest MSS. the wild imaginings of barbarous tribes may not have gathered round the indistinct form of a national hero, transferred him back to a mythic age, and endowed him with the attributes and surroundings of a god. As the Germans have decreed this, it is in vain to dispute it, and not worth while to attempt it here, as for our present purposes it is of the least possible consequence.

---

[1] 'Scriptores rerum Danicorum medii ævi,' 9 vols. folio, Hafniæ, 1722 et seqq.
[2] 'Historiæ Danicæ,' lib. xvi. Soræ, 1644, in fol.

About the Christian era there is said to have been a king, called Frode I., who, as he never was deified, may have had a tomb on earth, and might, if that could be identified, be allowed to head our list. Between him and Harald Harfagar, who, in 880, conquered Norway and came into distinct contact with British history in the Orkneys, we have several lists of kings, more or less complete, and with dates more or less certain.[1] That there were kings in those days, no one will probably dispute, nor perhaps is the succession of the names doubtful; and if the dates err to the extent of even fifty years or so, it is of little consequence to our argument. The monuments extend so far down, and to kings whose dates are so perfectly ascertained, that it is of no importance whether the earlier ones are assigned to dates forty or fifty years too early or too late. Their fixation may be left to future research, as it has no direct bearing on the theory we are now trying to investigate.

BATTLE-FIELDS.

The chief of the Scandinavanian monuments, and the most interesting for our present object, comprise those groups of stones which mark battle-fields. Not only are their dates generally known with sufficient precision to throw considerable light on the

---

[1] The following list of the kings of Denmark, copied from Dunham's, and giving the dates from Suhm, and Snorro's 'Heimskringla,' will probably suffice for our present purposes:—

	Suhm. A.D.	Snorro. B C.		Suhm. A.D.	Snorro. A.D.
Frode I.	35	17	Rolf Krake	522	479
Fridlief	47	—	Frode VII.	548	,,
Havar	59	—	Halfdan III.	580	554
Frode II.	87	—	Ruric	588	,,
Wermund	140	—	Ivar	647	587
Olaf	190	—	Harald Hildetand	735	,,
		A.D.	Sigurd Ring	750	—
Dan Mykillate	270	170	Rajnar Lothbrog	794	—
Frode III.	310	235?	Sigurd Snogoge	803	—
Halfdan I.	324	290	Herda Canute	850	—
Fridlief III.	348	300	Eric I.	854	—
Frode IV.	407	370	Eric II.	883	—
Ingel	436	386	Harald Harfagar	—	863
Halfdan II.	447	,,	Gorm the Old (died?)	941	—
Fode V.	460	,,	Harald Blatand	991	—
Helge and Roe	494	438	Sweyn	1014	—
Frode VI.	510	,,			

question of the antiquity of such monuments in general, but they also illustrate, if they do not determine, the use of many of the groups of stones we meet with in other countries. Sjöborg devotes ten plates in his first volume to these battle-fields, illustrating twice that number of battles which occurred between the fifth and the twelfth centuries after Christ.

The first of these, at Kongsbacka, near the coast in Halland, though of somewhat uncertain date, is worth quoting from its similarity to the alignments on Dartmoor, Ashdown, Karnac, and elsewhere, though, unfortunately, no plan or dimensions are given.

99.   View of Battle-field at Kongsbacka.   From Sjöborg.

On the hills beyond is a tumulus called the grave of Frode, and on the plain a conspicuous stone bears his name; but whether this was Frode V. (460) or some other Frode is not clear. Sjöborg assigns it to a date about 500, and there seems very little reason to doubt he is at least approximatively correct.[1]

The second battle-field illustrated is similar to the last, except in the form of the stones, which seem to belong to a different mineralogical formation.[2] They are plainly, however, seen to be arranged in circles and lines, and are even more like forms with which we are familiar elsewhere. It is said to represent a battle-field in which the Swedish king Adil fought the Danish Snio, and in which the latter with the chiefs Eskil and Alkil were slain. As all these names are familiarly known in the mediæval history of these countries there can be no great difficulty in ascribing this battle also to about the same age as that at Kongsbacka.

---

[1] 'Samlingar,' &c. i. plate 11, fig. 38, p. 104.   [2] *Loc. sup. cit.*, fig. 39.

With the third we tread on surer ground. No event in the history of these lands is better known than the fight on the Braavalla Heath, in Östergothland, where the blind old king, Harald Hildetand, met his fate in the year 736, or 750 according to others. As the Saga tells us, Odin had, when the king was young, taught him a form of tactics which gave him a superiority in battle over all his enemies; but the god having withdrawn his favour from him, he fell before the prowess of his nephew, Sigurd Ring, to whom the god had communicated the secret of the battle array. It does not appear to admit of doubt that the circles shown in the cut in the opposite page were erected to commemorate this event, and that they contain the bodies of those who were slain in this action; and if this is so, it throws considerable light on the battle-fields of Moytura, illustrated woodcuts Nos. 54 to 61. The circles on Braavalla are generally from 20 to 40 feet in diameter, and consequently are, on the average, smaller than those at Moytura; they are also more numerous, unless we adopt Petrie's suggestion,[1] that there must originally have been at least two hundred in the Irish field; and if so, it is the smaller ones that would certainly be the first to be cleared away, so that the similarity may originally have been greater than it now is— so great, indeed, as to render it difficult to account for the fact that two battle-fields should have been marked out in a manner so similar when so long a time as seven centuries had elapsed between them. As it does not appear possible that the date of the Braavalla fight can be shifted to the extent of fifty years either way, are we deceiving ourselves about Moytura? Is it possible that it represents some later descent of Scandinavian Vikings on the west coast of Ireland, and that the cairn on Knocknarea—

> "High and broad,
> By the sailors over the waves
> To be seen afar,
> The beacon of the war renowned"[2]—

which they built up during ten days—is really the grave of some Northern hero who fell in some subsequent fight at Carrowmore? That all these are monuments of the same class, and belong, if not to the same people, at least to peoples in close

---

[1] Stokes, 'Life of Petrie,' p. 260.   [2] Beowulf, *loc. sup. cit.*

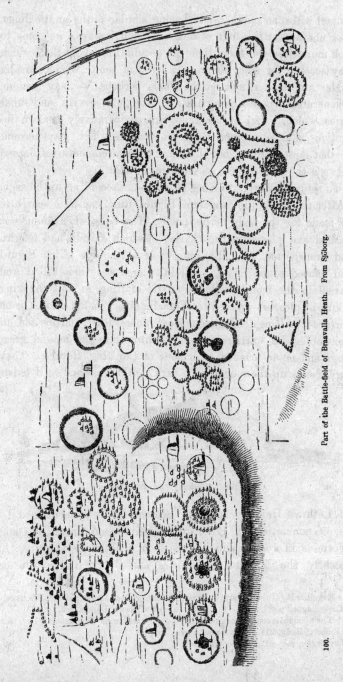

Part of the Battle-field of Bravalla Heath.　From Sjöborg.

100.

contact with one another, and having similar faiths and feelings,
does not appear to admit of doubt. When, however, we come to
look more closely at them, there are peculiarities about them which
may account for even so great a lapse of time. The Braavalla
circles are smaller, and on the whole perhaps, we may assume,
degenerate. There are square and triangular graves, and other
forms, which, so far as we know, are comparatively modern inventions, and, altogether, there are changes which may account
for that lapse of time; but that more than seven centuries elapsed
between the two seems to be most improbable.

To return, however, to King Hildetand. According to the saga,
"After the battle the conqueror, Sigurd Ring, caused a search to
be made for the body of his uncle. The body when found was
washed and placed in the chariot in which Harald had fought,
and transported into the interior of a tumulus which Sigurd
had caused to be raised. Harald's horse was then killed and
buried in the mound with the saddle of Ring, so that the king
might at pleasure proceed to Walhalla either in his chariot or on
horseback. Ring then gave a great funeral feast, and invited all
the nobles and warriors present to throw into the mound great
rings and noble armour, in honour of the king Harald. They
then closed up the mound with care."[1] This mound still exists

101.   Harald Hildetand's Tomb at Lethra.[2]

at Lethra's Harald, capital in Seeland. It was mentioned by
Saxo Grammaticus in 1236,[3] and described and drawn by Olaus
Wormius in 1643;[4] and no one ever doubted its identity, till
recently the Museum authorities caused excavations to be

---

[1] Engelhardt, 'Guide illustré du Musée
à Copenhague,' p. 33.

[2] The woodcut is copied from a drawing
in Sjöborg, ii. fig. 214. It is repeated by
Worsaae, loc. sup. cit., both copying from

some original I have not cared to trace.

[3] 'Historia Danica,' viii. p. 133.

[4] 'Danicorum Monument.' libri sex,
i. p. 12.

made. Unfortunately some "wedges of flint" have been found
in the earth which was extracted from the chamber, from
which Worsaae and his brother antiquaries at once concluded
that "it is beyond all doubt merely a common cromlech of the
stone period"[1]—a conclusion that seems to me the reverse of
logical. No one, I presume, doubts that King Hildetand was
buried in a tumulus with rings and arms; and if this tumulus
was regarded historically as his, for the last 600 years, and traditionally so from the time of his death, it is incumbent upon the
antiquaries to show how worthless these traditions and histories
are, and to point out where he really rests. To form an empirical
system and to assert—which they cannot prove—that no flint implements were used after a certain prehistoric date, and that consequently all mounds in which flint implements are found are prehistoric, seems most unreasonable, to say the least of it. It would
be surely far more philosophical to admit that flint may have been
used down to any time till we can find some reason for fixing a
date for its discontinuance. In this instance an "instantia crucis"
would be to dig into some of the circles at Braavalla, and see if
any flints are to be found there. No metal was found at Moytura,
though metal was, if history is to be depended upon, then commonly used, and flint implements were probably not found because
those who opened the tombs were not aware of its importance.
Pending this test, the form of the grave may give us some indication of its age. It is an oblong barrow, with an external dolmen
at one end, and with a row of ten stones on each side, the two end
ones being taller than the rest. A similar mound, known as the
Kennet long barrow, exists at Avebury,[2] so similar indeed that
if this tomb at Lethra is historical so certainly is the English
example. If, on the other hand, either can be proved to belong

---

[1] 'Primæval Antiquities of Denmark,'
p. 113.

[2] At one time I was, on the authority
of a Saxon charter, inclined to believe
that this tumulus was the grave of Cissa,
Saxon king of Winchester, who was
contemporary with Arthur. I am now
informed by the Rev. Mr. Jones, who
has carefully gone into the matter, that
the Charter No. 1094, which is taken

from the 'Codex Winton.' fol. 54, refers
to Overton in Hants, and not to Overton
in Wilts, because Tadanliage (Tadley) is
mentioned as part of it. As I cannot
dispute the competency of so eminent an
authority on such a question, its identification with the tomb of King Cissa must
for the present be withdrawn, but it by
no means follows in consequence that it
may not be of his age.

to the long forgotten past, the other must also be consigned to the same unsatisfactory limbo.

The barrow at West Kennet was carefully explored in 1859 by Dr. Thurnam, and the results of his investigation fully detailed in a paper in the 'Archæologia,' vol. xxxviii., from which the following particulars are abstracted, together with some others from a second paper, "On Long Barrows," by the same author, in vol. xlii. of the same publication.

Externally it is a mound measuring 336 feet in length by 75 feet at its broadest part. Originally it was surrounded by what is called a peristalith of tall stones, between which, it is said, a walling of smaller stones can still be detected. On its summit, as at Lethra, was an external dolmen over the principal chamber of the tomb. The chamber was nearly square in form, measuring 8 feet by 9, and approached by a passage measuring 15 feet by

102.   Long Barrow, Kennet, restored by Dr. Thurnam. 'Archæologia,' xlii.

3 feet 6 inches in width; and its arrangement is in fact the same as that of the Jersey tumulus (woodcut No. 11), and, as Sir John Lubbock remarks, "very closely resembles that of a tumulus" he had just been describing, of the Stone age, in the island of Möen, "and, in fact, the plan of passage graves generally."[1]

When opened, six original interments were found in the chamber, under a stratum of black, sooty, greasy matter, 3 to 9 inches in thickness, and which, Dr. Thurnam remarks, "could never have been disturbed since the original formation of the deposit" (p. 413). Two of these had their skulls fractured during lifetime; the others were entire. To account for this, Dr. Thurnam takes considerable pains to prove that slaves were sometimes sacrificed at the funeral of their masters, but he fails to find any instance in which they were killed by breaking their heads; and

---

[1] 'Prehistoric Times,' p. 153.

if they were to serve their master in the next world, even a savage would be shrewd enough to know that cracking his skull was not the way to render him useful for service either in this world or the next. No such mode of sacrifice was ever adopted, so far as I know.[1] But supposing it was so, all the six burials in this tomb seem to have been nearly equal, and equally honourable, and why, therefore, all their skulls were not broken is not clear. If on the other hand we assume that it is the grave of six persons who were slain in battle, two by blows on the head, and four by wounds in the body, this surely would be a simpler way of accounting for the facts observed. Even, however, if we were to admit that these men with the broken heads were sacrificed, this would by no means prove the grave to be prehistoric. Quite the contrary, for we know from the indisputable authority of a decree of Charlemagne that human sacrifices were practised by the pagan Saxons as late, certainly, as 789,[2] and were sufficiently frequent to constitute one of the first crimes against which he fulminated his edicts. The fact is that neither historians nor antiquaries seem quite to realise the state of utter barbarism into which the greater part of Europe was plunged between the collapse of the Roman Empire and the revival of order under Charlemagne. Christianity no doubt had taken root in some favoured spots, and some bright lights shone out of the general darkness, but over the greater part of Europe pagan rites were still practised to such an extent as easily to account for any heathen practice or any ancient form of sepulture which may be found anywhere existing.

To return, however, to our long barrow. Under a piece of Sarsen stone, but on the skull of one of the principal persons interred here (No. 4), were found two pieces of black pottery (fig. 8, page 415), which Dr. Thurnam admits may be of the Roman age. Other fragments of the same vessel were found in other parts of the tomb, and also fragments of pottery (figs. 14 to 17), not British, but to which he hesitates to assign an age. So far as I can judge, it seems just such pottery as the less experienced British potters would form, on Roman models, after

---

[1] The slaves of the Scythian kings were strangled (Herodotus, iv. 71 and 72).

[2] "Si quis, hominem diabolo sacrifi-caverit et in hostiam more paganorum dæmonibus obtulerit, morte moriatur."— Balusius, Capt. Reg. Franc. i. 253.

the departure of that people. But this is immaterial; for beyond the chamber, and deeper consequently into the tumulus, were found fragments of undoubted Roman pottery. So far, therefore, everything favours the view that it was the sepulchre of persons slain in battle, after the departure of the Romans; for we can hardly believe that a battle would be fought, and such a tomb raised over the slain, during their occupation; and if so, as the pottery proves it could not be before, a choice of a date is fixed within very narrow limits. It may either have been in 450, immediately after the departure of the Romans, or in 520, the date of the battle of Badon Hill, which is the time at which, I believe, it was reared. So far as the general argument is concerned, it is of no consequence which date is chosen. Against this conclusion we have to place the following facts. First, no trace of iron or bronze, or of metal of any sort, was found in the tomb. Secondly, at least 300 flint fragments were found in it. Some of these were mere chippings, some cones, but many were fairly formed flint implements (figs. 10 to 13),[1] not belonging to the oldest type, but such as antiquaries are in the habit of ascribing to the pre-metal Stone age. In addition to these, the quantity of coarse native pottery was very remarkable. No whole vessels were found, but broken fragments that would form fifty vessels were heaped in a corner; and there were corresponding fragments in another corner. Dr. Thurnam tries to explain this by referring to the passage in the grave scene in 'Hamlet,' where our great dramatist speaks of "shards, flints, and pebbles," which should be thrown into the graves of suicides; the use of which, he adds, "in mediæval times may be a relic of paganism." It does not, however, seem to occur to him that, if such a custom was known in the sixteenth century, it would be likely to have been in full force in the sixth. It is strange enough that such a custom, even if only referred to suicides, should have survived a thousand years of such revolutions and changes of religion as England was subjected to in those days; but that it should be known to Christians, after 3000 or 4000 years' disuse, seems hardly possible.

---

[1] The wood-blocks of these and other illustrations of Dr. Thurnam's paper were lent to Sir John Lubbock, and used by him in his 'Prehistoric Times,' Nos. 146-156, where they will be more accessible to many than in the 'Archæologia.'

No argument, it appears to me, can be drawn from the different kinds of pottery found in the tomb. If any one will take the trouble of digging up the kitchen midden of a villa built within the last ten years, in a previously uninhabited spot, he will probably find fragments of an exquisite porcelain vase which the housemaid broke in dusting the drawing-room chimney-piece. He will certainly find many fragments of the stoneware used in the dining-room, and with them, probably, some of the coarser ware used in the dairy, and mixed with these innumerable "shards" of the flower-pots used in the conservatory. According to the reasoning customary among antiquaries, this midden must have been accumulating during 2000 or 3000 years at least, because it would have taken all that time, or more, before the rude pottery of the flower-pots could have been developed into the exquisite porcelain of the drawing-room vase. The argument is, in fact, the same as that with respect to the flints. It may be taken for granted that men used implements of bone and stone before they were acquainted with the use of metal; but what is disputed is that they ceased to use them immediately after becoming familiar with either bronze or iron. So with earthenware: men no doubt used coarse, badly formed, and badly burnt pottery before they could manufacture better; but, even when they could do so, it is certain that they did not cease the employment of pottery of a very inferior class; and we have not done so to the present day. To take one instance among many. There are in the Museum of the Society of Antiquaries at Edinburgh a series of vessels, hand-made and badly burnt, and which might easily be mistaken —and often are—for those found in prehistoric tombs. Yet they were made and used in the Shetland Islands in the last and even in the present century.

The truth of the matter seems to be that, as in the case of a find of coins, it is the date of the last piece that fixes the time of the deposit. There may be coins in it a hundred or a thousand years older, but this hoard cannot have been buried before the last piece which it contains was coined. So it is with this barrow. The presence of Roman or post-Roman pottery in an avowedly undisturbed sepulchre fixes, beyond doubt, the age before which the skeletons could not have been deposited where they were found by Dr. Thurnam. The presence of flints and coarse pottery only shows, but it does so most convincingly, how utterly groundless the data are on which antiquaries have hitherto fixed the age of these monuments. It proves certainly that flints and shards were deposited in tombs in Roman or post-Roman times; and if there is no mistake in Dr. Thurnam's data, this one excavation is, by itself, sufficient to prove that the Danish theory of the three ages is little better than the "baseless fabric" of—if not "a vision"—at least of an illusion, which, unless Dr. Thurnam's facts can be explained away, has no solid foundation to rest upon.

If any systematic excavations had been undertaken in the Scandinavian long barrows, it would not, perhaps, be necessary to

adduce English examples to illustrate their age or peculiarities. Several are adduced by Sjöborg, but none are reported as opened. This one, for instance, is externally like the long

103.   Long Barrow at Wiskehärad, in Halland.
From a drawing by Sjöborg.

barrow at West Kennet, and, if Sjöborg's information is to be depended upon, is one of several which mark the spot where Frode V. (460-494) landed in Sweden, where a battle was fought, and those who fell in it were buried in these mounds, or where the Bauta stones mark their graves. If this is so, the form of the long barrow with its peristalith was certainly not unknown in the fifth century; and there is no improbability of its being employed in England also in that age. In settling these questions, however, the Scandinavians have an immense advantage over us. All their mounds have names and dates; they may be true or they may be false, but they give a starting-point and an interest to the enquiry which are wanting in this country, but which, it is hoped, will one day enable the Northmen to reconstruct their monumental history on a satisfactory basis.

In most cases antiquaries in this country have been content to appeal to the convenient fiction of secondary interments to account

for the perplexing contradictions in which their system everywhere involves them. In the instance of the Kennet long barrow
there is no excuse for such a suggestion. All the interments
were of one age, and that undoubtedly the age of the chamber
in which they were found, and the pottery and flints could not
have been there before nor introduced afterwards. Indeed, I do
not know a single instance of an undoubtedly secondary interment, unless it is in the age of Canon Greenwell's really prehistoric tumuli. When he publishes his researches, we shall be
in a condition to ascertain how far they bear on the theory.[1]
In the chambered tumuli secondary interments seem never to
occur; and nothing is more unlikely than that they should. As
Dr. Thurnam himself states: "In three instances at least Mr.
Cunnington and Sir R. C. Hoare found in long barrows skeletons
which, from their extended position and the character of the iron
weapons accompanying them, were evidently Anglo-Saxon."[2] A
simple-minded man would consequently fancy that they were
Anglo-Saxon graves, for what can be more improbable than that
the proud conquering Saxons would be content to bury their dead
in the graves of the hated and despised Celts whom they were
busy in exterminating.[3]

If the above reasoning is satisfactory and sufficient to prove
that the long barrow at West Kennet is of post-Roman times, it
applies also to Rodmarton, Uley, Stoney Littleton, and all the
Gloucestershire long barrows which, for reasons above given (*ante*,
page 164), we ventured to assign to a post-Roman period; and

---

[1] An argument for secondary interments has been attempted to be founded
(Lubbock, 'Prehistoric Times,' p. 156)
on an edict of Charlemagne, in which he
says:—"Jubemus ut corpora Christi-
anorum Saxonum ad coemeteria ecclesiæ
deferantur et non *ad* tumulos paganorum (Balusius, 'Cap. Reg. Franc.' i.
p. 154). If the expression had been "*in*
tumulos," there might have been something in it; but a fair inference from the
edict seems to me to be that even in
Charlemagne's time converted Saxons
insisted on being buried—probably in
tumuli—near where the tombs of their

fathers were, and probably with pagan
rites, in spite of their nominal conversion.

[2] 'Archæologia,' xlii. p. 195.

[3] Nothing would surprise me less than
the discovery of an interment in the upper
part of the barrow at West Kennet, between the roof of the chamber and the
dolmen. Many indications in the West
Country long barrows lead us to expect
that such might be the case, but it
by no means follows that it would be
secondary. On the contrary, it would
probably be, if not the first, at least the
chief burial in the mound.

à fortiori it carries with it King Hildetand's tomb at Lethra. It
is true we have not the same direct means of judging of its date
as we have of our own monuments. The Danes treat with such
supreme contempt any monument that does not at once fall
in with their system, that they will not even condescend to
explore it. So soon as Worsaae found some "flint wedges" in
the tomb, he at once decreed that it was prehistoric, and that it
was no use searching farther; and we are consequently left to
this fact and its external similarities for our identification. Here,
again, is a difficulty. The two drawings above given (woodcuts
Nos. 101 and 102) may show them too much alike or exaggerate
differences. The one is an old drawing from nature, the other a
modern restoration; still the essential facts are undoubted. Both
are chambered long barrows, ornamented by rows of tall stones,
either partially or wholly surrounding their base, and both have
external dolmens on their summit, and both contain flint implements. If this is so, the difficulty is rather to account for so little
change having taken place in 230 years than to feel any surprise
at their not being identical. The point upon which we wish to
insist here is that they are both post-Roman, and may consequently belong to any age between Arthur and Charlemagne.

The remaining battle-fields of which representations are given
in Sjöborg are scarcely so interesting as that at Braavalla, which
with the tomb of the king slain there are landmarks in our
enquiry. If those circles on Braavalla Heath do mark the battle-
field, and that tomb at Lethra is the one in which the blind
old king was laid—neither of which facts I see any reason for
doubting—all difficulties based on the assumed improbability of
the monuments being so modern as I am inclined to make them
are removed, and each case must stand or fall according to the
evidence that can be adduced for or against its age. To return,
however, to the battle-fields given by Sjöborg. Figures 43 and 44
represent two groups of circles and Bauta stones near Hwitaby,
in Malmö. These are said to mark two battle-fields, in which
Ragnar Lothbrok gained victories over his rebellious subjects in
Scania: Sjöborg says in 750 and 762, as he adopts a chronology
fifty years earlier than Suhm. But be this as it may, there does

not seem any reason for doubting but that these stones do mark fields where battles were fought in the eighth century, and that Ragnar Lothbrok took part in them. These groups are much less extensive than those at Braavalla, but are so similar that they cannot be distant from them in age.

At Stiklastad, in Norway, in the province of Drontheim, a battle was fought, in 1030, between Knut the Great and Olof the Holy; and close to this is a group of forty-four circles of stones, which Sjöborg seems, but somewhat doubtfully, to connect with this battle. But about the next one (fig. 49) there seems no doubt. The Danish prince Magnus Henricksson killed Erik the Holy, and was slain by Carl Sverkersson, in the year 1161, at Uppland, in Denmark; and the place is marked by twenty stone circles and ovals, most of them enclosing mounds and two square enclosures, 30 to 40 feet in diameter. They are not, consequently, in themselves very important, but are interesting, if the adscription is correct, as showing how this heathenish custom lasted even after Christianity must have been fairly established in the country. Another group (fig. 51) is said to mark the spot where, in 1150, a Swedish heroine, Blenda, overcame the Danish king Swen Grate, and the spot is marked by circles and Bauta stones; one, in front of a tumulus, bears a Runic inscription, though it merely says that Dedrik and Tunne raised the stone to Rumar the Good.

Only one other group need be mentioned here. On a spot of land, in the island of Freyrsö, off the entrance of the Drontheim Fiord, in the year 958, Hakon, the son of Harald Harfagar, overthrew his nephews, the sons of Erik Blodoxe, in three battles. The first and second of these, as shown in the plan (woodcut No. 104), are marked by cairns and mounds; and the third by eight large barrows, three of which are of that shape known in Scandinavia as ship barrows, and measure from 100 to 140 feet in length. There are also three tumuli at 4 in the woodcut, in one of which one of Erik Blodoxe's sons is said to be buried. It is not clear whether the five large mounds that stud the plain do not cover the remains of those also who fell in this fight. It does not appear that any excavations have been made in them. The interest of this battle-field to us is not so

much because it shows the persistence of this plan of marking
battle-fields at so late a date—later ones have just been quoted
—but because all the actors in the scene are familiar to us from
the part they took in the transactions in the Orkneys in the
tenth century. If they, in their own country, adhered to these
old-world practices, we should not be astonished at their having
erected circles or buried in mounds in their new possessions. It

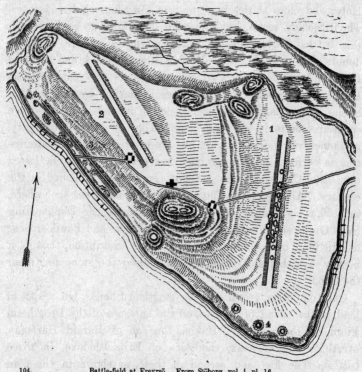

104.   Battle-field at Freyrsö.   From Sjöborg, vol. i. pl. 16.

is true that none of these Scandinavian circles can compare in
extent with the Standing Stones of Stennis or the Ring of
Brogar, but this would not be the first time that such a thing
has happened. The Greeks erected larger and, in proportion to
the population, more numerous Doric temples in Sicily than they
possessed in their own country; and the Northmen may have
done the same thing in Orcadia, where they possessed a conquered,
probably an enslaved, race to execute these works.

TUMULI.

The number of sepulchral mounds in Scandinavia is very great, and some of them are very important; but, so far as I can ascertain, very few have been explored, and, until interrogated by the spade, nothing can well be less communicative than a simple mound of earth. A map of their distribution might, no doubt, throw considerable light on the ethnography of the country, and tell us whether the Finns or Lapps were their original authors, or whether the Slaves or Wends were their introducers; and, lastly, whether the true Scandinavians brought them with them from other lands, or merely adopted them from the original inhabitants, in which case they can only be treated as survivals. Funereal pomp, or tomb-building of any sort, is so antagonistic to the habits of any people so essentially Teutonic as the Scandinavians were and are, that we cannot understand their adopting these forms, or indeed stone circles or monuments of any class, in a country where they had not previously existed. If we assume that the modern Scandinavians were German tribes who conquered the country from the Cimbri or the earlier Lapps and Finns, and did so as warriors, bringing no women with them, the case is intelligible enough. Under these circumstances, they must have intermarried with the natives of the country, and would eventually, after a few generations, lose much of their individual nationality, and adopt many of the customs of the people among whom they settled, using them only in a more vigorous manner and on a larger scale than their more puny predecessors had been able to adopt.[1] It is most improbable that the "Northmen," if Germans—as indeed their language proves them to be—should ever have invented such things as tumuli, dolmens, circles, or any other such un-Aryan forms, in any

---

[1] I have tried hard to follow Worsaae's argument in respect to this point ('Zur Alterthumskunde des Nordens,' 1847), but without success. As he is personally familiar with the country and its monuments, he may be perfectly correct in what he states, but as there are neither maps nor illustrations to this part of the work, it is almost impossible for a stranger to judge; and as, like all Danes, he is a devout believer in the three-age system, it is difficult to know how far this may or may not influence his view.

country where they had not existed previously to their occupying it; but that as immigrants they should adopt the customs of the previous occupants of the land is only what we find happening everywhere. The settlement of these points will be extremely interesting for the ethnography of Northern Europe, and ought not to be difficult whenever the problem is fairly grappled with. In the meanwhile, all that the information at present available will enable us to do here is to refer to some tumuli whose contents bear more or less directly on the argument which is the principal object of this work.

The first of these is the triple group at Upsala, now popularly known as the graves of Thor, Wodin, and Freya. It may illustrate the difficulty of obtaining correct information regarding these monuments to state that, even so late as 1869, Sir John Lubbock, who is generally so well informed, and had such means of obtaining information, did not know that they had been opened.[1] I was aware of a passage in Marryatt's travels in Sweden in which, writing on the spot, he asserts that one of them had been opened, and that "in its 'giant's chamber' were found the bones of a woman, and, among other things, a piece of a gold filagree bracelet, richly ornamented in spiral decoration, some dice, and a chessman, either the king or a knight." [2] Wishing, however, for further information, I obtained an introduction to Mr. Hans Hildebrand, who gave me the following information. Subsequently I received a letter from Professor Carl Säve, of Upsala, who kindly abstracted for me the only published accounts of the excavations as they appeared in a local paper at the time. These were forwarded to me by Professor Geo. Stephens, of Copenhagen, who also was so obliging as to translate them. They are so interesting that I have printed them, as they stand, as Appendix B. From these two documents the following account is compiled, and may be thoroughly depended upon.

One of the mounds, known as that of Wodin, was opened, in 1846, under the superintendence of Herr Hildebrand, the royal antiquary of Sweden. It was soon found that the mounds were situated on a ridge of gravel, so that the tunnel had to take

---

[1] 'Prehistoric Times,' p. 107.   [2] 'One Year in Sweden,' ii. p. 183.

an upward direction. At the junction of the natural with the artificial soil, a cairn was found of closely compacted stones, each about as large as a man could lift. In the centre of the cairn the burial urn was found in the grave-chamber, containing calcined bones, ashes, fragments of bronze ornaments destroyed by fire, and a fragment of a gold ornament delicately wrought. Within the cairn, but a little away from the urn, were found a heap of dogs' bones, equally calcined by fire, and fragments of two golden bracteates. "The workmanship of the gold ornaments," Herr Hildebrand adds, "closely resembles that of the gold bracteates of the fifth or sixth centuries, and, with the fragments of these peculiar ornaments themselves, settles a date before which these mounds could not have been raised." How much later they may be, it is not easy to conjecture, without at least seeing the bracteates, which do not seem to have been published. With a little local industry, I have very little doubt, not only that the date of these tombs could be ascertained, but the names of the royal personages who were therein buried, probably in the sixth or seventh century of our era.

"The tombs of Central Sweden," Herr Hildebrand adds, "are generally constructed in the same way, the urn containing the bones being placed on the surface of the soil, at the place of cremation or elsewhere, as the case may be. Generally, nothing is found with them but an iron nail, or some such trifling object"—a curious and economical reminiscence of the extravagant customs of their predecessors. According to him, "almost every village in Sweden, with the exception of those in some mountain-districts and the most northern provinces, has a tomb-field quite close to the side of the houses. The antiquities found in the mounds of these tomb-fields all belong to the Iron age. The tombs of the earlier ages have no connection with the homesteads of the present people."

How far these tombs extend downwards in date cannot be ascertained without a much more careful examination than they have yet been subjected to. It may safely, however, be assumed that they continued to be used till the conversion of the inhabitants to Christianity, and probably even for some considerable time afterwards, for such a custom is not easily eradicated.

It would be as tedious as unprofitable to attempt to enumerate the various mounds which have been opened, for their contents throw little or no light on our enquiry; and being distributed in cases in the museum, not according to their localities or traditions, but according to their systematic classes, it is almost impossible to restore them now to their places in history.

At Jellinge, however, on the east coast of Jutland, there are two mounds, always known traditionally as those of Gorm the Old and his queen Thyra Danebod—the Beloved. The date of Gorm's death seems now to be accepted as 950 A.D.;[1] but it is not clear whether he erected the tomb himself, or whether it is due to the filial piety of his son Harald Blaatand, or Blue-Tooth, and in which case its date would be 968.[2] Saxo Grammaticus at least tells us that he buried his mother in the tumulus, and then set a whole army of men and oxen at work to remove from the Jutland shore an immense stone— a little rock—and bring it to the place where his mother lay

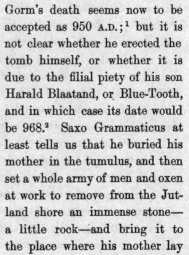

105.   Dragon on King Gorm's Stone, Jellinge.
From 'An. Nord. Oldkund.' xii. 1852.

inhumed.[3] That stone still exists, and has sculptured on one side a dragon, which calls forcibly to our mind that found on Maes-Howe (woodcut No. 85), and on the other side a figure, which is, no doubt, intended to represent Christ on the cross. On the two sides are Runic inscriptions, in which he records his affection for his father and mother and his conversion to the Christian faith.

So far as I can ascertain, the tomb of King Gorm has not yet been opened. That of Thyra was explored many years ago —in 1820 apparently; but no sections or details have been

[1] Engelhardt, 'Catalogue illus.' p. 33. Suhm makes it 991, but this seems more probably to have been the date of the

death of his son Harald Blaatand.
[2] 'Annalen for Nordk. Oldk.' xii. p. 13.
[3] 'Hist. danica,' x. p. 167.

published, so that it is extremely difficult to ascertain even the dimensions. Engelhardt reports the height as 43 feet, and the diameter as 240 feet;[1] Worsaae gives the height as 75 feet, and the diameter as 180 feet, and he is probably correct.[2] But in Denmark anything that cannot be put into a glass case in a museum is so completely rejected as valueless that no one cares to record it. When entered, it was found that it had been plundered probably in the middle ages, and all that remained were the following articles:—A small silver goblet, lined with gold on the inside, and ornamented with interlaced dragons on the exterior; some fibulæ, tortoise-shaped, and ornamented with fantastic heads of animals; some buckle-heads, and other objects of no great value. The chamber in which these objects were found measured 23 feet in length by 8 feet 3 inches in width, and was 5 feet high;[3] the walls and roof, formed of massive slabs of oak, were originally, it appears, hung with tapestries, but these had nearly all perished.

Not only are these monuments of Gorm and Thyra interesting in themselves, and deserving of much more attention than the Danes have hitherto bestowed upon them, but they are most important in their bearing on the general history of monuments of this class. In the first place, their date and destination are fixed beyond dispute, and this being so, the only ground is taken away on which any à priori argument could be based with regard to the age of any mound anterior to the tenth century. As soon as it is realised that sepulchral mounds have been erected in the tenth century, it is impossible to argue that it is unlikely or improbable that Silbury Hill or any other mound in England may not belong to the sixth or any subsequent century down to that time. The argument is, however, even more pertinent with reference to Maes-Howe and other tumuli in the Orkneys. If the Scandinavian kings were buried in "howes" down to the year 1000—I believe they extend much beyond that date—it is almost certain that the Orcadian Jarls were interred in similar mounds down at least to their conversion to Christianity (A.D. 986). Whether

---

[1] 'Guide ill.' p. 33.   [2] 'Primæval Ant. Denmark,' p. 104.
[3] Engelhardt, 'Cat. ill. du Musée,' p. 33.

Maeshowe was erected as a sepulchre for the sons of Ragnar Lothbrok, as John Stuart seems to infer from the inscriptions,[1] or of Havard Earl, as I have above attempted to show, is of little consequence to the general argument. That it was the grave of a Scandinavian Jarl, erected between 800 and 1000 A.D., seems quite certain, and my own impression is that it is almost as certainly the tomb of the individual Jarl to whom I have ventured to ascribe it.

As before mentioned, no argument against these views can be drawn from the fact that Thyra's tomb is lined with slabs of oak, while the chamber at Maes-Howe is formed with stone. The difference of the two localities is sufficient to account for this. Denmark has always been famous for its forests, and especially on the shores of the Baltic, at Jellinge, wood of the noblest dimensions was always available, whereas the stone of the country was hard and intractable. In the Orkneys, on the other hand, there is absolutely no timber of natural growth big enough to afford a good-sized walking-stick, and stone is not only everywhere abundant, but splits easily into slabs, self-faced, and most easily worked, so that stone, and stone only, would be the material employed in the Orkneys for that purpose, as wood would also be the best and most available material in Denmark.

If, before leaving this branch of the subject, we turn back for a few minutes to the Irish monuments, we are now in a position to judge more correctly of the probabilities of the case than we were. Assuming the three-chambered tumulus at New Grange to have been erected between the years 200 and 400, and Maes-Howe and Jellinge between 800 and 1000 A.D., we have a period of from five to six, it may possibly be seven, centuries between these monuments. Is this more than is sufficient to account for the difference between them, or is it too little? It is not easy to give a categorical answer to such a question, but judging from the experience gained from other styles, in different parts of the world, the conclusion generally would be that the time is in excess of what is required. That there was progress, considerable progress indeed, made in the interval between the Irish and Scandinavian monu-

---

[1] 'Proceedings Soc. Ant. Scot.' v. p. 265. If Ragnar was taken prisoner by Ella of Northumberland, it must have been in the latter half of the ninth century. Suhm places his death nearly a century earlier, 794.

ments, cannot be denied, but that it should have required five
centuries to achieve this advance is hardly what would be
expected, and it would be difficult to quote another example of
a progress so slow. Yet it is hardly possible to bring down New
Grange to the age of St. Patrick (A.D. 436), and as difficult to
carry back Maes-Howe beyond Ragnar Lothbrok (794 at the
extreme), and between these dates there are only 358 years; but
we must certainly add something at either one end or the other;
and if we do this, we obtain an amount of progress so slow that it
would be almost unaccountable, but upon the assumption that they
are the works of two different peoples. At the time the sepulchre
on the Boyne was erected, Ireland was energetically and rapidly
progressive, and her arts were more flourishing than might have
been expected from her then state of civilization. When Maes-
howe was erected, the native population was poor and perishing,
and as the lordly Vikings would hardly condescend to act as masons
themselves, they did the best they could with the means at their
disposal. Explain it, however, as we may, it seems impossible to
allow a longer time between the mounds at Jellinge and Stennis and
those on the Boyne than has been accorded above; and as it seems
equally difficult to bring them nearer to one another, the probability seems to be in favour of the dates already assigned to them.

To return, however, from this digression; besides those just mentioned, Denmark possesses a nearly complete series of royal tombs
such as are not to be found in any other country of Europe. Even
Worsaae acknowledges the existence of that of Frode Frodegode,
who lived about the Christian era, of Amlech, near Wexio—
Shakespeare's Hamlet, of Humble, and Hjarne,[1] besides those of
Hildetand, and Gorm and Thyra, already mentioned. If the
Danes would only undertake a systematic examination of these
royal sepulchres, it might settle many of the disputed points of
mediæval archæology. To explore tombs to which no tradition
attaches may add to the treasures of their museums, but can only
by accident elucidate either the history of the country or the
progress of its arts. If ten or twelve tombs with known names
attached to them were opened, one of two things must happen:

---

[1] 'Primæval Ant. of Denmark,' p. 112.

either they will show a succession and a progress relative to the age of their reputed occupants, or no such sequence will be traceable. In the first case the gain to history and archæology would be enormous, and it is an opportunity of settling disputed questions such as no other country affords. If, on the other hand, no such connection can be traced, there is an end of much of the foundations on which the reasoning of the previous pages is based, but in either case such an enquiry could not fail to throw a flood of light on the subject which we were trying to elucidate. The fear is that all have been rifled. The Northmen certainly spared none of the tombs in the countries they conquered, and our experience of Maes-Howe and Thyra's tomb would lead us to fear that after their conversion to Christianity they were as little inclined to spare those of their own ancestors. All they however cared for were the objects composed of precious metals; so enough may still be left for the less avaricious wants of the antiquary.

DOLMENS.

So far as is at present known, there are not any tumuli of importance or any battle-fields marked with great stones in the north of Germany; but the dolmens there are both numerous and interesting, and belong to all the classes found in Scandinavia, and, so far as can be ascertained, are nearly identical in form. Nothing, however, would surprise me less than if it should turn out that both barrows and Bauta stones were common there, especially in the island of Rügen and along the shores of the Baltic as far east as Livonia. The Germans have not yet turned their attention to this class of their antiquities. They have been too busy sublimating their national heroes into gods to think of stones that tell no tales. Whenever they do set to work upon them, they will, no doubt, do it with that thoroughness which is characteristic of all they attempt. But as the investigation will probably have to pass through the solar myth stage of philosophy, it may yet be a long time before their history reaches the regions of practical common sense.

No detailed maps having been published, it is extremely difficult to feel sure of the distribution of these monuments in any part of the northern dolmen region; but the following, which is abstracted from Bonstetten's 'Essai sur les Dolmens,' may convey some general information on the subject, especially when combined with the map (p. 275), which is taken, with very slight modifications, from that which accompanied his work.

According to Bonstetten there are no dolmens in Poland, nor in Posen. They first appear on the Pregel, near Königsberg; but are very rare in Prussia, only two others being known, one at Marienwerder, the other at Konitz. In Silesia there is one at Klein-Raden, near Oppeln; another is found in the district of Liegnitz, and they are very numerous in the Uckermark, Altmark, in Anhalt, and Prussian Saxony, as well as in Pomerania and the island of Rügen. They are still more numerous in Mecklenburg, which is described as peculiarly rich in monuments of this class. Hanover possesses numerous dolmens, except in the south-eastern districts, such as Göttingen, Oberharz, and Hildesheim. To make up for this, however, in the northern districts, Lüneburg, Osnabrück, and Stade, at least two hundred are found. The grand-duchy of Oldenburg contains some of the largest dolmens in Germany; one of these, near Wildesheim, is 23 feet long; another, near Engelmanns-Becke, is surrounded by an enclosure of stones measuring 37 feet by 23, each stone being 10 feet in height, while the cap stone of a third is 20 feet by 10. In Brunswick there were several near Helmstädt, but they are now destroyed. In Saxony some rare examples are found as far south as the Erzgebirge, and two were recently destroyed in the environs of Dresden. Keeping along the northern line, we find them in the three northern provinces of Holland, Groningen, Ober-Yssel, and especially in Drenthe, where they exist in great numbers, but none to the southward of these provinces, and nowhere do they seem to touch the Rhine or its bordering lands; but a few are found in the grand-duchy of Luxembourg as in a sort of oasis, halfway between the southern or French dolmen region and that of northern Germany.

From the North German districts they extend through Holstein and Schleswig into Jutland and the Danish isles, but are most numerous on the eastern or Baltic side of the Cimbrian peninsula, and they are also very frequent in the south of Sweden and the adjacent islands. Dolmens properly so called are not known in

Norway, but, as above mentioned, cairns and monuments of that class, are not wanting there.

The value of this distribution will be more easily appreciated when we have ascertained the limits of the French field, but meanwhile it may be convenient to remark that, unless the dolmens can be traced very much further eastward, there is a tremendous gulf before we reach the nearest outlyers of the eastern dolmen field. There is a smaller, but very distinct, gap in the country occupied by the Belgæ, between it and the French field, and another, but practically very much smaller one, between it and the British isles. This is a gap because the intervening space is occupied by the sea; but as it is evident from the distribution of all the northern dolmens in the proximity to the shores and in the islands that the people who erected them were a seafaring people, and as we know that they possessed vessels capable of navigating these seas, it is practically no gap at all. We know historically how many Jutes, Angles, Frisians, and people of similar origin, under the generic name of Saxons, flocked to our shores in the early centuries of the Christian era, and afterwards what an important part the Danes and Northmen played in our history, and what numbers of them landed and settled in Great Britain, either as colonists or conquerors, at different epochs, down to at least the eleventh century. If, therefore, we admit the dolmens to be historic, or, in other words, that the erection of megalithic monuments was practised during the first ten centuries after the Christian era, we have no difficulty in understanding where our examples came from, or to whom they are due. If, on the other hand, we assume that they are prehistoric, we are entirely at sea regarding them or their connection with those on the continent. The only continental people we know of who settled in Britain before the Roman times were the Belgæ, and they are the only people between the Pillars of Hercules and the Gulf of Riga who, having a sea-board, have also no dolmens or megalithic remains of any sort. All the others have them more or less, but the Northern nations did not, so far as we know, colonise this country before the Christian era.

As all the Northern antiquaries have made up their minds

that these dolmens generally belong to the mythic period of the Stone age, and that only a few of them extend down to the semi-historic age of bronze, it is in vain to expect that they would gather any traditions or record any names that might connect them with persons known in history. We are, therefore, wholly without assistance from history or tradition to guide us either in classifying them or in any attempt to ascertain their age, while the indications which enable us to connect them with our own, or with one another, are few and far between.

Among the few that give any sure indications of their age, one of the most interesting is at Herrestrup, in Zeeland, which has recently been disinterred from the tumulus that once covered

106.   Dolmen at Herrestrup.

it.[1] On it are engraved some half-dozen representations of ships, such as the Vikings were in the habit of drawing, and which are found in great quantities on the west coast of Gottenburg.[2] According to the best authorities, these representations range from about A.D. 500 to 900,[3] and some may perhaps be more modern. Those in this dolmen do not appear to be either among the most ancient or the most modern, and if we fix on the eighth century as their date, we shall not be very far wrong. That they are also coeval with the monument seems perfectly

---

[1] 'Annalen for Nord. Aldk.' vi. pl. x.
[2] Holmberg, 'Scandinavien Hallristingar,' p. 3.
[3] *Ibid.* p. 21. 'Soc. des Ant. du Nord,' ii. pp. 140 *et seqq.*

certain. We cannot fancy any Viking engraving these on a deserted dolmen, say even 100 years old, and then covering it up with a tumulus, as this one was till recently. Had it never been covered up, any hypothesis might be proposed, but the mound settles that point. Besides the ships, however, there are an almost equal number of small circles with crosses in them, on the cap stone. Whether these are intended to represent chariot-wheels, or some other object, is not clear, but if we turn back to woodcut No. 41, representing the side-stone of the dolmen at Aspatria, we find the identical object represented there, and in such a manner that, making allowance for the difference of style in the century that has elapsed between the execution of the two engravings, they must be assumed to be identical. No engravings—so far as I know—have been published of the objects found in this Danish dolmen, but in the English one, as already mentioned, the objects found belonged to the most modern Iron age; such things, in fact, as will perfectly agree with the date of the eighth century. Among them, as will be recollected, was the snaffle-bit, so like, though certainly more modern than, Stukeley's bit found in Silbury Hill. We have thus three tumuli which from their engravings or their contents confirm one another to a most satisfactory extent, and render the dates above assigned to them, to say the least of it, very probable. If the date thus obtained for the Aspatria monument is accepted, it is further interesting as giving that of those mysterious concentric circles, with a line passing through them from the centre, which have been found in such numbers on the rocks in the north of England and in Scotland.[1] These are, so far as I know, the only examples of these circles which were buried, and were consequently associated with other objects which assist in fixing their age.

As before hinted, many of the monuments engraved by Madsen [2] are so extremely like those in the field of Northern Moytura that it is almost impossible to believe that they were erected by a different race of people, or at any great distance of time. The one, for instance, at Halskov is so like the dolmen and circle

---

[1] Sir James Simpson, appendix, vol. vi. 'Proc. Soc. Ant. of Scotland,' *passim.*
[2] Madsen, 'Antiquités préhistoriques du Danemark,' 1869.

represented in woodcut No. 61 that the one might almost pass for the other, were it not that the photograph is taken from the wrong side, to bring out the resemblance, as it is seen on the spot, while in others the resemblance is as great, or even greater. It is very unsatisfactory, however, picking these points of similarity from books, some of the engravings in which are from imperfect drawings. In others, artistic effect has been more aimed at than truth, and some are taken from photographs, which, though they give a truthful, generally give an unintelligent representation of the object. It is only by personal familiarity that all the facts

107.   Dolmen at Halskov. From a drawing by Madsen.

can be verified and pitfalls avoided. But it is always useful to turn attention to any forms that may seem novel, and explain peculiarities in others which but for such means of comparison would remain unnoticed. Here, for instance, is one from Sjöborg, which resembles the Countless Stones at Aylesford, as drawn by Dr. Stukeley (woodcut No. 27). It is found at a place called Oroust, in Böhuslan,[1] and stands on a low mound encircled by twenty large stones at its base. The chamber is low, and semi-circular in form, and in front of it stands what the Germans call a sentinel stone. No date is given to this monument by Sjöborg, for he was so far indoctrinated in modern theories that he

---

[1] 'Samlingar,' i. pl. iii. fig. 6.

believed all dolmens to be prehistoric, though all the circles and
Bauta stones marking battle-fields were to him as essentially
historic as any monuments in his country. From its appearance,
the dolmen at Oroust may be of the same age as the Countless

108.   Dolmen at Oroust. From Sjöborg.

Stones at Aylesford, and if other monuments in the two countries
could be compared with anything like precision, their forms and
traditions might mutually throw great light on their real histories.

It is not only, however, from the analogies with similar monuments in this country, or from their bearing on their history, that
the Scandinavian dolmens are interesting to us. They have forms
and peculiarities of their own which are well worth studying.
If materials existed for mastering these differences, their aggre-
gate would make up a sum which would enable us to separate
the Scandinavian group from the British, as we can our own from
the French, and the French from that of Northern Germany. A
great deal more must, however, be published, and in a more accurate form, before this can be done; but, whenever it is possible,
it promises to afford most satisfactory results to ethnographical
science. The problem is similar to that which was known to
exist in reference to pointed Gothic architecture. That is now
admitted to be a Celtic-French invention, but it was adopted by
the Spaniards and Italians on the one hand, and by the Germans
and ourselves on the other; although always with a difference.
No antiquary would now for an instant hesitate in discriminating
between an Italian and a German or between a Spanish and an
English example, though the difference is so small that it can
hardly be expressed in words, and must be carefully represented
in order to be perceived. In like manner, the rude-stone style

of art seems to have been invented by some pre-Celtic people, but to have been adopted by Celts, by Scandinavian, by British, and Iberian races—perhaps not always pure in their own countries, but always with considerable differences, which, when perceived and classified, will enable us to distinguish between the works of the several races as clearly as we can between the mediæval styles that superseded them.

Among these peculiarities, the most easily recognised are the square or oblong enclosures which surround tumuli, and, some-times, one, at others two, or even three free-standing dolmens. In order to make the point clear, I have quoted a diagram from Sjöborg, though it is almost the only instance in this work in

109.   Diagram from Sjöborg, pl. i. fig. A.

which a woodcut does not represent a really existing object. I have no doubt, however, that it is correct, as old Olaus Wormius represents one of two similar ones which in his day existed near Roeskilde. Both had enclosures 50 paces square, enclosing one tumulus with a circle of stones round its base, another halfway up, and, the text says, an altar-dolmen on the top, though the woodcut does not show it. The other, on the road to Birck, in Zeeland, enclosed three tumuli in juxtaposition, the one in the centre similar to that just described, and with a dolmen on its summit; two smaller mounds are represented in juxtaposition on either side but with only a circle of stones round their base.[1] Other varieties

---

[1] Olaus Wormius, 'Danica Monumenta,' pp. 8 and 35.

no doubt exist, but modern antiquaries have not favoured us with
any drawings of them.   From the diagram and description it will
be perceived that in so far as the mound itself is concerned these
Danish tumuli are identical with those already quoted as existing
in Auvergne (woodcut No. 8), but so far as I know, the square enclosure does not exist in France, nor does it in this country.   These
square enclosures seem, however, to belong to a very modern date,
and the stones, consequently, are small, and may therefore have
been removed, which could easily be done; but still there seems
little doubt that many of them may still remain, and could be
found if looked for.

One of the most striking examples I know of, an oblong
rectangular enclosure, enclosing a single free-standing dolmen, is
that near Lüneburg, figured by Bonstetten [1] (woodcut No. 110); he

110.   Dolmen near Lüneburg.   From Bonstetten.

seldom, however, indulges in dimensions, and being perfectly
convinced that all are prehistoric, he never speculates as to dates,
nor condescends to notice traditions.   What we know of it is
therefore confined to the representation, which after all may be
taken from some other work, as he rarely favours us with references.   Two others are represented by von Estorff as existing near
Uelzen, in Hanover.[2]

A good example of two dolmens in a rectangular enclosure is
that at Valdbygaards, near Soröe, in Zeeland.   Here the enclosure is about 70 feet in one direction by 20 feet in the other
—outside measurement.   In this instance, the enclosing stones
are smaller in proportion to the dolmens than is usually the case.
On the same plate, Madsen represents a single dolmen in a much
squarer enclosure.[3]   It, like that at Halskov (woodcut No. 107),
is represented as standing on a knoll, but whether dolmens stand so

---

[1] 'Essai sur les Dolmens,' p. 9.
[2] 'Heidenische Alterthümer von Uelzen,' Hanover, 1846.
[3] Madsen, 'Antiquités préhist.' pl. 8.

or on the flat, like that at Valdbygaards, it is quite certain they never were enclosed in tumuli, but always stood free, as they now do.

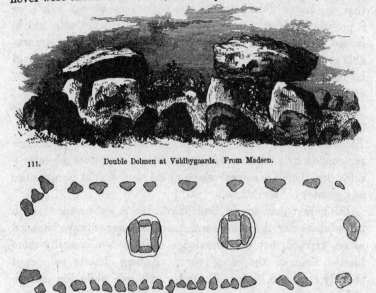

111.   Double Dolmen at Valdbygaards. From Madsen.

112.   Plan of Double Dolmen at Valdbygaards.

For three dolmens in one square enclosure we are obliged to go back to old Keysler, though, in this case, the engraving is so good that there can be very little doubt of its correctness.[1] It is situated near Hö-bisch, in Mark Brandenburg, consists of an outer enclosure

113.   Triple Dolmen, Höbisch. From Keysler.

of forty-four stones, and is 118 paces in circuit, and in the

---

[1] 'Antiquitates Septentrionales,' pp. 320 and 519, pl. xvii.

middle are twelve stones, of which six bear three large stones, placed transversely upon them. It is very much to be regretted that no better illustration of this curious monument exists, as it probably very closely resembles those in Drenthe, with which, indeed, he compares it; and as these form one of the most remarkable groups of this class of monuments on the continent, it would be most desirable to trace their connection with others farther east.

A similar monument to that at Höbisch is figured by Sjöborg (vol. i. pl. 6), but without the enclosure; and a third, Oroust, in Böhuslan (pl. 3); but in this instance the three long stones are surrounded by a circular enclosure with two sentinel stones outside; and there are several others which show similar peculiarities in a greater or less degree.

The buried dolmens in Scandinavia are, in some respects, even more interesting than those which are, and were always intended to be, exposed, but our knowledge of them is necessarily more limited than of the other class. Sjöborg deserts us almost entirely here, and Madsen illustrates only two, while the modern antiquaries have been more anxious to secure and classify their contents than to illustrate the chambers from which they were obtained. As a rule, they may be older than the free-standing examples, but they do not look old, though, as metal has not generally been found in them, it is assumed they all belong to the Stone age. One example will suffice to display the general features of the older group of this class of monuments. The next two woodcuts present an internal view and plan of one near Uby, in the district of Holbak, in Zeeland. It was opened in 1845, and measured then 13 feet in height, and had a circumference of upwards of 300 feet. The chamber measures 13 feet by 8 feet, and is walled in by nine great stones, which have been split or hewn, so as to obtain a flat surface towards the interior, and the interstices are filled in with smaller stones very neatly fitted. The entrance gallery is 20 feet in length, and is closed, or capable of being so, by two doors. From the disposition of the entrance it certainly does not appear that it was intended to be hid. The whole appearance is that of a dignified approach to the tomb. Had it been meant to be closed, the chamber would, no doubt, have been in the centre of the tumulus, instead of being near one side, as it is. The other monument of the same class,

114. View of Interior of Chamber at Uby. From Madsen.

illustrated by Madsen,[1] is near Smidstrup, in the district of Fredericksborg. It is very similar in dimensions and details, but has the peculiarity of having two chambers placed side by side, with two separate entrances, and the chambers affect a curve more

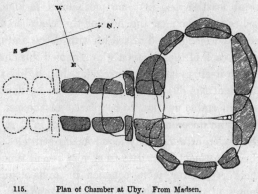

115. Plan of Chamber at Uby. From Madsen.

perfectly elliptical than is attained in that at Uby.

---

[1] Madsen, plates 13 and 14.

These last examples from Madsen's work are further interesting to us as illustrating the difference between dolmens or chambers always intended to be buried in tumuli and those which were always meant to be exposed. In the chambers at Uby and Smidstrup the stones are placed so closely together that very little packing between them was sufficient to keep out the earth, and the passages to them and other arrangements all indicate their original destination. The case, however, is widely different with the dolmens at Halskov and Valdbygaards, or those at Lüneburg or Höbisch, which evidently are now on their mounds as originally designed. With a very little study it seems easy to detect the original intentions in all these monuments; but there is this further difference. None of those intended to be exposed were ever buried, while many which were meant to have been covered up never received their intended envelope.

A monument having a considerable affinity to the two last quoted exists, or perhaps rather existed, at Axevalla, in Westergothland. It was opened apparently in 1805, and the representations are taken from drawings then made by a Captain Lindgren, who superintended the excavation by the king's command. It consists of one apartment 24 feet long by 8 feet wide and 9 feet high. The sides and roof are composed of slabs of red granite, which, if the plates are to be depended upon, were hewn or at least shaped in some mechanical fashion. Instead of the bodies being laid on the floor of the chamber as was usually the case, and being found mixed up with *débris* and utensils of various kinds, each of the nineteen who occupied this chamber had a little cist to itself, so small and irregular-shaped, like those at Rose Hill (woodcut No. 39), that the body had to be doubled up, in a most uncomfortable position, to be placed in the cist. This was by no means an uncommon mode of interment in those early ages, but if the skeletons were really found in the attitudes here represented, their interment must date from very recent times indeed. I know there is nothing more common in archæological books than to represent skeletons sitting in most free and easy attitudes in their boxes.[1] But if all the flesh had disappeared as completely as these

---

[1] Bateman, ' Ten Years' Diggings,' p. 23. Lewellyn Jowett, ' Grave Mounds,' pp. 14 and 15, &c.

drawings represent, the integuments must have gone also, and if
they were either rotted or reduced to dust, the skeleton must have
collapsed and been found in a heap on the floor. It would be
interesting to know how long, either in very dry or in moist places,
the integuments would last so as to prevent this collapse before
they were disturbed.   No qualified person has yet given an opinion
on such a subject, but the time could hardly extend to many

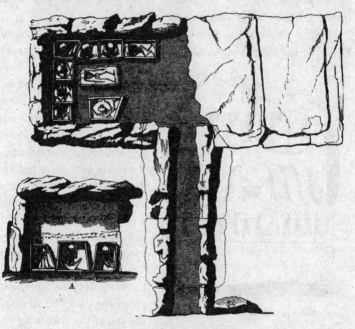

116.   Dolmen at Axevalla. From Sjöborg.

centuries.   But does the case really exist? are not all these queer
skeletons merely the imaginings of enthusiastic antiquaries?

Be this as it may, these elliptical and long rectangular dolmens,
with their arrangement of cists and entrances in the centre of the
longer side, seem so distinguished from those generally found in
other countries as to mark another province. It seems scarcely
open to doubt that the oval forms are the older, though what their
age may be is not so clear, nor have any descriptions of their
contents been published which would enable us to form distinct

opinion on the subject. Flint implements have been found in them, but, so far as I can gather, no bronze. According to the Danish system, therefore, they are all before the time of Solomon or the siege of Troy. It may be so, but I doubt it exceedingly. Those who excavated the Axevalla tomb reported that something like an inscription was found on one of the walls (woodcut No. 116, fig. A); but whether it was an inscription or a natural formation is by no means clear—at all events, as we have no copy of it, it hardly helps us in arriving at a date.

In some respects, the Axevalla tomb resembles the grave near Kivik, in the district of Cimbrisham, near the southern extremity

117. Head-stone of Kivik Grave. From Sjöborg.

of Sweden. This is the most celebrated of Swedish graves. It is mentioned as perfect by Linnæus in 1749, but was shortly afterwards opened, and drawings and illustrations of it have from time to time been published since, and given rise to the usual diversity of opinion. Suhm and Sjöborg seem to agree in connecting it with a battle fought in that neighbourhood by Ragnar Lothbrok, about the year 750, in which the son of the then king was slain.[1] This date appears probable; had it been later, there would almost certainly have been found Runes on some of its stones; if earlier, the representations of the human figure would hardly have been so perfect. One stone found elsewhere (woodcut No. 117),[2] which seems to have been its head-stone, has a curious resemblance to the head-stone of the Dol ar Marchant, at Locmariaker, illustrated farther on. The likeness may be accidental, but, as in all these cases, it is difficult to believe that five or six centuries can have elapsed between

---

[1] Sjöborg, *loc. sup. cit.*   [2] Now destroyed. Sjöborg, iii. pl. 10, p. 143.

two monuments which show so little progress; for whether this stone belonged to the Kivik grave or not, it certainly is of the same age and design, some of the figures on it being identical with those found in the tomb, and that can hardly be older than the date above quoted. Another of the stones of this tomb has two of those circles enclosing crosses which are seen on the Herrestrup dolmen and the Aspatria stone, all of which probably belong to the eighth century. The tomb itself is not remarkable for its dimensions, being only 14 feet long by 3 feet wide, and almost 4 feet in height. It is much too large, however, for any single warrior's grave, but we are not told whether it was occupied by a number of small cists like that at Axevalla. The probability, however, is that this was the case, but 120 years ago men were not accurate observers of antiquarian phenomena.

Besides these, there are two other forms of tombs which, so far as is yet known, are quite peculiar to the Scandinavian province. The first of these are the so-called ship graves, from their form. They consist of two segments of a circle joined together at the ends, so as to represent the deck of a vessel, and are of all sizes, from 20 or 30 feet to 200 or 300 feet. They are generally found on the sea-shore, and it seems hardly to be doubted that they mark the graves of Vikings.

The other form is quite as peculiar, but more difficult to explain. It is marked by a range of stones forming an equilateral triangle, sometimes straight-lined, but as frequently the lines curve inwards so as to restrict the internal space considerably. It is by no means clear what suggested this form, or what it was intended to represent. It is, however, found on battle-fields (woodcut No. 118), and solitary examples are frequent in Sjöborg's plates, sometimes with a Bauta stone in the centre. The one hypothesis that seems to account for this form, is that it is the "Cuneatus ordo" of Olaus Magnus, and that it marked a spot where a combined phalanx of horse and foot fought and conquered.[1] The probability is that where single it marks the grave of a particular rank either in the army or in civil life.

All these forms are shown in the next woodcut, from a group

---

[1] *Vide ante*, foot-note, p. 15.

found in the peninsula of Hjortehammer, in Bleking, in the south
of Sweden, but others are found in the island at Amrom, and in
many other places.[1] It has been disputed whether these represent battle-fields or are the ordinary graves of the inhabitants of
the district in which they are found. That those found on the
shore at Freyrsö (woodcut No. 104) mark the graves of those who

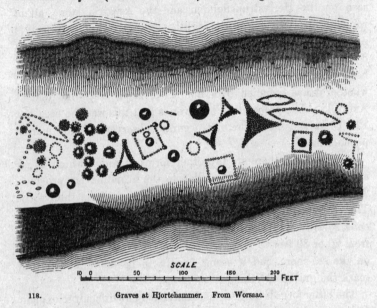

118.   Graves at Hjortehammer. From Worsaae.

fell in Blodoxe's battle there in the tenth century seems quite
certain, but whether this was always the case may be open to
doubt; but certainly a sandy peninsula, like that of Hjortehammer,
seems a most unlikely place for peaceful men to bury their dead,
especially at a time when not one-tenth part of the land around
could have been under cultivation.

For our present purposes it is of no great consequence which
opinion prevails, as these forms have no bearing on those of other
countries, especially as their date does not seem to be doubted.
Worsaae places them all between the years 700 and 1000,[2] or in

---

[1] The woodcut is reduced from a plate
in Worsaae's 'Alterthumskunde Scandi-
naviens,' but both it and the Amrom
group are found in the 'English Archæological Journal,' xxiii. p. 187.
[2] 'Archæol. Journal,' loc. sit. p. 185.

the second and latest Iron age, and as no one seems to dispute this, it may be accepted as an established fact. Their peculiarities of form, and the smallness of the stones of which most of them are composed, are such that the date here ascribed to them does not necessarily bring down that of the true megalithic remains to anything like the same age. It takes away, however, all improbability from the assertion that these may be much more modern than was supposed, and this much is certain that there was no break between the great English and Irish circles and the Viking graves; or, in other words, men did not cease to mark their sepulchres with circles and cairns, and then after a lapse of centuries revive the custom, and begin it again on a smaller scale. There may be a descent, but there was no solution of continuity, and any one can consequently form an idea how long a time must have elapsed before the great Wiltshire circles could have degenerated into those of Hjortehammer.

There is one other group of monuments it seems worth while to illustrate before leaving this branch of the subject. They are found in the extreme east of the province, on the banks of the Dwina, in Livonia. At a place called Aschenrade, about fifty miles as the crow flies from Riga, is a group shown in the accom-

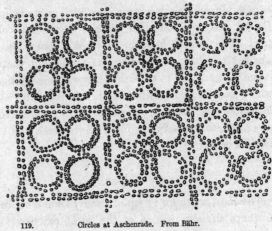

119.   Circles at Aschenrade. From Bähr.

panying woodcut.[1] The arrangement is unusual in Europe, but is met with in Algeria, and seems to be only such a combination

---

[1] Bähr, 'Die Gräber der Liven,' Dresden, 1850, pl. i. Unfortunately, as is too often the case, no scale is engraved on the plate, and no dimensions are mentioned in the text.

of the square enclosures of Scandinavia as we would expect to find
in a cemetery, as contradistinguished from a battle-field.

In these graves was found enormous wealth of bronze and other
metal and personal ornaments, many of which are engraved in Professor Bähr's book.   They resemble in many respects the celebrated
"find" at Hallstadt, in the Salzkammergut; [1] but mixed with these
Livonian treasures were great numbers of coins and implements
of iron of very modern form.   The coins are classified as follows:—

German coins, dating from	A.D. 936	to 1040.
Anglo-Saxon coins, dating from	„ 991	„ 1036.
Byzantine coins, dating from	„ 911	„ 1025.
Arabic or Kufic coins, dating from.. ..	„ 906	„ 999.

It is curious that the Eastern coins should be so much earlier than
the others, but they are only five in number, and may have been
preserved as curiosities.   The dates of the others prove, at all
events, that some of these tombs are not of earlier date than 1040,
and all, probably, are included in the century which preceded
that epoch.

Besides these, however, there are tumuli at a place called
Segewolde, and circles, sometimes with a stone in the centre, at
Bajard, and no doubt other remains of the same class in the district.   The purpose, however, of the only book I know on the subject
was not to illustrate the forms of tombs, but that of the objects
found in them, and to trace the ethnographic relations of the people
who possessed them with the other tribes who at various times
inhabited that district.   The dates of the whole, according to their
describer, may safely be included between the eighth and the
twelfth century.[2]

DRENTHE.

The most southern group of these monuments belonging to the
northern division is one of the most extensive, though unfortunately one of the least known.   It is situated almost exclusively
in the province of Drenthe, in North Holland, where the Hunebeds—giants' beds or graves, as they are locally called—are
spread over an area extending some twenty miles north and south,

---

[1] Not yet published, so far as I know.   [2] 'Die Gräber der Liven,' p. 51.

and probably ten or twelve miles in the opposite direction. This tract of country is a bare open heath, which even now is only partially cultivated, or indeed capable of cultivation, and at no time could have supported a population at all in proportion to so extensive a group of monuments.

As long ago as 1720, Keysler drew attention to them, and gave a representation of one in order to show its similarity to Stonehenge.[1] The engraving, however, is so defective that it is impossible to make out what it represents, and as no dimensions or statistics are given, it adds very little to our knowledge. A short paper on the subject appeared in the 'Journal of the Archæological Association' in 1870, but unfortunately without any illustrations,[2] and we are consequently dependent for our knowledge of them almost entirely to a work published at Utrecht in 1848, by the late Dr. Janssen, keeper of the antiquities in the museum at Leyden. This work is in many respects most painstaking and satisfactory; but, though it is hardly correct to say it, is without illustrations, the Hunebeds are represented by conventional symbols, which no one would guess were intended for buildings of any sort without a most careful study of the book. I have ventured to try to translate one of these into ordinary forms, in woodcut No. 120, but without at all guaranteeing its correctness. It is, however, sufficiently accurate to explain the general nature of the monuments.

Within the area above described, Janssen measured and described fifty-one Hunebeds still existing, and they were probably at one time much more numerous, as he regrets the loss of four which he remembers in his youth; and several others have been very much ruined in very recent times. This, fortunately, is not likely to happen again, as, with a liberality and intelligence not shown by any other government in Europe, the Dutch have purchased the Hunebeds and the ground on which they stand, with a right of way to the nearest road, so that, so far as possible, they will be protected from future depredations.

---

[1] 'Ant. Septent.' p. 5, pl. ii.

[2] It is by no means clear whether Mr. Sadler, who is the author of this paper, ever visited the spot, or compiled his information from Janssen's book, which, however, he never mentions. Be this as it may, it is the best paper I know of on the subject, and well worthy of perusal.

Of these fifty-one monuments only one is a dolmen, in the sense in which we usually understand it, meaning thereby a single cap stone, supported by three, or, as in this instance, by four uprights. This one is near Exlo, and is one of the few that formed a chamber in a tumulus. A few have three cap stones, and from that number they range up to ten or twelve, with at least double that number of supports. They are all, in fact, of the class which the French call "allées couvertes," or "grottes des fées;" Calliagh Birra's house (woodcut No. 80) and the dolmens at Glen Columbkill are of the same class. But the Drenthe dolmens have one peculiarity not found either in France or Ireland: that they are all closed at both ends, and the entrance, where there is one, is always on the longer side. In this respect they more resemble the Scandinavian examples, such as the tomb at Axevalla (woodcut No. 116), or that at Uby (woodcut No. 114).

The annexed attempted restoration of one near Emmen will give a fair idea of their general arrangements. It is 49 feet long over all, and inter-

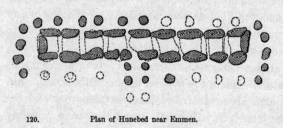

120.   Plan of Hunebed near Emmen.

nally from 4 to 6 feet in width. It is roofed with nine or ten stones, some of considerable dimensions. Some of these Hunebeds have a range of stones round them, not arranged in a circle or oval form, but, as in this instance, following the lines of the central chamber. This is the case with another near the same place, which is 125 feet in length over all. When closely examined, however, it does not seem to be one Hunebed, but three ranging in a straight line, with a small space between each. Two have five and one six cap stones. As a rule, each cap stone stands on two uprights, and though frequently they touch one another, as often they form really independent trilithons. It was no doubt this fact that induced Keysler to compare these monuments with Stonehenge, though in fact no two sets of rude-stone monuments could well be more dis-

similar either in arrangement or construction. As will be seen
from the annexed view of one near Ballo [1] (woodcut No. 121),
they are formed of unshaped granite boulders. Sometimes, it
may be, artificially split, but certainly untouched by the chisel.

121.   Dolmen at Ballo. From a Photograph.

All that has apparently been done has been to select those most
appropriate in form for the purposes to which they were to be
applied, and then rudely to heap them one upon the other, but
in such a manner as to leave wide gaps everywhere between the
stones composing the structure.

The first question that arises with regard to these Hunebeds
is, were they originally covered with earth or not? That some
of the smaller ones were and are is clear enough, and some of
medium size are still partially so; but the largest, and many
of the smaller, do not show a vestige of any such covering;
and it seems impossible to believe that on a tract of wretched
barren heath, where the fee-simple of the land is not now worth
ten shillings an acre, any one could, at any time, have taken
the trouble to dig down and cart away such enormous mounds
as would have been required to cover these monuments. It seems
here clearer than almost anywhere else that, even if it had been
intended to cover them, that intention, in more than half the
cases, was never carried into effect.

---

[1] The woodcut is from a photograph
kindly lent me by Mr. Franks. It is
sufficient to show the nature of the construction, but the camera is a singularly unintelligent interpreter of plan
or arrangements.

It may be taken for granted that these Hunebeds were at one time much more numerous in Drenthe than they now are, but it is a much more difficult point to ascertain whether they extended into the neighbouring provinces or not. One is found in Groningen, and one in Friesland, and none elsewhere. It may, of course, be that in these more fertile and thickly inhabited districts they have been utilised, or removed as incumbrances from the soil, while in Drenthe their component parts were of no value, and they are useful as sheep-pens and pigstyes; and to these uses they seem to have been freely applied. It may be, also, that there are no granite boulders in the neighbouring provinces, and that they are common in Drenthe. There certainly seem to be none in Guelderland, a country in which we would expect to find monuments of this class, as it is the natural line of connection with the German dolmen region; and unless it is that there were no materials handy for their construction, it is difficult to understand their absence.

As these Hunebeds have been open and exposed for centuries at least—if they were not so originally—and have been used by the peasantry for every kind of purpose, it is in vain to expect that anything will now be found in them which can throw much light on their age or use. We can only hope that an untouched or only partially plundered example may be found in some of the numerous tumuli which still exist all over the country. I confess I do not feel sanguine that this will be the case. I would hope more from the digging up of the floor of those which are known, and a careful collection of any fragments of pottery and other objects which may be found in them. Nothing of any intrinsic value will be found, of course; but what is perfectly worthless for any other purpose may be most important in an antiquarian sense. Judging them from a general abstract point of view, they do not seem of high antiquity, and may range from the Christian era down to the time when the people of this country were converted to Christianity, whenever that may have been. This, however, is only inferred from their similarity to other monuments mentioned in the preceding pages, not from any special evidence gathered from themselves or from any local tradition bearing on their antiquity.

When we have examined the megalithic remains of Brittany and of the north of France, we shall be in a better position than we now are to appreciate the importance of the gap that exists between the French and Scandinavian provinces; but in the meanwhile it may be convenient to remark even here that it hardly seems doubtful that the Hunebeds of Drenthe and the Grottes des fées of Brittany are expressions of the same feeling, and, generally, that the megalithic remains of the southern and northern divisions of the western parts of the European continent are the works of similar if not identical races, applied to the same uses, and probably are of about the same age.

These two provinces are now separated by the Rhine valley. It is probably not too broad an assertion to say there are no true Rude-Stone Monuments in the valleys of the Rhine or Scheldt,[1] or of any of their tributaries, or, in fact, in any of the countries inhabited by the Germans and Belgæ. The dolmen-building races were, in fact, cut in two by the last-named race on their way to colonise Britain. When that took place, we have no exact means of knowing. According to Cæsar, shortly before his time, Divitiacus ruled over the Belgæ of Gaul and Britain as one province;[2] and the inference from all we know—it is very little—is that the Belgian immigration to this island was of recent date at that time. Whether it was one thousand or ten thousand years, the fact that interests us here is that it took place before the age of the rude-stone monuments. If we admit that the peoples who, from Cadiz to the Cimbric Chersonese, erected these dolmens were one race—or, at least, had one religion—and were actuated by one set of motives in their respect for the dead, it seems impossible to escape from the conclusion that, whether they came direct from the east, or migrated from the south northward, or in the opposite direction, they at one time formed a continuous community of nations all along the western shores of Europe. They were cut across only in one place—between Drenthe and Normandy—and that by a comparatively modern people, the Belgæ. If this is so, the separation took

---

[1] There are several dolmens, as before stated, in rugged mountainous parts of Luxemburg, but they seem to belong to the old races that in those corners were not swept away by the Belgian current.

[2] Cæsar, 'Bell. Gall.' ii. p. 4.

place in the pre-dolmen period, whenever that may have been. If the original races in Belgium had been in the habit of erecting dolmens before they were dispossessed by the intruders, we should find remains at least of them there now, as we do both north and south of that district. As the case now stands, the conclusion seems inevitable that it was after their separation that the northern and southern families, though no longer in contact, adopted, each in its own peculiar fashion, those more permanent and megalithic forms which contact with a higher civilization taught them to aspire to, without abandoning the distinctions which separated them from the more progressive Celts and the thoroughly civilized Romans.

NOTE.

The map opposite is compiled partly from the two by M. Bertrand, mentioned p. 326, and partly from one which accompanies Baron de Bonstetten's 'Essai sur les Dolmens,' 1864. It has been corrected, in so far as the scale would allow, from the information since accumulated; and may be considered as representing fairly our knowledge of the distribution of dolmens at the present day. Till, however, the Governments of this country and of Denmark condescend to take up the subject, such a map must necessarily remain imperfect in its most vital parts.

CHAPTER VIII.

FRANCE.

It is only in very recent times that the French have turned their attention to the study of their Rude-Stone Monuments; but since they have done so, it has been in so systematic and scientific a manner that, had it been continued a few years longer, little would have been left to be desired by the students of that class of antiquities in France. War and revolution, however, intervened just as the results of these labours were about to be given to the world, and how long we may now have to wait for them, no one can tell. The Musée de St.-Germain was far from being complete in July last, and only the first parts of the great ' Dictionnaire des Antiquités celtiques ' had been published at that time. We can now hardly hope that the necessary expenditure will be continued which is indispensable to complete the former, and it is difficult to foresee in what manner the materials collected for the dictionary can now be utilised.

Even when much further advanced towards completion, it is hardly to be expected that the museums of St.-Germain and Vannes can rival the royal collections at Copenhagen; and if the French had confined themselves only to collecting, they would not have advanced our knowledge very much; but, while doing this, they have also gathered statistical information, and have been mapping and describing, so that our knowledge of their monuments is much more complete than of those of the Danes. To borrow a simile from kindred sciences, it is as if the Danes had attended exclusively to the mineralogy of the subject: collecting specimens from all parts, and arranging them according to their similarities or affinities, wholly irrespective of the localities from which they came. The French, on the other hand, have founded a science similar to that of geology on their knowledge of the minerals; they have carefully noted the distribution of the various classes of monuments, and, so far as possible, ascertained their relative superposition. The first is, no doubt, a most useful process, and one that must to a certain extent precede the other; but unless we map the various rocks on the surface and ascertain their stratification, it hardly helps us in studying the formation or history of our globe.

In 1864 M. Bertrand published in the ' Revue archéologique ' a small map of France, showing the distribution of dolmens as then known; and three years afterwards another, on a much larger scale, intended to accompany the ' Dictionnaire des Antiquités celtiques,' and containing all that was then known. Were a second edition of this map published now, it would, no doubt, be much more full and complete; but the main outlines must still be the same, and are sufficient for our present purposes. From these maps and the text which accompanies them we learn that the greater number of the rude-stone monuments in France are arranged at no great distance on either side of a straight line drawn from the shores of the Mediterranean, somewhere about Montpellier, to Morlaix, in Brittany. There are none east of the Rhone, none south of the Garonne, till we come to the Pyrenees, and so few north of the basin or valley of the Seine that they may be considered as wanderers.

Referring to the table at the end of this chapter, which is compiled from that of 1864, we find that thirty departments contain more than ten monuments. Thirty others, according to M. Bertrand, contain from one to eight or nine; and the remaining twenty-nine either contain none at all or these so insignificant as hardly to deserve attention.

From this table we learn, at least approximately, several facts of considerable interest to our investigation. The first is that, of the three divisions into which Cæsar divides Gaul, the northern in his day belonged to a race who who had no stone monuments. There are none in Belgium proper, and so few in French Flanders, or indeed in any part of Gallia Belgica, that we may safely assert that the Belgæ were not dolmen-builders. In the next place, I cannot help agreeing with M. Bertrand in his conclusion that the Celts properly so called have as little claim to the monuments as the Belgæ.[1] We know something of the provinces occupied by

---

[1] ' Revue archéologique,' August, 1864, 148 *et seqq.*

the Celts six hundred years before Christ from Livy's [1] description of the tribes who, under Bellevesus, invaded Italy. Their capital was Bruges, and they occupied the departments immediately around that city; but they had not then penetrated into Brittany, nor north of the Seine, nor into any part of Aquitania.[2] But they occupied the whole of the east of Gaul up, apparently, to the Rhine and the country on the east bank of the Rhone. According to the French statistics, there are 140,000 barrows or tumuli in the departments of the Côte-d'Or, Vosges, Haut-Rhin, Bas-Rhin, Doubs, Jura, and Ain, but not one single dolmen;[3] and there are none to the east of the Rhine. As we proceed westward, the tumuli become rarer, and the dolmens are gradually met with. The Averni, for instance, were one of the Celtic tribes that accompanied Bellovesus, and in their country dolmens are found; but perhaps we need only infer from this that in a hilly country like Auvergne the older people still remained, and followed their old customs in spite of its partial occupation by the conquering Celts. We do not know at what period the Celts first invaded Gaul, but there seems no reason for supposing that it could not be very long before they first came in contact with the Romans; and if we may judge from the rate of progress which they made in subduing the rest of the country in historic times, their first invasion could hardly have been a thousand years B.C. All the tumuli in the east of France which have been dug into have yielded implements of bronze and metal,[4] and if they belonged to the Celts, this would fairly accord with the conclusions at which archæologists have arrived from other sources with regard to the Bronze age. It is not, however, worth while following up the question here; for unless it could be proved that the dolmens either succeeded or preceded the tumuli, it has no bearing on our argument. The fact of their occupying different and distinct districts prevents any conclusion of the sort being arrived at from geographical or external considerations. Their contents, if compared, might afford some information, but up to the present time this has not been done, and all we can at present

---

[1] Livy, v. chap. 34.
[2] Walcknaer, 'Géographie des Gaules.' The earlier chapters and Map V.

[3] 'Revue archéologique,' new series, vii. 228.
[4] Ibid.

assume is that there were two contemporary civilizations, or
barbarisms, co-existing simultaneously on the soil of France. My
impression is, however, that the Celtic barrow-builders were earlier
converts to Christianity, and left off their heathenish mode of
burial long before the less easily converted dolmen-builders of the
west ceased to erect their Rude-Stone Monuments.

We are thus reduced to the third of the great provinces into
which Gaul was divided in Cæsar's time, to try and find the people
who could have erected the stone monuments of France, and at
first sight it seems extremely probable that they were erected by
the Aquitanians. Both Cæsar [1] and Strabo [2] distinctly assert that
the people of the southern province differed from the Celts in
language and institutions as well as in features, and add that
they resembled more the Iberians of Spain than their northern
neighbours. When, however, we come to look more closely into
the matter, we find that the Aquitania of Cæsar was confined
to the country between the Garonne and the Pyrenees, and where,
however, few, if any, dolmens now exist. They are rather frequent
in the Pyrenees [3] and the Asturias, where remnants of the dolmen-
building races may have found shelter and continued to exist after
their congeners were swept from the plains; and there are one or
two on the left bank of the Garonne, but except these there
are none in Aquitania proper. If, however, we apply the term
Aquitania to the province as extended by Augustus up to the
left bank of the Loire, we include the greater part of the provinces where dolmens are found; but here again, when we look
more closely into it, we find that the northern districts of this
great province were, in Augustus' time, inhabited by Celts, or, at
all events, that Celts formed the governing and influential bodies
in the states. Indeed, the fact seems to be that, during the six
centuries which elapsed between the invasions of Italy by the
Gauls and the return invasion of Gaul by the Romans, the Celts
had gradually extended themselves over the whole of central
France from the Garonne to the Seine, and had obliterated the
political status of the people who had previously occupied the

---

[1] 'De Bello Gall.' i. 1.   [2] Strabo, vi. 176, 189.
[3] 'Archæological Journal,' 1870, cviii. p. 225 et seqq.

country, though there is no reason to suppose they had then at
least attempted to exterminate them. It must thus be either that
the Celts were the builders of the dolmens, which appears most
improbable, or that there existed in these provinces a prehistoric
people to whom they must be ascribed.

Without at all wishing, at present at least, to insist upon it, I
may here state that the impression on my mind is every day
growing stronger that the dolmen-builders in France are the
lineal descendants of the Cave men whose remains have recently
been detected in such quantities on the banks of the Dordogne
and other rivers in the south of France.[1] These remains are
found in quantities in the Ardèche[2] and in Poitou.[3] If they
have not been found in Brittany, it may be that they have not
been looked for, or that the soil is unfavourable to their preservation; but they have been found in Picardy, though possibly
not exactly of the same class. It is, of course, dangerous to found
any argument on such local coincidence, as new discoveries may
be made in the east of France or elsewhere; but in the present
state of our knowledge the Cave men and the dolmens seem
not only conterminous but their frequency seems generally to be
coincident.

As we know next to nothing of the languages spoken in the
south-west of France before the introduction of the Romance
forms of speech, philology will hardly assist us in our enquiry.
There is, however, one particle, *ac*, which I cannot help thinking may prove of importance, when its origin is ascertained. In
the table at the end of this chapter, I have placed the number
of the names of the cities having this termination in each department[4] next to M. Bertrand's number of dolmens. The coincidence is certainly remarkable, more especially as it is easy to

---

[1] Lartet, Christy, and 'Reliquiæ Aqui-
tanicæ.' London, 1865 *et seqq.*

[2] 'Monuments mégalithiques du Viva-
rais,' p. Oll. de Marchand; Montpellier,
1870.

[3] 'Époques antéhistoriques du Poitou,' P. A. Brouillet; Poitiers, 1865.

[4] This list must be taken as only
tentative. All I have done was to take
the Atlas Joanne, and count the number

of names as well as I could. I feel far
from confident that I have counted all;
and, besides, the scale of the maps is too
small to feel sure that all, or nearly all,
are there. It is, however, sufficient for
present purposes of comparison. If it
is thought worth while to pursue the
investigation farther, it must be done on
the 80,000 scale map of France, which
would be work of great labour.

account for the comparative paucity of names with this termination in Brittany by taking into account the enormous reflex wave of Celtic population from England that overwhelmed that country in the fourth and fifth centuries, and changed the nomenclature of half the places in the district: still, Carnac and Tumiac, Missilac, and others, as names of monuments, and Yffignac, as the name attached to the port which I believe was the place of embarkation for England, with many others that remain, are sufficient to attest that more previously may have existed.

The question remains, what is this particle? The first impulse is to assume that it is the Basque definite article. The Basques, for instance, say *Guizon*, " a man," *Guizonac*, " the man," and *Guizónac*, " the men," besides using it in other cases, while their local proximity to the dolmen country would render such a connection far from improbable. Against this, however, it may be urged, that *ac*, as a terminal syllable, hardly ever occurs in the Basque provinces, and the names to which it is attached in France hardly seem to belong to that language. Another suggestion has been made,[1] that it is equivalent to the Greek word πόλις, which would be exactly the signification for which we are looking, though in what language this occurs is by no means clear. For our present purpose, however, it is of little consequence what it may or may not be. It is sufficient to know that its occurrence is, as nearly as may be, coincident with the existence of dolmens. It does not occur to the eastward of the Rhone, nor do dolmens, though both are frequent on the right bank of that river; and it is not to be found in the east of France, in those countries which we have reason to believe were at the dawn of history essentially Celtic, and where the tumuli of the Bronze period exist in such numbers. It does, however, occur in that part of Cornwall south of Redruth and west of Falmouth,[2] where all the rude-stone monuments of that province are found, but it is not found anywhere else in Great Britain or Ireland.

---

[1] Delpon, 'Statistique du Département du Lot,' i. p. 383.

[2] In the Ordnance Maps, 1-inch scale, the termination *ac* occurs at least 38 times in this corner, though in these maps always spelt with an additional *k*, as Botallack, Carnidjack; although this is by no means the usual or ancient spelling of the district.

Nor is it found in the Channel Islands, though dolmens abound there; but this may be accounted for by the subsequent colonisation of these islands, as of Brittany in more modern times, by races of a different origin, who have to a great extent obliterated the original nomenclature of the country.

Equally interesting, however, for our purposes is the fact that, though the *ac*-termination occurs frequently in the departments between the Garonne and the Pyrenees, no dolmens exist in that region except, as before mentioned, a few at the roots of the mountains. This, at first sight, might seem to militate against the universality of the theory; but I, on the other hand, only take it to express that the *ac*-people were driven from that country by Ibero-Aquitanians before they had adopted the fashion of stone monuments. If we knew when Aquitania was first occupied by the people whom Cæsar and Strabo found there, it would give us a date before which dolmens could hardly have existed; but as we have no materials for the purpose, all that can be said is that, just as the dolmen races were cut in two by the Belgæ before the use of stone for funereal monuments had been introduced, so here the same phenomenon occurred, and the people we have to deal with were driven north of the Garonne, west of the Rhone, and south of the Seine, before they took to building dolmens — assuming, of course, that they once had extended beyond those limits; but this, except in the case of Aquitania proper, does not at present seem capable of being proved.

Before the Romans came in contact with them, and our first written accounts describe them, they had ceased to be a nation politically, and their language also was lost, or, at least, except in the one syllable *ac*, we now know nothing of it. If, therefore, it may be argued, the nationality of this people was lost before the Christian era, and their language had become extinct, these monuments must belong to a long anterior period. There are, however, certain considerations which would make us pause before jumping too hastily to this conclusion. There are, throughout the whole dolmen region of the south of France, a series of churches whose style is quite distinct from that of central and northern France. The typical example of this style is the well-known church of St.-Front, Périgueux. But the churches at

Cahors, at Souillac, at Moissac, Peaussac, Tremolac, St.-Avit-Sénieur, and many others, are equally characteristic. The cathedral at Angoulême, the abbey church at Fontevrault, and St.-Maurice at Angers,[1] and the church at Loches—all these churches are characterized by possessing domes, and the earlier ones by having pointed arches which look very much more as if they were derived from the horizontal arches of the tumuli than from the radiating arches of the Romans, which the Celts everywhere adopted; and, altogether, the style is so peculiar that no one the least familiar with it can ever mistake it for a Celtic style. All belong to the same group, and as distinctly as, or even more so than, the *ac*-termination, mark out the country as inhabited in the eleventh and twelfth centuries by a people differing from the Celts. Though, therefore, both their nationality and their language may have been superseded by those of the more enterprising and active Celts before the time of Cæsar, it is evident they retained their old feeling and a separate internal existence to a period at least a thousand years later.

There is still another trait that marks this country as a non-Celtic country in historical times—it is in the south-west, and there only, in France that Protestantism ever flourished or took root. To the Celt, the transition was everywhere easy from the government of the hierarchy of the Druids to that of the similarly organized priesthood of Rome. But it required all the cruel power of the Inquisition—the crusades of Simon de Montfort—the exterminating wars against the Camisards of the Cevennes—and, in fact, centuries of the most cruel and unrelenting persecution down to the revocation of the Edict of Nantes, and, indeed, to the French Revolution—to exterminate this people and extirpate the faith and feelings to which they clung. If they have in their veins, as I fancy they must have, any of the blood of the Cave people, they belong to one of the least progressive people of the earth, and we should not therefore be surprised if it required two thousand years of Celtic aggressive-

---

[1] The whole of these churches are described in more or less detail by Félix de Verneilh in his 'Architecture byzantine en France,' 4to. Paris, 1851. Several of them are also illustrated in my 'History of Architecture,' i. 418-441.

ness, coupled with Celtic ferocity, entirely to obliterate this race, if, indeed, that is done even now, which I very much doubt.

Before leaving this part of the subject, there is one other question which it may be as well to allude to here, as these investigations into the distribution of the rude-stone monuments seem destined to throw a new and important light upon it. Few questions have been more keenly debated among the learned than the relationship stated to have existed between the Cimbri and the Gauls. A great deal has been, and can be, said on both sides,[1] but the difficulty appears to me to have arisen principally from the erroneous assumption that no other people except the Celts existed in France.

There is no trace of Celts or of a Celtic language in the Cimbric Chersonese or the north-west corner of Europe, which is generally assumed to be the country occupied by the Cimbri, and no such people as the Cimbri are found settled in any part of France in historical times. If, however, we assume that the relationship may have been between the Cimbri and the Aquitanians, the case assumes a totally different aspect. As we do not know what the language of the Aquitanians really was, no assistance can be obtained from it, but our very ignorance of it leaves the field open for any other evidence that may be adduced, and that of the monuments seems clear and distinct. It seems almost impossible that there should be so much similarity between the monuments of the two countries without some community of race, and the great likeness that exists between those on the southern frontier of the northern dolmen province and those on the northern edge of the southern dolmen field seems almost to settle the question.

From history we only know of the existence of this relationship by the mode in which they fought together against Marius in the late Roman wars. If they were then geographically separated by the Belgæ and the Celts having thrust themselves between

---

[1] The argument, which it is not necessary to enter on here, has been well summed up by Dr. Schmitz, in Smith's 'Dictionary of Greek and Roman Geography,' *sub voce* Cimbri.

them, the separation must have been recent, for a barbarian people could hardly be brought to acknowledge the ties and duties of relationship after a long interval of time.[1]

As may be gathered from the table, page 376, or the map opposite page 324, the rude-stone monuments are pretty evenly distributed over the whole of the area extending from the English Channel to the Mediterranean Sea. Our knowledge of them is, however, practically confined to the northern portion of this zone, known as Brittany. The information which is available regarding those of Languedoc and Guienne is of the most meagre description. Hundreds of English tourists have visited Brittany, and many of them have drawn the monuments there and at least described them intelligibly; but I do not know one English book that mentions those in the departments of Lot or Dordogne, and almost the only information regarding them is to be picked up from the local "Statistiques;" but as these are very rarely illustrated, they do not suffice. No form of words will convey a correct idea of any unknown architectural monument except by comparing it with one that is known; and unless both have some well-defined features of style, it is even then very difficult, and with rude unshaped stones, almost impossible, by words to convey what is intended.

It is to be regretted that we do not know more of the southern examples,[2] as they are different in several essential features from

---

[1] The existence of this line of dolmens and of a separate people, all the way from Brittany to Narbonne, may serve, perhaps, to explain the mode in which the tin of Britain found its way across France to the Mediterranean Sea. That the Veneti traded from the Côtes-du-Nord and the Morbihan to Cornwall and the Cassiterides, no one, probably, will dispute. Their vessels, according to Cæsar's account, were fully equal to carrying to France all the metal this country could produce. The road by which it reached Marseilles across France was always the difficulty. In later times, the Celtic trade-route across France was apparently up the Rhone, but on its left bank, and down the Seine, or on its right bank; passing then through Celtica, but round the Aquitania of Augustus, and reaching Britain through the country of the Morini, which was the route Cæsar followed. This does not, however, appear to have been the line which was taken by the trade in tin. It followed, so far as we know, the central line of the dolmen country; and the fact of one people and one language prevailing throughout the whole of that region takes away any improbability, and removes all the difficulties that have hitherto impeded the adoption of that hypothesis.

[2] My intention was to have spent last autumn in travelling through the southern departments of France with

those of the north; and it is probable that any one who was familiar with all could point out a gradation of style which would aid materially in determining their age. Whatever that may turn out eventually to be, no one will, I presume, contend that all are of one age or even of one century. It is far more probable that they extend over a considerable lapse of time, probably a thousand years, and if this is so, there must have been changes of fashion even among Cave races as their blood got more and more mixed; and it would be interesting to know where and—relatively at least —when this took place. My present impression is that the southern are the most modern, for this among other reasons.—I look on the sequence of a cist in a barrow to a dolmen or chamber in a tumulus as very nearly certain, and from that the sequence to the exposed free-standing dolmen, and from that to the dolmen on the tumulus, as nearly, if not quite as, probable. The latter form, so far as I know, never occurs in Brittany, while on the other hand it is common in the south of France.[1] If they are of the same

122.   Dolmen at Sauclières.

age as similar monuments in Scandinavia and Ireland, they must be of comparatively modern date. There are also some monu-

---

this intent; but the war rendered the position of an exploring and sketching foreigner so undesirable that I was forced to desist. Had this book been a "statisque" of the subject, as it was originally intended, I should have been obliged to defer its publication till I had accomplished this journey, or till the monuments had been illustrated. As, however, it has now assumed more the

form of an "argument," this is of comparatively little consequence.

[1] In a paper on the 'Monuments mégalithiques de l'Auvergne,' by M. Cartheilhac, in the Norwich volume of the Prehistoric Congress, he gives drawings of ten as types. Five of these, or one-half, are dolmens on tumuli, which is, however, probably more than a fair proportion. One has already been given, woodcut No. 8.

ments, trilithons of hewn or partially hewn stone, as this one at
Sauclières (woodcut No. 122), which at least look more modern
than their northern congeners.

The monument, however, that seems capable of throwing the
greatest amount of light on their age is the dolmen of St.-Germain-
sur-Vienne, near Confolens, in Poitou. As will be seen from the
woodcuts opposite, its cap-stone, measures 12 feet by 15 feet, and is
of proportionate thickness. The mass was originally supported by
five columns of Gothic design, but one having fallen away, it now
rests only on four; but their interest arises from the fact that
the style of their ornamentation belongs undoubtedly to the
twelfth century or thereabouts—certainly not earlier than the
eleventh. In order to explain away so unwelcome an anomaly, it
has been suggested, that some persons in the twelfth century cut
away all the rest of the original rude stones which supported the
cap-stone, and left only the frail shafts which we now see. If this
were so, it would in no way alter the argument to be derived
from it. If men could be found in the twelfth century to take
the trouble and run the enormous risk of such an operation, their
respect for the monument must have been quite equal to that im-
plied in its erection; but the fact is that each of the five columns
is composed of three separate pieces—a base, a shaft, and a capital,[1]
an we see them now as they were originally erected.[2]

There may be doubts about the tomb of the Moals at Ballina
(page 233), but doubt seems impossible with regard to this: it
is a dolmen pure and simple, and it was erected in the twelfth
century. In itself the fact may not be of any very great importance, but it cuts away the ground from any *à priori* argument
as to the age of these monuments. It does not, of course, prove
that they are all modern, but it does show that some of them at

---

[1] 'Statistique monumentale de la Charente,' 141. Richard, 'France monumentale,' p. 677. 'Mém. de la Société
royale des Antiquaires de France,'
vii. 26.

[2] The woodcuts are copied from
Michon, 'Statistique de la Charente.'
In describing it, he quotes the Edict
of the Council at Nantes with regard

to the destruction of these "venerated
stones." He (p. 141) gives the date of
this council as A.D. 1262, which would
almost make it appear that this was one
of the stones against which the decree
was fulminated. This date, however,
appears to be a mistake. The true date
I believe to be 658, as given above,
p. 24.

least were erected after the time of the Romans, and at an era extending even far into the middle ages.

123.　　　　　　Dolmen at Confolens.

It is amusing, however, to see how the French antiquaries resist such a conclusion. Dr. de Closmadeuc, for instance, one of the most distinguished antiquaries of Brittany, opened a perfectly virgin tumulus at Crubelz. After penetrating through three distinct but undisturbed strata, he reached the roof of the enclosed dolmen or chamber. In this he found the usual products of cremation and the inevitable flint arrow-heads, but he refers in triumph to the "absence de toute trace des métaux." "Aucun doute," he adds, "n'est donc possible. Ce dolmen appartient bien à cette classe de monuments primitifs de l'âge de pierre." So far all is clear;

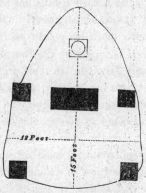

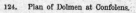
124.　　Plan of Dolmen at Confolens.

Z

but there are still difficulties, for he goes on to say: "Nous tenons peu de compte des débris de tuiles antiques rencontrées à la superficie du tumulus, et même sous les tables du dolmen. Il est raisonnable d'admettre que ces fragments de tuiles qui dénoncent l'industrie gallo-romaine, ont accidentellement pénétré dans l'intérieur."[1]

Let us pause a moment to consider what is involved in such a supposition. These tiles, which it is admitted are scattered in quantities over the surrounding plain, must have climbed to the top of the mound, penetrated through three undisturbed strata of earth, and finally penetrated " accidentally " between the close-fitting slabs forming the roof of the chamber. The hypothesis will not bear a moment's examination, but anything, however absurd, is to some minds preferable to admitting that any dolmen or tumulus can be subsequent to Roman times. It is astonishing, however, what effect that shibboleth, "no trace of metal," has on the mind of most antiquaries. It is, of course, true that before the metals were introduced no trace of them could be found in the prehistoric barrows of the rude savages that occupied Europe in the earliest times. We do not, at the present day, bury metal objects in our graves, and but for the coffin nails it would be as fair to argue that the graves in Kensal Green are pre-historic because the interments show no trace of metal implements. At all events, there are many burying races now existing who do not use coffins, nor bury metal objects in their graves; and all these this argument would make prehistoric. To me it seems much more logical to assume that, in those countries which had been occupied by the Romans, the natives, though reverting after their departure to their original modes of sepulture, had at least been so far civilized as to know that bronze daggers and spear-heads were not likely to be of much use in the next world, and had come to the conclusion that the personal ornaments of the dead might as well remain with their living friends. This hypothesis would at least account for the absence of metal in the long barrows of Gloucestershire, and at West Kennet, as well as at Crubelz, though Roman pottery was found in all these

---

instances. In fact, it is the merest negative presumption to assume that, because no metal is found in a grave, it must be prehistoric. It may be of any age, down to yesterday's, in so far as such proof is concerned.

Even the presence of metal, however, does not disturb the faith of some antiquaries. The Baron de Bonstetten, for instance, opened a tumulus not far from Crubelz. At one foot (30 centimetres) below the undisturbed surface the usual deposit of flint implements was found; and two feet (60 centimetres) below them two statuettes of Latona in terra-cotta and a coin of Constantine II. were found, but without this in the least degree shaking his undoubting faith in the prehistoric antiquity of the tomb![1]

Numerous other Roman coins have been found in these French monuments, but their testimony is disregarded. In the Manné er H'roëk, commonly called the Butte de César, about half a mile south from Locmariaker, near the surface, eleven medals of the Roman emperors, from Tiberius to Trajan, were found, together with fragments of bronze, glass, and pottery, but there were no signs of a secondary interment.[2] In like manner, in another monument at Beaumont-sur-Oise, Roman moneys were found, but, as M. Bertrand is careful to explain, in a stratum above the stone and flint implements, which, of course, he believed to mark the true date of the monument.[3] It seems impossible, however, that all these Roman coins can have been accidentally placed there. Those of Valentinian and Theodosius in the mound at New Grange were precisely in the same position as those of Titus, Domitian, and Trajan in the Butte de César or those of Beaumont, and so were those of Constantine found at Uley, in Gloucestershire (ante, p. 165). Those of Valentinian at Minning Lowe were in the tomb itself; so probably might others have been found in the other tombs had they not previously been rifled. It is not easy to assign a motive for placing these coins in the upper part of the mound externally. Their being found in that position at New Grange, Uley, Locmariaker, and Beaumont, is, however, sufficient to prove it was not

---

[1] 'Essai sur les Dolmens,' p. 38.

[2] Paper read by S. Ferguson, Q.C., before the R. I. A. 14th Dec. 1863. See also pamphlet by René Galles (Vannes, 1863), describing the exploration.

[3] 'Congrès préhistorique,' vol. de Paris, 1868, 42.

accidental, and their value is so small that they could not have been buried there for concealment. They must have had something to do with some funereal rite or superstition, the memory of which has passed away. No ancient British or Gaulish coins have ever been found in similar positions, and no Christian coins, which, had their presence been purely accidental, would probably have been the case. The inference seems to me inevitable that they were looked on as valued relics or curiosities, and placed there intentionally by those who raised the mounds it may be very long after the dates which the coins bear.

DOLMENS.

There is nothing specific in the Rude Stone Monuments of France sufficient to distinguish them from those of the other countries we have been describing. They are larger, finer, and more numerous there than in either Scandinavia or the British Isles, but except in the negative peculiarity of there being no circles in France there is little to distinguish the two groups. It can hardly even be absolutely asserted that there are no circles in France. There are some semicircles, which may possibly have been parts of circles never completed; there are some rows of small stones around or on tumuli; but certainly nothing that can for one moment be classed with the great circles of Cumberland and Wiltshire, or those of Moytura and Stennis, and certainly nothing like the innumerable Scandinavian examples.

We are hardly yet in a position to speculate why this should be so; but, so far as I can at present see, I would infer from this that the French examples are, as a rule, of earlier date than the British and Scandinavian. The circle I take to be one of the latest forms of rude-stone architecture—the skeleton of a tumulus, after the flesh of the sepulchral mound, which gave meaning to the group, had been thrown on one side as no longer indispensable. But of this we shall be better able to judge as we proceed.

Another characteristic, although not a distinction, is the fondness of the French for the "Allée couverte" or "Grotte des fées." No examples of this form have yet been brought to light in England, but one is engraved (woodcut No. 80) as the Hag

Birra's grave near Monasterboice, a second from the same neighbourhood, at Greenmount (woodcut No. 81), and they exist in
Scandinavia, but their home is Drenthe and the neighbouring
corner of Germany. As already mentioned, upwards of fifty
examples exist in that province. They are much ruder, it must
be confessed, than those of France; but this may arise from the
nature of the only material available; they have also the peculiarity of having the entrance always at the side instead of at the
end.

So far as their distribution in France has yet been ascertained,
the Grottes des fées exist only on the Loire, and to the north of
it, in fact in the most northern division of the French dolmen
region; while, on the other hand, as they are principally found in
Drenthe, or at the southern extremity of the German dolmen field,
we may assume that there is some connection between the two,
or that there would have been if it had not been severed by the
Belgians before those in either region were erected.

One of the finest of the French examples of this class of
monuments is that near Saumur, at Bagneux. The walls are
composed of only four stones on one side and three on the
other, yet it measures 57 feet 6 inches by 14 feet 4 inches across.
Another, near Essé, is even larger, though not so regular in plan,
nor so grand in the character of the stones. It measures, however, 61 feet by 12 feet at the entrance, increasing to 14 feet over
all at the inner end. There is a third at Mettray, near Tours,
which, though very much smaller, is curiously characteristic of
the form. The immense mass in the centre (woodcut No. 125)
and the two smaller which form the roof almost take from it the
character of rude-stone architecture. There is a fourth, of a less
megalithic character, at Locmariaker,[1] and several others are dispersed over Brittany. It is not possible to know whether the
intention may not have been that these, like all smaller chambers,
should have been buried in tumuli. These just quoted, however,
certainly never were so, but this may have arisen from their
having been left unfinished. That at Bagneux, however, could
hardly have supported a heavy mass without falling in, and that

---

[1] All these are represented in Gaillhabaud's 'Architecture ancienne et moderne,'
ii. plates 7 and 8.

at Mettray looks too like a finished monument for any one to
fancy its builders wished it hid.

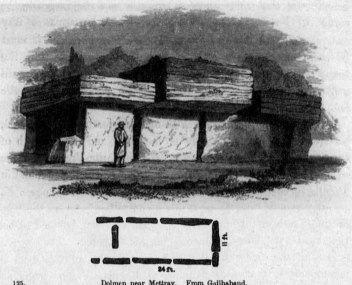

125.   Dolmen near Mettray.   From Gailhabaud.

The more usual form of French dolmens is either square or
slightly in excess of that form, seldom reaching two squares in

126.   Dolmen of Krukenho.

plan, and with a height equal to its breadth. One of the finest
specimens [1] of a monument of this class is in the middle of the

---

[1] The woodcut is from a publication privately printed by Dr. Blair and Mr. Ronalds.

village of Krukenho, halfway between Carnac and Erdeven, and is now used as a cart-shed or barn. It certainly never was covered up, though its entrance may have been closed ; indeed, the stones used for that purpose still lie in front of it. From this, which may be styled a first-class dolmen of the ordinary type, down to the simple dolmen of four stones, like Kit's Cotty house, every possible variety and gradation are to be found in France ; but, so far as I know, no classification has been hit upon which would enable us to say which are the oldest or which the more modern.

On the whole, however, I am inclined to look on the Grottes des fées as the more modern form. The stones of which they are composed are generally hewn, or at least shaped, by metal tools to the extent to which those of Stonehenge can be said to be so treated. They also look more like ordinary structures than other megalithic monuments, and seem rather sepulchral chapels than sepulchres. Even, however, if we were to determine to regard them as relatively the most modern of the northern dolmens, this would not settle the question of the southern external dolmens on tumuli, which may be even more modern. These questions, however, must, I fear, remain unanswered till our knowledge of the form of the whole group and of the materials of which the monuments are composed is more extensive and more accurate than it is at present.

The holed-stone variety occurs frequently in France, either in the form of simple four-stone dolmens, like that of Trie, Oise[1] (woodcut No. 127), or in a still more characteristic example at Grandmont, in Bas-Languedoc[2] (woodcut No. 128). Certainly neither of these was intended to be covered up, at least in the first instance, or, at all events, only partially ; or the use of the hole, which was, no doubt, to get access to the chamber, would have been destroyed. The umbrella form of the southern example is hardly such as would ever be used for a chamber in a tumulus, but as a pent-roof is singularly suitable for an open-air monument. The so-called Coves at Avebury were, I believe, in this form, and it prevails also in India[3] and elsewhere, and the

---

[1] Gailhabaud, 'Arch. anc. et mod.' i.

[2] Renouvier, 'Monuments de Bas-Languedoc.' No numbers to plates.

[3] See one published by Sir R. Colt Hoare, 'Modern Wiltshire,' iv. p. 57.

likeness between the two is so remarkable that it may well have given rise to speculations as to their common origin.

127.   Holed Dolmen, at Trie.   From Gailhabaud.

There is still a form of dolmen very common in France, but

128   Dolmen of Grandmont.

found also frequently in these islands, though I do not know if it occurs in Scandinavia. Mr. Du Noyer proposed to call them "earth-fast dolmens," [1] from one end of the cap-stones always resting on the ground, the other only being supported by a pillar or block. At first sight it might appear that they were only unfinished or imperfect dolmens, as it is more than probable that the mode of erection, in all instances, was to raise first one end of the cap-stone and then the other, as by this means the weight is

129.   Demi-dolmen.   From Malé, 'Antiquités du Morbihan.'

practically halved. If, however, any faith is to be placed in this representation of a monument by Malé,[2] it is clear that it was a deliberate mode of getting rid of half the expense and half the trouble of erecting a dolmen sepulchre. Generally speaking, however, they are more like the one near Poitiers (woodcut No. 130), where the stone either rests at one end on a bank or on a flat space sloping upwards. Those in Ireland and Wales seem all really to be only demi-dolmens, and as economy would hardly be a motive in the good old times, I look upon them as probably a very modern form of this class of monument. There is, indeed,

---

[1] 'Kilkenny Journal,' third series, vol. i. p. 40 et seqq.

[2] I have not seen the monument myself, nor do I know any one who has, but I cannot believe it to be a pure invention. Too much stress must not, however, be laid upon it.

one at Kerland, in Brittany (woodcut No. 131), which, in spite of
the shock such an idea will give to most people, I cannot help

130.   Demi-dolmen, near Poitiers.

thinking is and always was a Christian monument. At least it
is inconceivable to me from what motive any Christian could have

131.   Demi-dolmen at Kerland.

erected a cross on a pagan monument of this class, if it really
were one. It seems, on the other hand, perfectly intelligible

that long after their nominal conversion to Christianity the people would adhere to the forms so long practised by their ancestors, and there appears to be no great reason why even the most bigoted priest should object to it, provided the symbol of the cross made it quite clear that the "poor inhabitant below" died in the true faith.

I have purposely refrained from speaking of rocking stones, which play so important a part in the forms of Druidical worship invented by Stukeley, Borlase, and the antiquaries of the last century, because I believe that nine-tenths of those found in this country—if not all—are merely natural phenomena. So far from being surprised that this should be the case, the wonder is that they are not more frequent where loose boulders abound, either ice-borne or freed by the washing away of the underlying strata. That some of these should rest in an unstable equilibrium easily disturbed is only what might be expected, and that they would also be matters of marvel to the country people around is also natural; but it does not follow from this that any priests purposely and designedly placed, or could place, rude stones in such positions, or that they used them for religious purposes.

In France, however, there is one called the Pierre Martine, near

132.   Pierre Martine.

Livernon, in the department of the Lot, which was designedly balanced, if any one was. Its general appearance will be understood from the preceding woodcut, taken from 'La France monumentale et pittoresque,' which correctly represents its form and appearance.[1] The cap-stone measures 22 feet by 11 feet, and is 16 inches in thickness, and is so balanced on its two points of support that a slight pressure of the hand is sufficient to set it oscillating with a motion which it retains for some time.[2]

Another and more celebrated one, in Brittany, which is known as the Pierre branlante de Huelgoat, seems rather due to accident.

131.   Pierre Branlante, in Brittany.

It looks as if it formed, or was intended to form, part of a demi-dolmen, but happening to rest on one of its supports so as to oscillate, it has been allowed to remain so. Even assuming, however, that this was done designedly, what would it prove beyond the desire which pervades all these monuments, of exciting astonishment by *tours de force*. I believe it is correct to say that no passage exists in any book ancient or medieval which mentions rocking stones or their uses; nor has anyone

133.   Pierre Martine.   From Bonstetten.

[1] There is a woodcut in Bonstetten's work (p. 25) which, being taken endways, explains more clearly how, the cap-stone resting on two points only, it can be understood to oscillate. It is, however, much less correct as a representation.

[2] Delpon, 'Statistique du Dép. du Lot,' i. p. 388.

been able to explain how they delivered their oracles. A certain push produced an oscillation, not fitful or irregular, but always in proportion to the force applied ; so the answer must always have been the same and alike to all people. A still more important fact is that nowhere do the people appeal to them now. Neither at the Beltane nor at Halloween, nor at any of those festivals where country people revive every extinct superstition to aid them in prying into futurity, are these rocking stones appealed to ; and it seems almost impossible that, when so many other superstitions have survived, this one should be lost, and lost in presence of the rocks themselves, which still remain. Wonders they certainly are, but I question much if they ever were appealed to for any higher purpose than that of extracting sixpences from the pockets of gaping tourists.

CARNAC.

In a zone about twenty miles in extent, stretching from Erdeven on the north-west to Tumiac in a south-easterly direction, and nowhere more than five miles in width, there is to be found the most remarkable group of megalithic remains, not only in France, but perhaps in the whole world. Not only are examples of every class of monument we have been describing, except circles, to be found here, but they are larger and finer examples than are generally to be met with elsewhere. Another point of interest also is that within the zone are found—if I am not mistaken—both a cemetery and a battle-field. At least in the neighbourhood of Locmariaker, which there seems no reason for doubting was the Dariorigum of the Romans, the capital of the Venetes in Cæsar's times,[1] all the monuments are more or less sculptured, and all the stones fashioned, not to say hewn. On the other hand, no stone in the neighbourhood of Carnac is hewn, or even fashioned, beyond splitting, and no sculptures of any class have been traced. The distinction is too marked to be accidental, and unless it can be made out that they belong to different ages, which appears to me most improbable, goes far to establish the conclusion at which we have arrived in previous chapters.

---

[1] 'Ptolemæi Geo.' Amstel. 1605, p. 47.

To begin with the Carnac monument,[1] which is the best known
and the most important. As will be seen by the woodcut on
p. 352, it consists of two separate alignments, or great stone rows
—one, that of Carnac, extending for nearly two miles in a direction nearly east and west; the other, that of Erdeven, at a distance of two miles and a half from that at Carnac, being little more
than one mile in length. There is a third, but smaller, group at St.-
Barbe, about a mile and a half due south of Erdeven; and numerous
dolmens and tumuli are spread at intervals all over the plain.

In order to be understood, the Carnac monument must again
be subdivided into three portions. Beginning at Le Maenec (the
Stones), we have eleven rows of very fine stones, measuring from
11 feet to 13 feet in height from the ground, and still nearly
perfect. Gradually, however, they become smaller and more
sparse, till, when they reach the road from Auray to Carnac, there
are few of them that measure 3 feet in any direction, and
some are still smaller. Shortly after passing that road the
avenues cease altogether, for a distance of more than 300 yards,
there being nothing but a few natural boulders in the interval
between. When, however, we reach the knoll on which the
farm of Kermario stands, the avenues reappear, this time only
ten in number, but perfectly regular, and with stones as large
and as regularly spaced as those at Maenec. They diminish more
and more in size, however, and almost die out altogether before
they reach the mound (tumulus?) on which the windmill stands,

---

[1] The only survey of this monument
which has been published, and can be
depended upon, is that made by Mr.
Vicars, a surveyor of Exeter, for the
Rev. Dr. Bathurst Deane. It was published by him on a reduced scale in
vol. xxv. of the 'Archæologia,' and re-
engraved, with the principal parts on the
original scale, by Dr. Blair and Mr.
Ronalds, in the work before alluded to,
but unfortunately never published. The
original map, on a scale of 440 feet to
1 inch, is still in Dr. Deane's possession, at
Bath, and is so valuable a record of what
the monument was thirty-two years ago
that it is hoped it may be preserved by
some public body. Sir Henry Dryden and
the Rev. Mr. Lukis have been employed for
some years past exploring and surveying
in that neighbourhood, and have brought
back perfect plans, on a large scale, of all
the principal monuments; and if these
were published, they would leave little
to be desired in that respect. Meanwhile nothing can exceed Sir Henry's
kindness and liberality in allowing access
to his treasures, and the use of them by
any one who desires it; and I am indebted to him for a great deal of the
information in this chapter. The general
plans here published are from Messrs.
Blair and Ronalds' work, which is quite
sufficiently correct for my scale or my
present purpose.

and after that become so small and sparse that a stranger riding across the line could hardly remark that they were artificially disposed, but would merely regard it as a stony piece of land. They again cease entirely before we reach the brook, to recommence at Kerlescant, where thirteen rows are found; but these are composed of stones of less dimensions and more irregularly spaced than those at Maenec, and die out much more rapidly. At a distance of less than 500 yards from the head of the column they disappear entirely. It may be suggested that these gaps arise from the stones having been removed for agricultural and other purposes. I think, however, that any one who carefully examines the spot will be convinced that we really now possess all, or nearly all, that were ever placed here. They are thickest and best preserved in the village of Maenec, and at Kermario, where buildings are most frequent, and they disappear exactly in those places where there are no buildings or walls, but where the ground is an open, barren heath, without roads, and whence it would be very difficult to transport them; and in so stony a country it is very improbable that the attempt would be made. Besides this, the gradual way in which they diminish in size before disappearing shows a regularity of design, regarding which there can be no mistake. In addition to this, the heads of the three divisions are all marked by monuments of different kinds, but which are easily recognizable. At the head of the Maenec division there is a curvilinear enclosure of smaller stones, none of them being more than 6 feet in height, but set much closer together than the rows (woodcut No. 136). It probably was once complete, and, if so, joined the centre stone row. At Kermario, a dolmen stands in front of the alignment, not remarkable for its size, but conspicuous from its position; and at Kerlescant there is a quadrangular [1] enclosure, three sides of which are composed of stones of smaller size and set closely together, like those at Maenec. The fourth side is formed by a tumulus or long

---

[1] The form of this enclosure, as will be seen from the plan, is not an exact square, and some of the angle-stones being removed, it is difficult now to ascertain its exact form. Sir Henry Dryden makes it curvilinear. Messrs. Blair and Ronalds make the east side quite straight; the south and west were slightly curvilinear, but the whole figure is quadrangular; which is my own impression of its form.

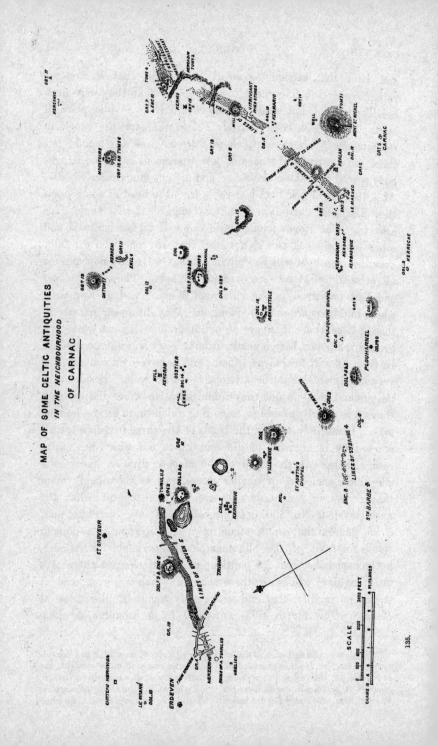

MAP OF SOME CELTIC ANTIQUITIES
IN THE NEIGHBOURHOOD
OF CARNAC

135.

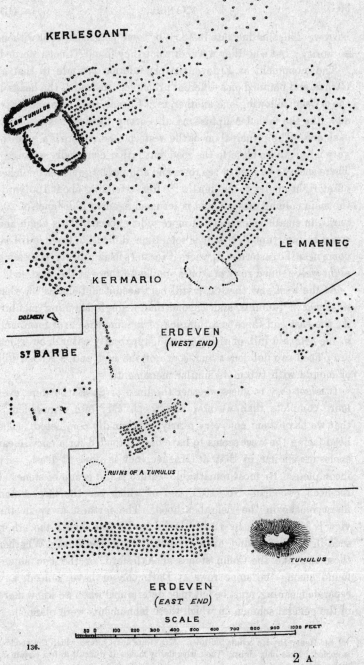

KERLESCANT

LOW TUMULUS

LE MAENEC

KERMARIO

DOLMEN

ERDEVEN
(WEST END)

S�||BARBE

RUINS OF A TUMULUS

TUMULUS

ERDEVEN
(EAST END)

SCALE

50 0   100   200   300   400   500   600   700   800   900   1000 FEET

2 A

barrow. This was dug into in 1851, by some persons with or without authority; but who they were, or what they found, is not recorded.

The monument at Erdeven is very inferior in scale to that at Carnac, and planned on a different principle. Instead of the heads of the division following one another, as at Carnac, they face outwards; and, like the fabled Amphisbena, this group has two heads, one at each end. The principal one is the western, where there is a group of very large stones close to the road, but rather confusedly arranged. There seem to be nine or ten rows, and a row of large stones branches off at right angles to the north. After extending about 100 yards the main column dies out, and is resumed again at a distance of 200 yards, in smaller stones much more widely spaced. It is again and again so interrupted, that it is sometimes difficult to trace it till we come near the eastern end, where it resumes its regularity, possessing eight well-defined rows of stones similar to those at the west end.[1]

At the west end there can still be traced the remains of what was once a tumulus, and, beyond that, a single standing menhir. At the east end there is a tumulus of a somewhat oval form, and in the centre, a hill, or rising ground, apparently natural, on which are placed two dolmens; and, south of the east end, a second hill or mound with two more similar monuments.

It is not easy to guess whether the lines of St.-Barbe were ever more complete than we now find them. My own impression is that we have them now very nearly as originally completed. The head facing the west seems to have been intended for a curvilinear enclosure similar to that at Maenec, but is now, at least, very incomplete. Its most remarkable feature is the group of stones at its head (woodcut No. 137), two of which are the largest and finest blocks in the neighbourhood. The farthest away in the view is 19 feet long by 12 feet broad, and 8 feet thick; the other, seen in the foreground, even exceeds it in dimensions. Whether these are like the Coffin stones at Aylesford, or the two stones found among the stone rows at Dartmoor, or have, indeed, any separate meaning, must be left to be determined when we know more of the general scheme on which these monuments were planned.

---

[1] Sir Henry Dryden counts ten rows. Mr. Vicars' survey, from which the woodcut is copied, makes only eight. Their irregularity makes it difficult to feel certain on such a point.

There is nothing at present but juxtaposition to justify us in connecting these great stone rows with the smaller groups of stones and the dolmens or tumuli which stud the plain where they are found. In respect to these, what we find at Carnac seems the exact converse of what exists at Stonehenge and Stennis. There the great stone monuments stand among the pigmy barrows of another race and age. Here all are megalithic and all seem to have been erected nearly at the same time, and to belong to one people, whoever they may eventually be proved to have been. In

137.　　　Head of Column at St.-Barbe.　　From Messrs. Blair and Ronalds' work.

so far as any argument as to their age is concerned, it is at present of little importance whether this is so or not, for they are all equally uncommunicative on this subject.

One of the tumuli known as Mont St.-Michel, is so situated with respect to the Maenec row that it seems impossible to dissociate the two. It was opened by M. René Galles in 1862, and an account of his researches, in the form of a report to the Préfet, was published shortly afterwards. The mound itself, at its base, is nearly 400 feet in length by half that dimension in width. In modern times its summit has been levelled, to form a platform for the church which now occupies its eastern summit. In front of the church, M. Galles sunk a shaft near the centre of the mound, and came upon a sepulchral chamber of irregular form, the side walls of which were formed of very irregular and bad masonry of small stones, similar to that of the dolmens at Crubelz. Its mean dimensions were about 6 feet by 5 feet, and 3 feet 6 inches in height. In it were found some magnificent celts of jade and tribolite, nine pendents in jasper, and 101 beads in jasper, with some in turquoise, all polished and pierced so as to form a necklace. The human remains in the principal cell seem utterly to have perished, owing probably to the continued penetration of water since, at least, the levelling of the summit, though some bones were subsequently found in a small chamber adjoining.

On the north side of the avenue at Kerlescant, at a distance of about 100 paces from it, is a second long barrow, consequently occupying the same relative position to it that Mont St.-Michel does to that at Maenec. It is so similar in external appearance and general arrangement to that forming the north side of the enclosure, which terminates the avenue, that there can be little doubt of their being of the same age and forming part of the same general arrangement. It had been opened some twenty years ago by a gentleman residing at Carnac, but was re-examined in 1867 by the Rev. W. C. Lukis.[1]

In the centre he found a long rectangular chamber, measuring 52 feet in length by 5 feet in width internally, and divided into two

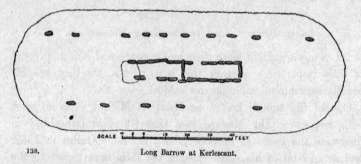

138.　　　　　　　　　Long Barrow at Kerlescant.

equal compartments by two stones cut away in the centre, so as to leave a hole 1 foot 6 inches wide by 3 feet high. A similar but smaller hole exists on the side, and is identical with those found in

---

[1] 'Journal of Archæological Association,' vol. xxiv. pp. 40 et seqq.

the long barrows at Rodmarton and Avening in Gloucestershire.[1]

Mr. Lukis, among other things, found an immense quantity of broken pottery, some of very fine quality. Two vases which he was enabled to restore are interesting from their general resemblance to the two which Mr. Bateman

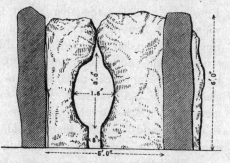

139.   Hole between Two Stones at Kerlescant.[2]

found in Arbor Low (woodcut No. 31). Though not exactly the same in form, there can be little doubt that they belong to the same age.

About a mile from this example, Mr. Lukis mentions a still larger one. It measures 81 feet in length by 6 feet in width, is divided into two compartments like the one just

141.   Vases found at Kerlescant.

---

[2] It is so difficult to realise these similarities, except by representation, that I give here a woodcut of that at Rodmarton. Allowing for the difference of drawing and engraving, the openings are identical, and it is so peculiar in form that the likeness cannot be accidental. If it does not occur anywhere else, or at any other time, it proves, as far as anything can prove, that the French and English long barrows were erected under the same inspiration. If one is post-Roman, so, certainly, is the other; or if one can be proved to be prehistoric, the other must follow.

140.   Entrance to Cell, Rodmarton.

described, and has also a holed entrance. He also measured two in
Finistère, one 76 feet, the other 66 feet, in length, and both 6 feet
wide. Both, however, had been rifled long ago, and are now mere
ruins. More, no doubt, would be found if looked for. Indeed, these
straight-lined "allées couvertes," or "Grottes des fées," without
cells, as the French call them, as before mentioned, are the most
characteristic, if not the most common, form of French rude-stone
monuments. The only other place where they are equally common
is Drenthe, and it may be that this side hole at Kerlescant is an
approach to the side entrance so usual in that province.

At Plouharnel, about a mile and a half westward from Mont
St.-Michel, a double dolmen was opened a good many years ago.
In it were found some beautiful gold ornaments, others in bronze,
and some celts or stone axes in jade[1]—all these, like those of
Mont St.-Michel, belonging evidently to what antiquaries call
the latest period of the Polished Stone age; but until it is
determined what that age is, it does not help us much to a date.

To the north of Kerlescant, at about the distance of half a mile,
is another long barrow, called Moustoir or Moustoir-Carnac, which

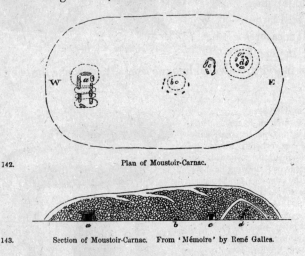

142.   Plan of Moustoir-Carnac.

143.   Section of Moustoir-Carnac. From 'Mémoire' by René Galles.

was opened in 1865, also by M. René Galles. It was found to

---

[1] These were exhibited in the inn in the village when I was there. Where they
are now, I do not know.

contain four separate interments, dispersed along its length, which exceeds 280 feet, the height varying from 15 to 20 feet. The western chamber is a regular dolmen, of the class called "Grottes des fées," and is apparently the oldest of the group. The centre one (*b*) is a very irregular chamber, the plan of which it is difficult to make out; the third (*c*) is a dolmen, irregular in plan, but roofed with three large stones; but the fourth (*d*) is a circular chamber, the walls of which are formed of tolerably large stones, the roof being built up into the form of a horizontal dome (woodcut No. 144), by stones projecting and overlapping, instead of the simpler ceiling of single blocks as on all the

144. Section of Chamber *d* of Moustier-Carnac.

earlier monuments. This, as well as the walls, being built with small stones, I take to be a certain indication of a more modern age. A considerable number of flint implements were found in the western chamber, with some beads and a partially pierced cylinder in serpentine, but no coins, nor any object of an age which can be positively dated. Here, however, these troublesome Roman tiles make their appearance as at Crubelz. "Ici, comme à Mané er H'roëk, nous trouvons les traces caractéristiques du conquerant (les Romains) : des tuiles à rebord ont croulé, au pied de notre butte funéraire, et plusieurs même se sont glissées à travers les couches supérieures des pierres, qui forment une partie de la masse." [1]

If these monuments are really prehistoric, it is to me incomprehensible that these traces of the Romans should be so generally prevalent in their structure. If it is objected that these are not found in the chambers of the tombs themselves, the answer seems only too evident that hardly one of them is virgin : all, or nearly all, have been entered before the time of recent explorers, and all their more valuable contents removed. Celts and beads and stone implements were not likely to attract the attention of early pilferers, and these they left; but except in the instance of the sepulchre at Plouharnel, metal is very rarely found in any. But

---

[1] 'Revue archéologique,' xii. p. 17.

the presence of Roman pottery, or other evidence of that people, in the long barrows in Gloucestershire, at Kennet, and at Carnac, are too frequent to be accidental. In so far as proving that the monument is not prehistoric, the presence of a single fragment of Roman pottery is as conclusive as a hoard of coins would be, provided it is found so placed that it could not have been inserted there after the mound was complete; and this I fancy is the case in all the instances mentioned above.

LOCMARIAKER.

It is rather to be regretted that no good survey exists of this cemetery. Not that much depends on the juxtaposition of the monuments, but that, as the French are continually changing their names, and most of them have two, it is not always easy to feel sure which monument is being spoken of at any particular time. Those on the mainland are situated in a zone about a mile in length, running north and south, between Mané Lud, the most northern, and Mané er H'roëk, the most southern. The first-named is a long barrow, 260 feet by about 165, but not, as in England, of one age or containing only one, but, like Moustoir-Carnac, several sepulchres, which may either be of the same age or erected at different though hardly distant periods, and joined together by being buried under one great mound. Of the three which Mané Lud contains, the most interesting is the partially covered dolmen at the west end. It consists of a chamber of somewhat irregular form, but measuring 12 feet by 10 feet, and covered by one enormous block of stone, measuring 29 feet by 15 feet, and with a passage leading to it, making the whole length from the entrance to the central block of the chamber 20 feet. According to Mr. Ferguson,[1] five of the blocks of this dolmen are sculptured; according to M. René Galles,[2] nine are so ornamented. The stone, however, is so rough and the place so dark that it is difficult at times to distinguish them and always so to draw them. The principal objects represented seem to be intended for boats

---

[1] 'Proceedings of Royal Irish Academy,' vol. viii. 1864, p. 298 et seqq.
[2] 'Revue archéologique,' vol. x. 1864, pl. iv.

and hatchets, but there are other figures which cannot be so classed, and, though it may be rash to call them writing, they may mean numbers or cyphers of some sort. Their great interest is, however, their similarity to the engravings on Irish monuments. If any one will, for instance, compare this woodcut (No. 145) and woodcut No. 68 from New Grange, he can hardly fail to see a likeness which cannot well be accidental; and in like manner the curvilinear forms of woodcut

145.   Sculpture at Mané Lud.

No. 146, in a manner hardly to be mistaken, resemble those from Clover Hill (woodcut No. 77).

Close by Mané Lud, but a little nearer to Locmariaker, stands what may be considered as the most interesting, if not the finest, free-standing dolmen in France. Its roof consists of two stones: one of these measures

146.   Sculpture at Mané Lud.[1]

18 feet by 9 feet,[2] and more than 3 feet in thickness. The second stone is very much smaller, and seems to form a sort of porch

147.   View of Dol ar Marchant.   From Blair and Ronald.

to it. The great stone rests, like that of most free-standing

---

[1] Woodcuts No. 145 and 146 are copied from Mr. Ferguson's paper in the 'Proceedings of Royal Irish Academy,' viii. 398 et seqq.

[2] These dimensions are from Richard; other authorities make it 18 feet by 12 feet.

dolmens, on three points, their architects having early learned
how difficult it was to make sure of their resting on more ; so that
unless they wanted a wall to keep out the stuff out of which the
tumulus was to be composed, they generally poised them on three
points like that at Castle Wellan (woodcut No. 7).

The great interest in this dolmen, however, lies in its sculptures. The stone which closes the east end is shaped into the form
of two sides of an equilateral spherical triangle and covered with
sculptures, which this time are neither characters nor repre-

148.   End Stone, Dol ar Marchant.   149.   Hatchet in roof of
                                                            Dol ar Marchant

sentations of living things, but purely decorative.   At one time I
thought the form of a cross could be traced on the stone.   The
central stem and the upper arm are shown clearly enough in the
drawing by Mr. Ferguson ; but all the drawings show a lower
cross-arm—though I confess I did not see it—which quite destroys
this idea.   On the roof a well-sculptured plumed[1] hatchet can
be traced very distinctly, as shown in the woodcut copied from
Mr. Ferguson.   He fancies he can also trace the form of a plough
in the sculptures of the roof, but this seems doubtful.

---

[1] The existence of the plume is doubted by Sir Henry Dryden, and he is so
accurate that he probably is right ; but as others say they have seen it, and nothing
depends upon it, I have allowed it to remain.

It is to this dolmen that the great fallen obelisk belongs. If it was one stone, it measured 64 feet in length and 13 feet across its greatest diameter; but I confess I cannot, from the mode in which it has fallen, rid myself of the idea that it was in reality two obelisks, and not one. Whether this was the case or not, it is a remarkable work of art for a rude people, for it certainly has been shaped with care, and with the same amount of labour might have been made square or round or any other shape that might have been desired. This, however, is one of the peculiarities of the style. No one will dispute that this obelisk and the stones of the Dol ar Marchant are hewn; but instead of adopting the geometrical forms, of which we are so fond, they preferred those that reminded them of their old rude monuments, and which to their eyes were more beautiful than the straight lines of the Romans. I do not feel quite sure that artistically they were not right.

If we compare this dolmen with that at Krukenho (woodcut No. 126), the difference between them appears very striking. The Dol ar Marchant is a regular tripod dolmen, carefully built of shaped stones and engraved. The other is a magnificent cist, walled with rude stones, and such as would form a chamber in a tumulus if buried in one, though whether this particular example was ever intended to be so treated or not is by no means clear. Be this as it may, there are two modes of accounting for the difference between two monuments so nearly alike in dimensions and situated so near to one another. The first would be to assume that the Krukenho example is the oldest, it being the rudest and approaching more nearly to the primitive form of the monuments: the second would be to assume that the one was the memorial of some warrior, erected in haste on the battle-field where he fell, by his companions in arms; and that the other was a royal sepulchre, prepared at leisure either by the king himself or by those who succeeded him in times of peace, and consequently who had leisure for such works. We must know more of these monuments before a satisfactory choice can be made between these two hypotheses. At present I rather incline to the belief that the circumstances under which they were erected may have more to do with their differences than their relative ages.

To return to Locmariaker. Close to the town there is, or was, a long allée couverte.[1]   It is 70 feet long, and divided towards its inner end into a square chamber, to which a long slightly curved gallery led, composed of fourteen stones on each side.   Five of

these are covered with ornaments, and characters engraved on them.   One might be considered as representing the leaf of a fern, or possibly a palm; the rest are ovals, circles, and similar ornaments, which may or may not have more meaning than those at New Grange or other monuments in the locality.

SCALE   FT

150.   Stone found inside Chamber at Mané er H'roëk.

On the other side of the village is the tumulus already mentioned as Mané er H'roëk, where the twelve Roman coins were found, and inside it an immense collection of polished celts, but all broken, and one slab, which apparently originally closed the door, and is covered with sculptured hatchets, similar in character to that on the roof of the Dol ar Marchant, but not so carefully drawn nor so well engraved.

Besides these there are several—probably as many as a dozen—monuments of the same class, within what may fairly be considered the limits of this cemetery; but of these the most interesting, as well as the most perfect, is that on

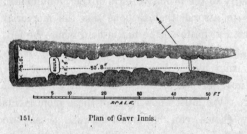

151,   Plan of Gavr Innis.

the island of Gavr Innis, about 2 miles eastward from Locmariaker.

The plan of the chamber of this monument will be understood from the

---

[1] It was in a very ruinous state when I saw it five years ago; and there is an ominous silence regarding it among subsequent tourists.   The measurements here quoted are from Richard, 'France monumentale.'

annexed plan.¹ The gallery of entrance measures 44 feet from
where the lining stones begin to the chamber, which is quadrangular in form, and measures 9 feet by 8 feet. All the six stones
forming the three sides of the chamber, and most of those
which line the entrance on either hand, are most elaborately
sculptured with patterns, the character of which will be understood from the annexed woodcuts. The pattern, it will be observed,
is not so flowing or graceful as those found at New Grange or
Dowth, and nowhere, I believe, can it be said to imitate vegetable

152. Sculptures at Gavr Innis. From a drawing by
Sir Henry Dryden.²

153. Holed Stone, Gavr Innis. From
a drawing by Sir Henry Dryden.

forms; and in the woodcut on the left-hand stone are some
seventeen or eighteen figures, which are generally supposed to
represent celts, and probably do so; but if they do, from their
position they must mean something more, either numbers or
names, but, whatever it may be, its meaning has not yet been
guessed. On other stones there are waving lines, which are very
generally assumed to represent serpents, and, I believe, correctly
so; but as that is somewhat doubtful, it is as well to refrain from
citing them. Besides these, the general pattern is circles within

¹ The plan here given is reduced from
one by Sir Henry Dryden, and may be
perfectly depended upon as far as the
smallness of the scale will allow.

² Sir Henry drew all these sculptures

first on the spot, and afterwards corrected his drawings from the casts at
St.-Germain. They are the only drawings existing which can thoroughly be
depended upon.

circles, and flowing lines nearly equidistant, but, except on one stone, never of spirals, and then less graceful than the Irish. The sculpture, however, on some of the stones at Lough Crew, and that in the centre especially of woodcut No. 75, is absolutely identical with the patterns found here; and altogether there is more similarity between these sculptures and those at Lough Crew than between almost any other monuments of the class that I know of.

In the chamber on the left-hand side is a stone (woodcut No. 153), with three holes in it, which have given rise to an unlimited amount of speculation. Generally it is assumed that it was here that the Druids tied up the human victims whom they were about to sacrifice. But, without going back to the question as to whether there ever were any Druids in the Morbihan, would any priest choose a small dungeon 8 feet square and absolutely dark for the performance of one of their greatest and most solemn rites? So far as we know anything of human sacrifices, they were always performed in the open day and in the presence of multitudes. Assuming for the moment, however, that these holes were intended for some such purpose, two would have sufficed, and these of a form much simpler and more easily cut. As will be seen from the woodcut, not only are the three holes joined, but a ledge or trough is sunk below them which might hold oil or holy water, and must, it appears to me, have been intended for some such purpose.

The existence of these holes seems to set at rest another question of some interest. Generally it has been assumed that the tattooing on the stones of the chambers, &c., may have been done with stone implements. This cannot be denied, though it seems improbable; but the undercutting of the passages between these holes and the formation of the trough could only be effected by a tool which would bear a blow on its head, and a heavy one too, or, in other words, by some well-tempered metal tool.

At Tumiac, opposite Gavr Innis, existed a very large tumulus, which was opened in 1853 by Messrs. Fouquet and L. Galles. It was found to contain a small chamber, partly formed of large slabs, partly of small stones. Some of the former had rude carvings upon them, but without any meaning that can now be made out.

The whole has the appearance of being considerably more modern than Gavr Innis.

Besides these, in the neighbourhood of Carnac and Loc-mariaker, there are at least three other groups of stones in France which deserve much more attention than has hitherto been bestowed upon them. The first is in the peninsula of Crozon, forming the southern side of the roadstead of Brest. It consists, among others, of three alignments of stones. The principal one is at a place called Kerdouadec, and consists of a single line of stones 1600 feet in length, arranged on a slightly curved plan, and terminating in a curious " Swastica"-like cross. The second, at Carmaret, is a

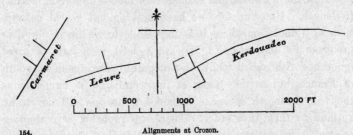

154.   Alignments at Crozon.

single line, 900 feet long, and with two branches at right angles to it, near its centre. The third, at Leuré, is likewise a single line with a slight elbow in the centre, from which starts a short branch at right angles.[1]

I am not able to offer a conjecture what these alignments repre-sent, nor why or when they were placed here. Whether an inspection on the spot might suggest some clue is not clear, but they are so unlike anything found anywhere else, either in France or any other country, that they must for the present, I fear, remain a mystery.

The second group, known as the Gré de Cojou, is situated about halfway between Rennes and Redon. The remains here consist of

---

[1] A plan of the first-named alignment was published by Freminville, ' Finistère,' part ii. pl. i., but the above particulars and the woodcut are taken from a dia-gram by Sir Henry Dryden in the last number of the ' Journal of the Anthrop. Inst.' He has perfect plans of the whole.

a short double alignment some 500 feet long, several tumuli—one at least surmounted by a circle of stones—several stone enclosures, and frequent dolmens. They have been imperfectly described by M. Ramé,[1] and planned, but not published, by Sir Henry Dryden. Until these are given to the world more in detail than has hitherto been done, it is impossible to say whether they represent a battle-field or a cemetery. From their position—a bleak, barren heath, far from any centre of population—I would guess the former; but I have not visited the place myself, and the information at my command is too meagre to enable me to speak with any confidence regarding them.

The third group is in the department of the Lot, near Preissac, in the parish of Junies, and extends over half a mile (800 metres) in length. Unfortunately we have nothing but verbal descriptions of it, and from these it is impossible to realise its form, or predicate its destination.[2] We are, indeed, in a state of great ignorance with regard to all these megalithic remains in the south of France, but as they seem as important and as numerous as those in the north, it is to be hoped some one will devote an autumn to their illustration. There are probably several other groups as important as those at Junies, but they are quite unknown to us at present. These groups must therefore be put aside for the present, and any argument regarding age or use of this class of monuments must be based wholly on what we know of those of the Morbihan.

So far as I know, no reasonable tradition attaches to any of the monuments in the Locmariaker cemetery which would enable us to fix their dates with anything like certainty, nor are there any local circumstances, except the Roman coins and tiles above alluded to, which aid us in our researches. We are thus left to such general inferences as the case admits of, and to a comparison with other similar monuments whose dates are nearer and better ascertained. No one, however, who is familiar with the two great cemeteries of Meath will probably hesitate in admitting that the

---

[1] 'Revue archéologique,' new series, ix. pp. 81 et seqq. I may mention that almost every other name in their neighbourhood ends in ac. See 'Joanne Atlas,' dép. Ille-et-Vilaine.   [2] Delpon, 'Statistique du Dép. du Lot,' i. 384.

two groups cannot be far separated in date. Of course, it is
impossible in a general work like the present to put the evidence
forward in anything like a complete state. In order to do this in
a satisfactory manner would require a large volume to itself, and
the illustrations both of the French and Irish examples should be
drawn by the same person. Even the few illustrations that have
been given are probably sufficient to show a similarity so great
that it can hardly be accidental, and I may be allowed to add,
from personal familiarity with both groups of monuments, that it
seems impossible to escape the conviction that they are monuments of the same class, probably of the same or a closely allied
race, and of about the same age. This last must always be the
most uncertain premiss of the three, as we can scarcely hope ever
to know the relative state of civilization of the two countries at a
given time; and consequently, even if we could prove that two
ornaments in the two countries were identical in form, this would
not prove that there might not be a difference of fifty or a hundred
years between them. Even at a later age, in the thirteenth century, for instance, the same form and the same style in France
and England did not prevent a difference of fifty years existing
between any two examples. In the fourteenth the two were
abreast, and in the fifteenth century they again diverged, so that,
although the architecture of both was still Gothic, a comparison of
style for this purpose became almost impossible.

In like manner, though the central ornament in the middle
stone at Lough Crew (woodcut No. 75) is almost identical with
some of the ornaments at Gavr Innis (woodcut No. 152), it
by no means necessarily follows that the two are exactly of the
same age. So, too, the foliage at New Grange (woodcut No. 67)
and that in the allée—now, I fear, destroyed—at Locmariaker are
evidently of one style, but still admit of a certain latitude of
date. On the whole, judging from style alone, I should feel
inclined to range Gavr Innis rather with the cemetery at Lough
Crew than with that on the Boyne; as well from its ornaments as
because I fancy that those monuments which are roofed with flat
stones only are earlier than those which make some attempt at
construction. But, on the other hand, I believe that Mané er
H'roëk and Mané Lud may more probably range with New Grange

and Dowth; and as I look upon it as quite certain that the monuments on the Boyne were all erected in the first four centuries after the birth of Christ, it seems impossible that the age of those at Locmariaker can be very distant from that date.

To many it will no doubt seem improbable that these monuments should have been erected during the occupation of the country by the Romans. If, however, they would take the trouble of studying what is now going on in India, their incredulity would, I fancy, soon disappear. The natives there at the present day are in many parts of the country building temples which it requires a practised eye to distinguish from those erected before any European settled in the land; and they follow their own customs, and worship their own gods, utterly irrespective of, and uninfluenced by, the strangers who have held the chief sway in the country for more than a hundred years. It must also be borne in mind that the Romans never really settled in Brittany. The country was poor then as now, and it led to nowhere. So long as the Bretons remained quiet, the Romans seem to have left them to themselves, and certainly have left no traces of any establishment of importance in their country—nothing that would lead us to suspect such intimate relations with the natives as would induce them to change their faith or fashions and copy the institutions of the foreigners.

On the other hand, it seems not only possible, but probable, that intercourse with the Romans may first have inspired the inhabitants of Brittany with a desire to attain greater durability and more magnificence, by the employment of stone, instead of earth or wood, for their monuments. This they might do, without its creating in their minds the smallest desire to copy either Roman forms or Roman institutions. On the contrary, we have every reason to believe that in these remote districts the Romans would be hated as conquerors, and that their religion and their customs would be held in abhorrence as strange and unsuited to the land they occupied.

Be this as it may, a comparison with the Irish examples reduces the questions at issue with regard to dates within very narrow limits. Either these monuments were erected immediately before or during the time of the Roman occupation or immediately after their departure, but prior to the conversion of the natives to Christianity. We are not yet in a position to decide positively between these two hypotheses, but the presence of Roman coins and Roman tiles in some of the mounds and the whole aspect of the argument seem to me to incline the balance in favour of their belonging to Roman times. Some may be anterior to the Christian era, but I am very much mistaken if it be not eventually admitted that the greater number of them are subsequent to that epoch.

Even, however, if the age of the monuments of the cemetery of Locmariaker could be ascertained, it would by no means necessarily carry with it that of the stone rows at Carnac. They belong to a different category altogether, and may be of a different age.

No one now, I presume, after what has been said above, especially with regard to the Scandinavian examples, will think it necessary that I should go over the ground to prove that they are not temples. Every argument that could be adduced to prove that Avebury or Stonehenge are not temples tells with tenfold force here. A temple extending over six or seven miles of country is more improbable than one covering only 28 acres. This one, too, is open everywhere, and has no enclosure or "temenos" of any sort, and there being an uneven number of equally spaced rows of stones in the principal monument is sufficient to show it was not intended and could not be used for processions. In fact I hardly know of any proposition that appears to me so manifestly absurd as that these stone rows were temples, and I feel sure that no one who thinks twice of the matter will venture again to affirm it.

It seems equally clear that they were not erected for any civic or civil purpose. No meetings could be held, and no administrative functions could be carried on in or around them. Nor are they sepulchral in any ordinary sense of the term. In the first place because, though men were buried in tumuli or under dolmens, or had single head-stones, nowhere were men buried in rows like this, extending over miles of heath and barren country. But the great fact is that the French savants have dug repeatedly about these stones and found no trace of burials. The most conclusive experiment of the sort was made by a road surveyor some six or seven years ago. Wishing to raise the road from Auray to Carnac, he dug out the sand and gravel on the east side of the road, over a considerable area, to a depth of from three to four feet; but being of a conservative turn of mind, he left the eleven rows of stones each standing on a little pillar of sand. It was then easy to trace the undisturbed strata of differently coloured earth round and almost under the stones, and to feel perfectly certain that it had never been disturbed by any inhumation. It, no doubt, is true that the long barrow at Kerlescant, the dolmen at Kermario, and the enclosure at Maenec, may have been, indeed most probably were, all of them, burying-places, but they can no more be considered the monument than the drums and fifes can be considered the regiment. They are only the adjuncts; the great rows must be considered as essentially the monuments.

If, therefore, they are neither temples, nor town-halls, nor even sepulchres, we are driven back on the only remaining group of motives which, so far as I know, ever induced mankind to expend time and labour on the erection of perfectly unutilitarian erections. They must be trophies—the memorials of some great battle or battles that at some time or other were fought out on this plain. The fact of the head of each division being a tomb is in favour of this hypothesis; but if it is considered as the principal part, it is like drawing a jackdaw with a peacock's tail—an absurdity into which these men of the olden time would hardly fall.

It is more difficult to answer the questions, Are Carnac and Erdeven parts of one great design, or two separate monuments? Is Carnac the march, St.-Barbe the position before the battle, Erdeven the scene of the final struggle for the heights that gave the victory, and the tombs scattered over the plain between these alignments the graves of those who fell in that fight? Such appears to me the only feasible explanation of what we here find; but the great question still remains, What fight?

There is, probably, no single instance in which the negative argument derived from the silence of the classical authors applies with such force as to this. If these stones existed when Cæsar waged war against the Veneti in this quarter, he must have seen them, and as it may be presumed that the monument was then more complete than it is now, he could hardly have failed to be struck with it, and, if so, to have mentioned it in his 'Commentaries.' Even, however, if he neglected them, the officers of his army must have seen these stones. They must have been talked about in Rome, and some gossip like Pliny, when writing about stones, must have heard of this wonderful group, and have alluded to it in some, way. The silence, however, is absolute. No mediæval rhapsodist even attempts to give them a pre-Roman origin. Such traditions as that of St. Cornely, or Cornelius the Centurion, though absurd enough, point, as such traditions generally do, to the transition time between paganism and Christianity, when, apparently, all mediæval chroniclers seem to have believed that all these rude-stone monuments were erected. Till, therefore, some stronger argument than has yet been adduced, or some new analogy be suggested, the pre-Roman theory must be set aside; and if this is so, we are tolerably safe in assuming that no battle of sufficient importance was fought which these stones could be erected to commemorate during the time when the Romans held supreme sway in the country.

If this is so, our choice of an event to be represented by these great stone rows is limited to the period which elapsed between the overthrow of the Roman power by Maximus, A.D. 383, and the time when the people of the country were completely converted to Christianity—which happened in the early part of the sixth century.[1] But if the history of England is confused and uncertain during that century and a half, that of Brittany is even more so, and has not yet been elucidated by the French authorities to the same extent as ours has been.

No one, I believe, doubts that Maximus, coming with an army from Britain, landed somewhere in Brittany, where he fought a great battle with the forces of Gratian, whom he defeated, and that

---

[1] " C'est en 465 que Vannes reçut pour premier évêque l'Armoricain St. Patern, qui mourut peu d'années après chez les Francs, où les Goths l'avoient forcé de se réfugier. Modestus en 511 mit tout en œuvre pour repandre le Christianisme parmi les Pagani de son diocèse, mais son zèle ne fut pas recompensé, car plus de trente ans après la mort de Patern les habitans de la Vénétie étoient encore presque tous païens. ' Erant enim tunc temporis Venetenses pene omnes Gentiles.'—Ap. Boll. ' Vita St. Melan.' vi. Jan. p. 311."—Courzon, 'Chartulaire de l'Abbaye de Redon,' cxliii.

afterwards, in a second battle near Lyons, he expelled the legitimate government of the Romans from Gaul.[1] I also see no reason for doubting that he was accompanied by a British prince Conan Meriadec, who afterwards settled in the country with thousands of his emigrant countrymen, over whom he was enabled to establish his chieftainship on the ruins of the Roman power.

If this is so, the battle which destroyed the Roman power, and gave rise to the native dynasty, would be worthy of such a monument as that at Carnac ; but so far as local traditions go, the place where Maximus and his British allies landed was near St. Malo, and the battle was fought at a place called Alleth, near St. Servan.[2] If this is so, it was too far off to have any connection with the Carnac stones. Two other wars seem to have been carried on by Conan, one in 410 against a people who are merely called barbarians,[3] a second against the Romans under Exuperantius in 416 ;[4] but we have no local particulars which would enable us to connect these wars with our stones. A war of liberation against Rome would be worthy of a national monument, and it may be that this is such a one, but I know of nothing to connect the two together, though local enquiries on the spot might remove this difficulty.

On the whole, however, I am more inclined to look among the events of the next reign for a key to the riddle. Grallon was engaged in two wars at least : one against the Roman consul Liberius in 439,[5] in which he succeeded in frustrating the attempts of that people to recover their lost power ; the other against the "Norman pirates ;"[6] and it is to this, as connecting the stone monuments with a Northern people, that I should be inclined to ascribe the erection of the Carnac alignments. From Grallon being the reputed founder of Landevenec, it might seem

---

[1] The authority for these events will be found at length in Gibbon, chap. xviii., and are too familiar to need quoting here.

[2] Daru's 'Histoire de la Bretagne,' vol. i. p. 58.　　[3] Ibid. p. 112.

[4] Dom. Bouquet, 'Recueil des Hist. des Gaules,' i. p. 629. "Exuperantius anno circa 416 Armoricos qui a Romanis defecerunt ad officium reducere tentavit."

[5] Daru, i. p. 112.

[6] "Gradlonus gratia dei rex Britonum necnon ex parte Francorum."—Chartulaire de Landevenec, quoted by P. Lobineau, ii. 17. And further : " 'Pervenit Sancti (Wingaboei) fama ad Grallonum regem Occiduorum Cornubiensium, gloriosum ultorem Normannorum qui post devictas gentes inimicas sibi duces subduxerat.'—Gurdestan, Moine de Landevenec, 'Vie de St.-Wingabois.' "—Daru, i. p. 69.

more probable that the alignments at Crozon marked the position of this battle, and I am not prepared to dispute that it may be so. The question is not of importance; if either group marked a battle-field of this period, the other certainly did so also, and I would prefer to refrain from offering any opinion as to what particular battle these stones commemorate. That must be determined by some local antiquary with much more intimate knowledge of the history and traditions of the province than I possess. All I wish to show here is that there was a period of a century and a half between the departure of the Romans and the time when the Bretons were so completely converted to Christianity as to abandon their old habits and customs, and that during that period there were wars with the Romans and the Northern barbarians of suffi-cient importance to justify the erection of any monuments within the competence of the people. If this is so, and we are limited to this period, enough is established in so far as the argument of this work is concerned, and the rest may fairly be left to be discussed and determined by the local antiquaries. All that it is necessary to contend for here is, that the alignments at Carnac are neither temples, nor tombs, nor town-halls, and that they were not erected before the time of the Romans. If these negative propositions are answered, there will not, probably, be much difficulty in admitting that they must be trophies, and that the battle or cam-paign which they commemorate was fought between the years 380 and 550 A.D.—in fact in the Arthurian age, to which we have ascribed most of those in this country.

The monuments in the cemetery at Locmariaker are probably older, but some of them extend down to the time when Carnac "closed the line in glory."

Number of Dolmens in Thirty-one Departments of France, according to M. Bertrand, 1864.[1]

	Dolmens.		Terminations in *ac*.
Lot	500	....	71
Finistère	500	....	3
Morbihan	250	....	26
Ardèche	155	....	16
Aveyron	125	....	35
Dordogne	100	....	75
Vienne (Haute et Basse)	82	....	41
Côtes du Nord	56	....	8
Maine-et-Loire	53	....	—
Eure-et-Loir	40	....	—
Gard	32	....	16
Aube	28	....	1
Indre-et-Loire	28	....	—
Charente	26	....	50
Creuse	26	....	6
Charente-Inférieure	24	....	21
Lozère	19	....	16
Corrèze	17	....	42
Vendée	17	....	—
Loire-Inférieure	16	....	11
Sarthe	15	....	—
Ille-et-Vilaine	15	....	18
Deux-Sèvres	15	....	—
Orne	14	....	—
Indre	13	....	3
Manche	13	....	—
Pyrénées-Orientales	12	....	2
Puy-de-Dôme	10	....	3
Oise	9	....	—
Cantal	8	....	37
Tarn-et-Garonne	7	....	16

[1] The information in this table must be received with great limitation. In the first place, What is a dolmen? Do the alignments at Carnac count as two, as seven, or as 700? Many also are mere estimates of local antiquaries. It is, for instance, very doubtful if Finistère contains more monuments than the Morbihan; and subsequent information may introduce great modifications into many of the numbers.

The value of the *ac* distinction does not come out clearly: first, because of the imperfect mode in which it has been obtained, but more because it does not make it clear that there are in France twenty-nine departments in which there are no dolmens, and no *ac*-terminations; in fact, the negative evidence which does not appear here is stronger than the positive.

CHAPTER IX.

SPAIN, PORTUGAL, AND ITALY.

It would not be easy to find a more apt illustration of the difficulty and danger of writing such a book as this than the history of how we acquired our knowledge of Spanish dolmens. When Ford published his interesting and exhaustive 'Handbook of Spain,' in 1845, he had travelled over the length and breadth of the land, and knew its literature intimately, but he did not know that there was a single "Druidical remain" in the country. The first intimation of their existence was in a pamphlet by Don Rafael Mitjana,[1] containing the description of one at Antequera; and since then Don Gongora ý Martinez [2] has published a work containing views and descriptions of thirteen or fourteen important monuments of this class in Andalusia and the south of Spain; and from other sources I know the names of at least an equal number in the Asturias and the north of Spain.[3] Had this work consequently been written only a very few years ago, a description of the dolmen at Antequera must have begun and ended the chapter. As it now is, we not only know that dolmens are numerous in Spain, but we have a distinct idea of their distribution, which may lead to most important historical results.

With regard to Portugal, the case is even more striking. Kinsey, in his 'Portugal Illustrated,' in 1829, gave a drawing of a " Druid's altar " at Arroyolos, and it was mentioned also by Borrow,[4] but there our information stopped, till the meeting of the International Prehistoric Congress at Paris in 1867, when S. Pereira da Costa described by name thirty-nine dolmens as still existing in Portugal. He also mentioned that as long ago as 1734 a memoir had been presented to the Portuguese Academy enumerating 314 as then to be met with; and though this is doubtful, it

---

[1] 'Memoria sobre el Tempio Druida de Antequera,' Malaga, 1847.

[2] 'Antegüedades prehistoricos de Andalucia,' Madrid, 1868.

[3] For a great part of the information regarding them, I am indebted to my friend Don J. F. Riaño, of Madrid.

[4] 'Bible in Spain,' ii. p. 35.

seems that they were at one time very numerous, and many, no
doubt, still exist which have escaped S. da Costa's enquiries.
Neither he nor any one else appears to have visited Cape Cuneus,
the most southern point of Portugal, where, if we read Strabo
aright, dolmens certainly existed in his day;[1] and if they do so
now, it would be a point gained in our investigation.

At present, according to S. da Costa, there are twenty-one
dolmens in Alentejo, two in Estramadura, nine in Beira, four in
Tras os Montes, and three in Minho. According to my information,
they are numerous in Gallicia, but have never been described.
Three at least are known by name in Santander, and as many in
the Asturias. One at least is known in Biscay, and two in Vitoria;
one in Navarre, and one in Catalonia. But I am assured that all
along the roots of the mountains they are frequent, though no
one has yet described or drawn them.[2] So far as is known, there
are none in the Castiles, in the centre of Spain, and only that
group above alluded to in Andalusia, where probably, instead of a
dozen, it may turn out that there are twice or thrice that number.

Assuming this distribution of the Spanish dolmens to be correct
—and I see no reason for doubting that it is so, in the main features
at least—it is so remarkable that it affords a good opportunity for
testing one of the principal theories put forward with regard to
the migrations of the dolmen-building people. According to the
theory of M. Bertrand, the dolmen people, after passing down
the Baltic and leaving their monuments there, migrated to the
British islands, and after a sojourn of some time again took to
their ships and landed in France and Spain, to pass thence into
Africa and disappear.[3] This seems so strange, that it is fortunate
we have another hypothesis which assumes the probability of an
indigenous population driven first to the hills and then into the
ocean by the advancing tide of modern civilization.

The first hypothesis involves the assumption that the dolmen
people possessed a navy capable of transplanting them and their
families from shore to shore, and that they had a sufficient know-

---

[1] Strabo, iii. p. 138.

[2] There is an interesting paper by
Lord Talbot de Malahide on this subject
in the 'Archæological Journal,' 108,

1870, illustrated by drawings of hitherto
unknown dolmens, by Sir Vincent Eyre.

[3] 'Revue archéologique,' new series,
viii. p. 530.

ledge of geography to know exactly whither to go, but at the same time possessed with such a spirit of wandering that so soon as they settled for a certain time in a given place, and buried a certain number of their chiefs, they immediately set out again on their travels. According to this view, they were so weak that they fled the moment when the original possessors of the land rose against them, though, strange to say, they had in the first instance been able to dispossess them. What is still more unlikely is that they should have possessed the organization to keep together, and to introduce everywhere their own arts and their own customs, but that, when they departed, they should have left nothing but their tombs behind. This hypothesis involves in fact so many difficulties and so many improbabilities that I do not think that either M. Bertrand or the Baron de Bonstetten would now, that our knowledge is so much increased, adhere to it. I at least cannot see on what grounds it can be maintained. It is so diametrically opposed to all we know of ancient migrations. They seem always —in so far as Europe is concerned—to have followed the course of the sun from east to west; and the idea that a people, after having peopled Britain, should have started again to land on the rugged coasts of the Asturias or in Portugal, and not have been able to penetrate into the interior, is so very unlikely that it would require very strong and direct testimony to make it credible, while it need hardly be said no such evidence is forthcoming.

The hypothesis which seems to account much more satisfactorily for the facts as we know them assumes that an ancestral worshipping people inhabited the Spanish peninsula from remote prehistoric times. If so, they certainly occupied the pastoral plains of Castile and the fertile regions of Valencia and Andalusia, as well as the bleak hills of Gallicia and the Asturias. Whether we call them Iberians, or Celtiberians, or, to use a more general term, Turanians, they were a dead-reverencing, ancestral worshipping people, but had not in prehistoric times learnt to use stone for the adornment of their tombs.

The first people, so far as we know, who disturbed the Iberians in their possessions were the Carthaginians. They occupied the sea coast at least of Murcia and Valencia, and if, according to their custom, they sought to reduce the natives to slavery, they probably frightened multitudes from the coast into the interior, but there is no proof that they ever made any extensive settlements in the centre of the country, nor on its west or north coast. It was different with the Romans: with them the genius of conquest was strong; they longed to annex all Spain to their dominions, and no doubt drove all those who were impatient of their yoke into the remote districts of Portugal and the rugged fastnesses of the Asturias and the northern mountains. It is also probable that many, to avoid their oppressions, sought refuge beyond the sea; but the great migrations are probably due to the intolerance of the early Christian missionaries. It thus seems that it was to avoid Carthaginian rapacity, Roman tyranny, and Christian intolerance, that the unfortunate aborigines were forced first into the fastnesses of the hills, and thence driven literally into the sea, to seek refuge from their oppressors in the islands of the ocean.[1]

Such an hypothesis seems perfectly consonant with all the facts as we now know them, and it also accounts for the absence of dolmens in the centre of Spain; for if this is correct, these migrations took place in the pre-dolmen period, and just as we find the Bryts beginning to use stones after having been driven from the fertile plains of the east into the fastnesses of Cumberland and Wales, so we find the Spaniards first adopting rude-stone monuments after having been driven into Portugal and the Asturias.

The one point which this theory does not seem to account for is the presence of dolmens in Andalusia. They however are, if I am not mistaken, an outlying branch of the great African dolmen field, and belong to the same age as these do, of which we shall be better able to judge presently. That there was a close or intimate

---

[1] " In the year B.C. 218, the second and fiercest struggle between the rival republics of Carthage and Rome was commenced by Hannibal taking Seguntum. The Peninsula thereafter became the theatre of a war afterwards carried by Hannibal into Italy, which was not concluded till 202 B.C., when Spain was added to the growing Italian Republic. But the nation of Spain did not willingly bow to the yoke. One of the bloodiest of all the Roman wars commenced in Spain 153, and did not finally terminate for twenty years, during which cities were razed to the ground, multitudes massacred and made slaves, and the triumphant arms of Rome borne to the Atlantic shores. Here, therefore, is an epoch in the history of the Spanish peninsula which seems completely to coincide with the ancient traditions of the Scoti, and the knowledge we possess of the period of their arrival in Ireland."—*Dan Wilson*, 'Prehistoric Annals of Scotland,' p. 475.

connection from very early times between the south coast of Spain and the north of Africa hardly admits of a doubt. The facility with which the Moors occupied it in the seventh century, and the permanence of their dominion for so many centuries, is in itself sufficient to prove that a people of the same race had been established there before them, and that they were not a foreign race holding the natives in subjection, but dwelling among their own kith and kin.

It seems in vain to look among the written annals, either of Spain or Ireland, for a rational account of these events. Both countries acknowledge to the fullest extent that the migration did take place; and the Spanish race of Heremon is one of the most illustrious of those of Ireland, and fills a large page in its history. So, too, the Spanish annalists fill volumes with the successful expeditions of their countrymen to the Green Island.[1] The mania, however, of the annalists of both countries for carrying everything back to the Flood, and the sons and daughters of Noah, so vitiates everything they say, that beyond the fact, which seems undoubted that such migration did occur no reliance can be placed on their accounts of these transactions.

One only paragraph that I know of seems to have escaped perversion. In his second chapter of his fourth book, D. O'Campo states :—" Certain natives of Spain called Siloros (the Siluri), a Biscayan tribe, joined with another, named Brigantes, migrated to Britain about 261 years before our era, and obtained possession of a territory there on which they settled." [2] This is so consonant with what we know of the settlement of the Silures on the banks of the Severn that there seems no good reason for doubting its correctness. It is more doubtful, however, whether any Spanish colonies reached Ireland at so early an age. Even allowing for the existence in the north-east of Ireland of the realm of Emania, the only kingdom in Ireland of which we have any authentic annals before the Christian era, there was plenty of room for the contemporary existence of the race of Heremon in the south and west. Tara did not then exist, and, in fact, according to the

---

[1] See a paper on the migration from Spain to Ireland, by Dr. Madden, 'Proceedings of Royal Irish Academy,' viii. pp. 372 et seqq.　　[2] Madden, l. s. c. p. 377.

annals of the 'Four Masters,' was founded by Heremon himself,
and took its first name, Teamair, from Tea, his wife, who selected
this spot. All this is perfectly consistent with what we know of the
history of the place. The earliest monument at Tara is the Rath
of Cormac[1] (218 A.D., or probably fifty years later). Though therefore chosen by Heremon as a sacred or desirable spot for residence, there is no proof that his race ever occupied it; and in the
two centuries that elapsed from his advent to the time of Cormac
his race had passed away from Meath at least, and was only to
be found in the south and west of Ireland. The one reminiscence
of the Milesian race that remained at Tara, in historical times, is
the Lia Fail, or Stone of Destiny, which these "veneratores lapidum" are said to have brought with them from Spain, but which,
with all due deference to Petrie, is not the obelisk still standing
there,[2] but may be the stone now in Westminster Abbey. The
Spanish colonists seem principally to have occupied the country
about Wexford and Galway,[3] and to these places, especially the
latter, a continual stream of immigration appears to have flowed
from the first century of our era down to the time of Elizabeth.
No one can travel in these counties without remarking the presence of a dark-haired, dark-eyed race that prevails everywhere;
but, strange to say, the darkest-complexioned people in the west
are those who still linger among the long-neglected dolmens of
Glen Malim More.

According to the annals of the 'Four Masters,' Heremon landed
in Ireland fifty years after the death of the great Dagdha. The
Irish historians say that the country was then ruled by three
princesses, wives of the grandsons of the Dagdha, and add that
the event took place 1002 years after Forann (Pharaoh) had been
drowned in the Red Sea.[4] If that event took place in 1312, as I
believe it did,[5] this would fix their advent in 310 B.C., which,
though less extravagant than the chronology of the 'Four
Masters, is still, I believe, at least three centuries too early.

---

[1] *Ante*, p. 193.
[2] Petrie, "Essay on Tara," 'Trans. R. S. A.' xviii.
[3] "The two provinces which the race of Heremon possessed were the pro-vince of Gailian (*i.e.* Leinster) and the

province of Olnemacht (*i.e.* Connaught)."
—*Petrie*, 'Round Towers,' p. 100.
[4] Reeves, translation of Nennius, p. 55.
[5] 'True Principles of Beauty in Art,' by the Author, appendix, 526.

All this may not be—is not in fact—capable of absolute proof; but it has at least the merit that it pieces together satisfactorily all we know of the history and ethnography of these races, and explains in a reasonable manner all the architectural forms which we meet with. It is hardly fair to expect more from the annals of a rude people who could not write, and whose history has never been carefully investigated in modern times. It is too early yet to say so, but the fact is, that it is these rude-stone monuments which alone can reveal the secrets of their long forgotten past. As they have hitherto been treated, they have only added mystery to obscurity. But the time is not far off when this will be altered, and we may learn from a comparison of the Irish with Spanish dolmens, not only what truth there is in the migrations of Heremon, but also at what time these Spanish tribes first settled as colonists in the Irish isle.

Dolmens.

The finest dolmen known to exist in Spain is that of Antequera, above alluded to; it will, indeed, bear comparison with the best in France or any other country in Europe. The chamber is of a somewhat oval shape, and measures internally about 80 feet

155.   View of the Interior of Dolmen at Antequera.   From Mitjana.

from the entrance to the front of the stone closing the rear. Its greatest width is 20 feet 6 inches, and its height varies between 9 and 10 feet.[1] The whole is composed of thirty-one stones:

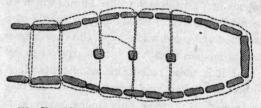

ten on each side form the walls; one closes the end; five are roofing, and three pillars support the last at their junction. The

156.   Plan of Dolmen called Cueva de Menga, near Antequera.

stone forming the roof of the cell or innermost part measures 25 feet by 21 feet, and is of considerable thickness. All the stones comprising this monument are more or less shaped by art—at least to the extent to which those at Stonehenge can be said to be so; while the three pillars in the centre, which seem to be part of the original structure, are certainly hewn. The whole was originally covered with a mound about 100 feet in diameter, and is still partially at least so buried. Its entrance is, however, and probably always was, flush with the edge of the mound, and open and accessible, and it is consequently not to be wondered at if nothing was found inside to indicate its age or use.

If we might assume—there is no proof—that the mound at Antequera was originally surrounded by a circle of stones like those at Lough Crew (woodcut No. 72), we should have a monument whose plan and dimensions were the same as those of Stonehenge, and, *mutatis mutandis*, the two would be, as nearly as may be, identical. There is the same circle of stone or earth 100 feet in diameter, and the same elliptical choir 80 feet in length, assuming that of Stonehenge to be extended to the outer circle. Antequera is, in fact, a roofed and covered-up Stonehenge, Stonehenge a free-standing Antequera. If both were situated in Wiltshire or in Andalusia, I should unhesitatingly declare for Antequera being the older. Men do what is useful before they indulge in what is merely fanciful. The two, in fact, bear exactly

---

[1] These dimensions are taken from Mitjana's book, merely turned into their equivalents in English feet. They do not, however, agree in scale with the plan, but are probably approximately correct.

the same relation to one another that Callernish does to New Grange; but when so widely separated geographically as the former two are, and belonging to two different races, it is difficult to say which may be the older. All we can feel sure of is that both belong to the same system, and that they are not far removed from each other in date. We must, however, know more than we do of the local history of Spanish dolmens before we can feel sure that Antequera may not be even considerably more modern than Stonehenge.

None of the other dolmens in Andalusia approach Antequera in magnificence, though they all seem to bear a similar character, and in appearance belong to the same age. The supporting stones seem to be all more or less shaped by art, and fitted to some extent to one another. The cap-stone is generally left in its natural state, largeness being the feature that the builders always aimed at. These peculiarities are well exhibited in the dolmen called de la Cruz del Tio Cogolleros, in the parish of Fonelas, near Guadix. Here the cap-stone mea- sures nearly 12 feet

157.   Dolmen del Tio Cogolleros.   From Gongora.

each way, and covers what was intended to be a nearly square chamber; one side, as at Kit's Cotty House, being left open; consequently it could hardly ever have been intended to be covered with a mound. Indeed, so far as we can gather from Don Gongora's drawings, none of those which he illustrates were ever so buried, nor does it appear that it was originally the intention ever to cover them with earth. Another monument, called only Sepultura Grande, in the parish of Gor, in the same neighbour- hood, is interesting from its resemblance to the Swedish sepulchre illustrated in woodcut No. 108, and to the Countless Stones at

2 c

Aylesford. Its cap-stone is 12 feet by 8 feet, and the side-stones fall away to a point in front. It evidently never was intended to be further roofed, nor to be buried in a mound, and, so far as can be judged from its appearance, is of comparatively modern date. .

The most interesting of Don Gongora's plates is one representing a dolmen near Dilar. This, if the drawing is to be depended upon, consists of a monolithic chamber, hollowed out of a stone of considerable dimensions, and hewn so as almost to look like an Egyptian cell. It is surrounded by twelve or fourteen rude-stone pillars, apparently 3 feet in height, and like those of

158.   Sepultura Grande.   From Gongora.

Callernish in shape. In the distance are seen two other circles of rude stones, but with nothing in their centre. If I understand Don Gongora rightly, these monuments are now very much ruined, if not entirely destroyed, and it is not clear how far the drawings are actual sketches or restorations. They may be correct, but without further confirmation it would hardly be safe to found any argument upon them.

So little is known—or at least so little has been published— regarding the dolmens of the north of Spain that it is very difficult and very unsafe to attempt any generalisation regarding them. There are three, however, which do seem to throw some light on our enquiries. The first is at Eguilar, in the district of Vitoria, on the road between that city and Pampeluna. It is of a horse-shoe form, like the Countless Stones at Aylesford, and measures 13 feet by 10 feet internally. Originally it was roofed by a single stone, measuring 19 feet by 15 feet, but which is now, unfortunately, broken. The side-stones and roof are closely fitted to one another, showing that it was always intended to be, and, in fact, is now, partially covered by a mound of earth.

At Cangas de Onis, in the Asturias, about forty miles east from Oviedo, there is a small church built on a mound which contains in it a dolmen of rather unusual shape. Its inner end is circular in plan, from which proceeds a funnel-shaped nave,

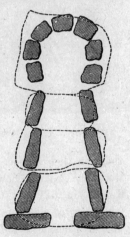

159.   Plan of Dolmen at Eguilar.

formed of three stones on each side, and with a doorway formed by two large stones at right angles to its direction. On the top of the mound a church was built, probably in the tenth or eleventh century,[1] to which this dolmen served as a crypt. From this it seems to be a fair inference that, when the church was built on the mound, the dolmen was still a sacred edifice of the aborigines. Had the Christians merely wanted a foundation for their building, they would have filled up or destroyed the pagan edifice, but it seems to have remained open to the present day; and though it has long ceased to be used for any sacred purpose, it still is, and always was, an essential part of the church which it supported.

160.   Plan of Dolmen at Cangas de Onis.

A still more remarkable instance of the same kind is to be found at a place called Arrichinaga, about twenty-five miles from Bilboa, in the province of Biscay. In the hermitage of St. Michael,

[1] There is a view of the mound and church in Parcerisa, 'Recuerdos y Bellezas de España, Asturias y Leon,' p. 30, but too small to enable us to be able to form any idea of its age from the lithograph.

at this place, a dolmen of very considerable dimensions is enclosed within the walls of what seems to be a new modern church. It may, however, be the successor of one more ancient; but the fact of these great stones being adopted by the Christians at all shows that they must have been considered sacred and objects of worship by the natives at the time when the Christians enclosed

161.   Dolmen of San Miguel, at Arrichiuaga.

them in their edifice. If the facts are as represented in the woodcut,[1] we can now easily understand why the councils of Toledo, in 681 and 692, fulminated their decrees against the "veneratores lapidum;"[2] and why also the more astute provincial priesthood followed the advice that Pope Gregory gave to Abbot Millitus, and by means of a little holy water and an

---

[1] The woodcut is copied from one in Frank Leslie's 'Illustrated News;' which is itself, taken from a French illustrated journal. I do not doubt that the American copy is a correct reproduction of the French original; but there may be exaggerations in the first. I see no reason, however, for doubting that the great stones do exist in the hermitage, and that they are parts, at least, of a dolmen—and this is all that concerns the argument. I wish, however, we had some more reliable information on the subject.   [2] Vide *ante*, p. 24.

image of San Miguel turned the sacred stones of the pagans into a temple of the true God. It is difficult to say when Christianity penetrated into the Asturias—not, probably, before the time of Pelayo (A.D. 720); but even this would be too early for such churches as those of Cangas de Onis and Arrichinaga. They, in fact, seem to carry down the veneration for big stones to almost as late a date as the age indicated by the dolmen at Confolens (woodcut No. 123), and bring the probable erection of some of them at least, if not of all, within the historic era.

PORTUGAL.

Only one drawing of a dolmen in Portugal has as yet, so far as I know, been published. It is situated on a bleak heath-land at Arroyolos, not far from Evora. Mr. Borrow describes it as one of

162.   Dolmen at Arroyolos. From Kinsey.

the most perfect and beautiful of its kind he had ever seen. "It was circular, and consisted of stones immensely large and heavy at the bottom, which towards the top became thinner, having been fashioned by the hand of art to something like the shape of scallop-shells. These were surmounted by a very large flat stone, which slanted down towards the south, where was a door. Three or four individuals might have taken shelter within the interior, in which was growing a small thorn-tree." [1]   Neither he nor Kinsey condescend to dimensions, and S. da Costa merely remarks that the dolmens which he has seen at Castello da Vide are of a similar construction to this one at Arroyolos.[2]

This, it must be confessed, is but a meagre and imperfect outline of one of the most important dolmen-fields in Europe, but it is probably sufficient to indicate its importance and its bearing on the history of megalithic remains in general.   When filled up, it promises to throw a flood of light on the subject in general, not only from being one of the connecting links serving to join the African dolmen-field to that of Europe, but more especially from the assistance it seems to afford us in understanding the hitherto mysterious connection of the Irish Milesians with Spain.   If the dolmens on the north and west coasts of the Spanish peninsula were carefully examined and compared with those in Ireland, their similarity would probably suffice to prove their affinity, and to establish on a broad basis of fact what has hitherto been left to the wild imaginings of patriotic annalists, more anxious for the fabled antiquity of their race than for the prosaic results of truthful investigations.

From such knowledge as we at present possess, I see no reason for supposing that any of the Spanish dolmens are as old as the Christian era; and the facts connected with the two at Cangas de Onis and Arrichinaga seem to prove that they were " venerated " as late at least as the eighth, it may be the tenth, century, and, if venerated, there is no reason why they should not also have been erected at that late age.

ITALY.

Although the experience we have just acquired with reference to dolmens in Spain ought to make any one cautious as to making assertions regarding those in Italy, still it probably is safe to

---

[1] Borrow, ' Bible in Spain,' ii. p. 35.
[2] ' Congrès international préhistorique,' Paris volume, p. 182.

assert that, with the exception of one group at Saturnia, there
are no dolmens in that country. In many respects Italy is very
differently situated from Spain. Her own learned societies and
antiquaries have for centuries been occupied with her antiquities,
and foreign tourists have traversed the length and breadth of the
land, and could hardly have failed to remark anything that called
to their recollection the Druids or Dragons of their own native
lands. As nothing, however, of the sort has been recorded, we
may feel tolerable confidence that no important specimens exist;
though at the roots of the hills and in remote corners there can
be little doubt that waifs and strays of wandering races will
reward the careful searcher for such objects. One, for instance,
is known to exist near Sesto Calende, in Lombardy. It is a circle
of small stones, some 30 feet in diameter, with an avenue 50 feet in
length touching it tangentially on one side, and with a small semi-
circle of stones 20 feet wide a few yards farther off.[1] The whole
looks like the small alignments on Dartmoor, and if several were
found and the traditions of the country were carefully sifted, this
might lead to some light being thrown on the subject. At present
it is hardly much bigger or more interesting than a sheep-fold.

The Saturnia group is thus described by Mr. Dennis:—" They
are very numerous, consisting generally of a quadrangular chamber
sunk a few feet below the surface, lined with rough slabs of rock
set upright, one on each side, and roofed over with two large slabs
resting against each other, so as to form a penthouse, or else a
single one of enormous size, covering the whole, and laid with
a slight slope, apparently for the purpose of carrying off the rain.
Not a chisel has touched these rugged masses, about 16 feet
square to half that size; some divided, like that shown in the
annexed woodcut, into two chambers over 18 feet across. To most
of them a passage leads, 10 or 12 feet long and 3 feet wide. All
are sunk a little below the surface, because each had a tumulus of
earth piled around it, so as to cover all but the cap stone."

One tumulus was observed with a circle of small stones set
round it, and Mr. Dennis suggests " that all may have been so
encircled, but that the small stones would be easily removed by

---

[1] 'Congrès international préhistorique,' Paris volume, p. 197.

the peasantry." "Nothing," he adds, "at all like them is seen in any other part of Etruria."[1] Saturnia is situated twenty miles from the sea, and if it is true that nothing of the sort is found elsewhere in Italy, these dolmens must be looked upon as exceptional—the remains of some stray colony of dolmen-builders, the memory of which has passed away, and may probably now be lost for ever.

If this is a correct representation of what took place in Italy, the conclusion seems inevitable that the chambered tumuli of that country—all of which are erected with hewn stones—did not

163.   Dolmen at Saturnia.   From Dennis' 'Etruria.'

grow out of rude-stone monuments. In no country in Europe are the tumuli so numerous or so important as in Etruria, and, as before mentioned, they certainly extend back to an era twelve or thirteen centuries before Christ. But if the dolmens of France or Scandinavia are prehistoric, or, in other words, extend back to anything like a thousand or fifteen hundred years before Christ, there is no reason whatever why dolmens should not be found also in Italy, if they ever existed there. Either it must be that Italy never

---

[1] 'Cities and Cemeteries of Etruria,' ii. p. 314.

possessed any or that those in the rest of Europe are very much more modern. If the northern dolmens are only one thousand to two thousand years old, the matter is easily explained. If they are three thousand or four thousand years old, they ought also to be found in Italy.

The fact seems to be that both the Pelasgi of Greece and the Tyrrheni of Italy came in contact either with Egypt or some early stone-hewing people before they left their homes in the East to migrate into Europe, and that they never passed through the rude-stone stage of architecture at any period, or at any place with which we are acquainted; and as they were, so far as we know, the earliest colonists of the countries they afterwards occupied, it seems in vain to look for dolmens where they settled. If Attila had lived five centuries before instead of after the Christian era, he and his Huns might have produced a rude-stone age in Italy. The inhabitants of Etruria were essentially a burying, dead-reverencing people, and if they had only been thrown back to that stage of barbarism which the rude monuments of our forefathers represent, we might have found dolmens there in thousands. The fate of Italy was different. Pressed by the Celts of Gallia Cisalpina in the north and by the Romans in the south, Etruria was squeezed out of existence, but by two races more civilized and progressive than herself. So far from throwing her back towards barbarism, Rome in adopting many of her forms advanced and improved upon them, and imparted to her architecture a higher and more intellectual form than she had been herself able to impress upon it. So, too, in Greece. The Dorian superseded and extinguished the Pelasgic forms, but after a longer interval of time. Four or five centuries elapsed between the last tomb we know of, at Mycenæ, and the earliest Doric temple at Corinth, and the consequence is that we see far fewer traces of the earlier people in the architecture of Greece than we do in that of Rome. But in neither instance was there any tendency to retrograde to a dolmen stage of civilization.

The case was widely different with such countries as Spain or France. There an aboriginal population had existed for thousands and tens of thousands of years, unprogressive and incapable, so far as we know, of progress within themselves, and only at last slowly and reluctantly forced by Roman example to adopt a more ambitious mode of sepulture than a mere mound of earth. No semi-civilized race ever settled in their lands, and the Carthaginians at Carthagena or Marseilles hardly penetrated into the interior, and were besides neither a building nor burying race, and had, consequently, very little influence on their modes of sepulture.

With Rome the case was different. She conquered and administered for centuries all those countries in which we find the earliest traces of rude-stone monuments, and she could hardly fail to leave some impress of her magnificence in lands which she had so long occupied. But when she withdrew her protecting care, France, Spain, and Britain relapsed into, and for centuries remained sunk in, a state of anarchy and barbarism as bad, if not worse than, that in which Rome had found them three or four centuries before. It was in vain to expect that the hapless natives could maintain either the arts or the institutions with which Rome had endowed them. But it is natural to suppose that they would remember the evidences of her greatness and her power, and would hardly go back for their sepulchres to the unchambered mole-hill barrows of their forefathers, but attempt something in stone, though only in such rude fashion as the state of the arts among them enabled them to execute.

CHAPTER X.

ALGERIA.

IT would be difficult to find a more curious illustration of the fable of "Eyes and no Eyes" than in the history of the discovery of dolmens in northern Africa. Though hundreds of travellers had passed through the country since the time of Bruce and Shaw, and though the French had possessed Algiers since 1830, an author writing on the subject ten years ago would have been fully justified in making the assertion that there were no dolmens there. Yet now we know that they exist literally in thousands. Perhaps it would not be an exaggeration to say that ten thousand are known, and their existence recorded.

The first to announce the fact to the literary world in Europe was the late Mr. Rhind. He read a paper on what he called "Ortholithic remains in North Africa," to the Society of Antiquaries in 1859, which was afterwards published in volume xxxviii. of the 'Archæologia.' It attracted, however, very little attention, perhaps in consequence of its name, but more from its not being illustrated. It was not really till 1863, when the late Henry Christy visited Algeria, that anything really became known. At Constantine he formed the acquaintance of a M. Féraud, interpreter to the army of Algeria, who took him to a place called Bou Moursug, about twenty-five miles south of Constantine, where, during a short stay of three days, they saw and noted down upwards of one thousand dolmens.[1] M. Féraud afterwards published an account of these in the 'Mémoires de la Société archéologique de Constantine' for 1863, and the subject having attracted some attention in Europe, a second memoir appeared in the following year, which contained a good deal of additional information collected from different district officers. Since then various memoirs have been published in Algeria and France. One by

---

[1] 'International Congress,' Norwich volume, 1869, p. 196.

the now celebrated General Faidherbe "speaks of three thousand tombs in the single necropolis at Roknia, and of another equally extensive within a few leagues of Constantine."[1] An excellent *résumé* of the whole subject will be found in the Norwich volume of the International Prehistoric Congress, by Mr. Flower. From all these we gather a fair general idea of the subject, but, unfortunately, none of the memoirs are written by persons combining extensive local experience with real archæological knowledge, except, perhaps, Mr. Flower. No plan of any one group has yet been given to the world, nor are any of the monuments illustrated with such details and measurements as would enable one to speak with certainty regarding them. This is especially the case with those represented in the 'Exploration scientifique de l'Algérie,' published by the French Government. There are in this work numerous representations of dolmens carefully and beautifully drawn, but very seldom with scales attached to them; and as no text has yet been published, they are of comparatively little value for the purposes of research. Had Mr. Christy lived a little longer, these deficiencies would doubtless have been supplied; but, unfortunately, his mantle has not fallen on any worthy successor, and we must wait till some one appears who combines leisure and means with the knowledge and enthusiasm which characterized that noble-minded man.

It need hardly be added that no detailed map exists showing the distribution of the dolmens in Algeria,[2] and as many of the names by which they are known to French archæologists are those of villages not marked on any maps obtainable in this country, it is very difficult to trace their precise position, and almost always impossible to draw with certainty any inferences from their distribution. In so far as we at present know, the principal dolmen region is situated along and on either side of a line drawn from Bona on the coast to Batna, sixty miles south of Constantine. But around Setif, and in localities nearly due south from Boujie, they are said to be in enormous numbers. The Commandant Payen reports the number of menhirs there as not less than ten

---

[1] Norwich volume of 'Prehistoric Congress,' p. 196.

[2] A very imperfect one appeared in the 'Revue archéologique,' in 1865, vol. xi. pl. v. It contained most of the names of places where dolmens were then known to exist, but our knowledge has been immensely extended since then.

thousand, averaging from 4 to 5 feet in height. One colossal monolith he describes as 26 feet in diameter at its base and 52 feet high.[1] This, however, is surpassed by a dolmen situated near Tiaret, described by the Commandant Bernard. According to his account the cap-stone is 65 feet long by 26 feet broad, and ·9 feet 6 inches thick; and this enormous mass is placed on other rocks which rise between 30 and 40 feet above the surface.[2] If this is true, it is the most enormous dolmen known, and it is strange that it should have escaped observation so long. Even the most apathetic traveller might have been astonished at such a wonder. Whether less gigantic specimens of the class exist in that neighbourhood, we are not told, but they do in detached patches everywhere eastward throughout the province. Those described by Mr. Rhind are only twelve miles from Algiers, and others are said to exist in great numbers in the regency of Tripoli.[3] So far as is at present known, they are not found in Morocco, but are found everywhere between Mount Atlas and the Syrtes, and apparently not near the sites of any great cities, or known centres of population, but in valleys and remote corners, as if belonging to a nomadic or agricultural population.

When we speak of the ten thousand or, it may be, twenty thousand stone sepulchral monuments that are now known to exist in northern Africa, it must not be understood that they are all dolmens or circles of the class of which we have hitherto been speaking. Two other classes certainly exist, in some places, apparently, in considerable numbers, though it is difficult to make out in what proportion, and how far their forms are local. One of these classes, called

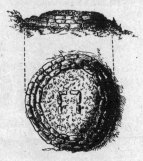

164.   Bazina.   From Flower's Paper.

Bazina by the Arabs, is thus described by Mr. Flower :—" Their general character is that of three concentric enclosures of stones

---

[1] 'Mémoires de la Soc. arch. de Constantine,' 1864, p. 127.

[2] Flower, in Norwich volume, p. 204.

[3] 'Mémoires, etc., de Constantine,' 1864, p. 124.

of greater or less dimensions, so arranged as to form a series of steps. Sometimes, indeed, there are only two outer circles, and occasionally only one. The diameter of the larger axis of that here represented is about 30 feet. In the centre are usually found three long and slender upright stones, forming three sides of a long rectangle, and the interior is paved with pebbles and broken stones.

"The Chouchas are found in the neighbourhood of the Bazinas,

165. Choucha. From a drawing by Mr. Flower.

and are closely allied to them. They consist of courses of stones regularly built up like a wall, and not in steps like the Bazinas. Their diameter varies from 7 to as much as 40 feet; but the height of the highest above the soil does not exceed 5 to 10 feet. They are usually capped and covered by a large flag-stone, about 4 inches thick, under which is a regular trough or pit formed of stones from a foot and a half to 3 feet in thickness. The interior of these little towers is paved like the Bazinas; and indeed M. Payen considers that they are the equivalents in the mountains of the Bazinas in the plains." [1]

In many instances the chouchas and bazinas are found combined

166.   Dolmen on Steps.   From 'Exploration scientifique de l'Algérie.'

in one monument, and sometimes a regular dolmen is mounted on steps similar to those of a bazina, as shown in the annexed woodcut, representing one existing halfway between Constantine

---

[1] Flower, in Norwich volume, pp. 201 et seqq.

and Bona. But, in fact, there is no conceivable combination which does not seem to be found in these African cemeteries; and did we know them all, they might throw considerable light on some questions that are now very perplexing.

The chouchas are found sometimes isolated, and occasionally 10 to 12 feet apart from one another in groups. In certain localities the summits and ridges of the hills are covered with them, while on the edges of steep cliffs they form fringes overhanging the ravines. .

In both these classes of monuments the bodies are almost always found in a doubled-up posture, the knees being brought up to the chin, and the arms crossed over the breast,[1] like those in the Axevalla tomb described above (page 312).

167.   Tumuli, with Intermediate Lines of Stones.

The most remarkable peculiarity of the tumuli and circles in Algeria is the mode in which they are connected together by

168.   Group of Sepulchral Monuments, Algeria.

double lines of stones—as Mr. Flowers expresses it, like beads on a string—in the manner shown in woodcut No. 167. What the object of this was has not been explained, nor will it be easy to guess, till we have more, and more detailed, drawings than we now possess. Mr. Féraud's plate xxviii.[1] shows such a line zigzagging

---

[1] 'Mémoires, etc., de Constantine,' 1864, pp. 109, 114.

across the plain between two heights, like a line of field fortifications, and with dolmens and tumuli sometimes behind or in front of the lines, and at others strung upon it. At first sight it looks like the representation of a battle-field, but, again, what are we to

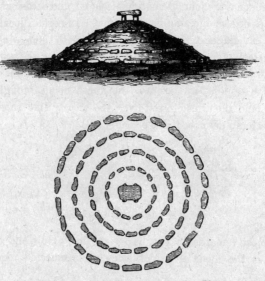

169.   Plan and Elevation of African Tumulus. From Féraud.

make of such a group as that represented in woodcut 168 on the previous page? It is the most extensive plan of any one of these groups which has yet been published, but it must be received with caution.[2] There is no scale attached to it. The triple circles with dolmens I take to be tumuli, like those of the Aveyron (woodcuts Nos. 8 and 122), but the whole must be regarded as a diagram, not as a plan, and as such very unsafe to reason upon. Still, as it certainly is not invented, it shows the curious manner in which these monuments are joined together, as well as the various forms which they take.

One of these (?) is represented in plan and elevation in the annexed woodcut 169.[3] It is, as will be observed, almost identical—

---

[1] 'Mémoires, etc., de Constantine.'

[2] Another is published by M. Bourguignal, in his 'Monuments symboliques de l'Algérie,' pl. i., but it is still more suspicious.

[3] I have been obliged to take some liberties with M. Féraud's cuts; the plan and elevation are so entirely discrepant, that one or both must be wrong. I have brought them a little more into harmony.

making allowance for bad drawing—with those of Aveyron just referred to, or with the Scandinavian examples as exemplified in the diagram (woodcut No. 109). As this class with the external dolmen on the summit seems to be very extensive in Algeria, indeed almost typical, an examination of their interior would at once solve the mystery of their arrangements, and tell us whether there was a second cist on the ground level, or where the body was deposited. Where the dolmen stands free, but on the flat ground, as is the case with that shown in this cut (No. 170), with two rows of stones surrounding it, the body was deposited in a cist formed

170.   Dolmen with Two Circles of Stones.   From Féraud.

between the two uprights that support the cap-stone, which are carried down some 5 or 6 feet into the ground for that purpose. My impression is that the same arrangement is met with in those which are raised, and that either the supports of the cap-stone are carried down to the ground for that purpose or that an independent cist is formed directly under the visible one.

The dolmen in this last instance is of the usual Kit's Cotty House style, consisting of three upright stones supporting the cap-stone. Sometimes the outer row of stones is replaced by a circular pavement of flat stones,[1] forming what may be supposed to be a procession path round the monument; but in fact hardly any two are exactly alike, and when we come to deal with

---

[1] 'Prehistoric Congress,' Norwich volume, p. 199.

thousands, it requires very complete knowledge of the whole before any classification can be attempted. Suffice it to say here that there is hardly any variety met with elsewhere of which a counterpart cannot be found in Algeria.

Of their general appearance as objects in the landscape, the annexed woodcut will convey a tolerable idea. They seem to

171. Dolmens on the Road from Bona to Constantine. From 'Exploration scientifique de l'Algérie.'

affect the ridges of the hills, but they also stretch across the plain, and in fact are found everywhere and in every possible position.

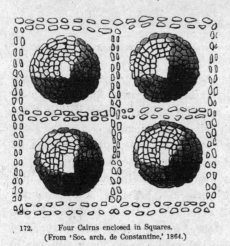

172.   Four Cairns enclosed in Squares.
(From 'Soc. arch. de Constantine,' 1864.)

Except apparently on the sea-coast, nothing like the Viking graves, so far as is known, is found in Algeria; whether this indicates that they were a sea-faring people or not is not quite clear, but it is a distinction worth bearing in mind.

One curious group is perhaps worth quoting as a means of comparison with the graves of Aschenrade (woodcut No. 119). It consists of four tumuli enclosed in four squares joined together like the squares of a chess-board. Single squares enclosing cairns are common enough in Scandinavia, but this conjoined arrangement is rare and remarkable, and its similarity to the Livonian example is so great that it can hardly be accidental. The Aschenrade graves, it will be recollected, contained coins of the Caliphs extending down to A.D. 999, and German coins down to 1040. There would, therefore, be no *à priori* improbability in these graves in Algeria being as late, if the similarity of two monuments so far apart can be considered as proving identity of age. Without unduly pressing the argument, the points of resemblance which exist everywhere between the Northern Europe and North African monuments appear to prove that the latter may be of any age down to the tenth or eleventh century, but any decision as to their real date must depend on the local circumstances attending each individual example.

The preceding woodcuts are perhaps sufficient to explain the more general and more typical forms of Algerian dolmens, but they are so numerous and so varied that ten times that number of illustrations would hardly suffice to exhibit all their peculiarities. Their study, however, is comparatively uninteresting, till we know more of their contents, and till something definite is accepted as to their age. When, however, we turn to examine that, we find the data from which our conclusions must be drawn both meagre and unsatisfactory. Such as they are, however, they certainly all tend one way. In the first place, the negative evidence is as complete here as elsewhere. The Greeks, the Romans, and the early Christians were all familiar with northern Africa, and there is not one whisper as to any such monuments having been seen by any of them. When we consider our own ignorance of their existence till some ten years ago, it may be said that such evidence does not go for much; but it is worth alluding to, as a hint in the opposite direction would be considered final, and as its absence, at all events, leaves the question open. On the other hand, all the traditions of the country as reported by M. Féraud, and others, and repeated by M. Bertrand and Mr. Flower, ascribe these monuments to the pagan inhabitants who occupied the country at the time of the Mahommedan conquest. Thus (page 127): "At the epoch the Mussulman invasion these countries were inhabited by a

pagan population, who elevated these vast ranges of stone to arrest
the invading host." Or, again, they even name the prince who
opposed the conquerors. Thus (page 117): "Formerly at Machira
lived a pagan prince called Abd en Nar—fire worshipper. He
married Zana, queen of a city now in ruins bearing that name.
When the Arabs conquered Africa, Abd en Nar abjured his
crown, became a Mussulman, and from that time called himself
Abd en Nour—worshipper of the light." [1]

This, too, must be taken for what it is worth; but in a cemetery
near Djidjeli, on the north coast, there is a curious tomb formed of
a circle of stones like those of the pagan cists, with a headstone
which, if it is not the turban-stone that is usually found in Turkish

173.   Tombs near Djidjeli.   From 'Exploration scientifique de l'Algérie.'

tombs of modern date, is most singularly like it. That the
cemetery belongs to the Mahommedans seems clear, but the circles
of stones, though small, indicate a very imperfect conversion—just
such as the tradition indicates.

These arguments, however, acquire something like consistency
when we come to examine the contents of the tombs themselves.
One of them (No. 4) is described by Mr. Féraud as surrounded by
a circular enceinte, 12 metres, nearly 40 feet, in diameter. The
chamber of the dolmen measured 7 feet by 3 feet 6 inches. At
the feet of the skeleton were the bones and teeth of a horse, and
an iron bridle-bit. In the same grave were found a ring of iron,
another ring with various other objects in copper (bronze?), some
fragments of pottery of a superior quality, and fragments of

---

[1] 'Mémoires, &c., de Constantine,' 1864.

worked flint implements, and lastly a medal of the Empress Faustina.[1] All the three ages were consequently represented in the one tomb, and yet it certainly belongs to the second century. None of the others give such distinct evidence of their age, but M. Bertrand, who is a strong advocate for the prehistoric age of French dolmens, sums up his impressions of M. Féraud's discoveries in the following words: " Ceux de la province de Constantine ne pouvaient, à en juger par les objets qui y ont été trouvés, être de beaucoup antérieur à l'ère chrétienne; quelques-uns même seraient postérieurs." [2]

In addition to what he found inside the tombs, M. Féraud discovered a Latin inscription in the cap-stone of a dolmen near Sidi Kacem. The letters are too much worn to enable the sense of the inscription to be made out, but quite sufficient remains to prove that it is in Latin, and, from the form of the letters, of a late type.[3]

Monsieur Leternoux found hewn stones and even columnar shafts of Roman workmanship among the materials out of which the bazinas at the foot of the Aures chain had been constructed, and he gives a drawing of a cippus of late Roman workmanship, bearing an inscription in Berber character, which he identifies with those on two upright stones of rude form, one of which forms parts of a circle near Bona.[4]

174.   Circle near Bona.

In addition to these there are numerous instances among the plates which form the volume of the ' Exploration scientifique de l'Algérie' where the rude-stone monuments are so mixed up with those of late Roman and early Christian character that it seems impossible to doubt that they are contemporary. As no text, however, has yet been published to accompany these plates, it is most unsafe

[1] ' Revue archéologique,' viii. p. 527.
[2] Ibid. l. s. c.
[3] ' Mémoires, &c., de Constantine,'
1864, p. 122, pl. xxx.
[4] Flower, in Norwich volume, pp. 202-206.

to rely on any individual example, which from some fault of the draughtsman or engraver may be misleading. The general impression, however, which these plates convey is decidedly in favour of a post-Roman date, and of their being comparatively modern. It requires, however, some one on the spot, whose attention is specially directed to the subject, to determine whether the rude-stone monuments are earlier than those which are hewn, or whether the contrary is not sometimes, perhaps always, the case. If M. Bertrand is right, and the Faustina tomb is of any value as an indication of age, certainly sometimes at least, the rude monuments are the more modern. Carthage fell B.C. 146, and the Jugurthan war ended B.C. 106, and it is impossible to conceive that a people like the Romans, would possess as they did the sovereignty of northern Africa, after that date, and not leave their mark on it, in the shape of buildings of various sorts. If we adopt the usual progressive theory, all must be anterior to B.C. 100; for on that hypothesis it would be considered most improbable that after long contact with Carthaginian civilization and under the direct influence of that of Rome anyone could prefer rude uncommunicative masses to structures composed of polished and engraved stones. It certainly was so, however, to a very great extent, and my impression is, for the reasons above given, that the bulk of these North African dolmens are subsequent to the Christian era, and that they extend well into the period of the Mahommedan domination, for it could not, for a long time at least, have been so complete as entirely to obliterate the feelings and usages so long indulged in by the aboriginal inhabitants of the country. Nothing, indeed, would surprise me less than if it were eventually shown that some of these rude-stone monuments extended down to the times of the Crusades. As, however, we are not yet in a position to prove this, it is only put forward here as a suggestion, in order that those who may hereafter have the task of opening these tombs may not reject any evidence of their being so late, as they probably would do if imbued with prehistoric prejudices.

It is to be feared that the question who the people were that set up these African dolmens must wait for an answer till we know more of the ethnography of northern Africa in ancient times than we do at present. The only people who, so far as we now see, seem to be able to claim them, are the Nasamones. From Herodotus we learn that this people buried their dead sitting, with their knees doubled up to their chins, and were so particular about this that, when a man was dying, they propped him up that he might die in that attitude (iv. 190). We also learn from him that they had such reverence for the tombs of their ancestors that it was their practice in their solemn form of oath to lay their hands on these tombs, and so invoke their sanction; and in their mode of divination they used to sleep in or on these sepulchres (iv. 172). All this would agree perfectly with what we find, but Herodotus unfortunately never visited the country nor saw these tombs, and consequently does not describe them, and we do not know whether they were mere mounds of earth, or cairns of stone, or dolmens such as are found in Africa. It is also unfortunate for their claim that, in his day, the Nasamones lived near the Syrtes and to the eastward of them (ii. 32), and it seems hardly possible that they could have increased and multiplied to such an extent in the four following centuries as to occupy northern Africa as far as Mount Atlas, without either the Greeks or the Romans having known it. They are mentioned again by Curtius (iv. 7), by Lucan (ix. v. 439), and by Silius Italicus (ii. v. 116 and xi. v. 180), but always as a plundering Libyan tribe, never as a great people occupying the northern country. Their claim, therefore, to be considered the authors of the thousands of dolmens which are even now found in the province of Algeria, seems for the present wholly inadmissible.

Still less can we admit M. Bertrand's theory alluded to above, that the dolmen-builders migrated from the Baltic to Britain, and thence through France and Spain to Africa. Such a migration, requiring long land journeys and sea voyages, if it took place at all, is much more likely to have been accomplished when commercial intercourse was established, and the North Sea and the Mediterranean were covered with sailing vessels of all sorts; but then it is unlikely that a rude people, as the dolmen-builders are assumed to be, could have availed themselves of these trade routes.

Still no one can look at such monuments as this of Aveyron (woodcuts Nos. 8 and 122) and compare them with those of Algeria, of which woodcut No. 169 is a type, without feeling that there was a connection, and an intimate one, at the dolmen period, between the people on the northern with those on the southern shores of the Mediterranean, which can only be accounted for in one of three ways.

Either it was that history was only repeating itself when Marshal Bougeaud landed in Algeria in 1830, and proceeded to conquer and colonise Algeria for the French. Or we must assume, as has often been done, that some people wandering from the east to colonise western Europe left these traces of their passage in Africa on their way westward. The third hypothesis is that already insisted upon at the end of the Scandinavian chapter, which regards these rude-stone monuments as merely the result of a fashion which sprung up at a particular period, and was adopted by all those people who, like the Nasamones, reverenced their dead and practised ancestral worship rather than that of an external divinity.

Of all these three hypotheses, the second seems the least tenable, though it is the one most generally adopted. The Pyramids were built, on the most moderate computation, at least 3000 B.C.[1] Egypt was then a highly civilized and populous country, and the art of cutting and polishing stones of the hardest nature had reached a degree of perfection in that country in those days which has never since been surpassed, and must have been practised for thousands of years before that time in order to reach the stage of perfection in which we there find it. Is it possible to conceive any savage Eastern race rushing across the Nile on its way westward, and carrying their rude arts with them, and continuing to practise them for four or five thousand years afterwards without change? Either it seems more probable to assume that the Egyptians would have turned them back, or if they had sojourned in their land like the Israelites, and then departed because they found the bondage intolerable, it is almost certain that they would have carried with them some of the arts and civilization of the people among whom they had dwelt. If such a migration did take place, it must have been in prehistoric times

---

[1] 'History of Architecture,' i. p. 81.

so remote that its occurrence can have but little bearing on the argument as to who built these Algerian monuments. But did they come by sea? Did the dolmen-building races embark from the ports of Palestine or those of Asia Minor? Were they in fact the far-famed Phœnicians, to whom antiquaries have been so fond of ascribing these structures. The first answer to this is that there are no dolmens in Phœnicia, and that they have not yet been found near Carthage, nor Utica, nor in Sicily, nor indeed anywhere where the Phœnicians had colonies. They are not even found at Marseilles, where they settled, though on the western bank of the Rhone, where they had no establishments, they are found in numbers. They may have traded with Cornwall, and discovered lands even farther north, but to assume that so small a people could have erected all the megalithic remains found in Scandinavia and the continent of France, and other countries where they never settled, perhaps never visited, is to ascribe great effects to causes so insignificant as to be wholly incommensurable. So wholly inadequate does the Phœnician power seem to have been to produce such effects, that the proposition would probably never have been brought forward had the extent of the dolmen region been known at the time it was suggested. Even putting the element of time aside, it is now clearly untenable, and if there is any truth in the date above assigned to this class of monuments, it is mere idleness to argue it.

The idea of a migration from France to Algeria is by no means so illogical. The French dolmens, so far as is now known, seem certainly older than the African—a fact which, if capable of proof, is fatal to the last suggestion—and if we assume that this class of monument was invented in western Europe, it only requires that the element of time should be suitable to establish this hypothesis. When the Celts of central Gaul, six centuries before the Christian era, began to extend their limits and to press upon those of the Aquitanians, did the latter flee from their oppressors to seek refuge in Africa, as at a latter period the dolmen-builders of Spain sought repose in the green island of the west? There certainly appears to be no great improbability that they may have done so to such an extent as to cause the adoption of this form of architecture after it had become prevalent elsewhere; and as the encroaching Celts, down to the prosecution of the middle ages, may have driven continual streams of colonists in the same direction, this would account for all the phenomena we find, provided we may ascribe that modern date to the Algerian examples which to me appears undoubted.

It is hardly probable, however, that the Aquitanians would have sought refuge in Africa unless some kindred tribe existed there to afford them shelter and a welcome. If such a race did exist, that would go far to get rid of most of the difficulties of the problem. We are, however, far too ignorant of North African ethnography to be able to say whether any such people were there, or if so, who their representatives may now be, and till our ignorance is dispelled, it is idle to speculate on mere probabilities.

We know something of the migrations of the peoples settled around the shores of the Mediterranean for at least ten centuries before the birth of Christ, but neither in Greek or Roman or Cathaginian history, nor in any of the traditions of their literature, do we find a hint of any migration of a rude people, either across Egypt or by sea from Asia, and, what is perhaps more to the point, we have no trace of it in any of the intermediate islands. The Nurhags of Sardinia, the Talayots of the Balearic Islands, are monuments of quite a different class from anything found in France or Algeria. So too are the tombs of Malta, and, as just mentioned, there are no such remains in Sicily.

We seem thus forced back on the third hypothesis, which contemplates the rise of a dolmen style of architecture at some not very remote period of the world's history, and its general diffusion among all those kindred races of mankind with whom respect for the spirits of deceased ancestors was a leading characteristic.

TRIPOLI.

Dr. Barth seems to be the only traveller who has in recent times explored the regions about Tripoli to a sufficient extent and with the requisite knowledge to enable him to observe whether or not there were any rude-stone monuments in that district. About halfway between Moursuk and Ghât, he observed "a circle laid out very regularly with large slabs, like the opening of a well; and, on the plain above the cliffs, another circle regularly laid out, "and," he adds, "like the many circles seen in Cyrenaica and in other parts of Northern Africa, evidently connected with the religious rites of the ancient inhabitants of these regions."[1] This is meagre enough; but fortunately, in addition to this, he observed and drew two monuments which are of equal and perhaps even of more importance to our present purposes.

One of these, situated at a place called Ksaea, about forty-five miles east by south from Tripoli, consists of six pairs of trilithons, similar to that represented in the annexed woodcut. No plan is given of their arrangement, nor does Dr. Barth speculate as to their use; he only remarks that "they could never have been intended as doors, for the space between the upright stones is so narrow that a man of ordinary size could hardly squeeze his way between them."[2]

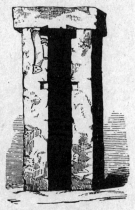

175.   Trilithon at Ksaea.

The other, situated at Elkeb, about the same distance from Tripoli, but south by east, is even more curious. It, too, is a trilithon, but the supports, which are placed on a masonry platform two steps in height, slope inwards, with all the appearance of being copied from a carpentry form, and the cap-stone likewise projects beyond the uprights in a manner very unusual in masonry. Another curious indication of its wooden origin is that the western pillar has three quadrangular holes on its inner side, 6 inches square, while the corresponding holes in the eastern pillar go quite through. These pillars are 2 feet square and 10 feet high, while the impost measures 6 feet 6 inches.

In front of these pillars lies a stone with a square sinking in it

[1] 'Travels and Discoveries in Northern Africa,' i. p. 204.   [2] *Ibid.* p. 74.
[3] *Ibid.* p. 59. The holes are not shown in the cut.

and a spout at one side. Whatever this may have been intended
for, it is—if the woodcut and description are to be depended upon
—the exact counterpart of a Hindu Yoni, and as such would not
excite remark as having anything unusual in its appearance if
found in a modern temple at Benares. Beyond these in the
woodcut are seen several other stones, evidently belonging to
the same monument, one of which seems to have been formed
into a throne.

These monuments are not, of course, alone. There must be
others—probably many others—in the country, a knowledge of
which might throw considerable light on our enquiries. In the
meanwhile the first thing that strikes one is that Jeffrey of Mon-

176.   Trilithon at Elkeb. From a Drawing by Dr. Barth.

mouth's assertion, that "Giants in old days brought from Africa
the stones which the magic arts of Merlin afterwards removed
from Kildare and set up at Stonehenge,"[1] is not so entirely
devoid of foundation as might at first sight appear. The removal
of the stones is, of course, absurd, but the suggestion and design
may possibly have travelled west by this route.

If we now turn back to page 100, it seems impossible not to

---

[1] 'British History,' viii. chap. ii.

177.
    Buddhist Monument at Bangkok.
From Mouhot's 'Travels in Indo-China, Cambodia, &c.' vol. i. p. 218.

be struck with the likeness that exists between woodcut No. 25 and woodcuts 175 and 176, especially the first. Such similarity is more than sufficient to take away all improbability from Dr. Barth's suggestion that "the traces of art which they display may be ascribed to Roman influence." It also renders it nearly certain that these African trilithons were sepulchral, and adds another to the many proofs adduced above that Stonehenge was both sepulchral and post-Roman.

The most curious point, however, connected with these monuments is the suggestion of Indian influence which they—especially that at Elkeb—give rise to. The introduction of sloping jambs, derived from carpentry forms, can be traced back in India, in the caves of Behar [1] and the Western Ghâts, to the second century before Christ, but certainly to no earlier date. The carpentry forms, but without the sloping jambs, continued at Sanchi and the Ajunta caves till some time after the Christian era, and where wood is used has, in fact, continued to the present day. "Mutatis mutandis," no two monuments can well be more alike to one another than that at Elkeb and the Buddhist tomb at Bangkok, represented in woodcut 177. The Siamese tomb may be a hundred years old; and if we allow the African trilithon to be late Roman, we have some fourteen or fifteen centuries between them, which, certainly, is as long as can reasonably be demanded. In reality it was probably less, but if the one was prehistoric, we lose altogether the thread of association and tradition that ought to connect the two.

To all this we shall have occasion to return, and then to discuss it more at length, when speaking of the Indian monuments and their connection with those of the West. In the meanwhile these two form a stepping-stone of sufficient importance to make us feel how desirable it is that the country where they are found should be more carefully examined. My impression is that the key to most of our mysteries is hidden in these African deserts.

---

[1] 'History of Architecture,' by the Author, ii. p. 483.

CHAPTER XI.

MEDITERRANEAN ISLANDS.

Before leaving the Mediterranean Sea and the countries bordering upon it, it seems desirable to say a few words regarding certain "non-historic" monuments which exist in its islands.   Strictly speaking, they hardly come within the limits assigned to this book, for they are not truly megalithic in the sense in which the term has been used in the previous pages; for though stones 15 feet and 20 feet high are used in the Maltese monuments, they are shaped and, it may be said, hewn with metal tools, and they are used constructively with smaller stones, so as to form walls and roofs, and cannot therefore be considered as Rude Stone Monuments.   Still they have so much affinity with these, and are so mixed up in all works treating of the subject with Druidical remains and prehistoric mysteries, that it certainly seems expedient to explain as far as possible their forms and uses.

The monuments are of three classes.   The first, found in Malta, are there called giants' towers—"Torre dei giganti"—a name having no meaning, but which, as also involving no hypothesis, it may be convenient to adhere to.   The second class, called Nurhags, are peculiar to Sardinia.   The third, or Talyots, are found only in the Balearic islands.   There may be some connection between the two last groups, but even then with certain local peculiarities sufficient to distinguish them.   The Maltese monuments however stand alone, and have certainly no connection with the other two, and, as it will appear in the sequel, none of the three have any very clear affinity with any known monuments on the continent of either Europe or Africa.

MALTA.

The best known monuments of the Maltese groups are situated near the centre of the Isle of Gozo, in the commune of Barbato.

When Houel wrote in 1787,[1] only the outside wall with the apse
of one of the inner chambers and the entrance of another
were known. He mistook the right-hand apse of the second pair
of chambers for part of a circle, and so represented it with a
dolmen in the centre, led to this apparently by the existence of
a real circle which then was found at a distance of 350 yards from
the main group. This circle was 140 feet in diameter, composed
of stones ranged close together and alternately broad and tall,
as shown in the next woodcut, which represents the rear of the
principal monument. The entrance was marked by two very tall
stones, apparently 20 feet high. The interior was apparently
rugged, but there is nothing in the plates to show from what
cause. When Houel made his plan,[2] it had all the appearance of
being what was styled a regular " Druidical circle," and might have
been used as such to support any Druidical theory. It is now
however evident that it really was only the commencement of the
envelope of a pair of chambers, such as we find in all the monuments of this class on these islands. If the plan is correct, it was
the most regular of any, which, besides its having every appearance
of never having been completed, would lead us to suppose that
it was the last of the series. This monument has now entirely
disappeared, as has also another of even more megalithic
appearance which stood within a few yards of the principal
group, but of which unfortunately we have neither plan nor
details. It is shown with tolerable distinctness in a view in
Mr. Frere's possession, and in the plates which are engraved from
drawings by a native artist, which Admiral Smyth brought home
in 1827,[3] and which are engraved in volume xxii. of the ' Archæologia.' Unfortunately the text that accompanies these plates
is of the most unsatisfactory character. This he partially explains
by saying that he had left his measurements with Colonel Otto
Beyer, who had just caused the principal pair of chambers to
be excavated.

The second pair of chambers was excavated by Sir Henry

---

[1] ' Voyage pittoresque en Sicile et
Malte,' 4 vols. folio, Paris, 1787.

[2] *Ibid.* pl. ccxli.

[3] The three formed part of a set of
nine, a duplicate of which has kindly
been lent to me by Mr. Frere, of Roydon
Hall, Norfolk. Unfortunately there is no
artist's name, and no date, upon them.

Bouverie when he was governor, some time before or about 1836, when a careful plan and drawings of the whole were published by Count de la Marmora.[1] It has been re-engraved by Gailhabaud and others, and is well known to archæologists.

The monuments thus brought to light consisted of two pairs of elliptical chambers very similar in dimensions and plan to those at Mnaidra (woodcut No. 179). The greatest depth internally from the entrance to the apse of the principal pair is 90 feet; the greatest width across both 130 feet. The right-hand pair as you enter is comparatively plain. The outer chamber of the left-hand pair still retained, when excavated, fittings that looked like an altar in the right-hand apse, which was separated from the rest by what may be called the choir-screen or altar-rail; and this was ornamented with spirals and geometric figures neatly and sharply cut. In the inner chamber was a stone, near the entrance,

178.   View of the exterior of the Giants' Tower at Gozo. From a drawing in the possession of Sir Bartle Frere, K.C.B.

on which was a bas-relief of a serpent, but no other representation of any thing living was found elsewhere.

The external appearance of the monument may be gathered

---

[1] 'Nouvelles Annales de l'Institut archéologique,' i.; Paris, 1836.

from the woodcut No. 178. The lower part of the wall is composed alternately—as in the circle just alluded to—of large stones laid on their sides and smaller ones standing perpendicularly between them. Above this the courses of stones are of regular masonry, and probably there was some kind of cornice or string-course before the beginning of the roof, but of this no trace now remains in any of these monuments.

The second group, known as Hagiar Khem, is situated near Krendi, on the south side of the island of Malta, and is the most extensive one known. The principal monument contains, besides the usual pair of chambers, four or five lateral chambers; and a short way to the north is a second monument, containing at least one pair; and to the south a third group, but so ruined it is difficult to make out the plan. Only the tops of the walls and the tall stones which still rise above the walls were known to exist of the monument, till in 1839 Sir Henry Bouverie authorized the expenditure of some public money to excavate it. An account of these excavations, with a plan and drawings, was published in Malta at the time by Lieutenant Foulis. The plan was repeated, in less detail however, in the 'Archæologia,'[1] and afterwards in the Norwich volume of the International Prehistoric Congress, by Mr. Furze, from a survey recently made by the Royal Engineers.

The third group, known as that at Mnaidra, is situated not far from the last, between it and the sea; and as it never has been published, a plan of it is given here[2] from a survey made by Corporal Mortimer, of the Royal Engineers. Like the Gozo monument, it consists of two pairs of oval chambers in juxtaposition. The right-hand pair, in this instance, is larger and simpler in design than that on the left, but it is so nearly identical, both in plan and dimensions, with the right-hand pair at Gozo that they are probably of the same age and served the same purpose. They are also, as nearly as may be, of the same

---

[1] With a paper by Mr. Vance, 'Archæologia,' vol. xxix. p. 227.

[2] For this plan and the photographs of it I am indebted to the kindness of Col. Collinson, R.E., who accompanied them by a very full description and notes on their history and uses, from which much of the following information is derived.

dimensions: both would be enclosed, with their side walls, by a
circle 75 feet in diameter. The left-hand cone at Mnaidra would
be nearly of the same diameter; but at Gozo the corresponding

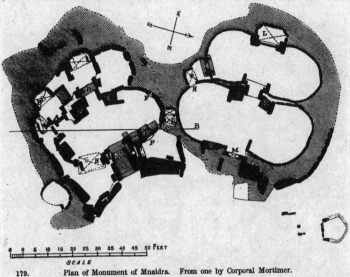

179.　　Plan of Monument of Mnaidra.　From one by Corporal Mortimer.

enclosure would require to be, and in fact was, 100 feet in diameter,
and the inner room, measuring 80 feet by 50 feet, including the
apse, was the largest and finest apartment of the class in the
islands.

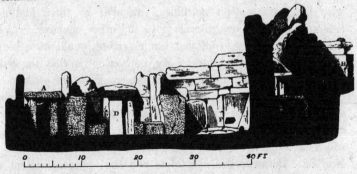

180.　　Section, on the line A B, through Lower Pair of Chambers, Mnaidra.

The section through the lower chambers (woodcut No. 180) will
suffice to explain the general appearance of these buildings in-

2 E 2

ternally, as they now stand.   A is the entrance into a small square
apartment in which the altar or table stands, shown more completely in the next woodcut (No. 181), from a photograph, which
also renders much mere clear the peculiar style of ornamenting

181.   Entrance to Chamber B, Mnaidra, showing Table inside.
                    (The Rod is divided into English feet.)

with innumerable "pit markings," peculiar to these Maltese
monuments.   D is the entrance into the other chamber, which
but for the interference of that last described, would have been
of the usual elliptical form. My impression is that the left-
hand apse was removed at some time subsequent to the erection of
the monument, to admit of its insertion. On each side of the
doorway are seats, C and E, which are always found in similar
situations. Beyond, at F, is one of those mysterious openings
which are so frequent; it is also seen with another in woodcut
No. 182. Between this apartment and the upper apartment H
are two tiers of shelves or loculi, which are also found at Gozo,
and for which it is difficult to suggest a meaning if they were not
used as columbaria for sepulchral purposes.

A difficult question here arises as to which of these two pairs of apartments is the older—the upper, with the simpler style and the smaller stones, or the apartments with the larger stones and more ornate arrangements. On the whole, I am inclined to think the simpler the older : among other reasons because the floor of the right-hand pair at Mnaidra is 10 feet above the level of the left-hand apartments. As the edifices are all placed on heights, it seems improbable that the first comer would have chosen a site commanded by a knoll 10 feet above him, and touching his half-buried building. But, besides this local indication, it seems probable that the style was progressive, and that this right-hand chamber at Mnaidra may be the oldest, and the great one at Gozo the last completed of all which we know.

182.   North End of Left-hand Outer Chamber at Mnaidra.   From a photograph.

The excavations at Mnaidra as well as those at Hagiar Khem have sufficed to settle the question of how these buildings were roofed. The above woodcut, from a photograph, shows the springing of the roof of the north end of the outer left-hand chamber, but, like photographs in general, does so unintelligently.

Colonel Collinson, however, informs me that they bracket outwards, at the rate of 1 foot in 10, and he calculates that they
would meet at a height of 30 feet so nearly that they could be
closed by a single stone. He, however, overlooks the fact that
all these horizontally-constructed domes, whether in Greece, or
Italy, or Sardinia, are curvilinear, their section being that of a
Gothic pointed arch, and consequently, if corbelling forward at
the rate of 1 in 10 near the springing, they would certainly meet
in this chamber at 15 or 20 feet from their base. When we
recollect that before the Trojan war the Pelasgic architects of
Greece roofed chambers 50 and 60 feet in diameter (*vide ante*,
page 33), we should not be surprised at the Maltese architects
grappling with apses of 20 feet span. This has generally been
admitted as easy, but several authors have been puzzled to think
how the flat spaces joining the two apses could have been so roofed.
A careful examination of the plans of the Maltese building seems
to make this easy. Looking, for instance, at the plan of Mnaidra,
a retaining wall will be observed on the extreme right, which is a
segment of a circle 75 feet in diameter, and continuing it all
round, it encloses both chambers. If a similar circle is drawn round
the left-hand chambers, it equally encloses them, and the circles
osculate, or have one party wall at a point where there is the
group of cells. This granted, it is easy to see that the external
form of the roof was a stepped cone, covering the inner roofs, and
so avoiding the ridges and hollows which would have rendered
independent roofing impracticable. The external appearance of
the building would thus have been that of two equal cones joined
together, and rising probably to a height of 50 feet above their
springing. To erect such a cone on an enclosing wall only 8 or
10 feet thick may appear at first sight a little difficult for such
rude builders as the Maltese were when they erected these domes,
but when we recollect that the cone was divided into two by a
cross party wall, which may have been carried the whole height,
all difficulty vanishes.

When we apply these principles to the ruins at Hagiar Khem,
their history becomes plain at once. Originally the monument
seems to have consisted of a single pair of chambers of the usual
form, A and B of the accompanying plan; but extension becoming

necessary, the central apse of the inner apartment was removed
and converted into a doorway, and the left-hand lateral apse was
also removed so as to make an entrance into four other ovoid
apartments, which were arranged radially so as to be covered
by a cone 90 feet in diameter.   Here again the difficulty, if any,
of constructing a cone of these dimensions is got over by the

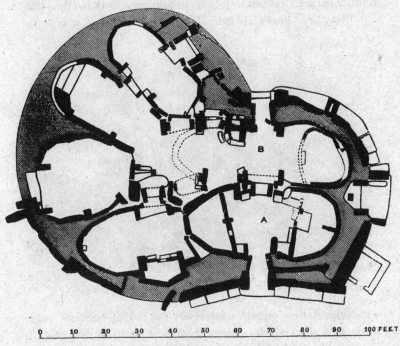

183.   Plan of Hagiar Khem, partially restored.

numerous points of support from perpendicular walls which
honeycomb the building. The external appearance of this
building would be that of one great cone 90 feet in diameter
covering the cells, and anastomosing with one 60 feet, or one-third
less, in diameter covering the entrance chambers.

Restored in this manner, the external appearance of these monuments would have been very similar to that of the Kubber
Roumeia near Algiers and the Madracen near Blidah. The
former was 200 feet in diameter, with a cone rising in steps to the
height of 130 feet, which was lower in proportion than suggested

above, but its interior was nearly solid, and admitted therefore of
any angle that might appear most beautiful. The Madracen looks
even lower, but no correct section of it has been published. The
Kubber Roumeia has now been ascertained to have been the tomb
of the Mauritanian kings down to the time of Juba II., or about
the Christian era.[1] Judging from its style, the Madracen may be a
century earlier. Be this as it may, it hardly seems to me doubtful
but that these tombs are late Roman translations of a type to

181.   View of Madracen.   From a plate in Blakesley's 'Four Months in Algeria.'

which the Maltese examples belonged; but the intermediate links
in the long chain which connects them have yet to be recovered.

Internally, these Maltese monuments are rude, and exhibit very
little attempt at decoration. The inner apartments, being dark,
are quite plain, but the outer, admitting a certain quantity of light
by the door, have a proportionate amount of ornament. At Gozo,
in the outer apartment, there are, as mentioned above, scrolls and
spirals of a style very much more refined than is found in Ireland
or in rude monuments generally, but more resembling that of those
found at Mycenæ and other parts of Greece. At Hagiar Khem
and Mnaidra the favourite ornament are pit markings. Whether

---

[1] Berbrugger, 'Tombeau de la Chrétienne—Mausolée des derniers Rois de Mauri-
tanie;' Alger, 1867.

these have any affinity with those which Sir J. Simpson so copiously illustrated,[1] is by no means clear.   In Malta they are spread evenly over the stone, and are such a decoration as might be used at the present day (woodcut No. 181).   An altar was found in one of the outer chambers at Hagiar Khem, and in both the Maltese monuments, stone tables from 4 to 5 feet high (one is shown in the woodcut No. 181), the use of which is not clearly made out.   They are too tall for altars, and, unless in the Balearic Islands, nothing like them is known elsewhere.

After what has been said above, it is hardly worth while to enter into the argument whether these buildings are temples or tombs. Their situation alone, in this instance, is sufficient to prove that they do not belong to the former class.   Men do not drop three or four temples irregularly, as at Gozo, within a stone's throw of one another, on a bare piece of ground, far away from any centres of population.   The same is the case at Hagiar Khem, where certainly three, probably four, sets of chambers exist; and Mnaidra may almost be considered a part of the same group or cemetery.

Malta, it is said, was colonised by the Phœnicians, at least was so in Diodorus' time,[2] though how much earlier they occupied it, we are not told, nor to what extent they superseded the original inhabitants.   We also learn incidentally that they possessed temples dedicated to Melkart and Astarte.   This is very probable, and if so, their remains will be found near their harbours, and where they established themselves; and Colonel Collinson informs me that remains of columnar buildings have been found both at Marsa Sirocco and near the dockyard creek at Valetta. These, most probably, are the remains of the temples in question, though possibly rebuilt in Roman times.   The little images found in the apartments at Hagiar Khem may be representations of the Cabeiri, though I doubt it; but little headless deformities, 20 inches high, some of stone and some of clay, are not the divinities that would be worshipped in such temples, though they might be offerings at a tomb.

If these buildings were tombs, they were the burying-places of a people who burnt their dead and carefully preserved their ashes,

---

[1] 'Proceedings Soc. Ant. Scot.,' vi., Supplement.   [2] Hist., v. 12, 3.

and who paid the utmost respect to their buried dead long after their decease. The inner apartments have shelves and cupboards in stone, and numerous little arrangements which it seems impossible to understand except on the supposition that they were places for the deposit of these sacred remains. Some of the recesses have doors cut out of a single slab 2 and 3 feet square at the opening, some are so small that a man could hardly squeeze himself through, and some are holes into which only an arm could be thrust,[1] but from the rebate outside of all, the intention seems to have been for them all to be closed.

Although from all these arrangements it may broadly be asserted that they are not temples in the ordinary sense of the term; the outer apartments may be considered as halls in which religious ceremonies were performed in honour of the dead, and, so far, as places of worship; but essentially they were sepulchres, and their uses sepulchral.

We know so little of the ancient history of Malta that it is extremely difficult even to guess who the people were who erected and used these sepulchres. Most people would at once answer, the Phœnicians; but, in order to establish their claim, one of two things is necessary—either we must have some direct testimony that they erected these monuments, or we must be able to show that they erected similar tombs either near their own homes or elsewhere. Neither kind of proof is forthcoming. No such tombs are found near Tyre or Sidon, or near Carthage, and classical authorities are absolutely silent on the subject. The monuments most like them are the tombs at Mycenæ, but the differences are so great that I would hesitate to lay much stress on any slight similarities that exist. The Greek monuments were always intended to be buried in tumuli. Those at Malta have so strongly marked and so ornamental a podium outside that it is evident they never were so covered up. It may be difficult to prove it, but I fancy if we are ever to find their originals, it is to Africa we must look for them. They are too unlike anything else in Europe.

It seems even more difficult to define their age than to ascertain their origin. Looking at the nature of the stone, their state of

---

[1] One at Mnaidra will be seen at F, in woodcut No. 180, and also in the view, woodcut No. 182.

preservation, and other circumstances, I cannot believe they are
very old. If they were in Greece, or in Europe, or anywhere
where they could be compared with other monuments, some
useful inferences might be drawn; but they are so unique that this
mode is unavailable. We have nothing we can confidently compare them with, and we are so entirely ignorant of the ancient
history of Malta that we cannot tell in the least at what age
she reached that stage of civilization which the workmanship of
these monuments represents. We are probably safe, however, in
assuming that they are pre-Roman, and as safe in believing that
they are not earlier than the monuments of Mycenæ and Thyrns;
in short, that they belong to some period between the Trojan and
the Punic wars, but are most probably much nearer to the former
than to the latter epoch in the world's history.

SARDINIA.

It is a curious illustration of the fragmentary nature of society
in the ancient world that Sardinia should possess a class of monuments absolutely peculiar to itself. It is not this time ten or a
dozen monuments, like those of Malta, but they are numbered by
thousands, and so like one another that it is impossible to mistake
them, and, what is still more singular, as difficult to trace any
progress or change among them. The Talyots of the Balearic
Islands may resemble them, but, excepting these, the Nurhags of
Sardinia stand quite alone. Nothing the least like them is found
in Italy, or in Sicily, or, indeed, anywhere else, so far as is at
present known.

A Nurhag is easily recognized and easily described. It is
always a round tower, with sides sloping at an angle of about
10 degrees to the horizon, its dimensions varying from 20 to
60 feet in diameter, and its height being generally equal to the
width of the base. Sometimes they are one, frequently two
and even three storeys in height, the centre being always occupied
by circular chambers, constructed by projecting stones forming a
dome with the section of a pointed arch. The chamber generally
occupies one-third of the diameter, the thickness of the walls
forming the remaining two-thirds. There is invariably a ramp or

staircase leading to the platform at the top of the tower. These peculiarities will be understood from the annexed section and plan of one from De la Marmora's work.[1]

185. Nurhag. From De la Marmora.

When the Nurhags are of more than one storey in height, they are generally surrounded by others which are attached to them by platforms, often of considerable extent. That at Santa Barbara has, or had, four small Nurhags encased in the four corners of the platform, to which access was obtained by a doorway in the central tower; but frequently there are also separate ramps when the platforms are extensive. The masonry of these monuments is generally neat, though sometimes the stones are unhewn, but

186. Nurhag of Santa Barbara.

nowhere does there appear any attempt at megalithic magnificence.

---

[1] 'Voyage en Sardaigne,' par le Cte. Albert de la Marmora; Paris, 1840. As this is not only the best but really the only reliable work on the subject, all, or nearly all, the information in this chapter is based upon it.

They are, at the same time, absolutely without any architectural ornament which could give us any hint of their affinities; and no inscriptions, no images, no sculptures of any kind, have been found in them. They are in this respect as uncommunicative as our own rude-stone monuments.

Written history is almost equally silent. Only one passage has been disinterred which seems to refer to them. It is a Greek work, generally known as 'De Mirabilibus Auscultationibus,'[1] and ascribed doubtfully to Aristotle. It is to the following effect:—"It is said that in the island of Sardinia there exist, among other beautiful and numerous edifices, built after the manner of the ancient Greeks,

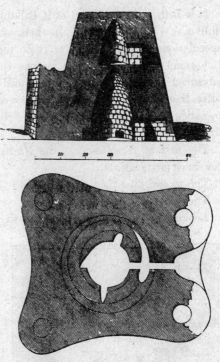

187.   Nurhag of Santa Barbara.   From De la Marmora.

certain domes (Θόλοι) of exquisite proportions. It is further said that they were built by Iolas, son of Iphicles, who, having taken with him the Thespiadæ, went to colonise this island." This certainly looks as if the Nurhags existed when this book was written, though the description is by a person who evidently never saw them. Diodorus so far confirms this that he says: "Iolaus, having founded the colony, fetched Dedalus from Sicily, and built numerous and grand edifices, which subsist to the present day, and are called Dedalean, from the name of their builder;"[2] and in another paragraph he recurs to the veneration

---

[1] Bekker, iii. p. 604, para. 100.   [2] Diodorus, iv. 30; v. 15.

"in which the name of Iolaus is held." This, too, is unsatisfactory, as written by a person who never visited the island, and had not seen the monuments of which he was speaking.

It is little to be wondered at if buildings so mysterious and so unlike any known to exist elsewhere should have given rise to speculations almost as wild as those that hang around our own rude-stone monuments. The various theories which have been advanced are enumerated and described by De la Marmora [1] so fully that it will not be necessary to recapitulate them here, nor to notice any but three, which seem really to have some plausible foundation.

The first of these assumes the Nurhags to have been watch-towers or fortifications.

The second, that they were temples.

The third, that they were tombs.

Looking at the positions in which they are found, the first of

188. Map of La Giara. From De la Marmora.

these theories is not so devoid of foundation as might at first sight appear. As a rule, they are all placed on heights, and at such distances as to be seen from one another, and consequently be able to communicate by signal at least. Take such an example, for instance, as that of Giara, near Isili (woodcut No. 188). Any engineer officer would be delighted with the manner in which the position is taken up. Every point of vantage in the circumference is occupied, and two points in the interior fortified, so as to act as supports. The designer of the entrenched camp at Linz might rub his eyes in astonishment to find his inventions forestalled by

[1] 'Voyage en Sardaigne,' chap. iv. pp. 117 to 159.

three thousand years, and by towers externally so like his own as hardly to be distinguishable to an unpractised eye. The form of the towers themselves lends considerable plausibility to the defensive theory. Such a Nurhag, for instance, as that of Santa Barbara (woodcuts Nos. 186, 187), surrounded by four lesser ones, connected by a platform, and dominated by the central tower, is a means of defence we might now adopt, provided we may assume the existence of a parapet, which has fallen through age.

When we come to look a little more closely at this military question, we perceive that we are attempting to apply to a people who certainly had no projectiles that would carry farther than arrows, principles adapted to artillery or musketry fire. The Nurhags are placed at such distances as to afford no support to one another before the invention of gunpowder, and though in themselves not indefensible, they possess the radical defect of having no accommodation for their garrisons. It is impossible that men could live, cook, and sleep in the little circular apartments in their interior, and the platforms added very little to their accommodation. Had the four detached Nurhags at Santa Barbara been connected with walls only, so as to surround the central tower with a court, the case would have been very different; but as in all instances this is filled up, so as to form a platform, it is evident that it was exposure, not shelter, that was sought in their construction.[1]

Another, and even stronger, argument is derived from their number. De la Marmora asserts that the remains of at least three thousand Nurhags can now be traced in Sardinia,[2] and there seems no reason to doubt the truth of his calculation, nor his assertion that they were once much more numerous, and that they are dispersed pretty evenly over the whole island. Can any one fancy a state of society in such an island which would require that there should be three thousand castles and yet no fortified cities as places of refuge? They were not erected to protect the island against a foreign

[1] The Scotch brochs, which are in their construction the erections most like these, have all courtyards in their centre, in which all the domestic operations of the garrison could be carried on conveniently, and they only needed to creep into the chambers in the wall to sleep.

[2] 'Voyage en Sardaigne,' pp. 46 and 116.

enemy, because most of them are inland. They could not be made to serve for the protection of the rich during insurrections or civil wars, nor to enable robbers to plunder in security the peaceful inhabitants of the plain. In short, unless the ancient Sardinians lived in a state of society of which we have no knowledge elsewhere, these Nurhags were certainly not military works.

When we turn to the second hypothesis and try to consider them as temples, we are met by very much the same difficulties as beset the fortification theory. If temples, they are unlike the temples of any other people. Generally it is assumed that they were fire temples, from their name *Nur*—in the Semitic languages signifying fire—but more from their construction. The little circular chambers in their interiors are admirably suited for preserving the sacred fire, and the external platforms as well adapted for that Sabean worship of the planets which is generally understood to be associated with fire-worship. But assuming this to be the case, why so numerous? We can count on our fingers all the fire-temples that exist, or were ever known to exist, in fire-worshipping Persia; and if a dozen satisfied her spiritual wants, what necessity was there for three thousand, or probably twice that number, in the small and sparsely inhabited island of Sardinia? Had every family, or little village community its own separate temple on the nearest high place? and did each perform its own worship separately from the rest? So far as we know, there is no subordination among them, nothing corresponding to cathedrals, or parish churches or chapels. Some are smaller, or some form more extensive groups than others, but a singularly republican equality reigns throughout, very unlike the hierarchical feeling we find in most religions. In one other respect, too, they are unlike the temples of other nations. None of them are situated in towns or villages, or near the centres of population in the island.

Must we then adopt the third hypothesis, that they were tombs? Here again the same difficulties meet us. If they were tombs, they are unlike those of any other people with whom we are acquainted. Their numbers in this instance is, however, no difficulty. It is in the nature of the case that sepulchres should accumulate, and their number is consequently one of the strongest arguments in favour of this destination. Nor does their situation militate against this view. Nothing is more likely than that a people should like to bury their dead, on high places, where their tombs can be seen from afar. In fact, there does not seem much to be said against this theory, except that no sepulchral remains have been found in them. It is true that De la Marmora found a skeleton buried in one at Iselle,[1] and apparently so placed that the interment must have taken place before the tower was built, or at all events finished; but the presence of only one corpse in two thousand nurhags tells strongly against the theory, as where one was placed more would have been found had this form of interment been usual, and amidst the hundreds of ruined and half-ruined nurhags some evidence must have been found had any of the usual sepulchral usages prevailed. To my mind the conclusion seems inevitable that, if they were tombs, they were those of a people who, like the Parsees of the present day, exposed their dead to be devoured by the birds of the air. If there is one feature in the nurhags more consistent or more essential than another, it is that of the stairs or ramps that give access to their platforms. It shows, without doubt, that, whether for defence, or worship, or burial, the platform was the feature for which the edifice was erected, and there it must have been that its purposes were fulfilled. But is it possible that such a practice ever prevailed in Sardinia? It is, of course, precipitate to answer that it did. But the custom is old. Anything so exceptional among modern usages is not the invention of yesterday, and it may have been far more prevalent than it now is, and it may in very ancient times have been brought by some Eastern colonists to this Western isle. I dare hardly suggest that it was so; but this is certain, that such towers would answer in every respect perfectly to the "Towers of Silence" of the modern Persians, and the little side chambers in the towers would suit perfectly as receptacles of the denuded bones when the time arrived for collecting them.

One argument against their being sepulchres has been drawn from the fact that frequently a different class of graves, called giants' tombs, is found in their immediate proximity. The conclusion I would draw from this is in a contrary sense. These giants' tombs are generally long graves of neatly fitted stones,

---

[1] 'Voyage,' p. 152.

with a tall frontispiece, which is formed of one stone, always carefully hewn and sometimes carved. On each side of the entrance two arms extend so as to form a semicircle in front, and when the circle is completed by detached menhirs, these are generally shaped into cones and carved. The whole, in fact, has a more advanced and more modern appearance than the nurhags, and, as I read the riddle, the inhabitants adopted this form, and that found in the nurhag at Iselle, after they had ceased to use the nurhag itself as a means of disposing of their dead, but were still clinging to the spots made sacred by the ashes of their forefathers.

That the nurhags are old scarcely seems to admit of a doubt, though I know of only one material point of evidence on the subject. It is that the pier of a Roman aqueduct has been founded on the stump of a ruined and consequently desecrated nurhag.[1] Some time must have elapsed before the primitive and sacred use of the nurhag had been so completely forgotten that it should be so used. But the passages above quoted from the ' Mirabilibus ' and Diodorus show that in the first and fifth centuries B.C. nothing was known of their origin by these authors, and no other has ventured to hint at their age. In classical times they seem to have been as mysterious as they are now :—

> " In the glimmer of the dawn
> They stand the solemn silent witnesses
> Of ancient days,—altars—or graves."

BALEARIC ISLANDS.

The third group of monuments indicated above are the Talyots of Minorca and Majorca. Unfortunately our guide, De la Marmora, deserts us here. He went to explore them, but ill health and other adverse circumstances prevented his carrying his intent fully into effect, and we are left consequently very much to the work of Don Juan Ramis,[2] which is the reverse of satisfactory.

Externally they generally resemble the nurhags in appearance, and apparently have always chambers in their interior, but De la

---

[1] De la Marmora, pl. v. p. 149.

[2] ' Antigüedades Celticas de la Isla de Menorca, &c.;' Mahon, 1818.

Marmora was unable to determine whether any of them had the internal staircase[1] leading to the summit which is the invariable and essential characteristic of the nurhag. If they had not this, they must

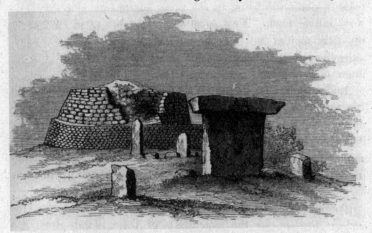

189.   Talyot at Trepucò, Minorca.   From De la Marmora.

be considered as more nearly approaching to our chambered cairns than to nurhags; and till this point is settled, and we know more about them, we must refrain from speculations on the subject. One characteristic feature they have, however, which it is useful to note. It is a bilithon, if such a term is admissible—an upright flat stone, with one across it forming a sort of table. In appearance it very much resembles those stone tables which are found in-

190.   Talyot at Alajor, Minorca.
From De la Marmora.

side the chambers of the Maltese sepulchres, but these are always larger, and placed, so far as is known, externally. What their use may have been, it is difficult to conjecture, but they were evidently considered important here, as in woodcut No. 190 one

---

[1] Voyage,' pp. 547 *et seqq.*

is shown surrounded by a sacred enclosure, as if being itself the
" Numen" to be honoured. At Malta, as before remarked, they
certainly were not altars, because pedestals, which were unmistakably altars, are found in the same apartments, and they are
very unlike them. They seem more like the great saucers in
the Irish tombs, and may have served the same purposes; but
altogether these Balearic outside tables are unlike anything we
know of elsewhere.

Rude-stone circles seem to be not uncommon in combination with
the talyots and tall altars, and on the whole they seem to bear as
much affinity to the monuments of Spain as to those of Sardinia,
but again till we know more it is idle to speculate on either their
age or uses beyond the conclusion drawn from all similar monuments—that their destination was to honour departed greatness.

It would be not only interesting but instructive to pursue the
subject further, for the monuments of these islands deserve a
more complete investigation than they have yet received; but
this is not the place to pursue it. Indeed, it is only indirectly
that they have any connection with the subject of this work.
They are not megalithic in the sense in which the word is
generally used. Nor are they rude, for all the stones are more
or less shaped by art, and all are used constructively. In none
of them is the stone itself the object and end of the erection.
In all it is only a means to an end.

It is their locality and their age that import them into our
argument if there is anything in the connection between the
monuments of France and Algeria, as attempted to be shown
above. Whether the African ones came from Europe, or *vice versâ*,
it must have been in consequence of long-continued intercourse
between the two countries, and of an influence of the dolmen
builders in the Western Mediterranean which could hardly have
failed to leave traces in the intermediate islands, unless they had
been previously civilized and had fixed and long-established modes
of dealing with their own dead.

Assuming that the nurhàgs and giants' towers extend back to the
mythic times of Grecian history, say the war of Troy—and some
of them can hardly be more modern—it will hardly be contended

now that the dolmens are earlier. If they were so, it must be by centuries or by thousands of years, if we are to assume that the one had any influence on the other, for it must have taken long before a truly rude-stone monument could have grown into a constructive style like that of Sardinia or Malta; and I do not think, after what has been said above, any one would now contend for so remote an antiquity. If neither anterior nor coeval, the conclusion, if we admit any influence at all, seems inevitable that the dolmens must be subsequent. But this is just the point at issue. The nurhags did not grow out of dolmens, nor dolmens out of nurhags. They are separate and distinct creations, so far as we know, belonging to different races, and practically uninfluenced by one another. Here, as elsewhere, each group must be judged by itself, and stand on its own merits. If any direct influence can be shown to exist between any two groups, there is generally very little difficulty in arranging them in a sequence and seeing which is the oldest, but till such connection is established, all such attempts are futile.

In so far as any argument can now be got out of these insular monuments, it seems to take this form. If the dolmen people were earlier than the nurhag-builders, they certainly would have occupied the islands that lay in their path between France or Spain and Africa, and we should find traces of them there. If, on the contrary, the nurhag-builders were the earlier race, and colonised these islands so completely as to fill them before the age of the dolmen-builders, the latter, in passing from north to south, or *vice versâ*, could only have touched at the islands as emigrants or traders, and not as colonists, and consequently could have neither altered nor influenced to any great extent the more practically civilized people who had already occupied them.

So far as we can see, this is the view that most nearly meets the facts of the case at present known, and in this respect their negative evidence is both interesting and instructive, though, except when viewed in this light, the monuments of the Mediterranean islands have no real place in a work treating on rude-stone monuments.

CHAPTER XII.

WESTERN ASIA.

———◦◆◦———

PALESTINE.

PALESTINE is one of those countries in which dolmens exist, not in thousands and tens of thousands, as in Algeria, but certainly in hundreds—perhaps tens of hundreds; but travellers have not yet condescended to open their eyes to observe them, and the Palestine Exploration Fund is too busy making maps to pay attention to a subject which would probably throw as much light on the ethnography of the Holy Land as anything we know of. Before, however, retailing what little we know about the monuments actually existing, it is necessary in this instance to say a few words about those which we know of only by hearsay. All writers on megalithic remains in the last century, and some of those of the present, have made so much of the stones set up by Abraham and Joshua that it is indispensable to try to ascertain what they were, and what bearing they really have on the subject of which we are treating.

The earliest mention of a stone being set up anywhere as a monument or memorial is that of the one which Jacob used as a pillow in the night when he had that dream which became the title of the Israelites to the land of Canaan. "And Jacob rose up early in the morning, and took the stone that he had put for his pillows, and set it up for a pillar, and poured oil upon the top of it."[1] The question is, What was the size of this stone? In the East, where hard pillows are not objected to, natives generally use a brick for this purpose. Europeans, who are more stiffnecked as well as more luxurious, insist on two bricks, and these laid one on the other, with a cloth thrown over them, form by no means an uncomfortable headpiece. The fact of Jacob being alone, and moving the stone to and from the place where it was used, proves that it was not larger

---

[1] Genesis xxviii. 18; xxxv. 14.

than, probably not so large as, the head that was laid upon it. It certainly, therefore, was neither the Lia Fail which still adorns the hill of Tara nor even the Scone stone that forms the king's seat in Westminster Abbey, and, what is more to our present purpose, it may safely be discharged from the category of megalithic monuments of which we are now treating.

The next case in which stones are mentioned is in Genesis xxxi. 45 and 46: " And Jacob took a stone, and set it up for a pillar. And Jacob said unto his brethren, Gather stones; and they took stones, and made an heap: and they did eat there upon the heap." This is not quite so clear; but the fair inference seems to be that what they erected was a stone altar, on which they partook of an offering, which, under the circumstances, took the form of a sacramental oath—one party standing on either side of it. The altar in the temple of Jerusalem, we know, down even to the time of Herod, was formed of stones, which no iron tool had ever touched,[1] and the tradition derived from this altar of Jacob seems to have lasted during the whole Jewish period. So there is nothing in this instance to lead us to suppose that " the heap" had any connection with the megalithic monuments of other countries.

The third instance, though more frequently quoted, seems even less relevant. When Joshua passed the Jordan, twelve men, according to the number of the tribes, were appointed, each " to take up a stone on his shoulder out of the Jordan, in the place where the priests' feet had stood, and to carry them and set them down at the place where they lodged that night, as a memorial to the children of Israel for ever."[2] Here, again, stones that men can carry on their shoulders are not much bigger than their heads, and are not such as in any ordinary sense would be used as memorials, inasmuch as they could be as easily removed by any one, as placed where they were. If ranged on an altar, in a building, this purpose would have been answered; but as an open-air testimonial such stones seem singularly inappropriate.

The only instance in which it seems that the Bible is speaking of the same class of monuments as those we are concerned with

---

[1] Josephus, ' Bell. Jud.' v. 6.

[2] Joshua iv. 2 to 8. There is some mistake in the 9th verse; either it is a mistranslation or the verse is an interpolation. It is to be hoped that the Revisers will look to it.

is in the last chapter of Joshua, where it is said (verse 26), he "took a great stone, and set it up there under an oak, that was by the sanctuary of the Lord," and said, "Behold, this stone shall be a witness unto us." It is the more probable that this was really a great monolith, as it seems to be the stone mentioned in Judges ix. 6 as "the pillar of the plain," . . . or "by the oak of the pillar which was in Shechem;" and if this is so, it must have been of considerable dimensions. It therefore alone, of all the stones mentioned in the Bible, seems to belong to the class of stones we are treating of; but even then its direct bearing on the subject is not clear. It by no means follows that because the Israelites in Joshua's time set up such a stone for such a purpose that either then or a thousand years afterwards the French or Scandinavians did the same thing with the same intention. It may be so, but both the time and locality seem too remote for us to rely on any supposed analogy.

As bearing indirectly on this subject, it is curious to observe that the rite of circumcision in these early days of Jewish history was performed with flint knives,[1] which, considering that bronze and iron were both familiarly known to the Israelites at that period, is a remarkable example of the persistence in an old fashion long after it might have been supposed it would have become obsolete. It is equally curious, if the Septuagint is to be depended upon, that they should have buried with Joshua in his grave those very flint implements (τὰς μαχαίρας τὰς πετρίνας) with which the operation was performed. This cannot of course be quoted as the latest or even a late example of flint being buried in tombs, but it is interesting as explaining one reason for the practice. It is at least one instance in which flint was used long after metal was known, and one tomb in which stone implements were buried for other reasons than the people's ignorance of the use of metal.[2] If the Jews used flints for that purpose in Joshua's time, and so disposed of them after the death of their chief, the only wonder is that they do not do so at the present day.

---

[1] Exodus iv. 25; Joshua v. 3.

[2] Herodotus (ii. 86) mentions that, in his day, the Egyptians, after extracting the brain with an iron instrument, cut open the body they intended to embalm with an Ethiopic stone, and Sir Gardner Wilkinson ('Ancient Egyptians,' iii. 262) found two flint knives in a tomb which might have been used for such a purpose.

To turn from these speculations, based on words, to the real facts
of the case. We find that the first persons who observed dolmens
in Syria were Captains Irby and Mangles. In their hurried journey
from Es Salt, in 1817, to the fords of the Jordan, apparently in a
straight line from Es Salt to Nablous, they observed a group of
twenty-seven dolmens, very irregularly situated at the foot of the
mountain. All those they observed were composed of two side-
stones, from 8 to 10 feet long, supporting a cap-stone projecting
considerably beyond the sides and ends. The chambers, however,
were only 5 feet long internally—too short, consequently, for a
body to be stretched out at full length. The contraction arose
from the two transverse stones being placed considerably within
the ends of the side-stones. One of these appears to have been

191.   Dolmens at Kafr er Wâl.   From a sketch by Mrs. Roberton Blaine.

solid, the other to have been pierced with what is called a door;
but whether this was a hole in one stone, or a door formed by two
jambs, is not clear.[1] No drawing or plan accompanies their
description; but the arrangement will be easily understood when
we come to examine those of Rajunkoloor, in India,[2] described
farther on (woodcut No. 206).

The only other reliable information I have is extracted for me
from his note-books by my friend, Mr. D. R. Blaine. In travelling
from Om Keis—Gadara—towards Gerash, at a place called Kafr er
Wâl, not far from Tibné, they met with one considerable group, a
portion of which is represented in the above woodcut (No. 191).
The size of the stones varies considerably; generally, however, they
are about 12 feet by 6 feet, and from 1 to 2 feet in thickness. One

---

[1] Irby and Mangles, 'Travels in Egypt, Nubia, &c.' 1823, p. 325.
[2] Colonel Meadows Taylor, in 'Trans. Royal Irish Academy,' 1865.

cap-stone was nearly 12 feet square, and the side-stones vary from
5 to 6 feet in height. On approaching Sûf, a great number of
dolmens were observed on either side of the road for a distance
of from three to four miles. Some of these seemed quite perfect,
others were broken down; but the travellers had unfortunately
no time to count or examine them with care.

This is a very meagre account of a great subject—so meagre,
indeed, that it is impossible to found any argument upon it that
will be worth anything; but it is interesting to observe that all the
dolmens as yet noticed in Syria are situated in Gilead, the country
of the Amorites, and of Og, king of Bashan. If it should prove
eventually that there are none except in this district, it would
give rise to several interesting ethnographical determinations. At
present all we can feel confident about is that there are no dolmens
west of the Jordan; but the Amorites were originally settled in
Hebron,[1] and there are certainly no dolmens there. So unless they
migrated eastward before the dolmen period, they can scarcely lay
claim to them. Then these dolmens may belong to the Rephaim,
the Emim, the Anakim, the Zuzim, and all those giant tribes that
dwelt beyond Jordan at the time of Chedorlaomer, the dreaded king
of Elam, who smote the kings of this district at the dawn of the
Bible history of these regions.[2] The speculation is a tempting one,
and if it should eventually be proved that they are confined to this
one district, it will no doubt find favour in some quarters. There
seems, however, nothing to support it beyond the fact that the
people in the region beyond the Jordan seem all and always to have
been of Hamite or Turanian blood, and therefore likely to adopt
this mode of burial whenever it may have been introduced, in
spite of the colonization of two tribes and a half of Israelites, who
could do but little to leaven the mass. I am afraid that, like the
theory which identified the Roman cities of the Hauran with
the giant cities of Og, king of Bashan, and his tall contemporaries,
this hypothesis will not bear examination. Every stone of these
cities, it is now known, was placed where we now find it, after the
time when Pompey extended Roman influence to these regions;
and nothing would surprise me less than to find that these dolmens

---

[1] Genesis, xiii. 18; xiv. 13.　　　[2] Gen. xiii. 5.

are even more modern.   Before, however, we venture to speculate
on such a subject, we must feel surer than we now do of their extent
and their distribution, and know something of their contents.   On
both these subjects we are at present practically entirely ignorant.

Gilead is almost the last safe resting-place at which we can
pause in our explorations eastward in our attempts to connect the
Eastern and the Western dolmen regions together.   But Gilead
is two thousand miles from Peshawur, where we meet the first
example of the Indian dolmens; and in the vast regions that lie
between, only one or two doubtful examples are known to exist.
We can creep on doubtfully a couple of hundred miles nearer,
in Arabia and Circassia; but that hardly helps us much, and
unless some discoveries are made in the intermediate countries,
the migration theory will become wholly untenable.

In the course of the recent ordnance survey of the peninsula of
Sinai in 1868-9, great numbers of circular buildings were discovered,
many of which were certainly tombs; and plans and drawings of
some of them have been engraved, and will be published by the
authorities at Southampton.   But as great bodies move slowly, it
may yet be a long time before they are accessible to the public.
Meanwhile the following particulars, gleaned from a paper by the
Rev. Mr. Holland,[1] will suffice to explain what they are.   The
buildings are of two classes: the first, which were probably store-
houses, were built in the shape of a dome, about 5 feet high and
5 or 6 feet in diameter in the interior.   The walls were often as
much as 4 feet thick, and a large flat stone formed the highest
portion of the roof, which appeared to have been covered with
loose shingle.   They had no windows, and one door, about 3 feet
high and 1½ foot broad.   The stones used in their construction
were often large, but never dressed, and no mortar was used.

The other kind of ruins, which is generally found in close
proximity to the former, often in separate groups, consists of
massively built circles of stones, of about 14 to 15 feet in
diameter, and 3 feet high, but without any roof.   "These," Mr.
Holland says, "were evidently tombs; for I found human bones

---

[1] 'Journal Royal Geographical Society,' 1868, pp. 243 et seq.

in all that I opened," which were never met with in the buildings of the first class; " and in one two skeletons lying side by side, one of them on a bed of flat stones. The rings of stones were apparently first half filled with earth ; the bodies were then laid in them, and they were then quite filled up with earth, and heavy stones placed on the top to prevent the wild beasts disturbing the bodies. Some of these rings are of much larger size: some 45, others 90, feet in diameter, and some contained a smaller ring in the centre. Near the mound of Nukb Hawy is one no less than 375 feet in diameter." From the above description it is evident that, except from the dimensions of the last-mentioned, these circles have much more affinity with the Chouchas and Bazinas of Algeria than with anything farther north or west, and there is probably some connection between them. But a wall of coursed masonry of small stones can hardly be compared with our megalithic structures, and, so far as is known, no dolmens, nor any examples of the great rude-stone monuments we are discussing, have been found in the peninsula. When the results of the survey are published, we may see reason to alter this opinion; but at present these Sinaitic tombs seem to belong to a class altogether different from the European examples, except in two points—that they are circular and sepulchral. These characteristics are, however, so important that eventually other points of comparison may be established.

The rude-stone monuments which Mr. Giffard Palgrave accidentally stumbled upon in the centre of Arabia are of a very different class from these. According to his account, what he saw was apparently one-half of what had once been a complete circle of trilithons; but whether continuous, like the outer circle of Stonehenge, or in pairs, like the inner circle there, is not quite clear. As he could just touch the impost with his whip when on his camel, the height was, as he says, about 15 feet—the same as Stonehenge; and the expression he uses would lead us to suppose that the whole structure was essentially similar. Allowance, however, must be made for his being in disguise, which prevented his making notes or writing down his observations; and writing afterwards from memory, his description may not be minutely correct. He is, however, so clear and acute an observer that he could hardly be deceiving himself; and we may take it for granted that exactly halfway between the Persian Gulf and the Red Sea, near Eyoon, in latitude 26° 20', there exist three rude-stone monuments —he saw only one, but heard of two others—of a class similar to those found in England and in the continent of Europe,[1] and what is more important to our present purpose, similar to those found in Tripoli, and illustrated above in woodcuts 175 and 176.

De Vogüé's plates of late Roman tombs in the Hauran, especially those represented in his plates 93 and 94,[2] take away all improbability from the idea that trilithons should have been erected for sepulchral purposes in this part of the world. That the one form is copied from the other may be assumed as certain; but whether the rude stones are anterior to or contemporary with or subsequent to those of the Roman order, every one must decide for himself. I believe them to be either coeval or more modern, but there is nothing in these particular monuments to guide us to a decision either way. If we could fancy that the savages who now occupy that country would ever allow it to be explored, it would be extremely interesting to know more of the Arabian examples, even if they should only prove to be an extension of Syrian or North African forms into Central Arabia. If, on the other hand, a migration theory is ever to be established, this probably would be the southern route, or at least one of the southern routes; though the imagination staggers when we come to consider how long it must have been ago since any wandering tribes passed through Central Arabia on their way westward.

Are there any dolmens in Asia Minor? It is no answer to this question to say that none have been seen by any of the numerous travellers who have traversed that country. Ten years ago, by a parity of reasoning, their existence in Algeria or in Syria might have been denied. My impression is that they will not be found in that region. I expect that Asia Minor was too completely

---

[1] S. Palgrave, 'Central and Eastern Arabia,' i. p. 251. These appear to be the same as those mentioned by Bonstetten. "Dernièrement encore un missionaire jésuite, le Père Kohen, a découvert en Arabie dans le district de Kasim, près de Khabb, trois vastes cercles de pierres pareils à celui de Stonehenge, et composés chacun de groupes de trilithes d'une grande élévation."—Essai sur les Dolmens, p. 27.

[2] One of them has already been given, woodcut No. 25, p. 100.

civilized in a pre-dolmen period to have adopted this form afterwards; but it is dangerous to speculate about a country of whose early history, as well as of whose modern geography, we really know so little.

It would be extremely interesting, however, if some traveller would open his eyes, and tell us what really is to be found there, as it would throw considerable light on some interesting problems connected with this subject. It would, for instance, be interesting to know whether there are or are not dolmens in Galatia. If there are, it would go far to assist the Celtic claim to their invention. If they do not exist, either the Celts must be asked to waive their claim or we must find out some other mode of accounting for their absence.

In like manner, it would be interesting to know if there are dolmens in Lydia. As mentioned before, there are numberless chambered tumuli in that country, and it would be curious to trace the existence or absence of any connection between these two forms of sepulchres. My impression is that the case of Lydia is very similar to that of Etruria. It was civilized before the dolmen era, and it will consequently be in vain to look there for any megalithic remains. The chambers in all the tombs yet opened are, so far as we at present know, constructed of small stones, and show no reminiscence of a rude-stone stage of art.[1]

When we cross the Black Sea to Kertch, we find a state of affairs very similar to that in Lydia—great numbers of chambered tumuli, but all of microlithic or masonic forms. The tombs seem to be the lineal descendants of those at Mycenæ, and to belong to a totally different class from those we are treating of, and, notwithstanding their similarity of purpose, have apparently sprung from a different source. Yet it is curious to observe that even here the inevitable flints reappear. In one tomb, known as Kouloba, or Hill of Cinders, were found the remains of a chief, with his wife, their servants, and a horse. He wore a cap ornamented with gold, a gold enamelled necklace, and gold bracelets, and his sword was of iron. An electrum plate, which had formed part of a quiver, was ornamented with figures of animals and

---

[1] *Ante*, p. 32.

inscribed with the Greek word Πόρναχο. The queen's ornaments were richer in metal and more elaborate in workmanship than her husband's, yet among all this magnificence were found a quantity of flakes and other implements of flint:[1] a tolerably convincing proof that flint implements were not buried in this tomb, any more than in Joshua's, because men did not know the use of metals, but for some symbolical reason we do not now understand. There is little doubt that other examples as striking as these will be found when looked for, and, at all events, these do away with all *à priori* arguments based on the probability or otherwise of their being modern.

192.   Holed Dolmen.   From Dubois de Montpereux.

.Combined with these are found, very sparsely on the shore of the Crimea, but frequently on the eastern shore of the Baltic and in Circassia, the forms of dolmens we are familiar with in other parts of the world. Nothing like a regular survey of them has yet been attempted, nor have we any detailed accounts of them; but from such information as is published,[2] the general type seems to be that of the holed dolmen, such as

193.   Holed Dolmen, Circassia.   From a drawing by Simpson.

those represented in the annexed woodcuts.

As far as can be judged from such illustrations as have been published, all the Caucasian or Circassian dolmens are composed of stones more or less hewn and shaped and carefully fitted together, giving them a more modern appearance than their

---

[1] Dubois de Montpereux, v. pp. 194 *et seqq.* pls. xx. to xxv. See also 'Journal Arch. Ass.' xiii. pp. 303 *et seqq.*

[2] Dubois de Montpereux, 'Voyage autour du Caucase,' i. p. 43. See also two dolmens from drawings by W. Simpson, in Waring's 'Stone Monuments,' pl. lx.

Western congeners. That, however, may be owing to other circumstances than age, and cannot be used as an argument either way till we know more about them. It would be extremely interesting if some one would make a special study of this group, as Circassia lies exactly halfway between India and Scandinavia, and if we adopt a migration theory, this is exactly the central resting-place where we would expect to find traces of the passage of the dolmen-builders. Their route probably would be through Bactria, down the Oxus to the Caspian, across Circassia, and round the head of the Sea of Azof to the Dnieper, and up that river and down the banks of the Niemen or Vistula to the Baltic.

If, on the other hand, we adopt a missionary theory, and are content to believe in an Eastern influence only, without insisting on a great displacement of peoples, this would equally be the trade route along which such influence might be supposed to extend, and so connect the north with the east, just as we may suppose a southern route to have extended through Arabia and Syria to the southern shores of the Mediterranean.

Even more important for our present purpose, however, than an examination of these Caucasian regions would be an exploration of the Steppes to the northward of the route just indicated. If there is any foundation for the theory that the dolmens are of Turanian origin, it is here that we should expect to find the germs of the system. It is one of the best-established facts of ethnology that the original seat of the Aryans was somewhere in Upper and Central Asia, whence they migrated eastward into India, southward into Persia, and westward into Europe. In like manner, the original seat of the Turanians is assumed to be somewhat farther north, and thence at an earlier period it is believed that they spread themselves at some very early prehistoric time over the whole face of the Old World. When we turn to the Steppes, whence this great family of mankind are supposed to have migrated, we find it covered with tumuli. As Haxthausen[1] expresses it, the Kurgans, as they are there called, are counted "non par des milliers, c'est centaines de milliers qu'il faudrait dire;" and Pallas equally gives an account of their astonishing

---

[1] Haxthausen, 'Mémoires sur la Russie,' ii. p. 291.

numbers.[1] These tumuli resemble exactly our barrows, such as
are seen on Salisbury plain, except that they are generally of very
much larger dimensions, and they have one peculiarity not known
elsewhere.   On the top of each is an upright stone, rudely carved,
but always unmistakably represent-
ing a human figure, and understood
to be intended for a representation
of the person buried beneath. Pallas,
Haxthausen, and Dubois, all give representations of these figures, but in
some instances at least they are re-
petitions of the same original. They
are perfectly described by the monk
Ruberquis, who visited these countries
in 1253. "The Comanians," he says,
"build a great tomb over their dead,

194.   Baba.
From Dubois de Montpereux.

and erect an image of the dead party thereon, with his face
towards the east, holding a drinking-cup in his hand before
his navel. They also erect on the monuments of rich men
pyramids, that is to say, little pointed houses or pinnacles. In
some places I saw mighty towers, made of brick, and in other places
pyramids made of stones, though no stones are found thereabouts. I saw one newly buried in whose behalf they hanged
up sixteen horse-hides, and they set beside his grave Cosmos
(Kumiss) to drink and flesh to eat, and yet they say he was
baptized. And I beheld other kinds of sepulchres, also towards
the east, namely, large floors or pavements made of stone, some
round and some square; and then four
long stones, pitched upright above the
said pavement, towards the four regions
of the world."[2]   The general correctness of this account is so fully confirmed
by more modern travellers that there
seems no reason for doubting it; but,

195.   Four-cornered Grave.
From Sjöborg.

as no one has described these "pavements," we dare not rely
too much on their manifest similarity to the Scandinavian square

---

[1] 'Voyage,' i. p. 495.   [2] 'Purchas his Pilgrims,' iii. p. 8.

and round graves, with four angle-stones, like the preceding one (woodcut No. 195).

It may not be satisfactory to be obliged to go back to a traveller of the thirteenth century, however much he may be confirmed by subsequent writers, for an account of monuments which we would like to see measured and drawn with modern accuracy. It is, on the other hand, however, a gain to find a trustworthy witness who lived among a people who buried their dead in tumuli and sacrificed horses in their honour, and provided them with meat and drink for their journey to the Shades; who, in fact, in the thirteenth century were enacting those things as living men which we find only in a fossil state in more Western lands.

196.　　　　　　　　Tumulus at Alexandropol.

The general appearance of these tumuli may be judged of by one of the most magnificent recently excavated by the Russians near Alexandropol, between the Dnieper and the Bazaolouk. It is about 1000 feet in circumference and 70 feet high, and was originally surmounted by a "Baba," which, however, is not there now. Around its base was a sort of retaining wall of small stones, and outside these a ditch and low mound, but no attempt whatever at lithic magnificence. Within it were several sepulchres. The principal one in the centre had apparently been already rifled, but in the subsidiary ones great quantities of gold ornaments were found, especially on the trappings of the horses which seem to have been buried here almost with more honour than their masters. Judging from the form of the ornaments and the style of the workmanship, the tomb belonged to the third or fourth century B.C.[1]

In Haxthausen's work[2] there is a woodcut which may give us a hint as to the genesis of circles. A kurgan, or tumulus, at

197.　　　Uncovered Base of a Tumulus at Nikolajew.

Nikolajew, in the government of Cherson, was cleared away, and though nothing was found in it to indicate its age and purpose, its base was composed of three or four concentric circles of upright stones, surrounding what appears to be a tomb composed of five stones in the centre. Similar arrangements have been found in Algerian tumuli, and it looks as if the first hint of a sepulchral circle may have arisen from such an arrangement having become familiar before being covered up, just as I believe the free-standing dolmen arose from the uncovered cist having excited such admiration as to make its framers unwilling to hide it.

It does not appear to me to admit of doubt that there is a connexion, and an intimate one, between these Scythian or Tartar tombs and those of Europe; but the steps by which the one grew out of the other, and the time when it took place, can only be determined when we have more certain information

---

[1] These particulars are taken from a Russian work, 'Recueil d'Antiquités de la Scythie,' 1866. Only one number, apparently, was ever published.

[2] 'Mémoires sur la Russie,' ii. p. 308.

regarding them than we now possess. It is important, however, to observe that, if they are the original models or congeners of the tumuli of the Western world, they are not of the dolmens or circles, except in such an indirect way as in the last example quoted from Haxthausen; nor are they of our menhirs, for all the stones we know of are carved as completely as the babas (woodcut No. 194); and we know literally of no rude stones connected with them, nor do we find any attempt in Scythia to produce effect by masses in unhewn stone, which is the fundamental idea that governed their use in Europe.

We tread on surer ground when we reach the Caubul valley, not that many proofs of it have yet been published, but the quantity of tumuli, topes, and similar monuments,[1] render it certain that circles and dolmens will be found there when looked for.

198.   Circle near Peshawur.   From a photograph.

Only one typical example has been published, but Sir Arthur Phayre, to whom we owe it, heard of other similar monuments existing in the neighbourhood. Fourteen of the stones composing this circle are still standing, and the tallest are about 11 feet in height, but others are lying on the ground more or less broken. The circle is about 50 feet in diameter, and there are appearances of an outer circle of smaller stones at a distance of about 50 to 60

---

[1] Introduction to Wilson's 'Ariana Antiqua,' *passim.*

feet from the inner one. The natives have no tradition about its erection, except the same myth which we find in Somersetshire, that a wedding party, passing over the plain, were turned into stone by some powerful magician.[1]

At present, these Eusufzaie circles, and those described by Sir William Ouseley at Deh Ayeh,[2] are almost the only examples we have to bridge over the immense gulf that exists between the Eastern and Western dolmen regions. Even the last, however, is only a frail prop for a theory, inasmuch as we have only a drawing of it by Sir W. Ouseley, who, in his description, says: "I can scarcely think the arrangement of these stones

199.　　　　Circle at Deh Ayeh, near Darabgerd.

wholly, though it may be partly, natural or accidental." Coupled with the stone represented as figure 13 on the same plate, in Sir William Ouseley's work, I feel no doubt about these belonging to the class of rude-stone monuments, but we must know of more examples and more about them before we can reason with confidence regarding them. Another example, which certainly appears to be artificial, is recorded by Chardin. In travelling between Tabriz and Miana, he observed on his left hand several circles of hewn stones, which his companions informed him had been placed there by the Caous—the giants of the Kaianian dynasty. "The stones," he remarks, "are so large, that eight men could hardly move one of them, yet they must have been brought from quarries in the hills, the nearest of which is twenty miles distant."[3] Numerous travellers must have passed that way since, but no one

---

[1] 'Journal Asiatic Soc. Bengal,' p. i. No. 1, 1870.

[2] 'Travels in Persia,' ii. p. 124, pl. lv. fig. 14.

[3] 'Voyages en Perse, &c.,' i. p. 267.

has observed these stones. It does not, however, follow that they are not still there, and hundreds of others besides; but while all this uncertainty prevails, it is obviously most unsafe to speculate on the manner in which any connexion may have taken place. It may turn out that the intervening country is full of dolmens, or it may be that practically we know all that is to be learned on the subject, but till this is ascertained, any theory that may be broached must be open to correction, perhaps even to refutation. It is not, however, either useless or out of place to make such suggestions as those contained in the last few pages. They turn attention to subjects too liable to be overlooked, but which are capable of easy solution when fairly examined, while their truth or falsehood does not practically in any essential degree affect the main argument. The age and uses of the Indian dolmens, as of the European examples, must be determined from the internal evidence they themselves afford. Each must stand or fall from its own strength or weakness. It would of course be interesting if a connexion between the two can be established, and we could trace the mode and time when it took place, but it is not necessarily important. If anyone cares to insist that there was no connexion between the two, he deprives himself of one of the principal points of interest in the whole enquiry, but does not otherwise affect the argument either as to their age or use. But of all this we shall be in a better position to judge when we have gone through the evidence detailed in the next chapter.

CHAPTER XIII.

INDIA.

THE number of rude-stone monuments in India is probably as great or even greater than that of those to be found in Europe, and they are so similar that, even if they should not turn out to be identical, they form a most important branch of this enquiry. Even irrespective, however, of these, the study of the history of architecture in India is calculated to throw so much light on the problems connected with the study of megalithic monuments in the West that, for that cause alone it deserves much more attention than it has hitherto received.

No one, it is presumed, will now be prepared to dispute the early civilization at least of the northern parts of India. Whether the Aryans crossed the Indus three thousand years B.C., as I believe, or two thousand B.C., as others contend, is of little consequence to our present purposes. It is generally understood that the Vedas were compiled or reduced to writing thirteen centuries before Christ, and the Laws of Menu seven or eight hundred years before our era, and these works betoken a civilization of some standing. Ayodia was a great prosperous city at the time of the incidents described in the Ramayana, and Hastinapura when the tragedy of the Mahabharata was being enacted; and these great events took place probably one or two thousand years before Christ, or between these two dates. Or to come a little nearer to our time, all the circumstances depicted in all the thousand and one legends connected with the life and teaching of Sakya Muni (623 to 543 B.C.), describe a country with cities and palaces, and possessing a very high state of civilzation; and these legends are so numerous and so consentaneous that they may fairly be considered, for this purpose at least, as rising to the dignity of history. Yet with all this we now know it for a fact that no stone building or monument of stone now exists in India that was erected before the time of Asoka, B.C.

250. But, besides negative proof, we have in the early caves, 150 to 200 B.C., such manifest proofs of the stone architecture being then a mere transcript of wooden forms that we know certainly that we have here reached the very *incunabula* of a style. Of course it does not follow from this that the cities before this time may not have been splendid or the palaces magnificent. In Burmah and Siam the palaces and monasteries are either wholly or mostly in wood, and these timber erections are certainly more gorgeous and quite as expensive as the stone buildings of the West, and the Indians seem to have been content with this less durable style of architecture till the influence of the Bactrian Greeks induced them to adopt the clumsier but more durable material of stone for their buildings.

With such an example before us, ought we to be surprised if the rude inhabitants of Europe were content with earth and the forms into which it could be shaped, till the example of the Romans taught them the use of the more durable and more strongly accentuated material? Nor will it do to contend that, if our forefathers got this hint from the Romans, they would have adopted the Roman style of architecture with it. The Indians certainly did not do so. Their early attempts at stone architecture are wooden, in the strictest sense, and retained their wooden forms for two or three centuries almost unchanged, and when gradually they became more and more appropriate to the newly adopted material, it was not Greek or foreign forms that they adopted, but forms of their own native invention. In Asoka's reign we have Greek or rather Assyrian ornaments in one of his lâts,[1] and something like a Persepolitan capital in some of the earlier caves,[2] but these died out, and it is not till after five centuries that we really find anything like the arts of Bactria at Amravati.[3] As the civilized race copied their own wooden forms with all the elaborateness of which wood carving is capable, so the rude race seems to have used the forms which were appropriate to their status, and which were the only forms they could appreciate.

---

[1] 'History of Architecture,' by the Author, ii. p. 459, fig. 968.

[2] 'Caves of Baja and Bedsa in Western Ghâts;' unpublished.

[3] 'Tree and Serpent Worship,' quotation from Hiouen Thsang, p. 135, and plates, *passim*.

Another peculiarity of Indian architecture is worth pointing out here as tending to modify one of the most generally received dogmas of Western criticism. In speaking of such monuments as New Grange or the tombs at Locmariaker, which are roofed by overlapping stones forming what is technically called a horizontal arch, it is usual to assume that this must have been done before the invention of the Roman or radiating arch form. So far as Indian experience goes, this assumption is by no means borne out. When Kutb u deen wished to signalise his triumph over the idolaters, he, in 1206 A.D., employed the Hindus to erect a mosque for him in his recently acquired capital of Delhi. In the centre of the screen forming the mosque, he designed a great archway 22 feet span, 53 feet in height, and formed as a pointed arch of two sides of an equilateral spherical triangle. This was the usual form of Saracenic openings at Ghazni or Balkh in the beginning of the thirteenth century, but it was almost beyond the power of the Hindus to construct it. They did so, however, and it still stands, though crippled; but all the courses are horizontal, like their own domes, except two long stones which form the apex of the arch.[1] In a very few years after this time the Mahommedan conquerors had taught the subject Hindus to build radiating arches, and every mosque or Mahommedan building from that time forward is built with arches formed as we form them; but, except a very few in the reign of the cosmopolite Akbar, no single Hindu building or temple, even down to the present time, has an arch in the sense in which we understand the word.

One of the most striking instances of this peculiarity is found in the province of Guzerat. There are still to be seen the splendid ruins of the city of Ahmedabad built by the Mahommedan kings of the province between the years 1411 and 1583.[2] There every mosque and every building is arched or vaulted according to one system. In the same province stands the sacred city of Palitana, with its hundreds of temples, some of a date as early as the eleventh, many built within the limits of the present century, and some now in the course of construction; yet, so far as

---

[1] 'History of Architecture,' by the Author, ii. p. 649.
[2] 'Architecture of Ahmedabad.' 120 photographs, with text. Murray, 1868.

is known, there is not a single arch within the walls of the city.
So it is throughout India: side by side stand the buildings of
the two great sects — those belonging to the Mahommedans
universally arched, those belonging to the Hindus as certainly
avoiding this form of construction.   This is the more remarkable as the moment we cross the frontier of India we find
the arch universally prevalent in Burmah, as early certainly
as the tenth or eleventh century, and in all the forms, round,
pointed, and flat, which we use in the present day.[1] But if we
extend our researches a little farther east, we again come to a
country full of the most wonderful buildings known to exist
anywhere, with bridges and viaducts and vaults; but not one
single arch has yet been discovered in the length and breadth
of the kingdom of Cambodia.

All this is no doubt very anomalous and strange, though, if it
were worth while, some of it might be accounted for and explained.
This, however, is not the place for doing so: all that is here
required is to point out the existence of the apparent anomaly, in
order that we may not too hurriedly jump to chronological conclusions from the existence or absence of arches in any given building.

Another most instructive lesson bearing on our present subject
that is to be derived from the study of Indian antiquities will be
found in that curious but persistent juxtaposition that everywhere prevails of the highest form of progressive civilization
beside the lowest types of changeless barbarism.   Everywhere in
India the past is the present, and the present is the past; not,
as is usually assumed, that the Hindu is immutable—quite the
contrary.   When contemporary history first dawned on us, India
was Buddhist, and for eight or nine centuries that was the prevalent religion of the state.   There is not now a single Buddhist
establishment in the length and breadth of the land.   The religions
which superseded Buddhism were then new, and have ever since
been changing, so that India now contains more religions and more
numerous sects than any portion of the world of the same extent.
Even within the last six centuries one-fifth of the population have
adopted the Mahommedan religion, and are quite prepared to follow

---

[1] Yule, 'Mission to the Court of Ava,' p. 43, pl. ix.

any new form of faith that may be the fashion of the day.   But
beside all this never ceasing change, there are tribes and races
which remain immutable.

To take one instance among a hundred that might be adduced.
Ougein was a great commercial capital in the days of the Greek.
It was the residence of Asoka, 260 B.C.[1]   It was the Ozene of the
Periplus, the capital of the great Vicramaditya in the middle of
the fifth century,[2] and it was the city chosen by Jey Sing for the
erection of one of his great observatories in the reign of Akbar.
Yet almost within sight of this city are to be found tribes of
Bhils, living now as they lived long before the Christian era.
They are not agricultural, hardly pastoral, but live chiefly by the
chase.   With their bows and arrows they hunt the wild game as
their forefathers did from time immemorial.   They never cared
to learn to read or write, and have no literature of any sort,
hardly any tradition.   Yet the Bhil was there before the Brahmin;
and the proudest sovereign of Rajpootana acknowledges the Bhil
as lord of the soil, and no new successor to the throne considers
his title as complete till he has received the tika at the hands of
the nomad.[3]   If India were a country divided by high moun-
tain-ranges, or impenetrable forests, or did impassable deserts
anywhere exist, this co-existence of two forms of society might be
accounted for.   But the contrary is the case.   From the Himalayas
to Cape Comorin, no obstacle exists, nor, so far as we know, ever did
exist, to the freest intercourse between the various races inhabiting
the country.   If we may believe the traditions on which the epic
of the Ramayana was founded, armies traversed the length and the
breadth of the land one thousand, it may be two thousand, years
before Christ.   The Brahmins carried their arms and their literature to the south at a very early age.   The Buddhists spread
everywhere.   The Jains succeeded them.   The Mahommedans
conquered and settled in Mysore and the Carnatic, but in vain.
The Bhil, the Cole, the Gond, the Toda, and other tribes, remain
as they were, and practise their own rites and follow the customs of
their forefathers as if the stranger had never come among them.

---

[1] 'J. A. S. B.' vii. p. 930.   [2] 'J. R. A. S.,' new series, iv. p. 88.
[3] 'Tods Rajastan,' i. p. 224.

EASTERN INDIA.

To turn from these generalities to two instances more directly illustrative of our European experience. The first is that of the Khonds, the Druids of the East, worshipping in groves, *priscâ formidine sacris*, and indulging in human sacrifices and other unamiable practices of our forefathers.[1] These tribes exist partly on a range of hills bounding the province of Cuttack on the western side and partly extend into the plains themselves. Almost within their boundaries there exists a low range of rocky hills known as the Udyagiri, in which are found a series of Buddhist caves, many of them excavated before the Christian era, and as beautiful and as interesting as any caves in India.[2] A little beyond this are seen the great tower of the Bobaneswar temple and of the hundred and one smaller fanes dedicated to the worship of Siva, which was established here in all its splendour in the seventh century;[3] and a little farther on, rises on the verge of the ocean the great tower of the temple of Juggernaut, at Puri, established in the twelfth century for the worship of that form of Vishnu.[4] Yet in defiance of all this, in close proximity to the shrines of the gentle ascetic who devoted his life to the prevention of the shedding of the blood of the meanest of created beings, in sight of Bobaneswar and Puri, Macpherson tells us, unconsciously almost repeating the words of Tacitus[5]: " The Khonds use neither temples nor

---

[1] The information regarding the Khonds is principally derived from a work entitled 'Memorials of Service,' by Major Charteris-Macpherson (Murray, 1865), and his papers in 'J. R. A. S.' xiii. pp. 216 *et seqq.* I quote by preference from the latter, as the more generally accessible.

[2] For several years past I have officially and privately been exerting all the influence I possess to try and get two bassi relievi that exist in these caves cast or photographed, or at least carefully copied in some form, but hitherto in vain. In 1869 the Government sent an expedition to Cuttack with draftsmen, photographers, &c., but they knew so

little what was wanted that they wasted their time and money in casting minarets and sculptures of no beauty or interest, and, having earned their pay, returned *re infecta.* I am not without hopes that something may be done during the present cold season. When representations are obtained, they will throw more light on the history of the Yavanas or Greeks in that remote part of India than anything else that could be done, and would clear up some points in the history of Indian art that are now very obscure.

[3] Sterling's account of Cuttack, 'Asiatic Researches,' xv. p. 306.

[4] *Loc. s. c.* p. 315.

[5] Tacitus' ' Germania,' 9.

images in their worship. They cannot comprehend and regard as absurd the idea of building a house in honour of a deity, or in the expectation that he will be peculiarly present in any place resembling a human habitation. Groves kept sacred from the axe, hoar rocks, the tops of hills, fountains, and the banks of streams, are in their eyes the fittest places for worship." It was in these sacred and venerable groves, that annually human victims were offered up to appease the wrath of the dreaded Tari, and to procure fertility for the fields. In 1836 we first interfered to put a stop to this, and before the Mutiny believed we had been successful. Perhaps we may have been so, but if our strong repressive hand were once removed, it cannot be doubted but the sacrifices would be instantly resumed. What the Buddhists and the Brahmins, working during at least two thousand years, have failed to accomplish, we strangers cannot expect to succeed in, in a few years, unless indeed we adopt the system followed by our fore-fathers, and are determined on extirpating those who obstinately adhere to such practices. Had it not been that first the Roman, and then the Celt, by sword and cord set vigorously to improve the older race, we might now have human sacrifices celebrated on the plains of Bauce in the neighbourhood of Chartres, and find people quietly erecting dolmens in the valley of the Dordogne.

The practices, however, of a Claudius or a Simon de Montfort are repugnant to the feelings of the Indians, and so long as no political issue is at stake, they rarely interfere with the religious proclivities of their neighbours.

When from the hills inhabited by the Khonds we cross the delta of the Ganges in a northerly direction, and come to the Khassia hills, we find a very different state of things, but equally interesting as an illustration of our present studies. These hills are situated between the valley of Assam and the plains of Sylhet, and, rising to a height of some 5000 to 6000 feet, catch the rains during the south-west monsoon, and but for this would be one of the most delightful sanitaria of the Bengal province. A country, however, where 300 inches of rain fall in three months is, for at least a quarter of the year, an undesirable abode, and it is difficult also to keep any soil on the rocks. Throughout the whole of the western portion of the hilly region, inhabited by tribes bearing the generic

name of Khassias, rude-stone monuments exist in greater numbers
than perhaps in any other portion of the globe of the same extent
(woodcut No. 200). All travellers who have visited the country
have been struck with the fact and with the curious similarity of
their forms to those existing in Europe.[1] So like, indeed, are they
that it has long been the fashion to assume their identity, and it
has consequently been often hoped that, if we could only find out
why the Indian examples were erected, we might discover the

200.   View in Khassia Hills.   By H. Walters.

motive which guided those in Europe who constructed similar
monuments, while at the same time there seemed every reason for
believing that it would not be difficult to discover the motives
which led to the erection of the Indian examples. The natives
make no mystery about them, and many were erected within the
last few years, or are being erected now, and they are identical in
form with those which are grey with years, and must have been
set up in the long forgotten past. Here, therefore, there seemed a
chance of at last solving the mystery of the great stones. Greater

---

[1] H. Walters, 1828, 'Asiatic Researches,' xvii. pp. 499 et seqq. Colonel
Yule, 'Proceedings, Soc. of Antiq. Scot.'
i. p. 92. Hooker's 'Himalayan Journals,' ii.
p. 276. Major Godwin Austen, 'Journal
Anthropological Institute,' vol. i. Part II.

familiarity with them has, however, rather tended to dispel these illusions.

The Khassias burn their dead, which is a practice that hardly could have had its origin in their present abodes, inasmuch as, during three months in the year, it is impossible, from the rain, to light a fire out of doors, and consequently, if any one dies during that period, the body is placed in a coffin, formed from the hollowed trunk of a tree,

201. Khassia Funereal Seats. From Yule.

and pickled in honey, till a fair day admits of his obsequies being properly performed.[1] According to Mr. Walters, the urns containing the ashes are placed in little circular cells, with flat tops like stools, which exist in the immediate proximity of all the villages, and are used as seats by the villagers on all state occasions of assembly; but whether one stool is used for a whole family, or till it is filled with urns, or whether a new stool is prepared when a great man dies, has not yet been ascertained.[2]

The origin of the menhirs is somewhat different. If any of the Khassia tribe falls ill or gets into difficulties, he prays to some one of his deceased ancestors, whose spirit he fancies may be able and willing to assist him. Father or mother, uncle or aunt, or some more distant relative, may do equally well, and to enforce his prayer, he vows that, if it is granted, he will erect a stone in honour of the deceased.[3] This he never fails to perform, and if the cure has been rapid, or the change in the luck so sudden as to be striking, others address their prayers to the same person, and more stones are vowed. It thus sometimes happens that a person, man or woman, who was by no means remarkable in life, may have five, or seven, or ten—two fives, for the number must always be unequal— erected in their honour. The centre stone generally is crowned by a capital, or turban-like ornament, and sometimes two are joined

[1] Schlagintweit, in 'Ausland,' No. 23, 1870, pp. 530 et seqq.
[2] 'Asiatic Researches,' xvii. p. 502.
[3] Major Godwin Austen, 'Journal Anthrop. Institute,' i. p. 127.

together, forming a trilithon, but then they apparently count as one. Major Austen mentions a set of five being erected in 1869 on the opposite side of the road to an original set of the same

202. Menhirs and Tables. From Schlagintweit.

number with which an old lady had previously been honoured, in consequence of the services which after her death she had rendered to her tribe.[1]

The origin of the stone tables or dolmens is not so clearly made

out. Like the tomb stools, they frequently at least seem to be places of assembly. One, described by Major Austen, measured 30 feet 4 inches by 10 feet in breadth, and had an average thickness

[1] 'Journal Anthrop. Inst.' i. p. 126.

of 1 foot; it had steps to ascend to it; and certainly it looks like a place from which it would be convenient to address an audience. The great stone of this monument weighed 23 tons 18 cwt., and another is described as measuring 30 feet by 13 feet, and 1 foot 4 inches in thickness, and others seem nearly of the same dimensions; and they are frequently raised some height from the ground, and supported on massive monoliths or pillars.

While this is so, we need not wonder at the masses employed in the erection of Stonehenge or Avebury, or any of our European monuments. Physically the Khassias are a very inferior race to what we can conceive our forefathers ever to have been. Their stage of civilization is barely removed from that of mere savages, and their knowledge of the mechanical arts is of the most primitive description. Add to all this that their country is mountainous and rugged in the highest degree. Yet with all these disadvantages they move these great stones and erect them with perfect facility, while we are lost in wonder because our forefathers did something nearly equal to it some fourteen centuries ago.

There are apparently no circles and no alignments on the hills, nor any of the forms which in the previous pages we have ascribed to battle-fields, and no tumuli nor any of their derivatives, and no sculptured stones of any sort. The real likeness, therefore, between the two forms of art is not so striking as it appears at first sight, but still presents coincidences that it is impossible to overlook.

One of the most curious points which an examination of these two Indian tribes brings to light with reference to the European congeners is that in Cuttack we have sacred groves, human sacrifices, an all-powerful priesthood indulging in divination, and various other peculiarities, all savouring of Druidism, but not one upright stone or stone monument of any sort. In the Khassia hills, on the other hand, we have dolmens, menhirs, trilithons, and most of the forms of rude-stone architecture, but no dominant priesthood, no human sacrifices, no groves, nor anything savouring of the Druidical religion.

To the European student the most interesting fact connected with the monuments on the Khassia hills is probably their date. We do not know how far back they extend, but we do know that many were erected within the limits of the present century, and some within the last few years. Yet this has taken place in presence of, and in immediate contact with, two far higher forms of civilization.

At the foot of the Khassia hills, to the north, lies the famous Hindu kingdom of Kamarupa. How far it extends back to, we do not know, but its foundation was certainly anterior to the Christian era; and when Hiouen Thsang visited it in the beginning of the seventh century, he found it rich and prosperous, and containing "temples by hundreds."[1] And now, in the jungles, ruins are continually being discovered of temples not so old perhaps as this date, but showing continued prosperity down to a far later period. All these temples are richly and elaborately carved and ornamented with that exuberance of detail characteristic of Hindu architecture.

At the foot of the southern slope of the hills lies Sylhet. When it became great, we do not know, but it certainly was occupied by the Mahommedans some centuries ago, and adorned with mosques and palaces and all that magnificence in which the Moslems indulged in the East. Yet the Khassia looks down on these new forms of civilization unmoved. As a servant or a trader he must have been for centuries familiar with both: but he clings to his old faith, and erects his rude-stone monuments, as his forefathers had done from time immemorial, and it is doubtful whether either our soldiers or our missionaries will soon wean him from this strange form of adoration.

Surely all this is sufficient to make us pause before arguing from our own European experiences, or deciding questions when so few facts have hitherto been available on which to base any sound conclusions.

WESTERN INDIA.

On the other side of India there are some groups of rude-stone monuments similar to those found in the Khassia hills, and apparently erected for similar purposes. They are, however, much less perfectly known, and are described or at least drawn by only one

---

[1] 'Mémoires sur les Contrées occidentales,' iii. p. 76.

traveller.[1] The most conspicuous of these is one near Belgaum.
It consists of two rows of thirteen stones each, and one in front of
them of three stones—the numbers being always uneven, as in
Bengal—and on the opposite side four of those small altars, or
tables, which always accompany these groups of stones on the
Khassia hills. These, however, are very much smaller, the central
stone being only about 4 feet high, and falling off to about a foot
in height at the end of each row.[2] Whether they were or were not
dedicated to the same purpose, Colonel Leslie does not inform us;
but their resemblance is so marked that there seems very little
doubt that they were dedicated or vowed to the spirits of deceased
ancestors.

Another class of circular fanes looks at first sight more promising
as a means of comparison with ours. Generally they seem to consist of one or three stones, in front of which a circular space—in
the largest instance 40 feet in diameter, but more generally 20 to
30 feet only—is marked out by a number of small stones, from 8
to 20 inches in height, while the great central stones are only
3 feet high. To compare these, therefore, with our great megalithic
monuments seems rather absurd. So far as can be made out, the
central stone seems to represent a local village deity, called Vetal
or Betal, who, like Nadzu Pennu, the village god, one of the inferior
deities of the Khonds, is familiarly represented merely by a rude
stone, placed under a tree.[3] In the instance of Vetal, it seems when
a sacrifice—generally of a cock—is to be made, all those who are
interested bring their own stones, and arrange them, in a circular
fashion, round the place where the ceremony is to be performed;
hence the superficial likeness. None, so far as is known, are ancient,
nor indeed has it at all been made out when and how the worship
of this deity arose. It is evidently a local superstition of some of
the indigenous tribes, which latterly under our tolerant rule has
become more prominent, for the sect is hated and despised by the
Brahmins; and so far as facts are concerned, it would be difficult

---

[1] Colonel Forbes Leslie, 'Early Races
of Scotland,' vol. ii. pls. lviii. lix. lx. They
have also been described by Dr. Steven-
son, 'J. R. A. S.' v. pp. 192 *et seqq.* It
would be extremely interesting, in an

ethnographic point of view, if some
further information could be obtained
regarding these stone rows.
[2] 'Early Races of Scotland,' ii. 459.
[3] 'J. R. A. S.' xiii. p. 268.

to carry back the history of this form of architecture for a hundred years from this time. It may be older, but there is nothing to show that it is so.

So far as the monuments above mentioned are concerned, there seems nothing in them that affords a real analogy or establishes any direct connexion between the European and Indian examples. The sacrifice of a cock to Vetal, when in sickness, looks like a similar sacrifice to Esculapius, and the human sacrifices and sacred groves of the Khonds are very Druidical in appearance; but no one probably will be found to contend that Vetal and Esculapius are the same god, or that the Khonds are Celts; and without this being established, the argument halts. The case, however, seems different when we turn to the sepulchral arrangements of the aboriginal tribes of India. Here the analogies are so striking that it is hard to believe that they are accidental, though equally hard to understand how and when the intercourse could have taken place which led to their similarity.

As in Europe, the sepulchral monuments of India may be divided into two great classes—the dolmens and the tumuli. In the present

205.   Dolmen at Rajunkoloor.   From a drawing by Colonel Meadows Taylor.

state of our knowledge it is difficult to say which are the more numerous. According to Colonel Meadows Taylor,[1] who is our best

[1] I quote from a paper by him, published in the 'Trans. R. Irish Academy,' xxiv. pp. 329 et seqq. There is an earlier paper by him in the 'J. B. B. R. A. S.' vol. iii. 179, but it is superseded by the later publication.

authority on the subject, the dolmens are of two kinds—those consisting of four stones, that is to say, three supporting stones and one
cap-stone—thus leaving one side open—and those in which the
chamber is closed by a fourth stone; in the latter case this fourth
stone has invariably a circular opening in it, like the Circassian
examples (woodcuts Nos. 192, 193), and the dolmen at Trie (No.
127). These forms are both shown in woodcut No. 205, representing two at Rajunkoloor, in the province of Sholapore, between
the Bheema and Kistnah, near their junction. The side-stones of
the larger monument measure 15 feet 3 inches by 9 feet in height,
and more than 1 foot in thickness. The cap-stone is 15 feet
9 inches by 10 feet 9 inches, and the internal space 8 feet by 6 feet,

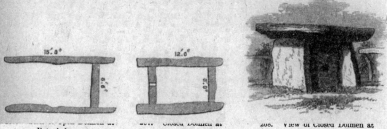

Rajunkoloor.   207. Closed Dolmen at   208. View of Closed Dolmen at
                             Raunkoloor.   Rajunkoloor.

the third slab being placed at some distance from the rear, and
between the two side-stones. The same arrangement is followed
in the closed dolmen, the cross slabs being inside, as shown in
the view (woodcut No. 208), and plan (woodcut No. 207). The
interior of the closed dolmen contained a little black mould on the
surface. Below this a greyish white earth, brought from a distance,
with which were found human ashes and portions of bones and
charcoal mixed, and pieces of broken pottery, red and black.
These rested on the solid rock on which the dolmen was erected.
Nothing whatever was found in any of the open dolmens; but
whether this arose from their being plundered, or from being
exposed, is not clear. It could hardly have been that they were
not sepulchral. They seem at least to be mixed up indiscriminately with the others, and except their being open, there is nothing
to distinguish them. The arrangement of these dolmens in plan
is peculiar. As will be seen from the next woodcut (No. 209),

they are as regular as in our cemeteries, and apparently in certain directions would have gone on extending *ad infinitum;* but in another direction are cairns irregularly spaced, and showing a distinction in the mode of burying which at present it is difficult to account for.

At a place in the Raichore Doab, called Yemmee Gooda, four of the dolmens of the first class were surrounded by double circles of stones; but this does not seem to be a usual arrangement.

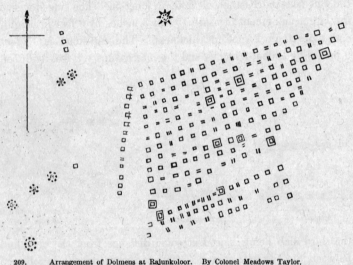

209.   Arrangement of Dolmens at Rajunkoloor.   By Colonel Meadows Taylor.

Almost more interesting than the dolmens are the cairns. The following plan of the group at Jewurgi, a place fifty miles, as the crow flies, north-east from Rajunkoloor, will explain their arrangement and juxtaposition. They, too, seem to divide themselves into two classes, as shown in the two sections—those with a summit-cist, like those in Auvergne, and those without; all, however, apparently have single and double circles of stones surrounding them. Two stones are generally found protruding slightly through the surface of the tumulus, and when an excavation is made between them, the cist is found laid in their direction at a depth of 9 to 10 feet below the surface. This seems to be generally double, and contains skeletons laid on their faces. At one end, but outside the cist, are quantities of pottery, and above the cist a number of skeletons, thrown in pellmell, and over these a thick layer of earth and gravel. Detached heads are found sometimes in the cists, sometimes outside

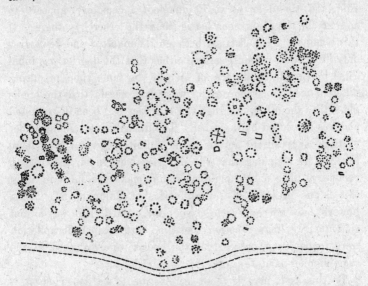

210.　　　Cairns at Jewurgi.　By Colonel Meadows Taylor.

among the pottery, which led Colonel Taylor to the conclusion that human sacrifices had been practised at the time these cairns

211.　　　Section of Cairn at Jewurgi.

were raised, and that these are the remains of the wives or slaves of the defunct. It may be so, but it may also be that, as in Europe

212.　　　Section of Cairn at Jewurgi.

we must make a distinction between battle-fields and cemeteries; and I confess the idea that the cairns at Jewurgi mark a battle-field, and the dolmens at Rajunkoloor a cemetery, appears to account for the phenomena better than the other hypothesis. If this is not so, as the distance between Rajunkoloor and Jewurgi is only fifty miles, we must assume either that the district was inhabited by two different races of men at the same time, practising different modes of sepulture, or we must concede that the one is older than the other, and that the one race had been dispossessed and was succeeded by the other. The difficulties attending either of these suppositions appear to me infinitely greater than those involved in assuming that the one is a battle-field, the other a cemetery. The only thing that would make me hesitate about this is the presence of several cairns at Rajunkoloor. These, however, do not appear to have been opened, and we do not consequently know whether the same instances of decapitation were to be found, or whether the bodies were arranged in the same manner as at Jewurgi.

Be this as it may, if these sections are to be depended on, it appears to be tolerably certain that these tombs cannot be old. It seems impossible that human bones could remain so entire and perfect as these are represented to be, so near the surface and in a recently disturbed soil, where rain and moisture must easily have penetrated at all times. A medical man on the spot might determine whether two or three or five centuries have elapsed since these bodies were laid where they are found; but I should be very much surprised if he raised their date beyond the last named figure. It is hazardous, however, to pronounce on such questions from the scanty data we have before us.

There is still another class of dolmens, or rather kistvaens, common on the Nilgiri hills and throughout the hill region of Malabar. In it the chamber is formed like those described above, but always buried in the earth, only showing the cap-stone flush with the surface of the soil. One of these, in the Coorg country, is worth quoting, from its possessing two circular apertures, like those of the Plas Newydd tumulus (woodcut No. 48). This one, however, has a diaphragm dividing it into two chambers. If the Welsh one was so partitioned, the wall has disappeared.

One other class of monument must be quoted, not as illustrating any of our examples, but because it is so nearly identical with the

213.　　　　　　　　Double Dolmen, Coorg.[1]

chouchas [2] of Northern Africa (woodcut No. 165), and when we try to find out whether there was any real connexion between the East

214.　　　　Tomb, Nilgiri Hills.　　From a drawing by Sir Walter Elliot.

---

[1] 'Proceedings, Asiat. Soc. Bengal, 1868,' p. 152.
[2] 'International Prehistoric Congress,' Norwich volume, p. 200.

and the West, such examples may afford valuable hints. According to Sir Walter Elliot,[1] they are the commonest, or rather, perhaps, the most conspicuous, being perched on the tops of hills or ridges. Their form is a circular wall of uncemented rough stones, 4 to 5 feet high, 3 feet thick, and 6 to 8 feet in diameter.

One other variety is interesting, not only from its similarity to those in Europe, especially in Scandinavia, but also from its bearing on the question of the age of those in India. The

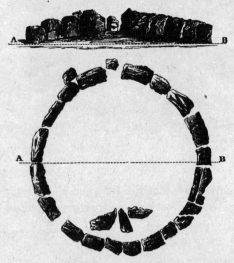

sepulchres of this class are all very like one another, and consist of small circles of rude stones, generally of two dimensions only, 24 and 32 feet in diameter, and have something like an opening on one side, and opposite this two or three stones within the circle, apparently marking the position of the sepulchral deposit.[2] Monuments

215.   Sepulchral Circles at Amravati.

very similar to these exist in the Nilgiri hills, and elsewhere in India,[3] but they are principally found at the roots of the hills round Amravati, where they exist literally in hundreds. No one, probably, who studies Colonel Mackenzie's map of that district[4] will doubt that they form the cemetery of the city of Dharani Kotta, to which the Amravati Tope is attached. As in China, burying in the fertile land was not allowed, and consequently the place selected for the graves of the inhabitants was the nearest uncultivated spot, which was the foot of the hills. So

[1] 'International Prehistoric Congress,' Norwich volume, p. 245.

[2] 'J. R. A. S.' new series, iii. p. 143.

[3] 'International Prehistoric Congress,'

Norwich volume, p. 257.

[4] Published on a reduced scale, 'Tree and Serpent Worship,' p. xlvi.

far as is at present known, these circular graves exist nowhere in
such numbers as here, and it can hardly be doubted but that they
have some connexion with the great circular rail of the Amravati
Tope. That rail is unique in India, whether we consider its extent,
the beauty of its sculptures, or the elaborateness of its finish.
Other rails exist elsewhere surrounding dagobas or sacred spots,
but none where the circle itself is relatively so much greater
and more magnificent than the surrounding objects. The question
thus arises, did the Amravati circle grow out of the rude-stone
graves that cluster round the hills in its neighbourhood, or are the
rude circles humble copies of that pride of the city? I have
myself no doubt that the latter is the true explanation of the
phenomena; but the grounds for this conclusion will be clearer as
we proceed. Meanwhile it is hardly worth while enumerating all
the smaller varieties of form which the rude-stone sepulchres of
the Indians took in former days. Their numbers in many classes
are few, and have no direct bearing on the subject of our enquiries.

Geographical Distribution.

Nothing would tend more to convey clear ideas on the subject
of Indian dolmens than a map of their distribution, were it possible
to construct one. As, however, no nation even in Europe, except
France, is in a position to attempt such a thing, it is in vain
to expect that sufficient information for the purpose should exist
in India, where the subject has been taken up only so recently in
so sporadic a manner.[1] The following sketch, however, is perhaps
not very far from the truth regarding them. They do not exist in
the valley of the Ganges, or of any of its tributaries, nor in the
valleys of the Nerbudda or Taptee; not, in fact, in that part
of India which is generally described as north of the Vindhya range
of hills. They exist, though somewhat sparsely, over the whole of

---

[1] The principal sources of information
on the subject are the papers of Sir
Walter Elliot and Col. Meadows Taylor,
so often referred to above. But I am
also indebted to Mr. M. J. Walhouse,
M.C.S., for a great amount of valuable
information on the subject. His private
letters to me are replete with details
which if he would only consent to
arrange and publish would throw a
flood of light on the subject.

the country drained by the Godavery and its affluents. They are very common, perhaps more frequent than in any other part of India, in the valleys of the Kistnah and its tributaries. They are also found on both sides of the Ghâts, through Coimbatore, all the way down to Cape Comorin; and they are also found in groups all over the Madras presidency, but especially in the neighbourhood of Conjeveran.

The first inference one is inclined to draw from this is that they must be Dravidian, as contradistinguished from Aryan; and it may be so. But against this view we have the fact that all the races at present dominant in the south repudiate them: none use similar modes of burial now, nor do any object to our digging them up and destroying them.

If we look a little deeper, we come to a race of Karumbers, to whom Sir Walter Elliot is inclined to ascribe the bulk of the rude-stone monuments.[1] From his own researches, and the various documents contained in the Mackenzie MSS.,[2] they seem to have been a powerful race in the south of India, from the earliest times to which our knowledge extends, and to have continued powerful about Conjeveran and Madras till say the tenth or eleventh centuries, when they were overpowered by the Cholas, and finally disappear from the political horizon before the rising supremacy of that triumvirate of powers, the Chola, Chera, Pandya, who governed the south till the balance of power was disturbed by the Mahommedan and Maharatta invasions.

A wretched remnant of these Karumbers still exists on the Nilgiri hills, and about the roots of the western Ghâts, but without a literature or a history, or even traditions that would enable us to identify or distinguish them from any of the other races of the south. The only test that seems capable of application is that of language, and this philologers have determined to be a dialect

---

[1] Norwich volume, 'International Prehistoric Congress,' pp. 252 *et seqq.* He places the destruction of the Karumbers as early as the seventh century, but the dates are, to say the least, often very doubtful. When, for instance, Hiouen Thsang visited Conjeveran in 640—the Buddhist establishment—they were still flourishing, and no signs apparent of the storm, which did not, I fancy, break out till at least a century after that time. See also 'The Seven Pagodas,' by Capt. Carr, Madras, 1869, p. 127.

[2] Second Report by the Rev. W. Taylor, 'Madras Lit. Jour.' vii. p. 311 *et passim.*

of the Dravidian tongues.[1] But, in such a case as this, language is a most unsafe guide. Within recent times the Cornish have changed their language without any alteration of race, and if intercommunication goes on at its present rate, English, in a century or two, may be the only language spoken in these islands. From the names of places we would know that Celtic races had inhabited many localities, but from the tongue of the people we should not know now that the Cornish, or then that the Welsh, were more Celtic than the inhabitants of Yorkshire or the Lothians. So in India nothing seems more likely than that, during the last eight or ten centuries, the Tamulian or Dravidian influence should have spread northward to the Vindhya, and that the Gonds, the Karumbers, and other subject half-civilized races, should have adopted the language of their conquerors and masters. It may be otherwise, but we know certainly that the southern Dravidians brought their style of architecture—as difficult a thing to change almost as language — as far north as Ellora, and carved the imperishable rocks there, in the eighth or ninth century, in the style that was indigenous at Tanjore;[2] and this, too, for the purpose of marking their triumph over the religion of Buddha, which they had just succeeded in abolishing in the south.

If this is so, there are still two distinguishing features which may help us to discriminate between the candidates for the rude-stone monuments. The true Dravidians — the Chola, Chera, Pandya—never were Buddhists, and never put forward a claim to have erected any monuments of this class. The Karumbers were Buddhists, and claim these monuments; and Buddhism and such structures must, I fancy, for reasons to be given hereafter, always have gone together.

Further researches may enable us to speak with precision on the subject, but all we can at present do is to except, first, the Aryans of the north, and all the people incorporated with them, from the charge of being builders of rude-stone monuments. We must

---

[1] Caldwell's 'Dravidian Grammar,' pp. 9 et seqq. 'The Tribes of the Nilgiri Hills,' by a German missionary (Madras, 1856)—the Rev. F. Metz, who probably knows more of their language than any one now living. Mr. Walhouse's letters are also strong on this point.

[2] See 'Rock-cut Temples,' by the Author, p. 50.

also except the Tamulians or pure Dravidians of the south. But between these two there must have been some race, whom, for the present at least, we may call Karumbers. One of their centres of power was Conjeveran, but from that they were driven, as far as I can make out, about the year 750. But it does not appear that they might not have existed as a power on the banks of the Upper Kistnah and Tongabudra to a much later period.

The limits of the Chalukya kingdom, which arose at Kalyan early in the seventh century,[1] and of that of Vijianagara, which was established in the Tongabudra in the fourteenth, are so nearly coincident with the limits of the dolmen region—except where the latter was compressed on the north by the Mahommedan kingdom of Beejapore—that it seems most probable that there must have been a homogeneity among the people of that central province of which we have now lost the trace.

This, however, like many other questions of the sort, must be postponed till we know something of the Nizam's country. In so far as the history or ethnography of the central plateau of India is concerned, or its arts or architecture, the Nizam's dominions are absolutely a *terra incognita*. No one has visited the country who had any knowledge of these subjects, and the Indian Government has done nothing to enquire, or to stimulate enquiry, into these questions in that country. Yet, if I am not very much mistaken, the solution of half the difficulties, ethnological or archæological, that are now perplexing us lies on the surface of that region, for anyone who will take the trouble to read them. Till this is done, we must, it is feared, be content with the vaguest generalities; but even now I fancy we are approaching a better state of knowledge in these matters, and I almost believe I can trace a connexion between our so-called Karumbers and the Singalese, which, if it can be sustained, will throw a flood of light on some of the most puzzling questions of Indian ethnography.

---

[1] Sir Walter Elliot, 'J. R. A. S.' iv. pp. 7 *et seqq.*; and new series, i. 250.

AGE OF THE STONE MONUMENTS.

A glimmering of light seemed to be thrown on this subject by a passage quoted by Sir Walter Elliot from a missionary report from Travancore, in which it was stated that an Indian tribe still continued to bury in "cromlechs," like those of Coimbatore, "constructed with four stones and a covering one." [1] If this were so, we might have got hold of one end of a thread which would lead us backwards through the labyrinth. It looked so like a crucial instance that Mr. Walhouse kindly wrote to Mr. Baker, the author of the report in question, and sent me an extract from his reply, which is curious. " The Mäla Arryians are a race of men dwelling in dense jungles and hills. Cromlechs are common among them, and they worship the spirits of their ancestors, to whom they make annual offerings. At the present day they are accustomed to take corpses into the sacred groves, and place small slabs of stones, in the form of a box, and, after making offerings of arrack, sweetmeats, &c., to the departed spirit, supposed to be hovering near, a small stone is placed in the model box or vault, and it is covered over with great ceremony. The spirit is supposed to dwell in the stone, which in many cases is changed at the annual feast into a rough silver or brass figure." As Mr. Walhouse remarks, this looks like an echo from megalithic times. The people, having lost the power of erecting such huge structures as abound in their hills and on the plains around, from which they may have been driven at some early period, are content still to keep up the traditions of a primæval usage by these miniature shams. There seems little doubt that this is the case, and it is especially interesting to have observed it here, as it accounts for what has often puzzled Indian antiquaries. In Coorg and elsewhere, miniature urns and miniature utensils, such as one sees used as toys in European nurseries, are often found in these tombs, and have given rise to a tradition among the natives that they belong to a race of pigmies : whereas it is evident that it is only a dying out of an ancient faith, when, as is so generally the case, the symbol supersedes the reality.

---

[1] Sir W. Elliot, 'Journal Ethnological Soc.,' new series, 1869, p. 110.

The articles found in the cairns and dolmens in India unfortunately afford us very little assistance in determining their age. The pottery that is found in quantities in them everywhere, is to all appearances, identical in form, in texture, and in glaze with the pottery of the present day. No archaic forms have, so far as I know, been found anywhere, nor anything that would indicate a progression. This might be used as an argument to prove how modern they were. In India, however, it would be most unsafe to do so. We have no knowledge as to how long ago these forms were introduced into or invented in that country, and no reason to suppose that they would change and progress as ours do. So far as our present knowledge extends, the pottery found in these tombs may have been made within the last few centuries, but it may also be a thousand or two thousand years old for anything we know to the contrary.

The same remarks apply to the gold and silver ornaments and generally to the trinkets found in the tombs. Similar objects may be picked up in the bazaars in remote districts at the present day, but they may also have been in use in the time of Alexander the Great. Iron spear-heads and iron utensils of the most modern shape and pattern are among the commonest objects found in these tombs; and if anyone were arguing for victory, and not for the truth, these might be adduced to prove that the tombs belonged to what the Germans call "the youngest Iron age." This reasoning has no application whatever to India. Flint implements are found there, and very similar to those of Europe, but never in the tombs. Bronze was probably known to the Indians at a remote age, but no bronze implements have been buried with the dead so far as we yet know, though iron has been, and that frequently; but its presence tells us nothing as to age. So far we know, the Indians were as familiar with the use of iron in the fourth century B.C. as the Greeks themselves were, and, for anything we know to the contrary, may have understood the art of extracting it from the ore and using it for arms and cutting-tools before these arts were practised in Europe.

One of the most curious and interesting illustrations of this is found in the existence of the celebrated iron pillar of Dhava, in the courtyard of the mosque at the Kutub, near Delhi. This

consists of a solid shaft of wrought iron, standing 22 feet 6 inches
out of the ground and is 5 feet 6 inches in circumference at about
5 feet from its base.   When I visited it, the report was that Colonel

216.   ,   Iron Pillar at the Kutub, Delhi.   From a photograph.

Baird Smith had dug down and found its base 16 feet below the
surface.   Lieutenant Cole[1] now brings home a report that it is
26 feet deep in the ground.   Taking, however, the more moderate

---

[1] Lieut. Cole, R.E., has brought home a cast of the upper part of this pillar,
which is now at the South Kensington Museum.

dimension, a single forging nearly 40 feet long and 5 feet circumference was not made, and could not have been made, in any country of Europe before the introduction of steam-machinery, nor, indeed, before the invention of the Nasmyth hammer.

There is an inscription on the pillar which, unfortunately, bears no date; but from the form of the characters, the nature of the event it describes,[1] coupled with the architecture of the capital of the pillar, it leaves no doubt that it was erected in the third or fourth century of our era.

It must be left to those practically skilled in the working of metals to explain how any human being could work in close proximity to such a mass heated to a welding heat, or how it was possible without steam-machinery to manipulate so enormous a bar of iron. The question that interests us here is, how long must the Hindus have been familiar with the use of iron and the mode of working it before they could conceive the idea of such a monument and carry it into execution? It could hardly have been centuries, it must have been nearer thousands of years, and yet they erect rude-stone monuments in India at the present day![2]

One other instance, at the lower end of the scale, may be quoted as also bearing directly on this subject. Of all the people of India the Khassias are probably the most expert in extracting iron from its ores and manufacturing it when made; and their mode of doing this is so original, and, though rude, so effective, that there can be no doubt that it is the result of long experience among themselves.[3] They have, in fact, practised the art from time immemorial; yet though possessing iron tools for, it may be, thousands of years, they at the present day adhere to the practice of using rude unhewn-stone monuments, like the Jews, in preference to those "which any iron tool had touched at

---

[1] 'Journal Asiatic Soc. Bengal,' vii. p. 629.

[2] The crack and bend in the upper part of the pillar are caused by a cannon shot, the dent of which is distinctly visible on the opposite side. I hope it was not fired by the English, but I do not know who else would, or could, have done it.

[3] Hooker's 'Himalayan Journals,' ii. p. 310. Percy's 'Metallurgy: Iron and Steel,' p. 254 et seqq. All the original authorities will be found referred to in the last-named work.

any time."[1] Nor can it be argued that they do this because they do not know better. As just mentioned, at any time, certainly within the last thousand years, they might have seen the Buddhist or Hindu stonemasons of Kamarupa erecting the most elaborately carved stone temples, and can now see the domes of the mosques which the Mahommedans erected in the cities of Sylhet three or four centuries ago.

Although it thus happens that all these *à priori* reasonings and mistaken analogies, drawn from our own progressive state, which are so familiar to European antiquaries, break down at once when applied to India, still there are a few indications from which approximate dates may be obtained, and many more could, no doubt, be found if looked for. One of these is, that the greater number of the dolmens of the Nilgiri hills are sculptured; but only one of the drawings on them, so far as I know, has been published,[2] and though it is ungracious to say so, I fear that it is not a very faithful representation. It is, however, sufficiently so to enable us to recognise at once a similarity to a class of monuments very common in the plains. These are called Viracull, if destined to commemorate men or heroes, and Masteecull if erected in honour of women who sacrifice themselves on their husband's funereal pile. Colonel Mackenzie collected drawings of more

217.   Sculpture on under side of Cap-stone of a Nilgiri Dolmen.

than one hundred of these, which are now in the India Office, and photographs of many others have been made but not published.

---

[1] Josephus, ' Bell. Jud.,' v. p. 6.   [2] ' Journal Madras Lit. Soc.' xiv. pl. 8.

The similarity in the costume and style of art displayed in the preceding woodcut with that of the memorial stones leaves little or no doubt of their being approximately of the same age. As most of the memorial stones are inscribed and their dates at least approximately known, if the identity can be established the date of the dolmens can also be determined. Till, however, some one will take the trouble of photographing the cairns, so as to enable us to compare them with the standing stones, no certainty can be obtained; but as none of the sculptured stones go back a thousand years, and those most like the woodcut cannot claim five centuries of antiquity, these sculptured cairns in the Nilgiris cannot be so very old as is sometimes assumed.

The second instance is curious and instructive. In the centre of

218.   Dolmen at Iwullee. From a photograph.

the courtyard of a now ruined Sivite temple at Iwullee, in Dharwar, in the very centre of the dolmen country, now stands a regular tripod dolmen of the usual shape (woodcut No. 218). The question is, how got it there? No one who knows anything of India will, I presume, argue that the Brahminical followers of Siva would erect the sanctuary of their god in front of the tomb of one of the despised aboriginal tribes, if still reverenced by them, or would

have neglected to utilize it if neglected. One of two things therefore only seems possible. Either a Korumber, or native chief of
some denomination, stipulated that on his conversion to the faith
of the Brahmins, if he erected a temple in honour of his newly-
adopted god, he should be allowed to be buried, " more majorum,"
in the courtyard. This is possible, but hardly probable. It seems
more likely that, after the temple was desecrated and neglected,
some native thought the spot fit and appropriate for his last
resting-place, and was buried there accordingly. From its architecture, there is no doubt that the age of the temple may be
carried back as far as the thirteenth century, but it more probably
belongs to the fourteenth. According to the first hypothesis, the
age of the dolmen would be that of the temple; according to
the second, one, two, or three centuries more modern.

A third indirect piece of evidence is derived from Colonel
Meadows Taylor's paper in the 'Irish Transactions.' He represents
a tolerably extensive
group of these monu-
ments as placed im-
mediately outside the
city gate at Shahpoor,
and from what he says
of them they are evi-
dently of the same age
as the other examples
he quotes. From their
position and arrange-
ment, it does not seem

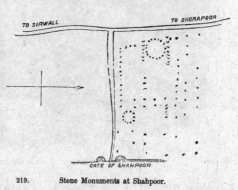

219.   Stone Monuments at Shahpoor.

doubtful that they are the usual extramural cemetery so generally
attached to Indian cities, and they are, in fact, subsequent in date
to the erection of the gate in front of which they are placed. The
gateway, I learn from a letter from Colonel Meadows Taylor,
undoubtedly belongs to the Mahommedan period. It is a regular
arch, of the usual pointed form, and consequently subsequent to
1347 A.D., when the Bahmany dynasty first established themselves in this quarter. This being so, the masons who built the
gate would certainly have utilized the tombs of the pagans had
they existed previously. They must, therefore, be subsequent to

the gate; and as it cannot be five centuries old, we have a limit
to their age beyond which we cannot go.

Our next example is still more curious and interesting. In
the cold weather of 1867-8, Mr. Mulheran, when attached to the
Trigonometrical Survey of India, came accidentally across a great
group of "cromlechs," situated on the banks of the Godavery,
near Nirmul, about half-way between Hyderabad and Nagpore,
in Central India. Some of these he photographed, and sent an
account of them to the Asiatic Society of Bengal,[1] from which the

220.　　　　　　　Cross at Katapur.　From a photograph.

following particulars are gleaned. "The majority of the cromlechs consist of a number of upright stones, sunk in the ground in
the form of a square, and covered with one or two large slabs of
sandstone. In some two bodies appear to have been interred, and
in others only one. The crosses are found in the neighbourhood
of Malúr and Katapur, two villages on the Nizam's side of the
river. The crosses at Katapur (woodcut No. 220) are, with one
exception, uninjured. All are situated to the right of the cromlechs
near which they have been erected. Judging from the one lying
exposed at Malúr, they are all above 10 feet in length, although

---

[1] 'J. A. S. B.' xxxvii. p. 116 et seqq.

only 6 to 7 feet appear above ground. They all consist of one stone, and are all of the latest form. No information of any kind could be obtained regarding the people by whom the crosses or cromlechs were erected. There can be no doubt, however, that the crosses are memorials of the faith of Christians buried in their vicinity." Close by is a cave, before which a cross was erected, which Mr. Mulheran assumes was thrown down by the Brahmins when they took possession of it; and he adds, "I enclose a note from Captain Glasfurd, who sent a packet of implements, rings, and utensils, found in two of the cromlechs he opened, to the

221.   Dolmen at Katapur.   From a photograph.

Asiatic Society." No such packet, however, ever arrived, and we are, therefore, left to his photographs and descriptions from which to draw our conclusions.

In the first place, I think it can hardly be doubted that the crosses are Christian emblems; and secondly, that the cromlechs and crosses are of the same date. Their juxtaposition and whole appearance render escape from this conclusion apparently inevitable. The question, therefore, is, when could any community of native Christians have existed in India who would bury in dolmens and use the cross as their emblems? Their distance from the coast and the form of the cross seem at once to cut them off from all connexion with St. Thomas's mission or that of the early apostles, even assuming that the records of these are authentic. My impression is that this form of cross was not introduced as an out-of-doors self-standing sign till, say, the sixth or seventh century.[1] On the other hand, it is extremely improbable that any such community could have existed after the Mahommedan invasion at the end of the thirteenth century. Between these limits we know that the Nestorians had establishments as far

222.   Dolmen with Cross in Nirmul Jungle.

east as China, and extending in a continuous chain westward as far at least as the Caspian;[2] and there seems to be no difficulty

---

[1] An elaborate paper by the Rev. Mr. Joyce, in the 'Archæological Journal,' 108, 1870, shows, I think clearly, that these crosses could not be earlier than 470 A.D.—all the crosses he quotes being of the usual Greek form, though possessing one longer limb. Indeed, I do not myself know of any crosses like those at Nirmul earlier than the 10th or 11th century; but, as my knowledge of the subject is not profound, I have allowed the widest possible margin in the text. I cannot prove it, but my impression is, that they belong to the 11th or 12th century.

[2] As it is wholly beside the object of this work I have not attempted to go into the history of the Siganfu Tables, nor the records of the early churches in the East. If the reader cares to know more, he will find the subject fully and clearly discussed in Col. Yule's 'Cathay, and the Way Thither,' published by the Hakluyt Society, 1866. It is the last work on the subject, and contains references to all the earlier ones.

in assuming that, between the seventh and the thirteenth centuries
a form of Taiping Christianity may have been introduced from the
north and established itself extensively in the western and central
parts of India, but, owing allegiance only to the potentate we
know of as Prester John, may have entirely escaped the knowledge
of the Western world. Besides helping to fix the date of the
dolmens in India, this discovery opens out a wide field for those
who would investigate the early history of the Christian Church
in India. There can be little doubt that this group is not
solitary. Many more will be found, when people open their eyes
and look for them. Meanwhile it is a curious illustration of the
policy of Pope Gregory in his advice to Abbot Mellitus, alluded
to in the Introduction (page 21). It is the same thing as the
dolmen at Kerland (woodcut No. 131), and that at Arrichinaga
(woodcut No. 161), repeated in the centre of India, though probably at a somewhat later date.

There is still another point of view from which these Indian
monuments may be regarded, so as to throw considerable light on
the history of their analogues in Europe, and perhaps to modify
to some extent our preconceived views regarding their history.
In Ceylon there is a class of dagoba, which, in some respects, is
peculiar to the island. Two of these will suffice for our present
purposes, both in the city of Anuradhapura, which was the capital
of the country from about B.C. 400 till the eleventh century.
The first of these, the Thupa Ramayana, was erected B.C. 161;
the second, the Lanka Ramayana, A.D. 231.[1] For the sake of the
argument it would be best to select the first for illustration; but
it was, unfortunately, so completely restored about forty years ago
that, as in the case of our unfortunate cathedrals, it requires
considerable knowledge of the style to discriminate between what
is old and what new. Notwithstanding the four centuries that
elapsed between their dates, however, they are so like one
another in all essentials that it is of little consequence which
we select. Neither is large, and both consist of nearly hemi-
spherical domes, surmounted by a square box-like appendage

---

[1] 'J. R. A. S.,' xiii. 164 et seq.

called a Tee, and both are surrounded by three rows of tall stone pillars, as shown in the accompanying woodcut.

That the domical part of the dagoba is the lineal and direct descendant of the sepulchral tumuli or cairns, which are found everywhere in Northern Asia and probably existed in India in primæval times, is hardly open to doubt. This the Buddhists early refined into a relic shrine, probably immediately after the

223.   Lanka Ramayana Dagoba, A.D. 231. From a photograph.

death of the founder of the religion, B.C. 543; and we know from numerous excavations [1] that the relic was placed in a cist in the centre of the mound, nearly on the level of the soil, exactly where, and in the same manner as, the body-containing kistvaens of our sepulchral tumuli. To this, however, the Buddhists added a square box on the top, which either was invented by them or copied from some earlier form; but no dagoba was complete without it, and all the rock-cut examples and sculptured representations of topes, with many structural ones, still possess it. That it represented a wooden relic-casket may be assumed as certain, but whether it was ever used as such is not quite clear. The

---

[1] Wilson's 'Ariana Antiqua,' Introduction *passim*. Cunningham, 'Bhilsa Topes,' &c., *passim*.

relics were sometimes accessible, and shown to the public on
festal occasions,[1] and unless they were contained in some external
case like this it is not easy to see how they could be got at. A
third indispensable part of a perfect dagoba was an enclosing
rail. All the early dagobas and all the sculptured representations
possess this adjunct. In the rock-cut examples and in the later
structural ones the rail becomes attached to the building as a
mere ornament, but is never omitted.

If we compare such a sepulchral mound as this at Pullicondah,
near Madras,[2] or that represented in section, woodcut No. 211,

224.   Dolmen at Pullicondah.[1]

with the Lanka or Thupa Ramayana dagobas, we cannot fail to
be struck with their similarity. Both possess the mound, the rail,
and the tee; and in this last instance it is a simulated tomb, such
as many in Europe are suspected of having been. That a people
might both bury in barrows and erect domical cairns to contain
relics would not necessarily involve a proof of the one form being
copied from the other; but that both should be surmounted by a
simulated sarcophagus or shrine, and both surrounded by one,
two, or three rows of useless stones, points to a direct imitation of
the one from the other which can hardly be accidental.

---

[1] Hiouen Thsang, 'Vie et Voyages,' p. 77.
[2] 'Madras Journal of Lit. and Science,' xiii. pl. 14.

Assuming for the nonce that the one is copied from the other, the ordinary mode of reasoning with which we are familiar in Europe would be then something like this. If the Thupa Ramayana were erected B.C. 161, this cairn at Pullicondah must probably be as old as B.C. 1000, for it would take many centuries before so rude a style of architecture could be reformed into so polished an example as the Thupa Ramayana, which, as before stated, we may assume as identical with the Lanka Ramayana (woodcut No. 223).

The conclusions I have arrived at are diametrically opposed to this view. As stated at the beginning of this chapter, the architectural material of India was wood, down to B.C. 250 or 300. It then became timidly lithic, but retained all its wooden forms and simulated carpentry fastenings down, at all events, to the Christian

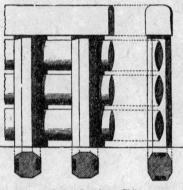

225.   Rail at Sanchi, near Bhilsa.

era. The rail at Sanchi, which was erected in the course of the two centuries preceding our era, is still essentially wooden in all its parts, so much so that it is difficult to see how it could be constructed in stone,[1] and these pillars round the Ceylonese dagobas are copies of wooden posts, and not such forms as in any number of centuries would have grown out of rude-stone forms. Had they been derived from the latter original they would have been thick, strong and massive, and never have assumed forms so curiously attenuated as we find here. It is difficult to see what these stone pillars or posts were originally intended for. It may have been either that garlands might be hung upon them on festal occasions, as we see represented in the sculptures, or that pictures might be suspended from them, as Fa Hian, who visited this place in the year 400, tells us was done all the way from Anuradhapura to Mehentele on the

---

[1] 'Tree and Serpent Worship,' p. 82, woodcut 8.

occasion of a great procession in honour of the Tooth relic which
was there exposed to public view.[1]

Be all this as it may, the question which this comparison raises
is simply this : If we admit the similarity between the Pullicondah
cairn and the Lanka Ramayana Tope, and that the one grew out
of the other, it seems to me perfectly evident that the adjunct of
the Tope grew out of a wooden and not out of a rude-stone
original. If this is so, and if the Tope did not grow out of the cairn,
the conclusion seems to me inevitable that the cairn is only a rude
copy of a polished original.

The same conclusion hinted at above was forced on me by the
examination of the rude-stone circles which crowd round the
elaborate tope at Amravati. Generally, I know of no hypothesis
by which the phenomenon of polished - stone buildings, with
known dates, existing in India for the last 2000 years side by
side with rude-stone monuments which are being erected at this
day, can be accounted for, unless we give up our favourite system
of sequence and are content to take facts as we find them.

It is quite certain there were no hewn-stone buildings in India
before the year 250 B.C., and my impression is that none of the
rude-stone monuments now existing there were erected till five, it
may be ten centuries from that time, and when they once began
that there is no break in the sequence to the present day.

I know nothing that can be fairly urged against this reasoning,
except our own ignorance, and that of the natives themselves,
with regard to the origin and date of these monuments. Neither
is much to be wondered at, as it is only so lately that Europeans
have turned their attention to the subject, and the natives know
so little about their own monuments that it would be strange
indeed if they knew anything at all about those of the hated and
despised Dasyus. Any one who has travelled in India knows
what sort of information he gets even from the best and most
intelligent Brahmins with regard to the dates of the temples they
and their forefathers have administered in ever since their
erection. One thousand or two or three thousand years is a

[1] 'Foe Kouć Ki,' p. 335.

moderate age for temples which we know were certainly erected within the last two or three centuries. Or ask any native about the date of the rock-cut temples at Ellora or Elephanta, he at once glibly answers, they were erected by the Pandus, 3101 B.C.; and if he breaks loose from that landmark, ten or twenty thousand years is the least you can expect. Yet we know now, from inscriptions and other data, that no rock-cut temple can be carried further back than the second century B.C.

In this infantile state of the native mind it costs them nothing to hide their ignorance in the mists of thousands of years when questioned about these rude stones, but their testimony is absolutely worthless, and it is only by processes like those just described that we can hope to arrive at the truth. Among races so unchangeable as some of those existing in India they may carry us back to a time prior to the Christian era with some classes of monuments; but, unless I am very much mistaken, it will be found that all those mentioned in the preceding pages are of comparatively recent date and are members of an unbroken series which continues to the present day.

Comparison of Eastern with Western Dolmens.

We are now in a position to approach one of the most interesting, but at the same time most difficult, branches of the inquiry we are engaged upon, which is the connexion, if any, that exists between these Indian rude-stone monuments and those we find in Europe. The difficulties, however, do not appear to be so much inherent in the essence of the subject as in its novelty. It has never fairly been approached by any modern writer, and would consequently require an amount of illustration incompatible with such a work as this to make it clear, or, on the other hand, it is necessary to assume an amount of information on the part of the public which it is feared hardly anywhere exists.

The architectural evidence, as detailed in the preceding pages, seems of a nature difficult to resist. It is easy and generally correct to assume that men in certain stages of civilization will do the same thing or things, in a manner so similar that it is difficult to discriminate between them. There would thus be no improbability in assuming that all men would raise a mound of earth over the dead bodies of their buried ancestors, or that they would protect their bodies from being crushed by the super-incumbent weight, by a cist or coffin more or less artificially formed of stone or wood. It may even further be granted that when having got so far they would naturally improve and enlarge this cist into a dolmen or chamber and provide it with an external entrance. All these things being found together would by no means prove a necessary connexion between two races using them, further than that the races using or inventing these forms must have belonged to the same family of tomb-building ancestral-worshipping people. But when we find two distinct people putting this cist outside, on the tumulus in the open air, and piercing one of the slabs in it with a circular hole 6 or 8 inches in diameter, we come to a coincidence that can hardly be considered accidental. As there was no writing and no post, either some tribe must have migrated from the east to the west and intro-duced the form, or *vice versâ*, some European must have taught the Indians the advantages of this hole, whatever they were; and having been once taught to adopt, they afterwards continued to employ it.

A still more striking instance is that already pointed out, of the combination of a central cistvaen containing a body inside a mound with a simulated cist on the top outside, and several circles of stones on or around the mound externally. All this is so com-plicated and shows so much design that it cannot possibly be the result of accident, if it is found in two distinct lands. The examples quoted above are perhaps sufficient to establish this similarity, but they are only a fraction of those which might be adduced if the subject were carefully followed out. It evidently was much more common in the East than we have hitherto had reason to suspect—for this reason alone, if for no other—that it continued to last so long. In this example from Burmah (wood-cut No. 226) we have first an external mound encircling the tope, then the circles of rude stones replaced by a complicated rail, and above all, in the centre, a simulated dagoba replacing the simu-lated cist. These are great changes, it must be confessed, but hardly so great as we might expect when we consider that the Senbya dagoba was only erected fifty-five years ago, and that the interval between it and the rude-stone monuments is consequently considerable. Another striking instance of the modern form this primæval sepulchre assumes is found in the celebrated tomb of Akbar the Great at Agra. There the king is buried in a vault below the level of the ground, but his simulated tomb is on the top of the pyramid, exposed to the air outside; and on each stage, externally, little pavilions replace the stones which his progenitors had previously employed for a like purpose.

These two—the holed stone and the simulated cist—are perhaps the most direct evidences of similarity between the East and the West, but the whole system affords innumerable points of contact, not sufficiently distinct perhaps to quote as evidence individually, but collectively making up such a case that it seems very difficult to refuse to believe that both styles were the product of one kindred race of men, and who at the time they erected them must have been more or less directly in communication with one another.

The literary evidence is much less complete or satisfactory. So far as I know, no paragraph has been detected in any classical authors which would lead us to suspect any connexion at any time between India and any country so remote from it, as France for instance, and still less with Denmark, unless it be the Woden myth belonging to the latter country. That, however, was either so indistinct originally, or has been so obscured by later additions, that it is now almost impossible to say what it is. Though so frequently insisted upon, it seems almost impossible that by any process, the gentle ascetic Sakya Muni could ever have become the fierce warlike Woden, and except some nominal similarities there seems nothing to connect the two. It may be that at some time about the Christian era, a chief of that name migrated from the Crimean Bosphorus to the Baltic, and may have brought with him some Asiatic practices, but the connecting link between him and India seems wholly wanting, and not likely to be now supplied.

The one passage that seems to bear directly on the subject, strange to say, comes this time from India itself. Among the edicts that Asoka engraved on the rocks in various parts of India,

View of the Senbya Pagoda, Burmah. From a photograph.

226.

the last or thirteenth is to the following effect, so far as it can be made out. It is unfortunately the nearest to the ground, and consequently in all the published copies appears more or less injured. Two more copies of the edicts are known to exist,—one in the Dehra Doon, the other in Orissa: when they are copied and published, perhaps a more perfect translation may be possible. Meanwhile, Mr. Prinsep's translation runs thus:—"There is not in either class of the heretics of men a procedure marked by such grace . . . nor so glorious nor friendly, nor even so extremely liberal, as Devanampiyo's (Asoka's) injunction for the non-injury and content of living creatures . . . And the Greek king besides by whom the kings of Egypt, Ptolemaios, Antigonus and Magas . . . Both here and in foreign countries wherever they go, the religious ordinances of Devanampiyo effect conversion. Conquest is of every description, but the conquest that bringeth joy, springing from pleasant emotion, becometh joy itself. The victory of virtue is happiness. Such victory is desired in things of this world and things of the next world."[1] In other copies of this edict the names of Antiochus and Alexander are found, making five well known names, and curiously enough all five are mentioned by Justin within a few lines of one another in the last chapter of his twenty-sixth book and the first chapter of his twenty-seventh book. There is thus no doubt who the kings were, nor of more than a year as to the date of this edict, which must have been within a year or so of 257 B.C.

The great interest, however, for our present purpose is that an Indian emperor, in the middle of the third century before Christ, should be in a condition to form an alliance with Magas of Cyrene so near the African dolmen-field. As before mentioned (*ante*, p. 410), we are still very deficient in our knowledge of the Megalithic remains of this country; but we do know that they exist, and that those which have been illustrated are of a singularly Indian type. It is also nearly certain that many of the rock-cut chambers about his capital are monasteries or temples, not tombs, as has always been too hastily assumed. Whether, on further investigation, these will prove to be so essentially Indian as they at present appear to be, remains to be seen, but meanwhile the possi-

---

[1] 'J. R. A. S.' xii. p. 233.   'J. B. A S.' vii. p. 261 *et seqq.*

bility of an alliance of this sort two or three centuries before Christ, takes away much of the improbability that would otherwise exist in assuming that Indian influence might have extended further westward at some subsequent period, and that the African dolmens might be proved to be allied to, and possibly contemporary with, those of India.

BUDDHISM IN THE WEST.

The great basis, however, on which any proof of the existence of a connexion between the East and West must eventually rest, will probably be found in the amount of pure Buddhism which crept into Christianity in the early age of the Church. The subject has not yet been fairly grappled with by any one capable of doing it justice. It has been frequently alluded to by travellers, who have been struck with resemblances which could hardly be accidental, and used sometimes by scoffers in order to depreciate Christianity; but no serious historian of the Latin Church has had sufficient knowledge of Buddhism or of its forms to be able to appreciate correctly either the extent or the cause of its introduction; and till some one does this, it will be treated by the general reader as an idle speculation. Yet it probably is not too much to assert, that at least nine-tenths of the institutions and forms which were engrafted on pure evangelical Christianity in the middle ages, are certainly derived from Buddhist sources.

Of these, one of the most striking is the introduction of monastic institutions, which exercised so important an influence on the forms of Christianity during the whole period of the middle ages. It is in vain to look for their origin in anything that existed in Europe before the Christian era. Nothing can be more forced than the analogies it has been attempted to establish between the Vestal virgins and the nuns of the middle ages, and no trace of conventual life can be found among the semi-secular priesthood of classical times. According to the usually received opinion, Antony (A.D. 305[1]) was the first monk, and from him and about his time a prolific progeny are traced to the Thebais, which is usually assumed to be the cradle of the institution. Monastic life was, however, absolutely anti-

---

[1] Gibbon, 'Decline and Fall,' iv. p. 392, where the original authorities are found.

thetical to the religious institutions of the ancient Egyptians, amongst whom the king was high priest and god, and where civil could hardly be distinguished from religious rank. It was equally opposed to the feelings of the Arabic or at least Semitic races, that superseded the Coptic in that country, and could consequently hardly have existed at all, unless introduced from some foreign source and maintained by some extraneous influence. The Essenes are the only sect to whom in the ancient world in the West anything like the peculiar institutions of monasticism can be traced; but unfortunately we do not know how or when they adopted them. Josephus represents them as only one of the three principal sects into which the Jews in his time were divided; but the silence not only of the Bible but of the Rabbis weakens the force of his statement, while his unfortunate omission of the name of their Lawgiver[1] leaves us in the dark on the most essential point. That it was not Moses, whose name is usually interpolated, is quite certain. He never inculcated any such doctrines, and one hardly dares to suggest the Indian name, which would clear up the whole mystery at once. Be this as it may, the sect only arose apparently in the time of the Maccabees, and practically disappeared with the destruction of Jerusalem by Titus; all which would accord perfectly with the hypothesis of their Indian origin, but would hardly suffice to support the idea that they were the sect from whom, in the fourth century, the Christian Church adopted the principles and practices of Asceticism.

When from these sparse indications we turn to the East, we are met by the difficulty that none of the books we possess were reduced to writing in their present form till the time of Buddhaghosa, A.D. 412,[2] or even later; and any one who knows what wild

---

[1] Josephus, 'B. J.,' II. viii. p. 9.

[2] "The prestige of such a witness as Buddhaghosa soon dwindles away, and his statements as to kings and councils 800 years before his time are, in truth, worth no more than the stories told of Arthur, by Geoffrey of Monmouth, or the accounts we read in Livy of the early history of Rome"—*Chips from a German Workshop*, i. p. 198. As a mere linguist, and dependent wholly on books,

Max Müller was perfectly justified in making this statement, while his ignorance of everything connected with the archæology or art of India, prevented his perceiving how these wild statements could be verified or controlled. Till he learns that there are other means of investigation than mere words his statements on these subjects are untrustworthy, and, in many cases, absolutely worthless.

imaginings can in the fertile East creep into works during the remodellings of a thousand years, will easily understand with what caution they must be used. Fortunately in this instance the monuments and inscriptions come to our assistance, and we are enabled to form a fair idea of the progress of monasticism in India from what they tell us.

Before the first monuments, the books tell us of three great convocations: the first held immediately on the death of the founder of the religion, B.C. 543, at Rajagriha; the second 100 years afterwards, at Vaisali; and the third by Asoka, 250 B.C., at Pataliputta, or Patna. These we are told were attended by thousand and tens of thousands of monks.[1] But Asoka's edicts give no countenance to any such extension of the system in his day. Shortly after this, however, the earlier caves show cells appropriated to hermits, or even for the reunion of a limited number of monks under one roof. These Viharas or monasteries are small at first, and insignificant as compared with the Chaityas or church caves to which they are attached, as at Karlee, Baja, Bedsa and elsewhere; but shortly afterwards, at Nassick and Jooneer, in the first or second centuries they become more important; and when we reach such a series as that at Ajunta or Baug, for instance, we find the Vihara becoming all important, the Chaitya sinking into comparative insignificance. This great change took place apparently about the end of the third or beginning of the fourth century of our era, and continued till Buddhism actually perished, smothered under the weight of its enormously developed hierarchy some three centuries later.

The sculptures tell the same story. There are no representations of priests in the form we afterwards find them in at Sanchi, in the first century of our era. Ascetics there are, dwelling in woods and lonely places, but not congregated in monasteries, nor jointly performing ceremonies. But at Amravati, three centuries later, we have shaven priests in their distinctive robes, and every symptom of a well developed system.

If this is so, it could hardly have been before the era of the Roman Empire that these peculiar institutions penetrated to the West; nor could they have done so during its supremacy without

---

[1] Turnour's 'Mahawanso,' 12 et seqq. 'J. A. S. B.,' vii. passim.

attracting attention. But in the great "débacle" which followed the change of the seat of government and the destruction of the old faith, it is easy to see how these forms may have crept in, together with the new Eastern faith, which an illiterate people were adopting, without much knowing whence it came, and without being able to discriminate what was Christian and what Buddhist in the forms or doctrines that were being presented to them.

Among the peculiarities then introduced, one of the most remarkable was the segregation of the clergy from the laity, and the devotion of the former wholly to the performance of religious duties. Still more so was their seclusion in monasteries, living a life of the most self-denying asceticism, subsisting almost wholly on alms, and bound by vows of poverty, chastity and temperance, to a negation of all the ordinary enjoyments of life. That the two systems are identical no one has doubted, and no one, indeed, can enter now a Buddhist monastery in the East and watch the shaven priests in the yellow robes at matins, or at vespers, issue from their cells and range themselves on either side of a choir, on whose altar stands an image of the Queen of Heaven, or of the three precious Buddhas, and listen to their litanies, chanted in what to them is a dead or foreign tongue, without feeling that he is looking in the East on what is externally the same as he had long been familiar with in the West.[1] If he follows these monks back to their cells and finds them governed by a mitred abbot, and subordinated as deacons, priests, and neophytes, learns that they are bound by vows of celibacy, live by alms, and spend their lives in a dull routine of contemplation and formal worship, he might almost fancy he was transported back into some Burgundian convent in the middle ages, unless he is prepared, like Huc and Gabet, to believe that it is a phantasm conjured up by the author of all evil for the confusion

---

[1] Huc and Gabet, in their 'Travels in Thibet,' give a most amusing account of their bewilderment on observing there these things :—"La crosse, la mitre, la dalmatique, la chape ou pluvial, que les grands Lamas portent en voyage, ou lorsqu'ils font quelque cérémonie hors du temple; l'office des deux chœurs, la psalmodie, les exorcismes, l'encensoir soutenu par cinque chaines, et pouvant s'ouvrir et se fermer à volonté; les bénédictions données par les Lamas, en étendant la main droite sur la tête des fidèles; le chapelet, le célibat ecclesiastique, les retraites spirituelles, le culte des saints, les jeûnes, les processions, les litanies, l'eau bénite : voilà autant des rapports que les Bouddhistes ont avec nous."—Vol. ii. p. 110.

of mankind. We know from the form and arrangement of the great Chaitya caves, that these forms prevailed as early at least as the first century B.C., and, as they are practised without change in the East to the present day, it seems clear that it is thence that they were introduced into Europe.

Canonization is another remarkable institution common to the Buddhist and Christian Churches, and to them only. It has frequently been attempted to draw a parallel between the demigods of Greece and Rome and the institution of Saints in the mediæval Church; but this argument has always failed, because in fact no two institutions could in their origin be more essentially different. The minor gods of the heathen pantheon, though sometimes remarkable for their prowess or virtues, were all more or less connected by ties of blood or marriage with the great Olympic family, and owed their rank rather to their descent than to their merits. It is true that in later times the deification of Roman emperors and others of that class, which the abject flattery of a corrupt age had introduced, was a nearer approach to the practice of Buddhism, which was then flourishing in the East, than anything before known in the pagan world. But canonization in its purity, as practised both in the East and West, is not to be attained through either birth or office, but by the practice of ascetic virtues on the part of the clergy, and by piety coupled with benefactions to the Church by those outside its pale. In these casteless institutions any man, however obscure his origin, by devotion to the interests of his adopted order, and the practice of the asceticism, heightened if possible by the endurance of self-inflicted tortures, might attain to Buddhahood or saintship. But such a path to adoration in this world, or to worship hereafter, was utterly unknown in Europe until it was introduced from the East, after the Christian era.

Relic-worship is another peculiarity which the mediæval Church certainly borrowed from the East. No tradition is more constant than that which relates that the relics of Buddha were, after cremation, divided into eight parts, and distributed to eight different kingdoms, and the history of some portions of these can be traced to comparatively modern times. Perhaps too much reliance should not be placed on these very early traditions, as no material evidence of them exists, nor in the often-repeated assertion that Asoka built 84,000 dagobas,[1] to receive relics. That he built several is quite certain. The fact of the relics of two of the favourite disciples of Buddha—Mogalana and Sariputra—and of ten of the principal dignitaries of the Buddhist Church in the time of Asoka having been found at Sanchi in topes certainly anterior to the Christian era,[2] is quite sufficient for our present purpose. As is well known, the Tooth relic, whose history can be traced back with certainty for more than fifteen centuries, is now worshipped under British protection in Ceylon.

No such form of worship existed in classical antiquity, nor is it quite clear how it came to be adopted by the Christian Church. Buddhism was a reform of a material, ancestral-worshipping, body-respecting form of religion. The sepulchral tumulus with them became in consequence a dagoba, or relic shrine, containing a bone, or a vessel, or rag, or something that belonged to Buddha or some of his followers; and all the grosser superstitions of the Turanian natives, whose faith he was trying to elevate and refine, were sublimated into something immaterial and more pure. But Christianity never could have wanted this, and its adoption of relic worship was either a piece of blind imitation adopted without thinking, among other things, for which there was more excuse, or it was one of the many instances of the toleration of foreign elements which characterized the Christian priesthood in the early age of the Church.

It is as little clear when this worship was introduced as why it was done, for Christian legends in regard to relics are not more to be depended upon than those of the Buddhists. It could not have been common in the days of Clemens of Alexandria, or he would not have mentioned as a wonder that the Indians worshipped a bone enclosed in a pyramid;[3] but shortly after Constantine's time the fashion became prevalent, and the miracles performed by the touch of relics became one of the favourite delusions of the middle ages. If this is correct, and we are justified in assuming

---

[1] 'Mahavanso,' p. 26.   [2] Cunningham, 'Bhilsa Topes,' p. 289 *et seqq.*
[3] Clemens, i. 194. Oxford, 1715.

that the Buddhism which we find in mediæval Christianity was
introduced after Constantine's time, we may take it for granted
that any influence which the East exercised on the Western rude-
stone monuments was also subsequent to that monarch's reign.   If
this is so, a considerable portion, at least, of those found in both
countries must also belong to the dark ages that closed with the
Crusades.

It would be easy to go on multiplying instances of Eastern
customs introduced into the Western Church were this the place
to do it.   All that is required here, however, is to adduce sufficient evidence to accentuate an assertion which no one, probably,
who knows anything of the subject would be found to dispute.
It is, that the mediæval Church borrowed many of its forms from
pre-existing Buddhism, and that these were introduced not before
but after the time of Constantine.   If, after having reached conviction on this point, we turn to our books to ascertain what light
they throw on the subject, we find them absolutely silent.   You
may wade through all the writings of the Fathers, all the ponderous tomes of the Bollandists, without finding a trace, or even
a hinted suspicion, that such a transference of doctrine took place.
Except from one or two passages in Clemens of Alexandria, we
should not be able to show that before the time of Constantine
the nations of the West knew even the name of Buddha,[1] much
less anything of his doctrines.   While this is so it is obviously
idle to ask for written evidence with regard to the influence
of either country on the architectural style of the other.   Men
write volumes on volumes with regard to doctrines and faiths, but
rarely allude to anything that concerns mere buildings; and
while written history is so absolutely silent respecting the introduction of Buddhist forms into the West, it is in vain to hope that
any allusion will be found to the influence Eastern forms may have
had on the sepulchral monuments of Northern Africa or Europe.
In this case, the "litera scripta" is not to be depended upon, but
the monuments and their inscriptions are, and it is from them
and them only, that either correct dates or reliable materials for
such an investigation can be obtained.   So far as I am capable of

[1] Clemens, i. 132.   Translation by Potter, ut sup. p. 504.

forming an opinion, their evidence is amply sufficient, in the first place, to take away all *à priori* improbability from the assumption that there may have been a direct influence exercised by the East on the Western rude-stone monuments. But it seems to me at the same time sufficient to render it extremely probable that while influencing to so great an extent the religious institutions of the country, they should also have modified their sepulchral forms so as fully to account for all the similarities which we find existing between them.

It may not be possible, in the present state of our knowledge, to explain exactly how this influence was exercised, and we must, consequently, rest content with the fact that as Buddhism did so influence the religion of the West in those early ages, the same agency may equally have acted upon the architectural or sepulchral forms of the same class in our population.

To explain this it is necessary to revert for a moment to a proposition I have often had occasion to advance, and have not yet seen refuted—that Buddhism is the religion of a Turanian race, using that word, as used by its inventors, in the broadest possible sense. The Persians say Iran and Turan, and Iran and Aniran, terms equivalent to our Aryan and non-Aryan; and Buddhism is not and never was, but exceptionally, the religion of the Aryan race, and is not now professed by any Aryan people in any quarter of the globe. It is essentially the faith of a quiescent, contemplative race, with no distinct idea of a god external to this world, or of a future state other than through transmigrations accomplished in this world, leading only to eternal repose hereafter; its followers, however, still believing in the direct influence of the temporarily-released spirits of their forefathers in guiding and controlling the destiny of their offspring, thus leading directly to ancestral worship. In India this primitive faith was refined and elevated into one of the most remarkable and beneficent of human institutions by the Aryan Sakya Muni and his Brahmin coadjutors, and did at one time nearly obliterate the Aryan faith which it superseded. After, however, a thousand years of apparent supremacy, the old faith came again to the surface and Buddhism disappeared from India, but still remains the only faith of all the

Turanian nations around it and wherever the Aryan races never seem to have settled.

If any Turanian blood remained in the veins of any of the various races who inhabited Europe in the middle ages, it is easy to understand how the preaching or doctrines of any Buddhist missionaries or Turanian tribes must have struck a responsive chord in their hearts, and how easily they would have adopted any new fashion these Easterns may have taught. As we have had occasion to point out above, the dolmen-builders of Europe certainly were not Aryan. Nor, if we may trust M. Bertrand and the best French antiquaries, were they Celts; but that an old pre-Celtic people did exist in those parts of France in which the dolmens are generally found appears to me indisputable. Though the more active and progressive Celts had commenced their obliteration of this undemonstrative people at the time when written history first began in their country, there is no reason to suppose that their blood or their race was entirely exterminated till a very recent period, and it may still have been numerically the prevalent ingredient in the population between the fourth and the tenth centuries of our era.

Of course, it is not intended to assert or even to suggest that the Western nations first adopted from the East the practice of using stone to accentuate and adorn their sepulchral monuments. The whole evidence of the preceding pages contradicts such an assumption. But what they do seem to have borrowed is the use or abuse of holed stones, and the arrangement of external dolmens on the summit of tumuli combined with two or three circles of rude stones. These I fancy to have been among the latest of the forms which rude-stone architecture adopted, and may very well have been introduced in post-Constantinian times; and when we become more familiar with the peculiarities of these monuments, both in the East and the West, there may be other forms which we may recognize as modern and interchangeable, while many others, such as the great chambered tumuli and the tall solitary menhirs, seem as original and as peculiar to the West.

Having now made the tour of the Old World, it will be

convenient to try to resume, in as few words as possible, the
principal results we have arrived at from the preceding investigation.

First, with regard to their age. It seems that the uncivilized,
ancestral-worshipping races of Europe first borrowed from the
Romans—or, if any one likes, from the Phœnicians or Greeks of
Marseilles—the idea of using stone to accentuate and adorn the
monuments of their dead. In like manner, it certainly was from
the Bactrian Greeks that the Indians first learned the use of stone
as a building material. How early the Eastern nations adopted
it in its rude form we do not know. In its polished form it
was used as early as the middle of the third century B.C., but
we have no authentic instance of the rude form till at least a
century or two after Christ; but, once introduced, its use continued to the present day. Its history in the West seems somewhat different. The great chambered tumuli at Gavr Innis, and
others in France, as well as those at Lough Crew, in Ireland,
seem to belong to a time before the Romans occupied the states
of Western Europe; but no stone monument of this class has yet
made out its claim to an antiquity of more than two centuries,
if so much, before the Christian era. Some of those in Greece
about Mycenæ, and those at Saturnia, may be earlier, but they
are as yet undescribed scientifically, and we cannot tell. From
shortly before the Christian era, till the countries in which they
are found became entirely and essentially Christian, the use of
these monuments seems to have been continual, whenever a
dolmen-building race—or, in other words, a race with any taint
of Turanian blood in their veins—continued to prevail. This, in
remote corners of the world, seems to have extended in France
and Britain down to the eighth or ninth century. In Scandinavia it lasted down to the eleventh or twelfth, and sporadically,
in out-of-the-way and neglected districts, as late both in France
and Great Britain.

These results do not, of course, touch the age of the earthen
tumuli or barrows, for the determination of whose age no scale has
yet been invented; still less do they approach the question of the
antiquity of the Cave men or the palæolithic stone implements,

the age of which we must, for the present at least, leave wrapped in the mists of the long prehistoric past.

Their uses seem more easily determined than their dates; with only a few rare and easily-recognizable exceptions, all seem originally to have been intended for sepulchral or cenotaphic purposes. Either, like the great chambered tumuli and the dolmens, they were actually the burying-places of the illustrious dead; or, like the greater circles and the alignments, they marked battle-fields, and were erected in honour of those slain there, whether their bodies were actually laid within their precincts or not; or, like the rude stone pillars of the Khassia hills, they were offerings to the spirits of the departed.

With the fewest possible exceptions[1] and these of the most insignificant character, their connexion with the relics of the dead can be proved from all having become places for ancestral worship and having under various forms been used for commemorating or honouring departed spirits. No single instance has been authenticated of either circles or dolmens in any other form, except perhaps single stones, having ever been used for the worship of Odin, or of the gods called Mercury, Mars, Venus, or the other gods of the Druids, still less is there any trace of the worship of the sun or moon or any of the heavenly host; nor, I am sorry to think, can the serpent lay claim to any temple of this class. Honour to the dead and propitiation of the spirits of the departed seem to have been the two leading ideas that both in the East and West gave rise to the erection of these hitherto mysterious structures which are found numerously scattered over the face of the Old World.

---

[1] The accidental resemblance of the microlithic temples of the Deccan mentioned above (p. 467) can hardly be quoted as an exception. They are said to be dedicated to Vetal, but it is not clear that the stones of the circle do not represent dead, as they certainly do absent persons, and the sacrifice, after all, is offered up to their departed spirits; it being a form of the present day we do not know how much its spirit may not be changed from the ancient rite which it was originally intended to typify.

CHAPTER XIV.

AMERICA.

IF this work had any pretension to being a complete history or statistical account of the Rude Monuments of the world, it might be necessary to describe somewhat in detail, and to illustrate those of the New World as well as those of the Old. In the form that it has now taken, however, nothing more is required than to point out as briefly as possible what the American monuments really are, with sufficient detail to show whether they have or have not any connexion with those we have been describing, and to point out what bearing—if any—their peculiarities may have on the main argument of this work.

In so far as the rude monuments of North America are concerned, there is fortunately no difficulty in speaking with confidence. In the first volume of the 'Smithsonian Contributions to Knowledge,'[1] the Americans possess a detailed description of their antiquities of this class such as no nation in Europe can boast of. The survey was carefully and scientifically carried out by Messrs. Squier and Davis, to whom it was entrusted. The text is tersely and clearly written, mere theories or speculations are avoided, and the plates are clearly and carefully engraved. If we had such a work on our own antiquities we should long ago have known all about them; but unfortunately there are no Smithsons in this country, and among our thousand and one millionaires, to whom the expense would be a flea-bite, there is not one who has the knowledge requisite to enable him to appreciate the value of such a survey, nor consequently the liberality sufficient to induce him to incur the expense necessary for its execution.

---

[1] 'Ancient Monuments in the Mississippi Valley;' Philadelphia, 1847.

NORTH AMERICA.

With this work before us, we feel justified in making the assertion that there are no rude-stone monuments on the continent of North America. There are extensive earth works of nearly all the classes found in the Old World, and some—especially the animal forms—which are peculiar to the New.

These earthworks Messrs. Squier and Davis classify as follows (page 7):—

1. Enclosures for defence.
2. Sacred and miscellaneous enclosures.
3. Mounds of sacrifice.
4. Mounds of sepulture.
5. Temple mounds.
6. Animal mounds.

With the first we have nothing to do: they are similar to those erected everywhere and in all ages of the world. They consist of a ditch, the earth taken in forming which is thrown up on its inner side, so as to form an obstacle to the advance of an enemy, and to become a shelter to the defenders. Some of these in America are of great extent, and show not only considerable proficiency in the art of defence, but indicate the presence of an extensive and settled population.

The so-called "sacred enclosures" are not only numerous and extensive, but are unlike anything met with elsewhere. In Ross county alone our authors state that there are 100 at least of various sizes, and in the State of Ohio 1000 to 1500, some of them enclosing areas from 100 to 200 acres in extent.

Their typical form will be understood from the annexed woodcut. All seem to have a forecourt either square or octagonal in form, with 4 or 8 entrances to it, and beyond this is a circle generally quite complete, and entered only by a passage

227. Enclosure in Newark Works.

or opening from the forecourt. These are enclosed by earthen mounds varying from 5 to 30 feet in height, with the ditch almost invariably on the inside.

The last peculiarity is in itself, as in the case of the English circles, quite sufficient to preclude the idea of their being fortifications or meant for defence, and they certainly are not sepulchral in any sense in which we understand the term. In the first place, because we know perfectly what the sepulchres of these people were, from the thousands and tens of thousands of tumuli which dot the plains everywhere; but also because, unlike the English circles, which are as a rule found in the most remote and barren spots, these American enclosures as generally occupy the flattest and richest spots in the country. They are most frequently situated near the rivers, and on the natural lines of communication; so much so indeed that many of the cities of the present occupants of the country stand on the same spots and within the enclosures of the earlier races who raised these mounds.

We are thus left to the choice between two hypotheses. Either they are sacred enclosures, as suggested by our authors, or they are royal residences—temples or palaces.

All the arguments, derived from its excessive size, that were urged against Avebury being a temple, apply with redoubled force to these American enclosures. Temples occupying 50 to 100 acres are certainly singular anomalies when we try to realise what these admeasurements imply. Our largest square, Lincoln's Inn Fields, occupies only 12 acres; the Green Park is 53; and all our parks together do not occupy the same space as the Newark enclosures, which, according to Messrs. Squier and Davis, cover more than four square miles.[1] Yet all these are circles and squares with connecting lines, and all with inside ditches. Temples of these dimensions, without divisions, or enclosures, or mounds, or permanent works of any kind, are anomalies difficult to understand, and must belong to some religion of which I, at least, have no knowledge; and no one, so far as I know, has yet suggested what that religion was, nor how these vast spaces could be utilized for any religious purpose.

---

[1] 'Ancient Monuments,' &c., p. 49. Hyde Park, including Kensington Gardens, occupies about one square mile.

If we adopt the idea that they were the residences of the chiefs of the people, the mystery does not seem so great. If the circular wigwam of the chief was erected in the centre of the circles, and the wigwams of his subordinates and retainers in concentric circles around him, it would account for their dimensions, and also for the disappearance of all traces of habitation. The forecourt would thus be the place of assembly of the tribe, the exercise ground or gymnasium, and for such purposes it is admirably adapted, and both the size and the situation of these enclosures seem easily explicable.

One curious circumstance tends to render this view more tenable. On plate xxi. of Messrs. Squier and Davis's work four groups of squares with circles are delineated, situated in different parts of the country; but all the four squares are almost identical in size, each side measuring 1080 feet. Why four temples should be exactly alike is a mystery, but that a tetrarchy of chiefs should be bound down to equal dimensions for their rival residences seems reasonable from a civil point of view.

It does not seem difficult to explain the meaning of the inside ditch when fortification was not intended, as it must have been almost a necessity with a people who had not arrived at the elevation of using brick drains or drain-pipes. Without some such arrangement all the rain that fell within these solid enclosures would have remained on the surface, or in the squares could only have escaped through the openings, but a deep and broad ditch all round would drain the whole surface without inconvenience, and secure the only mode which would prevent the enclosure, be it a temple or palace, from becoming a swamp.

Messrs. Squier and Davis divide the conical mounds which they excavated into two classes. The first they call " Mounds of sacrifice," because on digging into them they found on the level of the soil what appeared to be altars—raised floors which exhibited evidence of intense heat, and what they considered a long-continued practice of burning. It is evident, however, that such results might be produced in a week as well as in years, and it is very difficult to understand why at any time that which had been an altar should be buried in a tumulus. If it had been used for years, why, and on what occasion, was it agreed to bury it ? If it was the funereal pyre of some chief, and used for burning sacrifices for the time the funeral services lasted, and was then buried, the case is intelligible enough, but the other hypothesis is certainly not easy of explanation.

The true " Sepulchral mounds " are, as before mentioned, immensely numerous, and of all sizes, from a few feet up to such as the Grave Creek mound, 70 feet high and 1000 feet in circumference, or that at Miamisburgh, 68 feet high, and 852 feet in circumference at its base. The dead were buried in them apparently without coffins or cists, unless of wood, and generally in the contracted doubled-up position found so frequently in Scandinavia and in Algeria.

The " Temple mounds " are generally square or oblong truncated pyramids, with inclined planes leading up to them on three and frequently on all four sides. They are in fact in earth the same form as the Teocallis of the Mexicans, though the latter seem always to have been in stone. Whether in the one material or the other, they are of a perfectly intelligible templar form. If a human sacrifice or any great ceremonial is to take place before all the people, the first requisite is an elevated platform where the ministrants can stand above the heads of the crowd, and be seen by all; and the absence of this in the Ohio and in our English circles is one of the most fatal objections to the temple theory. In one or two instances a single earthen Teocalli is found within the circles, but this no further militates against the supposition that they were residences than the presence of a chapel or place of worship in any of our palaces would prove them to be temples also. It must, however, be borne in mind that it is always difficult to draw a hard and fast line between the House of God and the Palace of the King. In Egypt it is never possible, and in the middle ages royal monasteries and royal residences were frequently interchangeable terms. We should not therefore feel surprised if, in America, we found the one fading into the other. But, on the whole, the enormous number of these circular enclosures—1000 and 1500 in one State—their immense size, 100 and 200 acres being not unfrequent, and the general absence of all signs of preparations for worship, seem sufficient to prove that they must be classed among civil and not among sacred erections.

This seems to be the case even though sometimes three or four temple mounds are found together surrounded by a rampart just sufficient to enclose them with the necessary space for circulation all round; in which case, however, it is evident that they have passed the line separating the two divisions, and may, probably must, be classified as really sacred enclosures. These are generally found in the South, in Texas, and in the States most nearly bordering on Mexico, which looks as if they belonged to another race more nearly allied to the Toltecs or Aztecs than to the northern tribes.

The only remaining class of mounds are those representing "Animals," to which plates xxxv. to xliv. of Messrs. Squier and Davis's book are devoted. One of these, our authors have no doubt, represents a serpent 700 feet long as he lies with his tail curled up into a spiral form, and his mouth gaping to swallow an egg (?) 160 feet long by 60 feet across. This at first sight looks so like one of Stukeley's monstrous inventions that the first impulse is to reject it as an illusion on the part of the surveyors. When, however, we bear in mind that the American mound-builders did represent not only men, but animals, quadrupeds, and lizards, in the same manner, and on the same relative scale, all improbability vanishes. At the same time the simple fact that the form is so easily recognisable here is in itself sufficient to prove that our straight-lined stone rows were not erected with any such intention, and could only be converted into Dracontia by the most perverted imagination.

Though therefore we may assume that this mound really represents a serpent, it by no means follows that it was an idol or was worshipped. It seems to represent an action—the swallowing of something, but whether a globe or a grave is by no means clear, and must be left for further investigation. It is, however, only by taking it in connection with the other animal mounds in America that we can hope to arrive at a solution. They were not apparently objects of worship, and seem to have no connexion with anything found in the Old World.

The other mounds representing quadrupeds are quite unmistakable: they are a freak of this people whoever they were. But it seems difficult to explain why they should take this Brobdignagian way of representing the animals they possessed, or were surrounded by. If we knew more of the people, or of their affinities, perhaps the solution would be easy; at present it hardly interests us, as we have no analogue in Europe.[1]

It only now remains to try and ascertain if any connexion exists or existed between these American monuments and those of the Old World; and what light, if any, their examination may be expected to throw on the problems discussed in the preceding chapters. If it is wished to establish anything like a direct connexion between the two continents, we must go back to the far distant prehistoric times when the conformations of land and water were different from what they now are. No one, I presume, will be found to contend that, since the continents took their present shape, any migration across the Atlantic took place in such numbers as to populate the land, or to influence the manners or customs of the people previously existing there. It may be that the Scandinavians did penetrate in the tenth or eleventh centuries to Vinland, by the way of Greenland, and so anticipated the discovery of Columbus by some centuries; [2] but this is only a part of that world-pervading energy of the Aryan races, and has nothing whatever to do with the people of the tumuli. If any connexion really existed between the Old and the New World, in anything like historic times, everything would lead us to believe that it took place *viâ* Behring Strait or the Aleutian Islands. It seems reasonable to suppose that the people who covered the Siberian Steppes with tumuli may have migrated across the calm waters of the Upper Pacific, and gradually extended themselves down to Wisconsin and Ohio, and there left these memorials we now find. It may also be admitted that the same Asiatic people may have spread westward from the original hive, and been the progenitors of those who covered our plains with barrows, but beyond this no connexion seems to be traceable which would account

---

[1] I cannot help fancying that the great animals in stone that line the avenues leading to the tombs of the emperors in China may have some affinity with the American animal sculptures, which occur principally in Wisconsin and the farther West. I am unable, however, to obtain any information with regard to the Chinese or Siberian examples sufficiently reliable to found any argument upon.

[2] 'Annal. for Nordk. Oldkyndighed,' ii. p. 3 *et seqq.* See also C. C. Rafn, 'Antiquitates Americanæ,' &c., Hafniæ, 1837.

for anything we find. Nowhere, however, in America do these people ever seem to have risen to the elevation of using even rude stones to adorn their tombs or temples. Nor do they appear to have been acquainted with the use of iron or of bronze; all the tools found in their tombs being of pure unalloyed native copper—both of which circumstances seem to separate these American mound-builders entirely from our rude-stone people in anything like historic times.

Unfortunately, also, the study of the manners and customs of the Red-men, who occupied North America when we first came in contact with them, is not at all likely to throw any light on the subject. They have never risen beyond the condition of hunters, and have no settled places of abode, and possess no works of art. The mound-builders, on the contrary, were a settled people, certainly pastoral, probably to some extent even agricultural; they had fixed well chosen unfortified abodes, altogether exhibiting a higher state of civilization than we have any reason to suppose the present race of Red-men ever reached or are capable of reaching.

Although, therefore, it seems in vain to look on the Red Indians who in modern times occupied the territories of Ohio and Wisconsin as the descendants of the mound-builders, there are tribes on the west coast of America that probably are, or rather were, very closely allied to them. The Hydahs and the natives inhabiting Vancouver's Island and Queen Charlotte's Sound seem both from their physical condition, and more so from their works of art, to be just such a people as one would expect the mound-builders to have been. If this is so, it again points to Northern Asia, and not to Europe, as the country where we must look for the origin of this mysterious people; and it is there, I am convinced, if anywhere, that the solution of our difficulties with regard to this phase of North American civilization is to be found.

CENTRAL AMERICA.

When we advance a little farther south, we meet in Mexico and Yucatan with phenomena which are the exact converse of those in Ohio and Wisconsin. There everything is in stone; earth either never being used, or, if employed at all, it was only as a core to what was faced or intended to be faced with the more durable material. There is one fact, however, which takes the Mexican monuments entirely out of the category of the works contemplated in this book. All the stones in Central America are carved. So far as is known, no rude stones were ever set up there, even the obelisks which stand alone, and look most like our menhirs in outline, are, like the Babas of the Steppes, all carved, most of them elaborately; and though it may be true that they may, at some remote period, have been derived from some such rude originals as are found in Europe, still till we find some traces of these in Central America they cannot be said to belong to the class of monuments of which we are now treating; nor can they be used as affording any analogies or illustrations which it would be worth while citing in this place.

PERU.

The same remarks apply to what we find in Peru with equal force, but not with equal distinctness. No one will, I presume, contend that there was any direct communication between Europe and the west coast of South America before the time of Columbus. Yet there are similarities between the masonry of the Peruvian monuments and those of the Pelasgi in Greece and Tyrrheni in Italy which are most striking, and can only be accounted for, at present, on the assumption that nations in the same stage of civilization, and using similar materials, arrive nearly at the same results. Perhaps we ought to add to this, provided they have some taint of the same blood in their veins; and that, in this case, does not seem absolutely improbable.

Be this as it may, there are, so far as I know, no rude-stone monuments in Southern America. The ruins, for instance, of Tia Huanaco, which have often been quoted for their similarity to "Druidical remains," are as far removed as possible from that category. It is true that there are rows of squared stones that now stand apart, and in imperfect drawings look like our menhirs enclosing a square or circular space. In reality, however, as we learn from photographs, they are carefully squared stones, which formed pilasters in walls constructed with Adobes, or imperfectly burned bricks, or smaller stones which have been removed.[1] The doorways which led into this enclosure are hewn out of a single block of stone, and are more carefully cut and polished than anything else to be found anywhere out of Egypt, and there only in the best days of her great Pharaohs.

The same remarks may apply to the circles and squares illustrated by Mr. Squier.[2] I may be mistaken, but my impression is that like Houel's Druidical circles in Gozo, above alluded to, they are only the foundation courses of square and circular buildings, the upper parts of which have perished. At all events, till they are excavated, or some traditional or real use is found for them, I should be very unwilling to base any argument on their accidental similarity with our stone circles.

There can be no doubt that these earthen mounds and primitive carved stones of the American continent form in themselves a most interesting group of monuments, well deserving more attention than has yet been bestowed upon them, and that, when properly investigated, they will throw more light on the origin and migrations of the various aboriginal races of that country than can be expected from any other source. They are not, however, of the class we are treating of, nor do they seem to have any direct connexion with those of the Old World. As, besides this, their examination does not promise to solve any of our difficulties, they do not necessarily occupy an extended space in a work devoted to the elucidation of the Use and Age of Rude-Stone Monuments.

---

[1] 'History of Architecture,' by the Author, vol. ii. pp. 774 *et seqq.*
[2] 'The American Naturalist,' iv., March, 1870, figures 1, 8, and 9.

APPENDIX.

APPENDIX A.

(Referred to, page 225.)

DUNMINNING, GLARRYFORD, CO. ANTRIM,
August 18, 1871.

MY DEAR SIR,—I was unable to get to Glen Columbkille till this week, and I am afraid that I shall be too late to be of use to you. As, however, I did not forget to examine the monuments, I send the notes I made on them. All were written down at the stones themselves. Glen Columbkille is about 4 miles long and 3 broad. Its eastern boundary is a steep rocky mountain, from which the floor of the glen slopes down to the sea, and ends westward in Glen Bay. Glen Bay is of considerable width from its southern point, Rossan, to its northern, Glen Head, but it has only a short beach. There is also a dangerous bar, so that it is an almost impossible landing-place except for curraghs, and in smooth weather for boats. The north side of Glen Columbkille is rocky and steep, and is chiefly formed by the mountain Ballard. The south side, though in parts precipitous, and nowhere a very gradual slope, is not so steep as its opposite. The coast south and north of Glen Bay for miles is a range of cliffs, of from 1900 to 100 feet, with here and there a small beach, but no safe landing-places. South of Glen Columbkille is a smaller and shallower valley, Glen Malin. The sides of Glen Malin are all gradual; its coast is precipitous; on the south it is bounded by a mountain of large base, Leathan. Both Glen Columbkille and Glen Malin are in the parish of Glen Columbkille and barony of Banagh. Most of the great stone structures are in Glen Malin.

The monuments are of three kinds: (1) cromlechs;[1] (2) stone chambers; (3) solitary stones. They are in groups of various size and compactness. There are five distinct groups, a considerable distance apart, and with no apparent connexion of arrangement. Three groups are on the north and two on the south side of the glen. The stones in each have been more or less disturbed, and have been made to serve in lime-kilns and byres and as malt stores. While examining one set, I felt my foot sink, and, lifting the edge of a piece of heather, found an excavation filled with barley, soaking. On getting into another cavity, I found two black lambs inside, and in another some pigs, in another calves. The most remarkable general feature of the architecture that I noticed was that the stones in each group were much of a size, but that in some groups they were a good deal larger

---

[1] Throughout this paper Mr. Moore uses the term "Cromlech," as is usually done by English antiquaries, in the sense in which "Dolmen" is employed in the body of the work.

than in others. I shall speak of the groups as they are marked by
letters in a plan I made for my own use on the spot.

D. This group, which is that nearest the sea on the south side
of the river, consists of six cromlechs, arranged in line, with considerable intervals. A few yards west of this group are several
mounds of stones with some large blocks amongst them, but no blocks
more than 4 feet long. These extend for some 50 yards in line from
west to east. A few yards above them is a large pile of stones, in
the midst of which is a stone 6 feet high and 3 feet wide. These
heaps have been augmented by stones collected from the fields, but
I think there are indications that they were originally of the nature
of the cromlechs.

There are six cromlechs, and from the first the other five are in
sight. The line in which they are placed along the glen side is not
quite straight. The westernmost cromlech is some yards south of
the others, and the west to east line is not exact with regard to the
others, but is nowhere so much departed from as with the first pile.
The first is about half a mile from the sea. I shall describe them
from west to east.

I. This was a cromlech of five huge stones and a top. The top
stone has fallen to westward, and the uprights are all somewhat displaced. Three of the upright stones are still erect; two are fallen,
but not quite to the ground. At the west end are some smaller blocks
and another slab. These are hidden by small stones and earth; I
think there were two support stones and a slab. After examining
all the monuments of the two glens, I came to the conclusion that
this (D I.) was a cromlech with a stone chamber beside it. There
is a space 2 feet 6 inches wide be-
tween the two tallest uprights. The
annexed plan shows the arrangement of the uprights. The top slab
has fallen over e; d and e are fallen;
a, b, and c are upright, but slant more
or less. The dimensions are :—

228.   Plan of the Uprights of Cromlech D I.

			Ft.	In.
(a) Height ..	..	..	12	9
Breadth	..	..	9	4
Thickness	..	(about)	3	0
Widest girth	..	..	23	0
(b) Height ..	..	..	7	5
Breadth	..	..	4	3
Thickness	..	..	2	0
(c) Height ..	..	..	7	0
Breadth	..	..	2	10
Thickness	..	..	1	0
(d) Length ..	..	..	10	0
Breadth	..	..	5	0
Thickness	..	..	2	0
(e) Length ..	..	..	7	0

(a) slants somewhat to westward; the
height from its tip to the ground is 10 feet
2 inches.

(b) from tip perpendicular the height
is 6 feet 6 inches.

(e) is hard to measure, as it lies under
earth, stones, and the top slab.

All these are of a gritty stone, veined with quartz, a rock plentiful in Sliabh Liag, Sliabh Leathan, and the cliffs of the coast. Their shape is rugged.

The top slab is of pure quartz. It is about a foot thick, and is smooth on both sides. This sort of stone splits with a smooth surface, as may be seen on Sliabh Liag and in some of the cliffs. The slab is a tolerably regular oblong, 9 feet 8 inches by 6 feet 6 inches. The smaller slab alluded to above, and which was, I think, the top of the chamber, is about 6 feet by 3 feet.

D II. lies about 40 feet east of D I. It, too, is a cromlech, but the stones of which it is built are of smaller size than those of D I. There are no traces of a chamber, but otherwise it is constructed as D I. The highest standing stone is 4 feet high. There seem to have been five uprights. The top slab has fallen to the west side. It measures 6 feet 3 inches by 5 feet.

D III. is situate 55 feet east of D II. It is a cromlech of five uprights and one slab. One upright only is erect now. Its height is 5 feet, its width 3 feet. The slab which was atop is 8 feet by 7 feet, and averages 2 feet in thickness.

229. Plan showing the actual position of the Stones of D III.

D IV. is 31 feet east of D III. It is a small-sized cromlech. The uprights are all fallen. The slab measures 6 feet 8 inches by 6 feet. A series of low mounds with large stones sticking out here and there forms a sort of connexion with the next cromlech, which stands 48 feet farther east.

D V. Its slab has fallen to eastward, and the uprights in several directions. The tallest upright is 6 feet high. The slab is of quartz, and measures 10 feet by 7 feet, and is about 13 inches thick. Around this cromlech are numbers of loose stones. They are from 1 foot to 2 feet long, and are of mica-schist and quartz. They are not such as would be picked off the meadow, and seem to have been in some way connected with the cromlech.

D VI. stands 96 feet farther east. It is a very large cromlech. It is a good deal fallen; all the stones of which it is built have more or less the character of slabs. It is used as one side of a respectable byre. One great smooth piece of quartz seems to have been the roof. It measures 18 feet 7 inches by 11 feet. The biggest of the stones seems to have formed the east wall of the chamber. Its dimensions are 12 feet by 14 feet, and it is 4 feet thick. I took the dimensions of three others :—1. Length 5 feet 6 inches, width 4 feet; 2. Length 11 feet, width 8 feet; 3. Length 9 feet, width 3 feet, thickness 3 feet.

(Seven Stones in all.)

230. Plan (excl. Top Slab).

From the flat nature of the component stones, the chamber inside would have had few gaps in its walls. Near this cromlech is a low stony mound.

From a few yards east of D VI. a ridge runs slantwise up the side

of Leathan. Many stones stick up out of it, but I could make out
no arrangement. The highest projecting stone is not 4 feet high.
This ridge is about a quarter of a mile long. It might be natural,
but it has very much the look of a human work. Some 150 yards up
the ridge I noticed a slab projecting from the heather. It might
possibly be the top of a chamber, of which the walls are beneath the
earth. This seeming road does not lead to another group of stones,
but disappears a short way up the mountain side. Near the mountain top there is a small bare cliff, the only bare bit of rock on the
otherwise smooth slopes of Leathan. The rock exposed is quartz, and
the position of the little cliff leads one at a glance to imagine that
it may have been the quarry whence the slabs were brought. In
this case the ridge may have been the road down the mountain.
When one goes up to the crag, it looks less like a quarry than from
below, but at the same time I could perceive no geological reason
for the exposure of so small a surface of rock.

Some distance up Glen Malin, and on the same side of the river as
D, but not in sight from it, is another group, E, of stone monuments.

The large stones of this group are surrounded by numbers of
rough, weather-worn stone blocks, averaging 2 feet in length. The
monuments seem to be all cromlechs or chambers, and, as far as I
could tell, are about a dozen in number. One cromlech stands a good
deal higher than the rest. West of it are two stony mounds; these
seem to have been chambers. They are built of long flat slabs, with
similar slabs at the ends and top.

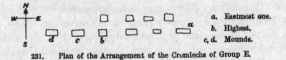

a. Eastmost one.
b. Highest.
c, d. Mounds.

231.   Plan of the Arrangement of the Cromlechs of Group E.

The ground beyond the cromlechs is moorland, and without loose
stones. The stony area is oval, and measures east to west 130 feet,
north to south 50 to 60 feet.

All the cromlechs are about the same size. In the construction of
all, the aim seems to have been a well shut-in chamber. The easternmost one is a chamber 9 feet 10 inches long. At each end it has a
flat stone 3 feet high. The side stones are 7½ feet long and 3 feet
high. The width of the chamber is 4 feet 6 inches. At each side,
and at each end, are heaps of loose small stones. The top slab is about
1 foot thick, and is almost a square of 9 feet.

On the north side of Glen Malin, there are three groups :—

A. This, which is the group furthest from the sea, is of five or six
cromlechs, but only one is in good preservation. It consists of a slab
resting on four flat blocks, and encloses a chamber. The side stones
are each 5 feet 8 inches long. This group stands on a small flat

piece of ground below a crag and above a stream. Leading from the chamber there seems to have been a passage, the sides of which were formed of slabs of stone, of which a few remain.

Some distance lower down the glen, on the north side, is a solitary pointed stone. It is 6 feet 1 inch high, and its girth is 5 feet 5 inches. Higher on the slope by 110 feet, and 18 feet farther west, group B begins.

B. The first of this group is a chamber cromlech. It is much buried in the heather. Some loose stones lie around the cromlech. What seems to have been the top slab is 10 feet across and nearly square, and 2 feet thick. One of the side slabs of the chamber is 10 feet 8 inches by 4 feet. The tallest stone is at the east end, and is in height 6 feet 8 inches. Lower down the slope, below this cromlech, are several low mounds, from which there are no projecting stones; 200 yards west in a straight line is a huge cromlech. It seems to have consisted of a gigantic slab, supported on three upright stones, not forming a closed chamber. The top slab is still on its supports; it is 3 feet thick, and measures 13 feet by 10 feet 9 inches. The tallest of the uprights is 9 feet high, and is rather pointed at top. The third upright seems to have been broken into several pieces. Some 10 yards from this is another cromlech of equal dimensions, and a little south of these several large loose stones are lying on the ground. Forty yards west is a chamber cromlech of small dimensions, and near it are many mounds with stones projecting, possibly artificial.

C. This group is some distance farther down on the same side of the glen; it consists of two cromlechs, separated by a short ridge, so that I think they are really parts of one structure. The eastern part is fallen; it consists of three uprights and a top slab. The western part consists of two stones leaning gablewise against one another. Between the two there is a short ridge, from which several stones stick out. Each of the western pair of stones is about 7 feet high by 6 feet broad. The dimensions of the eastern part of the monument are :—Top slab, 11 feet by 7 feet ; thickness, 1½ foot. Uprights : (a) 8 feet (and I think 2 feet below ground) by 7 feet 7 inches broad ; 2 feet 3 inches thick. (b) 9 feet 6 inches by 2 feet 8 inches ; thickness 2 feet 5 inches. (c) 9 feet 6 inches by 3 feet 5 inches ; thickness, 1 foot 9 inches.

The other groups do not command remarkable prospects, but from this last group there is a fine view of the sea, with the island of Rathlin O'Beirne close below, and beyond the mountainous coast line of Mayo as far as Belmullet.

So far the stone monuments of Glen Malin.

In Glen Columbkille is but one group. It stands in the townland of Farn MacBride, on the north side of the glen, and at the foot of the mountain Ballard. Its monuments are all of the chamber kind. The chambers are made of huge slabs, one at each side, one atop, one at each end. I measured one, and found the sides each 12 feet long and 4 feet broad. Most of the monuments project but little above the ground. One is used to keep calves in, one for pigs, and one for lambs. A native of the townland told me that his brother had dug up a skull and a piece of earthenware near one of the cromlechs. The skull was buried in the churchyard, and its grave is forgotten. The same man also told me that, digging to clear a cromlech for a malt-store, they found that the side slabs rested on a basement slab. The ground is very rugged about these monuments, and some are quite beneath ground, but I think there are altogether six.

I hope that, if these notes are too late to be of use for your book, they may yet be of some interest to you, and

I remain, my dear Sir, yours sincerely,

NORMAN MOORE.

James Fergusson, Esq.

On receiving the above communication, I forwarded to Mr. Moore an impression of the woodcut No. 80, representing Calliagh Birra's Tomb or House, and received the following reply :—

DUNMINNING, GLARRYFORD, Co. ANTRIM,
August 28, 1871.

MY DEAR SIR, — The cromlechs of Farn MacBride, as they stand apparently undisturbed, exactly resemble in plan that depicted in the woodcut. With one or two exceptions the cromlechs of Glen Malin, as far as one can tell in their fallen condition, are built on the same plan. The shape of the stones at the sides and of the top slabs of the cromlech in the engraving is exactly the shape of the stones of the cromlechs in both Glen Malin and Farn MacBride. In one or two of the cromlechs I noticed stones which might correspond to the buttress-like outside stones of the ground-plan in the cut.

The number of slabs in the side walls of the Glen cromlechs is smaller than the number in the woodcut.

The very large cromlech, easternmost of the group the first described in my letter, is in every particular, except the number of its component blocks, the counterpart of your engraving.

In fine, the plan of all the cromlechs of Glen Columbkille, except one or two, the variety of which may be owing to disarrangement, is that of the Meath cromlech.

NORMAN MOORE.

APPENDIX B.

THESE diggings were conducted by Riks Antiquary B. E. Hildebrand and Lieut.-Colonel Stât, chiefly in the days of August-September, 1846, and June 7-22, 1847. The only printed notices thereon appeared at the time, chiefly from the pen of B. E. Hildebrand, in the Upsala paper 'Correspondenten,' Nos. 75, 77, 79—September 12, 19, 26, 1846, and Nos. 50, 53—June 23 and July 3, 1847.

1. 'Correspondenten,' September 12, 1846.—Diggings going on, but prove more laborious than had been expected.

2. 'Correspondenten,' September 19, 1846.—A boarded gallery 7 Swedish feet 5 inches high and 5 feet broad has been constructed from the east side of the howe (Oden's Howe, the largest of the three so-called King-howes), towards the centre. After penetrating 68 feet (20 met.), a mighty wall of granite blocks was struck, probably a grave-chamber. The gently rising gallery abuts on the lowest stones of the chamber. During the diggings have been found unburnt animal bones, bits of dark wood, charcoal, burnt bones, &c. Thus this was evidently a sepulchral mound. The name *King-howes* is evidently correct. Diggings have also been made in the smaller cairns near by, and although they have been opened before, burial-urns have been found, burnt human bones, bones of animals and birds, bits of iron and bronze, &c.

3. 'Correspondenten,' September 26, 1846.—The great wall has proved to be the edge of a mighty chamber. Between 200 and 300 large granite blocks have been taken out. Some of them have traces of tooling. The gallery has been carried 16 Swedish feet through the stone mass, which lies on hard packed clay, over a layer of fine sand, resting on large stones above the natural soil. At the middle of the howe the grave-chamber is 9 feet above the level of the soil, 18 feet under the top of the howe. On the bed of clay under the great stones have been found an iron clinker 3 inches long, remains of pine poles partly burnt, a lock of hair chestnut coloured, &c. The numerous clusters of charcoal show that the dead had been burned on the layer of clay, and the bones have been collected in an urn not yet found. In one of the nearest small howes have been found a quantity of burnt animal and human bones, two little-injured bronze brooches, a fragment of a golden ornament, &c.

4. ' Correspondenten,' June 23, 1847.—The burial-urn has been found in the grave-chamber. Also have turned up bones of men, horses, dogs, a golden ornament delicately worked, a bone comb, bone buttons, &c.

5. ' Correspondenten,' July 3, 1847.—The gallery has been driven 4 feet farther, thereafter has been made a side gallery, 8½ feet wide and 8 feet long, up to the burial-urn. This was found 3 inches under the soil, and was covered with a thin slab. It was 7 inches high, 9 inches in diameter, filled with burnt bones, human and animal (horse, dog, &c.), ashes, charcoal (of needle and leaf trees), nails, copper ornaments, bone articles, a bird of bone, &c. In the mass of charcoal about were found bones, broken ornaments, bits of two golden bracteates, &c. Coins of King Oscar were then placed in the urn, and everything restored as before.

Frey's Howe was opened, and showed the same results.

The gallery remained for some years, and was visited by thousands of persons, but afterwards fell in, and the howe is now inaccessible.

CARL SÄVE.

Upsala, *March* 1, 1871.

========

APPENDIX C.

SINCE the sheets containing the account of the Scottish monuments were printed off, I have received from Sir Henry Dryden slips of two letters which he addressed to the editor of the *John o' Groat's Journal*, giving an account of some explorations he had made in Caithness during this autumn. One of these contains an account of certain chapels, brochs, and circles he had examined. The first two classes do not concern us here, and are therefore omitted; but the circles are of interest as probably belonging to the same category as those in the Orkneys, and the description of them is consequently printed with the other letter, which gives an account of four alignments which are so germane to our subject that Sir Henry's description is printed *in extenso*. The name of the first, "The Battle Moss, Yarhouse," is of itself singularly suggestive, and I have little doubt that, if properly inquired into, the peasantry could tell what battle was fought there, and what, consequently, these lines were erected to commemorate. Taken in conjunction with the horned cairns described by Mr. Anderson,[1] and the circles,

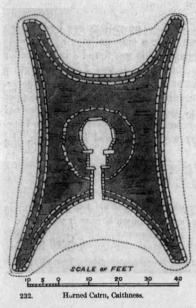

SCALE OF FEET

232.   Horned Cairn, Caithness.

it does not seem to me doubtful that the whole of this Caithness group belongs to the tenth century. The circles, and especially the horned cairns, are the exact counterparts of the fanciful forms of the Viking graves found at Hjortehammer (woodcut No. 118) and elsewhere in Scandinavia, which resemble them in more respects than one, and the alignments are such as those at Ashdown (woodcut No. 28). Nor need we go far for the events they commemorate. Between the years 970 and 996, A.D., two great battles, at least, are recorded to have taken place in Caithness, between the sons of Thorfin, and between Liotr, the victor of the first fight, and the Scots, who in vain attempted to avenge the death of Skiuli; and besides these there may have been many subordinate frays. It is probable that both brothers were buried in Caithness, and we are distinctly told that Laudver, the last surviving son of Thorfin, was certainly buried there.[2]

The fact of these alignments and horned cairns and semicircles being unlike what is found elsewhere in Scotland, separates this group from anything existing further south. Their similarity to the Viking graves of Scandinavia, avowedly of the tenth century, points to an age from which they cannot be distant; and when it is recollected that Caithness in the tenth century formed part of the Orcadian Jarldom, it does not seem that we have far to seek for an authentic explanation of all we find in that remote corner of the isle.   J. F.

---

[1] 'Proceedings Soc. Ant. Scot.,' vii. 480 et seqq.
[2] 'Barry's History of Orkney,' pp. 125-129.

LETTER FROM SIR H. DRYDEN, Bart.,

TO THE

Editor of the 'John o' Groat's Journal.'

———

Lines, Battle Moss, Yarhouse. Lines and Cist, Garry Whin. Lines, "Many Stones," Clyth. Lines, Camster. Circle (?) Achanloch. Circle, Guidebest, Latheronwheel.

GROUPS OF LINES.

I am not aware of any similar groups in Great Britain, though no doubt there are some, and have no books at hand to refer to any in Denmark, Norway, or Sweden. The groups of lines in France (of far larger stones and greater length than those in Caithness) have the largest stones and widest intervals and the highest ground (the heads) to the west or thereabouts, and the smallest stones and narrowest intervals and lowest ground (the tails) to the east or thereabouts. The Caithness groups differ entirely in principle. The one at Yarhouse Loch runs north and south, does not radiate, and is on nearly level ground; but the three others have the narrower intervals and higher ground to the north (which end we may call the head), and radiate towards the south and lower ground. The group at Battlemoss, near Yarhouse, is on ground falling slightly to north-west. It consists of eight lines placed north and south. The width at the south end is forty-four feet. The lines are somewhat irregular, and appear to radiate slightly towards the north, but this is uncertain. One line extends 384 feet, and another one 170 feet, but the remaining six now only extend 133 feet. The ground is covered with peat and heather, and other stones may be hidden below the surface. There is no cairn or other grave now visible in proximity to the lines. The largest stones are about 2 feet 6 inches high, 2 feet 6 inches wide, and 1 foot 3 inches thick.

The group at Garrywhin consists of six lines. The whole width at the head (north-east end) is 50 feet, and at the bottom 107 feet. The central line bears N.N.E. or S.S.W. The length of this line is 200 feet. The fall is 20 feet to the S.S.W. At the head is a cist of slabs 3 feet 6 inches by 2 feet 6 inches, and 2 feet 4 inches deep, placed east and west. As this grave is on the highest point of the knoll, and as the lines commence at it, it is fair to presume that they are connected. In the cist were found ashes, pieces of pottery, and flint chips, but no bones. As the cist is between the third and fourth lines, it is fair to presume that there never were more than six lines.

The group called "Many Stones" has the head on the top of a knoll, from which the ground falls on all sides. The lines are on the south

2 M

slope, and are 22 in number. The width at the head or north end is 118 feet, and at the bottom is 188 feet. The length in the centre is 145 feet, but there is no proof that this was the original length, and the presumption is the reverse. The average bearing is north and south, and the fall 10 feet 3 inches. The largest stones now remaining are about 3 feet high, 3 feet wide, and 1 foot 6 inches thick. There are numerous blocks of stone lying about the head, where, however, the rock is exposed, but the example of Garrywhin makes it probable that a cairn once existed on this knoll. There are no traces of any *sunk* grave, but the cairn may have contained a chamber above ground, like many in the vicinity.

The group at Camster is on the moor, on ground falling slightly to the south-west. A considerable depth of peat overlies the rock here, and many stones are below the surface. There are now six lines ascertained. The length is 105 feet, width at the head or north end 30 feet, and at the tail or lower end 53 feet. The average bearing is north and south. The stones are smaller than at the last mentioned group. There is no cairn or other grave apparent close to these lines, but in a direction due north, at 346 feet, is a chambered cairn. No stones are now traceable between; but as there are gaps in the lines themselves, this blank interval may once have had lines on it to connect the cairn with the existing group. No habitation *now* exists near the spot, but there were many in this strath, which may account for destruction of stones in former times. A few hundred feet farther north is the huge horned cairn described by Mr. Anderson, and at 436 feet N.N.E. from the small cairn is the round chambered cairn described in the same paper.

CIRCLE AT ACHANLOCH, ESTATE OF FORSE, IN PARISH OF LATHERON.

The name is spelt Achinloch and Auchinleck. These no doubt are wrong, and probably the name is derived from Gaelic words signifying " The Field at the Loch," or " The Field of the Stones," from these standing stones. The place is close to the new road from Lybster to Thurso. This series of standing-stones, entitled " circle," as a class-name, is in the form of a donkey's shoe, the length being N.N.W, and S.S.E., the open end to the latter. The sides are nearly parallel. The area is covered with heather and peat, on a substratum of rock of the slaty character common to the district. The ground falls from the area to the west, north, and east. In the latter direction, the ground falls only for a short distance, and then rises to much higher ground. On the north-east, at 700 feet or 800 feet, is the loch of Stemster.

There is no evidence that the two south ends were ever joined by a straight or curved line of stones; and as the sides are of equal length, we may infer that they never were joined, though possibly intended to be so. The highest point of the area is about 13 feet above the hollow on the east. This donkey-shoe-shaped series of stones is 226 feet long, and 110 feet wide in the middle, inside measure. The two extremities are 85 feet 3 inches apart.

There are now 36 stones existing, of which only one is down; but by filling up intervals at usual distances, it appears there were 54 stones, supposing the lower end vacant as now. The average interval seems to have been 8 feet. The highest stone is 5 feet 7 inches high above ground; the widest 5 feet 4 inches; and the thickest 1 foot 7 inches.

All these stones are of a slaty character, and have their sides parallel, so that in width (long sides) they are generally three or four times their thickness (short sides). But the singular characteristic of this series is that the stones are set with their long sides at right angles to the curve, projecting like cogs of a wheel.

In many circles some or all of the stones have no decided difference in the measures of width and thickness; but in all cases, when I have found a difference, the long sides are in the line of the curve.

Any notice of an arrangement similar to that at Achanloch would be a favour.

There is no appearance of any part of the area having been disturbed for burial or other purposes. There is a ruin of a chambered cairn south-east of the circle; and in the loch of Rangag, about a mile west, is the remain of a brough.

CIRCLE AT GUIDEBEST, LATHERONWHEEL, PARISH OF LATHERON.

The place is on the north bank of the burn, one mile and a half up the strath. The circle is nearly true in form, and though now imperfect, doubtless was once complete. It is 170 feet in diameter. The area is flat, covered with heather and peat, on a substratum of rock in some places, and of alluvial gravel in others. It is 15 feet above the brook, which has washed away the cliff very close up to the south-west stone, and appears likely, unless prevented, to dislocate the stones on that side.

There are now only seven stones existing—all erect—and by filling up the gaps at usual distances there were thirteen stones. The average interval seems to have been 45 feet. The highest stone is 5 feet 3 inches above ground; the widest 3 feet 2 inches; and the thickest 1 foot 10 inches. The stone is of the common argillaceous slate of the district.

The stones are nearer square or circular in plan than those at Achanloch, but (so far as they can be) are all set with the long sides to the curve. The south stone is a little beyond the line of the circle, but is evidently a moved and erected stone.

There are numbers of stones lying about the area; but no evidence of a cairn or other burial-place in or near the circle. From its soil, and the absence of remains, it was probably not sepulchral, though some antiquaries hold that all circles are sepulchral.

Lower down the strath on the same side of the brook were many circles which were destroyed in "improving" the land some years ago. These are stated to have been 20 or 30 yards across, of stones 2 feet to 4 feet high. No remains are known to have been found in them; but no observations or measures were made. It is probable that these circles were sepulchral—the absence of stones in the centres notwithstanding. Nearer the road and shore are other remains of broughs, cairns, cists, &c.

I remain your obedient servant,

H. DRYDEN,

Hon. Mem. of the Soc. of Antiquaries of Scotland.

Caithness, September 21, 1871.

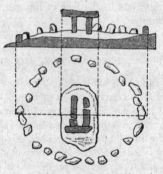

233.   Dolmen near Bona, Algeria.

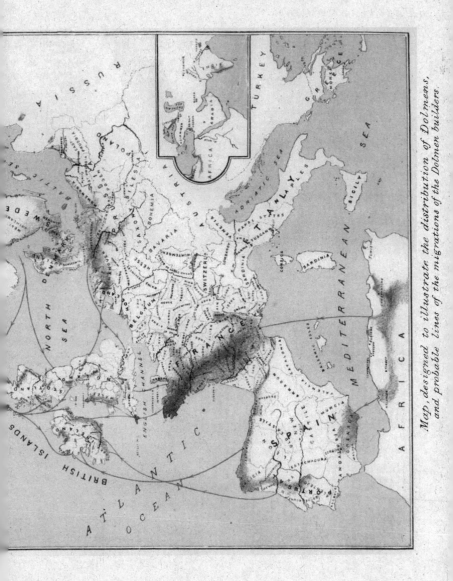

Map, designed to illustrate the distribution of Dolmens, and probable lines of the migrations of the Dolmen builders.

INDEX.

ABBEVILLE, museum at, 16.
Abbot Millitus, Pope Gregory's letter to, 21.
Abd en Nar and Abd en Nour, 404.
Aberdeenshire circles, 202 *et seq.*
Aberlemmo, stone at, with cross, 268; date, 270; memorial of what, 270.
Abraham, stone set up by, 438.
Ac, import of termination, 329, 330; its prevalence in West of France, 329; its coincidence with dolmens, 329; its occurrence in West of England, 330; names of cities with this termination in France, 328, 376.
Achemlock circle, 530.
Addington, groups at, 118; circles at, 119. *See* Aylesford.
Adil, Swedish king, defeats Snio, 279.
Africa. *See* Algeria, Tripoli. Its monuments may furnish key to solution of mysterious questions, 414.
African prince mentioned by Asoka, 498.
Age between exodus of Romans and Alfred, darkness of, 113-4; stones more eloquent than books then, 114.
Agra, tomb of Akbar at, 496.
Agricola, 20.
Ahmedabad, city of, 457.
Aix la Chapelle, decree of, 25.
Ajunta, importance of Vihara at, 501.
Akbar, sovereign of India, 459; tomb of, 47, 496.
Alajor, Talyot at, 435.
Aleutian Islands, route of peoplers of America, 516.
Alexander mentioned in edict of Indian prince, 498.
Alfred, 23-4; his victory at Ashdown, 123; how commemorated, 123.
Alaska, Hydahs in, 18.
Alentejo, dolmen in, 378.
Algeria, no Druids in, 6; long ignorance as to its numerous dolmens, 395; researches of Messrs. Rhind, Christy, and M. Féraud, 395; Bou Moursug, 395; Setif, 396; Tiaret, 397; Tripoli, 397; their ordinary position, 397; Bazinas, 397; Chouchas, 398; dolmen on steps, 398; tumuli with lines between, 399; sepulchral stones, 399; plan and elevation of African tumulus, 400; dolmen with two circles, 400, 471; others on road from Bona to Constantine, four

cairns enclosed in squares, 402; analogy to examples in Scandinavia, 403; age of Algerian examples, 403; of what race, 403; Djidjeli, tombs near, with circle, 404; find there, *ib.*; their age, *ib.*; Sidi Kacem, dolmeu near, and inscription, 405; circle near Bona, 405; Algerian monuments contemporary with early Christians, 405-6; their general age, 406; who erected them, 406 *et seq.*; date of, 403; compared to Aveyron, 407.
Alignment, at Shap, 130; Carnac, Erdeven, St.-Barbe, 354 *et seq.*; two heads, 354; singular head of column, 355; Crozon, Kerdouadec, Carmaret, Leuré, Gré de Cojou, 368; Preissac, 368; Stonehenge, why made, 110-1; Sesto Calende, 391. *See* Avebury, Avenues, Beckhampton, Caithness.
Alkil, Danish chief, 279.
Allées couvertes ou grottes des Fées in France, 340 *et seq.*, 358-9; at Lochmariaker, 365.
Alleth, battle at, 374.
Alphabetical writing, date of its introduction into Ireland, 189, 196, 271; interruption of use for centuries, 272.
Altars, 425.
Altmark, dolmen at, 301.
Alyattes, tomb of, 31.
Ambrius, convent of, 109.
Ambrosius Aurelius said to have erected Stonehenge, and why, 106; forces a peace upon Saxons, 107.
America, North, Smithsonian Contributions to Knowledge; survey of Messrs. Squiers and Davis, 510; absence of rude-stone monuments, *ib.*; earthworks, American peculiarity, 511; *enclosures for defence*, extent of, *ib.*; inference from, *ib.*; *sacred enclosures*, peculiarity and number of, size and form of enclosures, *ib.*; Newark Works, *ib.*; whether residences of chiefs, 513; *conical mounds*, mounds of sacrifice, finds, *ib.*; Grave Creek mound, Miamisburgh mound, 514; *temple mounds* compared to Teocallis of Mexicans, *ib.*; difficulty of distinguishing between temple and palace, *ib.*; were the mounds not civil? *ib.*; animal mounds, gigantic serpent form, doubt

whether animal object of worship, 515; whether European emigrants account for population of America, 517; way of communication, 516; material of tools found in America, 517; Redmen and mound-builders distinguished, these correspond with the "Hydahs," 517.

America, Central, and Peru, carved stone monuments, 517-8; Peruvian compared to those of Pelasgi and Tyrrheni, 518; no rude-stone monuments observed in South America, ib.; Tia Huanaco not like so-called Druidical remains, ib.; circles and squares, 519.

American Indians non-progressive, 18.

Amesbury, Hengist's meeting with British chiefs at, 107.

Amlaff, King, 253.

Amlech, or Hamlet, tomb of, 299.

Amorites, dolmens in country of, and perhaps nowhere else in Palestine, 442.

Amravati, arts of Bactria at, 456; sepulchral circles at, 474; tope and rail, 475, 493; representations of priests at, 501.

'Ancient and Modern Wiltshire,' 5.

'Ancient English Castles,' Mr. Clark's, 84.

Andalusia, dolmens in, 378.

Anderson, Mr., horned cairns described by, 528.

Angles, see Saxons.

Anglesea, Druids in, 5; circles in, 162.

Anhalt dolmen, 301.

Animal mounds in America, 515; whether of Chinese origin, 517 note.

'Annals of the Four Masters,' 176, 187-8.

Annandale, 129; circle, see Woodcastle.

Antequera dolmen, 383.

Antigonus } mentioned in edict of Asoka,
Antiochus }   498.

Antiquity, why caution necessary in assigning, 144; of rude and polished stone monuments, 508.

Antony, whether founder of Monasticism, 499.

Aquhorties circle, 263.

Aquitania in time of Cæsar, 328; of Augustus, 328; language of, unknown, 333; pressed upon by Celts, 409; whether they migrated to Africa, 410.

Aquitanians perhaps in Britain, 163, 238; and perhaps dolmen builders, 328; but few dolmens between Garonne and Pyrenees, 328.

Arabia, rude-stone monuments in, 444 et seq.

Arabs, their conquest of North Africa, 404; their feeling as to monasticism, 500.

Arborlowe, vallum and ditch of, 62. See Derbyshire.

Archæological Congress at Copenhagen, 10.

Arches not in use amongst Hindus, but Burmese, 458.

Architecture, meagreness of historical accounts of buildings between erection of Parthenon and Henry VII.'s Chapel, 114; Irish, 221 et seq.; law of progressive development, 222; when inapplicable, 222-3; sequence in monuments of Ireland, 237-8; three styles of three races perhaps simultaneous there, 238; of monuments at Stennis, 255-6; differences of style of similar monuments in different countries, 306; sequence of style in dolmens, 335; without drawings no words can describe style, 334; peculiarity of church architecture in south dolmen region in France, 332; Celtic, ib.; similarity of style no proof of synchronism, 369; different examples compared, 369; influences of Roman, 414; of Indian Art, ib.; of dolmens or nurhags and giants' towers, which the older, 437; sequence of style and material in India, 456 et seq.; wood, stone imitation of wood architecture, 456; Mahommedan mosque built by Hindus, 457; arches not used by Hindus, ib.; ruins of Ahmedabad, 457; Palitana, ib.; Burmah, Cambodia, 458; Hindu not immutable, 459; Indian unprogressive tribes, ib.; rude and refined architecture, co-existence of, in India, 482; early crosses in India, of what date? 486 et seq.; appropriation by Romanists of pagan forms, 489; connexion of Singalee dagobas and sepulchral tumuli, 491; Tee, what it represented, 490; wood and then stone forms—rails, 492-3; styles of Eastern and European dolmens compared, 494; points of similarity and dissimilarity, 495; cists outside tumuli, holed slabs, simulated summit cists, concentric enclosing circles, 496 et seq.; use of stone imitated by rude nations in Europe, from what nations, 508; and in India from what race, ib.; when introduced in the East in its rude form, and in its polished form, ib.; ditto in the West, ib.; age of introduction of tumuli or barrows unascertained, ib.; as also of Cave men and stone implements, ib.; uses sepulchral or cenotaphic, 509; or for battlefield, or offerings to spirits of the departed, ib.; connexion with relics of the dead, ib.; whether dedicated to God, sun or moon, &c., or serpents, ib.; twofold principle of erection of such structures, ib.; North America, 511; civil and sacred, royal and monastic, 514; animal, gigantic earthen forms, 515.

Ard-na-Raigh, place of execution, 233.

Ardèche, remains of Cave men in, 321.

Arfin, Prince of Norway, 250.

Argyllshire dolmens, 273.

Arles council, 24, 25.

Arnbjörg, wife of Sandulf, 272.

Art, King, where buried, 212.

Arthur, King, his existence doubted by some, 114, 132; round table, 62; contemporary history null, 114; his round table, 128 (see Penrith); probable history of Arthur, 133; his defensive war against invaders, 134; his supposed Scottish career, 134; ill-founded, 135; localities of his twelve battles, 135 et seq.; of his last battle, 86-7; views of the author, 152; fables respecting, likened to those about Alexander, 133; Arthur's pike at Shap, 130; Arthur's Quoit, 170. See Baden Mound, Bas Lowe, Caerleon, Caledonian Forest, Gain, Salkeld, Stanton Drew, Woodcastle Lyn.

Arrichinaga dolmen, 388.

Arroyolos dolmen, 377; described by Borrow, 389.

Aryans a progressive race, 18, 19; occupation of Greece, 39; when they crossed Indus, 445; penetrate into North America, by what route, 516; Aryan, non-Aryan, equivalents of what, 506.

Aschenrade, singular arrangement of circles, 317.

Ashdown, Sarsen stones at, 121-3; drawing of, 122; contrasted with Carnac, ib.; Druidical, 123; or monument of battle between Saxons and Danes, ib.

Asia Minor, dolmens not yet found in, 445.

Asoka, King, monument of, 47; introduction of stone monuments in India, 48, 455; his rock-engraved edict, 498; convocation, 501.

Aspatria, 155; compared to Herrestrup, 304. See Circles.

Asser cited as to battle between Saxons and Danes, 123.

Astarte, see Melkart.

Asturias, dolmens in, 378.

Atridæ, tombs of, 32; Atreus, 33.

Aubrey, 3; his account of Hakpen Hill, 76; cited, 104.

Auisle, King, 201.

Augustine, St., cession of temple at Canterbury to, 22-3.

Augustus, tomb of, 40; no coins of, found in Britain, 144.

Aurelius, see Ambrosius.

Axevalla, singular dolmen at, 312-3; find there, 312.

Aztecs, buildings of, 515.

Avebury, 1, 3, 6, 7, 61; age of, 17; pretended serpent worship, 4; represented, 62; vallum, ditch and circle, 62, 63; Sarsens, 62; Kennet avenue, 63; no curved avenues, 64; double circle or oval, 64; who interred there, 86; author's opinion, 86, 89; holes, 343; Beckhampton avenue, 64,

98; Silbury hill, 62; Waden hill. 62; object of structure, 65; theory of Druidical temples, 66; disputed, 66 et seq.; Avebury a burying-place, 72; charter of Athelstan as to, 73; stone row, 73; plan of, 81; sepulchral or battle-field, 116; attached to circles, 29, 51; with or without circles or dolmens, 29, 53; example at St. Helier, Jersey, 51; chamber there found buried, 54; at Merivale Bridge, on Dartmoor, ib.; why erected, ib.; what they represent, 56.

Avening, holes in chamber at, 357.

Avenue. See Alignments, Avebury, Aylesford.

Averni Celts mentioned by Livy, 327.

Aylesford, 110 et seq. Kit's Cotty House, what, 116; description of, 110; why erected, 119; erroneous view of Mr. Wright as to Belgian burials there, 119; Tollington, stones at, purpose of, 119; obelisks or coffin stones, 117; in memory of what, 119; circles of Addington abbey, ib.; Horstead, tumulus at, 120; explored by Colonel Fisher, ib.; absence of valuables or other articles in tombs there, accounted for, ib.; "Countless stones," 117; resembles Oroust, 305; drawing of, 117; a supposed avenue near, 117-8; other groups at Addington and near Kit's Cotty House, 118; Aylesford the stage of a battle between Vortigern and Saxons, 119; Bede's statement of locality of battle not conclusive, 121.

Baba, images of, buried, 449.

Babylon, age of its palaces, 1.

Bactrian Greeks, influence of, upon Indian architecture, 456, 508.

Badon Hill, Arthur's battle there, 138. See Battle.

Bähr, Professor, his book of Graves, 318.

Bahmany dynasty in India, 485.

Baker, Mr., his account of Aryan interments, 479.

Baille clough togal dolmen, 229.

Balk, Saracenic arches, 457.

Ballina, see Maols.

Ballo dolmen, 321.

Ballysadare, cairn at, 179.

Balor of the Evil Eye, 187.

Balquhain circle, 263.

Bang, importance of monastery at, 50.

Bangkok, Buddhist monument at, 413.

Banesdown battle, 87.

Barbarism of early Irish, 235.

Barbato, monuments in, 415.

Barbury Castle, siege of, 88.

Bards, 19; testify to Druids, 6.

Barrows, 11; of Roman period, 36 (see Bartlow Hills); British, 65; Silbury, ib.; conical, 83; their number and position, 102; age of, 104; Derbyshire, 138; Yorkshire, ib.; on Boyne,

200; in Orkneys at Stennis; bowl-shaped, 243; find, 243; Sandwick, *ib.*; conoid barrows, *ib.*; find, *ib.*; of what race the barrows, 243-4; *see* Maes-Howe; little barrows by thousands in Orkneys, of what race, 249; Halfdan's barrow, 250; Danish Royal barrow, *ib.*; *Long* barrow at Lethra, 282; and at West Kennet, 284; whose grave, 283; date, 285; explored by Thurnam, 283; find there, 285; inference from, 286-9; post-Roman, 286; long barrow at Wiskehärad in Halland, 288; what it marks, *ib.*; long barrows post-Roman, 289; ship barrows, 291-2; numerous in East France, 327; holed chambers in long barrows at Kerlescant and Rodmarton, 357.

Barry's 'Views in Orkneys,' 241.

Bartlow Hills barrow, 36; elevation, 14, 83.

Bas Lowe, Arthur's table, 137.

Basin, flat-bottomed, mysterious, 216-7.

Bassas, Arthur's battle on, 136.

Bateman, Messrs., diggings by, 138, 140-4; finds at Benty Grange, 145; and at Kenslow barrow, *ib.*; overlook monuments at Stanton Drew, 146.

Bateman, Mr., explores Arbor Lowe, 357; his and author's remarks on finds by, 13-4.

Bath, *see* Battles.

Battles.—Arthur's, 12, 135 *et seq*; Ashdown, 122; Aylesford, 119; Badbury, 87; Badon Hill, 86; place of Arthur's last battle disputed, 86-7; Banbury Hill, date of, 109; Banesdon, 87; Bath, 87; Battlemoss, Yarhouse, 526; Braavalla, 188, 280-2; Deorham, 88; Kongsbacka, 279; Moytura, South and North, 176 *et seq.*; Rollright, 126.

Battlefields marked by megalithic remains, 14.

Battlestones in Scotland, 240, 272; Kirkliston, 272.

Bauta stones, 60, 272.

Bazinas in North Africa, 397-8.

Beaumont-sur-Oise, find at, 339.

Beckhampton avenue, 64; position of stone, 98.

Bede, his division of Kent explained, 121.

" Beds " of Diarmid and Graine, 225.

Behring's Straits route of peoplers of America, 516.

Beira dolmens, 378.

Belgæ, absence of dolmens amongst, 302; their pre-dolmen immigration into Britain, 323-4; Belgæ or Firbolgs in Ireland, 176.

Belgaum, altars and tables at, 467.

Belgians, erroneous statement of interments at Kit's Cotty House, 119.

Bellovesus, his invasion of Italy, 327.

Benares, style of architecture at, 412.

Benty Grange barrow, 144. *See* Derbyshire.

Beowulf's poem contains incidents of Saxon burials, 120; Beowulf's victory over Wurm, *ib.*; his interment, *ib.*; his helmet, 145; his verses on Knock na Rea, 185.

Bernard, Commandant, his description of enormous dolmen at Tiaret, 397.

Bertrand, Alexander, attacks Celtic origin of megalithic monuments, 254.

Bertrand, M., 6; his essay upon dolmens, 324; his theory as to migration of dolmen race, 378-9, 407; as to builders in North Africa, 403.

Betal or Vetal, worship of, 467.

Bhils, Coles, Gonds and Toda, non-progressive tribes in India, 459; their tenacity to usages, *ib.*

Bilithons, 435.

Birck, dolmen enclosed in square, 307.

Birra the hag, 231; monastery, 231 *note.*

Biscay dolmens, 378.

Bits of Bridle, 81, 304. *See* Stukeley.

Blaine, Mr. D. R., his notes and sketch of dolmen at Kafr er Wâl, 441.

Blair, Dr., engraves Carnac, 350.

Blenda, Swedish heroine, her victory, 291.

Bluestones, if part of Stonehenge, 97; whence the stones, 108; story explained, 108-9. *See* Sarsens.

" Bluetooth," 296.

Boece and Fordun, their fables, 134.

Boinn, wife of Nechtan, 212; "her small hound" buried with her, *ib.*

Bollandists' work silent as to Buddhism, 505.

Bona, circle near, 405; dolmen, 532.

Bonstetten, cited, 308, 379; map, 324; according to, no dolmen in Poland, 301.

Borlase cited as to Boscawen circles, 160.

Borrow mentions monument at Arroyolos, 377.

Borther Lowe, find at, 12.

Boscawen, 160. *See* Circles.

Boucher de Perthes, collection by, 16.

Bouie's survey of New Grange, 204.

Bousquet, dolmen of, 46, 49.

Boyne, monuments on, 200, 290; burials, 212.

Braavalla Heath battle, 280-2. *See* Battle-fields.

Brachenbyr dolmen, 46, 49.

Brahmins, their domination in India, 459.

Breas' invasion of Ireland and defeat, 187.

Brest Menhir, 58.

Brigantes join Silures, 381.

British chiefs massacred by Hengist, where, 106.

British isles described by Diodorus, 8; not more prosperous before Roman invasion than in 5th century, 114-5; Spaniards, Silures, settle in, 383.

British Rude-Stone Monuments, how

affected by conquest by and withdrawal of Romans, 394.

Britons, 20, 21, 37 ; peace with Saxons, when, 89.

Brittany, monuments in, 6. See Carnac.

Broad-pated race, 306.

Brochs, Scotch, resemble Nurhags, 431 note.

Brodick Bay circles, 262.

Brogar, King of, in Orkneys, 241 ; failure of search there, 243 ; how to proceed, ib. ; tumuli. 252-3 ; compared to Stanton Drew circles, 256.

Bronze age, Stonehenge belongs to, 102 ; as also tumuli in South of France, 327.

Brouillet, M., his work on Poitou, 329.

Brown, Mr., his account of Hydahs, 18.

Bruges, capital of Celts, temp. Bellovesi, 327.

Brugh, burial-place of Kings of Tara, 190, 199, 212.

Brugh na Boinne, burials at, 191 et seq.

Brunswick dolmens, 301.

Bryce, Dr., his observations in Arran, 265.

Buckingham, Duke of, directs diggings at Stonehenge, 104.

Buddha, Dagobas or Stupas of, 41.

Buddhagosa, no written books before, 500.

Buddhism, 458 ; in India, 458 et seq. ; in the West, 499 et seq. ; in Christianity, 499 ; monastic institutions, ib. ; monasticism opposed to Egyptian institutions and Arab or Semitic feeling, 500 ; relation of Essenes to Buddhism, ib. ; monasticism in India apparent from monuments and inscriptions, 501 ; three convocations : cells : Viharas, Chaityas, 501 ; sculptures : Sanchi : Ascetics : Amravati shaven priests : date of similar institutions in West, ib. ; peculiarities of, separation of clergy from laity, 501 ; canonization, relic worship, 503 ; date, silence of the Fathers, eloquence of architecture, 506 ; Buddhism Turanian, ib. ; nature of the faith, ib. ; Turanians in Europe in Middle Ages, 507 ; what with respect to stone monuments the West borrowed from the East, 507 ; of what Buddhism was the reform, 504.

Buddhist architecture, 40-2.

Buddhist Topes. 46 ; rails, 48, 492 ; Lâts or Stambas, 57 ; convocations, 501.

Burials, usages of, in the Steppes, 449.

Burmah, date of temples at, 1 ; dagobas, 41.

Burmah and Siam, architecture of wood, 456.

Burn Moor, 159. See Circles.

Burton, Right Hon. W., describes cairn Knock na Rea, 184.

Butte de Cæsar, find there, 339.

Buxton, rude monuments near. See Derbyshire.

CABEIRI, images of, 425.

Caboul valley. 452.

Cæsar mentions Druids, but not their temples, 20 ; stood, perhaps, at Carnac, ib. ; inference from his and Pliny's silence, 373.

Caerleon, or Chester, Arthur's ninth battle at, 137.

Cairns at Rath Cruachan, 200 ; Lough Crew, 213 ; Glen Columbkille, 226 ; Freyrsö, 292 ; Norway, 302 ; the distribution of dolmens in Europe, 301-2 ; dolmens belong to a sea-faring race, 302 ; four cairns enclosed in squares, 402 ; compared to Aschenrade, 403 ; Jewurgi, 471-2 ; probably battle-field, 472 ; huge horned cairn Caithness, 528, 530 ; of "one Man," find there, 178-9.

Caldwell, Mrs, find in possession of, 210.

Caledonians like Germans, 162 ; Caledonian Forest, place of Arthur's battle, 137.

Callernish, age of, 52.

Calliagh Birra's House, 230.

Calvaries in Brittany, 59.

Cambodia, monuments of, not ancient, 1 ; style of buildings, 458.

Camden, his remark as to place of interments at Stonehenge, 105 ; as to Rollright and Rollo in England, 126 ; as to Long Meg, 127 ; as to ruins at Shap, 129 ; and Penrith, 132.

Camster alignment, 529.

Cangas de Onis, 387.

Cannibalism of early Irish, 235.

Canonization in the East, 503.

Canterbury, Roman Cathedral at, 22.

Canute forbids adoration of stones, 25.

Caons, or Giants' circles, 453.

Cape St. Matthieu, 59.

Carder Lowe, barrow opened at, 1.

Carl Sverkersson slays Danish prince, 291.

Carmaret, alignment at, 367.

Carnac, 1 ; Rev. Bathurst Deane's plan of, 6 ; Cæsar perhaps saw from it battle with Veneti, 20 ; described, 349 ; plan, 352.

Carnutes, Druids' chief seat amongst, 5.

Carrowmore, 181 ; field of battle, 187, 198, 223.

Carte, Mr., as to field of battle at Baydon hill, 87.

Carthaginians in Spain, 379 ; not building or burying race, 394.

Cartheilhac, M., his paper on megalithic monuments, 335.

Cas Tor avenue, 56.

Castern, find at, 13.

Castille, if dolmens in, 378.

Castle Wellan dolmen, 45.

Cat stones, 57, 146. See Derbyshire battle stones.

Catalonia, dolmens in, 378.

Cathair, or round fort, 235; of Tuatha de Danann, 193; of Cormac at Tara, 194.

Cathregomion, Cabregonnon, Catbregonnion, or Cathbregion, Arthur's 11th battle there, 138. *See* Stanton Drew.

Catigren, where buried, 144. *See* Kitt's Cotty House.

Cattle spoil of Cooley, 196.

Cave men, 17, 18, 329; like Red Indians, 17; or Esquimaux, *ib.*; under what circumstances found in France, 16; and England, 16, 17.

Cave races, gradations of style of monuments among, 335.

Caves, early, in India, 456; Buddhist, 460.

Ceallach, murder of, 233.

Cedric, Saxon chief, 88-9.

Celtiberians, *see* Iberians.

Celtic race, priests of, 3, 4; whether French megalithic monuments belong to, 6; their influence upon Etruria, 393.

Celts, ready converts to Christianity, 227; date of the first invasion of Gaul, *ib.*; were earlier converts than dolmen builders, 328; spread themselves through centre of France, *ib.*; either Celts or a prehistoric race built the dolmens, 329; the Cave men, *ib.*; who these were, *ib.*; dolmens and Cave men perhaps conterminous, *ib.*; Cimbri, Celts, and Gauls, 333; Cimbri and Aquitanians, relation of, *ib.*; their capital temp. Bellevesi, 327; described by Livy, *ib.*; Averni, *ib.*; if dolmens in Galatia, important bearing upon Celtic theory, 446; their invasions of other countries, 409.

Cemeteries of Ireland, 199; Cruachan, or Rathcrogen, *ib.*; circular mounds there, *ib.*; monument of Dathi, *ib.*; Relig na Riogh, 200; Red stone pillar, *ib.*; circle, *ib.*; cairns, *ib.*; burials, Queen Meave and Dathi, *ib.*; compared with Arbor Low and Salkeld, *ib.*; Knowth, *ib.*; New Grange, 201; plundered by Danes, *ib.*; first mentioned by Mr. Lloyd, *ib.*; Sir T. Molyneux's statement, *ib.*; Governor Pownall's, 202; engravings of by Bouie, 203; if uncovered, resemblance to Salkeld and Stanton Drew, *ib.*; sculpture, 204; reverses of stones elaborately carved, 205; how such came to be covered, *ib.*; entrance, position of, *ib.*; ornaments, 206-7; sculptured mark, 207; whether characters, *ib.*; Dowth, or perhaps Dubhad, plundered by Danes, 208; diggings, *ib.*; find there, 210; Netherville House, 209; tomb of the Dagdha, *ib.*; perhaps intact, *ib.*; find there, 209, 210; ornaments at Dowth, 211-2; written evidence respecting these three cemeteries, 212; and persons buried, *ib.*; author's con-

jecture as to New Grange, 213; Lough Crew, 213 *et seq.*; if cemetery of Talten, 219; choice of plan of cemetery amongst Irish, 220; 'Book of the Cemeteries' cited, 221; stone in cairn T, Lough Crew, 222; stones in sculptured graves, 223; Clover Hill, *ib.*; Shahpoor, 485.

Cetti, stone of, 173.

Ceylon dagobar, 41; Thupa Ramayana, and Lanka Ramayana, 489, 490.

Chaityas, *see* Church Caves.

Champollion's discoveries, 1.

Chardin cited as to circles at Tabriz and Miana, 453.

Chariot wheels sculptured on dolmens, 304.

Charlemagne condemns stone worship, 25.

Charleton, Dr., 15; Inigo Jones's theory attacked by, 3.

Chartham Downs, find at, 13.

Chartres Carnutes, 5.

Chester, *see* Caerleon.

China, monuments of, not ancient, 1.

Chinese not progressive, 19.

Chisel, early use of, in Ireland, 217.

Chorœa Gigantum, *see* Giants' Dance.

Chouchas in North Africa, 398-9; position of bodies in, *ib.*

Christian era, rude-stone monuments subsequent to, 27; according to Danes, iron introduced about commencement of, 9.

Christianity, according to Welsh and Irish writers, their Druids prior to, 6; date of introduction into Denmark, 10; into India, 489; in what respect influenced by Buddhism, 499 *et seq.*

Christians in India, *see* Crosses.

Christy, Mr., his researches in Algeria, 395-6.

Church caves at first more important than Viharas, 501.

Cimboeth marks date in Irish history, 189; founds Armagh, *ib.*

Cimbri, their cognate races, 333.

Cimbrian Chersonese visited by Pytheas, 38.

Circassia, dolmens in, of shaped stone, 447; importance of, to migration or missionary theory, 447-8.

Circles, 154; Englewood Wood, or Rosehill tumulus, *ib.*; platform, *ib.*; bilithons, 155; find, *ib.*; Aspatria, 156; barrow, *ib.*; find, 156-7; circle of cists in Isle of Man, *ib.*; Mule Hill, *ib.*; view and plan of, 158; openings to circle, 159; Burn Moor, Cumberland, *ib.*; find there, *ib.*; square enclosure there, 160; plan, 160; Boscawen not Temples nor "Things," *ib.*; plan of, 161; at Moytura, 183; triple, *ib.*; sculptured, enclosing crosses, 304, 315; mysterious concentric circles, with lines traversing them, 304; the use of circles and Viking graves cont:nuous in Ireland and England, 317; singular arrangement at Aschenrade and in Algeria, 317-8; circles with stone in centre at Bajard, 318; circular groups in India, 467 (*see* Bazina, Chouca); Alexandropol circles, 450; Nikolajen concentric circles, base of tumulus, 451; Western circles not imitation of Tartar, 452; Peshawur, 453; Deh Ayeh, near Darabgerd, *ib.*; circles attributed to Caons or Giants, *ib.*; enclosed circles in America, 511-3; at Caithness (*see* Scotland); Amravati, 474.

Circles, great English, peculiar, 153; and belong probably to Arthurian age, *ib.*; post-Roman, 154; of what race, *ib.*; in Wales and Anglesea no circles, 163; Giant's grave, Drumbo, 228; circle there object of, 224; in Scotland, 240; district of circles *par excellence* not on mainland, *ib.*; Orkneys, 241; King of Brogar and Stennis, 241-2; part of entire group, 254; date, 256; Callernish, 259; circle-building race, 274; opposite currents of migration, *ib.*; Braavalla Heath, 280; in France, 340; circle the skeleton of tumulus, 340; circle at Sesto Calende, 391; semicircle, *ib.*; circles, 397-9; triple and quadruple, 399; enclosed in squares, 402; at Djideli, 404; Bona, 405; Malta, 416; Sinai, 443-4; Arabia, 444.

Circles surrounding tumuli or dolmens, circles without tumuli or dolmens, 29, 47, 50; at Addington, 118-9; at Rollright, 124; Dartmoor, *ib.*; at Penrith, 126; concentric, 127 *note*; at Marden, 65, 85; at Shap, 130; Merivale Bridge, *ib.*; at Arbor Low, 139; Stanton Drew, 150.

Circular temple mentioned by Diodorus among Hyperboreans, 8.

Cissa, King, his tomb where, 283.

Cists, *see* Kistvaens.

Civil and sacred structures, where indistinguishable, 515.

Clark, Mr. George, his paper on Ancient English Castles, 84.

Clatford Bottom, 44; Sarsen stones at, 63; circles at, 161.

Claudian, verses of, as to disasters of Saxons, Picts, and Scots, in the North, 188.

Claudius Gothicus, coins of, 12, 36, 52; Claudius, 461.

Clava, 265; circles and mounds, *ib.*; perhaps burial-place of King Brude, 267.

Clemens of Alexandria, his surprise at relic-worship, 504; as to Buddhism, 505.

Clergy and laity, separation of, in the East, 502.

Closmadeuc, Dr., antiquary, 337.

Clover Hill, 223.

Cnodhba, cave of, identified with Knowth, 201.

Cock sacrificed to Betal, 467.

Cocumella, tomb at, 33.

Cœlus, God, Stonehenge ascribed to, 3.

Cœre, tomb at, 33-4.

Cogolleros, dolmen del Tio, 385.

Coibi, his conversion, 23.

Coilsfield, rubbing on stone at, 211; stone, 267.

Coins, Roman, of what Emperors generally found, 144; in Ireland, 166; inference from, *see* Finds.

Cojou, Gre de, alignment at, 367.

Cole, *see* Bhil.

Cole, Lieutenant, his report as to Kutub pillar, 181.

Collas barrow mentioned in Charter of Athelstan, 73.

Collinson, Colonel, finds columnar buildings in Malta, 425.

Columba, St., 59.

Columbus, America peopled by Europeans prior to, 516.

Columns, *see* Alignment.

Come Lowe, find at, 13.

Commerce of early Britons, with what races, 133-4.

Conaing, 201.

Conan, *see* Meriadec.

Concentric circles, *see* Circles.

Conchobhar McNessa, 197; husband of Queen Meave, 197, 221; his conversion, 221; where buried, *ib.*

Confolens, dolmen at, 337.

Cong, at Moytura, 177; place of battle, 198.

Conical form, Roman and Post-Roman, 84.

Conjeveran, city of Kurumbers, 478.

Conn of a Hundred Battles, 193-7, 212, 236. *See* Cormac MacArt.

Conor MacNessa, 193.

Constantine, Saxons defeated by, 109; his supposed interment at Stonehenge, and when, 109'; coins, 11, 12, 13.

Constantine Junior, coins of, 12.

Constantinople, coins of, 11.

Constans, coins of, 11.

Constantius, coins of, 11.

Conwell, Mr., exploration of Lough Crew, 199, 213, 222.

Copenhagen, congress at, 10; museum, 16, 325.

Cormack, son of Conn, 190; where buried, 212.

Cormack MacArt, 193; convert to Christianity, 196; orders tracts to be written, *ib.*; could he write? *ib.*

Cornelius, tradition as to, 373.

Cornwall, circles, 162; circle-building race in, 274.

Corpre, Etan's son, 191.

Costa, S. Pereira da, his account of Portuguese dolmens, 377.

Cotty or Coity House, *see* Aylesford.

Councils of Arles, Nantes. Rouen, Toledo. Tours, 24; their decrees as to stoneworship, 23-4.
Countless Stones, see Aylesford.
Court held at standing stones of Rayne by Bishop of Aberdeen, 264.
Cove, Long stone, 4.
Cremation amongst Saxons, 120.
Crew, Lough, 199.
Crichie, find at, 75.
Crimthann, when he lived, 190, 221; where buried, 192; seat of his dynasty, 194.
Croker, Mr., his survey of Stanton Drew, 150.
Crom, meaning of word, 44 note.
Cromlech, near Merivale, 55; among Mâla Aryans, 479. See Dolmen.
Cross Flats, 11.
Crosses, 270, 272; Irish, how distinguished from Scottish, 270; Isle of Man, with Runic inscriptions, 273; crosses in circles, 304; "Swastica"-like cross, 367; in India, and their date, 486 et seq.
Crozon, alignment at, 367; what battle there, 375.
Cruachan, ancient burial-place of Kings of Tara, find, 190-9.
Crubelz, 359.
Crusades, rude-stone monuments in time of, 406.
Cuchullin, 193-7.
Cumberland, no mention of Druids in, 5; rude monuments, 127, 128; circles in, probably of same age, 147; circle-building race in, 274.
Cumbhail (Fingal), 197.
Cumot, or Commensurate grave of Cairbre Lifeachaire, 213.
Cumrew, Salkeld and Mayborough, circles at, similar, 147.
Cuneus, Cape, unvisited by Portuguese writers, 378.
Cunningham, Lord Albert, finds by, at Dowth, 210.
Cunnington, Mr., his opinion as to Marden, 86; excavation by, at Stonehenge, 105-6; finds in long barrows, 289.
Curtius cited as to Nasomenes, 407.
Cuthbert, 22.
Cuttack, sacred groves at, 465.
Cyvragnon, pile of, mentioned in Welsh Triads, what, 173.

DABILLA, the hound, interment of, 212.
Daghda, the general, 187; and king, ib.; where buried, 191; when, 190; real name Eochy, 192; cairn of, ib.; residence, 195; his spit, ib.; family, 197, 212; his tomb where, according to author, 213; written evidence as to, 212.
Dagoba, Buddhist, 41, 79, 490 et seq.; relic, cists, Tee, rail, 490-1; compared to dolmen at Pullicondah, 491.

Dananns, Tuatha de, 177 et seq.; arrival in Ireland, 193; when, ib.; burial of, 212. See Ireland, Moytura.
Danes, cemeteries plundered by, 209.
Danish antiquaries, their opinion as to epoch of introduction of bronze and iron into Denmark, 9, 37; their system respecting, 9, 10, 28; too hastily adopted in France and England, 10, 388; their mistaken proceedings, 10-14, 16, 146, 257, 275; International Congress of Prehistoric Archæology, 276; merits of Sjöborg, 276.
Danish isles, dolmens in, 301.
Danish settlers in Greenland, 18; in Britain and Scotland before Roman invasion, 133-4; commerce, &c., 133.
Daoulas, menhir and cross at, 59.
Darabgerd, circle near, 453.
Dariorigum, standing stones of, 20.
Dartmoor parallel stones at Merivale Bridge, 54; circles and cromlechs, 55; avenues at Cas Tor, 56; circles compared with those at Rollright, 124.
Dasyus the despised, 493.
Date, priority of, in dolmens external or covered, 144.
Dates, found and corrected by architects, 113; comparative antiquity of certain classes of monuments, 261; rude-stone sometimes more modern, 407.
Dathi, monument of, 199.
Daviot circle, 263.
Dead, images of, 449.
Deane, Rev. Bathurst, adopts Stukeley's views, 6, 151; visits Carnac, 351.
Decrees of Councils respecting veneration of stone monuments, 24, 25.
Dedalean buildings in Sardinia, why so called, 429.
Deer Park, Sligo, monument in, 234-5.
Defence, see Mounds.
Deh Ayeh, circle at, 453.
Delhi, iron pillar near, 35; mosque of Kutb u deem, 457.
Demi-dolmens, 345.
Demons, see St. Patrick.
Denmark, megalithic remains in, 9; museums, ib.; bronze and iron, date of their introduction into, ib.; tombs of kings described by Olaus Magnus, 15; ignorance of Romans respecting, 38; tumuli in, 39; circles in, 47; Bauta or battle-stones, 60.
Dennis' 'Etruria' cited, 391.
Derbyshire dolmens, date of, 36; rude-stone monuments in, 138.
Derbyshire Rude-Stone Monuments, 138; Arbor Low, 139; description of, 139; similarity to Arthur's Round Table. 139; plan of, 140; circle, 140; dolmen, ib.; tumulus, ib.; excavations and find there, 140-1; Gib Hill tumulus, 141; excavation and find, 141-2; Minning Low, 142; plans of, 142-3; find there, 143; similarity to New Grange, ib.;

and Kit's Cotty House, 144; first
Roman, *ib.*; Benty Grange barrow, *ib.*;
find there, 144-5; Kentlow barrow,
145-6; Stanton Moor, 146; monuments
of earth and stone, *ib.*; Nine Ladies,
ib.; King Stone, *ib.*; other groups near
Arbor Low, *ib.*; cat stones, *ib.*; Derbyshire monuments not temples nor
tombs of inhabitants, 147; monuments
of what race? *ib.*; similar in purpose
and age to those in Cumberland, *ib.*;
find in former, 148; Stanton Drew, *ib.*

Devil's Quoits, 64.

Devonshire, circles in, 161.

Diarmid and Graine, *see* Beds.

Dinnsenchus, 233.

Diodorus, cited as to circular temple, 8;
text explained, *ib.*; as to barbarism of
Irish, 235; Phœnicians in Malta in his
time, 425; Dedalean buildings, 429.

Divitiacus, 323.

Djideli, tombs near, 404; whose, *ib.*;
find there, *ib.*

Dodwell, tombs of Atridæ discovered by,
33; that of Minyas explored, *ib.*

Dolicocephalic race, 35.

Dolmens, 29; freestanding, 29; on outside of tumuli, 29; progress of tomb-
building, 40-43; kistvaens, 43; chambers, *ib.*; with gallery, *ib.*; dolmens
covered, 44; uncovered, *ib.*; opinion
that all once covered with tumuli refuted, *ib.*; dolmen at Wellan, 45; de
Bousquet, 46; excavation suggested of
dolmen-crowned tumuli, *ib.*; at Kit's
Cotty House, 116; at Rollright, 124;
in Cumberland (*see* Penrith); at Arbor
Low, 140; France native country of,
161; few in England, *ib.*; and most of
English in Cornwall, 162; in Wales
more numerous, *ib.*; and Anglesea,
ib.; and Isle of Man, *ib.*; by whom
erected, *ib.*; where, 163; all not
originally buried; 163, 169; some
always intended to be covered, 164,
168; dolmen in Park Cwn tumulus,
164; find there, 165; Uley, *ib.*; find
there, *ib.*; judicious conclusions of Dr.
Thurnam from, *ib.*; Plas Newydd,
166-9; stone avenue leading to, 167;
holes in slab, 168; Pentre Ifan, *ib.*;
Arthur's Quoit, 170; whether originally in tumulus, 171-2; alleged avenue,
172; group of cairns there, 171; purpose, 172; not a cemetery, *ib.*; but
battlefield? *ib.*; Arthur's 8th battle
there? 173; the stone of "Cetti," *ib.*;
Hob Hurst's House, 172-3; dates of
dolmens, 173; at Moytura, 183; in
Ireland, how situated, 224; not on
battlefields, *ib.*; perhaps most on east
coast, *ib.*; beds of Diarmid, 225; elopement of, with Graine, *ib.*; legend as to
dolmens, *ib.*; legitimate inference from
legend, *ib.*; Glen Columbkill and Glen
Malin More, *ib.*; cairns there, 226;

age of, *ib.*; tradition as to St. Columba,
227; of what race the group, 227-8;
Spaniards or Iberians in Ireland, 228;
giant's grave, 228; circle there, 229;
object of, *ib.*; Town of the Stone of the
Strangers, *ib.*; dolmen at Knockeen, *ib.*;
Knockeen, plans of, 230; Calliagh Vera
or Birra, *ib.*; Greenmount tumulus, 231;
the "four Maols," Ballina, 232; dolmens
in Ireland do not mark battle-fields,
228; dolmens in Scotland, 240; many
dolmens erected by kings, &c., as their
burial-places, and covered after their
interment, 260 *et seq.*; comparative antiquity of Callernish and New Grange,
261; dolmens in North Germany, 300;
silence of German archæology, *ib.*; no
dolmens in Poland, 301; Prussia, *ib.*;
Silesia, *ib.*; Prussian Silesia, Pomerania, Rügen, *ib.*; Meckienburg, Hanover, Oldenburg, *ib.*; Wildesheim
and Engelmanns Becke, *ib.*; Helmstadt, *ib.*; Holland, *ib.*; Saxony, Grand
Duchy of Luxemburg, *ib.*; Holstein
Schleswig, Jutland, Danish isles, *ib.*;
Sweden, *ib.*; none in Norway, 302;
Herrestrup, 303; dolmen with representations of ships, and circles with
crosses, 304; analogous to dolmen at
Aspatria, *ib.*; Halskov, 305; Oroust,
306; dolmens in the different countries
have distinguishing features, *ib.*; oblong enclosures, 307; diagram from
Sjöborg, *ib.*; Roeskilde and Birck
dolmens with oblong enclosures, *ib.*;
Lüneburg, 308; Hanover, *ib.*; Valdbygaards, near Sorõe, double dolmen,
308-9; triple dolmens, Höbisch, 309;
sentinel stones, 310; buried dolmens,
ib.; Uby, 311; Smidstrup, *ib.*; Axevalla, and find there, 312-3; dolmens,
elliptical and oblong, 313; age of, *ib.*;
find, 314; inscription at Axevalla, *ib.*;
headstone with drawings on it, of Kivik
Grave, *ib.*; its resemblance to one at
Locmariaker, *ib.*; dolmen at Exlo,
320; peculiarity of Drenthe dolmens,
ib.; Ballo, 321; distribution of dolmens map, 324; pre-dolmen immigration of Belgæ into Britain, 323;
Luxemburg, *ib.*; Belgians and pure
Celts not dolmen builders, 326; sequences of dolmens, 335; Sauclières,
ib.; St. Germain-sur-Vienne or Confolens, 336; date of, *ib.*; demi-dolmens,
345; others in Ireland and Wales,
ib.; Poitiers and Kerland, 346; rocking
stones, Pierre Martine, 347; whether
accidental, 347-9; Pierre branlante de
Huelgoat, 348; double dolmen at
Plouharnel, and find, 358; dolmens,
&c., if built with small stones, more
modern, 359; Mané Lud, dolmen with
sculptured stones, similar to Irish,
360-3; Dol ar Marchant, sculpture
decorations, 361-2; Bertrand's list of

dolmens in France, 376; termination of names in ac, *ib.*; dolmens in Spain, Portugal, 377 *et seq.*; dolmen race, migration of, 378-9; Spain, Antequera, 383; its stone town once wholly buried, circle, 384; contrasted with Stonehenge, *ib.*; Tio Cogolleros, 385; Sepultura Grande, 386; compared to what, *ib.*; dolmen near Dilar, *ib.*; Eguilar, Cangas de Onis, 387; dolmen of San Miguel, Arrichinaga, 388; Portugal. Arroyolos. 389; Cangas de Onis, Arrichinaga, 390; why not so numerous in Italy, 392; influence of conquest and withdrawal of Romans upon, 394; distribution in Algeria, 396; principal dolmen region, *ib.*; Tiaret, enormous dolmen there, 397; Tripoli, *ib.*; Morocco, *ib.*; but not near populous centres, *ib.*; inference thence as to nomadic origin, 397; dolmen on steps, 398; on a circled tumulus, 400; with two circles of stones, 401; resemblance to Kit's Cotty House, *ib.*; dolmens on road from Bona to Constantine, 402; no dolmens in Phœnicia nor in their colonies, 409; Nurhags and giants' towers earlier than dolmens, 437; in Palestine, 441; in Gilead, whether of the giant tribe, 443; long interval from the first Indian dolmen at Peshawur, *ib.*; query as to dolmens in Asia Minor, 445; holed dolmen in Circassia, 447; migration theory of dolmens, 448; missionary theory, *ib.*; important bearing of searches in the Steppes upon theories, 448; Tartar tumuli not models of Western dolmens, 452; space unexplored for dolmens in East, 454; Rajunkoloor, 468, 470; dolmens with holes, find, 468; double circles round dolmens at Yemmee Gooda; arrangement of dolmens at Rajunkoloor, 470; Nilgiri hills : Courg double dolmens with circular openings, 473; tomb, *ib.*; sepulchral circles at Amravati, 474; rail there, 475; geographical distribution, 475 *et seq.*; of what race, 476 *et seq.*; age of, 479 *et seq.*; finds in Indian dolmens, 480; Nilgiri sculptured dolmen, 483; singular position of one at Iwallee, 484; stone monuments at Shahpoor, 485; Katapur, 487; find, *ib.*; dolmen with cross in Nirmul jungle, 489; illustration of Romish policy, *ib.*; dolmen at Pullicondah compared with Cingalese Dagoba, 491; Eastern and European dolmen compared, 494 *et seq.*; whether connexion between them to be inferred from similarity, 495; or from literature, or from rock - engraved edict of Asoka, 496. *See* Glen Columbkille; dolmen near Bona, Algeria, 532.

Dordogne, monuments in, insufficient knowledge of, 335.
Doric supersedes Pelasgic style, 393; earliest Doric temple, interval between and last Pelasgic tomb, 393.
Dowe Lowe, " find " in, 13.
Down, English tumuli on, 48.
Dowth Hill, 192, 200; the Dagdha's Rath at, 195; his son born there, *ib.*
Dracontia, 515. *See* Serpent, Stukeley.
Dragon in Maes-Howe, 245.
Drenthe, dolmens in, 301, 320; Hunebeds at, their extent, 319; compared by Keysler to Stonehenge, 319; described by Dr. Janssen, 319; Hunebeds, grottes des fées, 341.
Dresden, dolmens destroyed near, 301.
Drew, Stanton, circles at, 7, 161.
Drosten, name inscribed on stone, 273.
Druids, human sacrifices by, at Stonehenge, no longer believed, 1; Dr. Stukeley's fancy respecting their temples, 3; Cæsar's account of them, 4, 5; serpent worship supposed, 4; by Stukeley and Sir R. C. Hoare, 5; Druids in Mona met by Suetonius, *ib.*; none ever seen in regions of principal rude monuments, 6; nor in Algeria nor India, *ib.*; in Wales, according to Welsh writers, before Christianity introduced, *ib.*; controversy in France respecting so-called Druidical monuments, *ib.*; difficulty of connecting them with Druids, *ib.*; Stukeley's idea adopted by Deane, *ib.*; Stonehenge pretended to be their observatory, 7; remarks of author, 7, 20, 61; gods worshipped by Druids, according to Cæsar, 66; Druidical institutions in India, 465; Druids and serpents, freedom of Sjöborg from errors as to, 274.
Dryden, Sir Henry, explores Carnac, 350; near Emmen. 320; and Caithness, 530; letter from, to author, *ib.*; cited, 362; his drawings of Gavr Innis, 365; describes Gré de Cojou, 368.
Duald Mac Firbis, antiquary, 199.
Dubois, cited, 449.
Duglas or Dubglas River, Arthur's battle on, 136; meaning of word, *ib.*
Dunadeer Circle, 263.
Du Noyer, M., cited, 345; drawings, 225.
Dutthagamini, *see* Ellala.

Eadward, contemporary of Rollo, 126.
East, *see* Palestine.
Easter Island, images in, 53.
Eguilar dolmen, 387.
Egypt, iron when introduced into, 37.
Egyptians, tomb building race, 31; pyramids contained true and false tombs, 46; their feelings as to monasticism, 500; royal monasteries and residences indistinguishable, 514.
Eithlenn, daughter of Balor, 187.

Ellala, his defeat by King Dutthagamimi commemorated by Dagoba, 80.

Elliot, Sir Walter, cited on Indian interments, 479.

Elliptical dolmens, *see* Dolmens.

Ellis, Mr., his opinion that Stonehenge was an Observatory, 7.

Elopement of Diarmid with Graine, 225.

Ellora and Elephanta, dates of, 494.

Emmen, 320. *See* Hunebed.

Emmrys, work of, in Welsh Triads, what, 173.

Enclosures, dolmens with, 307 *et seq.*, 354; in America, for defence, 511; sacred and miscellaneous, 311.

End Low mound, 139. *See* Derbyshire.

England, circle-building race in, 274; dolmen-building race, *ib.*; old race in, improved by Celts and Romans, 461.

Englemanns Becke, dolmen near, 301.

English idolatry, letter of Gregory the Great concerning, 21.

Eochy, King, tradition as to his bath, 179; his death, *ib.*

Eochy the Daghda, 192 *note*.

Erdeven, 350.

Eric Blodoxe, 250; sons of, 291.

Eric the Holy, 291.

Eskil, 279.

Esquimaux, Cave men similar to, in what respects, 17.

Es Salt, dolmens near, 441.

Essenes, their connexion with Buddhism, 500.

Estremadura, dolmens in, 378.

Etan, poetess, 197; where buried, 212.

Ethelbert, cedes temple at Canterbury to Augustine, 22.

Ethnography, *see* Races.

Etrurians, tomb-building race, 31, 393; dead reverencing, 393; tomb of Commella, 33; of Regulini Galeassi, 34; contents of, 34; belong to age of bronze, 34; imitated at Rome, 40.

Europe, Northern, limited knowledge of, before Roman epoch, 38.

Eusufzaie circles, 453.

Fa Hian, his visit to Sanchi, 492.

Faidherbe, General, his remarks on tombs in Roknia, 396.

Family sepulchres marked by megalithic monuments, 15.

Faussett, Mr. Godfrey, his happy reference to Beowulf, 120.

Féraud, M., his researches in Algeria, 395; his opinion as to building-race, 403; respecting find at Djideli, 404.

Ferguson, Mr., drawings by, of sepulchres at Dol ar Marchant, 362.

Fiddes Hill circle, 263-5.

Fin, his conflict with Hengist, 120.

Finds : altar stone, 104; armour, 79, 104; amber beads, 218; amulet of iron, 14; arrow-head, flint, 11, 12; ditto, iron, 104-6, 337; awl, 13; axe-stone, 165; ball syenite, 217; batter dishes, 104; battle-axe, 156; basaltic celt, 11; and hammer head, 12; beads of glass, 13, 218, 359; and of amber, 218; bird of bone, 527; bluestone, chippings of, 103; bones, 74, 526; burnt, 13, 142, 159, 210, 526; charred, 217; calcined, 11; human bones, 155, 179, 182, 199, 216, 219, 446; bones of animals, 143-5, 182, 216; bones of mammalia, 210; of horse, 404, 446; dogs, 527; rats, 13; stags, 104; oxen, *ib.*; of men, *ib.*; bones incinerated, 264; bone bodkin, 210; comb, 527; box of bronze, 13; brass, 165; brass or copper pin, 12; spear-head, 103; bracelet, gold, 447, 527; bridle bit, 12, 80, 81, 148, 157, 404; bronze, 11, 13, 120, 141, 145, 184, 216, 318, 339, 358, 526; buckle, 43; and heads, 297; of gold, 156; burial urn, 527; cap ornamented with gold, 446; carvings. rude, 306; celt, basaltic, 11; stone, 11, 142; of bronze, 127; of jade, 358; chamber, rude, 159; charcoal, 103, 265, 469, 526; chief, and wife and children, remains of, 446; chippings of stones, 103; circular instrument, 13; circumcision, instruments of, 440; c'sts, 12, 140-1, 155-6; coal, Kimmeridge, 13; coins (*see* Roman Coins); coins, German, 318; Anglo-Saxon, *ib.*; Byzantine, *ib.*; Arabic or Kufic, *ib.*; coins, Roman, 74; brass coins, 11; Claudius, Gothicus, 12, 33, 143; Constantine, 11, 12, 143, 165; family of, 11; Constans, 11; Constantine II., 11, 339; Constantinopolis, 11; Constantine Junior, 12, 143; Gratian, 11; Hadrian, 84; from Tiberius to Trojan, 339; Theodosius, 209; Urbs Roma, 11; Valens, 11; Valentinian, 11, 12, 36, 143, 144, 209; combs, engravings on, 218; compass, leg of, 218; comb, 527; copper, 120; cromlechs, 143; cylinder partially pierced, 359; dagger, bronze, 145; brass or bronze, 12, 13, 14; dart or javelin point, 142; dog's bones, 527; drinking cup (fragments', 12, 145, 297; earthenware, 525; electrum plate, part of quiver ornamented with figures of animals and Greek inscription, 446-7; enamels, 145; engraved dagger and Wurm knot, 245; fibula, 11, 13, 142, 210, 297; fibula, gold, 156; flat basin, large, 217; flint, 11, 12, 14, 146, 165, 182, 218; fragments of, 286; flakes, and instruments of, 447; flowers, silver, 156, 339; Faustina, medal of, 405; garnets, 11; giant, remains of, 130, 156; glass, 13, 339; glass beads, *ib.*; glass, molten drop of, 218; gold-enamelled necklace and bracelets, 440; gold cross, 11;

necklace, 12 ; brooch, 212 ; ornaments, 13, 358, 451 ; goblet, silver, 297 ; gold, traces of, 155 ; hair, human, chesnut-coloured, 526 ; hammer - head, 12 ; handle of knife, 13 ; helmets ornamented with bronze and silver, 114 ; hone of sandstone, 12 ; horns, 74 ; stags', 13, 105 ; of other animals, 105. 150 ; horse, 446 ; bones and teeth of, 404 ; teeth, 12 ; bones, 183, 527 ; human remains, 165, 209, 217, 356, 444 ; ashes and bones, 469 ; hair, 526 ; human interments, 185, 359 ; original or secondary, 209, 284 ; inscriptions, 246, 314 ; implements of flint and bone, 145, 184, 185, 217, 218, 359 ; of iron, 218 ; of modern form, 318 ; of flint, 286 ; inscriptions, 246, 314 ; instruments, 13 ; ironstone, 12 ; ivory tweezers, 103 ; jade, axes in, 358 ; jet bracelet, 210 ; ornaments, 217 ; knife, 11, 146 ; knife with iron sheath, 12 ; iron, 212 ; knife-shaped articles, 218 ; lacrymatory, Roman, 165 ; medal, 404 ; metal, lump, 155 ; nails, 527 ; ornaments, Anglo-Saxon, 11 ; rude, 185 ; more refined, 211 ; of goblet, 297 ; dragons, tortoise, fantastic heads of animals, 297 ; in gold and bronze, 358, 526 ; and copper, 527 ; oyster shells, 74 ; pebbles, 218 ; pin, iron, 13 ; bronze ditto, 141, 216 ; copper, 210 ; pine poles partly burnt, 526 ; point, flint, of dart or javelin, 142 ; pottery, fine, broken, 357 ; pottery, rude, 12, 217, 218, 285, 339 ; Roman, 105, 106 ; black, 285 ; fine, 404 ; red and black, rude British, 105, 285 ; Roman British, or Mediæval, 165 ; precious stones, traces of, 142 ; punch, iron, 218 ; rat's bones, 13 ; ring, gold, 210 ; iron, ib. ; bronze, 218, 487 ; Runes, 244 ; representations of stag and camels, 218 ; shield, fragments of, 156 ; silver-flower sword-ornaments, 156 ; slate, 525 ; spear heads, flint or stone, 182 ; skulls, human, 155, 525 ; snaffle bridle, 156 ; sword, iron, 148, 156, 184 446 ; syenite, 217 ; sea shells, 218 ; silver, 13, 243 ; skeletons, human, 11, 14, 17, 76, 145, 148, 165, 209, 289, 313 ; sling-stones, 210 ; spear-head, 11, 12 ; of brass, 103 ; sculptured slab, 365 ; stained fragments, 218 ; stag's bones, 216 ; statuettes, 339 ; stone, 11, 165 ; polished stones, 218 ; stone button, 210 ; stone shot, ib. ; studs of coal, 13 ; tiles, Romano-Gallic, 338 ; others, 359 ; teeth of animals, 12 ; human, 155, 216 ; of horse, 404 ; tweezers, ivory, 103 ; terra cotta, 339 ; torques, gold, 210 ; silver, 243 ; urns, 11-13, 143, 179, 264 ; with ashes, 184, 210 ; of stone, 210 ; for burial, 527 ; vases, 140-1, 357 ; whetstone, 13 ; wood, coals, 74 ; wood, burnt, 182 ; wood, dark, 526.

Finds in Denmark, 10 ; Derbyshire, 11 ; Winster Moor, ib. ; Pegges Barrow, ib. ; Long Rood, ib. ; Haddon Field Barrow, ib. ; Gib Hill, ib. ; Cross Flats, ib. ; Galley Lowe, 12 ; Minning Lowe, ib. ; Borther Lowe, ib. ; Rolley Lowe, ib. ; Ashford Moor, ib. ; Carder Lowe, ib. ; New Inns, ib. ; Net Lowe, 13 ; Castern, ib. ; Chartham Downs, ib. ; Stand Lowe, ib. ; Wetton and Ilam, ib. ; Middleton Moor. ib. ; Come Lowe, ib. ; Dowe Lowe. ib. ; valley of Somme, 16 ; Abbeville, ib. ; Gray's Inn Lane, ib. ; Nineveh, 34 ; at Avebury, 74 ; at Crichie, 75 ; at Hakpen, 76 ; contents of, 250 ; tumuli, analysis of contents of, 11 ; finds at Stonehenge, 103-5 ; at West Kennet, 285 et seq. ; inferences from, 288 ; inference from nature of, 106 ; from coins, 338 ; from absence of British, Gallic, and Christian coins, 340 ; from Roman pottery, 360 ; few inferences of age possible from finds in India, and why, 480 ; no iron or bronze, but copper, in North America, 517 ; and tools only of copper, 517.

Finn, suitor of Graine, 225.

Firbolgs, or Belgæ, in Ireland, 176 ; when, 193 ; defeat at Moytura, 179 ; how long in Ireland, 193 ; whence they came thither, 193.

Fire, worship of, forbidden by Councils, 25.

Flann, son of Conaing, 201.

Flint remains found at Abbeville, 16 note ; inference from. 166 ; symbolic of what, 447. See Finds.

Flower, Mr., account of African monuments, 396 ; and their builders, 403.

Ford, Mr., his 'Handbook of Spain.'

Fordum, see Böece.

Formorians, from Africa, settled in Ireland, 176 ; dispossessed by Belgæ, 176 ; of same race as Dananns, 187.

Forres, Sweno's stone at, 59.

Fountains, worship of, 24-5.

Fouquet, M., see Galles, M.

Four-cornered grave, 449.

"Four Masters" cited, 213, 225, 382.

France, climate of, at epoch of "Cave men," 17 ; finds in, 16 ; menhirs, 59 ; a single sculptured stone there, 59 note ; French study of rude-stone monuments, recent, but scientific, 325 ; 'Dictionnaire des Antiquités Celtiques,' ib. ; Bertrand, M., his map of France, 326 ; general distribution of French monuments, ib. ; no dolmens in East of France, 327 ; date of Celtic first invasion of Gaul, 327, 334 ; two early contemporary races in, 328 ; the 'ac' termination, 329 ; church architecture in dolmen region of the South of France, 331 ; form of dolmen distinguishes dolmens in Brittany from those in South of France, 335 ; Confolens, 337 ; plan of, *ib.*; error of French antiquaries, *ib.*; find, 337-9; dolmens, 340; size, number, and beauty of, *ib.*; few and imperfect circles, *ib.*; "Allée couverte" or "Grotte des Fées," *ib.*; examples of, elsewhere than in France, *ib.*; their distribution here, 340; Saumur, Essé, Locmariaker, Bagneux, Mettray, 341; form of French dolmens, 342; Krukenho, *ib.*; comparative age of, 343; demi-dolmens, rocking stones, &c., 345 *et seq*; Carnac, cemetery and battlefield, 349; alignments, Carnac and Erdeven, St. Barbe, 350; Maenec and Kermario, 351; map, 352-3; stone rows, 354; differ how, from Stonehenge and Stennis, 355; head of column of St. Barbe, Mont St. Michel, *ib.*; find, 356; Kerlescant, find, 357; Plouharnel, double dolmen and find, 358; long barrow, Moustoir-Carnac, *ib.*; find, 359; Locmariaker, cemetery, dolmen, 360; sculptured stones at Mané Lud, 361; dolmen, Dol ar Marchant, *ib.*; end stone and roof, sculptured, 362; fallen obelisk, 363; compared to dolmen at Krukenho, *ib.*; allée couverte, 364; ornamented stones, *ib.*; Mané er H'roëk, and find, *ib.*; Gavr Innis, sculptured stones, 365; resemble sculptures at Lough Crew, 366; three-holed stone, tools used, *ib.*; Tumiac, tumulus and find, *ib.*; Crozon alignments, their origin and purpose obscure, 367; Gré de Cojou, double alignment, circle, enclosures, dolmen, 367-8; Preissac, *ib.*; date and object of monuments at Carnac, 370 *et seq.*; Carnac, Erdeven, and St. Barbe, are they parts of one whole? 372; argument against their existence in Cæsar's time, 373; not pre-Roman, *ib.*; early history not satisfactory, *ib.*; battle between Maximus and Gratian, *ib.*; Conan Meriadec, 374; author's view as to origin of Carnac monuments, 374-5; Grallon's war with Liberius and Northern pirates, 374; Romans never settled in Brittany, 370; effect there of Roman building-style, *ib*; and of withdrawal of Romans, 394.

Franks, M., his photograph of Ballo dolmen, 321.

French antiquaries, errors of, 337.

Frere, Mr., his find at Abbeville, 16 *note*.

Freyrsö, battle at, 276.

Frey's Howe, opened, 527.

Friar's Heel stone at Stonehenge, 7.

Frode Frodegode, tomb of, 299.

Frode V., 278, 288.

GALATIA, importance of dolmens there, if any, to Celtic theory, 446.

Galles, M. René, explores Mont St. Michel,

354; with M. Fouquet explores Tumiac, find, 366.

Galley Low, find at, 12.

Gallicia, dolmens in, 378.

Ganora, *see* Guinevere.

Gariock, Newton stone at, 57.

Garrywhin alignment, 529.

Gaul, Pliny's tale of snakes in, 4; no stone temples in, mentioned by Cæsar or Tacitus, 20.

Gavr Innis, in Morbihan, 43, 364; sculptures, holed stone, 365; compared to Lough Crew, 366; holes and trough below, *ib.*; object of it.

Geraldus Cambrensis, his statement as to removal of stones to Stonehenge, 107; how fable originated, 108.

Germans, worship of, in groves only, 20.

Germany, North (*see* Scandinavia); dolmens in, 301.

Gervaise mentions cemetery at Canterbury, 22.

Ghazni, Saracenic arches at, 457.

Giant tribes in Palestine, builders of dolmens? 442; circles, 453.

"Giant's dance," Geraldus and Ware cited as to, 107 *note*.

Giant's grave, 229; circle there, *ib.*

Giants' towers, 415.

Giara, plan of, Nurhag of, 430. *See* Mediterranean Islands.

Gib Hill, find at, 11, *see* Derbyshire; analogue of Silbury Hill, 147.

Gildas cited, 87; as to interments at Stonehenge, 110.

Gilead, dolmens in, 442; last safe place for dolmens before India, 443.

Gizeh, date of pyramid of, 31.

Glasfurd, Capt., find by, 487.

Glem, or Glein, river, Arthur's battle near, 135.

Glen Columbkille, 225.

Glen Columbkille and Glen Malin, survey of Mr. Norman Moore, 520; cromlechs or dolmens, stone chambers, solitary stones, 320; plan of one, 521; groups of, 523-4; find, 525; resemblance of one to Calliagh Birra's tomb, 525.

Glen Malin More, 225.

Godmundingham, destruction of church at, 23.

Gond, *see* Bhil.

Gongora y Martinez, Don, his work cited, 377.

Gordon, Principal, anecdotes of, respecting holed stones at Stennis, 255.

Gorm, monument of, 27; date of, 126, 296 *et seq.*; dragon on, 245.

Gothland perhaps mentioned by Diodorus, 8.

Göttenburg, drawings of ships on stones at, 303.

Göttingen, no dolmens in, 301.

Gower caves, 16.

Gozo, spirals and scrolls at, compared to those at Mycenæ, 424.

Graine, daughter of Cormac Mac Art, see Beds.

Grallon, king of Briton. his wars, 374.

Grandmont, holed dolmen at, 343.

Grange, New, cairns at, 52.

Gratian, defeat of, in Brittany, 374.

Grave, four cornered, 449.

Greece, Aryan occupation of, 39; early tombs in Greece, ib.; succession of architectural styles, 393. See Bactrian.

Greeks of Bactria introduce usage of stone monuments in India, 48; Greek kings mentioned by Asoka, 498.

Greenland, route of early peoplers of America, 516.

Greenmount, tumulus at, 231; diggings at, ib.; date, 232.

Greenwell, Canon, his researches as to prehistoric tumuli, 289.

Gregory the Great, letter of, respecting English idols, 21.

Gröningen, dolmens in 301.

Grottes des Feés, see Alleés couvertes.

Groups of stones in England, 56.

Groves, sacred, 465.

Guest, Dr., accuracy of his dates, 86; opinions as to place of Arthur's last battle, 87.

Guidebert circle, 531.

Guin, Arthur's 8th battle there, 137, 172.

Guinevere, where born and buried? 134.

Guzerat, ruins in, of Mahommedan city, 457.

HACAS PEN, see Hakpen Hill.

Hadrian, mausoleum of, 40; coins of, 84.

Hagiar Khem, plan of cone, 423; pitmarkings, 424; altar, 425; headless image, ib.

Hag's Hill, 213. See Slieve na Calliage.

Haken, his victory, 291.

Hakpen Hill, circle and avenue, 4; double circles, 64; Dr. Stukeley's theory as to, 4; dimensions, 65; mentioned in Charter of Athelstane, 73; dimensions of ovals, 75; stones, 76; find, 76; date of interments, 77; Camden's account, 78; Saxon and Danish burials, ib.; Roman road at, 83.

Hale Farm, 117.

Halkor, 305; dolmen, with drawing of ships, circles with crosses or chariot-wheels, 304.

Hamlet, citation from, 286.

Hannibal in Spain, 380.

Hanover dolmen, 301; with enclosure, 308.

Harald Blaatand, 296.

Harald Hildetand, his defeat, 280; grave, 282.

Harold Harfagar, 248; when took the Orkneys, 250.

Haugagerdium, 249.

Havard the Happy, 250.

Havard, Earl, where interred, 298.

Hauran, Roman tombs in the, 445.

Haxthausen, cited as to Steppes, 448-9.

Headstone, see Kivik.

Hecatæus cited, 8.

Height of mound an indication of its age, 142 note.

Helmstadt, once dolmens were near, 301.

Hengist and Horsa, 119; Hengist's grandson, 57; his treachery, 107.

Henry of Huntingdon cited as to triliths at Stonehenge, 94.

Heracleidæ, return of, what figured by, 39.

Heraldic symbolism, 273.

Heremon, Spanish race of, in Ireland, 381 et seq.; kings of this race in Ireland, where buried, 200.

Herodotus, his descriptions of tomb of Alyattes, 31; his account of the Nasomenes, 407.

Herrestrup, dolmen at, 303; ships, and circles with crosses engraved upon, 303.

Hesiod, his statement as to respective antiquity of brass or iron, 35.

Hiero's temple at mouth of Loire, 21.

Hildebrand, his account of diggings and find at Oden's Howe, 526.

Hildesheim, no dolmen at, 301.

Hindu Goni, 412.

Hindus as builders, 457; did not employ the arch, 457; not immutable, 458.

Historic, monuments not, 416.

Hjarnæ, tomb of, 299.

Hjortehammer, singular form of graves at, 316; date of, according to Worsae, 316; Viking graves at, 528.

Hoare, Sir R. C., 5; his work on Wiltshire, ib.; his authority, in what questionable, 10; his account of Hakpen, 77; etymology of Marlborough, 84; surveyed Marden, 85; his opinion of, 86; plan of Stonehenge, 91; cited as to Stonehenge, 101-5, 110; Stanton Drew, 150; find by long barrows, 289.

Hob Hurst's house, 172.

Höbisch, double dolmen at, 309.

Hock Norton, defeat of English at, 126.

Holback, 310.

Holes in dolmens, 161; Plas Newydd monolith at Stennis, 255; ceremony connected with, ib.; date of, 256; certainly Scandinavian, 258; in France, Trie, Grandmont, Bas Languedoc, 343-4; umbrella form has analogues in India, &c., 343; holes as entrances to chambers at Kerlescant and Rodmarton, 357; others at Finistère, 358; Gavr Innis, 365; objects of holes there, trough below, 366; in trilithon, 411; in dolmen in Circassia, 447; at Rajunkoloor, 469; inference of connexion of race from, 495. See Tumulus.

Holland, dolmens in, 301. See Drenthe, Hunebeds.

Holland, Rev. Mr., cited as to Sinai, 443; find by, 444.

Holstein, dolmens in, 301.

Holy Land, *see* Palestine.

Horsa, his burial-place, 119-21; battle between and Vortigern, 119.

Horses, sacrifices of, in the Steppes, 449-52.

Horstead, Horsa perhaps there buried, 121.

Houel's monuments in Malta, 416.

Howes, Danish and Saxon burials in, 104; British ditto, to what date, *ib.*; Danish kings buried, 250; to what date, argument from, 297.

Hoxay, 249-50.

Hubba the Dane, his era, 104.

Huc and Gabet cited as to monasticism in the East, 502.

Human remains, *see* Finds.

Human sacrifices amongst Anglo-Saxons, 284-5; and Khonds in India, 460; in Cuttack, 465.

Humble, tomb of, 299.

Hunebeds, 318, *et seq.*; Emmen, 320-1; Ballo, 321; were they originally covered, 321; Groningen and Friesland, 322; use and date, *ib.*

Hunestadt, dragon at, 245.

Hwitaby circles and Bacta stones, 290.

Hydahs in Alaska, 18; compared to Cave men, *ib.*; accounts of, 18 *note*; whether of race of mound builders, 517.

Hy Fiachrach cited, 233.

Hyperboreans, mentioned by Diodorus, 8; circular temples amongst, *ib.*; falsely supposed to be inhabitants of Britain, *ib.*

Iberians, or Celtiberians, 227; in Britain, 162; in Donegal, 227; dolmens, 228; Irish dolmens, 238; not very ready converts to Christianity, 228.

Idols, worship of, Councils forbidding, 24, 25.

Ilam, find at, 13.

Images, headless, 425; of dead on tombs, 449.

India, temples of, 1; no Druids in, 6; observations on, 7; when iron first known in, 35; tombs in, 41; holed stones, 343; westernmost dolmen, 443; rude-stone monuments, 455; dates of Aryans crossing Indus, of Vedas and laws of Menou, 455; no existing stone building prior to Asoka, *ib.*; progress of Indian architecture contrasted with that of other countries, 457; Hindu not immutable, 459; but other races are so, 459-461; Khassia Hills, 462; rude monuments there similar to European examples, *ib.*; cremation amongst Khassias, 463; funereal seats, *ib.*; origin of menhirs there, stone turbans, 464; menhirs and

tables, *ib.*; turban-stone, stone-table, trilithon, *ib.*; no circles and alignments, tumuli, nor sculptures, but coincidences with Western nations, 465; points of similarity and of dissimilarity to Druidical institutions, *ib.*; date of monuments, *ib.*; Kamarupa, 466; Sylhet, *ib.*; Western India, *ib.*; Belgaum altars or tables, 467; small circles, central stones, worship of Betal, *ib.*; dolmen at Rajunkoloor, 468; closed dolmen, 469; find, 470; cairns, *ib.*; Raichore Doab dolmens surrounded by double circles, 470; arrangement of dolmens at Rajunkoloor, *ib.*; cairns at Jewurgi, find, 471; purpose of each set of dolmens, 472; their ages, *ib.*; double dolmen, Coorg, 473; tomb, Nilgiri Hills, *ib.*; sepulchral circles at Amravati, 474; circular rail, 475; distribution of dolmens in India, *ib.*; Karumbers Buddhists, 477; Dravichans or Tumulians, 478; Karumbers and Singalese, connexion of, *ib.*; importance of the unexplored territory of Nizam, *ib.*; Travancore cromlechs, 479; mode of interment, offerings to departed spirits, explanation of miniature utensils, 479; finds, 480; age of monuments, iron how long known in India, iron pillar at Kutub, Delhi, 481; sculptured Indian dolmen, 483; Iwallee, 484; group at Shahpoor, 485; cross and dolmen at Katapur, 486-7; dolmen with cross at Nirmul Jungle, 488; dagobas in Ceylon, 489, 490; dolmen at Pullicondah, 491; Sanchi, rail near, 422; author's view as to dates of hewn and rude-stone buildings, ignorance of natives, 493-4; Eastern and Western dolmens, similarities between, how far proof of connexion, 495; tomb of Akbar at Agra, 496; proof from literature inconclusive, 496; from Asoka's rock-engraved edict, 498.

Indian Buddhists, rails of, 48; art influences elsewhere, 414.

Indian origin of Essenes, 500.

Inhumation, different kinds and history of, 30.

Inigo Jones, his treatise on Stonehenge, 23.

Inquisition, 332.

Inscriptions in Maes-Howe, 246; Newton Stone, perhaps earliest Scotch inscription, 271; Kirkliston, 271; Ogham inscription, 271,

Interments, place of, in case of circles, 132, 151; at Shap, Hakpen, and Crichie, 131-2; Saxon (*see* Beowulf); articles deposited by Saxons, 145-6; theory of successive interments, 146; secondary interments, 165-6; fallacy as to, 288-9; Sir John Lubbock's argument respecting summit interments, 166.

International Prehistoric Congress at Paris, 337.

Iolaus with Thespiadæ colonizers of Sardinia, 429.

Iorsala Farer or pilgrims, 244.

Iran and Turan or Aniran, of what these words the equivalents, 500.

Irby and Mangles, Captains, observe dolmens in Syria, 441.

Ireland, tomb-building in, 43; dolmens in, 45; external ditto, 46; menhirs in, 58; no symbolage in, 59; bluestones from, transported to England, 108; rude-stone monuments in, 175; best illustration of megalithic remains, *ib.*; obstruction of the study of Irish monuments, *ib.*; services of Dr. Petrie, *ib.*; materials for history of, *ib.*; copious literature, 176 (*see* Moytura); King Eochy, 178; Firbolgs or Belgians, 179; tradition of the " One Man," *ib.*; Queen Misgan Meave, 184-6; Dananns who? 188; King Nuada of the Silver Hand, 186; Fomorians, 186-7; Breas, 186; Balor of the Evil Eye, 187; the great Daghda, *ib.*; Fomorians and Dananns alleged to be of same Scandinavian race, *ib.*; their very early intercourse with Irish, 188; Dananns were Danes, *ib.*; chronology of early events, 188 *et seq.*; places of royal interment, 190; race of Crimthann, 132; introduction of alphabet, 189, 196; division into kingdoms, 189; early accounts of its peopling, *ib.*; Irish history doubtful until Cimboeth, *ib.*; burial-places of ancient kings, 190; first influx of civilization, when, according to Dr. Todd, 193 *note*; Oghams, 196; authentic history of Ireland, when commences, according to Petrie, *ib.*; legend of the Beds of Diarmid, 225; tradition as to (*see* Cemeteries); St. Colomba, 227; Iberians in Ireland, monuments of, 227; murder of Dathi by foster-brothers, 233; barbarism of Irish before St. Patrick, 235-6; their civilization progressive, 236; stages of architecture, 237-8; marks of triple system of monuments, 238; importance of them to history, 238; age and sequence of its monuments, 237-8; circle-building race in, 274; dolmen-building ditto, 274, 381; Spanish migration to, Heremon, 381; where Spaniards settled, 382; date, *ib.* *See* Glen Columbkille.

Iron, when known to Greeks, Israelites, Etruscans, 35; argument from absence of iron in tombs considered, 37; when introduced into Denmark, England, Egypt, *ib.*; iron, early manufacture of, in India, 482: and now by Khassias especially, *ib.*

Iron pillar at Kutub, 481; date of, 482.

Italy, tomb-building in, 40; dolmen at Saturnia, 391-2; chambered tumuli, 392; hewn stones, *ib.*; Etruria, *ib.*; why dolmens not so uniform in Italy as in France and Scandinavia, 393; earliest colonists, the Pelasgi and Tyrrheni, in contact with merely stone-hewing peoples, *ib.*; reverence of Etrurians for dead, *ib.*; their effacement by more progressive races, *ib.*; Rome adopts and improves Etruscan architecture, *ib.*; and forces Spain and France to a more ambitious sepulture, 394; their relapse into rude-stone monuments, *ib.*

Iwallee, singular place of dolmen, 484.

JACOB, stone set up by, 438-9.

Jains succeeded Buddhists in India, 459.

James I. directs researches respecting Stonehenge, 3, 104.

Janssen, Dr., his work on Hunebeds, 319.

Jarl Ragnvald, his expedition, 244.

Jarls, Orcadian, how buried, 297.

Jeffrey of Monmouth cited, 88; account by, of Stonehenge, 106 and of Merlin, are justified, 412; his character as writer, 106.

Jellinge, King Gorm's tomb at, 245, 296 *et seq.*

Jersey, tumulus in, 51; circle, 52.

Jewurgi, cairns at, 471-2.

Jey Sing, observatories of, 7, 459.

John, St., Baptistery of, at Canterbury, erected, 22.

Jones, *see* Inigo.

Joshua, stone set up by, 438-40; flint instruments of circumcision interred with him, 440.

Joyce, Rev. Mr., on crosses, 488.

Juggernaut, temple of, 460.

Junies, remains there, 368.

Jutes, settle in and trade with Britain before Cæsar's time, 133.

Jutland, dolmens in, 301.

KAFR ER WÂL, dolmen at, 441.

Kamarupa, Hindu kingdom, 466.

Karl Lofts, if circle there, 130.

Karumbers, 476 *et seq.*; originators of rude monuments in India, 478.

Katapur, cross and dolmen at, 486-7.

Kemble cited, 64, 73; as to historical value of poem of Beowulf, 120.

Kemp How, 130.

Kennet Avenue at Avebury, 63-4; called " stone row " in charter of Athelstan, 74; river, station of Saxons upon, 88; long barrow similar to Lethra, 283. *See* River Kennet.

Kens Low, 139; barrow, find at, 145.

Kent, division of, by Bede, 120.

Kent's Hole, 16.

Kerdouadec alignment, 367.

Kerland demi-dolmen, 336.

Kerlescant, 351, 356; long barrow opened, find, 356.

Kermario avenues, 350.

Keyna, traditions respecting, 151.
Keysler, citations from, 24, 25; compares Drenthe to Stonehenge, 319.
Khassia Hills, rude-stone monuments, 462 et seq.; tribes practise cremation, 463; funereal usages, 463; iron manufacture, 482.
Khatoura, tomb of Isidorus at, 100.
Khónds (see Gonds), usages of, resemblance to Druids, 460; Major Macpherson's remarks respecting their worship, 461; difficulty of putting an end to their human sacrifices, ib.
King Stone, 146. See Stanton Drew.
Kings of Denmark, tombs of, 15.
Kinsey, his 'Portugal Illustrated,' 377.
Kistvaens, or cists, how composed, 43; contents of, ib.; when covered, 43-4; passages into, 43; sculpture in, ib.; New Grange, ib.; Gavr Innis, ib.; Maes-Howe, ib.; Arbor Low, 140; Gib Hill, 141; Plas Newydd, 166.
Kit's Cotty House, 116; whether ever covered, 44.
Kivik grave, headstone of, 314; figures upon, ib.; date assigned to, ib.; resembles one in France, ib.
Klein-Raden, 301. See Cotty House.
Knock na Rea, 184; cairn at, 280. See Queen Misgan Meave.
Knockeen, dolmen at, 229.
Knowth, cairn of, 192, 200; identified by Petrie with cave of Cnodhba, 201; searched by Danes, ib.
Knut, the great battle between and Olof, 291.
Kongsbacka battle-field, 279.
Königsberg, dolmens near, 301.
Konitz, dolmen at, 301.
Krukenho, allée couverte at, 342; dolmen compared with Dol ar Marchant, 36.
Kubber Roumeia, tomb of Mauritanian kings, 423-4.
Kurgans or mounds in the Steppes, 448.
Kutb u Deen, his mosque at Delhi, 457.
Kutub iron pillar, 35, 481.

Laity, see Clergy and Laity.
Landevenec founded by Grallon, 374.
Landver, son of Thufin, where buried, 528.
Largs, battle of, 58; stone to mark, 58.
Larking, Rev. Mr., his visit to Aylesford, 118.
Latheronwheel, 530 et seq.
Lean Low mound, 139. See Derbyshire.
Lecan, book of, cited, 233.
Lech, meaning of word, 44.
Ledwich, Dr., his description of New Grange, 143.
Lefroy, General, his diggings at Greenmount, 231.
Leoghaine, 212-3.
Leslie, Col. Forbés, 264; his paper upon Aberdeenshire circles, 263; Belgian group described by, 467.

Lethra, tomb at, of Harold, 282, 289.
Leure, alignment at, 367.
Lia Fail, 382, 439. See Stone of Destiny.
Liberius, Consul, defeat of, 374.
Liegnitz, dolmen at, 301.
Lifeachair Cairbre, his grave, 213.
Linn ⎱ see Linuis; meaning of word, 136;
Lyn ⎰ perhaps Lake country, 136.
Linuis, where, 136; locality of a battle of Arthur, different opinions respecting locality, 136.
Liotr, or Landver, sepulchre, 254.
Listoghil cairn, 181; mentioned by Petrie, ib.; find there, 182.
Llwyd, Mr., 201.
Lockmagen, 129. See Wood Castle.
Locmariaker, allée couverte at, 341; Dariorigum, capital of Venetes, 349; long barrow, Mané Lud 360; Mané er H'roëk, 360; dolmen and sculpture, 360-1; Dol ar Marchant, 361; allée couverte near, 364; date, 370.
Loire, grottes des fées along, 341.
Loncarty, defeat of Danes at, 270.
Long Stow Cove, 64.
Long-headed race, superior antiquity of, 36.
Longroads, barrow at, 11.
Lot, department of, 334.
Lothbrok Ragnar, victories of, 290; sepulchre of, 298; battle fought by, 314.
Lough Crew, 199, 213; excavations, 213; cairn T, 214; Hag's Chair, 215; two stones, 216; cairn L, 217; cairn H, ib.; find there, 218; cairn D, 219; other monuments at, ib.
Lubbock, Sir John, analysis by, of contents of numerous tumuli, 11; Park Cwn tumulus described by, 164.
Lucan cited as to Nasomenes, 407.
Lug, grandson of Balor, 187.
Lukis, Rev. Mr., explores Carnac, 350, 356-7.
Lumberdale House, cist at Gib Hill removed to, 141.
Lüneburg, dolmen near, with enclosures, 308.
Luxembourg, Grand Duchy, dolmens in, 301, 323; to whom referred, 323.
Lyons, battle near, 374.

Mackenzie, Col., his map cited, 474; his drawings of Viraculls and Masteculls, 483.
Macpherson, Major Charteris, his work, memorials of service in India cited, 460.
Madracen, 423; of same type as Maltese examples, 424.
Madsén, his 'Antiquités prehistoriques du Danemark,' 188; gives examples of buried dolmen, 310.
Maenec, Le, 350 et seq.
Maes-Howe tumulus, 244; opened, ib.; early spoliation of, ib.; runes descriptive

of origin, *ib.*; the spoilers, who, *ib.*; inference from runes, *ib.*; engraving of dragon, similar to Danish, 245, 246 *et seq.*; Wurm knot, 245; inscription, 246; age of, *ib.*; architecture of howe, 247; chamber and loculi, *ib.*; resemblance of mound to those on Boyne, 248; of what race and age, 249-256; unique monument must have belonged to most magnificent race, 258.

Magas mentioned by Asoka, 498.

Magh Mor, King of Spain, his connexion with Ireland, 187.

Magnus Henricksson, Danish Prince, 291.

Magnus Olaus, description by, of megalithic remains in Sweden, 15, 101.

Mahabharata, date of the, 455.

Mahommedans could not influence the nonprogressive tribes of India, 459.

Mahommedanism, aversion to, in India, 459.

Majorca and Minorca, *see* Mediterranean Islands, 434.

Mal Lumkun, cross erected by, 272.

Male, M., his example of demi-dolmen, 345.

Malmor, or Malmurn, 272.

Malta, tombs of, 410; giants' towers, 415; Maltese monuments, *see* Mediterranean Islands.

Man, Isle of, circles in, 162; crosses in, 273.

Mané er H'roëk, find there, 339, 360, 364; singular sculptured slab, 364.

Mané Lud, 360.

Mangles, Captain, *see* Irby.

"Many Stones," group, 529.

Maols, or Murderers, graves of four, at Ballina, 233, 336; certain date of, 233.

Marden, 63; circle, plan, 85.

Marienburg, dolmen at, 30.

Marlborough, etymology of word, 84.

Marmora, Count de la, his work on Sardinia, 428 *et seq.*

Marsa Sirocco, remains at, 425.

Masses, immense, moved by rude peoples, 465.

Masteeculls, what, 483.

Mauritanian kings, tombs of, 424.

Maximus, overthrow of Roman power by, 373; his battle, 374.

Mayborough (*see* Penrith and Cumrew); circle at, compared to Little Salkeld, 127.

Meave Misgan, Queen, *see* Misgan.

Mecklenburg, dolmens in, 301.

Mediterranean islands, non-historic monuments of, shaped stones, 415, 436; Malta, giants' towers, circles, 416; Gozo, 417; Hagiar Khem, 419, 423; Mnaidra, 418-22; roofing of Maltese monuments, 422; these compared to Kubber Roumeia and Madracen, 424; Gozo scrolls and spirals compared to those of Mycenæ and Greece, *ib.*;

pit-markings, *ib.*; altars and stone tables, 225; monuments not temples but sepulchres, 425-6; Phœnicians in Malta, 425; the monuments, of what race and age, 426, 437; prior to dolmens, 437; Sardinic Nurhags, 427; storeys of Nurhags and groups, plan of, *ib.*; Santa Barbara, 428, 431; silence of history as to them, 429; Dedalean buildings according to Diodorus, *ib.*; La Giara, 430; what Nurhags were, 431; derivation of, 432; view of author as to purpose of Nurhags, 433; Balearic islands, Talaiots at Trepuco, Minorca bilithon, 435; Alajor, *ib.*; stone tables, 435-6; rude-stone circles, 432.

Megalithic monuments at Moytura, 180 *et seq.*; every kind of, except avenues, 180-1; monument in Deer Park, Sligo, 234; its anomalous nature, 235; Celts had nothing to do with, according to Bertrand, 254; gap of, between France and Scandinavia, 323; none in valleys of Rhine or Scheldt, *ib.*; distribution of, 334; map, 324; table, 376; demi-dolmens, rocking stones, 345 *et seq.*; Carnac, 350; Tiaret, 397.

Megalithic remains, how to study, 19; rarely in this country contain flint, bronze, or iron, 19; style uniform, 36; age of, 37; resemblance to Buddhist structure, 42 (*see* Kistvaens); mark battlefields, family sepulchres, or graves of distinguished men, 15; great light as to, derivable from Irish remains, 175.

Melkart and Astarte, temple in Malta dedicated to, 425.

'Memorials of Service,' work of Major Charteris-Macpherson, 460.

Menhirs, 29; derivation of word, 57; where, *ib.*; purpose, *ib.*; single stones in Scripture, Greece, Etruria, *ib.*; rarely inscribed, *ib.*; in Ireland, Wales, Scotland, 59; France, *ib.*; at Lochrist, *ib.*; Denmark, 60 (*see* Monoliths); purpose of menhir in Khassia, 463; Western not after Tartar models, 452.

Menou, laws of, date of, 455.

Meriadec Conan, British Prince in France, 374; wars of, *ib.*

Merivale, bridge at, 55-6; parallel lines of stones at, 54; their purpose, *ib.*; avenue, circles, and cromlech at, 55-6.

Merlin, his bury, 84; his connexion with Stonehenge, 107; fable about, 133; explained, 412.

Mettray, allée couverte at, 341.

Mexican temples, 514; race non-progressive beyond a certain point, 19.

Mexico, carved stone monuments in, 517.

Miamisburgh, sepulchral mound at, 514.

Miana, circle at, 453.

Microlithic remains, 40, 41, 47.

Miegle, alleged burial-place of Guinevere, 134.

Migration from France to Algeria, 409; of people settled around Mediterranean, 410.

Migration theory, how proved or disproved, 443, 445.

Minho, dolmens in, 378.

Miniature urns and utensils in Indian tomb, use of, explained, 479.

Minjana, Don Rafael, pamphlet by, 377.

Minning Low, 130, 142-3. *See* Derbyshire.

Minorca, *see* Mediterranean.

Minyas, tomb of, 33.

'Mirabilibus Auscultationibus, De,' work ascribed to Aristotle, 429, 434.

Miscellaneous, *see* Mounds.

Misgan Meave, Queen, cairn of, 183; killed by whom, 184 (*see* Moytura); poem of her life and adventures, 196; her husband, 197.

Mnaidra, elliptical chambers, 417; plans of monuments at, 418-22; cones, 419; pit-markings, 420; openings in walls, shelves or loculi or columbaria? 420; roofs, 421.

Modestus, his zeal of proselytism unsuccessful in Brittany, 373.

Mogalana and Sariputra, disciples of Buddha, 504.

Mogols, domes of, 40.

Molyneux, Sir Thomas, 202.

Monasticism in the West, 499; Vestal Virgins, Antony, *ib.*; Essenes, 500; history silent as to monasticism in the East, not so architecture, 501; imitated by the West from the East, *ib.*; peculiarities introduced, 502.

Monoliths at Stennis, 242; holed, 242, 255; Setif, 397.

Mont St. Michel, possibly occupied by Cæsar, 20; find, 356.

Montfort, Simon de, 481.

'Monumenta Britannica' cited, 87.

Monuments, *see* Rude-Stone.

Moon worship forbidden, 25.

Moore, Norman, Mr., his visit to Glen Columbkille, 225; letters from, respecting, *Appendix*, 520-3.

Moors in Spain, 381.

Motes, or places of judgment, stones to mark, 26.

Mounds of sacrifice in North America, 513; of sepulture, 514; temple, *ib.*; animal mounds, 515; conical mounds, 513.

Moustoir Carnac, long barrow and find, 358-9.

Moytura, 176; two battles at, 175; narrative of, by O'Donovan, 176; first battle at North Moytura, 176-7; second battle at South Moytura, 177-9; circles, 177; cairns, *ib.*; cairn of "One Man," 178; importance and varieties of monuments at Northern Moytura, 180; map, 181; plan of circles, 182-3; dolmen, 183; tomb of Misgan Meave, 184;

locality of it doubted, 185; account of battle of Northern Moytura, 186; dates of battles, 188, 197; when accounts first written, 197; localities of battles, 198; monuments at, contrasted with English and Scandinavian examples, 198; resemblance of, to Braavalla, 280, 304.

Muir Divock, 130; circles at, 130.

Mule Hill, 157-8. *See* Circles, Small.

Mulhevan, Mr., account of Katapur, 487.

Mull of Cantyre circles, 262.

Munch, Professor, his observations as to spoilers of Maes-Howe, 244; mentions Halfdan's barrow, 250.

Mycenæ, tombs of Atridæ at, 32, 36; analogous to Jersey circles, 52, 53; scrolls and spirals there resemble those of Gozo, 424.

Nablons, dolmens on road to, 441.

Naper, Mr., excavations by, 213.

Nasamones, who, 407; Herodotus mentions their veneration of dead, *ib.*; a plundering tribe, *ib.*

Navarre, dolmens in, 378.

Nemedh, three sons of, 179.

Nennius, his account of origin of Stonehenge, 107; of Arthur's battles, 135.

Nestorians, how far to the east, 488.

Net Lowe, find, 13.

Netterville House, tumulus, 209.

New Craig circle, 263.

New Grange, 43, 52; Royal cemetery, 192, 201.

New Inn, 12.

Newark Works in America, 511.

Newton, 263; sculptured stone, 263, 271.

Niall, father of Leoghaire, 212.

Nicol, Dr., his observations in Kincardine, 265.

Nikolajew, uncovered base of tumulus, 451.

Nilgiri Hills tombs and dolmens, 472-3; sculptured dolmens, 483.

Nine Ladies, circle of, at Stanton Moor, 48-9, 140.

Nineveh, dates of buildings at, how ascertained, 1, 34.

Nirmul Jungle dolmen with cross, 488.

Nizam's unexplored territory important to art and history, 478.

Nonhistoric monuments, 415.

Norman pirates, Grallon's war with, 374.

North Germany, *see* Scandinavia.

Norway, no dolmens in, but cairns and such like monuments, 302.

Nuada, king, "of the silver hand," battle and death, 187.

Nur, meaning of, 432.

Nurhags of Sardinia, 410, 415, 427 *et seq.*; derivation of word, *see* Sardinia.

Oak used in Thyra's tomb, 298.

Obelisk, development of, 59; at Ayles-

ford, 117, 119; at Rollright, 124; at Dol ar Marchant, 363.
Oberhartz, no dolmens in, 301.
Oberyssel, dolmen in, 301.
O'Brian, wild speculations of, 175.
Observatories in India, 459.
Ochaim, Niall's burying-place, 212.
O'Curry, his account of battle cited, 188; his view as to date of Ogham writing, 196.
Oden's Howe, exploration of, 526; find, *ib.*
O'Donovan, his account of Moytura, 176; his confession of uncertainty of Irish chronology, 190; remarks as to dolmen of four Maols, 233.
Og, king of Bashan, 442.
Oghams, 29; on menhirs, 58; date of introduction, 196; little used, and for what, *ib.*; on Newton Stone, 271.
Ohio, sacred enclosures in, 511; district of, how first peopled, 516.
Oise, holed dolmen at, 343.
Olaus, *see* Wormius, Magnus.
Old Testament, stones mentioned in, 57.
Oldenburg, dolmens in, 301.
Olfers, Dr., tomb of Alyattes examined by, 32.
Olof the Holy, 241.
Ophite theory, 4, 7.
Oppeln, dolmen near, 301.
Orchomenos, sepulchre explored by Dodwell, 33; lined with bronze, 34; inference from, as to civilization, 39.
Orkneys (*see* Maes-Howe, Scotland, Stennis); no timber in, 298.
Orkhow, treasure there, 252.
Oroust, dolmen at, 305-6; resembles Countless Stones, 305; in enclosure, 310.
Osnabrück, dolmen in, 301.
Ougein, observatories in, 7; commercial capital of Asoka, 459.
Ousely, Sir W., cited as to Eastern circles, 453.
Oval dolmens, *see* Dolmens.
Ozene, or Ougein, which see.

PAGAN temples, similarity of, to Christian, 22-3.
Palestine and the East, dolmens, 438; of stones mentioned in Scripture but one of megalithic class, 438-40; monolith, 440; dolmens between Es Salt and Nablous, 441; and Kafr-er-Wâl, *ib.*; whether dolmens outside of Gilead, 442; of what tribe known examples are, *ib.*; age of, 443; Peshawur, *ib.*; circular-domed tombs at Sinai, and stone circles, *ib.*; find, 444; Nukb Hawy ring, *ib.*; resemblance to Bazinas and Chouchas, *ib.*; Arabia, near Eyoor, rude-stone monuments mentioned by Palgrave, resembling those of the West and at Tripoli, 445; interest attaching to Arabian examples, *ib.*; Asia Minor, unsolved problems respect-

ing, 446; Kertch, chambered tumuli, and finds, 447; dolmens of shaped stones, holed in Circassia, Crimea, and on shore of Baltic, 447.
Palgrave, Mr. Giffard, rude-stone monuments seen by him in Arabia, 444.
Pallas cited, 449.
Pancras, St., temple at Canterbury dedicated to, 22.
Pandus, temples popularly assigned to, 494.
Pape and Peti, early inhabitants of Orkneys, 248.
Parallel lines or avenues, 50. *See* Avenues.
Park Cwn tumulus, 164; meant to be visible, 164; find at, *ib.*
Parkhouse circle, 263.
Pataliputta, *see* Patna.
Patan, Emperors, domes of, 40.
Patna, convocation at, 501.
Pausanias, tomb of Atridæ described by, 32, 33.
Pegges Barrow, 11.
Pelasgi and Tyrrheni, in contact with only stone-hewing races, 393.
'Pelasgic Remains,' work by Dadwell, 33; style superseded by Doric in Greece, 393.
Pembroke, Philip, Earl of, his testimony as to Stonehenge, 104.
Pen, prefix, meaning of, 64.
Pennant cited as to Mayborough, 128-9.
Penrith, Arthur's Round Table at, 82; Long Meg and her Daughters, 126 *et seq.*; mentioned by Camden, 127; Mayborough, *ib.*; monolith, 128; King Arthur's Round Table, *ib.*; plan of, *ib.*; history of monuments, 131; Shap alignment not Druidical, *ib.*; nor sepulchral, *ib.*; at least not the cemetery of Shap, *ib.*; marks battle-field, 132; victory over Saxons, perhaps, *ib.*; objections, 132-3; monuments near, mark victories of Arthur, 132.
Pentre Ifan dolmen, 168.
'Periplus,' the, cited, 459.
Perthes, M. Bouche de, "find" by, on the Somme, 16.
Peru, carved stone monuments in, 518; resemble Pelasgic and Tyrrhenian, *ib.*
Peshawur dolmen, 443; circle, 452; and at Deh Ayeh, 453; hewn-stone circles ascribed to Caons or giants, 453; if other dolmens in the East? 454.
Peti or Picts, 248-9. *See* Pape.
Petrie, Dr., his useful but interrupted services in Ireland, 175; observations of, as to cairn Listoghil, 181; Moytura, 181 *et seq.*; Tara, 193; introduction of writing into Ireland, 196; Oghams, *ib.*; Knowth, 201; cited as to Talten, 219; style of Irish monuments, 238; his excavations in the Orkneys, 249; his suggestion as to Moytura, 280.

Phayre, Sir Arthur, on circle at Peshawur, 452.

Phœnicians, Romans, and Greeks of Marseilles, their influence upon architecture of rude nations, 508.

Phœnicians, voyages of, to Cornwall, 38; written characters at New Grange, 207; not builders of rude-stone monuments, 409.

Picardy, remains of Cave men in, 329.

Pictland, features of, 58.

Picts, origin and relations with Irish and Gauls, 267; their capitals, 271; language, ib.

Pierre branlante, Brittany, 348.

Pierre Martine, rocking stone, 347-8.

Pilgrim Scandinavian pirates, 244.

Pit-markings, 424.

Plas Newydd dolmen, 167-9.

Pliny, see Cæsar.

Plouharnel, double dolmen at, 358.

Poitiers, demi-dolmen, 346.

Poitou, Cave men's remains in, 329.

Poland and Posen, no dolmens in, 301.

Pomerania, dolmens in, 301.

Portugal, writers on its rude-stone monuments, 377; dolmens, ib.; Strabo, an authority for its dolmens, ib.; Cuneus, 378; distribution of dolmens, ib.; throws light upon theories, ib.; course taken by dolmen race, 378 et seq.; Arroyolos, dolmen at, 389.

Posen, see Poland.

Pownall, Governor, his disquisition upon marks at New Grange, 202, 207.

Pregel, dolmens on, 301.

Prehistoric prejudices, 406. See International.

Preissac, alignment at, 368.

Pre-Roman theory, 373.

Progressive theory, 406.

Prussia, dolmens rare in, 301.

Prussian Saxony, see Saxony.

Priam's house of brass, 35.

Prinsep, Mr., his translation of an edict of Asoka, 498.

Priority of dates, see Dates.

Ptolemy, mentioned in edict of Indian Prince, 498.

Pullicondah, cairn or dolmen, 491.

Puri, temple of Juggernaut at, 460.

Pyramids, inference as to climate from pictures in, 17; date of that at Gizeh, 31; antecedent structures supposed, ib.; contain tombs true and false, 46; probable date of, 408.

Pytheas, visit of, to Cimbrian Chersonese, 38.

Queen Charlotte's Sound, whether natives a race of mound-builders, 517.

RACE, inference as to, from use of circles, 163; of dolmens, ib.; of circles and dolmens, ib.; divisions of, in Britain by Tacitus, 162; inference from simulta-neous monuments of three kinds in Ireland as to races, 238; relations of Picts with Irish and Gaels, shown by comparison of monuments, 267, 271; circle-building and dolmen-building races, 274; whence each came, and course which each took, ib.; dolmens, historic, 302; distribution of, ib.; prehistoric theory leaves subject of races obscure, ib.; dolmen-building race not so ready converts to Christianity as the Celts, 328; inference from church architecture in South of France, 332; and Protestant feeling in South of France, ib.; non-progressive, ib.; Cimbri, Celts, and Gauls, 333; Cimbri and Aquitani related, ib.; race traced by dolmens from Brittany to Narbonne, 334; Iberians, Celtiberians, Turanians, 379; disturbed by Carthaginians, 379; Romans, 380; Moors, their easy conquest of Spain, how accounted for, 381; Spanish settlers in Ireland and Britain, ib.; Tara, 382; Lia Fail, ib.; Heremon, 381-3; ethnography of North Africa, 406, et seq.; different theories as to, ib.; connexion between races on the northern and southern sides of Mediterranean, 408; chief race in India, 458; Bhil, Cole, Gond, and Toda, non-progressive, 459; Hindus not immutable, ib.; inference from style of architecture, 495; peopling of America, 516; by what way, 516; Mound-builders, Redmen, Hydahs, 517; Aztecs and Toltecs, 515; Pastoral or Agricultural races, ditto Hunters in North America, ib.

Race-course, notion that alignments at Stonehenge were, 111.

Raguhilda, wife of Eric, 250.

Rail, Sanchi, 492.

Rajagriha, convocation at, 501.

Rajpootana, pertinacity of Bhil usages, 459.

Rajunkoloor, 468 et seq.

Ramayana, the date of, 455.

Ramé, M., describes alignment at Gré de Cojou, 377.

Rath at Dowth, residence of the Dagdha, 195.

Rath of Leoghaire, 195; singular direction by him as to his burial, ib.

Rath of Queen Meave, 193.

Rath na Riogh, 194; resembles Avebury, ib.

Rathcrogan, supposed burial-place of Queen Meave, 183.

Rayne, old circle at, 263.

Rectangular dolmens, 313. See Dolmens.

Redmen of North America, 517; not mound-builders, ib.

Redstone pillar, 200.

Relic worship in the East, 503.

Relig na Riogh, Dati's burial-place, 200.

Rhind, Mr., his bequest for Professorship

of Archæology in Scotland, 239 ; paper on ortholithic remains in Africa, 395-7.

Ribroit, Arthur's tenth battle there, 137.

Rickman, his perception of progress and sequence in monuments, 113 ; value of his process in fixing dates, 114.

Ring Sigurd, 280 ; saga as to, 282.

Ringham Low, group, 139. *See* Derbyshire.

Rocking stones, 347.

Rodmarton, chambered tumulus, 166 ; post-Roman, 289 ; holes in entrance, resembles Kerlescant, 357.

Roeskilde, dolmen in square, 307.

Rolley Lowe, 12.

Rollo in England, 126.

Rollright, circle at, 124 ; obeliscal stone, *ib.*; dolmen, *ib.*; examined by R. Sheldon, 125 ; unimportance of monuments there, *ib.*; whether sepulchral, *ib.*; assigned by Camden to Rollo, 126.

Roman coins, find of, in Ireland, 166. *See* Coins, Finds.

Roman pottery found at Stonehenge, 105 ; inference from, 106. *See* Finds.

Roman road at Silbury Hill, 81 ; argument from its state, 82 ; and of that at Hakpen Hill, 83.

Romans, Stonehenge assigned to, by Inigo Jones, 3 ; in England, 96 ; effect of Roman art upon British civilization, *ib.*; and architecture, 394 ; in Africa, 414 ; pressure of, upon Eturia, 393.

Ronalds, Mr., his engraving of Carnac, 350.

Rooke, Mr., his account of Stanton Moòr, 146 ; snaffle-bit found by, 156.

Rose Hill tumulus, 155. *See* Circles, Small, 155.

Ros-na-righ, who buried there, 212.

Ross County, North America, sacred enclosures in, 811.

Rothiemay circle, 263.

Round tower, *see* Tower.

Roy's, General, 'Military Antiquities of Romans' cited as to circle at Wood Castle, 129.

Rude-stone monuments erected even where letter inscriptions and carving practised, 273 ; none in the valleys of Scheldt and Rhine, 323 ; sometimes comparatively modern, 406 ; result sometimes of fashion, 408 ; Aryans and pure Dravidians or Tamulians not builders of, in India, 447-8.

Rudeness of monument, what it proves, 100.

Rugen, island of, dolmens in, 301.

Runes on menhirs, 29 ; Maes-Howe, 246-8, 251 ; Isle of Man, 273.

SABÆAN worship of planets, 432.

"Sabrinum ostium," meaning of words, 87 ; Arthur's last battle fought near, *ib.*

Sacrifices, *see* Human.

Sagas, 254 ; as to Harald Hildetand, 280.

Sakya Muni, date of, 455 ; influences Buddhism, 506 ; is not Woden, 496.

Salkeld, Arthur's seventh battle, 137. *See* Cumrew.

Sanchi rail, 492 ; gate, 94 ; no images of priests, 501 ; relics of saints, 504 ; dagobas and stupas, 41.

Sandulf the Swarthy, 272.

Santa Barbara, Nurhags at, 428 *et seq.* *See* Mediterranean Islands.

Santander dolmens, 378.

Sardis, tombs at, 32 ; age of, 32.

Sariputra, see Mogalana.

Sarsen stones, at Ashdown, 122 ; what they represent, *ib.*; at Avebury, 73, 86 ; whence they came, 95 ; at Stonehenge, 94.

Saturnia, dolmen at, 391-2.

Sauclières dolmen, 335.

Saumur, grotte des feés near, 341.

Säve, Karl, letter from, respecting diggings at Oden's Howe, 526-7.

Savernake Forest, 87.

Saxo-Grammaticus as to Gorm's son, 296.

Saxons, defeat of, by Vortimer, 106 ; battle with Vortigern, 119.

Saxons, march of, in the West, 88 ; encounter Arthur, 88-9, 132 ; their defeat near Penrith, 132 ; traded with and settled in Britain before Cæsar's time, 133-4 ; grave mounds in England, 36 ; articles supposed Saxon at Stand Lowe, 13.

Saxons, Prussian, 301.

Saxony, dolmens in, 301.

Scandinavia and North Germany, 275 ; Danes, their megalithic remains little known, *ib.*; false route of their antiquaries, 276 ; except Sjöborg, 277 ; their early historians little reliable, *ib.*; Scandinavian history prior to Christ, *ib.*; Odin, fable as to, *ib.*; Frode I., date of, 278 ; and of Harald Harfagar, *ib.*; list of kings, *ib.*; battle-fields, *ib.*; Kongsbacka, 279 ; its analogy to Dartmoor, Ashdown, and Karnac alignments, *ib.*; view of, *ib.*; grave of Frode, but which Frode ? *ib.*; battlefield of Swedes and Danes, *ib.*; Braavalla Heath, 280 ; resemblance to Moytura, *ib.*; circles, *ib.*; doubt as to date of, *ib.*; square and triangular graves, 282 ; King Harald Hildetand, saga of, and Sigurd Ring, 283 ; tomb of former, 282 ; find of flints, 283 ; erroneous inference, *ib.*; form of grave, *ib.*; Hwitaby circles and Bauta stones at, 290 ; battle-fields, whose, *ib.*; Lothbrok, 291 ; Stiklastad, and circles there, *ib.*; circles and ovals, mounds and square enclosures, *ib.*; victory of Blenda, *ib.*; Freyrsö cairns, mounds, and ship barrows, *ib.*; tumuli, to what race due, aboriginal or invading, 293; Scandinavians, of what race, *ib.*; Worsae's argument, *ib.*; triple group at Upsala, 294; find, *ib.*; mound of Wodin, *ib.*; Jellinge, tombs of Gorm and Thyra, 296; importance of, 297; diggings in the latter, 296; find, 297; date, *ib.*; compared to Maes-Howe, 299; comparative dates of Danish, Irish, and Stennis monuments, *ib.*; series of Royal Danish tombs, *ib.*; might furnish dates of styles, 300. *See* Scotland, Caithness.

Scandinavian antiquaries commended, 15.

Scandinavians in Ireland, 187; different tribes of, 187; Vikings, *ib.*; in Scotland, Orkneys, 244; pilgrims, Christian, and pirates, *ib.*; conoid graves, 243; ship graves, 315; equilateral triangles, *ib.*; meaning of the latter form, 315-6; singular arrangement of circles at Aschenrade, 317; resembles Algerian example, 318; finds, *ib.*; no Druids amongst, 6; ignorant of iron, 37.

Schleswig dolmens, 301.

Scone stone, 439.

Scotland, menhirs in, 57; megalithic remains in, 239; Wilson's 'Prehistoric Annals' of, *ib.*; scanty means of studying monuments in, *ib.*; cat or battle-stones, dolmens, circles, 240; distribution of, *ib.*; Orkneys, 241; circles, tumuli, *ib.*; Stennis, *ib.*; dolmens, 241, 355; monoliths, 242; holed monument, 242, 255; bowl-shaped barrows, 243; find, *ib.*; conoid barrows, *ib.*; find there, *ib.*; Maes-Howe, *ib.*; spoliation of, *ib.*; runes, *ib.*; dragon and Wurm knot, 245; inscription at Maes-Howe, 246; chamber there, 247; and loculi, 248; resemblance to Boyne monuments, *ib.*; red sandstone material, *ib.*; conquest of Island by Harold Harfagar, *ib.*; Pape and Peti, who these races were, *ib.*; what is Maes-Howe, 248-9; and what the barrows, *ib.*; Haugagerdium, perhaps How of Hoogsay, who buried there, *ib.*; Halfdan's Barrow, 250; similarity to Danish royal tumuli, *ib.*; account of conquest of Orkneys by the Norwegians, *ib.*; Stennis, scene of what battle, 250-1; runic inscriptions, 251; scantiness of, accounted for, 252; an inscription confirmed by a find, *ib.*; Maes-Howe, whether it has connexion with circles, 253-4; dates of early invasions of Northmen, 255; Brogar, 254; less ancient than Stennis, 255; conversion of Northmen to Christianity, *ib.*; date of group of monuments at Stennis, 256; analogy of to Stanton Drew, *ib.*; author's reasons justifying date assigned to group at Stennis, 257-8; Callernish circles, *ib.*; cruciform grave, 259; avenue, 260; Tormore,

Isle of Arran, cist circles, 261-2; Brodick Bay circle, and obelisk, 262; Mull of Cantyre, *ib.*; Aberdeenshire circles, 263; Fiddes Hill, 264; circle at Rayne and find, 263; post Christian date of, 264; moat and entrances, 265; uses merely sepulchral, *ib.*; Clava mounds and circular chambers, 266; find, *ib.*; their use, 267; stone at Coilsfield, *ib.*; stone at Aberlemmo, 268-9; its purpose, 270; Caithness alignments differ from British and French, 529; horned cairn, 530; circles inferred by Sir H. Dryden not always to be sepulchral, 532; date, 528; similarity to Viking graves, 528.

Scott, Sir Walter, his description of holed monolith in Orkney, 242.

Scrolls and spirals in Irish sculpture, 222.

Sculpture, 29; difficulty of reasoning from gradation of style as to Irish or Scottish, 59; chiselled, engraved, pricked, 217; what tools employed, *ib.*; at Mané Lud, imitations of boats, hatchets, writing, 361; at Dol ar Marchant, hatchet, plume, 362.

Secondary, *see* Interment.

Semitic race, their feeling to monasticism, 500.

Senbya dagoba, 496-7.

Sentinel stones, 310.

Sepultura Grande dolmen, 386.

Sepulture, *see* Cairns, Circles, Cists, Dolmens, Mounds, Tombs, Tumuli.

Seringham, monoliths of, 96; monstrous size of, *ib.*; work there, how interrupted, *ib.*

Serpent temples, false theory as to, 4, 21, 64; gigantic serpent-forms in earth in America, 515; serpent knot, *see* Wurm.

Sesto Calende, rude-stone monuments at, 391.

Setil, dolmen near, 396.

Shahpoor stone monuments, 485.

Shap avenue, counterpart of Kennet, 147. *See* Penrith.

Ship graves, 316.

Ships sculptured in dolmens, 303.

Siam, 456; dagobas and stupas in, 41.

Siberian Steppes, America peopled from, 516.

Side-stone, Aspatria cist, 157.

Siganfu tables, 488 *note*.

Sigurd, converted by Olaus, 250.

Silbury Hill, Roman writers silent as to monuments, 20; their purpose and age, 65, 84; description of, 78; dimensions, 79; researches there, *ib.*; negative results, *ib.*; accounted for, *ib.*; find in, 81; mound, who raised, 86; near Wansdyke, 88; Arthur's last battle, 89; mound, why created, *ib.*; analogue of Gib Hill, 147.

Silesia, dolmens in, 301.

Silius Italicus cited, 407.

Silures in Britain, 162-3; in Wales and
Anglesea, 163; Cornwall, ib.; join
with Brigantes, 381.
Simpson, Sir J., cited as to Vetta, 271;
as to pit-markings, 425.
Sinai, monuments at, 443-4.
Sing, Jey, observatory, 7.
Sivite temple, ruined, at Iwullee, 484.
Sjöberg, 276; his merits, 276-9; treats
dolmens all as pre-historic, 306.
Skailbay, 252.
Skaili, death of, 528.
Skene, see Stuart, Glennie.
Slieve na Calliagh, 213 (see Hengist and
Horsa); when first remarked, 213;
illustrations of, 214 et seq.; style of
sculpture, 215; find at, 215-6; mys-
terious great stone saucer, 216; find,
217-8; absence of circles, alignments,
and rude-stone monuments, 219.
Sligo trilithon, 108; cairn of Bally-
sadare, King Eochy's tomb, 179.
Smidstrup, buried dolmen at, 311.
Smith, Colonel Baird, his excavation
at Kutab pillar, 481.
Smith, Dr., his astronomical theory, 7.
'Smithsonian Contributions to Knowledge' cited, 510 et seq.
Smyrna, date of tombs at, 32.
Smythe, Piazzi, his theories, 31, 91.
Snake theory, see Stukeley, Dr.
Snio, king, where slain, 279.
Spain, writers on its rude-stone monuments, 377; dolmens there, ib.; dolmen race, 378; its navigation, in which
direction, 378 et seq.; prehistoric race
in Spain, 379; its characteristics, ib.;
and non-use of stone in prehistoric
times, ib.; Iberians, Celtiberians, Turanians, ib.; Carthaginians, Romans,
381; Moors' easy conquest proves
earlier settlements in Spain, ib.;
Spanish race of Heremon in Ireland,
ib.; Spaniards, Siloros, migrate to
Britain, ib.; part occupied by them in
Ireland, 382; date of Heremon, 383;
light thrown by rude-stone monuments on connexion of Spain and Ireland, ib.; Roman architecture, its
influence upon rude-stone monuments,
394.
Spaniards in Ireland, 227.
Spring Farm, 117.
Square enclosures in North America,
511-12.
Squares in Algeria, 399; four cairns enclosed in squares, 402.
Squier and Davis, Messrs., their survey
of America, 510 et seq.
St. Augustine's monastery, 23.
St. Barbe, 354; head of column at,
355.
St. Columba, 227; converts Picts, 248;
visits King Brude, 267; language of
Picts unknown to, 271.
St. Front, Périgueux, church, 330.

St. Germain-sur-Vienne, 336. See Con-
folans.
St. Helier, cells at, 52.
St. Jerome cited as to barbarism of Irish,
235.
St. Malo, Maximus and British landed
there, 374.
St. Pancras, heathen fane consecrated to,
22.
St. Patern, a Breton, his death, 373.
St. Patrick fails to convert Leoghaire,
195; legend of him and demons, 227.
St. Servan, battle near, 374.
St. Vigean's stone, 273.
Stand Low find, 13.
Stanton Drew circles, 64; not observatories, 7; circles at, 148; similar to
those in Derbyshire and Cumberland
in purpose and date, ib.; plan of, 149;
oval, ib.; avenues, 150; Kingstone,
ib.; Stukeley's interpolation of serpentine avenues, ib.; ruins of dolmens,
151; tradition as to Keyna, ib.; date
of, 151-2; belongs to Arthurian age,
152; scene of Arthur's 9th battle, ib.;
meaning of "Stanton," ib.; Maes
Knoll, 153; meaning of word Maes,
ib.; similarity to Stennis, 256-7.
Stanton Moor circle, 48, 49.
Stanley, Hon. W. C., circles enumerated
by, 162; cist found by, at Plas Newydd,
166.
Stawell, Lord, excavation directed by, at
Avebury, 74-5.
Stennis, 241; dolmen, ib.; great circle
like English ones, 161; like Stanton
Drew, 257; date, ib.; countless barrows,
ib.; magnificent effect of group, ib.;
circles and barrows belong to different
and what races, ib.; dates thereof, ib.
Steppes, importance of exploring with
reference to Turanian origin of dolmens, 447 et seq.; tumuli, 448-9; images
of dead on tombs, 449; usages as to
interments and sepulchres, ib.; four-
cornered grave, ib.; tumulus at Alexandropol, 450; find, 451; uncovered
base of tumulus, ib.; genesis of circles,
ib.; Tartar and European tombs cognate, but not of same origin as Western
dolmen or circles, or menhirs, 452;
Haxthausen s example an exception,
ib.; examples in the Steppes carved,
ib.
Stiklastad in Norway, battle at, 291.
"Stone of Destiny," where now, 382.
Stone tables, 425.
Stone temples, no classical writer connects Druids with, 20.
Stonehenge, theories respecting, 3, 4;
not an observatory, 7; not alluded to
by Diodorus, 8; ill-judged proceedings
as to, 15; age of, 17; not mentioned
by Roman writers, 20; plans, 89, 90,
91, 92, 93; circles, 100-3; Sarsen or
bluestones, 92-7; trilithons, 95, 98,

100; means of transport, 95-6; who erected, 97; intermediate circle, *ib.*; mere stones more numerous, 98; was Stonehenge a temple, 99; why hewn stones there, *ib.*; erected leisurely, *ib.*; trilithons called gates by Olaus, 101; question as to priority in time of the barrows or stone monuments, *ib.*; connexion between circles and British villages, 102; diggings there, 104; map of country around, 102; its builders not Christians, 104; whether sepulchral, 112, 116; why erected and by whom, 106, 116. *See* Alignments, Avenues, Barrows, Bluestones, Finds, Sarsens.

Stones, worship of, forbidden, 24-6.

Stoney Littleton, chambered tumulus, 166; grave intended to be covered, 164; post-Roman, 289.

Strabo, account of Druids by, 5; of temple by, 21; barbarism of early Irish, 235.

Stuart, Glennie, and Kendal, W., assign Scottish birthplace and campaign to Arthur, 134.

Stuart, J., cited, 52, 239; as to diggings at Rayne, 264-5.

Stukeley, Dr., wild theory of, 3, 4, 15, 21, 64; adopted by Sir R. C. Hoare, 5; misunderstands text of Diodorus, 8; drawings by, 44; his visit to Shap, 129; compared in one respect to Boece, 135; his serpent interpolation at Stanton Drew, 150; his snake bit, 151.

Stupas in India, 41.

Suetonius, Druids met by, 5.

Sûf, dolmens near, 442.

Suhm, cited as to date of Lothbrok victories, 290.

Summit interments, 166. *See* Interments.

Sun worship forbidden, 25.

Sutherland, Duchess of, her etchings of ruins in Orkneys, 241.

Swansea, Arthur's Quoit at, 170.

Sweden, South, megalithic remains in, 15; circles, 47; dolmens in, 301.

Swen Grate, King, 291.

Sylhet, Mohammedan kingdom, 466.

Symbol stage, none in Ireland, 59.

Syria, trilithons in, 100.

TABLE-STONES, 435-6.

Tabris circle, 453.

Tacitus cited as to three races in Britain, 162.

Tailton, Talton, or Telltown, burial of Irish kings there, 199; of Lough Crew, 219 *et seq.*; fair in honour of Magh Mor, King of Spain, 186.

Táin Bó Chuailgne, 196.

Talyots, or talayots, 434 *et seq.*; in Balearic isles, 410, 415.

Tamulians not builders of rude-stone monuments in India, 477.

Tantalais tumulus, 32.

Tara, Hill of, remains at, 193; early celebrity of, *ib.*; capital of Firbolgs and Dananns, 190, whence the name, 382.

Tartar tombs, 451.

Taylor, Col. Meadows, cited as to Indian dolmens, 469; and Shahpoor monuments, 485.

Teamair, wife of Herimon, 382.

Tee in Tope, 46; in rock at Ajunta, 47, 491; as connecting links between Eastern and Western dolmens, 489-90.

Temples, what structures not, 512; megalithic remains not, 20 *et seq. See* mounds.

Teocallis, Mexican, what, 514.

"Things," meaning of word, 26.

Thomas, Lieut., his account of monuments in the Orkneys, 241, 248.

Thorfin, 250; sons of, 528; where buried, 249; battle between them and Liotr, 528.

Three Ages, Danish doctrine of, 9; illusive application of, 10.

Thunderstone at Shap, 129, 130.

Thurnam, his work on British Skulls, 35, 35, 72; his inference from finds, 165, 286; as to West Kennet, 287.

Thyra, monument of Queen, 27, 250; finds, 297.

Tia Huanaco, ruins at, not like those attributed to Druids, 518; what they were, 519.

Tigernach, his date of Queen Meave's death, 184; of Crimthann's, 190.

Tika received by Rajahs from Bhils, 459.

Tin, route of ancient British commerce in, 334.

Toda tribe in India, 459. *See* Bhil.

Toltecs, buildings of, 515.

Tollington, supposed avenue at, 117-9; obelisks at, 117.

Tombs—of Alyattes, 3; Atridæ, 32, 33; Cocumella, 33; Cœre, 33; Regulini Galeassi, 34; of great men marked by megalithic monuments, 15; of Isidorus, 100; Tartar, 451; Nilgiri hills, 473.

Toope, Dr., his letter to Aubrey respecting Hakpen Hill, 76, 77.

Tooth-relic, worship of, 504.

Topes in India found blind, 80. *See* Dagoba.

Tormore, 261.

Towers, round, at Brechin and Abernethy, 271.

Town of the Stone of the Strangers, 229.

Tras os Montes dolmens, 378.

Tree-worship forbidden, 24, 25.

Trepuco talyot, 435.

Triads, Welsh authority for interments at Stonehenge, 110; as to stone of Cetti, 173; value of, as authority, *ib.*

Triangular monuments, 315; perhaps cuneatus ordo of Olaus Magnus, *ib.*

Trie, holed dolmens, 343.

Trilithons at Stonehenge, 99 ; connexion with dolmens, 100 ; in Sligo, 108 ; at Ksaea at Elkeb, 412 ; Hauran, 445.

Tripoli, trilithons at Ksaea, 411 ; Elkel with holes, 411-2 ; compared to Hindu Yoni, 412 ; Buddhist monument at Bangkok, 43.

Tuatha de Dananns, see Dananns.

Tuathal, authentic history begins with, 196 ; " the accepted," 197.

Tumiac tumulus and find, 366.

Tumuli, 29 ; different kinds of, ib. (see Barrows, Pyramids,Tombs) ; history of inhumation, 30 ; Troy, 32 ; Roman, 84 ; truncated cones, ib. ; spoliation of their own ancestors' tombs by Northmen, 300 ; Kemp How at Shap, 130 ; find at, ib. ; chambered tumuli, 166, 168 ; Freyrsö, 291 ; certain Danish, identical with some in Auvergne, 323 ; tumuli by thousands in the east of France, 327 ; finds, ib. ; numerous in Etruria, 392 ; peculiarity of tumuli in North Africa, 399 ; plan and elevation of two sepulchral monuments, ib. ; not battle-field, 400 ; quadruple circles, ib.; tumuli chambered in Lydia and Kertch, 446 ; kouloba on hill of cinders, ib.; find there, 446-7 ; tumuli in the Steppes, 448 ; at Alexandropol, 450 ; finds there, ib. ; uncovered base of, at Nikolajew, 451 ; Tartar tumuli perhaps models of Western, 452.

Turanian origin of dolmens, theory of, how to be proved or disproved, 448 ; Turanian race in Europe, 507.

Twining's strange map theory, 76.

Tynebagger, circle at, 263.

Tynwald Mount, 71.

Tyrrheni, see Pelasgi.

Uby, buried dolmen at, 310 ; chamber, 311.

Udyagiri Hills, Buddhist caves in, 460.

Uekermark, dolmen at, 301.

Uelzen, dolmen with enclosures near, 308.

Uffington Castle, monuments near, 121 ; why constructed, 123.

Uley, 163 ; chambered grave, 163, 166 ; post-Roman, 289.

Ultonians, tombs of, 219, 220.

Upland, Danish prince killed at, 291.

Urn found in cairn of One Man, 179.

Vaisali, convocation at, 501.

Valdbygaards, two dolmens in enclosure, 308.

Vallancy, wild speculations of, 175, 207.

Vancouver's Island, natives of, whether mound-builders, 517.

Vannes, Museum of, 326.

Vedas, date of, 455.

Veneti, Cæsar's naval battle with, 20, 37 ; hence what inference of age of monuments, 372 ; iron nails used by, 37.

Verneilh, Felix de, his ' Byzantine Architecture in France,' 332.

Vestal Virgins, no just analogy of Nuns to, 499.

Vetta, his name on Cat stone, 57 ; supposed grandfather of Hengist and Horsa, 271.

Via Badonica, under Silbury Hill, 20.

Vicars, Mr., surveys Carnac, 350.

Vicramaditya, his capital, 459.

Viharas, early date and growth of, in India, 501.

Vikings, 303-4 ; grave, 315, 317.

Vinland, America peopled through, 516.

Viraculls, what, 483.

Vitoria, dolmens in, 378.

Voguë's, De, plates of Roman tombs in the Hauran, 445.

Vortigern, victory of, at Aylresford, 119.

Vulci, tomb at, 33.

Waden Hill, where and what it is, site of what battle, 88-9.

Wales, Druids in, when 6 ; dolmen-building race, 274.

Walhouse, Mr., cited, 479.

Walker, Mr., his find at Knock na Rea, 185.

Wansdyke, barrier against Welsh, 87, 88, 89.

Ware, statement of, as to Giant stones in Kildare, 108 ; circles in, 162.

Waterloo, mound at, 56.

Wayland Smith's Cave in Berkshire, used by Scott in ' Kennilworth,' 122 ; what it was, 123-4 ; great circle there, 161.

Webb's reply to Dr. Charleton respecting Stonehenge, 3.

Welsh Gate, what and where it was, 87-89.

Welsh Triads, see Triads.

West Kennet, 4 ; its similarity to barrow in Denmark, 283 et seq. See Barrow.

Western Islands, no Druids in, 6.

White Horse, near Uffington, described by Mr. T. Hughes, 121.

Wilde, Sir W., his residence at Moytura, 176 ; his work, 177, 202 et seq.

Wildesheim, dolmen at, 301.

Wilkinson, Sir Gardner, observations on Long Meg, 127 ; on Arbor Low, 139, and Gib Hill, 141 ; his corrections to Croker's survey of Stanton Drew, 150 ; dolmen at Gower opened by, 171.

Wilson, Captain, his survey of Clava, 265.

Wilson, Daniel, dolmen mentioned by, in Argyllshire, 273.

Wilson's ' Prehistoric Annals,' 239 ; his remarks upon Daw's theory as to origin, 253.

Wiltshire, Sir R. C. Hoare's work on, 5.

Wisconsin and Ohio, how first peopled, 516.

Woden myth, its allusion to Indian

origin, 496; Woden not Sakya Muni, 496.

Woking, principle of selection of, as cemetery, 131; not applied by ancients, 131.

Wood worship forbidden, 25; early employment of, in Indian architecture, 492.

Wood Castle, circle at, 129 *note*; Arthur's battle there, 135.

Wormius Olaus, correspondence with Dr. Charleton respecting Stonehenge, 3; mentions dolmens with square enclosures, 307.

Worsae cited as to Scandinavian monuments, 297 *et seq.*

Wright, Mr., account of monuments at Aylesford, 118. *See* Aylesford.

Written history, errors of, 113; deficiency of, supplied by monuments, 113; and by architectural study, 113; uncertain accounts of King Arthur, 114.

Wurm Knot in Maes-Howe, 245.

YARHOUSE, battle at, 529.

Yarrow, inscription in stone at, 272.

Yucatan, 516; carved stone monuments, 517.

Yule, Col., his 'Cathay,' 488 *note*.

ZANA, Queen, 404.

Zealand, *see* Birk Valdbygaards.

THE END.

WORKS BY THE SAME AUTHOR.

HISTORY OF ARCHITECTURE IN ALL COUNTRIES, FROM THE EARLIEST TIMES TO THE PRESENT DAY. With 1200 Illustrations. 2 vols. 8vo. 84s. London, Murray, 1865-7.

HISTORY OF THE MODERN STYLES OF ARCHITECTURE. FORMING THE THIRD VOLUME OF THE 'HISTORY OF ARCHITECTURE.' With 312 Illustrations. 8vo. 31s. 6d. London, Murray, 1862.

ILLUSTRATIONS OF THE ROCK-CUT TEMPLES OF INDIA. 18 Plates in Tinted Lithography, folio: with an 8vo. volume of Text, Plans, &c. 2l. 7s. 6d. London, Weale, 1845.

PICTURESQUE ILLUSTRATIONS OF ANCIENT ARCHITECTURE IN HINDOSTAN. 24 Plates in Coloured Lithography, with Plans, Woodcuts, and explanatory Text, &c. 4l. 4s. London, Hogarth, 1847.

AN ESSAY ON THE ANCIENT TOPOGRAPHY OF JERUSALEM; with restored Plans of the Temple, and with Plans, Sections, and Details of the Church built by Constantine the Great over the Holy Sepulchre, now known as the Mosque of Omar. 16s. London, Weale, 1847.

AN ESSAY ON A PROPOSED NEW SYSTEM OF FORTIFICATION, with Hints for its Application to our National Defences. 12s. 6d. London, Weale, 1849.

AN HISTORICAL INQUIRY INTO THE TRUE PRINCIPLES OF BEAUTY IN ART, more especially with reference to Architecture. Royal 8vo. 31s. 6d. London, Longmans, 1849.

THE PALACES OF NINEVEH AND PERSEPOLIS RESTORED: An Essay on Ancient Assyrian and Persian Architecture. 8vo. 16s. London, Murray, 1851.

THE PERIL OF PORTSMOUTH. FRENCH FLEETS AND ENGLISH FORTS. Plan. 8vo. 3s. London, Murray, 1853.

PORTSMOUTH PROTECTED: with Notes on Sebastopol and other Sieges during the Present War. Plans. 8vo. 3s. London, Murray, 1856.

OBSERVATIONS ON THE BRITISH MUSEUM, NATIONAL GALLERY, and NATIONAL RECORD OFFICE; with Suggestions for their Improvement. 8vo. London, Weale, 1849.

THE ILLUSTRATED HANDBOOK OF ARCHITECTURE. Being a Concise and Popular Account of the Different Styles prevailing in all Ages and all Countries. With 850 Illustrations. 8vo. 26s. London, Murray, 1859.

NOTES ON THE SITE OF THE HOLY SEPULCHRE AT JERUSALEM. An answer to 'The Edinburgh Review.' 2s. 6d. London, Murray, 1861.

THE MAUSOLEUM AT HALICARNASSUS RESTORED, IN CONFORMITY WITH THE REMAINS RECENTLY DISCOVERED. Plates. 4to. 7s. 6d. London, Murray, 1862.

THE HOLY SEPULCHRE AND THE TEMPLE AT JERUSALEM. Being the Substance of Two Lectures delivered in the Royal Institution, Albemarle Street, on the 21st February, 1862, and 3rd March, 1865. Woodcuts. 8vo. 7s. 6d. London, Murray, 1865.